Contemporary Topics in Finance

Contemporary Topics in Finance

A Collection of Literature Surveys

Edited by Iris Claus and Leo Krippner

Registered Offices
John Wiley & Sons, Inc., 111 River Street, Hoboken, NJ 07030, USA
John Wiley & Sons Ltd, The Atrium, Southern Gate, Chichester, West Sussex, PO19 8SQ, UK

Editorial Office
9600 Garsington Road, Oxford, OX4 2DQ, UK

For details of our global editorial offices, customer services, and more information about Wiley products visit us at www.wiley.com.

Wiley also publishes its books in a variety of electronic formats and by print-on-demand. Some content that appears in standard print versions of this book may not be available in other formats.

Library of Congress Cataloging-in-Publication data is available for this book.

9781119565161 (paperback)

Cover Design: Wiley
Cover Images: Lee Yiu Tung/Shutterstock, © Golden House Studio/Shutterstock

Set in 10/12pt TimesLTStd by Aptara Inc., New Delhi, India
Printed in Singapore by C.O.S. Printers Pte Ltd

10 9 8 7 6 5 4 3 2 1

CONTENTS

1.   Contemporary Topics in Finance: A Collection of Literature Surveys   1
   Iris Claus and Leo Krippner

2.   A Survey of the International Evidence and Lessons Learned about
   Unconventional Monetary Policies: Is a 'New Normal' in our Future?   11
   Domenico Lombardi, Pierre Siklos and Samantha St. Amand

3.   Implicit Bank Debt Guarantees: Costs, Benefits and Risks   41
   Sebastian Schich

4.   Financial Fraud: A Literature Review   79
   Arjan Reurink

5.   Estimating Inflation Risk Premia Using Inflation-Linked Bonds: A Review   117
   Alexander Kupfer

6.   Finance and Productivity: A Literature Review   151
   Mark Heil

7.   Business Angels Research in Entrepreneurial Finance: A Literature Review and
   a Research Agenda   183
   Francesca Tenca, Annalisa Croce and Elisa Ughetto

8.   Venture Capital Internationalization: Synthesis and Future Research Directions   215
   David Devigne, Sophie Manigart, Tom Vanacker and Klaas Mulier

9.   Is Relationship Lending Still a Mixed Blessing? A Review of Advantages and
   Disadvantages for Lenders and Borrowers   249
   Andi Duqi, Angelo Tomaselli and Giuseppe Torluccio

10.   Determinants of the Performance of Microfinance Institutions: A Systematic
    Review   297
    Niels Hermes and Marek Hudon

11. Crowdfunding and Innovation 331
Fabrice Hervé and Armin Schwienbacher

12. Crypto-Currencies – An Introduction to Not-So-Funny Moneys 351
Christie Smith and Aaron Kumar

Index 383

1

CONTEMPORARY TOPICS IN FINANCE: A COLLECTION OF LITERATURE SURVEYS

Iris Claus

University of Waikato

Leo Krippner

Reserve Bank of New Zealand

"*For there was once a time when no such thing as money existed .... But it did not always and so easily happen that when you had something which I wanted, I for my part, had something that you were willing to accept. So a material was selected which, being given a stable value by the state, avoided the problems of barter by providing a constant medium of exchange.*"

Julius Paulus Prudentissimus, about 230 A.D. (translation by A. Watson, 1985)

Finance has always played a critical role in economies, given it is at the heart of consumption, saving, and investment decisions by individuals, firms, and governments. As a practical and professional field, finance facilitates the efficient exchange of funds within economies between lenders, investors, and borrowers. Therefore, it is understandable that finance is continually evolving in practice.

However, it is important that the practical evolution of finance is complemented by active academic and policy related research. As a simple historical example, money, which lies at the core of finance and economics, has existed in practice for thousands of years, as has the temptation for its exploitation by authorities. The introductory quote is actually part of an academic argument on the key properties of money (an efficient medium of exchange, a secure store of value, and a stable unit of account) that successfully convinced Gordian III at the time against debasing the currency of Rome.

Following the theme of best practice being complemented by best research, this book comprises a collection of up-to-date reviews on eleven contemporary topics in finance. We have broadly grouped these into the three categories discussed in the following paragraph.

Contemporary Topics in Finance: A Collection of Literature Surveys, First Edition. Edited by Iris Claus and Leo Krippner.
Chapters © 2019 The Authors. Book compilation © 2019 John Wiley & Sons Ltd. Published 2019 by John Wiley & Sons Ltd.

Developments in finance practice, research, policy, and regulation can be triggered by many catalysts. One such catalyst is exceptional financial and economic events that can lead policy makers, researchers, and society in general to question and revisit the parameters and limits under which the finance industry operates. A broader avenue, for research in particular, is the passage of time, which allows previously new forms of financing to be bedded in, while new empirical methods and data become available for quantitative analysis. A third catalyst is technological innovations, which can alter the efficiency of existing financial transactions and flows of funding, or create new ones.

The most exceptional financial and economic event in recent history is, of course, the Global Financial Crisis (GFC) and the associated Great Recession. The first three articles in this book relate to those events. They review the literature on the effectiveness of unconventional monetary policy, the costs of implicit bank debt guarantees, and drivers of financial fraud. Estimation of inflation risk premia, advances in finance and productivity, and less traditional forms of finance including business angels, venture capital, microfinance, and relationship lending are reviewed in the next six articles. The last two reviews are on new topics in finance that have arisen from technological advances; crowdfunding and innovation and an introduction to crypto-currencies.

The immediate challenges of the GFC and Great Recession were to stabilize financial markets and the economy, and ultimately setting them on a course for an eventual recovery. Hence, in "A survey of the international evidence and lessons learned about unconventional monetary policies: Is a 'new normal' in our future?" Pierre Siklos, Domenico Lombardi, and Samantha St. Amand discuss the effectiveness of unconventional monetary policy (UMP) and implications for the future. UMP is defined as any policy action, other than the conventional setting of short-term interest rates undertaken prior to the GFC of 2007/08 that influences economic activity and/or moderates shocks to the financial system to achieve a stated monetary policy objective. UMP therefore includes the well-known quantitative easing (QE) actions, where central banks change the size and/or composition of their balance sheet, forward guidance policies, where central banks change market expectations of interest rates by sending signals about the future policy path, and inflation target announcements that can change expected inflation and hence real interest rates.

The authors find considerable evidence that UMP can be powerful in offsetting the negative economic effects of a financial crisis. In that context, the evidence suggests that a successful monetary policy response should be forceful, that a joint response from both the fiscal and monetary authorities is desirable, and that the policy response should be persistent until confidence and the conditions for full recovery are in place. From these perspectives, the authors provide a retrospective on the case of UMP in Japan, given that it so far shows few signs of producing the aimed-for economic outcomes despite long and varied attempts. They also raise related questions for the euro area, given that the specific structure of its financial system and macroeconomic policy making processes may limit the desired co-ordinated response.

Regarding the aftermath of a financial crisis, the authors interpret the evidence as showing that UMP is not necessarily sufficient or capable of promoting stronger long-term economic growth on its own. Consistent with this, central banks have been reluctant to claim that they can restore growth to pre-crisis conditions without supporting fiscal and structural policies also being enacted.

The GFC was also a catalyst for revisiting the topic, and policy framework, around implicit government guarantees for banks, given that the banking system and many individual banks received unprecedented government support at the time, although the topic also has plenty of pre-GFC history. "Limiting implicit bank debt guarantees" by Sebastian Schich reviews the literature, noting that implicit government guarantees exist for banks essentially due to the expectation by market participants that public authorities might bailout the creditors of banks that are considered to be "too big to fail" (TBTF). The policy response to the GFC might have further entrenched that perception.

While implicit bank debt guarantees might benefit some stakeholders in the short term, they create economic costs as well as additional risks. In particular, they tend to weaken market discipline, encourage bank leverage and risk-taking, and distort competition between banks and non-banks, between small and large banks, and between banking sectors from different countries. They also create contingent liabilities for the sovereign and the taxpayer.

Policy measures to limit the value of implicit guarantees, and hence their costs, differ from country to country. One overarching goal is to strengthen bank balance sheets, thus making guarantees less valuable. Another avenue is to make bank failure resolution smoother and more effective, thus reducing the perception that implicit guarantees exist. Explicitly charging a user fee, as a disincentive for banks to "use" such guarantees, is considered less attractive, given the difficulty of making appropriate valuations and also potentially reinforcing the perception that guarantees exist. The approach of identifying some banks as globally systemically important and subjecting them to a special and more intrusive regulatory treatment may be seen as an indirect charge for the "use" of implicit guarantees. However, Schich finds little evidence that this specific approach has been successful so far.

Schich summarizes the measures of implicit guarantees which, while inherently difficult to value, can be used to assess progress regarding limiting TBTF. There is evidence that the values of implicit bank debt guarantees for banks have declined from their peaks attained during the GFC, but it is not clear whether the values have fallen below those prevailing before the crisis.

Open questions that remain are how much further should the value of implicit bank debt guarantees be reduced? And at what point can their level be considered low enough so that the costs of further efforts to reduce them would outweigh the benefits of doing so?

Another topic that has been given a new lease of life in the onset and the wake of the GFC is financial fraud, given the role of the subprime mortgage markets in that event, although the topic has had a long and colourful pedigree prior to the GFC. In "Financial fraud: A literature review", Arjan Reurink surveys the empirical literature on financial fraud from three perspectives. The first is financial statement fraud, which involves false statements about investment entities, the second is financial scams, which are deceptive and fully fraudulent schemes, and the third is fraudulent mis-selling practices, where the product or service is knowingly unsuitable for clients' needs.

Reurink finds that financial fraud is widespread throughout the financial industry, including the frequent involvement of established financial institutions, and is not simply attributable to a few "bad apples". Indeed, the literature review highlights four recent developments that scholars think have facilitated the occurrence of financial fraud. First, financial deregulation has resulted in new conflicts of interest and perverse incentive structures, facilitated by incentive-based compensation structures in financial firms at all levels (and new layers of intermediaries, such as fund managers and financial advisers). Perverse incentive structures can orientate firms towards short-term profit-making and stock-price maximization, irrespective of the legal implications, and legal penalties can simply be seen as a cost of doing business. Second, financial markets have seen an influx of relatively unsophisticated investors during the last few decades, which has provided fraudulently predisposed market players with a larger pool of more easily exploitable investors. Third, the increasing complexity involved in financial market transactions provides opportunities for fraudsters to deceive other market participants. Fourth, the veil of secrecy and mystique surrounding some collective investment funds which have been on the rise over recent decades can facilitate fraud. The secrecy is justified in the context of proprietary trading models used by fund managers, but financial scams and financial statement frauds associated with the funds can thrive in the environment of incomplete disclosure.

Future research in the area, building on some existing work, could investigate the impact of fraud on the functioning of markets and the stability of financial systems, the political and economic structures that facilitate financial fraud, and the relationship between deregulation and financial fraud. Particularly relevant in the present environment of unusually low interest rates is how that might encourage excessive risk taking and facilitate Ponzi like schemes.

Within the second main category of existing topics in finance that have benefited from new research, we include six papers.

Alexander Kupfer in "Estimating inflation risk premia using inflation-linked bonds: A review" surveys studies investigating the premia in inflation-linked bonds (ILBs), which have grown in number with the availability of new data, notably in the United States over the past 20 years. Inflation expectations are an unobserved variable that are an important economic quantity for policy makers and investors. In principle, nominal bonds and ILBs should allow high frequency readings of implied inflation expectations for different horizons (unlike surveyed inflation expectations). However, nominal-ILB spreads are biased by inflation risk premia, liquidity premia, lags on indexing ILBs to inflation outturns, and embedded deflation options (some ILBs rule out indexation below face value). Allowing for those biases improves implied inflation expectations nominal-ILB spreads, and is also important for decisions on nominal versus ILB sovereign debt issuance. The sign of the inflation risk premium also offers some intuition about the state of the economy.

Kupfer finds that strategies to estimate the inflation risk premium vary considerably throughout the literature, including regression-based approaches, term structure models (with and without inflation data), and macro-finance term structure models. These studies generally find that the magnitude and variation in the inflation risk premium is material. Regarding the liquidity premium, it was highest in the first years of ILB issuance and around the time of the GFC. The indexation lag and deflation option are found to be negligible, apart from during the GFC in the latter case.

The survey also presents potential directions for future research. One is building on limited work so far using term structure models that allow for the effective lower bound in nominal yields, while ILB yields are free to evolve to negative values. Similarly, further and in-depth analysis is needed on ILB liquidity premia and their determinants because eliminating that premium would present a large fiscal saving when issuing ILBs. Finally, a further area for future research is to extend recent term structure approaches that gauge the equilibrium real rate using ILBs, and to investigate two-(or multi-)country term structure models that include ILB data.

Another topic that has evolved rapidly in the past decade, due in part to greater availability of firm-level and plant-level data and policy agenda priorities, is the relationship between finance and productivity. In "Finance and productivity" Mark Heil surveys the empirical literature, after providing an introduction to the long-term trends in productivity and finance, and a stylized view of key policy mechanisms that influence productivity.

Regarding empirical results, mounting evidence shows that financial development has been an important contributor to productivity growth. Conversely, financial frictions that impede the efficient flow of finance can mitigate the positive effects through a variety of channels. For example, inefficient insolvency regimes that impede the exit of low-productivity firms inhibits productivity growth. The magnitudes of frictional costs in general appear to be modest in financially developed economies, but are considerably larger in developing economies.

A primary driver of productivity growth is knowledge production, yet evidence that the availability of financing facilitates higher educational attainment is tenuous. On the whole, merger and acquisition activity is associated with gains in productivity, but the direct contributions of the financial sector to productivity are mixed; improvements during the late 1990s were substantial, but might be associated with the tech bubble at the time. Cross-country and single-country studies agree that financial liberalization, such as stock market opening and lifting of foreign capital controls, is associated with economically meaningful aggregate productivity gains.

The research suggests that the availability of equity financing is particularly valuable for the growth of young and small enterprises and it remains the primary external source for funding research and development. Recent studies of both periods of economic decline and booms suggest that business cycle influences on productivity are inconclusive.

As the author notes, the recent empirical literature provides fresh insights that may inform policy development to help enact finance related measures that more effectively promote productivity growth. However, it will be important in future research to identify empirical regularities, as well as differences across countries.

Angel finance is a non-traditional source of funds that has become more commonplace in recent decades, in practice and in the literature. In "Business angels research in entrepreneurial finance: A literature review and a research agenda", Francesca Tenca, Annalisa Croce, and Elisa Ughetto provide a summary of findings of prior literature and a bibliometric analysis. Business angels are high wealth individuals who provide seed or growth capital, advice, and hands-on assistance to business start-ups in exchange for ownership equity. They invest at the earliest stages of ventures' lifecycle typically long before institutional investors. Business angels play a complementary role to venture capitalists. They are typically more involved in the selection phase and first contact with entrepreneurs, while venture capitalists head the deal-structuring phase. In the post-investment phase, business angels are more involved in mentoring while venture capitalists are more engaged in monitoring through contracts and supervisory board involvement.

The authors categorize the literature on business angels into three thematic areas. The first is business angel characteristics, which was the first research stream to emerge. The second is business angel market, and the third is business angel investment process, which has become the most extensive research stream following increased growth in the number of papers published since 2011. However, a significant research gap has emerged between developed and emerging economies. Emerging markets are often characterized by political uncertainty, corruption, lack of supporting institutions for early stage investment, and legal protection for minority shareholders. Business angels manage such difficulties by adopting investment strategies of informal networking and co-investment. In emerging countries business angels co-invest to reduce high levels of financial, legal, currency, political, economic, and market risks while in developed economies they typically co-invest to reduce financial risks.

Quantitative analysis is the most frequent methodology used in business angel research. However, a key challenge is that business angels are often anonymous and invisible and hence difficult to identify which makes sampling problematic and most studies rely on convenience samples.

Venture capital is another non-traditional source of funds, sometimes described as the 'business of building businesses', which is reviewed by David Devigne, Sophie Manigart, Tom Vanacker, and Klaas Mulier in "Venture capital internationalization: Synthesis and future research directions". Venture capital investments are long-term, illiquid, minority equity investments for the launch, growth, or expansion of privately held companies. In recent years the importance of foreign investments in venture capital has been increasing. But foreign venture capital firms face geographical, cultural, and institutional distance which constrains domestically used strategies to reduce information asymmetries. The authors review the literature on venture capital internationalization and suggest avenues for future research. They discuss which venture capital firms invest across borders and in what countries, how venture capital firms address liabilities of foreign investing, and the outcomes of international venture capital investments.

Foreign venture capital firms source, fund, syndicate, and monitor portfolio companies differently than domestic venture capital firms. A venture capital firm's internationalization strategy is typically influenced by the institutional environment in target countries and determined by the experience of its managers (human capital), and its network of syndication partners including international technical communities of immigrants (social capital). Investment deal features and legal contracts are used to reduce problems of information asymmetries, monitoring, and resource transfer. Another strategy of foreign venture capital firms is syndication with local venture capital firms which outsources monitoring and value adding functions to local co-investors who do not face geographical, cultural or institutional distance. Regarding outcomes of international venture capital investments in terms of development of portfolio companies and financial returns earned by venture capital investors upon exit from portfolio companies the authors find that the evidence is mixed and conclude that more research is needed.

A more traditional source of funding is through relationship lending, which Andi Duqi, Angelo Tomaselli, and Giuseppe Torluccio address in "Is relationship lending still a mixed blessing? A review of advantages and disadvantages for lenders and borrowers". A key challenge for small businesses is that they generally do not have audited financial statements and traded debt or equity. A common lending technology is relationship lending which can help overcome these information difficulties because banks use proprietary information obtained over time through contact with firms, their owners, and local community to decide whether or not to lend to a firm and at what terms. Relationship lending thus differs from transactions based lending (or arm's length lending) where banks mostly use verifiable and hard information derived from financial statements, credit scoring or guarantees. In the review, the authors assess how the main determinants of relationship lending impact on benefits and costs for lenders and borrowers. They find that relationship lending helps banks screen out bad from good borrowers and reduces credit rationing compared to arm's length lending to small and medium-sized businesses but the benefits for borrowers appear to depend on borrowers' ability to signal their reputation in the market. In particular, it is not optimal for firms to have many banks because this sends a signal of low quality to the market.

Relationship lending is typically practiced by small banks that are located near their customers, while large banks tend to rely on transactions based lending, possibly because they have the tools to implement and benefit from transactions based lending. During times of crisis the evidence suggests that relationship banks extend credit at better terms than transactions banks possibly because they charge higher interest rates in good times to compensate for during a crisis.

Relationship lending may lead to two problems. The first problem is a soft budget constraint which arises when a borrower is in financial distress or a project becomes more risky and the bank extends lending to avoid bankruptcy of the firm. The second problem is a hold-up problem which occurs when relationship lending gives banks a monopoly on information allowing them to charge higher interest rates.

Under the various Basel accords, which are a series of recommendations on banking laws and regulations, banks are increasingly adopting screening technologies that rely on the use of hard information. The authors venture that the Basel accords will discourage banks from gathering and processing soft information and recommend further research on optimal banking practices and their links with regulation, bank stability, and the real economy.

Microfinance is a recent introduction to the field of finance that now has more data and research available for analysis. Marek Hudon and Niels Hermes review the literature on the performance of microfinance institutions in "Determinants of the performance of microfinance institutions: A systematic review". Microfinance institutions provide financial services to poor households who are excluded from the formal financial system. Their performance has typically been evaluated by their success in improving the lives of the poor and their independence of donor support in the long run. However, more recently there has been a shift in focus from social to financial performance. The attention is mainly on cost efficiency because lower costs of providing financial services maximize the contribution that the provision of financial services can make to reducing poverty.

Hudon and Hermes draw some conclusions from the literature. The size and scale of operations positively affect financial but not always social performance of microfinance institutions. The impact of subsidized funding on financial performance is mixed, but subsidies tend to improve social performance. Most studies focus on subsidies probably because most microfinance institutions are still dependent on subsidies from governments and only a few studies consider other funding sources, e.g. deposits, equity, and debt. The lack of attention to deposits as a funding source has consequences for the social performance of microfinance institutions because deposits and savings help manage fluctuations in income. Only a few studies have considered the relationship between the development of the domestic financial system and microfinance institutions' performance. Regarding governance most papers focus on the role of boards and few discuss the importance of transparency and disclosure.

The last two papers are on new topics in finance that have arisen from technological advances. Technology can lead to innovations in finance through efficiencies that facilitate latent markets that might otherwise not be viable. Or pure technological advances can lead to entirely new financial products.

Fabrice Hervé and Armin Schwienbacher in "Crowdfunding and innovation" review a new form of finance called crowdfunding for small firms. Crowdfunding campaigns take place on dedicated platforms that facilitate the launch of campaigns by standardizing processes and create greater visibility of projects. A broad range of projects now raise money through crowdfunding and different types have emerged ranging from rewards based, donations based, loans based, and equity crowdfunding. Many projects financed by crowdfunding are artistic and social.

Crowdfunding can provide equity financing to small, innovative firms that often is not available from professional investors, and it has some important differences with business angels and venture capital also surveyed in this issue. Crowd investors do not purchase equity *per se* but securities such as participating notes. In contrast, angel investors and venture capital funds typically purchase common shares and convertible preferred shares. Crowd investors, in addition to providing financial resources, may also participate in the development of projects by providing feedback and ideas to entrepreneurs.

Obtaining information and feedback from the crowd however may not always support the development of innovative projects, for example, when entrepreneurs have to spend significant time interacting with the crowd. Moreover, crowdfunding discloses more information about a project in the public domain than projects funded by professional investors because of the participation of a large number of individuals. As a result, projects that are difficult to replicate or only marginally innovative may be more likely to seek crowdfunding. Research on crowdfunding has mainly been theoretical and predictions remain to be tested empirically.

An example of a pure technological advance that has led to a new financial product is the use of computer encryption technology to create so-called crypto-currencies. In "Crypto-currencies: An introduction to not-so-funny moneys", Christie Smith and Aaron Kumar provide an introduction to the key concepts and what to look out for with potential future developments. Smith and Kumar summarize the rise and potential future implications of crypto-currencies and distributed ledger technology, in particular highlighting some of the risks associated with crypto-currencies, and discussing some of the potential implications of these technologies for payments systems, financial institutions, markets, and regulators.

The authors conclude that crypto-currencies do not have the three basic attributes of money, given they are not yet generally accepted or used as a unit of account, and their volatility makes them an uncertain store of value. However, crypto-currencies possess some features that make them attractive, which help to explain the growing demand for them. For example, crypto-currencies allow quicker cross-border transactions, possibly lower transaction fees, transaction irreversibility, and pseudo-anonymity (even while related prosecutions illustrate there is no guarantee of absolute anonymity).

Crypto-currencies currently facilitate a very small proportion of global transactions, and so do not yet pose material competition to traditional financial systems and intermediaries. Similarly, while some efforts have been made to adapt crypto-currencies to the provision of credit, the economies of scale that financial intermediaries have for evaluating and monitoring borrowers means that those intermediaries will likely continue to play a dominant role in facilitating credit.

The future growth of crypto-currencies and their use as transaction media is by no means clear. Crypto-currencies and decentralized ledger technology could well become an important part of global payment systems (and distributed ledgers and the use of cryptography also have wider uses). But the wide-scale adoption for transactions would depend on competition from alternative transaction technologies, and scalability issues would need to be addressed in order to compete in intermediating the volume of transactions undertaken globally. What does seem clear is that the regulatory and legal status of crypto-currencies must be resolved if crypto-currencies are to play a prominent role in exchange. Regulatory and legal reform will need to account for the decentralised nature of most crypto-currencies, and for their capacity to transcend national borders. Undoubtedly there will be more to review on crypto-currencies in future given the relatively brief time since inception and common usage.

The eleven articles in this book provide up-to-date surveys on contemporary topics in finance—a field that continues to evolve in practice and research. We hope the reviews will prove useful to academics, governments and policy makers, financial analysts and anyone interested in critical insights into developments in finance.

References

Devigne, D., Manigart, S., Vanacker T. and Mulier, K. (2018) Venture capital internationalization: Synthesis and future research directions. This book.

Duqi, A., Tomaselli, A. and Torluccio, G. (2018) Is relationship lending still a mixed blessing? A review of advantages and disadvantages for lenders and borrowers. This book.

Heil, M. (2018) Finance and productivity: A literature review. This book.

Hervé, F. and Schwienbacher, A. (2018) Crowdfunding and innovation. This book.

Hudon, M. and Hermes, N. (2018) Determinants of the performance of microfinance institutions: A systematic review. This book.

Kupfer, A. (2018) Estimating inflation risk premia using inflation-linked bonds: A review. This book.

Reurink, A. (2018) Financial fraud: A literature review. This book.

Schich, S. (2018) Limiting implicit bank debt guarantees. This book.

Siklos, P., Lombardi, D. and St. Amand, S. (2018) A survey of the international evidence and lessons learned about unconventional monetary policies: Is a 'new normal' in our future? This book.

Smith, C. and Kumar, A. (2018) Crypto-currencies: An introduction to not-so-funny moneys. This book.

Tenca, F., Croce, A. and Ughetto, E. (2018) Business angels research in entrepreneurial finance: A literature review and a research agenda. This book.

Watson, A. (1985) *The Digest of Justinian: Volume 2*. University of Pennsylvania Press.

2

A SURVEY OF THE INTERNATIONAL EVIDENCE AND LESSONS LEARNED ABOUT UNCONVENTIONAL MONETARY POLICIES: IS A 'NEW NORMAL' IN OUR FUTURE?

Domenico Lombardi

Banca di San Marino S.p.A.

Pierre Siklos

Wilfrid Laurier University

Samantha St. Amand

Centre for International Governance Innovation

1. Introduction

We are approaching a decade since the expressions quantitative easing (QE) and unconventional monetary policies (UMPs) became household words. Central bankers, however, have frequently repeated the need to pursue a 'looser for longer' stance in monetary policy, even after years of ultra-low interest rates and noninterest-rate forms of monetary easing. This study surveys the empirical literature on the effectiveness of UMP in responding to financial crises and boosting economic activity. In doing so, it considers the circumstances under which these policies have been found to be successful and examines cases where their impact remains questionable.

Before the 2007–2009 global financial crisis (GFC), an increasing number of central banks adopted a short-term interest rate setting as the main, if not sole, instrument of monetary policy. However, owing to the severity of the crisis and its potential implications on the real economy, the central banks that were most directly affected by the crisis quickly lowered their policy interest rates near zero. These policy settings were initially referred to as the 'zero lower bound' (ZLB) because it was argued that interest rates could not, for practical reasons, go below zero.[1]

Contemporary Topics in Finance: A Collection of Literature Surveys, First Edition. Edited by Iris Claus and Leo Krippner.
Chapters © 2019 The Authors. Book compilation © 2019 John Wiley & Sons Ltd. Published 2019 by John Wiley & Sons Ltd.

However, several central banks implemented negative interest rates alongside UMPs. Thus the ZLB expression became the 'effective lower bound' (ELB) in recognition that the article of faith once held by many policymakers had been abandoned (see Lombardi *et al.*, forthcoming, and references therein).

For the purpose of this analysis an UMP tool is defined as any policy instrument, other than the setting of short-term interest rates, that aims at achieving a stated monetary policy objective either by influencing economic activity or by moderating shocks to the financial system. An unconventional policy need not only be used when the ELB has been reached. It may also be implemented to prevent reaching that threshold or to provide targeted policy support to specific segments of the financial system. In addition, unconventional tools need not be used exclusively to provide monetary stimulus, though there are few examples of their use during periods of monetary tightening. We provide in Section 2.1 listing of UMP tools that have been used in practice or discussed theoretically.

There has been significant scepticism about the economic benefits of UMP type policies. Some of the criticism arises because the ELB and the objectives of UMP seem to differ across central banks and across time, creating uncertainty about what purpose these policies are supposed to serve. Furthermore, the scale of interventions has been extraordinary, amounting to trillions of U.S. dollars in some economies, and their scope is also unprecedented. This has raised concerns about inducing distortions in financial markets (e.g. Borio and Disyatat, 2010). Similarly, at the macro-economic level, there are concerns that low policy interest rates and further stimulus through UMP have amplified both domestic and international spillover effects (e.g. Rajan, 2014). As a result, central banks have been accused of risking the loss of their hard-earned credibility in managing inflation expectations (e.g. Taylor, 2014).

In the wake of the GFC, policymakers argued that using these policy tools was necessary to prevent an even worse contraction. Once the crisis passed, they argued that the continued application of such policies could speed up the recovery from crisis conditions. In light of the received macro-economic wisdom about what monetary policy can (or cannot) accomplish in the medium term, it is important to review the evidence concerning the economic effects of UMP.

The present paper surveys the financial-market and macro-economic effects of UMP in the economies where these policies were introduced as well as their spillover effects across borders. This is not the only survey of its kind. However, the present survey considers the range of international experiences and implications of UMP, while others have focussed more on the outcomes in specific countries (see Bhattarai and Neely, 2016 for the U.S. experience). It also considers a wider range of UMP, rather than the impact of specific policy instruments (as in Gagnon, 2016, Haldane *et al.*, 2016 and Reza *et al.*, 2015, who focus on QE; and Charbonneau and Rennison, 2015, who focus on forward guidance). Our survey comes closest to Borio and Zabai (2016). However, our survey emphasizes the diversity of experience and outcomes in using UMP. We provide a retrospective on the important but often neglected case of Japan beginning in the late 1990s, where UMP were first attempted and, so far, show few signs of producing the aimed-for economic outcomes. We also consider whether the Eurozone's experience with UMP is substantively different from that of other jurisdictions, given the specific structure of its financial system and its macro-economic policymaking process.

Finally, we present some evidence that underscores one of the main claims made by central bankers about UMP: that they were essential in preventing much worse economic outcomes after the 2008 financial crisis, at least in advanced economies (AEs). This conclusion is important because it suggests that UMP should not be considered as part of a 'new normal' but are best thought of as a set of policies to be applied only under exceptional circumstances. We return to this point in the conclusions.

The next section establishes the economic and financial context within which central banks needed to resort to UMP and provides a typology of UMP. Section 3 evaluates the evidence of the short-term impact of UMP on financial markets. Section 4 turns to an analysis of the relatively smaller literature dealing with the macro-economic impact of UMP. Section 5 concludes.

2. The Transition to Unconventional Policies

2.1 *The 2008 GFC*

Financial crises are nothing new, as Reinhart and Rogoff (2009) remind us. Yet, at the time their work was published, UMP had not yet entered the vocabulary of the central bankers (indeed, neither term appears in their book's index). Was there something fundamentally different about the events that began in 2007? There are at least two notable differences between the GFC and all the crises that preceded it, save perhaps for the Great Depression of the 1930s. First, the crisis began and was centred in AE. Previously, financial crises were phenomena typically seen as being restricted to developing or emerging market economies (EMEs).

Financial crises have been classified in several ways, including: currency crises (exceptionally large depreciations or devaluations in the nominal exchange rate), inflation crises (persistently high inflation rates that exceed historical norms), sovereign debt crises, stock market crashes and, of course, banking crises.[2] Aggregating all types of financial crises we observe – since the 1980s – that the median frequency of crises in EMEs was at least as high, or higher than, in AEs until the GFC. Similarly, the most recent banking crises erupted in AEs, while the last string of banking crises in EMEs were in the 1980s. Of course, banking crises were not unheard of in AEs prior to 2007 (see Siklos, 2017, chapter 3). However, the shock emanating from systemically important US and UK financial markets, combined with the imbalances in several economies through property-market bubbles or over-leveraged financial institutions, created the conditions for the eventual GFC.

Second, although central banks in the economies most directly affected by the GFC entered the crisis period with relatively low policy interest rates, their, inflation rates were also relatively low. Policy rates for three key central banks began at around 5% at the beginning of 2007. The Bank of Japan (BoJ) is the exception – its policy rate had been near zero since the late 1990s. The low starting point may have contributed to some hesitancy in rapidly lowering interest rates. Indeed, the Bank of England (BoE) only lowered its policy rate by 75 basis points over the period from the peak of its earlier tightening cycle in July 2007 to September 2008; it then lowered its policy interest rate another 450 basis points to the then ZLB of 0.5% over the subsequent six-month period from October 2008 to March 2009. The European Central Bank (ECB) actually increased interest rates in July 2008 to 4.25%, and did not effectively reach the ZLB even two years after the GFC. Only the U.S. fed funds rate was reduced relatively quickly, from 5.25% in August 2007 to the mid-point of a range between 0 and 0.25% by December 2008. Also influencing central banks may have been their success with lowering policy rates earlier in the decade when the threat of the deflation was on the minds of policy makers in several AEs (see IMF, 2003).

Widespread introduction of UMP came shortly after the height of the crisis in the fourth quarter of 2008. Much has been written about the Fed's large balance sheet, and the impression is sometimes given that the Fed has been more aggressive than its counterparts elsewhere. Figure 1 shows that this has not been the case. The top portion (Figure 1A) shows the size of balance sheets of the four major central banks as a per cent of GDP during the years surrounding

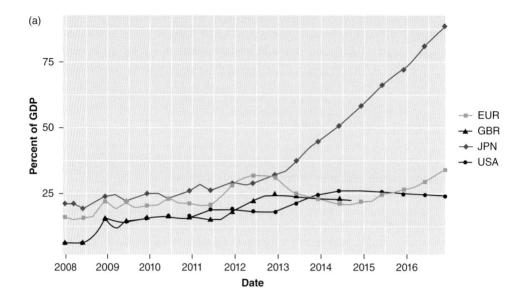

(a)

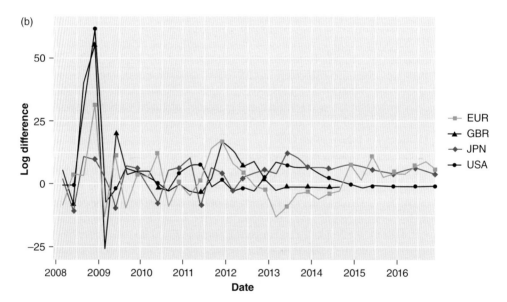

(b)

Figure 1. (a) Central Bank assets as a per cent of GDP. (b) Quarterly rate of change in Central Bank assets as a per cent of GDP.

Note: Data source is CEIC. Sample size is from 2007Q4 to 2016Q4. The Bank of England changed its methodology for reporting its balance sheet in October 2014; the series therefore ends 2014Q3.

[Color figure can be viewed at wileyonlinelibrary.com]

the worst of the GFC. While the U.S. data show a sharp increase in late 2008, the ratio of Fed assets to the size of the U.S. economy rose only modestly thereafter. Indeed, increases of similar magnitude occurred more or less simultaneously at both the ECB and the BoE. Even the BoJ expanded its balance sheet at the time, despite its share of assets being higher than elsewhere, owing to the on-going legacy of its banking crisis in the 1990s. Finally, notice that by 2012 the share of assets to GDP at both the BoE and the ECB increased sharply once again, as the impact of the Eurozone crisis began to take hold in that part of the world. The most dramatic increase occurred in Japan in 2013 when its program of Qualitative and Quantitative Easing (QQE) was introduced (see Section 3.2 below). When we instead examine the rate of change in assets of the same central banks as displayed in Figure 1(B), it is immediately clear that the largest interventions via the central bank balance sheet took place in late 2008 and early 2009. The rate of accumulation in central bank assets subsided shortly thereafter except at the BoE and the ECB in 2011, during the Eurozone crisis. The interventions by the BoJ after 2013 show steady increases, producing noticeable growth in the balance sheet-to-GDP ratio.

Figure 1, however, contains another important message. The Fed and the BoE began to shift emphasis away from the policy interest rate to the composition of their balance sheets *before* they approached the ZLB. Balance sheet policies were being used as a way of restoring confidence and easing the flow of credit in the financial sector. This outcome is also seen in the sharp deterioration of lending conditions in the four economies being reviewed (see Siklos, 2015; Siklos and Lavender, 2015; Filardo and Siklos 2018). The deterioration was largest for the United States, but was also significant in the euro area and the United Kingdom. Only Japan, mired in a low inflation and growth, seemed to escape the trend. Since the potential contraction of loans affects a key element of the transmission of monetary policy the threat to economic activity was potentially large.

2.2 *A Brief Typology of UMP*

Space limitations prevent a detailed discussion of different types of UMPs. For a more extensive account of these policies see, for example, Ball *et al.* (2016) and IMF (2013).

A UMP is defined as any policy instrument, other than the setting of short-term policy interest rates, that aims at achieving a stated monetary policy objective either by influencing economic activity or by moderating shocks to the financial system. It need not only be used when the ELB has been reached; it might, for example, be implemented to prevent reaching that threshold or to provide targeted policy support to specific segments of the financial system or economy. Table 1 provides a summary of the types of UMPs employed in AEs. Note that we present one of several ways to categorize UMP; there are many different typologies for these policies and there are also no neat separations among policies.

The term QE is often used to refer to any policy decision that aims to change the size and/or composition of the balance sheet. But these policies can take several forms. With QE, the central bank targets the liabilities side of its balance sheet by changing the level of reserves held by financial institutions. The aim is to change the money supply via the monetary base. Credit easing (CE) is another balance sheet policy that changes the composition of the central bank's assets. The aim is to improve liquidity conditions in one or more segments of the financial system, but it need not lead to a change in the size of the central banks' balance sheet (i.e. asset purchases may be sterilized by the sale of other types of assets). A third balance sheet policy creates incentives for the recipients of funds from central bank operations, namely commercial banks, to increase loan activity in an effort to stimulate economic activity.

Table 1. Unconventional Monetary Policies in Advanced Economies (Chronological by Type).

Policy type	Economy	Policy name	Time period
Forward Guidance[1]			
Qualitative	Japan	Zero interest rate policy (ZIRP)	April 1999 to August 2000
	United States	n/a	August 2003 to December 2005
	United States	n/a	December 2008 to July 2011
	Euro area	n/a	July 2013 to present[2]
Calendar-Based	Canada	n/a	April 2009 to March 2010
	United States	n/a	August 2011 to November 2012
State-Based	Japan	n/a	March 2001 to March 2006
	Japan	n/a	October 2010 to March 2013
	United States	n/a	December 2012 to February 2014
	Japan	n/a	April 2013 to present[2]
	United Kingdom	n/a	August 2013 to January 2014
Balance Sheet Policies			
Quantitative Easing	Japan	Quantitative Easing (QEJ)	March 2001 to March 2006
	United States	Large Scale Asset Purchase Program (LSAP1)	January 2009 to March 2010
	United Kingdom	Asset Purchase Facility – Gilt (BQE1)	January 2009 to February 2010
	Japan	Comprehensive Monetary Easing (CME)	October 2010 to March 2013
	United States	Large Scale Asset Purchase Program (LSAP2)	November 2010 to June 2011
	United Kingdom	Asset Purchase Facility – Gilt (BQE2)	October 2011 to October 2012
	United States	Large Scale Asset Purchase Program (LSAP3)	September 2012 to October 2014
	Japan	Quantitative and Qualitative Monetary Easing (JGB purchases)	April 2013 to present[2]
	Euro area	Public Sector Purchase Programme	January 2015 to present[2]
	United Kingdom	Asset Purchase Facility – Gilt (BQE3)	August 2016 to present[2]
	Switzerland	Expansion of Sight Deposits (Reserves)	August 2011
	Sweden	Government bonds	February 2015 to present[2]

(Continued)

Table 1. *Continued*

Policy type	Economy	Policy name	Time period
Credit Easing	United States	Commercial Paper Funding Facility	October 2008 to February 2010
	United States	Mortgage-Backed Securities Purchases (see also LSAP1)	November 2008 to March 2010
	Switzerland	Private Sector Bond Purchases	March 2009 to July 2009
	United Kingdom	Asset Purchase Facility – Commercial Paper	March 2009 to November 2011
	United Kingdom	Asset Purchase Facility – Secured Commercial Paper and Corporate Bond Secondary Market Scheme	March 2009 to August 2016
	United States	Operation Twist	September 2011 to June 2012
	Euro area	Securities Markets Programme	May 2010 to September 2012
	Euro area	Outright Monetary Transactions Programme	September 2012 to present[2]
	Euro area	Asset Backed Securities Purchase Programme	September 2014 to present[2]
	Euro area	Covered Bond Purchase Programme	July 2009 to June 2010; November 2011 to October 2012; October 2014 to present[2]
	Japan	Quantitative and Qualitative Monetary Easing (ETF and J-REIT purchases)	April 2013 to present[2]
	Euro area	Corporate Sector Purchase Programme	June 2016 to present[2]
	United Kingdom	Asset Purchase Facility – Corporate Bond Purchase Scheme	September 2016 to April 2017
Subsidized Lending to Banking System	Euro area	Longer-term refinancing operations (LTRO)	6 month: March 2008 to March 2010; August 2011 12 month: May 2009 to December 2009; October 2011 3 year: December 2011
	United States	Term Asset-Backed Securities Loan Facility (TALF)	November 2008 to June 2010

(Continued)

Table 1. *Continued*

Policy type	Economy	Policy name	Time period
	Japan	Loan Support Program	June 2010 to present[2]
	United Kingdom	Funding for Lending Scheme	July 2012 to present[2]
	Euro area	Targeted longer-term refinancing operations (TLTRO)	September 2014 to March 2017
	United Kingdom	Term Funding Scheme	September 2016 to present[2]

[1]Forward guidance only refers to the ad-hoc use of central bank communication of future policy path during crises or periods of high market uncertainty. The release of conditional forecasts (e.g. at the Reserve Bank of New Zealand, Norges Bank and Riskbank) are not included in this analysis (see, e.g. Kool and Thornton, 2012).
[2]As of 31 October 2017.
Source: Individual country central banks accessible via the BIS's Central Bank Hub (https://www.bis.org/cbanks.htm).

Readers are referred to European Central Bank (2015), Borio and Zabai (2016) and Stone *et al.* (2011), for more detailed discussions and alternative classifications of balance sheet policies. For example, excluded from this analysis are foreign exchange interventions or the provision of foreign exchange liquidity, which are included in other classifications of balance sheet policies.

While balance sheet policies involve direct intervention in the monetary system, another set of UMP tools aim to change expectations by sending signals about the future policy path. Forward guidance policies (FG) use communication to affect policy outcomes. They were introduced by the BoJ almost two decades ago (see, inter alia, Filardo and Hofmann, 2014). FG can take several forms. Qualitative guidance involves communicating the central bank's views about future policy actions but stops short of offering any sort of commitment. Two examples include the US FOMC's statement, starting in December 2008, that 'weak economic conditions are likely to warrant low levels of the federal funds rate for some time' and the ECB Governing Council's guidance, introduced in July 2013, that they 'expect the key ECB interest rates to remain at present or lower levels for an extended period of time'. The other two types of FG link a commitment to a certain policy path – usually promising to keep interest rates low – during a specified time period (calendar-based FG) or at least until a specified economic threshold is reached (state-based FG). In practice, the distinction between different forms of FG is somewhat arbitrary, as central banks may use a mix. For more details on FG policies, refer to Moessner *et al.* (2017), who examine whether central banks actually make commitments in practice, and Charbonneau and Rennison (2015).

There are several other policy actions that might be classified as 'unconventional'. Until the GFC the possibility of negative interest rates was regarded as an interesting possibility, but unlikely to be seen in practice. But the GFC ushered in negative interest rates that persist to this day. Significantly, the U.S. Fed and the BoE have explicitly ruled out allowing their policy rates to turn negative for fear of distorting capital markets in a manner that would not offset the potential benefits of the further easing brought about by such a strategy (e.g. Burke *et al.*, 2010; Turner, 2014). The evidence on the effectiveness of this tool is not discussed below, as it remains conventional according to our definition.

Two UMPs that have yet to be implemented are: helicopter money and changing the inflation objective.[3] The term 'helicopter money' was coined by Milton Friedman (1969), and essentially involves the transferring of funds directly into the hands of the public (e.g. via injections of cash or bank deposits). It has been given serious consideration by scholars (e.g. Buiter, 2014; Turner, 2016, chapter 14) and, in some circumstances, QE and helicopter money are fiscally equivalent (Reichlin *et al.*, 2013; Cohen-Setton, 2015). However, there are few indications that any countries are anywhere near considering such an option even if the global economy reverts to recession. Since some countries (e.g. China, India, Sweden) are already exploring a future where the central bank issues digital money (see, inter alia, Rogoff, 2016a; Camera, 2017; Engert and Fung 2017), this could open up the possibility of helicopter money being more readily available as an additional instrument of monetary policy, though only as a last resort.[4]

In the 1980s, there was a shift towards the adoption of explicit inflation targets. As inflation targeting spread to EMEs, the target levels were typically set higher and tolerance zones wider than in AEs. In light of the near miss with the ZLB in the early 2000s when some AEs – notably the United States – faced the possibility of a protracted deflation, it became apparent that hitting the ZLB was becoming more likely with sustained low inflation rates (see Chung *et al.*, 2012). This spurred largely theoretical work to investigate, among other issues, the economic consequences of the ZLB and its implications for the financial system (Williams, 2014, and references therein).

On the presumption that the ZLB should be avoided if possible, some scholars made the case for raising inflation targets (Blanchard *et al.*, 2010). Others argued that if inflation was below target for an extended period of time, then a credible commitment to letting inflation rise above target during the recovery could help prevent a liquidity trap (Woodford, 2012). See Ball *et al.* (2016) for an extensive discussion of the benefits and costs of raising the inflation rate.

More recently, Bernanke (2017) has suggested that a future monetary policy regime could combine some of the virtues of price-level targeting and inflation targeting. In normal times inflation targeting has proved successful, while price-level targeting promises to overshoot a future price level in case current prices evolve too slowly. In this fashion central banks have an argument for maintaining policy rates lower for longer when they are near or at the ZLB. How one might credibly switch from one type of inflation control regime to another remains unclear.

In what follows, we do not discuss the potential financial system and economic implications of financial repression or macro-prudential policy strategies, occasionally also thought of as unconventional, so as to retain focus on UMPs with more direct central bank involvement. See, however, Edison *et al.* (2004), Lombardi and Siklos (2016) and Reinhart *et al.* (2011), and references therein.

3. The International Evidence to Date: Financial Markets

3.1 *Measurement Challenges*

There are at least two challenges in evaluating the impact of UMP on financial markets. First, there is usually considerable speculation about an upcoming announcement ahead of the actual announcement. Next, UMP announcements are infrequent. As a result, the number of available 'observations' is generally small. These features likely explain a preference among researchers for relying on event-type studies to investigate the impact of UMP on financial markets.[5]

Since there are potentially many news items that can take place simultaneously with an announcement of an UMP action, identifying the isolated impact of, for example, the launch of a QE program is not straightforward. In part for this reason a growing number of studies rely on ultra-high frequency data (intra-daily or even tick by tick; see Rogers *et al.*, 2014). The finely chosen timing of events also ignores the real possibility that agents, even those in financial markets, are rationally inattentive or do not react to news at the very moment an event takes place. Such a possibility could bias estimates from even the most careful event study. MacKinlay (1997) is a well-known survey of the advantages and limitations of event studies.

Empirical contributions that adopt an event study approach include Aït-Sahalia *et al.* (2012), Acharya *et al.* (2017), Bastidon *et al.* (2016), Chen *et al.* (2014), Gagnon *et al.* (2011), Christensen and Rudebusch (2012) and Rogers *et al.* (2014). The events investigated can range from the announcement of QE-style policies to the whole gamut of UMP. This methodology treats policy announcements and/or interventions as events whose effects can be individually measured and the cumulative response to events associated with a specific policy captures the policy's total impact. In what follows we focus mainly on the impact of UMP on bond yields, especially those of long-term government bonds, since these are the main target of large-scale asset purchases made by central banks under the aegis of QE policies.

Swanson and Williams (2014a, 2014b) argue that in order to test whether UMPs can be effective at the ZLB one must first confirm that markets are responsive to surprises. The authors ask whether the responsiveness of financial markets to macro-economic news surprises changed after the GFC, relative to the pre-crisis period. If macro-economic news surprises no longer effect interest rates along the yield curve, then monetary policy may also be unable to impact markets, thereby losing its effectiveness. Data for the U.S., the U.K. and Germany suggest that market responsiveness has diminished at the short end of the yield curve. However, monetary policy is found to remain effective at the longer end of the yield curve. Lombardi *et al.* (2017, forthcoming) concur, relying on a wider array of countries, more recent data, as well controlling for the verbal and written communication of central banks.

Figure 2 shows the distribution of estimates of the impact of balance sheet policies on long-term government bond yields in the Eurozone, Japan, the United Kingdom and the United States across both time series and event studies. While the range of estimates across a large number of studies can be large it is almost unambiguously negative, implying that UMP could be successful in reducing bond yields even at the longer end of the term structure.

3.2 *Learning from Japan's Experience*

Two characteristics of Japan's experience with QE make it a particularly important case study: the BoJ was the first central bank to introduce QE in 2000; and, as shown in Figure 2, the BoJ's QE policies were the least effective at lowering government bond yields. We may never know conclusively why QE seems to have had a different outcome in Japan than elsewhere, but it seems that the combination of a lack of commitment to QE and early withdrawal from such programs were key factors.[6] Koo (2015, p. 64) describes the conflicting views inside and outside the BoJ that limited the effectiveness of QE. Policymakers were concerned about a 'QE trap', that is, the economic and financial risks of exiting from a massive expansion of the balance sheet. A somewhat related argument is that the BoJ did not adequately exploit its balance sheet by providing the necessary additional stimulus to halt the economic contraction (McCauley and Ueda, 2009; Ueda, 2011).

In the early 1990s, Japanese equity and property bubbles burst, putting intense deflationary stress on the domestic financial system. In response, the BoJ reduced the uncollateralized overnight call rate – the key policy interest rate – from a peak of 8.5% in 1991 to 0.5% in

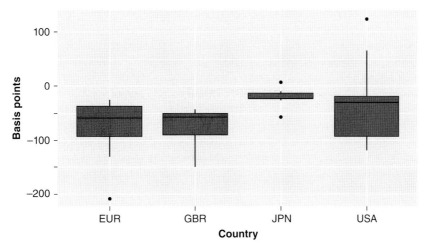

Figure 2. Summary of selected empirical studies: The impact of UMP on long-term government bond yield.

Note: $N = 62$. Impact on government bonds expressed in basis points. When the study reports several estimates, the minimum and maximum estimates, or estimates using various techniques are recorded. Euro area (EUR): $N = 13$. Studies include Altavilla *et al.* (2016), Andrade *et al.* (2016), De Santis and Holm-Hadulla (2017), Fic (2013), Eser and Schwaab (2016), Fratzscher *et al.* (2016), *et al.* (2015), Middledorp (2015) and Middledorp and Wood (2016). United Kingdom (GBR): $N = 11$. Studies include Breedon *et al.* (2012), Caglar *et al.* (2011), Bridges and Thomas (2012), Christensen and Rudebusch (2012), Fic (2013), Churm *et al.* (2015), Gros *et al.* (2015), and Joyce *et al.* (2011). Japan (JPN): $N = 9$. Studies include Fic (2013), Fukunaga *et al.* (2015), Gros *et al.* (2015), Lam (2011), and Ueda (2012). United States (USA): $N = 29$. Studies include Christensen and Rudebusch (2012), D'Amico and King (2013), Bauer and Rudebusch (2014), Engen *et al.* (2015), Gagnon *et al.* (2011), Fic (2013), Fratzscher *et al.* (2018), Gros *et al.* (2015), Krishnamurthy and Vissing-Jorgensen (2011), Hamilton and Wu (2012), Ihrig *et al.* (2012, 2013), Neely (2010), Swanson (2011), and Li and Wei (2013). [Color figure can be viewed at wileyonlinelibrary.com]

1995. Subsequently, the call rate was reduced to zero in early 1999. Around the same time, Japan began to experience sustained periods of consumer price deflation. The BoJ then began adopting UMP. In April 1999, the BoJ committed to maintaining a zero-interest rate policy (ZIRP) 'until deflationary concerns are dispelled'. This was the first use of forward guidance. ZIRP was lifted in August 2000, only to be reintroduced in March 2001. The BoJ then adopted QE and increasing purchases of longer-term Japanese Government Bonds (JGBs) but it ended the QE program in March 2006 and began to downsize its balance sheet.

Harrigan and Kuttner (2004) conclude that deflation was anticipated around early 1993 and question why the BoJ did not further ease interest rates prior to 1995. Ahearne *et al.* (2002) suggest that deflation was not anticipated until as late as 1995. Given Japan's circumstances it is not surprising that the literature provides competing recommendations for the BoJ (see, inter alia, Ahearne *et al.*, 2002; Harrigan and Kuttner, 2004; Fujiwara *et al.*, 2007; Leigh, 2010). Counterfactual simulations suggest that more aggressive monetary policy in the early 1990s would not have avoided a deflationary slump, but setting a higher inflation target, combined with a stronger emphasis on output stabilization or following a price level targeting rule might have been successful at avoiding deflation and improving output.

The results from a variety of event studies suggest that ZIRP and QE may have been effective at decreasing expected future short-term interest rates and therefore yield curves (Bernanke *et al.*, 2004; Kuttner and Posen, 2004). Baba *et al.* (2005) find that ZIRP was effective at decreasing the expectation component of future short-term interest rates, but had little impact on risk premiums.

The foregoing only scratches the surface of studies that explore Japan's early experience with QE. Nevertheless, there is evidence that by becoming avant-garde in the use UMP the BoJ was able to at least cushion the blows from the bursting of the 1990s asset price bubble. Nevertheless, in a review of the BoJ's early efforts with UMP, Ueda (2012) concludes that entrenched deflationary expectations underpinned the failure to secure an economic recovery. By acting either too slowly or too cautiously, or a combination thereof, Japanese monetary policy failed to stifle the recession.

Perhaps for all of the foregoing reasons the BoJ did not immediately follow other large economies by implementing UMP once the GFC was underway in 2007–2008. Former BoJ Governor Shirakawa lamented that Japan had pioneered some forms of UMP but that these policies were unable to help the country's growth rate reach escape velocity (Shirakawa, 2012).[7] Still, the BoJ introduced a new program – comprehensive monetary easing (CME) – in October 2010. This program not only included purchases of long-term JGBs but also more risky assets such as exchange-traded funds and Japan real estate investment trusts, in an effort to reduce risk premiums. The CME program was found to be effective at reducing interest rate spreads and risk premiums, as well as raising equity prices, consumer and business confidence and corporate bond issuances. However, the policy was ineffective at influencing inflation expectations or foreign exchange rates (Lam, 2011; Ueda, 2012).

Shirakawa's successor, Governor Kuroda, launched Qualitative and Quantitative Easing (QQE) shortly after his appointment in April 2013. To date, there have been three phases of QQE: a determination to reach a 2% inflation target together with a massive expansion of the BoJ's balance sheet (see below); the breaching of the ZLB into negative short-term interest rate territory; and the on-going phase of pushing yields along the yield curve to zero through the aggressive purchases of JGBs, which had expanded the BoJ's balance sheet by an additional 55% of Japan's GDP as of the fourth quarter of 2016 (see Figure 1A). The BoJ's own assessment three years into the policy shift acknowledged its failure to shift inflation expectations to towards the 2% target (Bank of Japan, 2016). Gertler (2017) argues that presumptions about the effectiveness of FG under QQE cannot succeed as theory would predict because expectations are not rational. Nishino *et al.* (2016) show that inflation expectations in Japan are adaptive and highly sensitive to exogenous factors. They do not dismiss the importance of credibility altogether, but instead assume the BoJ has experienced a persistent negative credibility shock (see also De Michelis and Iacoviello, 2016). The current state of play may indeed reflect the erosion of BoJ credibility (Bordo and Siklos, 2016b) while Japan is said to have 'lost' two decades of potentially higher economic growth and inflation.[8]

3.3 *The GFC and Its Aftermath*

The United States first introduced an outright asset purchase program in November 2008, purchasing agency mortgage-backed securities and agency debt to help stabilise the housing market and the underlying financing structure. In March 2009, the program was extended to include Treasury securities; this program is referred to as the first Large-Scale Asset Program

(LSAP1), and asset purchases totalled around $1.75 trillion. The U.S. Fed later embarked on three other major balance sheet programs. The second (LSAP2) was announced in November 2010 and consisted of the purchase of $600 billion in longer-term U.S. treasuries with the objective of reducing their yields. The third, the Maturity Extension Program (MEP; also known as Operation Twist), was announced in September 2011. The MEP swapped the U.S. Fed's holdings of Treasuries with shorter residual maturities for Treasuries with longer maturities. The final program (LSAP3) had no *ex ante* determination of the duration or total size of asset purchases, with pre-announced monthly purchases of Treasuries and mortgage-backed securities. LSAP3 was announced in September 2012, and asset purchases ceased in October 2014.

Based on median estimates in the empirical literature, and unlike the BoJ's experience, LSAP1 had the largest impact. All in all, the literature on the Fed's experience with balance sheet policies suggests that there were diminishing returns to its asset purchases, largely owing to the important role of changing market expectations through the signalling channel (Ihrig *et al.*, 2012).[9] Similarly, the impact of LSAP2 was quite large, and there is some debate over whether purchasing non-treasury securities (specifically, mortgage-backed securities) is more effective at lowering yields because the purchase of scarce and/or distressed assets affects markets through additional channels (see Krishnamurthy and Vissing-Jorgensen, 2011, 2013).

In the United Kingdom, the Government established the Asset Purchase Facility in January 2009, providing a framework for the BoE to purchase assets, which the central bank began doing in March 2009. The first round of asset purchases (BQE1) occurred in 2009, and totalled $200 billion of mostly medium- and long-term gilts, but also included the purchase of some commercial paper and corporate bonds. The second round of purchases (BQE2) occurred in the background of the neighbouring euro area crisis from 2011 to 2012, and included an additional $175 billion of gilt purchases. Figure 2 suggests that the U.K.'s experience with QE appears to have been the most effective at reducing long-term yields. As is the case with the U.S. Fed's asset purchases, the effectiveness of the U.K.'s purchases exhibited diminishing returns. Evidence suggests that while the reduction in U.S. Treasury yields operated mainly through the signalling channel (i.e. changing market expectations about future short-term interest rates), the dominant channel in the U.K. was through portfolio rebalancing (Joyce *et al.*, 2011; Christensen and Rudebusch, 2012).

A few central banks in small open economies, such as the Swedish Riksbank and the Swiss National Bank, have also used balance sheet programs. The impact of asset purchases in these economies is believed to be smaller, in large part owing to their inability to affect global term premiums (Diez de los Rios and Shamloo, 2017). Central banks in small open economies may have limited influence on domestic term premiums (Kabaca, 2016).

There are a few important elements of these countries' UMP that are missing in some of the studies used to construct Figure 2, namely, a role for central bank communication. Hansen *et al.* (2014), Acosta and Meade (2015), Bennani (2015), Lombardi *et al.* (2017, forthcoming), Malmendier *et al.* (2017) and Meade *et al.* (2015) are examples of studies that apply different algorithms and techniques to quantify the content of central bank policy statements, minutes, speeches and other central bank written publications. These studies explore the impact of written communications on anything from inflation expectations to the stance of monetary policy more generally. All of these efforts are also at the core of the FG approach to policy.

In 2009, with the Bank of Canada's (BoC's) policy rate was near the ZLB, the BoC altered course by forcefully announcing in the April 2009 Monetary Policy Report that it would promise to leave the overnight rate at the ZLB for a year unless conditions warranted removing the promise. The BoC removed the promise and raised the policy rate in April 2010, one meeting before FG was due to expire. Although subsequent empirical investigations suggest that the removal of the conditional commitment by the BoC was successful (He, 2010; Siklos and Spence, 2010) based on financial markets' reactions, one must wonder whether the success may have been short-lived. It has been suggested that the success of the BoC's policy at changing market expectations is related to the fact that FG was used as an unorthodox policy, that is, communicating information the BoC typically does not provide, which may have made the conditional commitment more credible (He, 2010; Woodford, 2012). Indeed, the current Governor of the BoC, Stephen Poloz, came to believe that FG should only be used in crisis conditions (Poloz, 2015).

The United States was also quick to add FG to its arsenal of UMPs in the aftermath of the GFC. The Fed is the only major central bank to use qualitative, calendar-based and state-contingent FG in the aftermath of the GFC, thus making it a good case for comparative analysis.[10] The use of date-based guidance was found to significantly reduce the volatility of interest rate expectations and may have changed expectations about the U.S. Fed's policy reaction function (Campbell *et al.*, 2017; Raskin, 2013).

Not all scholars are convinced about the effectiveness of FG beyond the near-term (e.g. Kool and Thornton, 2012; Filardo and Hofmann, 2014). Moessner *et al.* (2017) suggest that central banks do not make commitments of the kind that is discussed in theory. Precisely because of the conditionality of the language used by central banks, there have been concerns that UMP may impair any hard-won credibility that central banks had prior to the GFC. For example, event studies do not consider the extent to which there was any loss of trust or credibility in central banks in the lead up to these policy announcements.

3.4 *Is Europe Different?*

The answer is both yes and no. The succession of programs that began in October 2008 with the fixed-rate full allotment, long-term financing operation (LTRO), followed by the purchases of debt securities held by banks (covered bond purchases or CBPP) in 2009, were akin to the operations to ease liquidity that other central banks also introduced around that time. Of course, the details of these programs reflected some of the specific financial problems that some individual euro-area member states faced after 2008.

As the Eurozone crisis unfolded, the ECB adopted government bond purchase programs. The first of these programs – the Securities Markets Program (SMP) – was announced in 2010. Purchases under this programme were aimed at reducing high risk premiums. The ECB's second government bond purchase program – the Outright Monetary Transactions (OMT) program – introduced in the third quarter of 2012 – had similar technical features. It was not until January 2015 that the ECB adopted a QE program which included outright purchases of government bonds across euro-area member states, and debt instruments issued by international or supranational institutions located in the euro area.

The ECB initially referred to these undertakings as 'non-standard' policies (Coeuré, 2013) although, by 2014, the expression 'unconventional' was more widely used. The strictures imposed by the Maastricht Treaty, at least in principle, forbade a bailout of individual member governments via monetary policy actions. This meant that the ECB had to be scrupulous in not favouring some euro-area member states over others even if the effects of the sovereign debt crisis were clearly asymmetric across different countries in the single currency area.

Unsurprisingly then, the events since 2008 created a heated debate over how much intervention the ECB was permitted and whether it amounted to favouring some member states over others (e.g. Sinn, 2014).

Although the ECB's UMP actions were criticized as being 'too little, too late' (see Wyplosz, 2011; Kang *et al.*, 2016), the evidence shows that the ECB's policies were just as effective at lowering long-term yields and more effective at lowering short-term yields than the policies implemented in the U.S. and the U.K. (see Figure 2). An important caveat is that the ECB's first two government bond purchase programs were aimed at reducing risk premiums in countries under stress (Altavilla *et al.*, 2016; Fratzscher *et al.*, 2018). Indeed, the SMP and OMT were effective in reducing spreads among euro area member countries (Wafte, 2015), while the PSPP appears to have been effective in reducing yields across the euro area (De Santis and Holm-Hadulla, 2017).

Similar delays in policy action were observed in the ECB's use of communication as a policy tool: FG was first introduced in July 2013. The ECB proceeded cautiously by using qualitative guidance. The purpose was to better align financial markets, specifically money market rates, with the ECB's policy stance. It has been deemed successful both at aligning market expectations with the Governing Council's policy intentions and at reducing market uncertainty in short-term rates (European Central Bank, 2014).

Generally, it appears that Europe took a slightly different approach to implementing UMP than other major AEs. In particular, the timeline differed from the actions of the U.S. and U.K., which were mainly in response to the GFC. However, legal restrictions in future might hamper the ECB's ability to do 'whatever it takes' in the event of a future crisis.[11]

3.5 *International Spillovers from UMP*

The impact of UMPs introduced by major AEs on exchange rates and exchange rate volatility was particularly controversial. It seems difficult to ignore the cross-border effects of UMP on economies that needed to react to shocks emanating from AEs in crisis. Textbook descriptions presume that flexible exchange rates insulate an economy from external shocks. However, even before the GFC doubts were raised about this conclusion, because de facto regimes seemed at variance from the stated exchange rate regimes (Cook and Devereux, 2016). Moreover, the predicted effects of exchange rates on the trade of goods and services differed from the impact on financial flows (Ilzetzki *et al.*, 2017).

Overall, however, the evidence linking QE and UMP to exchange rates is far from conclusive (see Gagnon *et al.*, 2017). Figure 3 shows the range of estimates in the literature on the impact of spillovers from QE to exchange rates and sovereign bond yields. Both positive (appreciation) and negative (depreciation) effects on the exchange rates of domestic currencies in EMEs have been identified. The evidence suggests that the Fed's so-called 'taper tantrum' in the second and third quarters of 2013 caused a depreciation in the currencies of EMEs (Mishra *et al.*, 2014; Eichengreen and Gupta, 2015; Aizenman *et al.*, 2016). In contrast, as also shown in Figure 3, the impact on sovereign bond yields was relatively more consistent in that UMP in AEs lowered yields in EMEs.

The success of QE appears to have put a floor under a potential economic collapse in AEs, and likely did not hurt EMEs. Nevertheless, the literature is unable to reach a firm conclusion that QE actually harmed EMEs in particular. As Bayoumi *et al.* (2017) point out, the arithmetic of adding up the global costs and benefits of UMP remains a work in progress.

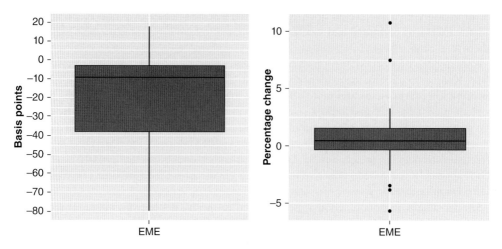

Figure 3. Summary of selected empirical studies: Spillovers of UMP on EMEs. (a) Long-term sovereign bond yields. (b) Exchange rates.

Note: NForex = 25; *N* Long-term yields = 24. Impact on government bonds expressed in basis points, and impact on foreign exchange rates is expressed as percentage change with a positive value referring to a domestic currency appreciation against the benchmark currency (mainly U.S. dollar). Studies include Chen *et al.* (2013), Chua *et al.* (2013), Aizenman *et al.* (2016), Falagiarda *et al.* (2015), Fic (2013), Fratzscher *et al.* (2016; 2018). [Color figure can be viewed at wileyonlinelibrary.com]

4. The International Evidence to Date: Macro-Economic Effects

4.1 *Can UMP Have Real Economic Effects?*

Many tests of the impact of QE on real economic outcomes rely on some variant of a vector autoregressive (VAR) model, which we will evaluate in this section. Another approach is to use cross-sectional studies that rely on microeconomic data (e.g. lending by banks) to investigate the real effects of UMP (Bowman *et al.*, 2015; Acharya *et al.*, 2017). Alternatively, various macro-economic models may be used, such as Real Business Cycle variants (Farmer, 2012) or dynamic stochastic general equilibrium (DSGE) models (discussed in Section 4.2).

Empirical applications of a VAR model generally ask whether and how monetary policy shocks in the period since the GFC have changed, or whether the introduction of UMP has changed any of the relationships under investigation (see Weale and Wieladek, 2016). Other studies consider how macro-economic variables such as real GDP growth and inflation responded to QE-like shocks (Bridges and Thomas, 2012; Altavilla *et al.*, 2016). These shocks are often considered to be one-time occurrences and are assumed to exert only transitory effects on the macro-economy. In any case, the investigator must take a stand not only on the exogeneity of UMP-style interventions, but also concerning the restrictions needed to identify the structural parameters of interest.

Neely (2014) concludes that the likelihood of parameter instability over any sample that includes the GFC implies serious reservations about the reliability of estimates based on these kinds of econometric models. Unfortunately, no clear alternative is provided.[12] Until the relevant econometric lacunae are overcome, if a cross-section of models and estimates that rely on different identification techniques points in the same direction concerning the impact of UMP then we can have some confidence about the macro-economic impact of QE.

The empirical evidence to date suggests that UMPs have real economic effects, but that these are limited in size and occur with a significant lag. Monetary policy shocks in the form of QE are found to increase real GDP growth and inflation in the U.S. and U.K.; with the peak impact estimated to occur between two and six years after these central banks first introduced UMPs (Bridges and Thomas, 2012; Engen *et al.*, 2015). In the euro area, targeted government bond buying programs during the sovereign debt crisis increased credit and economic growth in the countries under stress (Altavilla *et al.*, 2016).

An illustration of the VAR approach to examining the effects of QE is Haldane *et al.* (2016). Eschewing the use of dummy variables to identify QE episodes, they rely instead on the size of a central bank's balance sheet (as a per cent of GDP). Haldane *et al.* (2016) find that QE effects are state dependent but that spillovers across AEs are relatively strong; see Ball *et al.* (2016), Haldane *et al.* (2016) and Weale and Wieladek (2016) for references to several other studies of this kind. While most VAR models are for single economies, some of the VARs are of the global variety wherein VARs for individual economies are 'stacked' to create a global VAR (GVAR).[13] Chen *et al.* (2017) is an example that combines data from AEs and EMEs to investigate the global impact of QE. Spillover effects can then readily be estimated from such models. The authors conclude that U.S.-style QE had the largest impact, while the adverse spillover effects on EMEs claimed by some policymakers are exaggerated.

Since there is considerable scepticism about the macro-economic effects of QE it is worth further exploring the potential impact of UMP style policies. To illustrate, we focus exclusively on the US experience. Suppose that we can summarize the sources of real shocks to the economy by a vector of variables that includes inflation (we use the personal consumption expenditures (PCE) deflator), forecasts of inflation and real GDP growth, real GDP growth, the unemployment rate and oil price inflation. We then reduce the dimensionality of the problem of evaluating the effects of UMP by estimating the first principal component of these variables. The resulting scores, essentially a linear combination of the variables described above, define the evolution of the real economy in the United States.[14]

The same logic is used to define a monetary policy factor and a financial factor. The former consists of foreign exchange reserves, changes in the Fed funds rate and the growth in the money supply. We also estimate separately a version that includes the size of the Fed's balance sheet as a per cent of GDP. Finally, the vector that is used to generate scores that define the evolution of financial conditions in the economy includes: credit growth, the return on the Wilshire 5000 stock market index, the VIX, the three-month Treasury bill yield and the yield on 10-year Treasuries, and growth in housing prices.

Figure 4 shows partial results from the estimation of a VAR model that consists of real, monetary and financial factors.[15] We then apply a shock to the monetary factor equivalent to one standard deviation to identify how the real and financial factors respond. In estimating these relationships we consider three variants. The top set of impulse responses is for estimates that end in 2006Q4, that is, before the onset of the GFC. The next two sets are for the full sample that ends in 2016Q4. The difference between the two estimates is that the bottom set of impulse responses incorporates UMP effects (primarily QE) into the monetary factor while the middle set of impulse responses does not.

Two conclusions emerge from the set of impulse responses. First, monetary shocks do not appear to have exerted any real effects either before or after the crisis, whether or not we include the UMP proxy. All the reasons noted previously apply. However, perhaps most importantly, the monetary factor can also have prevented a fall in the real factor while monetary policy was, as theory would suggest, largely neutral in real economic terms during the Great Moderation.

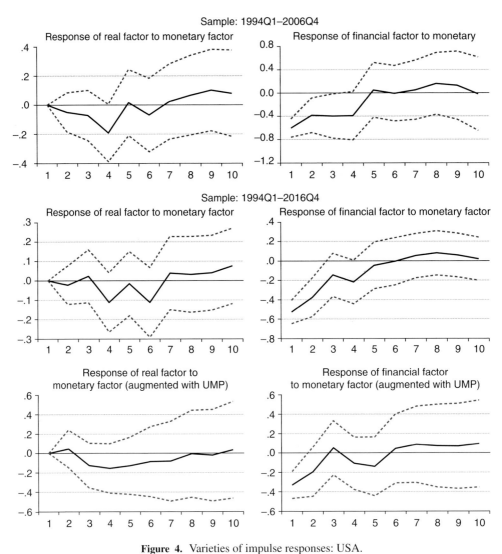

Figure 4. Varieties of impulse responses: USA.
Note: A vector autoregression of order 2 is estimated for the samples shown above. The VAR consists of a real factor, a financial factor and a monetary factor, in that order. Confidence intervals are estimated via bootstrapping (1000 replications). [Color figure can be viewed at wileyonlinelibrary.com]

Turning to the financial factor we observe, as noted above, that an improvement or loosening of financial conditions is associated with a loosening of monetary policy. While the impulse responses become insignificant after three quarters for the pre-crisis sample, the effect disappears after two quarters when the monetary factor excludes the central bank assets to GDP ratio and only after one quarter when the UMP proxy is incorporated. Therefore, QE may have helped to improve financial conditions, but the impact deteriorated over time. This result broadly parallels some of the findings discussed earlier about the size and duration of QE effects using data sampled at a much higher frequency.

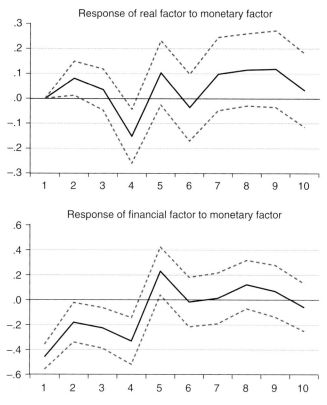

Figure 5. Counterfactual experiment: What if the crisis never happened?
Note: See the notes to Figure 4 for estimation details. The counterfactuals are described in the main body of the paper. [Color figure can be viewed at wileyonlinelibrary.com]

Finally, Figure 5 considers a counterfactual. Suppose that the economy evolved as if the estimates of the VAR until the end of 2006Q4 remained unchanged until the end of the available sample (2016Q4). How would real and financial factors respond to a monetary shock? We observe that a positive monetary shock produces a small but statistically significant temporary boost to real activity that lasts two quarters and partly reversed after the fourth quarter. The improvement or loosening of financial conditions reported earlier remains as in the pre-crisis sample shown in Figure 5, although the effect persists for a little longer (four quarters). Once again, it appears that the policy interventions undertaken after 2008 may have prevented a decline in real activity but did not provide the boost that some expected.

4.2 *DSGE Alternative*

An alternative to the estimation of VAR-like models is estimation using DSGE models that are widely used by many central banks. They have been criticized because they used to ignore a role for the financial system and were based on stringent assumptions about the rationality of inflation expectations, among other issues.[16]

The strength of DSGE models lies in their ability to provide a coherent explanation for what might happen under certain economic conditions when the channels through which monetary policy is thought to operate are clearly spelled out. Their weakness is that such models typically fail to explain macro-economic facts very well. This is partly due to the technical difficulties that DSGE models face when the ELB is breached. However, each failure with such models spurs a search for improvements, and critics of the DSGE methodology often do not fully appreciate the progress made in less than a decade (Binder *et al.*, forthcoming). Jones (2015), for example, overcomes DSGE model difficulties in the presence of the ZLB by treating the economy as subject to a sequence of contractionary shocks that can ostensibly be overcome with FG. On this basis, FG does produce benefits for output and inflation that otherwise would not have been observed. This is only one of many other examples that have led to improvements in DSGE models' ability to explain macro-economic facts. Nevertheless, there is the risk that such models become too complex; the experience of large scale models of a few decades ago that were eventually discarded as 'incredible', led to a new generation of more compact and econometrically sensible econometric models – a reminder of how a once promising research agenda can be transformed.[17]

4.3 *Central Bank Credibility and Inflation Expectations*

An important consideration is whether central bank credibility has taken a hit since the GFC. Bordo and Siklos (2016ba, 2016ab) have noted that there is no consensus on how to measure central bank credibility. Nevertheless, there is an expectation that actual inflation performance ought to be closely associated with a broad set of inflation expectations. Bordo and Siklos (2016b), relying on a large panel of countries, conclude that central bank credibility was adversely affected by the GFC. However, monetary authorities with strong institutional features (e.g. countries with an inflation target, central banks with greater transparency and autonomy) fared much better.

Other studies that focus on particular events or economies have reached somewhat different conclusions. Moessner (2014) does not find that the ECB's credibility changed by the events of recent years. Raynard (2012) indicates that if QE is supposed to raise inflation expectations, in part to avoid a deflationary outcome, the data suggest that the GFC has not changed the relationship between money growth and inflation. Campbell *et al.* (2012) highlight a role for FG in influencing inflation expectations and conclude that private sector forecasters did respond to central bank communication policies.

Monetary policy rules also play an important role in Engen *et al.*'s (2015) study that examines U.S. Blue Chip forecasts. While the Fed's FOMC was found to successfully influence inflation expectations, the continued delay in the economic recovery tempered the potential real economic impact of QE. Whether this outcome can be linked to Orphanides' (2015) claim that the Fed 'procrastinated' when it reversed course away from continuing to implement an ultra-loose monetary policy is unclear.

5. Conclusions: Lessons Learned, the Exit and the 'New Normal'

The body of evidence that seeks to measure the economic and financial repercussions of the GFC has accumulated very quickly. There is already considerable evidence that UMPs can be powerful tools to blunt the negative economic effects of a financial crisis. Financial crises come in different forms; if their impact and origins are heterogeneous (Bordo and Haubrich, 2017; Romer and Romer, 2017), so too must be the policy responses.

Some policymakers have a tendency to insist on a 'never again' attitude towards financial crises; but this approach is unrealistic. Perhaps we should instead borrow from the Dutch, most of whom live at or below sea level and face infrequent but potentially devastating floods they have chosen to live *with* water, not to fight it. In other words, we should abandon the thought that we can prevent all manner of financial crises and learn instead to live with smaller crises – a common occurrence in history as Reinhart and Rogoff (2009) have clearly demonstrated – while seeking to avoid crises of the kind that produced the Great Depression or the Great Recession of 2008–2009.

The events that began in 2007 also teach us that any successful monetary policy response should be forceful (see also Geithner, 2016), that a joint response from both the fiscal and monetary authorities is essential, and that the policy response should be persistent until confidence and the conditions for full recovery are in place. Moreover, depending on the size and the spread of the financial crisis, a premium ought to be placed on a mechanism that allows for a rapid and at least cooperative, if not coordinated, international response.

It remains in the realm of a counterfactual to ask whether a faster and more aggressive easing of policy might have restored confidence more quickly. Even more intriguing is whether this kind of approach might have made the exit back to normal conditions less time-consuming and difficult. Clearly, complicating the exit is not the technical element in removing policy accommodation. Instead, it is how the accumulated loss of credibility and trust in central banks may have affected public uncertainty and scepticism about whether economic activity has returned to normal. UMP has demonstrated that it can reduce the economic costs of a financial crisis. However, the monetary authorities have been reluctant to claim that it can restore growth to pre-crisis conditions unless other policies, in the realm of fiscal and structural policies, are also enacted. As a result, they are caught in a trap where their policies may actually contribute to delaying a return to more normal conditions. The fact that some central banks are beginning to reverse course on policy rates in spite of inflation rates that remain below target may well be an indication that they are aware of the dilemma they face.

Finally, it is worth asking, if the old normal is not in our future, whether the new normal in monetary policy should routinely include the panoply of instruments and interventions that make up what are now referred to as UMP? To the extent that the wide variety of interventions is a product of past failures and greatly complicates the task of monetary policy, the answer should be in the negative. Using a wide range of instruments that can prevent economic collapse, but are not designed to promote adequate economic growth, does not appear to be a sound monetary policy strategy. Far better to utilize new communication devices together with standard monetary policies to deliver not just low and stable inflation but to do so in a credible fashion. This might also prevent future policy makers from asking – or expecting – too much from their central banks.

Acknowledgements

This is a CIGI-sponsored research project. The opinions in the paper are those of the authors and not the institutions that supported this research. Domenico Lombardi was Director of the Global Economy program at CIGI when the paper was written, Samantha St. Amand is Senior Research Associate and Pierre Siklos is a CIGI Senior Fellow, and Professor of Economics at Wilfrid Laurier University and the Balsillie School of International Affairs. Dylan Clarke provided excellent research assistance. Comments by the Editor and an anonymous referee are gratefully acknowledged. A longer version of the paper is available, together with an appendix that includes material omitted due to space limitations.

Notes

1. Belongia and Ireland (2017) remind us that reverting to alternative monetary rules – for example, targeting the monetary base or monetary aggregates, as opposed to an interest rate rule – avoids the zero bound and, in principle, can be more effective at stabilizing nominal income than negative interest rates. Other studies in this monetarist vein also support the view that monetary policy around this time helped cushioned the blow from the GFC (e.g. Beckworth, 2017; Congdon, 2010; Hetzel, 2009; Sumner, 2011).

2. There is no unique definition of a financial crisis but the ones adopted by Reinhart and Rogoff (2009) are arguably the best known. Our interpretation on data from Bordo and Landon Lane (2013), who build on the earlier work of Bordo *et al.* (2001) and Laeven and Valencia (2012). There is disagreement about the incidence of financial crises (see Bordo and Meissner, 2016). The latest addition is due to Romer and Romer (2017). Their chronology for AEs also departs from the one proposed by Reinhart and Rogoff (2009).

3. This would be unconventional for the AEs but not all EMEs. Nevertheless, since the GFC, not even the EMEs have changed their inflation targets.

4. Paralleling this development is the suggestion that, except for small denominations, cash should be removed altogether especially in AE. See, for example, Rogoff (2016b).

5. There may also be a problem with identifying the timing of certain events. Should one date the event when an intention to do something is announced as opposed to when the action is taken? For example, Draghi's 'whatever it takes' pronouncement in London in July 2012 caused a major market reaction, but the actual OMT policy details were announced September 6th.

6. The Japanese example has come to be called a case of a balance sheet recession (Koo, 2015).

7. The term 'escape velocity' was coined by BoE Governor Mark Carney (2014) and refers to 'the momentum necessary for an economy to escape from the many headwinds following a financial crisis'.

8. After factoring in demographic factors, Borio *et al.* (2015, Box 2) argue that only the 1990s can be characterized as a lost decade, as growth in GDP per capita exceeded that of the U.S. after 2000.

9. Of course, as elaborated by Haldane *et al.* (2016), asset purchases are likely to have a larger effect during times of market turmoil; a feature we also observe for the euro area's experience to be discussed below.

10. The BoJ used a combination of calendar-based and state-contingent FG as part of its QQE program; but the discussion in Section 3.2 shows why it may not be the best case for analysing the effectiveness of FG.

11. The ECB may not be the only central bank that suffers from a potential loss of flexibility in a future crisis. The Dodd-Frank reforms of 2010 also placed new limits on the Fed. Geithner (2016) argues that a future crisis will reduce the margin of the Fed to ease financial conditions in the manner it did in 2008 and 2009.

12. A referee suggested that a time-varying estimation approach is preferable. This is undoubtedly true. However, time-varying VARs of various kinds (whether of the Bayesian variety or not) are unlikely to be conclusive at this point because existing sample spans provide a limited number of time-varying coefficients that can be estimated with reasonable precision especially when quarterly data are employed.

13. Chudik and Pesaran (2016) is a recent survey of the GVAR technique. This modelling approach consists in attempting to estimate a model for N economies in the VAR framework for the express purpose of recognizing that macro-economic linkages exist between the countries in a dataset. It is ideally suited to explore questions of financial integration and cross-country spillover effects. Nevertheless, since the technique requires a large number of restrictions GVARs can be difficult to estimate and the identification of some shocks may not always have a readily available economic interpretation. Another alternative is the panel VAR approach.

14. Statistical testing (not shown) reveals that the first principal component accounts for the overwhelming proportion of the total variation across the estimated principal components.

15. Six lags are specified based on several lag selection criteria. The results are largely unaffected if we reverse the order of the monetary and financial factors.

16. Among the most prominent critics are Buiter (2009), and Krugman (2016), though the criticisms are often levelled at earlier generations of such models. A more recent critique by Romer (2016) raises broader criticisms of central bank modelling strategies. In all of these cases, there is insufficient recognition that judgement still plays a dominant role in central bank decision-making (Siklos, 2017). Some of the criticisms of this approach, especially the difficulty of modelling heterogeneity across firms, financial institutions and individuals, does continue to have some resonance.

17. Blanchard (2016) also offers a sharp critique of DSGE modelling while defending its usefulness. Interestingly, given the importance central banks place on communication, one of his chief concerns is how such models fail in this regard.

References

Acharya, V.V., Eisert, T., Eufinger, C. and Hirsch, C. (2017) Whatever it takes: The real effects of unconventional monetary policy. Sustainable Architecture for Finance in Europe Working Paper 152.

Acosta, M. and Meade, E. (2015) Hanging on every word: Semantic analysis of the FOMC's postmeeting statement. Board of Governors of the Federal Reserve System, FEDS Notes, 30 September.

Ahearne, A., Gagnon, J., Haltmaier, J. and Kamin, S. (2002) Preventing deflation: Lessons from Japan's experience in the 1990s. Board of Governors of the Federal Reserve System, International Finance Discussion Papers No. 729.

Aït-Sahalia, Y., Andritzky, J., Jobst, A., Nowak, S. and Tamirisa, N. (2012) Market response to policy initiatives during the global financial crisis. *Journal of International Economics* 87(1): 162–177.

Aizenman, J., Binici, M., and Hutchison, M.M. (2016) The transmission of federal reserve tapering news to emerging financial markets. *International Journal of Central Banking* 12(2): 317–356.

Altavilla, C., Giannone, D. and Lenza, M. (2016) The financial and macroeconomic effects of the OMT announcements. *International Journal of Central Banking* 12(3): 29–57.

Andrade, P., Breckenfelder, J., De Fiore, F., Karadi, P. and Tristani, O. (2016) The ECB's asset purchase programme: An early assessment. ECB Working Paper Series 1956.

Baba, N., Nishioka, S., Oda, N., Shirakawa, M., Ueda, K. and Ugai, H (2005) Japan's deflation, problems in the financial system, and monetary policy. Bank of Japan's Institute for Monetary and Economic Studies No. 47–112.

Ball, L., Joseph Gagnon, J., Honohan, P., and Krogstrup, S. (2016) What else can central banks do? *Geneva Reports on the World Economy* 18. London: CEPR Press.

Bank of Japan. (2016) *Comprehensive Assessment: Developments in Economic Activity and Prices as well as Policy Effects since the Introduction of Quantitative and Qualitative Monetary Easing (QQE): The Background*. Tokyo: Bank of Japan.

Bastidon, C., Huchet, N. and Kocoglu, Y. (2016) Unconventional monetary policy in the eurozone: A lack of forward guidance? *Emerging Markets Finance & Trade* 52(1): 76–97.

Bauer, M.D. and Rudebusch, G.D. (2014) The signaling channel for federal reserve bond purchases. *International Journal of Central Banking* 10(3): 233–289.

Bayoumi, T., Gagnon, J., Londono-Yarce, J.M. and Saborowski, C. (2017) Direct and spillover effects of unconventional monetary and exchange rate policies. *Open Economies Review* 28(2): 191–232.

Beckworth, D. (2017) Permanent versus temporary monetary base injections: Implications for past and future fed policy. *Journal of Macroeconomics* 54A: 1–48.

Belongia, M.T. and Ireland, P.N. (2017) Circumventing the zero lower bound with monetary policy rules based on money. *Journal of Macroeconomics*, 54: 42–58.

Bennani, H. (2015) The art of Central Banks' forward guidance at the zero lower bound. Working Paper, 25 June.

Bernanke, B.S. (2017) Monetary policy in a new era. Prepared for Rethinking Macroeconomic Poliy, Peterson Institute for International Economic, Washington, D.C., October.

Bernanke, B.S., Reinhart, V.R. and Sack, B.P. (2004) Monetary policy alternatives at the zero bound: An empirical assessment. *Brookings Papers on Economic Activity* 2: 1–100.

Bhattarai, S. and Neely, C. (2016) A survey of the empirical literature on U.S. unconventional monetary policy. Federal Reserve Bank of St. Louis Working Papers 2016–21.

Binder, M., Lieberknecht, P., Quintana, J. and Wieland, V. (forthcoming) Model uncertainty in macroeconomics: On the implications of financial frictions. In D. Mayes, P. L. Siklos and J.E. Sturm (eds.), *Handbook of Central Banking*. Oxford: Oxford University Press.

Blanchard, O. (2016) Do DSGE models have a future? PIIE Policy Brief August.

Blanchard, O., Dell'Ariccia, G. and Mauro, P. (2010) Rethinking macroeconomic policy. IMF Staff Position Note 10/03.

Bordo, M., Eichengreen, B., Klingebiel, D. and Martinez-Peria, M.S. (2001) Is the crisis problem growing more severe? *Economic Policy: A European Forum* 32: 51–75.

Bordo, M.D. and Haubrich, J.G. (2017) Deep recession, fast recoveries, and financial crisis: Evidence from the American record. *Economic Inquiry* 55(1): 527–541.

Bordo, M.D. and Landon-Lane, J. (2013) Does expansionary monetary policy cause asset price booms: Some historical and empirical evidence. NBER Working Paper No. 19585.

Bordo, M.D. and Meissner, C.M. (2016) Fiscal and financial crises. NBER Working Paper No. 22059.

Bordo, M.D. and Siklos, P.L. (2016a) Central Bank credibility: An historical and quantitative exploration. NBER Working Paper No. 20824.

Bordo, M.D. and Siklos, P.L. (2016b) Central Bank credibility before and after the crisis. NBER Working Paper No. 21710.

Borio, C. and Disyatat, P. (2010) Unconventional monetary policies: An appraisal. *The Manchester School* 78(s1): 53–89.

Borio, C., Erdem, M., Filardo, A. and Hofmann, B. (2015) The costs of deflations: A historical perspective. *BIS Quarterly Review*, March.

Borio, C. and Zabai, A. (2016) Unconventional monetary policies: A re-appraisal. BIS Working Paper No. 570.

Bowman, D., Cai, F., Davies, S. and Kamin, S. (2015) Quantitative easing and bank lending: Evidence from Japan. *Journal of International Money and Finance* 54: 15–30.

Breedon, F., Chadha, J.S. and Waters, A. (2012) The financial market impact of UK quantitative easing. BIS Papers No. 65.

Bridges, J. and Thomas, R. (2012) The impact of QE on the UK economy — Some supportive monetarist arithmetic. Bank of England Working Paper No. 442.

Buiter, W.H. (2009) The unfortunate uselessness of most 'state of the art' academic monetary economics. MPRA Paper No. 58407.

Buiter, W.H. (2014) The simple analytics of helicopter money: Why it works – Always. Kiel Institute for the Worl Economy, Economics Discussion Papers No. 2014–24.

Burke, C., Hilton, S., Judson, R., Lewis, K. and Skeie, D. (2010) *Reducing the IOER Rate: An Analysis of Options*. Washington, DC: Federal Reserve Board of Governors.

Caglar, E., Chadha, J.S., Meaning, J., Warren, J. and Waters, A. (2011) Non-conventional monetary policies: QE and the DSGE literature. In J.S. Chadha and S. Holly (eds.), *Interest Rates, Prices and Liquidity: Lessons from the Financial Crisis* (pp. 240–273). Cambridge: Cambridge University Press.

Camera, G. (2017) A perspective on electronic alternatives to traditional currencies. *SverigesRiksbank Economic Review* 1: 126–148.

Campbell, J.R., Evans, C.L., Fisher, J.D.M. and Justiniano, A. (2012) Macroeconomic Effects of Federal Reserve Forward Guidance. *Brookings Paper on Economic Activity* Spring: 1–80.

Campbell, J.R., Fisher, J.D., Justiniano, A. and Melosi, L. (2017) Forward guidance and macroeconomic outcomes since the financial crisis. In M. Eichenbaum and J.A. Parker (eds.), *NBER Macroeconomics Annual 2016*, Vol. 31 (pp. 283–357). Chicago: University of Chicago Press.

Carney, M. (2014) Remarks delivered at Davos CBI British Business Leaders Lunch, Davos, 24 January.

Charbonneau, K. and Rennison, L. (2015) Forward guidance at the effective lower bound: International experience. Bank of Canada Staff Discussion Paper No. 2015-15.

Chen, J., Mancini-Griffoli, T. and Sahay, R. (2014) Spillover from United States monetary policy on emerging markets: Different this time? IMF Working Paper No. 14/240.

Chen, Q., Filardo, A., He, D. and Zhu, F. (2013) International spillovers of central bank balance sheet policies – An update. Paper prepared for the 2013 Bank of Canada Annual Conference "International Macroeconomic Policy Cooperation: Challenges and Prospects", Ottawa, 4 November.

Chen, Q., Lombardi, M., Ross, A. and Zhu, F. (2017) Global impact of US and euro area unconventional monetary policies: a comparison. BIS Working Paper No. 610.

Christensen, J.H.E. and Rudebusch, G.D. (2012) The response of interest rates to US and UK quantitative easing. *Economic Journal* 122(564): 385–414.

Chua, W.S., Endut, N., Khadri, N. and Sim, W.H. (2013) Global monetary easing: Spillovers and lines of defence. Bank Negara Malaysia Working Paper Series No. WP3/2013.

Chudik, A. and Pesaran, M.H. (2016) Theory and practice of GVAR modelling. *Journal of Economic Surveys* 30(1): 165–197.

Chung, H., Laforte, J.-P., Reifschneider, D. and Williams, J.C. (2012) Have we underestimated the likelihood and severity of zero lower bound events. *Journal of Money, Credit and Banking* 44(1): 47–82.

Churm, R., Joyce, M., Kapetanios, G. and Theodoridis, K. (2015) Unconventional monetary policies and the macroeconomy: The impact of the United Kingdom's QE2 and Funding for Lending Scheme. Bank of England Staff Working Paper No. 542.

Coeuré, B. (2013) Nonstandard monetary policy measures: where do we stand? Speech presented at the International Monetary Seminar "Sovereign Risk, Bank Risk and Central Banking", Banque de France, Paris, 10 July 2013.

Cohen-Setton, J. (2015) Permanent QE and helicopter money. Bruegel Blog, 5 January. Electronic copy available at: http://bruegel.org/2015/01/permanent-qe-and-helicopter-money/.

Congdon, T. (2010) Monetary policy at the zero bound. *World Economics* 11: 11–48.

Cook, D. and Devereaux, M.B. (2016) Exchange rate flexibility under the zero lower bound. *Journal of International Economics* 101: 52–69.

D'Amico, S. and King, T.B. (2013) Flow and stock effects of large-scale treasury purchases: Evidence on the importance of local supply. *Journal of Financial Economics* 108(2): 425–448.

De Michelis, A. and Iacoviello, M. (2016) Raising an inflation target: The Japanese experience with Abenomics. *European Economic Review* 88: 67–87.

De Santis, R.A. and Holm-Hadulla, F. (2017) Flow effects of central bank asset purchases on euro area sovereign bond yields: Evidence from a natural experiment. European Central Bank Working Paper Series No. 2052.

Diez de los Rios, A and Shamloo, M. (2017) Quantitative easing and long-term yields in small open economies. IMF Working Paper No. 17/212.

Edison, H.J., Klein, M., Ricci, L. and Sløk, T. (2004) Capital account liberalization and economic performance: Survey and synthesis. *IMF Staff Papers No.* 51: 220–256.

Eichengreen, B. and Gupta, P. (2015) Tapering talk: The impact of expectations of reduced Federal Reserve security purchases on emerging markets. *Emerging Market Review* 25: 1–15.

Engen, E.M., Laubach, T.T. and Reifschneider, D. (2015) The macroeconomic effects of the Federal Reserve's unconventional monetary policies. Board of Governors of the Federal Reserve System, Finance and Economics Discussion Series No. 2015-005.

Engert, W. and Fung, B.S.C. (2017) Central Bank digital currency: Motivations and implications. Bank of Canada Staff Discussion Paper No. 2017-16.

Eser, F. and Schwaab, B. (2016) Evaluating the impact of unconventional monetary policy measures: Empirical evidence from the ECB's Securities Markets Programme. *Journal of Financial Economics* 119(1): 14–67.

European Central Bank. (2014) The ECB's forward guidance. ECB Monthly Bulletin, April (pp. 65–73).

European Central Bank. (2015) The transmission of the ECB's recent non-standard monetary policy measures. ECB Economic Bulletin No. 7/2015 (pp. 32–51).

Farmer, R.E.A. (2012) The effect of conventional and unconventional monetary policy rules on inflation expectations: Theory and evidence. NBER Working Paper Series No. 18007.

Fic, T. (2013) The spillover effects of unconventional monetary policies in major developed countries on developing countries. DESA Working Paper No. 131.

Filardo, A. and Hofmann, B. (2014) Forward guidance at the zero lower bound. *BIS Quarterly Review* (March): 37–53.

Filardo, A. and Siklos, P. (2018) The cross-border credit channel and lending standards surveys. BIS Working Paper No. 723, May.

Fratzscher, M., Lo Duca, M. and Straub, R. (2016) ECB unconventional monetary policy: Market impact and international spillovers. *IMF Economic Review* 64(1): 36–74.

Fratzscher, M., Lo Duca, M. and Straub, R. (2018) On the international spillovers of US quantitative easing. *The Economic Journal* 128(608): 330–377.

Friedman, M. (1969) *The Optimum Quantity of Money.* London: Macmillan.

Fujiwara, I., Hara, N., Hirakata, N., Kimura, T. and Watanabe, S. (2007) Japanese monetary policy during the collapse of the bubble economy: A view of policymaking under uncertainty. Bank of Japan's Institute for Monetary and Economic Studies No. 89–128.

Fukunaga, I., Kato, N. and Koeda, J. (2015) Maturity structure and supply factors in Japanese Government Bond Markets. Bank of Japan's Institute for Monetary and Economic Studies No. 45–96.

Gagnon, J. (2016) Quantitative easing: An underappreciated success. PIIE Policy Brief No.16-4.

Gagnon, J.E., Bayoumi, T., Londono, J.M., Saborowski, C. and Spariza, H. (2017) Unconventional monetary and exchange rate policies. Board of Governors of the Federal Reserve System, International Finance Discussion Papers No. 1194.

Gagnon, J.M.R., Remache, J. and Sack, B. (2011) The financial market effects of the Federal Reserve's large-scale asset purchases. *International Journal of Central Banking* 7(1): 3–43.

Geithner, T. (2016) Are we safer? The case for strengthening the Bagehot Arsenal. Per Jacobsson Lecture delivered at Annual Meeting of the International Monetary Fund and World Bank Group, Washington, D.C., 8 October.

Gertler, M. (2017) Rethinking the power of forward guidance: Lessons from Japan. NBER Working Paper No. 23707.

Gros, D., Alcidi, C. and De Groen, W.P. (2015) Lessons from quantitative easing: Much ado about so little? CEPS Policy Brief No. 330.

Haldane, A.G., Roberts-Sklar, M., Wieladek, T. and Young, C. (2016) QE: The story so far. Bank of England Staff Working Paper No. 624.

Hamilton, J.D. and Wu, J.C. (2012) The effectiveness of alternative monetary policy tools in a zero lower bound environment. *Journal of Money, Credit and Banking* 44(1): 3–46.

Hansen, S., McMahon, M. and Prat, A. (2014) Transparency and deliberation within the FOMC: A computational linguistics approach. CEPR Discussion Paper No. 9994.

Harrigan, J. and Kuttner, K. (2004) Lost decade in translation: Did the US learn from Japan's post-bubble mistakes? NBER Working Paper No.10938.

He, Z. (2010) Evaluating the effect of the Bank of Canada's conditional commitment policy. Bank of Canada Discussion Paper No. 2010–11.

Hetzel, R. (2009) Monetary policy in the 2008–2009 recession. *Federal Reserve Bank of Richmond Economic Quarterly* 95: 201–233.

Ihrig, J., Klee, E., Li, C., Schulte, B. and Wei, M. (2012) Expectations about the Federal Reserve's balance sheet and the term structure of interest rates. Federal Reserve Board Staff Working Paper No. 2012–57.

Ilzetzki, E., Reinhart, C. and Rogoff, K. (2017) Exchange arrangements entering the 21st century: Which anchor will hold? NBER Working Paper No. 23134.

IMF. (2003) *Deflation: Determinants, Risks, and Policy Options—Findings of an Interdepartmental Task Force*. Washington, DC: International Monetary Fund.

IMF. (2013) *Unconventional Monetary Policies—Recent Experience and Prospects—Background Paper*. Washington, DC: International Monetary Fund.

Jones, C. (2015) Forward guidance at the zero lower bound. Working Paper, New York University.

Joyce, M.A.S., Lasaosa, A., Stevens, I. and Tong, M. (2011) The financial market impact of quantitative easing in the United Kingdom. *International Journal of Central Banking* 7(3): 113–161.

Kabaca, S. (2016) Quantitative easing in a small open economy: An international portfolio balancing approach. Bank of Canada Staff Working Paper No. 2016-55.

Kang, D.W., Ligthart, N. and Mody, A. (2016) The ECB and the Fed: A comparative narrative. VoxEU.org, 19 January. Electronic copy available at: http://voxeu.org/article/ecb-and-fed-comparative-narrative.

Koo, R. (2015) *The Escape from Balance Sheet Recession and the QE Trap: A Hazardous Road for the World Economy*. New York: John Wiley & Sons.

Kool, C.J.M. and Thornton, D.L. (2012) How effective is Central Bank forward guidance? Federal Reserve Bank of St. Louis Working Paper No. 2012-063A.

Krishnamurthy, A. and Vissing-Jorgensen, A. (2011) The effects of quantitative easing on interest rates: Channels and implications for policy. *Brookings Papers on Economic Activity* 2: 215–287.

Krishnamurthy, A. and Vissing-Jorgensen, A. (2013) The ins and outs of LSAPs. Economic Policy Symposium Proceedings 'Global Dimensions of Unconventional Monetary Policy' (pp. 57–111). Jackson Hole, WY: Federal Reserve Bank of Kansas City.

Krugman, P. (2016) The State of Macro Is Sad (Wonkish). *New York Times*, 12 August. Electronic copy available at: https://krugman.blogs.nytimes.com/2016/08/12/the-state-of-macro-is-sad-wonkish/.

Kuttner, K.N. and Posen, A.S. (2004) The difficulty of discerning what's too tight: Taylor rules and Japanese monetary policy. *North American Journal of Economics and Finance* 15: 53–74.

Laeven, L. and Valencia, F. (2012) Systemic banking crises database: An update. IMF Working Papers No. 163.

Lam, R.W. (2011) Bank of Japan's monetary easing measures: Are they powerful and comprehensive? IMF Working Papers No. 264.

Leigh, D. (2010) Monetary policy and the lost decade: Lessons from Japan. *Journal of Money, Credit, and Banking* 42(5): 833–857.

Li, C. and Wei, M. (2013) Term structure modelling with supply factors and the Federal Reserve's large-scale asset purchase programs. *International Journal of Central Banking* 9(1): 3–39.

Lombardi, D. and Siklos, P.L. (2016) Benchmarking macroprudential policies: An initial assessment. *Journal of Financial Stability* 27: 35–49.

Lombardi, D., Siklos, P.L. and St. Amand, S. (2017) Exchange rates, central bank news and the zero lower bound. *Applied Economic Letters* 24(4): 269–272.

Lombardi, D., Siklos, P.L. and St. Amand, S. (forthcoming) Government bond yields at the effective lower bound: International evidence. *Contemporary Economic Policy*, available online 16 June 2017.

MacKinlay, A.C. (1997) Event studies in economics and finance. *Journal of Economic Literature* 35(1): 13–39.

Malmendier, U., Nagel, S. and Yan, Z. (2017) The making of Hawks and Doves: Inflation experiences on the FOMC. NBER Working Paper No. 23228.

McCauley, R. and Ueda, K. (2009) Government debt management at low interest Rates. *BIS Quarterly Review* (June): 35–51.

Meade, E.E., Burk, N.A. and Josselyn, M. (2015) The FOMC meeting minutes: As assessment of counting words and the diversity of views. Board of Governors of the Federal Reserve System, FEDS Notes, 26 May.

Middledorp, M. (2015) Very much anticipated: ECB QE had a big impact on asset prices, even before it was officially announced. Bank Underground, 14 August. Electronic copy available at: https://bankunderground.co.uk/2015/08/14/very-much-anticipated-ecb-qe-had-a-big-impact-on-asset-prices-even-before-it-was-officially-announced/

Middledorp, M. and Wood, O. (2016) Too eagerly anticipated: The impact of the extension of ECB QE on asset prices. Bank Underground, 4 March. Electronic copy available at: https://bankunderground.co.uk/2016/03/04/too-eagerly-anticipated-the-impact-of-the-extension-of-ecb-qe-on-asset-prices/

Mishra, P., Moriyama, K., N'Diaye, P. and Nguyen, L. (2014) Impact of fed tapering announcements on emerging markets. IMF Working Paper No.14/109.

Moessner, R. (2014) Effects of ECB balance sheet policy announcements on inflation expectations. DNB Working Paper No. 416.

Moessner, R., Jansen, D.-J. and de Hann, J. (2017) Communication about future policy rates in theory and practice: A survey. *Journal of Economic Surveys* 31(3): 678–711.

Neely, C.J. (2010) The large-scale asset purchases had large international effects. Federal Reserve Working Paper No. 2010–018C.

Neely, C.J. (2014) How persistent are monetary policy effects at the zero lower bound? Federal Reserve Bank of St. Louis Working Paper Series No. 2014-004A.

Nishino, K., Yamamoto, H., Kitahara, J. and Nagahata, T. (2016) Developments in inflation expectations over the three years since the introduction of quantitative and qualitative monetary easing (QQE). Bank of Japan Review October: 1–7.

Orphanides, A. (2015) Fear of Liftoff: Uncertainty, rules, and discretion in monetary policy normalization. *Federal Reserve of St. Louis Review* (Third Quarter): 173–196.

Poloz, S. (2015) Central Bank credibility and policy normalization. Remarks delivered at the Canada-United Kingdom Chamber of Commerce, London, 26 March.

Rajan, R. (2014) Containing competitive monetary easing. Project Syndicate, 28 April. Electronic copy available at: https://www.project-syndicate.org/commentary/raghuram-rajan-calls-for-monetary-policy-coordination-among-major-central-banks?barrier=accessreg

Raskin, M.D. (2013) The effects of the Federal Reserve's date-based forward guidance. Board of Governors of the Federal Reserve System, Finance and Economics Discussion Series Working Paper2013-37.

Raynard, S. (2012) Assessing potential inflation consequences of QE after financial crises. Peterson Institute for International Economics Working Paper No. 12–22.

Reichlin, L., Turner, A. and Woodford, M. (2013) Helicopter money as a policy option. VoxEU.org, 25 March. Electronic copy available at: https://voxeu.org/article/helicopter-money-policy-option.

Reinhart, C.M., Kirkegaard, J.F. and Sbrancia, M.B. (2011) Financial repression redux. *IMF Finance and Development* June: 22–26.

Reinhart, C.M. and Rogoff, K.S. (2009) *This Time is Different: Eight Centuries of Financial Folly*. Princeton, NJ: Princeton Press.

Reza, A., Santor, E. and Suchanek, L. (2015) Quantitative easing as a policy tool under the effective lower bound. Bank of Canada Staff Discussion Paper No. 2015-14.

Rogers, J.H., Scotti, C. and Wright, J.H. (2014) Evaluating asset-market effects of unconventional monetary policy: A cross-country comparison. Board of Governors of the Federal Reserve System, International Finance Discussion Papers No. 1101.

Rogoff, K. (2016a) *The Curse of Cash*. Princeton, NJ: Princeton University Press.

Rogoff, K. (2016b) The Case Against Cash. Project Syndicate, 5 September 5, 2016.

Romer, C.D. and Romer, D.H. (2017) Why some times are different: Macroeconomic policy and the aftermath of financial crises. NBER Working Paper No. 23931.

Romer, P. (2016) The trouble with macroeconomics. Mimeo, Stern School of Business, New York University, 14 September. (Forthcoming in The American Economist).

Shirakawa, M. (2012) Future of Central Bank and Central Banking. Speech delivered at the 2010 International Conference, Institute for Monetary and Economic Studies, Bank of Japan, Tokyo, 26 May.

Siklos, P.L. (2015) Macroeconomic implications of financial frictions in the euro zone. *Comparative Economic Studies* 57: 205–221.

Siklos, P.L. (2017) *Central Banks: Into the Breach: From Triumph to Crisis and the Road Ahead*. Oxford: Oxford University Press.

Siklos, P.L. and Lavender, B. (2015) The credit cycle and the business cycle in Canada and the United States: Two solitudes? *Canadian Public Policy* 41: 109–123.

Siklos, P.L. and Spence, A. (2010) Faceoff: Should the Bank of Canada release its projections of the interest rate path? —The cases for and against. C.D. Howe Institute Backgrounder No. 134.

Sinn, H.-W. (2014) *The Euro Trap*. Oxford: Oxford University Press.

Stone, M., Fujita, K. and Ishi, K. (2011) Should unconventional balance sheet policies be added to the Central Bank Toolkit? A review of the experience so far. IMF Working Paper No. 11/145.

Sumner, S. (2011) Why Japan's QE didn't work. The Money Illusion, 25 March. Electronic copy available at: http://www.themoneyillusion.com/why-japans-qe-didnt-work/.

Swanson, E.T. (2011) Let's twist again: A high-frequency event-study analysis of operation twist and its implications for QE2. *Brookings Papers on Economic Activity* (Spring): 151–188.

Swanson, E.T. and Williams, J.C. (2014a) Measuring the effect of the zero lower bound n yields and exchange rates in the U.K. and Germany. *Journal of International Economic* 92(Sup 1): S2-S21.

Swanson, E.T. and Williams, J.C. (2014b) Measuring the effect of the zero lower bound on medium- and longer-term interest rates. *American Economic Review* 104(10): 3154–3185.

Taylor, J.B (2014) Causes of the financial crisis and the slow recovery: A ten-year perspective. In M.N. Bailey and J.B. Taylor (eds.), *Across the Great Divide: New Perspectives on the Financial Crisis* (pp. 51–66). Stanford: Hoover Institution Press and Brookings.

Turner, A. (2016) *Between Debt and the Devil: Money, Credit, and Fixing Global Finance*. Princeton, NJ: Princeton University Press.

Turner, P. (2014) The exit from non-conventional monetary policy: What challenges? BIS Working Papers No. 448.

Ueda, K. (2011) Japan's deflation and the Bank of Japan's experience with non-traditional monetary policy. Centre for Advanced Research in Finance Working Paper 235.

Ueda, K. (2012) The effectiveness of non-traditional monetary policy measures: The case of the Bank of Japan. *Japanese Economic Review* 63(1): 1–22.

Wafte, G. (2015) The impact of the ECB's asset purchase programmes on sovereign bond spreads in the euro area. Bruges European Economic Research Papers No. 35/2015.

Weale, M. and Wieladek, T. (2016) What are the macroeconomic effects of asset purchases? *Journal of Monetary Economics* 79: 81–93.

Williams, J.C. (2014) Monetary policy at the zero lower bound: Putting theory into practice. The Hutchins Center on Fiscal & Monetary Policy Working Papers January.

Woodford, M. (2012) Methods of policy accommodation at the interest-rate lower bound. Economic Policy Symposium Proceedings 'The Changing Policy Landscape' (pp. 185–288). Jackson Hole, WY: Federal Reserve Bank of Kansas City.

Wyplosz, C. (2011) They still don't get it. VoxEU.org, 25 October. Electronic copy available at: http://voxeu.org/article/eurozone-leaders-still-don-t-get-it

3

IMPLICIT BANK DEBT GUARANTEES: COSTS, BENEFITS AND RISKS

Sebastian Schich

OECD

1. Introduction

The expectation by market participants that public authorities might bail out the creditors of banks that are considered too big or important for another reason to be allowed to fail, is commonly referred to as an implicit guarantee. It is implicit because public authorities do not have any explicit commitment to intervene, but may do so nonetheless. In fact, they may even honestly state that they not want to do so *ex ante*, but may feel compelled to do so *ex post*. The support provided by public authorities is not explicitly stated but only perceived. If the perception is strong and shared by everyone, the *ex ante* value of an implicit guarantee is similar to that of an explicit guarantee.

Implicit guarantees create costs, as no fee is charged in exchange for them, at least not directly or openly, meaning that the guarantee is too cheap. Funding costs for banks benefitting from it are artificially low and insensitive to bank risk-taking. The implicit subsidies generated imply that too many resources are being channelled into such banks as compared to a situation without the existence of implicit bank debt guarantees, although it is less clear how the subsidies are shared among different bank stakeholders.

The immediate policy response to the global financial crisis has further entrenched the perceptions that banks benefit from such implicit guarantees, although more recent policy initiatives aim at limiting that perception. A key challenge in this context is to ensure that banks of any size and structure can fail and will be allowed to do so if they experience financial distress. To the extent that such efforts are credible, the perception that debt of banks is protected would diminish. As long as such efforts are not credible, however, implicit bank debt guarantees will continue to have an economic value.

Implicit guarantees are closely related to the concept of 'too-big-to-fail' (TBTF). In particular, TBTF in the case of banks implies that some uninsured bank creditors benefit from an implicit guarantee. Thus, measures of implicit guarantees can be used to assess progress regarding limiting TBTF, which is one of four core aims of the G20 financial regulatory reform

Contemporary Topics in Finance: A Collection of Literature Surveys, First Edition. Edited by Iris Claus and Leo Krippner.

Chapters © 2019 The Authors. Book compilation © 2019 John Wiley & Sons Ltd. Published 2019 by John Wiley & Sons Ltd.

agenda. Before discussing recent policy initiatives (especially as part of Section 6.1), Section 2 provides some background regarding the fundamental cause for the presence of implicit guarantees, that is the presence of the financial safety net. Section 3 discusses how the funding costs advantage arising from implicit bank debt guarantees benefits different bank stakeholders and Section 4 discusses the various economic costs created by these guarantees. Section 5 describes the factors influencing the value of implicit guarantees and the difficulties in monitoring developments in their value. Section 6 discusses what policy makers say and do about this phenomenon; it also places particular attention on the somewhat novel approach of identifying some banks as globally systemically important and subjecting them to a special and more intrusive regulatory treatment and asks what have been the financial market reactions to that approach so far. Section 7 concludes and raises a number of questions considered useful for further study.

2. Why Do Implicit Bank Debt Guarantees Arise?

2.1 Why Do Explicit Bank Debt Guarantees Exist?

Guarantees, options and other contingent arrangements play a powerful role in financial markets and are key to risk management. To the extent that financial market participants are risk averse, such arrangements allow them to share risk with others rather than having to seek actions to avoid risk altogether. The ability to do so in turn enhances investors' readiness to engage in risky activities, and they might decide to provide funding for specific types of activities that they would not have done in the absence of a guarantee of other form of credit enhancement, thus supporting real activity growth. Against the background of the powerful effect of guarantees and other contingent arrangements on incentives and activities, public authorities support and use such arrangements to achieve a variety of financial policy objectives. Such objectives include facilitating risk-taking and transactions that would otherwise not have taken place, such as bank lending to small enterprises with unknown track record and limited collateral. Yet, others are to instil assurance in the presence of specific risks, such as is the case for publicly supported deposit guarantee arrangements.

Guarantees are an important element of the financial safety net that aims to preserve the functioning of 'the system' and is provided by public authorities including fiscal authorities, the central bank and bank regulators and supervisors. As regards the beneficiaries of safety net provisions, banks have traditionally been considered by policy makers as 'special' among financial institutions for two main reasons. First, they play a key role in the payment and settlement system and the transmission of monetary policy. Second, they feature particular balance sheet structures, which involve making long-term loans funded by deposits that can be withdrawn on short notice. As a result of this mismatch in maturities between its assets and liabilities, a bank is typically unable to satisfy all legitimate claims for deposits at any one time, which implies that there is a first-mover advantage for any depositor should there be concerns about the solvency of a bank. In fact, confidence by depositors can erode quickly, and this situation can result in a run on bank that may have a severe effect even on relatively healthy institutions. To avoid such runs and maintain confidence, depositors are being given assurance regarding the safety and availability of their deposits and claims through a deposit insurance arrangement. To counterbalance the potential effects of such a guarantee on the risk-taking on the part of the bank, a premium is charged in exchange for such insurance, and bank activities are being regulated and the adherence to the regulation being supervised. The regulatory and supervisory functions are the quid-pro-quo for the deposit insurance and lender-of-last-resort functions, which all together constitute the so-called financial (system) safety net meant to ensure the safety of the (financial) system.

What exactly entails the financial safety net policy is not clear *ex ante*, as long as public authorities cannot commit to provide a specific response *ex post*. This situation in turn implies that it is desirable to restrict safety net access to a specific group of entities, for example, banks rather than financial intermediaries more generally, as the lack of commitment implies that public authorities provide too much support to protected financial institutions *ex post* (Bengui *et al.*, 2016). In practice, as the recent global financial crisis reminds one, in situations of extreme financial market stress and uncertainty, public authorities tend to err of the side of providing too much assurance in an attempt to avoid the threat of a system crisis. That observation does not come as a surprise; as succinctly put well before the most recent global financial crisis by Volcker (2004):

> '*Faced with the clear and present danger of a severe fallout from a large bank failure, on the one hand, against the more amorphous and certainly more distant risk of losing market discipline, on the other hand, official judgements may be biased toward the "not on my watch" syndrome'*.

The financial systemic safety net was at the core of the policy response to the recent financial crisis and its design was arguably significantly adjusted as part of that response. The boundaries of the safety net were extended in terms of the institutions covered (for example, including money market mutual funds) and the scope of coverage of bank liabilities. The response involved the extension of a variety of existing – and the introduction of new – explicit guarantees for the liabilities of banks (and sometimes even their assets).

Arguably, a functional adjustment occurred as well as part of the policy response to the crisis. In particular, the scope of the lender-of-last-resort and deposit insurance functions were effectively extended, as was reflected in increases of central bank balance sheets and the assurance that liquidity would always be ample, the introduction of new officially supported guarantees and the expansion of existing ones. The government and the central bank together, in line with their roles as ultimate providers of capital and liquidity in a situation of a systemic crisis, acted effectively as *guarantor of last resort* for financial claims on banks (and, incidentally, also on other types of financial institutions). As a result, effectively, the traditional definition of the financial safety net changed (Figure 1).

2.2 *Differences between Explicit and Implicit Bank Debt Guarantees*

There is widespread agreement that the extension of the scope of the financial safety net was necessary to avoid a worsening of the systemic financial crisis, but that this response was not costless. This response, consisting of the emergency extension of explicit guarantees for some bank liabilities and policy announcements implying the existence of additional protection for other liabilities, might have further entrenched the perception that bank liabilities benefit from an *implicit guarantee* provided by public authorities.

What distinguishes an implicit guarantee from an explicit one is the nature of the obligation on the part of the guarantor. In the case of an explicit guarantee, the obligation is explicitly stated in a contract or is recognized by law. By contrast, in the case of an implicit guarantee, the guarantee is not plainly or directly stated; it is implied, understood or suggested in some

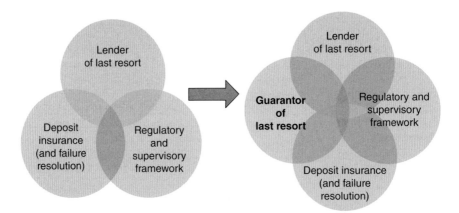

Figure 1. *De Facto* Change in the Traditional Financial Safety Net Definition.
Source: Schich (2011). [Color figure can be viewed at wileyonlinelibrary.com]

wording or past actions. The entity seen as the guarantor might even expressly negate the existence of the guarantee, although that announcement might not be credible.

Thus, the support provided by public authorities to banks through implicit guarantees is qualified by two attributes; it is perceived and potential support. These two attributes imply that any attempt to measure the value of implicit bank debt guarantees faces considerable challenges. In fact, while the contingent nature of an explicit guarantee already complicates valuation to some extent, the valuation of an implicit guarantee is further complicated by the difficulty to know to what extent the 'guarantor' is intent on vindicating the perceived guarantee.

2.3 *Why Do Implicit Bank Debt Guarantees Arise?*

There is no obvious stress threshold beyond which public authorities will provide the expected support. Public authorities are likely to make available the financial safety net provisions already when they perceive the *threat* of a crisis of the system, with severe adverse consequences for real economic activity. Such a threat might (be perceived to) exist when considerable distress characterizes an entity that is large, complex and internationally connected, thus making the entity systemically important and, hence, 'TBTF' (see also Section 6.1). That role 'for the system' might refer to a global, national or regional level. Alternatively, a systemic threat might arise because a number of banks simultaneously enter into difficulties. Banks are much more leveraged than other firms and they are closely linked to each other through lending and derivatives transactions, so that a bank's failure may trigger a chain of subsequent failures (Rochet and Tirole, 1996). Moreover, even beyond direct links, the failure of one bank can quickly undermine the confidence in other banks that are seen as presenting similar vulnerabilities and trigger runs on those banks (Chen, 1999). In practice, it is notoriously difficult to neatly distinguish between individual bank failures and systemic crises (Avgouelas and Goodhart, 2014), which makes it difficult to know for sure that any bank failure would remain an idiosyncratic event.

Beyond concerns for the stability of the system, public authorities might decide to prevent banks from defaulting on their debt for other reasons, having considered that the costs of such a default would be unacceptable high (Kaufman, 2014). Such situations can arise, for example, if the bank is seen as playing an important role as counterparty in specific financial market segments worth protecting for other financial policy reasons (for example, as the development of specific segments of securitized mortgage markets is being supported), when public authorities are concerned that a bank failure would damage their own reputation as a bank regulator or supervisor (Boot and Thakor, 1993), or when bank counterparties or creditors are entities considered particularly worthy of protection for social considerations (for example, if considerable parts of creditors are small and presumably unsophisticated households; see Cariboni *et al.*, 2016).

Insofar as the policy concern is the systemic threat, the bank failure resolution framework plays a crucial role. Effective and credible frameworks would allow one to smoothly resolve the failure of a bank of any size and structure without any wider economic consequences. By contrast, as long as a disorderly failure of a bank could cause instability of the wider system in the absence of public support, however, public authorities might feel compelled to provide support under some circumstances. Special insolvency laws or administrative procedures for banks that go beyond conventional corporate insolvency laws have been developed in response to the financial crisis to better promote both the objective of efficiency and stability. Efficiency requires that some creditors must face the risk of losses so as to incentivize them to discipline bank risk-taking, while stability requires that the risk of losses must not be a source of systemic risk. In this regard, there is an obvious dilemma as the threat of losses must be credible to generate effective market discipline, while that same credible threat also creates incentives for creditors to 'run' on a bank in distress (Wihlborg, 2017).

Absent an effective and trusted failure resolution framework capable of smoothly resolving any bank without wider adverse repercussions, a time inconsistency problem is likely to exist. In particular, even in cases where the presumed guarantor does have an expressed intent *ex ante* not to provide any support to any bank, subsequent events might make it optimal to renege on such announcements *ex post*. As long as it is not possible to definitively rule out such scenarios and the possibility of support (either to avoid a systemic threat or harm to bank counterparties for other reasons), an implicit guarantee will have an economic value. Whether and to what extent these perceptions *should* be vindicated *ex post* is another issue. Under some circumstances, some form of regulatory forbearance (Morrison and White, 2010) or direct transfer of funds from public authorities (Casey and Posner, 2015) to banks to prevent them from defaulting on their debt, might be provided ('bail-out'). Of course, as highlighted by the case of Icelandic banks in 2008 (see, for example, Baldursson *et al.*, 2017), there can be situations where banks may simply be too large compared to the size of the domestic economy to be saved.

3. Who Benefits from Implicit Bank Debt Guarantees?

3.1 *Bank Creditors*

The effect of a guarantee on risky bank debt is to transfer risk from the creditor to the guarantor, although in the case of an implicit guarantee the transfer is not certain but perceived. Nonetheless, the creditor accepts a lowering of the nominal return in exchange for that belief. The extent to which the nominal return is lowered reflects the value of the guarantee. Thus, the guarantor subsidizes the funding costs of the bank, while receiving no financial compensation from the debtor. There might be some indirect compensation for public authorities in the sense that the achievement of the policy goal of financial stability is facilitated over the short term, especially if lenders were to run on the bank in the absence of the presence of a guarantee. That said, such advantages are at best short-term and are more than outweighed over the medium to long term by the additional risk-taking that is triggered on the part of the bank by the presence of an under-priced guarantee. As a general rule, no compensation is received by the guarantor so that the implicit guarantee becomes a subsidy reducing the bank funding costs. How this advantage benefits the various stakeholders in the success of the bank is not clear *a priori*. Benefits may occur to the banks' creditors, owners, their customers, their employees or other stakeholders. Thus, an important question is who ultimately benefits from implicit bank debt guarantees?

What types of bank debt benefits from an implicit guarantee is not clear *a priori*, and the perimeter appears to be changing over time. Among the various bank creditors, the perception that their claims benefit from an effective government guarantee is probably strongest for insured depositors, even if the insurance arrangement is a private one. There seems to be a perception that governments always stand behind deposit insurance arrangements, even if they do not have to do so. In this context, the European Free Trade Association Court (2013), for example, decided that there is no obligation for public authorities to backstop private deposit insurance regimes whenever their funding turns out to be insufficient to cover the amounts of deposits insured. But as a matter of general practice, insured deposits seem to be *de facto* benefiting from special protection and, with the notable exception of Cyprus in 2013, are typically exempt from the burden sharing associated with bank failure resolution. Even in the United States, where the Federal Deposit Insurance Corporation (FDIC) does inflict losses on shareholders and subordinated creditors as a general rule and expects creditors, uninsured depositors and itself to take losses as part of failure resolutions (Bennett *et al.*, 2014), the FDIC favours 'purchase and assumptions' resolutions that keep insured and other depositors fully protected. While the desirability of protecting small retail depositors is not much disputed today, the discussion leading to the introduction of a formal deposit insurance supposedly covering such depositors in the United States in the early part of the 20th century was intensely and controversially discussed.

Remarkably, the perceived protection for uninsured depositors appears to be almost as strong as for insured depositors. For example, the comprehensive database of deposit insurance arrangements established by Demirgüç-Kunt *et al.* (2014) distinguishes between explicit and implicit deposit insurance arrangements. Where deposit insurance arrangements are explicit, the database provides additional information on design characteristics, such as management, coverage or funding. Where no explicit deposit insurance coverage exists, coverage is assumed to be implicit. The authors of the database succinctly explain: 'Indeed, implicit coverage [for deposits] always exists, regardless of the level of explicit coverage'. This assessment is however not so astonishing given that deposits, especially to the extent that they held by households, are the focus of the traditional financial safety net discussed in Section 2. Also, it reflects the historical record, which includes very few examples where uninsured depositors and even fewer examples where insured depositors have incurred losses as part of bank failure resolution cases.

Protection goes beyond deposits, however. Senior unsecured creditors and often even subordinated creditors also benefit from implicit guarantees, which is problematic as these types of creditors would be expected to be a helpful source of bank monitoring and disciplining the risk-taking of banks. According to standard principles of failure resolution, the principle of absolute legal liquidation priority implies that junior debt holders absorb losses before senior debt holders if aggregate losses were to be distributed among creditors of an insolvent firm. Against this background, considerable hopes to ensure market discipline had been pinned on subordinated debtholders during the 1990s and early 2000s, although it turned out that the involvement of the latter in the funding of bank failure resolution following the global financial crisis was however rare, although not as rare as that of senior debt holders (Schich and Kim, 2012).

More recently, new regulation foresees the systematic involvement of subordinated bank debt holders in the burden sharing associated with bank failure resolution, although there are still considerable challenges in practice. For example, in some cases, retail households were identified as being significant holders of the claims to be written down as part of bank failure resolution. This situation has complicated and delayed failure resolutions, as policy makers felt compelled to adjust resolution principles to the nature of debt holders. One solution has been to involve the subordinated debt in the financing of resolution, but to promise to compensate the retail holders of such debt subsequently through fiscal transfers.

3.2 Bank Owners

The perceived protection of the bank's liabilities typically pertains to debt but might go even beyond it and include part of its equity. In particular, there might be the perception that the implicit guarantee pertains to the survival of the bank in its present form, which would imply that not just current depositors and creditors but also shareholders would be directly perceived to be protected to some extent. In fact, while public authorities agree that shareholder dilution or wipe-out in the case of bank failure resolution should be the norm, a total wipe-out of shareholders was avoided in many cases, and this situation might have confirmed a perception that shareholders are more directly sharing the value of implicit guarantees for bank liabilities. That benefit might be limited to the extent that public authorities make good on the guarantee by injecting equity capital, thus diluting the value of existing shareholders.

Bank equity holders benefit from an implicit guarantee on bank debt, which represents a subsidy for equity holders. The value of that subsidy is maximized by taking more risks and raising leverage. While the increase in assets might lower average return on assets, shareholders are also compensated for the higher risk taken by higher average returns. In fact, the share of financial companies in total stock market capitalization has increased based on some broad indices such as the S&P 500, although this pattern has been partly reversed after the global financial crisis. Further investigation of who holds bank equity might be worthwhile. Stock market wealth is more unequally distributed across households in different income groups than income, with top earners holding the overwhelming share of stock market wealth (Guiso et al., 2002; and, more recently, Guiso and Sodini, 2013, for the United States, and Denk and Cazenave-Lacroutz, 2015, for Europe). If bank stocks are distributed proportionally to overall stock market wealth, the higher rate of return on bank equity as a result of implicit bank debt guarantees would benefit primarily investors at the top of the income (and wealth) distribution.

3.3 Selected Other Stakeholders

Part of the benefits from implicit bank debt guarantees may accrue to bank debtors, especially in situations where competition between banks for lending is strong. It would lower interest rates on loans, which in turn would likely increase the overall amount of credit in the economy. There is some evidence that interest rates might be lowered, although this situation does not seem necessarily to be reflected in wider credit availability. For example, Afonso *et al.* (2015) show that banks benefitting from higher values of implicit guarantees tend to accumulate more impaired loans as a share of total assets, consistent with a view that they had charged too low interest rates or accepted too many risky borrowers. Gadanecz *et al.* (2012) study the pricing of loans in which banks that benefit from implicit bank debt guarantees act as senior arrangers and the loan portfolios that they retain on their books. They find that the activity of supported banks is associated with lower loan spreads, reflecting a 'more relaxed' attitude toward credit risk, although supported banks are 'not very special and do not seem to seek out borrowers that are shunned by others'. Considering the well-known debt-favouring distortion induced by the tax exemption of debt interest payments, Groenewegen and Wierts (2017) argue that insofar as the funding costs advantages are passed on to equity holders, such subsidies will be subject to taxation. Thus, there is an incentive to pass on the subsidy to other stakeholders. As regards household creditors, Denk and Cazenave-Lacroutz (2015) observe that the distribution of household credit is more unequal than the distribution of household disposable income, with higher-income households receiving disproportionally large shares of bank credit. Thus, to the extent that part of the value of implicit bank debt guarantees was to be equally distributed among debtors, its effect would be to widen the distribution of household wealth, which is undesirable.

Bank employees including managers might also benefit in terms of higher salaries obtained (Figure 2). Earnings, including wages and bonuses, are higher in finance than elsewhere. Moreover, there is evidence for the existence of a 'financial sector wage premium' that raises wages above the compensation levels usually associated with the profiles of employees in terms of education age, experience, etc. Denk *et al.* (2015) show that financial sector employees are concentrated at the upper end of the income distribution and wage premia are especially large for the top earners. Thus, insofar as implicit guarantees benefit bank employees contribute to financial sector wage premia, they tend to widen the income distribution.

4. What Are the Economic Costs of Implicit Bank Debt Guarantees?

4.1 *Weakened Market Discipline*

As long as debtors are exposed to the risk of loss on their claims (or delayed access to funds), they can be expected to impose market discipline on their debtor. Implicit guarantees tend to weaken market discipline, however. They not only distort the incentives of bank owners and managers leading them to take additional risks, but they also distort the incentives on the part of creditors and other bank counterparties to monitor and discipline the former. The guarantees immunize banks' creditors against the consequences of default, leading to a lower level of interest rate demanded on bank debt as well as a lower level of incentive for monitoring banks on the part of bank creditors and other counterparties. Which types of bank liabilities are affected by such (perceived) protection is not clear *a priori*, although it might reflect the regulators' fear of economic disruptions from not protecting these counterparties. The greater the fear of greater collateral damage, the more a given counterparty will be counterparties (Kaufman, 2014). The author provides a stylized description of the liability side of a bank balance sheet, illustrating that as more types of liabilities (small depositors, large depositors, short-term creditors, long-term creditors, etc.) are partially or fully protected against more types of losses (considering 'credit losses', defined as shortfall of recovery proceeds from the claim as of the par value of that claim and 'liquidity losses', defined as delays in the receipt

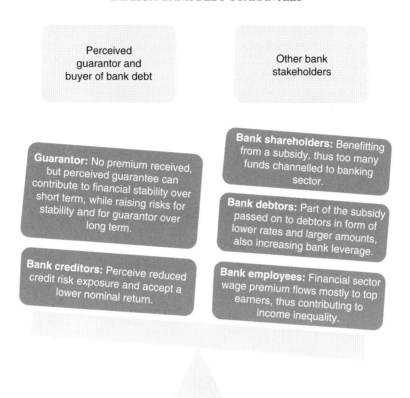

Figure 2. Selected Considerations Regarding Costs, Benefits and Risks of Implicit Bank Debt Guarantees. [Color figure can be viewed at wileyonlinelibrary.com]

of the proceeds), the more comprehensive and costly is the protection, and the weaker market discipline is likely to be overall. By contrast, market discipline is functioning where the probability increases that bank debt holders will incur losses as banks take higher risks (Beyhaghi *et al.*, 2013).

Where effective market discipline is absent, however, an essential tool to control risk-taking is lost (Calomiris, 1997, 1999), which results in more banking services being produced and consumed than would otherwise be the case. In fact, banking sector growth has been large by some measures. For example, growth might have become outsized compared to real activity growth. Some recent empirical studies have run regressions relating economic growth to bank credit relative to GDP in cross-country samples covering several decades and documented a tight association between more bank credit and *lower* GDP growth. This result differs from studies produced before the global financial crisis, which tended to find that deeper financial markets, often measured by intermediated credit relative to GDP, are associated with *higher* GDP growth. The differences in results reflect sample choices to some extent. Rousseau and Wachtel (2011) show that the *positive* association of financial market depth and economic growth disappears when the empirical analysis focuses on the period since 1990. This situation might reflect that the relationship under investigation is hump-shaped, with financial deepening being correlated with higher GDP growth at low levels of financial development and lower GDP growth after some threshold (Beck *et al.*, 2014). For a sample of 34 OECD countries,

Cournède and Denk (2015) show that this negative link is stronger for bank credit than non-bank credit. These results leave open the question which specific channels more bank credit induces lower growth, but they are consistent with the hypothesis that a part of implicit bank debt guarantees results in too much banking sector growth.

4.2 Increased Risk-Taking

Most empirical evidence is consistent with the hypothesis that banks tend to increase their risk-taking in the presence of implicit guarantees for their debt, thus leading to 'too much' of an increase in bank balance sheet size (Morrison, 2011; IMF, 2014). For example, Marques et al. (2013) suggest that under-priced government support arrangements are associated with more risk-taking and Dam and Koetter (2012) study actual cases of bail-outs to show that higher bailout probabilities increase risk-taking. The availability of under-priced guarantees tends to create an incentive for both additional bank risk-taking as well as sector leverage, and this situation gives rise to negative externalities emanating from the banking sector to the rest of the economy in the form of higher probability of default and higher level of systemic risk (Admati et al., 2013). Hagendorff et al. (2017) provide empirical evidence consistent with the view that implicit bank debt guarantees are one explanation for the observation that relatively large banks expose themselves to higher tail risks.

Admittedly, implicit guarantees on bank debt not only reduces the market discipline exercised by bank creditors but also increase the charter value of bank equity and this latter effect could in principle lead bank owners to limit risk-taking to protect future rents (Marcus, 1984). Monopolistic rents derived from imperfect competition in a highly regulated banking industry create bank charter values, which can have a disciplinary effect on bank risk-taking incentives. By contrast, when the *explicit* government guarantees for German Landesbanken were removed, thus perhaps resulting in a loss in franchise value, the previously protected banks increased their risk-taking by more than their never-protected peers (Fischer et al., 2014). Dell'Ariccia and Ratvnoski (2013) argue that strengthening the charter value of a bank can have such a disciplinary effect when the guarantees protect against risks that banks cannot control. By contrast, assuming shareholders fully control bank risks, they will take excessive risks in situations where they obtain some benefit whenever implicit guarantees protect debtholders, given that they control the risks against which they are effectively insured (Cordella et al., 2017). Schenck and Thornton (2016) show that the effects of bailout promises, that is of perceived guarantees, on bank risk taking are non-monotonic. They increase risk-taking incentives for bailout recipients relative to non-recipients for 'weak' institutions with low charter values and high leverage. By contrast, the opposite is true for 'strong' institutions with high charter values and low leverage.

4.3 Competitive Distortions

Implicit guarantees are typically not priced, at least not directly, and policy makers are reluctant to accept the idea of explicitly charging for the benefits of implicit bank debt guarantees (Section 6.1). Consequently, as with any guarantee for which there is no adequate fee, several distortions to incentives and competition are being created, which reinforce each other. A fundamental problem is that losses of excessive risk-taking are expected to, and may actually be, eventually socialized, while the gains accruing in the meantime remain private. This situation invites excessive risk-taking on the part of bank owners and managers and, as a result, too many resources flow into the banking as compared to other corporate sectors. Moreover, in the presence of implicit guarantees for some banks, even non-protected banks adjust their risk-taking upwards for competitive reasons (Gropp *et al.*, 2010).

The value of the implicit guarantee differs from one bank to another. This observation reflects various bank-specific characteristics as well as the strength of the sovereign seen as providing the guarantee (Section 5.1). This situation has received special attention in Europe, where the presence of implicit bank debt guarantees supposedly being provided by domestic sovereigns has tended to reinforce the close and adverse interrelationships between the values of domestic sovereign and banking sector debt. To break that link, efforts to advance the European banking union have been intensified (see, for example, Gropp, 2014), based on the view that as long as substantial values of implicit guarantees for bank debt persist and the value of that guarantee for a bank systematically continues to reflect the identity and strength of its domestic sovereign, banks do not compete with each other on a level-playing field (Cardillo and Zaghini, 2012). An undesirable sovereign-banking sector link was observed already when governments responded to the financial crisis by providing explicit guarantees for newly issued unsecured bank bonds so as to instil confidence and help banks gain time: The spreads at launch were not monotonically related to bank ratings: better-rated banks in some countries paid larger spreads than weaker banks in other countries. In other words, the spread seemed to reflect the nationality of banks rather than their soundness (Levy and Schich, 2009; Grande *et al.*, 2011; Levy and Zaghini, 2011).

4.4 *Creating Perceived Contingent Liabilities for the Sovereign*

Another aspect of the relationship between sovereign and banking-sector debt is that implicit guarantees can also have potentially adverse effects on the perceived guarantor. Admittedly, the bank debt guarantees are only implicit and perceived by market participants, and thus do not imply direct fiscal costs. Nonetheless, they are seen as creating contingent liabilities for the 'guarantor', as illustrated by the significant effect of (country averages of) the value of implicit bank debt guarantees on the CDS spreads of the respective sovereigns (Zhao, 2017). An adverse feedback loop can arise as sovereign credit risk increases, given that the market value of sovereign debt that is held in large amounts by domestic banks loses value (Acharya *et al.*, 2014). Moreover, the perceived contingent fiscal liabilities can be substantial (Snethlage, 2015; Blix Grimaldi *et al.*, 2016; Benczur *et al.*, 2017) and can become real contingent liabilities if events force the conversion of the implicit guarantee into an explicit one. In addition, they can become actual liabilities if the bank in question fails to pay its own debt. The experience of some countries with banking sectors that are large compared to the domestic economy have highlighted how quickly banking sector problems can become sovereign problems under adverse circumstances, although policy choices regarding resolution of bank failures matter (Markúsdóttir, 2011).

5. What Factors Influence the Value of the Perceived Guarantee?

5.1 *The Credit Strengths of the Debtor and the 'Guarantor'*

Merton (1974) uses an option pricing approach to show that the value of a guarantee increases with the risk of the debtor. Estrella and Schich (2015) derive predictions regarding the value of implicit guarantees from a sovereign for bank debt on the basis of a contingent claims model in which, however, not only the bank but also the sovereign is risky. The value of the guarantee is higher the weaker and larger the debtor and the stronger and larger the guarantor, although the credit strength of the bank and the sovereign strength are economically more important for the value of implicit bank debt guarantees than the size of bank and sovereign. For any given bank strength, the credit uplift obtained from a sovereign guarantee is greater the lower the correlation between bank and sovereign strength. Also, the authors illustrate that the credit uplift, or value of bank debt guarantee, is more sensitive to changes in bank strength than it is to changes in sovereign strength.

Empirical results using data for credit rating uplifts for international banks suggest that the value of implicit guarantees is higher when the bank is larger and weaker and when the country in which the bank is headquartered is larger and more creditworthy. The empirical relationship between the strength of the sovereign and the value of banking debt seems robust to differences in specifications and sample choices (Estrella and Schich, 2011; Cariboni *et al.*, 2013; Toader, 2015). It also seems to extend to bank equity valuations. When sovereigns in several countries experienced downward credit rating pressures, the stocks of banks considered more likely to receive government support significantly under-performed in the broad market (Correa *et al.*, 2013). Against the background of the relationship between the identity of the sovereign and the value of implicit bank debt guarantees, an observed decline in the latter, while *a priori* to be welcomed for the various reasons discussed before, needs to be viewed in a nuanced way. In particular, to the extent that the decline results from a weakening of the fiscal or other strength of the perceived guarantor, the underlying cause of the decline is obviously less desirable.

5.2 Collective and Idiosyncratic Risk

Interpreting implicit guarantees as (perceived) put options, yet another caveat needs to be considered when interpreting estimated changes in the value of implicit bank debt guarantees. Even if the belief prevails that an implicit bank debt guarantee exists, market-price-based estimates of its value might suggest a declining value when the likelihood of a crisis recedes. The guarantee simply moves further out-of-the-money similar to a put option (Schweikhard and Tsesmelidakis, 2012).

Distinguishing between collective and idiosyncratic risk provides some further insight in this regard. Kelly *et al.* (2016) consider an implicit government guarantee that 'promises that' banking sector equity index holders will not experience losses that exceed a specific percentage, while idiosyncratic risk affecting individual bank stocks is not directly covered by such a guarantee. In the presence of such a guarantee, the behaviour of the spread between out-of-the money put options on (i) a basket of individual bank stocks and (ii) a banking sector ETF stock index during the recent global financial crisis could be reconciled with standard option pricing theory. For example, Merton (1974, 1973) shows that the price of a basket of put options is always as high as an index option on the same basket of stocks. The spread between the two is driven by the volatility of individual stocks and by the correlation between them. Correlation tends to be high in a crisis and when correlation goes towards one, the basket-versus-index spread goes towards zero. The opposite was however observed during the recent crisis, where the insurance of the basket became more expensive than that of the index, and this observation can be explained by the presence of a type of systemic risk insurance as mentioned above. The intuition is that the (free) guarantee drives down the price that investors are willing to pay for the private, traded version of the insurance against sector-wide risks (that is the put on the index), while individual bank puts that protect against idiosyncratic risk are less affected by the implicit guarantee.

5.3 *Estimating the Value of Implicit Bank Debt Guarantees*

Empirical attempts to (more or less) *directly* measure the value of implicit bank debt guarantees typically focus on the costs of funding for banks by using observed market prices of bank debt. As discussed before, the effects of implicit debt guarantees can spill over to the value of the equity of the bank concerned, which is why some event studies also focus on the value of bank equity, although the effect on the latter is indirect rather than direct. When estimating the debt funding cost advantages, it is useful to distinguish between the probability of financial distress of a bank (abstracting from the possibility of some form of external support) and the probability that the bank in distress obtains support from public authorities involved in the provision of the financial safety net.

5.3.1 *Funding Cost Advantages Estimated from Interest Rate Spreads*

Estimates of the effect of implicit guarantees are obtained from observations of the yield spread differentials for debt securities that have similar characteristics but are issued by entities that differ only in the extent to which they benefit from an implicit guarantee. Such debt securities are difficult to find, however, as important features, such as term to maturity, coupon or currency, often differ from one bond to another. Moreover, yield spread differentials for different debt securities reflect not only credit-risk premia but also liquidity and other premia and it is difficult to disentangle the various factors and isolate the effect of implicit guarantees. For example, such an analysis of funding cost advantages might suggest that the value of implicit guarantees is insignificant, as was arguably the case for G-SIBs in the United States (Goldman Sachs, 2013). G-SIBs have however generally higher leverage ratios and controlling for the leverage difference by restricting the sample to banks with a leverage ratio similar to G-SIBs reveals a significantly positive estimate of the value of implicit bank debt guarantees (IMF, 2014). This example highlights the need to control for factors affecting the probability of distress in the absence of any guarantee, which essentially requires one to effectively control for factors influencing the probability that the bank receives support if in distress. Assessing the influence of the various factors remains a challenge (including in particular the presumed willingness and capacity of the perceived guarantor to vindicate the guarantee); however, and in many studies, the potential empirical determinants are chosen *ad hoc*, based on reduced form models rather than fully specified structural models.

A careful choice of control groups is helpful, where the control groups are other banks or non-financial firms that can reasonably be assumed not to receive any debt support if in distress. For example, Santos (2014) finds that large banks versus small banks benefit from a larger funding cost advantage than large versus small non-financial firms once one controls for riskiness, as judged by issuer credit rating. Acharya *et al.* (2016), using a sample of unsecured bonds traded in the United States between 1990 and 2012 including financial as well as non-financial institutions as control group, document that for the largest financial institutions in the United States, yield spreads are less sensitive to risk than for smaller peers (and that a similar relation does not exist for the non-financial sector). Moreover, the authors show that financial institutions' 'issuer ratings' affect their funding costs, while their 'stand-alone ratings' do not. Also, larger financial firms have significantly better issuer ratings, but not stand-alone ratings.

Deposit funding cost advantages have also been considered. Jacewitz and Pogach (2014) show that the differences in interest rates paid on uninsured deposits at small and large banks in the United States during the crisis were considerable at an average of 39 basis points during 2007–2008, consistent with an implicit guarantee on deposits at large banks. The cost advantage subsequently declined to about 20 basis points during 2009–2010, remaining however significant. Kumar and Lester (2014) observe that the large bank deposit funding cost advantage decline to a few basis points by 2012. Moreover, they argue that the differentials between rates on uninsured deposits might be affected by factors such as the wider variety of services that large banks can offer relative to those offered by small banks and the lower cost at which they can provide those services. These factors are unlikely to have changed considerably over time, so that the observed decline in the estimated value of implicit guarantees reflects either the perception of a reduced likelihood of distress or extraordinary firm-specific support in the event of such distress.

5.3.2 *Funding Costs Advantages Inferred from Credit Rating Assessments*

An alternative to using financial market data to assess the extent of funding costs advantages is to rely on credit rating agency assessments. Rating agencies may not always prove to be correct in their assessments, but market participants do take them into account when valuing bank debt, as reflected in the significant correlation between these assessments and issuers' debt funding costs (Morgan and Stiroh, 2005). As long as bank creditors extract information from such ratings, they are helpful in estimating the value of implicit bank debt guarantees. Rime (2005) observes that credit rating agencies produce credit ratings that are homogenous measures of perceived credit risk of banks that can be easily compared across banks. Moreover, credit rating agencies explicitly distinguish between an issuer 'all-in' credit rating and a 'stand-alone' (or intrinsic strength) credit rating, with the former but not the latter including the rating agency's assumption regarding the external support provided for bank debt (Packer and Tarashev, 2011). The difference between the two ratings is typically referred to as the credit rating uplift and reflects the value of assumed support from public authorities in case the bank is in distress. In the case of Moody's, the difference reflects mostly sovereign support but also institutional support from other parts of the financial firm, while Fitch Ratings allows one to extract a measure of the sovereign support assumption only (Afonso *et al.*, 2015), although credit rating methodologies can change, which makes it challenging to construct consistent time series. Translating these credit rating uplifts to bond yields, one obtains a measure of the bank funding cost advantages in basis points of interest rates (for example, Schich and Lindh, 2012; Ueda and Weder di Mauro, 2012).

Acharya *et al.* (2016) find that 'issuer ratings' but not 'stand-alone ratings' matter for funding costs, which provides support for the approach of using credit rating uplifts to measure the value of implicit bank debt guarantees. That said, the exact relationship between 'issuer ratings' and funding costs is not stable over time, and it might have been closest at the peak of the global financial crisis (Noss and Sowerbutts, 2012). Thus, the function for translating observations for the credit rating uplift into a basis point savings in funding costs or to US dollar equivalents needs to be adjusted over time. Currently, there is an effort on the part of policy makers co-ordinated by the Financial Stability Board (FSB) to de-emphasize the role of credit agency ratings in financial regulation and in particular the mechanical reliance on such ratings by some market participants, so that the role of credit ratings might change in the future.

Considering information from credit rating agencies, including in particular estimates of a positive credit rating uplift, to identify TBTF banks has some attractive features. Unlike measures of the size of the bank, which are often used in the empirical literature, credit rating agency assessment in principle should reflect also other factors than size, such as its interconnectedness, that makes a bank TBTF. Moreover, when considering size measures, it is not clear what is the threshold beyond which a bank would be considered either TBTF or a candidate for the control group. By contrast, a positive credit rating uplift reflecting the assumption of external support from public authorities provides one objective measure of TBTF perceptions. Unfortunately, however, extraction of these support assumptions is not always straightforward and the required approach differs across rating agencies. Related to these difficulties, estimates of basis points of funding costs advantages differ depending on *which* credit rating agency is considered (Siegert and Willison, 2015).

5.3.3 *Contingent Claims Method to Compare Observed and Hypothetical CDS Spreads*

Based on the observation that guarantees are similar in structure to options, contingent claims approaches have been used to explain the economic value of guarantees. One approach is to view the banking sector as a residual claimant on the government, receiving a pay-off equal to that of a hypothetical put option that allows the owner to sell the banking sector assets at a quasi 'strike price' given by the trigger point at which the banks fail (Noss and Sowerbutts, 2012). In response to Haldane (2010), an Oxera study (2011), commissioned by the Royal Bank of Scotland, applies a standard Black Scholes option pricing approach to estimating the value of a guarantee for the United Kingdom banking sector and obtains substantially lower estimates than Haldane (2010). Noss and Sowerbutts (2012) reconcile the different results and show that funding cost advantages in the United Kingdom attained a peak of 175 basis points in 2010. One drawback of the approach is that it requires one to make the (strong) assumption that government support will be provided with certainty once a specific threshold is reached, that is, the probability that public authorities provide support for a bank, once in distress, is assumed to be equal to one.

Another approach uses data on the price paid for credit default swaps (CDSs) on bank bonds, that is CDS spreads, and compares the latter with hypothetical so-called 'fair-value' CDS spreads calculated from equity price information. Both equity and debt prices can be interpreted as derivatives on the bank value, although the pivotal characteristics of bank bailouts is the rescue of bondholders (Hett and Schmidt, 2016). Observed CDS spreads reflect both the probability of bank distress and the possibility that public authorities provide support for the bonds on which the CDS are written. Assuming that equity holders are wiped out in the event of default, information on the probability of default on bonds can be extracted from equity prices. That information allows one then to calculate a 'fair-value' CDS spread that by definition abstracts from the possibility of external support for bank debt. The difference between the observed and the 'fair-value' spread measures the value of implicit bond debt guarantee, which is estimated to have peaked during 2009 for international banks (IMF, 2014). Values for the sample of so-called G-SIB and top-3 banks per country declined subsequently on average, although with considerable differences across countries. Estimates tend to be highest for the euro area. Gudmundsson (2016) provides more recent estimates, extending the standard Black Scholes option pricing model to allow for negative jumps in asset prices. Considering a sample of eleven G-SIBs, the author finds that the value of implicit guarantees peaked during 2008–2009 for that sample, attaining a maximum of 170 basis points. Estimates decline subsequently to a value of between 30 and 40 basis points, broadly similar to the pre-crisis period (Table 1).

5.3.4 *Investigating Asset Price Reactions to Events*

Event studies have focused on the effect of specific events on bank bond or equity returns to see whether returns or asset values increase as a result of them, assuming that such events make the

Table 1. Estimates of Value of Implicit Bank Debt Guarantees in Terms of Basis Points Funding Cost Advantages.

Study, sample or approach	'Weight'	Implicit subsidy in basis points of interest rates									
		2007	2008	2009	2010	2011	2012	2013	2014	2015	2016
Haldane (2010), UK large banks sample	0.7		100	200							
UK small banks sample	0.55		100	100							
Oxera (2011), contingent claims	0.25				8						
Sveriges Riksbank (2011)	0.5	86	86	86	86	86	86				
Noss and Sowerbutts (2012), ratings-based	0.7				54						
Contingent claims, assumption I	0.5				175						
Contingent claims, assumption II	0.5				36						
Contingent claims, assumption IIII	0.5				29						
Li et al. (2011), European banks	0.6	3	50	50	50						
Ueada and Di Mauro (2012), ratings-based	0.8	60		90	50						
Schich and Lindh (2012), ratings-based	1	111	120	157	156	109	110				
Bijlsma and Mocking (2013)	1		5	16	15	31	30				
IMF (2014), Euro area, ratings-based	0.25	21	45	92	74	74	61	62			
Japan, ratings-based	0.25	18	31	65	53	44	25	24			
UK, ratings-based	0.25	8	18	35	23	22	17	16			
USA, ratings-based	0.25	6	8	19	19	13	14	12			
Euro area, contingent claims	0.25	10	16	22	14	-10	91	86			
Japan, contingent claims	0.25	29	99	137	115	79	80	63			
IMF (2014), UK, contingent claims	0.25	10	34	22	-3	0	79	62			
USA, contingent claims	0.25	3	19	43	24	15	15	13			
PWC (2014), bond-spread-based	1			27	7	-5	11	1			

	Weight									
Gudmundsson (2016), contingent claims min	0.5	34	38	37	33	35	33	32	32	31
contingent claims, max	0.5	39	146	170	38	41	38	38	37	37
Zhao (2017), international banks and insurers	1	1	13	13	26	26	26	26		
Groenewegen and Wierts (2017), European banks	1		401	180	254	343	148	94	91	100
Weighted average of all studies		**39**	**59**	**105**	**65**	**77**	**82**	**49**	**64**	**100**
Arithmetic average of all studies		**29**	**55**	**89**	**55**	**51**	**66**	**45**	**54**	**53** / **100**

Note: Author updates since 2013 from Kloeck (2014), although with minor modifications from the latter in the case of some reported estimates. 'Weight' denotes the weight assigned to the respective study in calculating the weighted average of all studies by year, following Kloeck (2014) for studies published until 2013. The latter author determines the weight as a function of his assessment of robustness, transparency and sample coverage of each study's estimate. Weights for the updates after 2013 are chosen to be equal to one for each study, although lower weights are given for regional sub-sample results or where sample minima or maxima but not averages are available in order to obtain a single point estimate per study and year. IMF (2014) considers G-SIB banks plus the three largest banks by asset side in each country if these are not G-SIBs. Zhao (2017) reports mean estimates for 35 banks (and 11 insurance companies) for three different periods (2005 to mid-2007, 2008 to 2009, and 2010 to 2013) that are transformed here into annual data (with the observation for 2007 obtained from the first average, etc.). Estimates reported for Groenewegen and Wierts (2017) refer to the weighted average of funding advantages in basis points for banking sectors in France, Germany, Italy, the Netherlands and the United Kingdom.

implicit guarantees more or less valuable. An advantage of this approach is that, provided the probability of bank financial distress is unaffected by the event, the asset price change reflects the change in the assumed probability of support for the bank *if* in distress. An early example is O'Hara and Shaw (1990), who find that positive wealth effects accrued to shareholders of the eleven banks that were considered 'TBTF' when that terminology was introduced in the bank regulatory debate by the United States Comptroller of the Currency. Other examples of such events are the bailout of banks (Pop and Pop, 2009) or their collapse (Warburton *et al.*, 2013), or changes in sovereign credit ratings (Correa *et al.*, 2013). Yet, other studies that could be subsumed under the broad header of event studies focus on mergers and acquisitions that can be expected to make the merged entity more likely to be 'TBTF'. For example, Brewer and Jagtiani (2007) find that the merger premium is higher to the extent that the merger increases the perception of an implicit guarantee.

One shortcoming of studies considering the effect of events on bank equity, as opposed to bond returns, is that the results are difficult to interpret. As explained in Section 4, the economic effect of an increase in the value of implicit bank debt guarantees consist of weakened market discipline and increased risk-taking on the part of the bank. As a result, bank leverage tends to rise, which generates higher equity returns in 'good times'. These advantages are partly offset by potentially larger equity losses in 'bad times', however, although the net expected effect on shareholder returns should be positive as long as bank managers act in their shareholder interest. That said, increased bank risk-taking tends to increase the probability of the shareholders being partly or fully wiped out as part of bank failure resolution. In the United States, equity holders have traditionally been wiped out as part of the failure resolution of small and medium-sized banks. In Europe, the Bank Recovery and Resolution Directive makes the absorption of losses from within the bank, and involving equity holders, mandatory as part of bank failure resolution as of 1 January 2016. Another, more general, issue related to all event studies, that is also to those that consider bond returns, is that the result from any of them is by definition difficult to generalize and verify through continued monitoring, as it would require the occurrence of similar events for results to be updated. Obviously, an event-study approach is particularly useful if the question addressed is to identify what has been the effect of specific regulatory or other policy actions or announcements on the value of implicit bank debt guarantees, as discussed in Section 6.

5.3.5 *Combining Different Approaches to Obtain More Robust Estimates*

There is no *single* measurement approach that is widely used and accepted. Four different types of methods can be distinguished, measuring the value of implicit bank debt guarantees more or less directly and requiring different data as well as making different assumptions. All methods present some shortcomings and the choice of the method depends on the question raised. To the extent that one is interested in estimates of the *magnitude* of the phenomenon and developments over longer stretches of time, rating-based methods seem to be the preferred choice by policy makers (figure 3 in Schich and Aydin, 2014a). A ratings-based approach is straightforward to implement even across different countries or markets. It also benefits from the simplicity of methodology and easy availability of required data. That being said, the usefulness of rating-based approaches to valuing implicit guarantees, in terms of basis-point or US-dollar-equivalent funding advantages, crucially hinges on the quality of the mapping from credit rating uplifts into funding cost advantages. This link is, however, time-varying and reflects in particular the wider financial market condition,

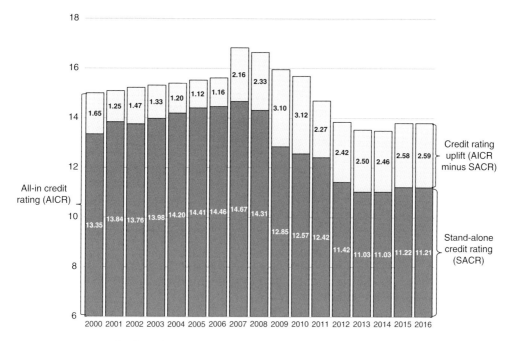

Figure 3. Credit Rating Uplifts of Large Banks due to Assumed External Support.
Notes: Horizontal axis shows numerical equivalents of credit rating in notches, where a triple-A rating corresponds to a value of 20, double-A to a value of 19 and so on. The bars indicate annual average values of stand-alone credit rating (SACR) and the difference between the all-in credit rating (AICR) and SACR, which defines the credit rating uplift due to assumed external support. Sample of 204 banks. Based on data publicly available from Moody's. Note that other rating agency assessments might be consistent with a more substantial decline in credit rating uplifts over the most recent years than is suggested by the estimates shown in the above figure.
Source: Update from Schich and Toader (2017). [Color figure can be viewed at wileyonlinelibrary.com]

including the level of collective risk, the influence of which on this relationship is difficult to assess.

Direct estimates of funding costs advantages based on observed market prices are difficult to implement, especially if the intent is to consider cross-country evidence, which is typically the case as a large part of the reforms are internationally co-ordinated. Moreover, it requires one to be confident in one's ability to isolate the effects of the implicit guarantee from those of changes in the debtor's creditworthiness and other factors affecting prices such as general market conditions.

Contingent claims analysis is conceptually attractive and allows one to distinguish between idiosyncratic and collective risk, but it tends to produce estimates that can be highly volatile as a result of small changes in assumptions and are thus sometimes difficult to interpret. It should also be noted that estimates that use historical data to calibrate a baseline are biased downwards as bail-out expectations are already reflected in the market pricing (Kelly *et al.*, 2016; Gudmundsson, 2016). Thus, the observed volatility, which was particularly high during 2008 and 2009 would have been much higher in the absence of the presence of the guarantor-of-last-resort function (see also Section 2.1), and standard methods thus underestimate the value of implicit bank debt guarantees in such situations. As a general rule, considering more than one approach in parallel (as done by Noss and Sowerbutts, 2012; IMF, 2014) is likely to generate more robust results than relying on any individual method.

Table 1 provides summary estimates from different studies, building on Kloeck (2014) and updating the latter to include more recent estimates of funding cost advantages in terms of basis points of interest rates. The picture that is emerging is that estimates seem to have peaked during the heights of the global financial crisis in 2008 and 2009 for worldwide banks. Distinguishing between regions, estimates for Europe tend to be higher than those for Japan and the United States. Estimates of funding cost advantages in terms of basis points of interest rates have declined from their peaks, although it is not so clear how the value of implicit guarantees for the most recent period compares to the pre-crisis period. Estimates are not strictly comparable across different studies and few estimates are available that stretch over long time periods of a decade or so, covering both pre-crisis and a very recent period. Estimates of credit rating uplifts due to assumed external support are available for comparatively longer periods (Figure 3). Using such estimates to assess developments in the value of implicit bank debt guarantees for large international banks, it appears that such values have declined since their peak, but not necessarily below values observed before the global financial crisis.

6. How Do Markets React to What Policy Makers Say and Do about Implicit Guarantees?

6.1 How Do Policy Makers Communicate about the Issue of Implicit Bank Debt Guarantees?

Communication on the part of policy makers regarding the value of implicit bank debt guarantees is a challenge. At the peak of the recent global financial crisis, numerous policy announcements were made that aimed at instilling confidence and that suggested the presence of implicit bank debt guarantees. By contrast, during normal times, policy makers tend not to make any announcement that could be interpreted as confirming the notion that such guarantees exist. More recently, numerous policy makers have clearly announced their intentions to rid banks of the benefits of such implicit guarantees given that they create costs on their own (see, for example, Dombret, 2013) and that they reflect other economic distortions (Haldane, 2011): 'Indeed, eliminating this subsidy has been taken as a bellwether of the authorities' success in tackling the too-big-to-fail problem'.

Robust measures of the value of implicit guarantees are required to assess bank regulatory and failure resolution progress (for example, Noss and Sowerbutts, 2012; Schich, 2013; Siegert and Willison, 2015). As discussed in Section 5.3.5, unfortunately, there is no single measurement approach that is widely used and accepted as the standard approach. Moreover, as a general rule, public authorities do not have *official* estimates of the value of implicit bank debt guarantees. They do not have *official* views on the value of such guarantees in particular as they do not intend to provide such guarantees and wish to avoid taking measures or making assessments that might be interpreted as confirming the existence of such guarantees. For example, as a general rule, the value of implicit bank debt guarantees is not recognized in the government's fiscal budget and this situation makes it difficult to hold governments accountable for these guarantees. Transparency about not just actual but also contingent liabilities is, however, an important factor that facilitates accountability and sound decision making; in principle, knowing that the public is aware of the consequences of policy decisions should instil additional incentives on the part of policy makers to avoid making poor decisions.

That said, several public authorities have produced estimates of the value of implicit bank debt guarantees or are aware of credible estimates of such values (for example, Noss and Sowerbutts, 2012; Deutsche Bundesbank, 2016). Discussions of the results of a survey of self-assessment among public authorities of the effects of bank regulatory reform on the value of implicit bank debt guarantees conducted by the Committee on Financial Markets of the OECD concluded (Schich and Aydin, 2014a):

'Despite the measurement difficulties, there was consensus that a reasonably robust measure of implicit bank debt guarantees is a key input to assessing the success of regulatory reform, including changes in resolution methods, in reducing the perception that banks are too-big, too interconnected or otherwise important to be allowed to fail'.

Such measures could be used, in principle, not only for monitoring bank regulatory and failure resolution reform progress, but also to calibrate an explicit premium in exchange for implicit bank debt guarantees. Such a 'user fee' would disincentive banks' 'usage' of the guarantor of last resort function discussed in Section 2.1. In fact, to limit the value of implicit guarantees, in principle, three policy options are available. First, to strengthen banks, for example, by requiring larger and better-quality capital and liquidity buffers and improved governance and risk management, so that the value of implicit guarantees declines. Second, to strengthen the capacity of public authorities to withdraw the implicit guarantees, in particular by making failure resolution more effective and credible. Third, to charge an explicit premium in exchange for the market perception of an implicit guarantee, thus incentivizing banks to reduce their 'use' of this guarantee and making themselves safer and more resolvable. Asked pointedly to what extent a mix of these three policy approaches describes their specific regulatory reforms, respondents to the above-mentioned OECD survey considered strengthening banks (first option) and withdrawing guarantees (second option) appropriate descriptions. Less so the third option, that is 'charging a user fee' (Figure 4). Moreover, a list of specific policy choices was offered in the survey, grouped by the three policy options mentioned above. Again, among the altogether 33 specific policies, respondents considered *'producing estimates of the value of implicit bank debt guarantees and charging directly for them'* the least adequate description of their domestic policy (see Appendix A and Schich and Aydin, 2014b, figure 1). By contrast, more than three quarters of respondents considered appropriate to describe measures of their bank regulatory reform as indirectly charging by *'imposing other costs such as extra capital charges that rise with measures of "systemicness" of bank'* so as to incentivize banks to reduce their use of implicit bank debt guarantees. This assessment is consistent with the discussion in Section 2.3, which suggests that given the complex nature of implicit guarantees and time-inconsistency problems, simply 'charging' for their value is not a feasible option to eliminate them.

'TBTF' is a fundamental reason why implicit guarantees exist and, against the background of this assessment, 'ending TBTF' is a declared objective and key element of financial regulatory reform (FSB, 2017a, 2017b). The TBTF terminology dates back to at least 1984 when 11 banks in the United States were singled out by the Comptroller of the Currency as being 'TBTF'. No specific charge was involved then, which was criticized by O'Hara and Shaw (1990). Also, no precise definition for TBTF was provided, except that it meant that all deposits of the 11 banks considered TBTF were effectively protected by an implicit bank debt guarantee. Thus, the concepts of TBTF and implicit guarantees are closely related to each

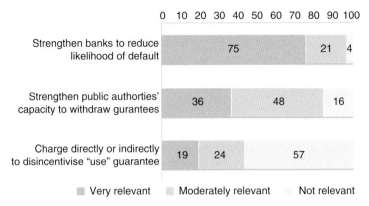

Figure 4. Description of Mix of Regulatory Reforms Undertaken with a Bearing on the Value of Implicit Bank Debt Guarantees (according to Self-Assessment by Policy Makers).

Note: Percentages of responses. Responses from 33 of (then-) 34 OECD member countries and two partner countries to a survey by the OECD Committee on Financial Markets on 'policy responses to the issue of implicit bank debt guarantees'. Respondents were asked to describe the overall thrust of the mix of policy measures that they have either implemented, where three categories were offered alternatively for the responses. The questionnaire acknowledged that even if many of the regulatory reform measures were not exclusively geared towards reducing the value of implicit guarantees, they would be expected to have an effect on the value as they affect the costs, returns and risks of bank business activities.

Source: Schich and Aydin (2014b). [Color figure can be viewed at wileyonlinelibrary.com]

other, and the value of implicit guarantees might thus be a good measure to assess progress in limiting TBTF (Haldane, 2011; Siegert and Willison, 2015).

TBTF is however a broad concept and means different things to different people (Kaufman, 2014); often, TBTF, implicit guarantees and bail-out are used almost interchangeably, which is why it is useful to explain the relationships between these concepts. A narrow definition of TBTF is that failure of the entity would have adverse consequences for the functioning of the financial 'system', either a national or global one. Regulators have identified banks considered either globally or domestically systemically important. But implicit guarantees go beyond such entities and include entities where market participants perceive that other policy-maker objectives might be relevant, such as those of supporting specific regional activities, financial market segments or protecting specific types of investors. For example, in the case of some stressed Spanish and Italian banks, retail households turned out to be significant holders of subordinated bank debt claims, and expectations that such holders of claims would not be fully bailed in as part of bank failure resolution was reflected in the dynamics of the pricing of such claims. A hierarchy of types of banks can thus be said to exist with respect to the degree of *ex ante* strength of perception of implicit guarantees (Figure 5), which corresponds to the expectations that creditors of the bank under consideration would be bailed out *ex post*.

'Ending TBTF' is part of the wider financial regulatory reform, which aims at making the system safer, simpler and fairer (FSB, 2017c). The finalization of Basel III in December 2017 completes that package of reforms and the agenda is now changing to implementation and evaluation of reforms. Making it safer involves making institutions safer, especially those considered to be systemically important, in particular by requiring them to hold larger and qualitatively better capital and liquidity buffers. In addition, it involves limiting any potential

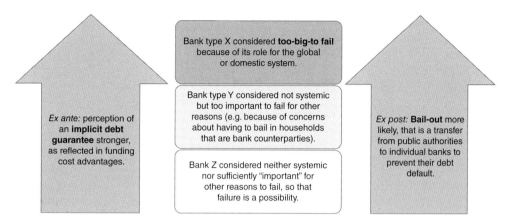

Figure 5. Implicit Guarantees, Too-Big-to-Fail and Bail-Out: Strength of Selected *Ex Ante* and *Ex Post* Considerations Depending on 'type of bank'.
Notes: Arrows indicate the direction in which the strength of respective perceptions tend to be increasing as a function of the considerations regarding the 'type of bank', as described by one of three stylized descriptions (referred to as bank X, Y or Z, respectively). A bail-out is defined here as a transfer from public authorities to individual banks to prevent a debt default that is considered to impose such severe negative externalities upon other economic actors that outweigh the potential moral hazard effects created by the transfer. [Color figure can be viewed at wileyonlinelibrary.com]

adverse spill-overs that might arise from the behaviour or the failure of individual institutions for the stability of the system as a whole. Making it simpler involves in particular simplifying the network of relations created through derivatives transactions and shifting the bulk of these to central clearing systems. It also involves strengthening the resilience and resolvability of these systems, as well as ideally the entities interacting with each other as part of them. This situation includes that banks of any size would be allowed to fail, if the risks taken by them turned out to be excessive, without having wider adverse spill-overs for the system as a whole. In defining what is involved in making the system fairer, the FSB explicitly refers to large banks at the centre of the financial system that did not internalize the social costs that their excessive risk-taking created. In fact, it is pointed out that the gains of such risk-taking activities were privatized and losses socialized. A fairer system involves funding conditions that are more closely aligned with the riskiness of the entities. In other words, there would be no room for implicit bank debt guarantees.

6.2 *How Do Financial Markets React to What Policy Makers Say and Do?*

A number of empirical recent studies assess the effect of regulatory and other policy actions and announcements on indicators of the value of implicit bank debt guarantees, based on the idea that these events would be expected to influence the value of implicit bank debt guarantees. For example, Zhao (2017) considers a measure of implicit debt guarantees based on price differentials of bank bond CDS spreads (stipulating that senior but not junior bonds are protected) and regresses the measure on a number of control variables and a dummy taking on the value of one from the date of announcement of Basel III in November 2010. The dummy variable turns out to be significantly positive, thus different from the direction desired by regulatory reform. Unfortunately, the study does not differentiate between banks that do and those that do not benefit from implicit guarantees, thus making it difficult to conclude that Basel III has not had an effect on the value of implicit guarantees. As implicit bank debt guarantees reflect market perceptions rather than the result of an explicit policy, a robust analysis must identify on the basis of *a priori* considerations a group of banks that may be benefiting from an implicit guarantee, as well as a comparison group of banks or other firms that can be reasonably assumed not to be protected by a similar guarantee. No strong consensus has yet emerged among researchers of how best to define these groups, but a growing number of suggestions are becoming available. Schäfer *et al.* (2016) study CDS premiums and their reactions to bank failure resolution cases, distinguishing whether only junior or also senior debtholders were involved in the burden sharing in these cases ('bail-in'). Overall, they find that creditor bail-in events imply an increase in CDS spreads and hence a reduction in the value of implicit bank debt guarantees. The reaction is found to differ across countries, with the effects stronger for banks in fiscally weak countries, and over time, with early bail-ins in Denmark and Spain not having as significant an effect as the later bail-ins in the Netherlands and Cyprus. The finding is interpreted by the authors as suggesting that policy actions speak louder than words. This interpretation is consistent with Schich and Kim (2012), who suggest resolution practises have more powerful effects on perceptions of government support (as reflected in credit ratings) than mere changes in regulation or legislation, which may or may not be followed by changing practises.

Equity price reactions to actions and announcements have also been analysed. For example, Bongini *et al.* (2015) conduct an event study considering stock market reactions for a sample of 70 of the largest banks worldwide subsequent to the publication of the consultative papers on 19 July 2011 and the disclosure of the first and second list of G-SIBs on 4 November 2011 and 1 November 2012, respectively. Subsequent to the first event, the authors identify significantly positive cumulative abnormal daily stock market prices for banks from Europe (both G-SIBs and non-G-SIBs) but not for banks from other regions, which the author explain as perhaps reflecting the greater perceived rescue propensity of public authorities in Europe compared to other regions. The second event did not result in any discernible and robust patterns in terms of bank nationality or G-SIB status and the third was considered non-event. Moenninghoff *et al.* (2015) analysed the stock market reaction in terms of cumulative abnormal returns for G-SIBs and other banks to announcements regarding the designation and special 'treatment' of globally systemically important banks. They consider altogether 12 policy or regulatory announcements between November 2008 and November 2011, most of which were related to G20 summits. Many announcements were found to result in negative abnormal returns for G-SIBs (two of which were even significant), consistent with the view that market value declines for banks that are exposed to more costly and intrusive regulation arising from G-SIB status. By contrast, the designation of banks as G-SIBs in November 2011 is found to have an offsetting positive effect as compared to these other events. The authors conclude that designating G-SIBs eliminated ambiguity about the presence of government guarantees, and thereby may have run counter to the regulators' intent to contain the effects of TBTF at that point in time. As explained in Section 5.3.4, the validity of the interpretation of these empirical results requires that bank equity value unequivocally increases with the value of implicit bank debt guarantee. That assumption is not justified as a general rule; hence, these results need to be interpreted with some caution.

One drawback of event studies is the difficulty in precisely attributing a change in the regulation or resolution framework to a specific date. Such changes are typically the results of long-term processes and it is difficult to identify which dates were the most relevant in providing 'news' about framework changes. A similar issue complicates the interpretation of results for actual resolution cases. Bank failure resolutions do not occur on a specific day without forewarning, but are parts of processes, some of which can be long and drawn-out. Another major drawback of event studies is that they can only interpret the financial market's reaction on the actual day of the announcement or for a short period after. Market participants' assessment of a specific piece of regulation or interpretation of policy action might, however, change during the weeks or months after the initial 'event'. Event studies only capture the short-term response to 'news' and, thus, it would be problematic to assess regulatory reform progress based on such snapshots.

6.3 *What Has Been the Response to the 'Special Treatment' Administered to G-SIBs So Far?*

Parts of the overall financial reform package are equivalent to effectively imposing an *indirect* charge for the 'use' of implicit guarantees. Such a characterization seems to describe, for example, the regulatory approach that is to designate some banks as so-called globally systemically important banks (henceforth, G-SIBs), based on an internationally agreed methodology, and then to subject these banks to a special regulatory, supervisory and failure resolution regime. This approach comes close to charging extra costs in exchange for the special privileges that the designated banks benefit from.

To clarify, the term 'designate' is used here somewhat loosely, as strictly speaking the process involves at least three distinct steps. First, the Basel Committee on Banking Supervision (BCBS) defined a methodology in 2011 on the basis of which the FSB and the BCBS established a list of banks identified as G-SIBs, published in November 2011. Incidentally, the methodology for identifying G-SIBs was revised in November 2012, and so was the composition of the list, although only marginally. Second, the FSB, in consultation with the BCBS and national authorities, uses that methodology annually to subject this list to changes and publishes a list of banks identified as G-SIBs in November of each year. Third, national authorities decide to implement the policy measures agreed upon. For simplicity, the remainder of this paper refers to these various steps just as 'G-SIB approach'.

According to the FSB, the G-SIB approach is motivated by the view that G-SIBs pose greater risks to the global financial system than other financial institutions. Beyond identifying a list of such entities, the designated entities are subjected to the following 'special treatment' as compared to other financial institutions (FSB, 2011): (i) a new international standard as a point of reference for reforms of national resolution regimes, to strengthen authorities' powers to resolve failing financial firms in an orderly manner and without exposing the taxpayer to the risk of loss; (ii) specific requirements for resolvability assessments, recovery and resolution plans and institution-specific cross-border co-operation agreements for G-SIBs; (iii) specific requirements for additional loss absorption capacity above the Basel III minimum for global systemically important banks; and (iv) more intensive and effective supervision through stronger supervisory mandates, and higher supervisory expectations for risk management functions, risk data aggregation capabilities, risk governance and internal controls. The various elements of the special treatment were foreseen to, and did enter at different dates that were known in advance. Starting in January 2016, the requirements were phased in with full implementation foreseen by January 2019.

What has been the effect of this 'special treatment' so far? Schich and Toader (2017) consider G-SIB designation in November 2011 as the beginning of the treatment of G-SIBs,

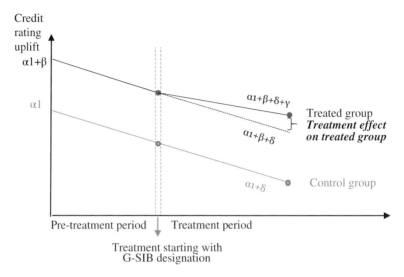

Figure 6. Interpretation of Difference-in-Difference Parameter Estimates. [Color figure can be viewed at wileyonlinelibrary.com]

considering a sample of 27 G-SIBs and a control group of 177 other large banks from 23 countries from 2007 to 2015. The authors estimate the following equation (for the interpretation of parameters, see also Figure 6):

$$UPLIFT_{it} = \alpha_1 + \beta Treatment\_group_i + \delta T_t + \gamma(Treatment\_group_i \ x \ T_t) + \alpha_2 X_{it} + \varepsilon_{it}$$

where $UPLIFT_{it}$ is the value of implicit bank debt guarantee for bank i in year t (credit rating uplift calculated as shown in Figure 3), and $Treatment\_group_i$, T_t and $Treatment\_group \ x \ T$ are binary variables. $Treatment\_group_i$ is equal to one for the group of treated banks, that is, banks that have been included in the list of G-SIBs, and it is equal to zero for banks never included in that list (henceforth referred to as other banks). T_t describes the timing of the treatment; it is equal to zero for the period until the designation of G-SIBs, that is, until the first publication of that list (or, alternatively, the publication of the revised list one year later) and equal to one afterwards. The binary variable $Treatment\_group_i \ x \ T_t$ takes the value of one only for the treatment group in the post-treatment period. X_{it} is a vector of explanatory variables, including the strengths of the bank and its domestic sovereign as well as control variables in the form of dummies identifying changes in resolution regimes and practises (see Appendix B), and α_2 is the vector of estimation parameters for these variables. The coefficient β measures the differences across groups that are constant over time, δ the differences over time that are common to both groups and γ the effect of the treatment on the treated group. Figure 6 illustrates the interpretation of the various parameters.

The G-SIB approach might, in principle, have two consequences. First, the additional regulatory, supervisory and failure resolution failures requirements might make the concerned banks more stable and more easy to resolve should they experience substantial stress. Both of these effects would tend to lower the value of implicit bank debt guarantees for the concerned banks as compared to other banks, all other aspects being equal. The probability of distress would decline together with the probability of bail-out if in distress. This is the desired effect.

Second, by identifying some banks as different from others by including them in a list of banks considered to constitute a greater risk to the financial system in the event of failure, the perception that these banks are 'TBTF' might become further entrenched, that is, the probability of bail-out if in distress would increase. If this was the case, the value of implicit guarantees for those banks compared to other banks would not change, or might even increase. This would be an undesirable effect. The empirical results regarding these potential effects, considering data until 2016, are as follows (Table 2):

- First, the signs of the key control variables are all significant in the expected direction. In particular, the coefficient of the banks' own strength, *SACR*, is found to be negative and highly significant. That is, weaker banks benefit from greater values of implicit guarantees. The coefficient of the strength of the domestic sovereign, *SCR*, is significantly positive. That is, banks headquartered in countries with a stronger sovereign benefit from higher values of implicit guarantees. Both observations are consistent with empirical findings in several previous empirical studies (for example, Estrella and Schich, 2011; Toader, 2015; Schäfer *et al.*, 2016) and conceptual work on the role of the strengths of the debtor and the guarantor in the valuation of risky guarantees discussed in Section 5.1.
- Second, the coefficients of the other control variables, capturing changes in resolution frameworks or practises are almost always significant in the expected direction. The coefficient for the variable capturing the introduction of a new resolution regime, *NRF*, is negative as expected and highly significant in one but not the other specification. The results regarding changes in resolution practises, that is, *DL*, are highly significant in the expected direction, as is the result regarding *NRF* x *DL* capturing situations where both a new resolution regime was introduced and debt holders were included in the burden sharing. Thus, once losses are effectively being imposed on debt holders in a country that had adopted a new failure resolution framework, the value of implicit bank debt guarantees for banks in that country subsequently declines (see also Schäfer *et al.*, 2016; and Schich and Kim, 2012).
- Third, the results regarding the effects of G-SIB status are mixed. Banks designated as G-SIBs benefit from higher values of implicit guarantees than other banks, on average, over the sample. The coefficient of the variable *Treatment group* is positive and statistically significant. Also, the coefficient δ of the variable *Treatment* is negative, implying that the value of implicit guarantees declined during the treatment period for all banks. The estimated parameter for the variable *Treatment_group$_i$ x T$_t$*, that is, the effect of the treatment on the treated is however not significant.

Thus, while there has been overall progress in reducing the perception of government support for large banks worldwide, the G-SIB approach – that is, identifying and then subjecting to special treatment a sub-set of banks that are considered to pose a particular threat to global financial stability – has not been effective. The liabilities of G-SIBs continue to benefit from a higher level of government support assumption than those of other banks. One interpretation is that there has been no practical experience with the resolution of a G-SIB in practise and that resolution regimes for G-SIBs are not yet fully credible. For example, the credibility of the so-called living wills intended to render the default of these institutions manageable and submitted by the banks themselves has been questioned by regulators (Fed and FDIC, 2016). Allowing firms to fail and involving bank debtors in the burden sharing seems, however, the most effective approach to limiting the value of implicit bank debt guarantees. In other words (borrowed from Schäfer *et al.*, 2016), actions speak louder than words.

Table 2. Difference-in-Difference Estimates on Credit Rating Uplift (Data from 2007 to 2016; Considering G-SIB Designation in 2011).

Dependent variable: Credit rating uplift, i.e. all-in minus stand-alone credit rating	(1)	(2)	(3)	(4)	(5)
Independent variables:					
Treatment group (=1 if bank is on FSB G-SIB list)	0.57***	0.65***	0.79***	0.79***	0.71***
	(4.97)	(5.70)	(6.70)	(6.68)	(5.88)
Treatment (=1 if year is > 2010)	−0.64***	−0.28***	−0.44***	−0.46***	−0.29***
	(−6.86)	(−2.95)	(−5.11)	(−4.87)	(−3.33)
Treatment group × Treatment (=1 if bank is on FSB G-SIB list and year >2010)	0.18	0.23	0.15	0.15	0.27*
	(1.24)	(1.61)	(1.03)	(1.01)	(1.78)
Strength of bank (stand-alone credit rating)	−0.37***	−0.39***	−0.39***	−0.39***	−0.39***
	(−21.16)	(−22.17)	(−23.93)	(−23.22)	(−24.11)
Strength of sovereign (domestic sovereign credit rating)	0.26***	0.28***	0.25***	0.25***	0.25***
	(18.25)	(19.98)	(19.46)	(18.74)	(19.12)
New resolution framework (NRF=1 if new resolution framework implemented)		−0.74***		0.03	
		(−8.74)		(0.36)	
Debtholders losses (DL=1 if bank failure resolution involved debtholder losses)			−1.33***	−1.34***	
			(−16.96)	(−14.63)	
NRF × DL (=1 if new resolution framework in place and debtholders incurred losses)					−1.40***
					(−16.12)
Constant	2.55***	2.57***	3.21***	3.22***	3.11***
	(12.78)	(12.82)	(15.48)	(15.58)	(14.89)
Observations	2,026	2,026	2,026	2,026	2,026
R^2 adjusted	0.28	0.30	0.37	0.37	0.37
F	109.3	106.7	166.7	143.4	157.1

Notes: Dependent variable is the credit rating uplift, UPLIFT, defined as the difference between an issuers' all-in credit rating and its stand-alone credit rating according to Moody's in numerical equivalents. The treatment considered is the designation of G-SIB status in November 2011. Alternatively considering 2012 (or 2009 and 2010 when an unofficial, supposedly, 'leaked' list was published in the Financial Times), the results are very similar. Data for 204 banks and 10 years, although some missing, resulting in a dataset of 2026 observations. Robust t-statistics in parentheses. Significance at 1%, 5%, 10% identified by ***, **, and *, respectively.
Source: Update from Schich and Toader (2017).

7. Concluding Remarks and Open Issues

Implicit bank debt guarantees reflect perceptions by financial market participants that policy makers do not allow the bank to fail on its debt, thus avoiding to cause losses to its counterparties. Implicit bank debt guarantees create economic costs and while they might benefit some stakeholders in the short-term, they create additional economic costs over the long-term as well as additional risks. In particular, they tend to weaken the functioning of market discipline and encourage an increase in bank leverage and risk-taking. They also distort competition between banking sectors and other corporate sectors, between small and large banks as well as between banking sectors from different countries. They also might affect income distributions in undesired ways and they do create potential contingent liabilities for the sovereign and the taxpayer. The policy response to the global financial crisis might have further entrenched perceptions that at least many banks are TBTF.

Against the background of these various observations, policy makers have announced their intention to limit the value of implicit bank debt guarantees, even if not directly targeting such values. Most recently, related efforts have been framed by the FSB as an attempt to make the financial system 'fairer'. To achieve that policy objective, the preferred mix of policy measures chosen differs slightly from one country to another, although an overarching goal is to strengthen banks, thus making guarantees less valuable. Yet, another one is to taking measures that allow policy makers to withdraw the guarantees such as by making bank failure resolution more smooth and effective, thus reducing the perception that implicit guarantees exist. The third policy option available in principle, which is to use measures of the value of implicit bank debt guarantees to calibrate and charge a user fee on such guarantees, so as to disincentivize banks' 'use' of such guarantees, is considered less attractive. The rationale given is that there is no widely agreed preferential measure of the value of implicit guarantees and any official announcement regarding such estimates might be reinforcing the perception that such guarantees exist. Moreover, calibration of such a premium is challenging, given the complex nature of perceptions of guarantees and the feedback loops between such perceptions and what policy makers say and do.

That said, the approach of identifying some banks as globally systemically important and subjecting them to a special and more intrusive regulatory treatment ('the G-SIB approach') could be seen as an example of an indirect charge for the 'use' of implicit guarantees. So far, there is little evidence that this approach has been effective, however. There is evidence that the values of implicit bank debt guarantees for banks have declined from their peaks attained during the global financial crisis. Even if this observation might reflect in particular changed perceptions regarding banks that are not necessarily considered globally or domestically systemically important, it is nonetheless consistent with the desired effect of bank regulatory, supervisory and failure resolution reforms.

Several questions remain. According to many empirical estimates it is not clear whether the value of implicit bank debt guarantees has fallen below the values prevailing before the global financial crisis. The question then arises how much further should the value of implicit bank debt guarantees be reduced? At what point can their level be considered low enough so that the costs of further efforts to reduce them would outweigh the benefits of doing so? A related question is to what extent measures of the value of implicit bank debt guarantees are informative about perceptions that a guarantee exists? Or, to what extent might a decline in estimates just reflect the value of the guarantee moving further out of the money (just like a put option)? Also, some of the observed declines in measures of implicit guarantees seem to reflect a weakening capacity of the sovereign to provide the guarantee, but not necessarily a perceived increased resolve on the part of public authorities to withdraw the guarantee. As regards the latter, actions speak louder than words. Perceptions of implicit guarantees are most effectively limited by using some of the newly available failure resolution instruments and involve the creditors of a failing bank in the burden sharing associated with its resolution. Progress towards such a scenario appears to be some way off for creditors of large banks, and a long way off for those of the few 'G-SIBs'.

Acknowledgements

The author would like to thank Arturo Estrella for helpful suggestions on an earlier draft and Tryggvi Gudmundsson for discussions. Figure 3 and part of the results described in Section 6.3 draw on collaborative work with Oana Toader. The data shown in Table 1 for IMF (2014) are kindly made available by Oksana Khadarina and Frederic Lambert, and for Groenewegen and Wierts (2017) by the latter authors. The author also acknowledges the constructive suggestions from two anonymous referees, which have greatly improved the structure and clarity of the survey; the author is responsible for all remaining errors and interpretations.

References

Acharya, V.V., Drechsler, I. and Schnabl, P. (2014) A pyrrhic victory? Bank bailouts and sovereign credit risk. *Journal of Finance*, 69: 2689–2739.

Acharya, V.V., Anginer, D. and Warburton, A.J. (2016) The end of market discipline? Investor expectations of implicit government guarantees. NYU-Stern Working Paper, May. Retrieved from https://pages.stern.nyu.edu/~sternfin/vacharya/public_html/pdfs/Acharya%20Anginer%20Warburton%20May%2026,%202016%20paper.pdf.

Admati, A.R., DeMarzo, P.M., Hellwig, M.F. and Pleiderer, P. (2013) Fallacies, irrelevant facts and myths in the discussion of capital regulation: Why bank equity is not expensive. Working Paper No. 2065, Stanford Graduate School of Business. Retrieved from https://www.gsb.stanford.edu/faculty-research/working-papers/fallacies-irrelevant-facts-myths-discussion-capital-regulation-why.

Afonso, G., Santos, J.A.C. and Traina, J. (2015) Do 'too-big-to-fail' banks take on more risk? *The Journal of Financial Perspectives*, 3(2): 41–58. July.

Avgouelas, E. and Goodhart, C. (2014) A critical evaluation of bail-ins as bank recapitalisation mechanisms. CEPR Discussion Paper, No. 10065, Centre for Economic Policy Research. Retrieved from https://www.law.ed.ac.uk/includes/remote_people_profile/remote_staff_profile?sq_content_src=%2BdXJsPWh0dHAlM0ElMkYlMkZ3d3cyLmxhdy5lZC5hYy51ayUyRmZpbGVfZG93bmxvYWQlMkZzwdWJsaWNhdGlvbnMlMkYyXzI3NF9hY3JpdGljYWxldmFsdWF0aW9ub2ZiYWlsaW5zc2FzYW5rcmVjVjYXBpdGBkZiZhbGw9MQ%3D%3D.

Baldursson, F.M., Portes, R. and Thorlaksson, E.E. (2017) Iceland's capital controls and the resolution of its problematic bank legacy. SSRN Working Paper, 3 July. Retrieved from https://ssrn.com/abstract=2996631.

Beck, R., Georgiadis, G. and Straub, R. (2014) The finance and growth nexus revisited. *Economics Letters*, 124(3), September: 382–385.

Benczur, P., Cannas, G., Cariboni, J., Di Girolamo, F., Maccaferri, S. and Petracco Giudici, M. (2017) Evaluating the effectiveness of the new EU bank regulatory framework: A farewell to bail-out? *Journal of Financial Stability*, 33: 207–223, https://doi.org/10.1016/j.jfs.2016.03.001.

Bengui, J., Bianchi, J. and Coulibaly, L. (2016) Financial safety nets. NBER Working Paper 22594, September. Retrieved from https://www.nber.org/papers/w22594.pdf.

Bennett, R.L., Hwa, V. and Kwast, M.L. (2014) Market discipline by bank creditors during the 2008-2010 crisis. FDIC Center for Financial Research Working Paper, FDIC CFR WP 2014-03, March.

Beyhaghi, M., D'Souza, C. and Roberts, G.S. (2013) Funding advantage and market discipline in the Canadian banking sector. Bank of Canada Working Paper 2013-50. Retrieved from https://publications.gc.ca/site/archivee-archived.html?url=https://publications.gc.ca/collections/collection_2013/banque-bank-canada/FB3-2-113-50-eng.pdf.

Bijlsma, M. and Mocking, R. (2013) The private value of too-big-to-fail guarantees. Triburg University, TILEC Discussion Paper, May.

Blix Grimaldi, M., Hofmeister, J., Schich, S. and Snethlage, D. (2016) Estimating the size and incidence of bank resolution costs for selected banks in OECD countries. *OECD Journal: Financial Market Trends*, 2016/1, https://doi.org/10.1787/fmt-2016-5jlvbslktw7j.

Bongini, P., Nieri, L. and Pelagatti, M. (2015) The importance of being systemically important financial institutions. *Journal of Banking & Finance*, 50: 562–574.

Boot, A.W.A. and Thakor, A. (1993) Self-interested bank regulation. *American Economic Review*, 83(2): 206–212. Retrieved from https://www.jstor.org/stable/2117665.

Brewer, E. and Jagtiani, J. (2007) How much would banks be willing to pay to become 'too-big-to-fail' and to capture other benefits. Retrieved from https://ssrn.com/abstract=1003163 or https://doi.org/10.2139/ssrn.1003163.

Calomiris, C.W. (1997) The postmodern bank safety net – Lessons from developed and developing economies. The AEI Press, Publisher of the American Enterprise Institute, Washington, D.C.

Calomiris, C.W. (1999) Building an incentive-compatible safety net. *Journal of Banking & Finance*, 23: 1499–1519.

Cardillo, A. and Zaghini, A. (2012) The recent trends in long-term bank funding. Questioni di Economia e Finanza (Occasional Papers), No. 137, Bank of Italy, Economic Research and International Relations Area.

Cariboni, J., Joensson, H., Kazemi Veisari, L., Magos, D., Papanagiotou, E. and Planas, C. (2013) Annex A4.2: Size and determinants of implicit state guarantees to EU banks. JRC Scientific and Policy Reports, JRC84687. Retrieved from www.cdep.ro/afaceri_europene/CE/2014/SWD_2014_30_EN_DOCUMENTDETRAVAIL_f.pdf

Cariboni, J., Fontana, A., Langedijk, S., Maccaferri, S., Pagano, A., Petracco Giudici, M., Rancan, M. and ... Schich, S. (2016) Reducing and sharing the burden of bank failures. *OECD Journal: Financial Market Trends*, 2015/2, https://doi.org/10.1787/fmt-2015-5jm0p43ldl30.

Casey, A. and Posner, E.A. (2015) A framework for bailout regulation. Coase-Sando Working Paper in Law and Economics, No. 724.

Chen, Y. (1999) Banking panics: The role of the first-come, first-served rule and information externalities. *Journal of Political Economy*, 107(5): 946–968.

Cordella, T., Dell'Ariccia, G. and Marquez, R. (2017) Government guarantees, transparency, and bank risk-taking. Policy Research Working Paper, No. WPS 7971, World Bank. Retrieved from https://documents.worldbank.org/curated/en/468401487165710483/Government-guarantees-transparency-and-bank-risk-taking

Correa, R., Lee, K.H., Sapriza, H. and Suarez, G. (2013) Sovereign credit risk, banks' government support, and bank stock returns around the world. Board of Governors of the Federal Reserve System, International Finance Discussion Papers (2012-No. 1069). Retrieved from www.federalreserve.gov/pubs/ifdp/2012/1069/default.htm

Cournède, B. and Denk, O. (2015) Finance and economic growth in OECD and G20 countries. OECD Economics Department Working Papers, No. 1223, OECD Publishing, Paris. https://doi.org/10.1787/5js04v8z0m38-en.

Dam, L. and Koetter, M. (2012) Bank bailouts and moral hazard: Evidence from Germany. *The Review of Financial Studies*, 25(8): 2343–2380. Retrieved from https://rfs.oxfordjournals.org/content/25/8/2343

Dell'Ariccia, G. and Ratvnoski, L. (2013) Bailouts and systemic insurance. IMF Working Paper WP/13/233, International Monetary Fund, November. Retrieved from https://www.imf.org/external/pubs/ft/wp/2013/wp13233.pdf

Demirgüç-Kunt, A., Kane, E. and Laevenet, L. (2014) Deposit insurance database. IMF Working Paper WP/14/118, International Monetary Fund, July. Retrieved from https://www.imf.org/external/pubs/ft/wp/2014/wp14118.pdf

Denk, O. and Cazenave-Lacroutz, A. (2015) Household finance and income inequality in the euro area. OECD Economics Department Working Papers, No. 1226, OECD Publishing, Paris. https://doi.org/10.1787/5js04v5wh9zs-en.

Denk, O., Schich, S. and Cournède, B. (2015) Why implicit bank debt guarantees matter: Some empirical evidence. OECD Journal: Financial Market Trends, 2014/2. https://doi.org/10.1787/fmt-2014-5js3bfznx6vj.

Deutsche Bundesbank. (2016) Magnitude and development of implicit government guarantees for banks. Financial Stability Review, 41–42. Retrieved from https://www.bundesbank.de/Redaktion/EN/Downloads/Publications/Financial_Stability_Review/2016_financial_stability_review.pdf?__blob=publicationFile

Dombret, A. (2013) Systemic risk, too big to fail and resolution regimes. Speech by Dr Andreas Dombret, Member of the Executive Board of the Deutsche Bundesbank, at the Salzburg Global Seminar "Out of the Shadows: Should Non-banking Financial Institutions Be Regulated?", Salzburg, 19 August 2013. Retrieved from https://www.bis.org/review/r130820c.pdf>

Estrella, A. and Schich, S. (2011) Sovereign and banking sector debt: Interconnections through guarantees. OECD Journal: Financial Market Trends, 2011/2. https://doi.org/10.1787/fmt-2011-5k9cswn0sfxt.

Estrella, A. and Schich, S. (2015) Valuing guaranteed bank debt: Role of strength and size of the bank and the guarantor. Journal of Economic and Financial Studies, 3(5): 19–32. Retrieved from https://EconPapers.repec.org/RePEc:lRc:lAreco:v:3:y:2015:i:5:p:19-32

European Free Trade Association Court. (2013) Judgment of the Court: 28 January 2013 (Directive 94/19/EC on Deposit-guarantee Schemes – Obligation of Result – Emanation of the State – Discrimination), Case E-16/11, EFTA Surveillance Authority v. Comm'n v. Iceland". Retrieved from www.eftacourt.int/.

Fed and FDIC. (2016) Agencies announce determinations and provide feedback on resolution plans of eight systemically important, domestic banking institutions. Joint Press Release of the Board of Governors of the Federal Reserve and the Federal Deposit Insurance Corporation, April 2016. Retrieved from https://www.federalreserve.gov/newsevents/pressreleases/bcreg20160413a.htm

Fischer, M., Hainz, C., Rocholl, J. and Steffen, S. (2014) Government guarantees and bank risk taking incentives. CESifo Working Paper, No. 4706, March.

FSB. (2011) Policy measures to address sistemically important financial institutions. Financial Stability Board, November. Retrieved from https://www.fsb.org/wp-content/uploads/r_111104bb.pdf?page_moved=1.

FSB. (2017a) Implementation and effects of the G20 financial regulatory reforms: Third annual report. Financial Stability Board, 3 July. Retrieved from https://www.fsb.org/2017/07/implementation-and-effects-of-the-g20-financial-regulatory-reforms-third-annual-report/.

FSB. (2017b) Ten years on: Taking stock of post-crisis resolution reforms. Sixth Report on the Implementation of Resolution Reforms, Financial Stability Board, 6 July. Retrieved from https://www.fsb.org/2017/07/ten-years-on-taking-stock-of-post-crisis-resolution-reforms/.

FSB. (2017c) Safer, simpler, fairer: G20 reforms explained. Financial Stability Board, 3 July. Retrieved from https://www.fsb.org/multimedia/safersimplerfairer/

Gadanecz, B., Tsatsaronis, K. and Altunba, Y. (2012) Spoilt and lazy: The impact of state support on bank behavior in the international loan market. International Journal of Central Banking. Retrieved from https://www.ijcb.org/journal/ijcb12q4a6.pdf.

Goldman Sachs. (2013) Measuring the TBTF Effect on Bond Pricing. New York: Goldman Sachs Global Markets Institute.

Grande, G., Levy, A., Panetta, F. and Zaghini, A. (2011) Public guarantees on bank bonds: Effectiveness and distortions. OECD Journal: Financial Market Trends, 2011/2, December. https://doi.org/10.1787/fmt-2011-5k9cswn0qg6l.

Groenewegen, J. and Wierts, P. (2017) Two big distortions: Bank incentives for debt financing. European Systemic Risk Board Working Paper Series No.53, August. Retrieved from https://www.esrb .europa.eu/pub/pdf/wp/esrb.wp53.en.pdf?9e481e87024eee87e31182773c128f70.

Gropp, R. (2014) Discussion of Correa, Lee, Sapriza, and Suarez. *Journal of Money, Credit and Banking*, Supplement to Vol. 46, No. 1, February. Retrieved from https://onlinelibrary.wiley.com/ doi/10.1111/jmcb.12081/abstract.

Gropp, R., Hakanes, H. and Schnabel, I. (2010) Competition, Risk Shifting and Public Bailout Policies. *Review of Financial Studies*, 22: 2084–2120.

Gudmundsson, T. (2016) Whose credit line is it anyway: An update on banks' implicit subsidies. IMF Working Paper WP/16/224, International Monetary Fund, November. Retrieved from https://www .imf.org/en/Publications/WP/Issues/2016/12/31/Whose-Credit-Line-is-it-Anyway-An-Update-on-Banks-Implicit-Subsidies-44406.

Guiso, L. and Sodini, P. (2013) Household finance: An emerging field. *Handbook of the Economics of Finance*, 2(B): 1397–1532.

Guiso, L., Haliassos, M. and Jappelli, T. (2002) (eds.) *Household Portfolios*. Cambridge, MA/London: MIT Press.

Hagendorff, J., Keasey, K. and Vallascas, F. (2017) When banks grow too big for their national economies: Tail risks, risk channels, and government guarantees. *Journal of Financial and Quantitative Analysis*, ISSN 0022-1090. Retrieved from https://www.cambridge.org/core/journals/ journal-of-financial-and-quantitative-analysis.

Haldane, A. (2010) The $100 billion question. BIS Review 40/2010. Retrieved from www.bis.org/review/ r100406d.pdf.

Haldane, A. (2011) Control rights (and wrongs). Wincott Annual Memorial Lecture, Westminster, London.

Hett, F. and Schmidt, A. (2016) Bank rescues and bailout expectations: The erosion of market discipline during the financial crisis. SAFE Working Paper No. 36, 24 October 2016. Retrieved from https://ssrn.com/abstract=2018830 or https://doi.org/10.2139/ssrn.2018830.

IMF. (2014) How big is the implicit subsidy for banks considered too important to fail? Global Financial Stability Report, Chapter 3, April.

Jacewitz, S. and Pogach, J. (2014) Deposit rate advantages at the largest banks. FDIC Working Paper 2014-02, February.

Kaufman, G.G. (2014) Too big to fail in banking: What does it mean? *Journal of Financial Stability*, 13: 214–223.

Kelly, B., Lustig, H. and Van Nieuwerburgh, S. (2016) Too-systemic-to-fail: What option markets imply about sector-wide government guarantees. *American Economic Review*, 106(6) June: 1278–1319.

Kloeck, A. (2014) Implicit subsidies in the EU banking sector. Intermediary report prepared for "Banking Structural Reforms: A Green Pperspective". Study commissioned by the Greens/EFA group in the European Parliament, January 2014. Retrieved from https://www.sven-giegold.de/ wp-content/uploads/2014/01/Implicit-subsidies-in-the-EU-banking-sector.pdf.

Kumar, A. and Lester, J. (2014) Do deposit rates show evidence of too big to fail effects? An updated look at the empirical evidence through 2012 among US banks. Oliver Wyman, March. Retrieved from https://www.theclearinghouse.org/~/media/files/press%20room/oliver%20wyman_deposit%20 rates%20study_031814.pdf.

Levy, A. and Schich, S. (2009) The Design of government guarantees for bank bonds: Lessons from the recent financial crisis. *OECD Journal: Financial Market Trends*, 2010(1). https://doi.org/ 10.1787/fmt-2010-5km7k9tp8t40; https://www.oecd.org/dataoecd/46/47/45636972.pdf.

Levy, A. and Zaghini, A. (2011) The pricing of government-guaranteed bank bonds. *Banks and Bank Systems*, 6(3): 16–24.

Li, Z., Qu, S. and Zhang, J. (2011) Quantifying the value of implicit government guarantees for large financial institutions. Moody's Analytics Quantitative Research Group, January.

Marcus, A. J. (1984) Deregulation and bank financial policy. *Journal of Banking & Finance*, 8(4): 557–565.

Markúsdóttir, E.V. (2011) Ireland's Too Big to Fail vs. Iceland's Too Big to Bail. B.SC. Thesis, Reykjavik University. Retrieved from https://skemman.is/bitstream/1946/9931/1/BSc%20Ritger%C3%B0%20Eva%20V.%20Mark%C3%BAsd%C3%B3ttir.pdf.

Marques, L.B., Correa, R. and Sapriza, H. (2013) International evidence on government support and risk taking in the banking sector. IMF Working Paper WP/13/94, International Monetary Fund, May. Retrieved from https://www.imf.org/external/pubs/ft/wp/2013/wp1394.pdf.

Merton, R. (1973) Theory of rational option pricing. *The Bell Journal of Economics and Management Science*, 4(1): 141–183.

Merton, R.C. (1974) On the pricing of corporate debt: The risk structure of interest rates. *Journal of Finance*, 29(2): 449–470.

Moenninghoff, S.C., Ongena, S. and Wieandt, A. (2015) The perennial challenge to counter too-big-to-fail in banking: Empirical evidence from the new international regulation dealing with global systemically important banks. *Journal of Banking & Finance*, 61, December: 221–236.

Morgan, D.P. and Stiroh, K.J. (2005) Too big to fail after all these years. Federal Reserve Bank of New York Staff Reports, No. 220, September. Retrieved from https://www.newyorkfed.org/medialibrary/media/research/staff_reports/sr220.pdf.

Morrison, A.D. (2011) Systemic risks and the 'too-big-to-fail' problem'. *Oxford Review of Economic Policy*, 27(3): 498–516.

Morrison, A.D. and White, L. (2010) Reputational contagion and optimal regulatory forbearance. European Central Bank Working Paper 1196, May. Retrieved from https://www.ecb.europa.eu/pub/pdf/scpwps/ecbwp1196.pdf?2487d72e479b527fbaeef430766528ba.

Noss, J. and Sowerbutts, R. (2012) The implicit subsidy of banks. Bank of England Financial Stability Paper, No. 15, Bank of England. Retrieved from www.bankofengland.co.uk/publications/Documents/fsr/fs_paper15.pdf.

O'Hara, M. and Shaw, W. (1990) Deposit insurance and wealth effects: The value of being 'too big to fail'. *Journal of Finance*, 45(5): 1587–1600.

Oxera. (2011) Assessing state support to the UK banking sector. Prepared at the request of The Royal Bank of Scotland, March 2011. Retrieved from www.oxera.com/Oxera/media/Oxera/downloads/reports/Assessing-statesupport-to-the-UK-banking-sector.pdf?ext=.pdf.

Packer, F. and Tarashev, N. (2011) Rating methodologies for banks. BIS Quarterly Review, June. Retrieved from https://www.bis.org/publ/qtrpdf/r_qt1106f.pdf.

Pop, A. and Pop, D. (2009) Requiem for market discipline and the specter of TBTF in Japanese banking. *The Quarterly Review of Economics and Finance*, 49: 1429–1459. Retrieved from https://congres.afse.fr/docs/PopPop.pdf

Pricewaterhouse Coopers (PWC). (2014) Bank structural reform study: Supplementary Report 1- Is there an implicit subsidy for EU banks? November. Retrieved from https://www.pwc.com/gx/en/banking-capital-markets/pdf/pwc-supplementary-report-1.pdf.

Rime, B. (2005) Do 'too big to fail' expectations boost large banks issuer ratings? Swiss National Bank.

Riksbank, Sveriges. (2011) Appropriate capital ratio in major Swedish banks: An economic analysis. Sveriges Riksbank, December.

Rochet, J.-C. and Tirole, J. (1996) Interbank lending and systemic risk. *Journal of Money, Credit and Banking*, 28(4): 733–762. Retrieved from https://www.jstor.org/stable/2077918.

Rousseau, P.L. and Wachtel, P. (2011) What is happening to the impact of financial deepening on economic growth?. *Economic Inquiry*, 49(1): 276–288.

Santos, J.A.C. (2014) Evidence from the bond market on banks' 'too-big-to-fail' subsidy. *Federal Reserve Bank of New York Economic Policy Review*, 20(2): 29–39. Retrieved from https://www.newyorkfed.org/research/epr/2014/1412sant.html.

Schäfer, A., Schnabel, I. and Weder di Mauro, B. (2016) Bail-in expectations for European banks: Actions speak louder than words. ESRB Working Paper Series, No.7, April.

Schenck, N.A. and Thornton, J.H. Jr (2016) Charter values, bailouts and moral hazard in banking. *Journal of Regulatory Economics*, 49(2), April 2016: 172–202. Retrieved from https://link.springer.com/article/10.1007/s11149-015-9292-0.

Schich, S. (2011) The government as guarantor of last resort: Benefits, costs and the case for premium charges. In L. Brosse (ed.), *Managing Risk in the Financial System*. Edward Elgar, Cheltenham, United Kingdom, June.

Schich, S. (2013) How to reduce implicit bank debt guarantees? A framework for discussing bank regulatory reform. *Journal of Financial Regulation and Compliance*, 21(4), November. Retrieved from https://www.emeraldinsight.com/journals.htm?articleid=17098675.

Schich, S. and Aydin, Y. (2014a) Measurement and analysis of implicit guarantees for bank debt: OECD survey results. *OECD Journal: Financial Market Trends*, *2014/1*. https://doi.org/10.1787/fmt-2014-5jxzbv3r9rf4.

Schich, S. and Aydin, Y. (2014b) Policy responses to the issue of implicit bank debt guarantees: OECD survey results. *OECD Journal: Financial Market Trends*, *2014/1*. https://doi.org/10.1787/fmt-2014-5jxzbv3r1x9x

Schich, S. and Kim, B.-H. (2012) Developments in the value of implicit guarantees for bank debt: The role of resolution regimes and practices. *OECD Journal: Financial Market Trends*, *2012/2*. https://doi.org/10.1787/fmt-2012-5k4c7r8dvhvf.

Schich, S. and Lindh, S. (2012) Implicit guarantees for bank debt: Where do we stand? *OECD Journal: Financial Market Trends*, *2012/1*. https://doi.org/10.1787/fmt-2012-5k91hbvfkm9v.

Schich, S. and Toader, O. (2017) To be or not to be a G-SIB: Does it matter?. *Journal of Financial Management, Markets and Institutions*, 2/2017, July-December. https://doi.org/10.12831/88826.

Schweikhard, F. and Tsesmelidakis, Z. (2012) The impact of government interventions on CDS and equity markets. Working Paper, University of Oxford.

Siegert, C. and Willison, M. (2015) Estimating the extent of the 'too big to fail' problem: A review of existing approaches. Bank of England Financial Stability Paper, No. 32.

Snethlage, D. (2015) Towards putting a price on the risk of bank failure. New Zealand Treasury Working Paper 15/03, New Zealand, March.

Toader, O. (2015) Quantifying and explaining implicit public guarantees for European banks. *International Review of Financial Analysis*, 41, October, 136–147, Elsevier. Retrieved from www.sciencedirect.com/science/article/pii/S1057521915001234.

Ueda, K. and Weder di Mauro, B. (2012) Quantifying structural subsidy values for systemically important financial institutions. IMF Working Paper No. 12/128, International Monetary Fund.

Volcker, P.A. (2004) Foreword. In Stern and Feldman (2004) *Too Big to Fail: The Hazard of Bank Bailouts*. Brookings Institution Press, Washington, D.C.

Warburton, J., Anginer, D. and Acharya, V. (2013) The end of market discipline? Investor expectations of implicit state guarantees. SSRN Paper, March 2013. Retrieved from https://papers.ssrn.com/sol3/papers.cfm?abstract_id=1961656.

Wihlborg, C. (2017) Bail-ins: Issues of credibility and contagion. SUERF Policy Note, Issue No. 10, The European Money and Finance Forum (SUERF).

Zhao, L. (2017) Market-based estimates of implicit government guarantees in European financial institutions. *European Financial Management*, John Wiley & Sons, https://doi.org/10.1111/eufm.12124.

Appendix A: Reform policies either implemented or being considered for implementation

Strengthen Banks (Reduce the likelihood of bank default):

Policy 1 Enhance the quantity and quality of capital at the level of the bank

- 1.1 Implement internationally agreed capital standards
- 1.2 'Top-up' internationally agreed capital standards by introducing additional capital charges
- 1.3 Change the risk-weighting of specific asset classes
- 1.4 Introduce binding leverage ratios
- 1.5 Introduce other measures that effectively limit the overall size of bank balance sheet

Policy 2 Enhance the quantity and quality of liquidity at the level of the bank

- 2.1 Implement internationally agreed liquidity standards
- 2.2 'Top-up' internationally agreed liquidity standards by introducing additional liquidity charges

Policy 3 Improve governance, risk management and disclosure of banks

- 3.1 Enhance on-going efforts to improve governance risk management and disclosure by banks
- 3.2 Disclose supervisory ratings and/or stress test results to strengthen market discipline

Policy 4 Tighten micro-prudential supervision to strengthen banks directly

- 4.1 Tightening on-site supervision
- 4.2 Tightening off-site supervision
- 4.3 Devoting more resources to supervision

Policy 5 Introduce or refine macro-prudential supervision to 'strengthen banks indirectly'

Policy 6 Introduce structural restrictions to avoid undesired cross-subsidization between parts of banking groups

- 6.1 Disallowing banking groups to engage in certain activities altogether
- 6.2 Requiring different types of activities to be conducted in separate and fully capitalized subsidiaries
- 6.3 Requiring subsidiarization of certain activities when specific thresholds of the extent of such activities are reached
- 6.4 Other structural measures

Strengthen the Capacity to Withdraw Guarantees:

Policy 7 Facilitate mote effective resolution

- 7.1 Establish new or make more effective existing bank failure resolution regimes
- 7.2 Strengthen unsecured creditor bail-in mechanisms
- 7.3 Mandatory issuance of specific amounts of instruments (for example, subordinated debt or debt to be converted into equity under specific circumstances)
- 7.4 Establish separate industry-financed funds for systemic crisis resolution to have funds available when required

Policy 8 Introduce structural restrictions to limit failure resolution costs and better protect claims considered worth protecting

8.1 Impose full structural separation of different business activities to facilitate resolution

8.2 Introduce structural restrictions or ring-fence specific activities

8.3 Require or encourage the adoption of specific corporate structures to facilitate resolutions

8.4 Require banks to develop plans how their operators could be dismantled

Policy 9 Strengthen deposit insurance directly

9.1 Strengthen deposit insurance arrangements and their funding

9.2 Introduce depositor preference

9.3 Introduce insured depositor preference

Policy 10 Improve financial market infrastructure

Charge a user fee to incentivize banks to reduce their 'use' of implicit guarantees:

Policy 11 Directly: produce estimates of the value of implied guarantees and charge banks for it (thus making them explicit)

Policy 12 Indirectly: impose other costs thus incentivizing banks to make less 'use' of guarantee

12.1 Impose other costs such as extra capital charges that rise with measures of 'systemicness' of banks

12.2 Charge deposit insurance premiums that rise with measures of riskiness

12.3 Establish separate systematic crisis resolution funds with risk-based premiums

Legend:

| | Policies implemented or considered by at least 75% of respondents. | | Policies implemented or considered by 50% to 75% of respondents. | | Policies implemented or considered by less than 50% of respondents. |

Note: The different patterns at the beginning of each row relate to the sum of respondents (in percentages) either i) having implemented or ii) considered implementation of the specific policy, with the alternative answer allowed to that question being 'not considered helpful'. Dark-grey shading indicates policies implemented or considered by at least 75% of respondents. Light-grey shading refers to policies either implemented or being considered for implementation by 50% to 75% of respondents. Cells with vertical stripes refer to policies implemented or considered for implementation by less than 50% of respondents. The percentages shown for broad policy categories (e.g. Policy 1) are obtained as the unweighted average of all responses to the specific policy choices in that category.

Source: Schich and Aydin (2014b).

Appendix B: Changes in resolution regimes and practises by country

Country	Number of banks	2007	2008	2009	2010	2011	2012	2013	2014	2015	2016
Australia	7										
Austria	7										
Belgium	4										
Canada	6										
Denmark	6										
Finland	3										
France	9 incl. 4 GSIBs										
Germany	19 incl. 1 GSIB										
Greece	4										
Ireland	5										
Italy	13 incl. 1 GSIB										
Japan	18 incl. 3 GSIBs										
Luxembourg	2										
Korea	9										
Netherlands	9 incl. 1 GSIB										
New Zealand	4										
Norway	9										
Portugal	6										
Spain	10 incl. 1 GSIB										
Sweden	6 incl. 1 GSIB										
Switzerland	8 incl. 2 GSIBs										
United Kingdom	15 incl. 4 GSIBs										
United States	25 incl. 8 GSIBs										

Legend: New resolution regimes introduced (NRF) / Losses imposed on unsecured debtholders (DL) / Both, new resolution regimes introduced and debtholder losses imposed.

Notes: The table illustrates the timing considered for constructing variables NRF, DL and NRF x DL contained in Table 2 of the main text. NRF (new resolution framework) is a dummy variable that takes on the value of one if a new bank failure resolution regime has been adopted in the home country of a bank. DL (debtholders losses) is a dummy that takes on the value of one for a bank whenever the bank failure resolution practises in the home country changed to the effect that failure resolution included situations where holders of either subordinated or senior unsecured debt instruments incurred losses. NRF x DL is an interaction dummy variable that takes on the value of one for a bank whenever both bank failure resolution regimes and practices changed in the home country. The table also indicates the number of banks in the sample from each country, including G-SIBs. Cells with vertical stripes indicate that a change in the bank failure resolution regime has occurred in the respective country at the beginning of the thus indicated period, cells with dots indicate that unsecured bank debtholders have been exposed to losses as part of actual bank failure resolution practices and dark-grey shaded cells indicate that both these types of events have occurred in the respective country at the beginning of the thus marked period.

Source: Update from Schich and Toader (2017).

4

FINANCIAL FRAUD:
A LITERATURE REVIEW

Arjan Reurink

Max-Planck-Institut fur Gesellschaftsforschung

1. Introduction

This paper explores the phenomenon of fraud in the financial services industry. Increasingly, it appears, fraud has moved from the fringes of the financial market activity to become a type of behaviour that is widespread throughout the industry. Despite the clear observability of this trend in the news media and its obvious empirical implications, mainstream academic research on financial markets has until now largely failed to account properly for this trend. As a first step in bringing the phenomenon of financial fraud closer to the centre of academic research on financial markets, this paper describes the empirical universe of financial fraud as it has been documented in the literature across a wide variety of disciplines.[1] The main purpose is not to present an all-encompassing analysis of the literature on financial fraud, but to provide a descriptive account of the different forms of fraudulent behaviour in the context of financial market activities,[2] the prevalence and consequences of such behaviour as identified by previous research, and the market structures that scholars believe facilitate this behaviour.

Before presenting the results of the literature review, it might be useful to demarcate the boundaries of the phenomenon under study. Fraud is a complex and elusive concept, both as a behavioural category[3] and as a legal one. In the context of financial market activities – banking, securities, and insurance – however, fraud can be attributed a more specific meaning and is best understood as the unlawful falsification or manipulation of financial information (Fligstein and Roehrkasse, 2013). Financial information acts as the linchpin for financial market transactions. Participants in financial markets merely exchange intangible rights (and obligations), the present and future value of which depends entirely on the status and future performance of the issuer of those rights (Lomnicka, 2008). To assess the current status and future performance of the issuer and ultimately to establish the perceived value of a financial instrument, both accurate information and the expertise necessary to interpret that information are essential.

Contemporary Topics in Finance: A Collection of Literature Surveys, First Edition. Edited by Iris Claus and Leo Krippner.
Chapters © 2019 The Authors. Book compilation © 2019 John Wiley & Sons Ltd. Published 2019 by John Wiley & Sons Ltd.

To facilitate the provision of information to the market, to safeguard the integrity of such information, and to protect market participants that lack the necessary expertise from being exploited by more sophisticated market participants, state authorities issue legal rules – regulatory rules, statutory laws, civil laws, and criminal laws – and prescribe sanctions that are then enforced by the courts and the designated authorities. Three sets of legal rules are of specific significance with regard to the phenomenon of financial fraud. First, to facilitate the provision of information to the market and to ameliorate the problem of information asymmetries, financial regulators have imposed *disclosure requirements* as a central pillar of financial market regulation in all developed financial markets (Seligman, 1983; Coffee, 1984; Mahoney, 1995; Selden, 2006). Disclosure requirements prescribe that issuers of financial instruments and providers of financial services disclose to the market and their counterparties all relevant information, that they do so in a timely manner, and that they make sure that all market participants have equal access to this information.

Second, to protect those financial market participants who are deemed to have insufficient expertise to interpret the available information from being exploited by more sophisticated market players, legal systems may impose *fiduciary duties* or *suitability requirement* on certain market participants. Fiduciary duties and suitability requirement, which exist in both retail (Mundheim, 1965; Lowenfels and Bromberg, 1999; BIS, 2008; Engel and McCoy, 2002, pp. 1317–1363) and wholesale (Schmedlen, 1995; Geckeler, 1996; Roberts, 1996; Pardieck, 2006; Davidoff Solomon *et al.*, 2012) financial markets, prescribe that financial service providers and financial advisers share some of the knowledge and expertise they hold so that clients or customers can make informed decisions with regard to financial transactions. Whether or not a fiduciary duty or suitability requirement applies, as well as the nature and extent of the duty in any particular case, is established by reference to the character of the parties involved in a specific transaction or cooperation and the underlying contractual relationship between those parties.

Third, legal systems prohibit certain deceptive behaviour through *general fraud laws*, which may appear in both civil and criminal bodies of law (Podgor, 1999; Buell, 2006, 2011; Ryder, 2011, pp. 93–139; Harrison and Ryder, 2013, pp. 61–90). In many jurisdictions the law also provides a number of legal statutes that target certain kinds of financial fraud more specifically. Most importantly, financial fraud in the securities markets is usually targeted by countries' securities law regimes. Other statutes may specifically target financial fraud in the banking or insurance sector, fraud perpetrated using mail and wire communications, or fraud perpetrated through the use of a computer or the Internet.

Where financial market participants willingly and knowingly provide the market or counterparties in specific transactions with false, incomplete or manipulative information in a way that violates any of the three sets of legal rules mentioned above we enter the domain of financial fraud. Fraud is thus understood here as a characteristic of a course of action that provides sufficient grounds for a regulatory enforcement action, successful private litigation, criminal prosecution in the courts, or all of these. For the purpose of this study, financial frauds can then be defined as *acts and statements through which financial market participants misinform or mislead other participants in the market by deliberately or recklessly providing them with false, incomplete or manipulative information related to financial goods, services or investment opportunities in a way that violates any kind of legal stipulation, be it a regulatory rule, statutory law, civil law, or criminal law.*

Concrete acts of financial fraud vary widely in their representations, depending on the market segments in which they are perpetrated, the financial instruments they pertain to, and the

Table 1. A Typology of Financial Fraud.

	Nature of the deception	Nature of the enterprise	Primarily prohibited by
False financial disclosures	Plain lies/mis-statements of facts	Legitimate	Disclosure requirements & General fraud laws
Financial scams	Plain lies/mis-statements of facts	Illegitimate	Disclosure requirements & General fraud laws
Fraudulent financial mis-selling	Misleading impressions	Legitimate/ Illegitimate	Fiduciary duties & Suitability requirements

actors involved. To make the empirical universe of financial fraud intelligible and to structure the survey presented in this paper, a conceptual distinction is made here between three types of financial fraud (see Table 1). The first of these, which will be referred to as *false financial disclosures*, groups together a variety of behaviours in which financial market participants make false statements about the performance or financial health of an investment outlet – that is a company, fund, borrower, or investment product. Notwithstanding the involvement of plain lies, false financial disclosures pertain to otherwise legitimate enterprises, actors, or products. This distinguishes them from *financial scams*, which constitute the second type of financial fraud. Financial scams are fully fraudulent schemes in which fraudsters induce people to voluntarily interact with the fraudster and, ultimately, to willingly hand over funds or sensitive information related to their personal finances. Like false financial disclosures, financial scams involve plain lies. Differently from false financial disclosures, however, financial scams are designed not as a legitimate enterprise, but as a true confidence game. Finally, *fraudulent financial mis-selling* refers to the deceptive and manipulative marketing, selling, or advising of a financial product or service to an end user, in the knowledge that the product or service is unsuitable for that specific end user's needs. Where both false financial disclosures and financial scams involve plain lies, financial mis-selling practices evolve around suggestive communications that create misleading impressions, but do not involve mis-statements of facts.

It needs emphasis that these are ideal types in a Weberian sense. The boundaries between these categories are blurry and not all real world cases fit neatly and unequivocally within one of the categories. For example, whether a specific communication involves plain lies, and thus qualifies as a false financial disclosure, or 'merely' suggestive statements, and therefore constitutes an act of financial mis-selling, is not always clear-cut. Similarly, it is not always as easy to determine whether a fraudulent act or statement pertains to an otherwise legitimate entity, and thus qualifies as a false financial disclosure, or whether the entity as a whole operates as a financial scam. This indeterminacy of the typology is further augmented by the fact that financial frauds may present themselves as courses of action in which behaviours that fall under different types of financial fraud are combined into elaborate fraud *schemes*.

The paper proceeds as follows. Each of the following three sections of the paper will first spell out in more detail the specific characteristics of one of the above types and then move on to a more detailed description of the specific fraudulent acts that are subsumed under it. Specifically, it will describe how these acts are executed, identify the actors and financial instruments involved, present some estimations on the prevalence of these frauds as well as the social and economic costs and consequences they incur, and explain the market structures and dynamics that facilitate these fraudulent conducts.[4] The conclusion then summarizes the general findings of the literature review and suggests possible directions for future research.

2. False Financial Disclosures

The term *false financial disclosures* is used here to group together a variety of behaviours in which financial market participants make false statements about the performance or financial health of an investment outlet – that is a company, fund, borrower, or investment product. False financial disclosures thus exploit the information asymmetry that exists between different parties in a financial transaction. By combining the illusion of disclosure with false information, false financial disclosures increase this information asymmetry while appearing to minimize it (Black, 2006). Notwithstanding the deceptive element, false financial disclosures pertain to otherwise legitimate enterprises, actors or products. This distinguishes them from investment scams, which are designed as con games from the start. False financial disclosures are also distinct from financial mis-selling practices. Whereas financial mis-selling practices merely create misleading impressions, false financial disclosures disseminate plain lies and untrue facts.

In most cases, false financial disclosures concern misrepresentations made by representatives of an organizational entity. Such misrepresentations may have either one of two objectives. First, misrepresentations may be used to cover up the misuse, misappropriation or misapplication of funds. Organizational insiders who misuse or embezzle funds may alter accounting ledgers and supporting documentation to conceal their deeds. Alternatively, false financial disclosures may be issued by managers to mislead investors or regulators about the financial health and future prospects of an enterprise.[5] Misrepresentations by organizational actors may be communicated through presentations, prospectuses, financial reports, or financial statements with the regulator. Although at times this involves misrepresentations of the nonfinancial characteristics of the company – for example, the credentials or ownership interests of executive management – most often these misrepresentations pertain to the financial health of a company or one of its subunits, as documented in the accounts. Hence, many authors speak of false financial disclosures in organizational contexts more specifically in terms of *accounting fraud*.[6]

Like organizational entities, individuals may also misrepresent their financial affairs. Usually, this is done in an attempt to ensure better terms for a financial contract. For example, loan applicants may make false disclosures about their income, assets, or liabilities in order to induce a lending institution to make a loan it would have otherwise refused. Alternatively, parties seeking insurance may misrepresent a true state of affairs in order to negotiate better terms for an insurance policy.

2.1 *Rogue Traders: False Financial Disclosures at the Proprietary Trading Desks of Financial Firms*

One context in which false financial disclosures have repeatedly surfaced over past decades is at the proprietary trading desks of securities firms and investment banks. Securities traders working at these trading desks have repeatedly been found to have manipulated accounts and internal control systems to make their trading activities look either more profitable or less risky than they actually were. Although such 'rogue traders' are in no sense a new phenomenon, the 1990s witnessed a remarkable number of consecutive high-profile cases in which financial firms lost billions of dollars. The increasing availability of derivatives at that time not only enabled traders to take trading positions of a size that had previously been unheard of, it also undermined the capacity – or willingness – of senior managers to supervise traders' trading activities (Hudson, 1998; Krawiec, 2000; Partnoy, 2002). Although arguably rogue traders never truly disappeared from the stage, the aftermath of the financial crisis of 2007–2008 witnessed what one observer acclaimed to be 'the return of the rogue' (Krawiec, 2009).[7]

Typically, rogue trader scandals begin with traders executing unauthorized trades that result in trading positions that exceed risk- or loss limits set by the firms they work for (Krawiec, 2000; Fisher QC, 2015). Rather than unwinding their deteriorating positions and accepting losses when they find the market moving against them, rogue traders often extend their unauthorized positions in an attempt to 'double down' on their losses. In doing so they accumulate risks and losses up to a point where they find themselves forced to cover up their activities through fraudulent accounting, forged documentation, and active circumvention of internal control systems. In some cases, rogue traders managed to hide their losses over extended periods of time by creatively misrepresenting their true trading activities and deceiving their colleagues and managers. Toshide Iguchi, for example, managed to hide his losses from his employer – Daiwa Bank – for nearly eleven years (Wexler, 2010).

2.1.1 Prevalence, Costs and Consequences

Rogue trading scandals have been described as 'low-frequency, high-impact events' (Krawiec, 2009). Although the number of detected cases of traders gone rogue is relatively low, the costs and consequences of their schemes can be enormous. A review of the literature reveals that banks victimized by rogue traders found themselves forced to readjust their financial statements, correcting for losses associated with these scandals ranging from $118 million up to $7.2 billion. At times, rogue trading scandals may even constitute a direct threat to the stability and existence of established financial institutions (Krawiec, 2009). For example, the British investment bank Barings, which had been in business for more than 200 years, was instantly brought down when the rogue trading activities of one of its derivatives traders at the bank's Singapore branch, Nick Leeson, were uncovered, resulting in losses of over a $1 billion (Kane and DeTrask, 1999; Körnert, 2003).

2.1.2 Perpetrators, Motivations and Opportunities

In trying to understand what drives some traders to cross the boundaries of what is permissible, scholarly research has focused on a number of themes. One of these themes concerns the 'psychological picture' of traders (Laffort and Cargnello-Charles, 2014). In general, these individuals are described as risk-seekers who are 'motivated by the rewards, both intrinsic and extrinsic, of pushing outwards into the danger zone where others do not have the skills to operate' (Wexler, 2010, p. 4). They often do not see their activities as rooted in a casino-like notion of chance but insist that they have special skills that allow them to beat the odds and stay in control in the midst of growing uncertainty, disorder and chaos (Wexler, 2010).

Another theme concerns the working environment and incentive structures in which these actors operate. The stereotypical image of the rogue trader is that of a deviant actor, an undersocialized member of an occupational community where most members do not cross the line. In the scholarly literature; however, this image of the rogue trader as a 'bad apple' has repeatedly been challenged (Krawiec, 2009; Wexler, 2010; Laffort and Cargnello-Charles, 2014). Instead it is suggested that the securities industry induces traders to cross the line. It has been emphasized that traders are not only in charge of enormous sums of corporate funds, enabling them to make profits for the firm, they are also encouraged to use these funds to maximize their own wealth in the form of year-end bonuses (Krawiec, 2000). It has also been said that traders are strongly driven by a pursuit of esteem and status, and the trading floors on which they operate have been described as 'superstar environments', where a disproportionate share of benefits is accrued by the star trader. These benefits not only come in the form of higher bonuses and intrinsic rewards. Equally important, managers confer benefits on superstar traders in the form of more accommodating risk and loss limits and less scrutiny in terms of oversight (Krawiec, 2000; Stein, 2000; Wexler, 2010). Traders, it is suggested, thus feel quite invited by their employees to cross the line (Wexler, 2010).

A third theme concerns the lack of controls to prevent traders from perpetrating their harmful schemes. Managers typically explain failures to detect rogue trading activities by the fact that rogue traders possess insider knowledge which allows them to draw up sophisticated cover-up schemes and cleverly bypass internal controls. For example, Jerome Kerviel, whose rogue trading activities caused his employer Société Général a loss of $7.2 billion, was said to have relied on his intimate knowledge of back-office operations, which he had acquired while working there, to perpetrate his scheme. The academic literature, however, rather emphasizes the absence of effective managerial oversight in many security firms. The literature is rife with examples of management's failures to see, or at least act upon, obvious red flags. For example, a major warning sign ignored by Société Général was that Jerome Kerviel's earnings grew sixfold between 2006 and 2007, instantly amounting to a substantial percentage of total desk (59%) and division (27%) earnings (Krawiec, 2009). Another example of an often-ignored warning sign is the reluctance of traders to take vacations – presumably for fear that their fraud will be detected. In one extreme case, Toshide Iguchi of Daiwa Bank refused to take a single day off during his eleven-year tenure at the bank (Krawiec, 2009). The literature proposes three reasons for which managers may refrain from questioning their star traders. First, proprietary trading has the potential to bring enormous profits to the company, resulting in large bonuses not only for traders, but also for their superiors (Krawiec, 2000; Weber, 2011). Nick Leeson, whose name has become almost synonymous with the term 'rogue trader', would himself say that the biggest crime he was guilty of was trying to protect people and ensure that the bonuses they expected were paid (Leeson, 1996). A second reason for which managers may refrain from scrutinizing their star trader stems from group psychological dynamics at work amongst an organization's senior management. It has been suggested that senior managers of financial institutions that face a crisis because of changes in their external environment may vest all their hope of getting out of the crisis in one star trader. Those senior managers may then create an organizational structure and culture that gives that star trader great leeway and in fact encourages him to 'go rogue'. The star trader is thus identified as a 'saviour' who, when sufficiently left alone, can individually 'rescue' the organization (Stein, 2000). Third, because of the increasing complexity of proprietary trading activities, largely due to the spread of derivative instruments, managers are said to not fully comprehend their subordinates' activities (Hudson, 1998; Instefjord et al., 1998; Partnoy, 2002; Körnert, 2003).

2.2 Mortgage Origination Fraud: False Financial Disclosures in the Context of Loan Applications

In the housing bubble that preceded the financial crisis of 2007–2008, a significant undercurrent of financial crime existed in the form of mortgage fraud. Analytically the mortgage industry can be thought of as consisting of two distinct segments. In the 'primary mortgage market', mortgage originators, with the interference of brokers, escrow agents, and appraisers, originate and provide loans to borrowers. In the 'secondary mortgage market', investment banks, government-sponsored enterprises, and credit rating agencies engage in the business enterprise of securitizing and managing loans originated in the primary mortgage market (Collins and Nigro, 2010; Nguyen and Pontell, 2010). As will be revealed below, fraud has been rampant in both segments of the mortgage industry.

In the literature, fraudulent behaviour in the primary mortgage market is generally discussed under the heading of *mortgage fraud*, (e.g. Carswell and Bachtel, 2009; Barnett, 2013) or *mortgage origination fraud* (e.g. Collins and Nigro, 2010; Nguyen and Pontell, 2010). Mortgage origination fraud has been defined as 'the material misstatement, misrepresentation, or omission by an applicant or other interested parties, relied upon by an underwriter or lender to fund, purchase or insure a loan' (FBI, 2007, cited in Nguyen and Pontell, 2010, p. 592). Mortgage fraud consists of a great variety of behaviours. A common thread running through all such behaviour is that the purpose is to induce a lending institution to make a loan it would have otherwise refused (Gans, 2011). Following government authorities and industry organizations, researchers usually group these different types of behaviour under two broad categories: *fraud for housing* and *fraud for profit*.

Fraud-for-housing schemes are relatively straightforward. They involve loan applicants who make minor misrepresentations, usually on a single loan, with regard to their income, employment status, or outstanding liabilities. This is done in the hope that a lender will fund the loan or will provide a better rate on a loan for a property of primary residence. Ultimately, however, the borrower intends to repay the loan. Fraud-for-profit schemes are often more complex. They typically involve multiple loans and elaborate schemes designed to gain illicit proceeds from property sales and real estate transactions. They are usually perpetrated by a number of cooperating parties, which may include mortgage brokers, home appraisers, and so-called 'straw borrowers', who make gross misrepresentations concerning appraisals, loan documents, and even the identity of the borrower. Of the two, fraud-for-profit schemes are of greater concern to law enforcement and the mortgageindustry (Nguyen and Pontell, 2010). Table 2, adopted from Carswell and Bachtel (2009), lists some common fraud-for-profit schemes.

Mortgage origination fraud is believed to have been a major contributor to the collapse of the subprime mortgage market in the United States and the subsequent global financial crisis of 2007–2008 (Nguyen and Pontell, 2010; Baumer *et al.*, 2013; Ryder, 2014). Investigations into the causes of these events revealed that fraud was rampant throughout the entire industry, especially the subprime sector, during the pre-crisis boom in the US housing market. In fact, the FBI had already identified the threat to the financial system posed by increasing levels of mortgage origination fraud in 2004. However, since the Bush administration had prioritized the tackling of terrorism over that of white-collar crime, both the agency and the Department of Justice lacked the resources to respond because all resources were being devoted to the war on terror (Ryder, 2014). Although these priorities were reversed after the collapse of the subprime mortgage market in 2007 and the start of the Obama administration in January 2009, rates of mortgage fraud did not really decline. Perpetrators simply adapted to the changed market conditions by developing new schemes and modifying older ones. As a result, even in the postcrisis period, mortgage fraud has been said to be 'the number one white collar crime in the United States' (Smith, 2010, p. 473).

2.2.1 *Prevalence, Costs and Consequences*

There is wide agreement in the literature that the period from the late 1990s until today has witnessed an explosion of mortgage fraud, especially in the United States[8] (e.g. Smith, 2010;

Table 2. Common Fraud-for-Profit Schemes (adopted from Carswell and Bachtel, 2009).

Fraud offenses	Description
Illegal flipping	Seller inflates the value of the property using an illegitimate appraisal. Once the mortgage is delivered, the home is then sold with the mortgage taken over by another buyer, who unwittingly believes that the house is of higher quality than it truly is. Ultimately, the buyer is left to repay a high mortgage on a property whose mortgage value exceeds the market value, a situation which usually results in default.
Real estate title fraud	Through identity theft, a mortgage fraud perpetrator is able to secure a mortgage loan using an assumed identity and presumably an untarnished credit file and history.
Straw buyer	Similar to the title fraud offense, a strawbuyer is someone who has knowingly given credit information to an interested party for a fee, usually totalling several thousand dollars. Months after the mortgage fraud has been committed, the straw buyer is left with the outstanding mortgage, much to his or her surprise.
Silent second mortgages	Buyer of the property borrows the down payment through an undisclosed second mortgage (usually through the seller). If the second mortgage is not recorded, this can allow the seller to inflate the actual value of the house, beyond its market value.
Foreclosure rescue/equity skimming	This situation occurs when a financially strapped homeowner is urged to sign over the deed of the property to a 'specialist' who can help sell the house quickly, sometimes with an upfront fee involved. The rescue buyer may collect rents on the property without making any mortgage payments. This forces the lender to foreclose on the property, holding the original owner and mortgage holder liable in the process
Air loans	The property in question is either misrepresented, does not exist, or is not what the loan says it is. The dishonest broker fabricates borrowers and properties, creates accounts for payments and maintains custodial accounts for escrows.
Double sales scam	This form of fraud occurs in areas where the recording of the transactions takes several weeks to several months. In essence, the owner of the house (who may operate under the guise of a shell company) takes advantage of this delay in deed recording to sell the home more than once. When the ruse is uncovered, actual title to the property becomes cloudy as a result.

Ryder, 2014). The most frequently used indicator for the prevalence of mortgage (origination) fraud in the United States is the number of mortgage-related Suspicious Activity Reports (SARs) filed with the US Treasury Department's Federal Financial Crimes Enforcement Network (FinCEN).[9] In a 2006 report, FinCEN reported that this number has increased by approximately 1400% over the period between 1997 and 2006 (FinCEN 2006, cited in Nguyen and Pontell, 2010). This number has continued to rise since the collapse of the subprime mortgage market. In 2011, FinCEN received 92,028 SARs, up from 37,313 for the period 2006–2007 (Ryder, 2014). The continuing pervasiveness of mortgage origination fraud also becomes clear if one considers law enforcement actions. Already in 2006, the FBI warned that mortgage fraud was 'pervasive and growing' (FBI 2006, cited in Barnett, 2013, p. 110). The subsequent years witnessed a 400% increase in the number of mortgage fraud-related investigations undertaken by the FBI (Ryder, 2014). In 2008, the FBI reported that it was investigating 14 corporations as part of its Subprime Mortgage Industry Fraud Initiative (Nguyen and Pontell, 2010). In that same year, 'Operation Malicious Mortgage', a multiagency enforcement action, identified more than 400 defendants associated with $1 billion in losses. Two years later, the Financial Fraud Enforcement Task Force completed its enforcement action called 'Operation Stolen Dreams', which involved 1517 criminal arrests, resulting in 525 indictments that represented estimated losses of over $3 billion (Barak, 2012).

Estimates of the monetary costs of mortgage origination fraud fall within a wide range and are difficult to compare. For example, while the US Mortgage Bankers Association has estimated that fraud costs the mortgage industry between $946 million and $4.2 billion in 2006 (Mortgage Bankers Association 2007, cited in Nguyen and Pontell, 2010, p. 593), the Mortgage Asset Research Institute estimated 2008 losses at between $15 and $25 billion. However, even though it is difficult, if not impossible to determine the exact monetary cost of mortgage origination fraud (Ryder, 2014), the literature identifies at least three groups of actors for whom such fraud has serious economic consequences. First, mortgage origination fraud results in direct losses to *lenders* and *investors* through higher default rates on loan portfolios. For example, Piskorski *et al.* (2013) found that loans with a misrepresented borrower occupancy status or misreported second lien have a significantly higher likelihood to default when compared with otherwise similar loans. Because these higher risks are hidden, the authors emphasize, they are not compensated for in terms of higher yields. Second, mortgage fraud poses adverse economic consequences for *tax payers* (Gans, 2011). Through securitization and derivatives trades, the hidden risks associated with mortgage origination fraud are spread throughout the financial system. Ultimately, these systemic risks are borne by taxpayers who pay for bailouts. Third, mortgage origination fraud has significant consequences for *homeowners* and *communities*. High levels of mortgage fraud in a given geographical area have been found to be a significant predictor of foreclosures in that area as well as in bordering areas (Nguyen and Pontell, 2011; Baumer *et al.*, 2013).

2.2.2 *Perpetrators, Motivations and Opportunities*

The primary perpetrators of mortgage origination fraud can be divided into two groups. First, *loan applicants* themselves are often involved. According to a 2008 analysis by FinCEN, about 60% of all reported mortgage fraud involved the willing participation of borrowers (FinCEN 2008, discussed in Gans, 2011, p.148). However, it is important here to distinguish between fraud-for-housing and fraud-for-profit schemes. In the case of the former, the involvement of loan applicants is obvious. In order to secure a loan, genuine applicants misrepresent their financial health or employment status. In fraud-for-profit schemes the situation is different. These schemes often involve 'straw borrowers' – persons who have knowingly conveyed their identity and credit information to other perpetrators of the scheme for a fee, usually totaling several thousand dollars – or perpetrators who, through identity theft, assume someone else's identity and untarnished credit file and history (Carswell and Bachtel, 2009, p. 350).

The second group of primary perpetrators are *mortgage industry intermediaries*. According to the FBI, 80% of all reported mortgage fraud losses involve collaboration or collusion by mortgage industry insiders (FBI, 2007, cited in Smith, 2010, p.479). This includes corrupt mortgage brokers, real estate appraisers, escrow agents, title officers, builders and land developers (Collins and Nigro, 2010; Gans, 2011). Scholars have pointed out that for corrupt intermediaries mortgage fraud schemes constitute a 'low-risk and high-return activity' (Gans, 2011, p.150). Especially prior to the collapse of the US housing market, there was much to gain and little to lose for those involved in mortgage fraud. Before it collapsed in 2006, the mortgage industry, and especially the subprime part of it, represented an enormous and grow-ing industry,[10] making it a tempting target for fraudsters. At the same time, perpetrators had little to fear, neither from law enforcement agencies – sentences were light and the chance of getting caught was low[11] (Smith, 2010, p. 475) – nor from the lending institutions that they seemingly victimized with their devious schemes. In fact, as will be discussed below, these lending institutions acted as important facilitators of mortgage origination fraud.

2.3 Mortgage Securitization Fraud: False Financial Disclosures in the Context of Structured Finance Investments

Mortgage origination fraud was only the beginning of a chain of lies that ran through the entire mortgage industry (see Figure 1). In the secondary mortgage market, investment banks, acting as underwriters for securities issued by structured investment vehicles, have been accused of making false statements to investors and other market participants about the quality and char-acter of those securities (Barnett, 2013; Fligstein and Roehrkasse, 2013; Piskorski *et al.*, 2013). Structured investment vehicles are contractual entities that pool portfolios of loans – residential mortgages, student loans, car loans etc. – and then issue bond-like securities for which the prin-cipal and interests paid on those portfolios of loans serve as collateral. The process of issuing these structured finance products – primarily residential mortgage-backed securities (RMBSs), asset-backed securities (ABSs) and collateralized debt obligations (CDOs) – usually involves, besides the issuer, the service of an underwriter. The job of the underwriter, most often an investment bank, is to raise capital from institutional investors who are willing to invest in the security issued by the structured investment vehicle (Fligstein and Roehrkasse, 2013). It has been found that, during the pre-crisis boom, many underwriters misrepresented the character-istics of these securities and the quality of the loans underlying them to investors and sellers

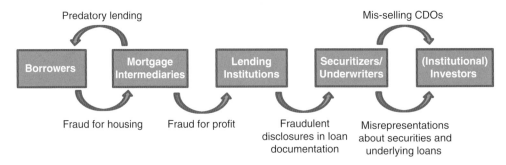

Figure 1. Chain of Lies in the Mortgage Industry

The lower part of the figure identifies instances of false financial disclosures in the US mortgage industry prior to the financial crisis of 2007–2008. The upper part identifies instances of mis-selling in that same industry. Predatory lending will be discussed in more detail in Section 3.1 of this paper. For a discussion of the mis-selling of CDOs, see Reurink (2016, pp. 73–76). [Color figure can be viewed at wileyonlinelibrary.com]

of insurance on those securities – issuers of so-called credit default swaps (CDSs). This included misrepresentations about the quality of the loans in the portfolios that provide collateral for these securities – for example fraudulent property appraisals, misrepresented loan-to-value ratios, misstatements about the sort of loans underlying the security, and misrepresentations about the delinquency status of the loans in the portfolio – or misrepresentations about the credit rating on them.

2.3.1 Prevalence, Costs and Consequences

False financial disclosures in the context of structured finance investments were especially widespread in the United States, the epicentre of the subprime mortgage boom. According to one observer, 'almost all the prospectuses and sales material on mortgage-backed bonds sold from 2005 through 2007 were a compound of falsehoods' (Ferguson, 2012, p. 191). Recent legal developments seem to support such allegations. It has been reported that the top 10 underwriting firms, which together represented 74.1% of the market share, have all been implicated in securities fraud cases. Eight of them have settled with regulators or investors over underwriting-related fraud allegations (Fligstein and Roehrkasse, 2013). Academic attempts to quantify the prevalence of false financial disclosures in the underwriting of structured finance products point in a similar direction. Piskorski *et al.* (2013) found that about 1 out of every 10 loans in their dataset involved some sort of misrepresentation. These misrepresentations existed across all underwriters involved in the sale of RMBSs.[12]

The ultimate victims of the fraudulent misrepresentations by underwriters were the unsuspecting investors that bought the RMBSs, ABSs and CDOs – that is midsized European banks, public pension funds, and hedge funds (Ferguson, 2012; Nesvetailova and Sandu, 2015). Although in their defence banks have maintained the opposite, in the literature it is generally assumed that these buyers were not as 'sophisticated' as the investment banks that sold these products, giving the latter an informational advantage in the transaction (Piskorski *et al.*, 2013). In their earlier mentioned study, Piskorski *et al.* found that misrepresentations by underwriters had significant economic consequences for these investors. The delinquencies of misrepresented loans were 60–70% higher than the delinquency rate of otherwise similar loans, potentially impacting RMBSs with a combined outstanding balance of up to $160 billion (Piskorski *et al.*, 2013).

2.3.2 Perpetrators, Motivations and Opportunities

The primary perpetrators of mortgage securitization fraud were the *broker-dealers* who worked for the investment banks and brokerage firms that underwrote, marketed, and sold these complex investment products to institutional investors. As underwriters, investment banks have a legal obligation to perform due diligence on the loans they receive from originators before selling them on to investor. In fact, the prospectus of a structured finance security such as a RMBS or CDO typically assures investors that, prior to acquiring the loans, the underwriting firm would conduct a review of the seller of the loans – its credit risk, its senior-level management, its mortgage loan origination processes, historical loan level loss experiences etc. (Barnett, 2011). As we now know, they often failed to do so. In the literature, the failure to perform due diligence has generally been explained as a result of the structures of *competition* and *compensation* in the mortgage industry. Under the so-called 'originate to distribute' (OTD) model, originators and lending institutions passed most of the risks associated with the mortgages they originated along to securitizers, who in turn passed the risks on to bullish and often naïve investors. Under the OTD model securitizers thus generated most of their revenues from fees rather than returns on investment. Hence they were principally concerned with volume, rather than quality, that is whether or not the loans that went into the securitization products were well documented or likely to be repaid (Fligstein and Roehrkasse, 2013). Compensation structures for the individual investment bankers who engineered and marketed the securitized loans largely mirrored the motivations of their firms to deal deceptively in high quantities of low-quality debt (Barnett, 2011; Fligstein and Roehrkasse, 2013).

Notwithstanding the fact that legal liability for misrepresentations in the context of structured finance investments rests primarily with the banks that securitized and underwrote these products, actors from outside the banks have been involved in these schemes as well. Attention has especially focused on the role played by the credit rating agencies (CRAs) in mortgage securitization fraud (Bussani, 2010; Dorn, 2011; Maas, 2011; Barak, 2012). In February 2013, the US Department of Justice filed civil charges against Standard & Poor's (S&P) for allegedly engaging in a scheme to defraud investors in RMBSs and CDOs. Civil fraud claims against the CRAs have also been filed by private litigants. Most of these claims allege that the agencies fraudulently inflated their ratings of structured finance investment products, and that the CRAs lied to investors about their independence and objectivity in the construction of those ratings. Academic scrutiny of the involvement of CRAs in securitization fraud has especially problematized the business model and limited accountability, especially in criminal law, of the CRAs (Bussani, 2010; Johansson, 2010; Cane et al., 2012; Lehmann, 2014).

3. Financial Scams

Financial scams are deceptive and fully fraudulent schemes in which fraudsters, often assuming a false identity or exhibiting a misplaced aura of trustworthiness, convince, mislead, or induce people to voluntarily interact with the fraudster and, ultimately, to willingly hand over money or sensitive information related to their personal finances.

Financial scams do not simply victimize their targets by exploiting existing information asymmetries that could impossibly have been bridged by the victims. In most cases, cautious investors could have easily known or found out that the opportunity or invitation was a scam (Pressman, 1998). The skill of the con artist lies in the ability to induce the investor to make a leap of faith. Financial scams are thus different from financial mis-selling practices in that they go beyond misleading and suggestive communications. Financial scams are built on blatant lies and completely fabricated facts. Financial scams are also different from false financial disclosures in that, unlike the latter, they are designed not as a legitimate enterprise, but as a true confidence game.[13]

Genuine financial scams typically proceed according to a well-delineated pattern. First, the potential victims – the 'marks' – must be approached and their interest piqued. The mark's attention may be caught by offering high returns at low risks or by threatening that the mark's bank account will be shut off if the mark does not cooperate. The perpetrators of the scam – the 'operators' – may communicate this message in different ways. In some cases, operators work with lists that contain telephone numbers or e-mail addresses of individuals, usually people with high disposable incomes or individuals who have been successfully defrauded before (Shover et al., 2004; Policastro and Payne, 2014). Such 'lead lists' or 'mooch lists' can be easily purchased on the Internet for a relatively small price. In other cases, scam artists take advantage of affinities and social networks, which quickly generate interest in the scam by word of mouth (Baker and Faulkner, 2003; Nash et al., 2013). Affinity relationships between the scammers and their victims may also play an important role in the second step, in which operators try to garner trust (for a detailed discussion of the construction of trust in the Madoff Ponzi scheme see Stolowy et al., 2014). In this phase scam artists may hijack trusted brand names and misrepresent themselves as being representatives of legitimate companies. Finally, the marks must be enticed to participate in the scheme. To undercut the marks' perceived need for due diligence, operators appeal to trust and visceral triggers. They may, for example, appeal to the marks' greed or distressed financial situation by promising high returns and stressing the need to make the decision urgently.

3.1 Investment Scams: Sham Business Ventures and Ponzi Schemes

Investment scams are fraudulent schemes that try to deceive investors into investing their money in a specific investment opportunity that, in fact, is nonexistent or that will most certainly not live up to expectations. Such investment opportunities may consist of shares, equity stakes, or debt issued by fake or dubious companies, often backed purportedly by a hot new product, technology, or business opportunity. Alternatively, investment scams might offer participations in collective investment vehicles, real estate projects, or insurance plans.

Investment scams can be designed in either one of two ways. In some cases the operators of the scam simply collect the money and then disappear. Investment scams designed in this way frequently make use of shell companies registered in secrecy jurisdictions. The anonymity provided by these jurisdictions enables the operators to collect the money and then disappear without leaving any traces for duped investors to recover their losses (Tillman, 2002). In most cases, however, investment scams are designed to live a longer life and take the form of a *Ponzi scheme*. Ponzi schemes are often characterized as investment scams wherein investors' returns are generated by capital coming in from new investors rather than the success of the underlying business ventures. A somewhat more nuanced understanding of Ponzi schemes, however, recognizes that the rollover of investments made by new investors is not the only mechanism that helps to keep the scheme going. Often, operators provide earlier investors with fictitious paper earnings[14] that are then re-invested in another investment cycle (Frankel, 2012; Lewis, 2012). Thus, in Ponzi schemes the returns promised to investors do in fact materialize initially, at least on paper. However, even though the seeming realization of returns enables Ponzi schemes to last for some time without being discovered, in the long run they are doomed to collapse; as soon as new investors stop joining or earlier investors want to redeem their investments and/or paper profits, the scheme starts to collapse (Trahan et al., 2005).

To lure victims into participating, investment scams appeal to a variety of needs and emotions such as greed, ego, the fear of losing opportunities (Will, 2013). Typically, they draw the marks' attention with promises of steady returns, often above the market rate, at low risk. The exact rates of return vary widely between schemes. There are examples in the literature of scammers offering returns of up to 40% within six to eight weeks, or 100% within a month (Frankel, 2012). On the other hand, the scheme perpetrated by Bernard Madoff, supposedly the largest Ponzi scheme ever, offered investors modest but steady returns of 10–12% per year, regardless of market conditions (Nolasco et al., 2013).

The success of investment scams also depends on an effective diffusion system. This is especially pertinent in the case of Ponzi schemes, which need a constantly expanding investor base to survive. The literature identifies two different ways in which the investment opportunity is made known among investors. First, the scam can be disseminated through *impersonal methods.* Operators of investment scams may use paid sales forces to promote the scam. They may, for example, recruit telemarketing teams to run through mooch lists or salesmen to go from door to door to sell a certain 'investment opportunity' (see Baker and Faulkner, 2003; Shover *et al.*, 2003; Shover *et al.*, 2004). Also, con artists may recruit registered broker-dealers who advertise the fund or company with their clients. Ponzi schemes that play out in the fund industry may recruit so-called 'feeder funds': investment advisers and money managers, backed by prominent financial institutions, who direct their clients' funds directly towards the Ponzi fund (Lewis, 2012). For example, established financial institutions throughout the world had been known to accept payments from Madoff for recruiting investors (Frankel, 2012). Second, the scam might be promoted to investors through wort-of-mouth within *social networks* (Baker and Faulkner, 2003; Comet, 2011; Nash *et al.*, 2013). Frequently, such scams take the form of an 'affinity fraud' (Perri and Brody, 2012; Blois, 2013), in which operators take advantage of a shared identity with the victims, be it as part of a religious organization (e.g. Bernard Madoff), an immigrant community (e.g. Charles Ponzi), exclusive clubs, or simply a group of family or friends. Often a fortunate group of early investors become the 'songbirds' that sing the praises of the scam to others. To provide credibility and induce the songbirds to bring friends, family members or business colleagues into the scam, operators make regular dividend payments to those early investors, giving the scam an appearance of profitability and legitimacy (Frankel, 2012; Lewis, 2012).

3.1.1 *Prevalence, Victims, Costs and Consequences*

Discussions of investment scams in the financial press tend to focus on rare high-impact cases. Examples are the multibillion-dollar schemes operated by Bernard Madoff and Allen Stanford. However, the scholarly literature on investment scams is rife with examples of smaller and less well-known albeit for the victims equally destructive scams. Investment scams appear to be so pervasive that some have even suggested they have reached the proportion of an epidemic (Frankel, 2012). In the years 2008 and 2009 alone, 190 Ponzi schemes collapsed in the United States (Lewis, 2012, p. 294), and a 2007 study conducted by the Canadian Securities Administration noted that about one in twenty Canadians had been victimized by investment fraud (CSA, 2007, cited in Lokanan, 2014, p. 226).

Although precise figures on the monetary costs associated with investment scams are scarce, they are generally believed to be significant. For example, the costs associated with global investment fraud in the year 2001 have been estimated to be around $35 billion (Frankel, 2012). The majority of these costs fall on those who invested their money in the scheme. However, investors are not the only ones injured by investment schemes. Victims may also include financial institutions that have unwittingly facilitated the scheme. For example, feeder funds that directed their clients to the scheme not knowing it was a scam, brokerage firms that executed transactions for the Ponzi fund, and banks that offered accounts to the operator etc. These institutions might be affected in their daily operations and often suffer from tainted reputations (Frankel, 2012).

3.1.2 *Perpetrators, Motivations and Opportunities*

Operators of investment scams tend to exhibit certain character traits. On the one hand, con artists are said to be charming and captivating individuals (Lewis, 2012). On the other hand, they are said to frequently have a narcissistic character and to lack any concern or empathy for their victims, sometimes even blaming them for being duped into the scheme (Frankel, 2012). Their motivation is often intrinsic and comes from more than greed alone. They may have grandiose dreams of making a fortune but also of gaining recognition and respect. In pursuing their dream, they behave very much like legitimate entrepreneurs and might even believe their scheme to be true 'businesses' (Frankel, 2012). This not only helps to make the investment opportunity appear 'trustworthy' in the eyes of investors, a crucial element of a successful investment scam (Stolowy *et al.*, 2014), it also explains a tendency amongst operators of investment scams not to want to see certain things, such as the unsustainable structure of the scheme (Naylor, 2007).

It has been suggested in the literature that a number of institutional arrangements in present-day finance capitalism are especially conducive to investment scams. Building on Robert K. Merton's theory of the anomic society, some scholars have pointed to *the American dream* as a factor driving both perpetrators and victims of investment scams (Trahan *et al.*, 2005; Young, 2013). Most importantly, they point at the way in which the American dream emphasizes the importance of success and de-emphasizes the methods of acquisition. Scholars have also indicated the way in which investment scams take advantage of institutionalized practices in financial markets. In the hedge fund industry, where the mystique of alpha returns reigns supreme, trading models are generally clouded in secrecy for fear that competitors will imitate them. Perpetrators of investment scams take advantage of this *justified secrecy*, using it primarily to keep investors at bay and avoid detection (Frankel, 2012; Blois, 2013; Shapiro, 2013; Stolowy *et al.*, 2014). It has also been suggested that *technological advancements* have given fraudsters a greater range of vehicles and opportunities to perpetrate investment scams. Especially the Internet has reduced the need to finance a large sales force, and the anonymity it provides shields con artists from detection (Frankel, 2012). Finally, the success of investment scams has also been said to depend on a *lack of efficient oversight*. At one level, scholars have pointed to the lack of serious scrutiny by external auditors (Geis, 2013; Shapiro, 2013). At another level, observers have emphasized the failure of regulatory authorities to police the market and detect, at an early stage, large-scale investment scams such as those perpetrated by Bernard Madoff and Allen Stanford (Markopolos, 2010; Shapiro, 2013). An interesting point in this regard is that regulatory investigations are usually theory-driven, that is to say, investigators do not approach a case with an open mind but with a hypothesis in mind. This may direct their attention away from what they should be looking for. In the Madoff case, for example, the SEC had been tipped off by a hedge fund but was blinded by the idea that Madoff was engaged in insider trading (Lewis, 2012).

3.2. *Financial Identity Scams: Phishing, Pharming and Payment Scams*

The term *financial identity scams* is used here to refer to fraudulent schemes that try to induce potential victims to hand-over personal identifying information related to their financial accounts and credit scores. Once the operator has succeeded in inducing the mark to surrender the information – which may include account numbers, credit card details, passwords, user IDs etc. – the operator then uses this information to perform fraudulent money transfers. Thus understood, the term financial identity fraud refers to both the *obtaining* of the victim's financial identifying information, often through scam-like schemes, and the subsequent fraudulent *use* of that information for financial gain.

To obtain the identifying information, operators of financial identity frauds use different techniques. In the literature, a conceptual distinction has been made between *technical subterfuge schemes* and *social engineering schemes* (Vittal, 2005; Button *et al.*, 2014). *Social engineering schemes* contact their marks with 'spoofed' e-mails – e-mails with forged sender-addresses – that prompt recipients to visit counterfeit websites designed to trick them into divulging their financial identity voluntarily. The most common social engineering scheme technique is what is called *phishing* (see Lynch, 2005; Jagatic *et al.*, 2007). In a typical phishing scheme, the operator, pretending to be an agent from a bank or credit card company, sends out e-mails in which he prompts customers of the bank to click on a hyperlink that brings them to a website, controlled by the phisher, where they will be asked to further process their account details (Vittal, 2005). To appear credible and to trick the recipient's into participating in the scheme, the scam artist's e-mails may contain company logos or use scare tactics – such as threats of account closure – and urgency cues that short-circuit victims' elaboration on clues that could reveal the deceptive nature of the invitation (Lynch, 2005; Vishwanath *et al.*, 2011).

Technical subterfuge schemes, in comparison, are more technical in nature and rely much less on persuasion to entice victims into the scheme. This enables a much wider victim base. For example, in what is generally referred to as *pharming* (Vittal, 2005; Brody *et al.*, 2007), fraudsters send out e-mails which, when opened, plant malware – malicious software – in the victims' personal computers. The malware then directs traffic from those PCs that is destined for a legitimate website, say, a bank, to the pharmer's bogus website, which looks just like the real one. Without the victim's knowledge or consent, all the information the victim thinks is being sent to the bank's website is sent directly to the pharmer. Another possible mode of operation for pharmers is to alter a website's Internet protocol (IP) address in the domain name server (DNS). In so doing, pharmers redirect all users who type in the web address of, say, a bank to the illegitimate website controlled by the pharmer.

After having obtained the victim's financial credentials, operators of financial identity scams then fraudulently use this information to realize financial gain.[15] Here, again, operators choose from a menu of different techniques, which can be thought of as falling along a continuum. At the least sophisticated and low-cost end of the spectrum are traditional payment frauds, or credit card frauds, whereby perpetrators make unauthorized use of one or several of the victim's existing bank and credit card accounts by withdrawing cash or buying merchandise. These kinds of frauds are generally detected at an early stage by victims or financial institutions' fraud detection systems and hence are generally limited to a few transactions. At the more sophisticated end of the spectrum are fraud schemes that take longer to be detected and, accordingly, involve much larger costs to the victims. Here, fraudsters not only make unauthorized use of the victim's existing accounts, but open up and deplete new credit accounts and credit lines using the victim's identity, without the victim being aware of it. Between those ends of the continuum are 'account takeover frauds', whereby fraudsters establish complete control over an existing account in order to extract the entire balance in a deposit account or to access the full credit line of a credit account, and 'fictitious identity frauds', in which pieces of real data from one or more consumers are combined with made-up information to fabricate an identity and establish a credit line that does not belong to any real person[16] (Cheney, 2005).

3.2.1 *Prevalence, Victims, Costs and Consequences*

There is widespread agreement in the literature that financial identity scams and identity abuses in general constitute a serious and growing threat for financial systems today. Identity abuses have been said to form the number one and fastest growing economic crime in a range of countries as diverse as the United States (Brody *et al.*, 2007; Pontell and Geis, 2007), China (Bai and Chen, 2013) and India (Geeta, 2011). In the United States, losses from financial identity scams have been estimated to be as high as $49.3 billion for the year 2006 (Javelin, 2007, cited in Epstein and Brown, 2008). In the United Kingdom, estimated losses caused by identity-related crime have been calculated around 1.3 billion British pounds per year. For Australia estimates vary from 1 to 3 billion US dollars (Pontell and Geis, 2007; Ozaki, 2008).

A review of the literature (Vittal, 2005; Brody *et al.*, 2007; Anderson *et al.*, 2008; Ozaki, 2008; Ram, 2008; Geeta, 2011) reveals that the adverse consequences of financial identity scams are born by three groups of victims. The first of these consists of the *consumers and businesses* whose financial identities misappropriated and abused by the fraudsters. Adverse consequences experienced by this group of victims may include having to spend time and money in sorting out the fraud, a loss of access to credit due to credit score deteriorations, as well as psychological and emotional consequences. A second group consists of the *merchants and credit providers* who have been tricked into delivering money or goods based on fraudulent payments. These companies generally bear the costs of investments in fraud detection technologies and may forgo potential revenues due to their refusal to accept valid transactions because they look suspicious or due to growing consumer reluctance to engage in e-commerce. The third group of victims consists of the *banks, credit card companies and e-retailers* whose brand names are hijacked by phishing schemes. These companies may suffer from costs associated with increased surveillance and prevention as well as negative effects on stock prices and trading volume.

3.2.2 *Perpetrators, Motivations and Opportunities*

Financial identity scam operations are organized as highly professionalized, global criminal networks. These networks involve a wide variety of criminal entrepreneurs and exhibit a highly developed division of labour (Lovet, 2006; Brody *et al.*, 2007; Pontell and Geis, 2007; Moore *et al.*, 2009). For example, at the front end of the value chain, where the collection of identifying information takes place, *phishermen* – criminal actors that operate a copy of a genuine bank website – hire *spammers* to drive customers of the bank to their fake websites. In contacting customers, spammers use the services of *botnet herders*, people who manage large collections of virus-infected personal computers that can be controlled remotely under a common command and control infrastructure (Ianelli and Hackworth, 2007). Spammers, phishermen and botnet herders all make use of malware that has been developed by *malware developers*. Once the identifying information has been obtained, the fraudsters may obtain the service of *information specialists* who fill in the gaps when identity data are incomplete. One step further down the line in the 'production chain', the fraudulently obtained information might be used in several ways. In the case of traditional payment card frauds, *runners* use the information for online purchases of expensive goods, which are then delivered at the address of a *drop*; someone who allows delivery of items at their home. The drop then forwards the goods to the runner who finally sells them to *complicit retailers* for a price below market value. In other cases, the information obtained by the phishermen is sold to *cashiers*, who use the information to transfer money from the victim's account to an account controlled by a *money mule*. The money mule fulfils a role similar to that of a drop; he receives and subsequently forwards the money, usually through irrevocable payment services such as Western Union. Both money mules and drops are often duped into cooperating in the scheme. They are recruited via job ads sent in spam e-mails or on websites, where they have been offered opportunities to work from home as 'transaction processor' or 'sales executives'. After the fraud is discovered, they often become personally liable for the buying and laundering of stolen goods and money.

A number of developments are believed to have facilitated the proliferation and professionalization of financial identity fraud. To begin with, information and communication technologies, most notably the networked computer, have created *new channels* through which financial identities can be fraudulently obtained. Especially the proliferation of electronic means for personal banking and the rise of e-commerce are believed to have opened up new ways of perpetrating financial identity scams and allowed these scams to be perpetrated on an industrial scale (Pontell and Geis, 2007; Smith, 2010). Parallel to this, the *economic value of identifying information* has increased significantly. In this regard, scholars have pointed to the specific nature of modern payment systems, and specifically to the increased reliance on identification in those systems (Anderson *et al.*, 2008; Ozaki, 2008). In response to this, organized crime groups increasingly look at identifying information as profitable business opportunity (Smith, 2010). Thus, it has been maintained that another important reason for the proliferation and professionalization of online identity fraud is the *increased involvement of organized crime groups*, which has greatly increased the financing available to hackers and other scam artists (Brody *et al.*, 2007).

4. Fraudulent Financial Mis-Selling

The term *fraudulent financial mis-selling* is used here to refer to the deceptive and manipulative marketing, selling or advising of a financial product or service to an end user, in the knowledge that the product or service is unsuitable for that specific end user's needs. Similar to the other forms of fraud discussed here, fraudulent mis-selling practices illegally exploit information asymmetries that exist between transacting parties. In the case of mis-selling, however, this information asymmetry is of a different character. It involves not so much an asymmetry in access to financial facts directly related to the transaction, but rather an asymmetry of more general financial expertise, that is, the capability of interpreting the available information and extracting meaning from that information with regard to the future performance of a financial product. Contrary to false financial disclosures and financial scams, mis-selling cases thus do not necessarily involve false representations of facts. At the heart of fraudulent financial mis-selling are deceptive sales practices in which the seller of a financial product or service or the financial adviser advising on it makes misleading and highly speculative statements with regard to the future performance of the products or service and/or fails to communicate in a balanced manner the suitability of the financial product or service for the specific end user.[17]

Fraudulent mis-selling practices are generally perpetrated by agents who fulfil a double role as sales agent and adviser in financial transactions. In its most innocent form, mis-selling involves cases in which such agents – direct salesmen, brokers, financial advisers, broker-dealers –provide their clients with unsuitable advice because they lack the advisory competence required by regulations. More devious and fraudulent forms of mis-selling, and of primary concern in this section, involve cases in which sales agents and financial advisers abuse their role by deceptively inducing clients to engage in financial contracts that, given full information and devoid of behavioural and cognitive biases, they would not have engaged in. Especially in the retail financial market, the relative ignorance and limited financial literacy of most consumers puts the sales agents at a considerable informational advantage. Mis-selling agents exploit this informational advantage by providing their clients with biased advice or utilizing aggressive and manipulative marketing strategies.

The financial products involved in financial mis-selling practices typically have relatively far-off horizons and complex contract structures and therefore are associated with high levels of uncertainty. Typically, these are financial products that provide insurance against possible life- or market-events in a relatively distant future. Examples of such products are pension saving plans, life insurance plans, interest rate swaps, or foreign exchange swaps. Because the benefits of such products for the user only become clear long after the transaction has taken place, determining whether a certain product is beneficial for the consumer involves a lot of guesswork and speculation. Through misleading promotional materials, high-pressure sales techniques, and inaccurate or suggestive statements, mis-sellers overemphasize beneficial scenarios, while underemphasizing those that are less beneficial to the buyer.

Although mis-sellers typically target relatively 'unsophisticated' investors – most often retail consumers or small and medium enterprises – increasingly mis-selling practices target more sophisticated market players as well.[18] Especially derivatives have proven to be useful instruments for investment bankers attempting to 'out-mathematize and sweet-talk' (Goldmann, 2010) supposedly sophisticated clients into deals they really don't understand.[19]

4.1. *Predatory Lending: The Mis-Selling of Mortgage Loans*

The mis-selling practices that have probably received most attention in the recent literature are those that have been associated with the selling of mortgage loans. Commonly referred to as *predatory lending*, the mis-selling of mortgage loans involves a wide range of practices that include charging excessive fees; steering borrowers into bad or unaffordable loans that net higher profits; inducing a borrower to repeatedly refinance a loan in order to charge high points and fees (Nguyen and Pontell, 2011; Barnett, 2013).

In the majority of cases predatory lenders target subprime borrowers with little prior experience in the credit market (Engel and McCoy, 2002; Delgadillo *et al.*, 2008). They capitalize on these borrowers' limited financial literacy and lack of access to unbiased financial advice (Engel and McCoy, 2002). Descriptions of the predatory lending process described in the literature suggest that the predatory lending process can be divided into three phases: the *solicitation phase*, the *closing phase*, and the *exploitation phase*. In the solicitation phase, predatory lenders conduct aggressive door-to-door solicitations in target neighbourhoods. In this phase they 'endear themselves with charm and solicitude that mask their guile. They consciously exude an aura of expertise and success, intimidating customers from questioning the advisability of the loans they are offering' (Engel and McCoy, 2002, p. 1283). During the loan closing that marks the second phase of the predatory lending process, predatory lenders impose on these borrowers exploitative loan conditions that often differ from what the borrowers thought they would get, based on their communications with the lender in the solicitation phase. To induce borrowers to sign their overpriced and overly risky mortgage loan contracts, predatory lenders create excessively complex contracts and make use of consumer psychology (McCoy, 2005; Willis, 2006). For example, predatory lenders may persuade borrowers to close a deal as soon as possible under the pretext that their opportunity to borrow will soon vanish (Engel and McCoy, 2002, p. 1283). In the final exploitation phase, the 'friendly veneer' with which predatory lenders have initially approached their victims yields to aggressive exploitation of the precarious situation that the loan contract got the borrower into. Often this is where a new round of high-pressure solicitations to refinance the loan starts (Hill and Kozup, 2007).

4.1.1 *Prevalence, Costs and Consequences*

The diversity of practices subsumed under predatory lending, the different credit markets involved, and the lack of a common definition of predatory lending make it difficult to quantify its prevalence and costs. There is, however, a shared understanding in the literature that, at least in the United States, predatory lending practices were widespread during the housing boom that preceded the financial crisis of 2007–2008 and that hundreds of thousands of homeowner have been victimized in the past decade (Willis, 2006; Fligstein and Roehrkasse, 2013; Ryder, 2014). Interestingly, a review of the literature on the phenomenon reveals that scholars had already identified the problem of widespread predatory lending practices and their adverse social and economic consequences well before the financial crisis of 2007–2008 (e.g. Engel and McCoy, 2002; Renuart, 2004; Willis, 2006).

Quantifications of the monetary costs of predatory lending are similarly hard to find. One estimate for the United States suggests that predatory lending of all kinds – including predatory lending by payday lenders, credit card companies, and the like – costs borrowers $25 billion annually. A 2001 report by the Coalition for Responsible Lending estimated that excessive fees and interest rates alone cost those US borrowers who fell victim to predatory lending specifically in the area of mortgage loans around $9 billion annually (Stein, 2001). Given the fact that predatory lending practices often trick borrowers into loans they cannot actually afford, the ultimate social and economic costs associated with predatory lending come in the form of increased foreclosure rates (Ryder, 2014). These costs go beyond those who have obtained a predatory loan and may affect entire communities and neighbourhoods (Engel and McCoy, 2002; Ryder, 2014). In this process, the elderly, poor and minority populations are said to be hit the hardest (Engel and McCoy, 2002; Nguyen and Pontell, 2011).

4.1.2 *Perpetrators, Motivations and Opportunities*

The main perpetrators of predatory lending practices in the mortgage industry are mortgage brokers and mortgage originators who, driven by fees and enabled by significant information asymmetries between lenders and borrowers, an abundance of credit, and a lack of regulatory oversight, took advantage of vulnerable borrowers. Incentives structures that in the literature are believed to have motivated predatory lenders are similar to the ones that have been discussed in relation to mortgage origination fraud. The OTD model that prevailed in the mortgage industry operated under a fee structure by which mortgage brokers and originators profited from maximizing the volume of the loans they originated, irrespective of loan quality. Moreover, as Fligstein and Roehrkasse (2013, p. 27) point out, 'when brokers were compensated in terms of yield-spread premiums – the difference between the rate charged and the par rate – brokers had incentives to inflate that rate through deception or discrimination. When mortgage brokers were compensated through fees, they had incentives to conceal add-ons and penalties'. Under such a compensation structure, brokers and originators thus have obvious economic incentives to originate as many loans as possible, to refinance them as often as possible, and to originate loans with high interest rates, irrespective of whether this was in the best interest of borrowers, and irrespective of whether borrowers would be able to carry the burden of their debts over the long run.

Predatory lenders have been greatly facilitated in their egregious practices by two major changes in the mortgage industry that have taken place over the last few decades. First, widespread *securitization* of subprime mortgage loans made possible a constant flow of money to the subprime mortgage market and allowed nonbank lenders to enter that market. This resulted in the rise of thinly capitalized and barely regulated mortgage banks that were not regulated by financial institution regulatory agencies and have relatively little to fear from reputational risk (Engel and McCoy, 2002). Indeed, the majority of cases of predatory lending are said to have occurred among such independent mortgage banks[20] (Delgadillo *et al.*, 2008; Nguyen and Pontell, 2011). Moreover, for mortgage lenders, the increased availability of funds opened up the possibility to serve a new market segment of 'subprime' borrowers who had previously been excluded from the credit market because of credit rationing and discrimination. Most of these borrowers were inexperienced and had low levels of financial literacy, resulting in a substantial information asymmetry between lenders and borrowers in the subprime market (Engel and McCoy, 2002). In reaching out to these new borrowers, mortgage lenders, facilitated by the deregulatory policies of the industry's regulators and governmental policies that aimed at increasing homeownership, engendered a *proliferation of mortgage products* that were difficult for inexperienced and unsophisticated borrowers to understand. This further impaired the decision-making capacity of borrowers (Willis, 2006). The combined result of the proliferation of products and the lack of financial literacy amongst the new class of borrowers was a further increase in information asymmetries ready to be exploited by unscrupulous mortgage lenders (Engel and McCoy, 2002; Willis, 2006).

4.2 *The Mis-Selling of Life Insurance and Pension Schemes*

Another segment of the financial services industry that has been repeatedly plagued by episodes of large-scale mis-selling is the life-insurance and private pensions industry. Widespread mis-selling of life insurance and pension plans resulted in major scandals and regulatory actions in the United States in the 1980s (Fischel and Stillman, 1997; Egler and Malak, 1999), in the United Kingdom in the 1990s[21] (Black and Nobles, 1998; Ryley and Virgo, 1999; Schulz, 2000; Ward, 2000) and in the Netherlands[22] and India in the 2000s (Anagol *et al.*, 2013; Halan *et al.*, 2014).

Previous research on the abovementioned mis-selling scandals suggests that they all occurred against the backdrop of a gradual withdrawal of government support for state pension provision and a secular move away from traditional, collective 'defined benefit' pensions towards personal 'defined contribution' accounts, which essentially are investment products based on the investment performance of an underlying portfolio (Black and Nobles, 1998; Ryley and Virgo, 1999; Ericson and Doyle, 2006; Mitchell and Smetters, 2013). Governments in those countries allowed, through legislation, and encouraged, through tax incentives and advertising, individuals to substitute personal pension plans provided by life insurance companies for collective occupational pension schemes. To facilitate the provision of personal pensions by private companies, governments coupled the reforms with a deregulation of retail financial services sectors, allowing all sorts of financial institutions to provide an increasingly large menu of pension plans (Black and Nobles, 1998). The political rhetoric behind these reforms was one of increased efficiency and flexibility of pension systems, enhanced individual control over life savings, higher returns, and decreased government pension costs (Schulz, 2000). In reality, however, the reforms turned out to create the perfect conditions for widespread mis-selling of life insurances and pensions.

Existing literature also identifies a number of market dynamics that played a role in the abovementioned scandals. In all cases, life insurance companies experienced an intensification of competition as government deregulatory policies allowed banks and other financial services providers to enter the life insurance market. The entrance of new competitors into the industry prompted life insurance companies to rapidly expand their sales forces and adopt more aggressive sales techniques (Black and Nobles, 1998; Egler and Malak, 1999). In an attempt to sell as many plans as possible, poorly trained sales agents driven by perverse incentives exploited consumers' ignorance about pension and life insurance products on a massive scale. In many cases, sales agents did not sufficiently inquire about the risk profile of the client, failed to properly explain risks, created overly optimistic projections of the future performance of the plans, or failed to properly disclose charges and commissions. Sales agents particularly exploited the uncertainty stemming from the strong investment component of personal pension plans, which significantly increases the guesswork and speculation involved in establishing the suitability of the plan for the specific consumer. A widespread practice in the industry, for example, is to have sales agents suggest that, thanks to the investment component of the plan, the product would pay for itself over time (Ericson and Doyle, 2006). In reality, however, consumers frequently ended up seeing much of their premiums leak away to hidden costs and fees, subtracting from the amount of capital over which return can be achieved and resulting in investment results that failed to meet expectations.

4.2.1 Prevalence, Costs and Consequences

Although it is has been suggested in the literature that mis-selling in the life insurance industry is widespread (Ericson and Doyle, 2006), exact numbers concerning the prevalence and monetary costs of the phenomenon are hard to come by. As Ericson and Doyle (2006) point out, it is often difficult to discern when or how often the deceptive behaviour of insurance salespeople might violate the law. In many cases, plan holders of mis-sold insurance plans are themselves not even aware that they have been victimized. Nor do regulatory investigations provide much conclusive results with regard to the exact scope of the problem. This is due largely to the fact that only a case-by-case examination can determine whether a product has been fraudulently mis-sold.

However, whatever estimates can be found in the literature do indicate that the scale of the problem is considerable, both in terms of the number of victims involved and the costs associated with it. For example, a review of life insurance selling practices in the United Kingdom during the early 1990s, commissioned by the UK securities market regulator at the time, found that 91% of a representative sample of files failed to prove substantial compliance (Ryley and Virgo, 1999). More specifically, the review found that 61% of the files indicated that the adviser did not adequately determine the investor's risk profile, 85% of the files showed no evidence of alternative pension arrangement having been considered and in only 23% of the files was there an adequate analysis supporting the recommendation (Black and Nobles, 1998). It is generally assumed that around 2 million people were involved in the scandal, which involved costs totalling some £11 billion (Ward, 2000). In an audit study on the advice given by financial advisers in the Indian life insurance market, Anagol et al. (2013) found that in 60–80% of the cases agents provided unsuitable advice. The costs associated with this scandal have been estimated at $28 billion (Halan et al., 2014). However, such estimates focus primarily on the costs associated with fines and customer redress, which are borne by shareholders of mis-selling firms. Excluded from such estimates are the emotional and psychological costs associated with the economic insecurity that plan holders have to cope with as a result of mis-sold life insurance products (Schulz, 2000; Tombs, 2013).

4.2.2 *Perpetrators, Motivations and Opportunities*

Scholarly research enumerates a number of factors that have contributed to the 'institution-alization of deceptive sales in life insurance' (Ericson and Doyle, 2006). With regard to the supply side of the market, scholars have pointed to the remuneration of life insurance agents. The earnings of sales agents are said to be based almost exclusively on *commissions*, creating a strong incentive to adopt aggressive marketing techniques and to sell the highest commission product rather than the product that is most suitable for the consumer (Black and Nobles, 1998; Ericson and Doyle, 2006). Another factor that has been highlighted in the literature is the fa-cilitating effects of an *aggressive sales culture* that prevails in many life insurance companies. Agents, it has been suggested, 'face a constant barrage of motivational messages aimed at aug-menting their production' (Ericson and Doyle, 2006, p. 1005). Embedded in these messages are a number of beliefs, or interpretive frames, that are thought to facilitate, if not encourage, mis-selling among agents (MacLean, 2008). Scholars have, for example, mentioned the way in which customers are depicted by agents as perpetually underinsured (Ericson and Doyle, 2006; MacLean, 2008) and the way in which compliance regulations are described in formal company documents as empty rituals (MacLean, 2008). Third, scholars have named vulnera-bilities in the *recruitment, training and supervision of sales agents* as a source of mis-selling practices (Black and Nobles, 1998; Ericson and Doyle, 2006). In what has been referred to as a 'revolving doors' policy, insurance firms capitalize on agents' networks of sales prospects and then cut them loose when their networks are exhausted, so that 'recruitment is not based on the recruit, but on the prospect list that the recruit can come up with among his family and friends' (Ericson and Doyle, 2006, p. 1003). One consequence of such a policy is that life insurance sales agents generally go through little training, and what little training time they do have is used primarily to focus on sales techniques and the specificities of the firm's in-house products, rather than on life insurances in general or the requirements of regulatory rules and compliance procedures relating to the selling process.

The demand side of the market has also been said to feature certain characteristics that fa-cilitate mis-selling by agents. One issue that repeatedly comes up in the literature is the *public ignorance* with regard to life insurance products and the investment value of money. Con-sumers have been said to have difficulties comparing an ever-widening menu of products, all of which involve different risks, potential benefits, and costs (Black and Nobles, 1998; Ericson and Doyle, 2006). It is maintained that life insurance firms and their agents exploit consumers' ignorance by providing them with deceptive projections of the future performance of insurance and pension plans that are based on highly speculative assumptions, by downplaying risks, and by hiding the mechanisms through which fees are charged by the insurance companies (Ericson and Doyle, 2006).

Finally, the literature finds that *regulatory authorities* have done little to ameliorate the prob-lems. Conform to the neoliberal approach to market regulation, regulators have downloaded responsibility with regard to compliance to companies themselves. Regulatory actions have been largely reactive to public complaints, an approach that becomes problematic when the majority of consumers that have been mis-sold life insurance plans are not even aware they have been victimized (Ericson and Doyle, 2006). Even when regulatory institutions did step in, they continued to delegate authority to the industry itself. Rather than punishing and ex-cluding offenders, regulators have generally commissioned firms to internally re-evaluate their sales procedures and identify and compensate possible victims. However, in both the United Kingdom and the Netherlands, the failure of firms to properly redress victims and their

attempts to reach secretive agreements with select groups of victims in an attempt to minimize legal costs have led to great public controversy.

4.3 *The Mis-Selling of Interest Rate Derivatives*

Because of their complexity and opaqueness, derivatives have proven to be useful devices for
mis-selling practices. From the mid-1990s onwards, derivatives have become the subject of
a number of mis-selling claims in the securities industry, in which not only retail consumers
but also small and medium enterprises and at times even supposedly sophisticated institutional
investors have been victimized. One category of derivative contracts that has repeatedly been
involved in allegations of fraudulent mis-selling by financial service firms is the *interest-rate
hedging product* (IRHP). IRHPs, colloquially referred to as *interest rate swaps*, are derivative
contracts that are intended to protect against interest rate risk associated with an underlying
loan. The first accusations of IRHP mis-selling began to emerge in the mid-1990s and involved
IRHPs that were allegedly mis-sold to a number of large corporate, and presumably sophisticated, clients of the American investment bank Bankers Trust (Overdahl and Schachter, 1995).
A more recent wave of IRHP mis-selling claims emerged in the aftermath of the financial crisis
of 2007–2008. In the run-up to the crisis, banks had been targeting much smaller and definitely
less sophisticated clients with their aggressive and manipulative derivative-selling practices.
Banks in Belgium, the Netherlands, and the United Kingdom, for example, have been found to
have mis-sold large numbers of IRHPs to small and medium enterprises (SMEs) and semipublic entities (Zepeda, 2013; Marshall, 2014; Bavoso, 2015).

Many SMEs in those countries had obtained business loans that had floating rates attached
to them. To hedge against fluctuations in these rates, loan officers at banks and sales agents
advised those SMEs to purchase IRHPs in connection with their business loans. In some cases,
the purchase of an IRHP was made a condition for a loan. In their simplest form, IRHPs set a
fixed rate and oblige the parties in the contract – the borrower and the bank – to make payments
to each other that offset the variability of the interest rate paid on the underlying loan *vis a vis*
the fixed rate. When the relevant benchmark rate – and thus the interest rate that needs to be
paid over the loan – is higher than the fixed rate agreed upon, the bank pays the difference to
the SME. When interest rates fall below it, the SME pays the difference to the bank. Often,
however, loan applicants were talked into purchasing the more complex and more risky types
of IRHPs. In the United Kingdom, for example, this frequently involved so-called 'structured
collars'.[23]

During the initial period when most of the SMEs signed these contracts, central bank rates
were relatively stable (Zepeda, 2013). However, when postcrisis monetary conditions led central banks to drastically lower interest rates to historic lows, many SMEs were prompted to
make large and unexpected payments to the banks or to pay exorbitant exit fees to terminate
the IRHPs (Zepeda, 2013), causing major financial difficulties for many SMEs. Later, studies
into the matter by regulators in different countries revealed that many of the SMEs had been
mis-sold the IRHPs by the banks and that large-scale mis-selling had taken place. For example, the FSA, the UK financial regulator at the time, said it had found 'serious failings' by
several banks in the sale of IRHPs. These concerns related to evidence of inappropriate sales
of IRHPs, poor sales practices, poor record-keeping by banks, and sales incentive schemes that
were likely to exacerbate the risk of poor sales practices (FSA, 2012, referred to by Zepeda,
2013). It was found that many IRHPs had been 'over-hedged' – meaning that the amounts or
the duration of the IRHP, or both, did not match the underlying SME loan – and that banks

had included excessive break costs – costs to prematurely exit the contract – in the contracts; these costs sometimes exceeded 40% of the value of the underlying loan. Moreover, in many cases sales agents had failed to ascertain the customer's understanding of these costs as well as other risks involved in the contract (Zepeda, 2013; Marshall, 2014). Another key issue identified by the financial conduct authority in the Netherlands was that banks had not made it sufficiently clear to their clients and customers that they were not acting as advisers in the sale of IRHPs, as they usually do in other transactions with their clients, but merely as sales persons (AFM, 2013). Clients thus assumed the banks were advising them on IRHPs, while in fact the banks were acting as counterparties in an arms-length transaction, which frees them from their fiduciary duties towards clients.

In addressing the issue, regulators in Belgium, the Netherlands and the United Kingdom all urged or forced banks to come to a suitable solution and offer appropriate redress and compensation on a case-by-case basis.[24] To the dismay of many, these solutions allowed banks to settle claims out of court. Thus, claims have been settled privately and away from public scrutiny.[25] Some have suggested that the watering down of findings in regulatory investigations and the low-profile solutions suggested by regulators have come into being under the pressure of governments and banks, for whom the mis-selling scandals would be 'a scandal too far' (Zepeda, 2013).

4.3.1 *Prevalence, Costs and Consequences*

At the time of writing, not much is said in the scarce literature about the extent of mis-selling of IRHPs. The Dutch regulator has stated that about 17,000 IRHP contracts have been sold to SMEs (FTM, 2014a) and in the United Kingdom this number is estimated at about 60,000 SMEs (Khalique, 2015). However, what proportion of these IRHPs has been fraudulently mis-sold is not clear. In Belgium, the government regulatory agency did not reveal the exact extent of the mis-selling of IRHPs but did say the problem had not reached the proportions it has in the Netherlands and the United Kingdom (FTM, 2015). Nevertheless, an indication of the extent of fraudulent mis-selling that has been offered in the literature refers to a 2012 FSA pilot study. The study, which looked at 173 sales of IRHP to nonsophisticated clients by eight different banks, found that over 90% of these sales did not comply with one or more regulatory requirements (FSA, 2012, cited in Zepeda, 2013).

For individual SMEs, the costs and consequences of mis-sold IRHPs are substantial and have resulted in a great number of bankruptcies. The unprecedented low interest rates in the postcrisis period forced many SMEs to either make large payments to the banks who sold them the IRHP or pay exorbitant exit costs to terminate the contract. These termination costs could amount to 50% of the value of the loan, in addition to the value of the loan itself (Bavoso, 2015). In some cases, SMEs that were unable to make such payments saw their credit lines with the bank being blocked because the negative value of their IRHP was accounted for by the banks as a claim of the bank on the SMEs. The mis-selling episode has also resulted in significant costs to the firms who sold the IRHPS. In the United Kingdom, as of February 2015, banks have already paid out £1.3 billion in redress and compensation (Khalique, 2015). However, despite this large number, it has been argued that redress is unlikely to ensure full and fair compensation for all victims. SMEs face major challenges in providing evidence that they are eligible for redress and, even when they manage to do so, are likely to be grateful for whatever redress is proposed by the banks, even though, according to some, this might be 'considerably less than what they should receive in the interest of fairness' (Zepeda, 2013, p. 11).

4.3.2 *Perpetrators, Motivations and Opportunities*

Reports of regulatory authorities and journalists, as well as the scarce academic literature on the topic, suggest that rewards and incentives for sales agents acted as the main motor driving the mis-selling of IRHPs. Loan officers were subjected to perverse incentives in the form of targets and bonuses to sell as many IRHPs as possible and preferably the types of IRHPs most profitable for the bank in connection with the loans they extended to SMEs (FTM, 2014b; Bavoso, 2015). It has also been emphasized that the mis-selling of IRHPs has been facilitated by the fact that interest rates had been relatively stable throughout the period from 2001 to 2008, the period during which most of the IRHPs were sold. According to one observer, it is possible or perhaps even likely that this stability was used by banks' salespeople to persuade SMEs that the potentially high payment obligations for the knock-in floor strike rate would never be triggered (Zepeda, 2013).

5. Conclusion

When recapitulating the literature review presented in this paper, it appears that financial fraud is widespread throughout the financial industry. What makes the pervasiveness of financial fraud especially worrying is the frequent involvement of established financial institutions. Large banks such as Goldman Sachs and Deutsche Bank, accountancy firms like Ernst & Young and Deloitte, and insurance conglomerates such as Lloyds and AIG, were deeply involved in many of the financial scandals discussed in this paper. The industry itself has usually responded to revelations of their involvement in financial fraud by suggesting that fraudulent dealings are the work of a few bad apples within the organization. The findings of this literature review, however, suggest that the 'bad apples theory' provides a partial explanation at best. Rather, the findings lend support to the criminogenic markets hypothesis (Needleman and Needleman, 1979), which postulates that markets and organizations can be criminogenic in the sense that they structurally facilitate or even promote illegal behaviour. Although the specific market structures and arrangements that have been identified in the literature as being responsible for financial fraud differ between different types of fraud, it is possible to distil from the findings of this literature review four recent developments that are believed to have been important explanatory factors for the occurrence of financial fraud.

First, scholars have repeatedly pointed out the problematic consequences of financial deregulation for prevailing structures of competition and compensation. Financial deregulation has repeatedly been said to have intensified competitive dynamics in previously protected industries and allowed *new fundamental conflicts of interest and perverse incentive structures* to develop in both vertically and horizontally integrated financial conglomerates and throughout industries.[26] Parallel to this, the institutionalization of incentive-based compensation structures (e.g. stock options, bonuses, commission fees) in financial firms, not only at the top but at all levels, has been said to have created perverse incentives throughout the entire financial value chain. As a result, business models of financial firms have become increasingly oriented towards short-term profit-making and stock-price maximization, irrespective of the legal implications of such business models. Fines and other legal penalties are built into such business models as simply a cost of doing business. The incentive problem has been further exacerbated by the introduction of new layers of intermediaries (e.g. fund managers, financial advisers, mortgage brokers, insurance agents) in the financial value chain and the new forms of compensation that have come with it.

Second, over the last few decades financial markets have seen an *influx of relatively unsophisticated investors*. As a consequence of a general trend towards the privatization of social security and the financialization of Western economies, consumers, small and medium enterprises, local governments, and semipublic institutions in those economies increasingly started to engage in financial market activities. The findings of this literature review suggest that this influx of relatively unsophisticated investors has provided fraudulently predisposed and more financially sophisticated market players with a large pool of unexperienced and thus easily exploitable investors. This seems especially to have facilitated the occurrence of a number of large-scale mis-selling scandals.

A third development that has repeatedly surfaced throughout the paper is the *increasing complexity involved in financial market transactions*. Rapid technological, legal, and financial innovation (e.g. derivatives, securitization, special purpose vehicles) and an ever-widening menu of financial products have greatly reduced the transparency, comprehensibility, and controllability of financial transactions and increased the opportunities available to fraudsters to deceive other market participants.

Fourth and finally, the veil of secrecy and mystique surrounding many financial market activities further facilitates the occurrence of fraud in financial markets. The *increased use of justified secrecy* in the form of a mystification of the trading models adopted by fund managers has been on the rise over recent decades. Especially financial scams and false financial disclosures in the context of collective investment funds appear to thrive in this fertile soil of incomplete disclosure.

Most academic work on financial markets to date treats financial fraud as no more than a circumstantial issue with only tangential relevance to a number of mainstream issues. The findings of this literature review, however, suggest that financial fraud deserves to be a mainstream focus in its own right. For economists studying financial markets, there is still much uncovered terrain with regard to financial fraud as a subject for research. A number of directions for future research appear to be especially fruitful. To begin with, future research could look at the impact of fraud on the functioning of markets and investigate the way in which financial frauds have an impact on the stability of financial systems. Recent research going in this direction (Blanqué, 2003; Sen, 2009; Huisman, 2011; Nesvetailova and Palan, 2013; Nesvetailova and Sandu, 2015) has found meaningful points of departure in the works of Hyman Minsky and Charles Kindleberger. More research could also be done on the political and economic structures that facilitate financial fraud. What has been especially lacking so far is comparative research on the nature and character of financial fraud across different political economic systems. How do levels of financialization of national economies and degrees of institutionalization of financial systems affect the occurrence and control of financial fraud? Also, to what extent does the occurrence of financial fraud differ between different legal systems? Such work could build on existing work in the field of comparative political economy and on literature in law and finance (e.g. La Porta *et al.*, 1998; Coffee, 2005; Deakin *et al.*, 2015). Another interesting issue for future research concerns the relationship between deregulation and financial fraud. What are the causal mechanisms establishing the observed link between deregulation and financial fraud? Finally, economists could study the way in which prevailing interest rates affect the occurrence of financial fraud. To what extent do low interest rates encourage excessive risk taking and facilitate Ponzi-like investment schemes? This question is especially relevant when considered against the backdrop of the secular stagnation thesis, which predicts a sustained period of unusually low interest rates (Summers, 2014).

Recognizing and giving due consideration to the illegal dimensions of financial market activities is essential if we are to further our understanding of the dynamics that drive financial markets and safeguard the integrity and soundness of financial systems in the future to come.

Acknowledgements

I would like to thank two anonymous reviewers and the editors of this book for their incisive comments. I would also like to thank Jens Beckert, Renate Mayntz, Patrick Köppen, Tod van Gunten and Benjamin Braun for helpful comments on previous versions of this paper.

Notes

1. A few notes on the scope of the literature review are in order here. First of all, only the English language literature on financial fraud has been included in the literature review. This has had implications for the scope of the findings of the literature review. The English language literature on financial fraud displays a strong bias towards incidences of financial fraud in the financial markets of the United States and Western Europe. This bias should not come as surprise, since these jurisdictions, and especially the United States and the United Kingdom, harbor the biggest and most important financial markets globally. Precisely for this reason, whatever discussions of financial fraud in other, less prominent financial markets do exist in the English language literature are not given much prominence in the present paper. Second, to secure that the literature review has significance for our understanding of financial fraud in contemporary financial markets, only the literature dealing with financial frauds in the last couple of decades is included in the review.

2. Note that the literature review's focus on 'fraudulent behavior in the context of financial market activities' implies that (accounting) frauds in the context of nonfinancial corporations are excluded from the analysis presented in this paper. Corporate (accounting) frauds are dealt with elsewhere in this book.

3. Researchers approaching fraud as a behavioral category have proposed many definitions of fraud, ranging from such cursory ones as 'the obtaining of goods and/or money by deception' (Levi, 2009, p. 224) to more elaborate ones that claim fraud is 'a human endeavor, involving deception, purposeful intent, intensity of desire, risk of apprehension, violation of trust, rationalization, and so on'. (Ramamoorti and Olsen, 2007). The law is just as ambiguous about the phenomenon. Legal scholars have repeatedly stressed the ambiguity of the legal concept of fraud and have at times even referred to the body of law dealing with fraud as a 'conceptual morass' (Podgor, 1999; Green, 2007).

4. The primary concern of the literature review presented in this paper is with the fraudulent acts, rather than the victims and perpetrator of those acts. Perpetrators and their motivations are discussed insofar as they contribute to our understanding of the reasons for the occurrence of the fraudulent act. However, matters that are related to the phenomenon of financial fraud, but that do not bear direct relevance for the occurrence of the fraudulent acts themselves, such as victims' coping strategies or perpetrators' postfraud rationalizations are not discussed in the present paper.

5. Arguably, a third objective of false financial disclosures may be the facilitation of other forms of financial crime, such as money laundering operations or the execution of elaborate tax evasion schemes (see Platt, 2015). The role of accounting fraud in the facilitation of these crimes will not be dealt with in this paper.

6. A look at accounting fraud in more detail reveals that, in carrying out their schemes, perpetrators resort to an enormous variety of fraudulent accounting techniques. A review of the literature (e.g. Mulford and Comiskey, 2002; Jones, 2011; Zack, 2013), however, shows that this myriad of techniques can be broken down into five broad categories. The first two of these, *revenue-based schemes* and *expense-based schemes*, aim at artificially boosting a firm's current profitability as reported on the income statement. The third and fourth categories, *asset-based schemes* and *liability-based schemes*, involve the fraudulent strengthening of the balance sheet through misrepresentations of asset values and risk exposures, in order to increase a company's financial health and perceived future earnings power. The final category, *other financial statement schemes*, represents a residual one.

7. High-profile rogue trading scandals that erupted in the aftermath of the global financial crisis of 2007–2008 include those of Jerome Kerviel of Société Générale, Kweku Adoboli of UBS and Bruno Iksil, a.k.a. 'the London Whale', of JP Morgan.

8. Because of its centrality to the recent financial crisis, the vast majority of the literature on mortgage fraud is concerned with the US mortgage market. Mortgage fraud is, however, not unique to the United States. It has been said to be a serious threat as well in countries such as the United Kingdom (Ryder, 2014) and the Netherlands (Van Gestel, 2010).

9. Note that SAR filings do not reveal the full extent of mortgage fraud. Not only does much fraud go undetected or unreported, institutions that are not federally insured, such as independent mortgage lenders and mortgage brokers, are not required to file SARs (Smith, 2010; Gans, 2011).

10. According to Barnett (2013, p. 108), the subprime mortgage market grew by 324% from $190 billion in 2001 to $615 billion in 2016.

11. It has been suggested by several observers that one important explanation for the low levels of law enforcement is that, despite warnings by the FBI that mortgage fraud was endemic and that a major crisis was pending, the Bush administration decided to focus attention on the War on Terror. As a consequence, the FBI saw the staffing of its white-collar crime unit reduced by 36% in 2001 (Ferguson, 2012).

12. As the authors of the study emphasize, these results are complicated by the fact that it is difficult to determine where exactly in the supply chain of credit – be it at the level of the borrower, the lender or the underwriter – the misrepresentation took place. Theoretically at least, it is possible that underwriters were unable to detect misrepresentations that had occurred at the level of the loan origination process, despite their genuine efforts to perform due diligence.

13. In some cases, what begins as a false financial disclosure may over time evolve into a true financial scam. Entrepreneurs running an otherwise legitimate enterprise may, as their business gets into difficult times, turn to false financial disclosures to paint an artificially rosy picture of the business' profitability and financial health to investors and creditors. In some cases, the necessity of fraudulent disclosures may disappear as time passes and the business becomes profitable again. In other cases, however, the business continues to falter. Unwilling to admit to failure and declare bankruptcy, some entrepreneurs may then slide further down the 'slippery slope of fraud', leading their business to evolve into a true scam.

14. Paper earnings are earnings that are not actually paid out to investors but that accumulate within in the scheme.

15. Stolen financial identities are also used in the perpetration of other types of financial crimes such as money laundering and terrorist financing (Acoca, 2008, p. 77; Ozaki, 2008,

pp. 12–14). The use of identity abuses in these kinds of crimes are not discussed in this paper.

16. Because of the fictitious nature of the identity, there are no consumer-victims involved in this type of fraud. The primary victims are the financial service providers that extend the credit lines.

17. Note that legal systems prohibit financial mis-selling practices primarily through the imposition of fiduciary duties and suitability requirements. As no material misstatements of facts are involved in genuine financial mis-selling cases, general fraud laws generally do not apply.

18. In the United States, as well as in most other countries with developed financial markets, regulators employ a two-track regulatory system in which they distinguish between 'sophisticated' and 'nonsophisticated' or 'unsophisticated' investors. Under such a regulatory regime, sophisticated investors (mostly institutional investors and big corporations) are largely exempted from protective regulation, allowing them to engage in tailored contracts that help them to fulfill needs stemming from their specific investment strategies (see Markham, 1995). Unsophisticated investors (mostly retail consumers and small and medium enterprises), are protected against exploitative practices by a relatively paternalistic regulatory regime that relies on legal concepts such as fiduciary standards and suitability requirements.

19. One prominent example of a mis-selling scandal in which the victims were considered sophisticated investors is the Goldman Sachs ABACUS transaction, a $2 billion synthetic CDO deal that the bank allegedly tricked investors to invest in, even though it knew the deal to be a bad investment. Although the ABACUS transaction represents one of the most compelling occurrences of the mis-selling of structured finance products in the wake of the credit crunch, it is not an isolated case. Similar cases have been mentioned in the literature that involve Deutsche Bank (Scopino, 2014), JP Morgan (Ryder, 2014), Merrill Lynch (Taibbi, 2009) and Citigroup (Ryder, 2014).

20. In fact, many of these 'independent' mortgage banks later became subsidiaries of 'respectable' banks that operated as securitizers and underwriters in the secondary mortgage market (Rosoff *et al.*, 2014, p. 48).

21. More recently, the issue of mis-sold life insurances has resurfaced in both the United States and the United Kingdom. Driven by presumably faulty and misleading advice, many people in the United States over the last decade have rolled-over from 401(k) pension plans to so-called individual retirement accounts (IRAs), which give more freedom to individuals to make decisions about their own investments. The deceptive sales practices have resulted in regulatory actions by the Department of Labor and FINRA, the financial industry's self-regulatory authority (Turner and Klein, 2014). In the United Kingdom, a new mis-selling scandal is in the making that involves annuities (FCA, 2015). In many cases, pensioners in poor health have been mis-sold regular annuities while in fact they were entitled to so-called 'enhanced annuities', which provide higher payments to compensate for shorter life expectancies (Dyson, 2014; Hyde and Morley, 2014; Morley, 2015).

22. The mis-selling affair in the Netherlands, in the country itself usually referred to as the '*woekerpolisaffaire*', involved not only life insurance policies but also mortgage-related payment-protection insurance policies, study saving plans, and other kinds of investment-related insurance plans.

23. In the Netherlands, the majority of IRHPs that were (mis-)sold to SMEs involved plain vanilla swaps. In Belgium, investigations by the financial market regulator focused on the

mis-selling of so-called 'Bermudan callable swaps', which had been sold to SMEs during the period 2007 to 2009 (FTM, 2015).

24. In the United Kingdom, the FSA reached an agreement with eight banks that had been involved in the scandal – most notably Barclays, HSBC, Lloyds, and RBS – that forced these banks to provide redress and compensation to customers who had been mis-sold IRHPs. As was the case in the United Kingdom, the Belgian financial market regulator FSMA used its authority to force banks to re-evaluate their most questionable IRHPS sales to SMEs, that is, those that involved so-called 'Bermudan callable swaps', and provide suitable redress to the SMEs (FTM, 2015). The regulator in the Netherlands (the AFM) did not use its authority to force banks to re-evaluate their sales of IRHPs to SMEs but nevertheless said that the advice given by banks to SMEs was often inadequate and urged banks themselves to come up with a suitable solution to the problem (AFM, 2014).

25. Nevertheless, some SMEs have filed private and collective suits against the banks that sold them the IRHPs, accusing them of misleading marketing and sales practices in regard to these products.

26. Note that the observation that deregulation has been identified in the literature as a facilitator of financial fraud scandals that have occurred in the past decades is different from saying that deregulation has been a cause of a general increase in the occurrence of financial fraud across the board.

References

Acoca, B. (2008) Online identity theft: a growing threat to consumer confidence in the digital economy. In D. Chryssikos, N. Passas, and C.D. Ram (eds), *The Evolving Challenge of Identity-Related Crime: Addressing Fraud and the Criminal Misuse and Falsification of Identity* (pp. 71–86). Courmayeur Mont Blanc, Italy: ISPAC (International Scientific and Professional Advisory Council of the United Nations Crime Prevention and Criminal Justice Programme).

AFM (Authoriteit Financiële Markten) (2013) *AFM Rapportage Rentederivaten: Dienstverlening aan semipublieke instellingen en het professionele MKB*. Available at: http://www.afm.nl/~/media/Files/rapport/2013/dienstverlening-rentederivaten.ashx (Accessed on January 12, 2016).

AFM (Authoriteit Financiële Markten) (2014) *Aanbevelingen rentederivatendienstverlening: Voor een passende dienstverlening aan het niet-professionele MKB*. Available at: http://www.afm.nl/~/media/Files/publicatie/2014/aanbevelingen-rentederivatendienstverlening.ashx (Accessed on January 12, 2016).

Anagol, S., Cole, S.A. and Sarkar, S. (2013) *Understanding the advice of commissions-motivated agents: evidence from the Indian life insurance market*. Working Paper 12–055, Harvard Business School, Boston.

Anderson, K.B., Durbin, E. and Salinger, M.A. (2008) Identity theft. *The Journal of Economic Perspectives* 22(2): 171–192.

Bai, F. and Chen, X. (2013) Analysis on the new types and countermeasures of credit card fraud in Mainland China. *Journal of Financial Crime* 20(3): 267–271.

Baker, W.E. and Faulkner, R.R. (2003) Diffusion of fraud: intermediate economic crime and investor dynamics. *Criminology* 41(4): 1173–1206.

Barak, G. (2012) *Theft of a Nation: Wall Street Looting and Federal Regulatory Colluding*. Lanham, MD: Rowman & Littlefield.

Barnett, H.C. (2011) The securitization of mortgage fraud. In M. Deflem (ed), *Economic Crisis and Crime*. Bingley: Emerald.

Barnett, H.C. (2013) And some with a fountain pen: mortgage fraud, securitization, and the subprime bubble. In S. Will, S. Handelman and D.C. Brotherton (eds), *How They Got Away with It: White*

Collar Criminals and the Financial Meltdown (pp. 104–129). New York: Columbia University Press.

Baumer, E.P., Arnio, A.N. and Wolff, K.T. (2013) Assessing the role of mortgage fraud, confluence, and spillover in the contemporary foreclosure crisis. *Housing Policy Debate* 23(2): 299–327.

Bavoso, V. (2015) *Financial innovation, derivatives and the UK and US interest rate swap scandals: searching for lessons and drawing a way forward. Draft March 2015.* Available at: http://papers.ssrn.com/sol3/papers.cfm?abstract_id=2467006 (Accessed on January 18, 2016).

BIS (Bank for International Settlements) (2008) *Customer Suitability in the Retail Sale of Financial Products and Services.* Basel: Basel Committee on Banking Supervision. Available at: http://www.bis.org/publ/joint20.pdf (Accessed on January 23, 2016).

Black, J. and Nobles, R. (1998) Personal pensions misselling: the causes and lessons of regulatory failure. *The Modern Law Review* 61(6): 789–820.

Black, W.K. (2006) Book review: control fraud theory v. the protocols. *Crime, Law and Social Change* 45(3): 241–258.

Blanqué, P. (2003) Crisis and fraud. *Journal of Financial Regulation and Compliance* 11(1): 60–70.

Blois, K. (2013) Affinity fraud and trust within financial markets. *Journal of Financial Crime* 20(2): 186–202.

Brody, R.G., Mulig, E. and Kimball, V. (2007) Phishing, pharming and identity theft. *Academy of Accounting and Financial Studies Journal* 11(3): 43–56.

Buell, S.W. (2006) Novel criminal fraud. *New York University Law Review* 81: 1971–2043.

Buell, S.W. (2011) What is securities fraud? *Duke Law Journal* 61(3): 511–581.

Bussani, M. (2010) Credit rating agencies' accountability: short notes on a global issue. *Global Jurist* 10(1): 1–13.

Button, M., Nicholls, C.M., Kerr, J. and Owen, R. (2014) Online frauds: learning from victims why they fall for these scams. *Australian & New Zealand Journal of Criminology* 47(3): 391–408.

Cane, M.B., Shamir, A. and Jodar, T. (2012) Below investment grade and above the law: a past, present and future look at the accountability of credit rating agencies. *Fordham Journal of Corporate & Financial Law* 17: 1063–1126.

Carswell, A.T. and Bachtel, D.C. (2009) Mortgage fraud: a risk factor analysis of affected communities. *Crime, Law and Social Change* 52(4): 347–364.

Cheney, J.S. (2005) *Identity theft: do definitions still matter?* Federal Reserve Bank of Philadelphia Payment Cards Center Discussion Paper (Available at SSRN).

Coffee Jr, J.C. (1984) Market failure and the economic case for a mandatory disclosure system. *Virginia Law Review* 70(4): 717–753.

Coffee Jr, J.C. (2005) A theory of corporate scandals: why the USA and Europe Differ. *Oxford review of economic policy* 21(2): 198–211.

Collins, M.C. and Nigro, P.J. (2010) Mortgage origination fraud. *Criminology & Public Policy* 9(3): 633–640.

Comet, C. (2011) Anatomy of a fraud: trust and social networks. *Bulletin de Méthodologie Sociologique* 110(1): 45–57.

Davidoff Solomon, S.M., Morrison, A.D. and Wilhelm Jr, W.J. (2012) The SEC v. Goldman Sachs: reputation, trust, and fiduciary duties in investment banking. *The Journal of Corporate Law* 37(3): 529–553.

Deakin, S., Gindis, D., Hodgson, G.M., Kainan, H. and Pistor, K. (2015) *Legal Institutionalism: Capitalism and the Constitutive Role of Law.* University of Cambridge Faculty of Law Legal Studies Research Paper Series (Paper No. 26/2015).

Delgadillo, L.M., Erickson, L.V. and Piercy, K.W. (2008) Disentangling the differences between abusive and predatory lending: professionals' perspectives. *Journal of Consumer Affairs* 42(3): 313–334.

Dorn, N. (2011) Reconstructing 'conflict of interest' in financial markets: private management, public challenges, future prospects. *International Journal of Law, Crime and Justice* 39(3): 161–173.

Dyson, R. (2014) Annuity mis-selling scandal: could it be as big as PPI? *The Telegraph*, December 11, 2014. Available at: https://www.telegraph.co.uk/finance/personalfinance/pensions/ 11286965/Annuity-mis-selling-scandal-could-it-be-as-big-as-PPI.html (Accessed on January 18, 2016).

Egler Jr, F.N. and Malak, P.J. (1999) The individual life insurance sales practice case: a litigation primer. *FICC Quarterly* 50(1): 1–28.

Engel, K.C. and McCoy, P.A. (2002) A tale of three markets: the law and economics of predatory lending. *Texas Law Review* 80(6): 1255–1367.

Ericson, R.V. and Doyle, A. (2006) The institutionalization of deceptive sales in life insurance: five sources of moral risk. *British Journal of Criminology* 46(6): 993–1010.

FCA (Financial Conduct Authority). (2015) *Retirement Income Market Study: Final Report – Confirmed Findings and Remedies*. Market Study 14/3.3 London: Financial Conduct Authority. Available at: https://www.fca.org.uk/your-fca/documents/market-studies/ms14-03-3 (Accessed on January 12, 2016).

Ferguson, C. (2012) *Predator Nation*. New York: Crown Business.

Fischel, D.R. and Stillman, R.S. (1997) The law and economics of vanishing premium insurance. *Delaware Journal of Corporate Law* 22(1): 1–36.

Fisher QC, J. (2015) Risk, recklesness, and policing the financial markets. In N. Ryder, U. Turksen and S. Hassler (eds), *Fighting Financial Crime in the Global Economic Crisis*. New York, NY: Routledge.

Fligstein, N. and Roehrkasse, A. (2013) *All the incentives were wrong: opportunism and the financial crisis*. Paper presented at the American Sociological Association Annual Meeting, Hilton New York and Sheraton New York, New York, NY.

Frankel, T. (2012) *The Ponzi Scheme Puzzle: A History and Analysis of Con Artists and Victims*. New York, NY: Oxford University Press.

FTM (Follow the Money) (2014a) *AFM Voert Druk op Banken op om Verkoop Swaps aan MKB*. May 28, 2014. Available at: www.ftm.nl/exclusive/afm-voert-druk-banken-op-om-verkoop-swaps-mkb/ (Accessed on January 12, 2016).

FTM (Follow the Money) (2014b) *Oud Rabo-bankier: 'Perverse Prikkels voor Verkoop van Renteswaps'*. December 24, 2014. Available at: www.ftm.nl/exclusive/oud-rabo-bankier-perverse-prikkels-voor-verkoop-van-renteswaps/ (Accessed on January 12, 2016).

FTM (Follow the Money) (2015) *Belgische Toezichthouder Grijpt Hard in om 'Plofderivaten' bij MKB*. May 22, 2015. Available at: www.ftm.nl/artikelen/belgische-toezichthouder-grijpt-hard-in-om-plofderivaten-bij-mkb (Accessed on January 12, 2016).

Gans, K. (2011) Anatomy of a mortgage meltdown: the study of the subprime crisis, the role of fraud, and the efficacy of the Idaho safe act. *Idaho Law Review* 48: 123–174.

Geckeler, P.M. (1996) Municipal derivatives use and the suitability doctrine. *Washington University Journal of Urban and Contemporary Law* 49(1): 285–314.

Geeta, D.V. (2011) Online identity theft: an Indian perspective. *Journal of Financial Crime* 18(3): 235–246.

Geis, G. (2013) Unaccountable external auditors and their role in the economic meltdown. In S. Will, S. Handelman and D.C. Brotherton (eds), *How They Got Away with It: White Collar Criminals and the Financial Meltdown* (pp. 85–103). New York, NY: Columbia University Press.

Goldmann, P. (2010) *Fraud in the Markets: Why It Happens and How to Fight It*. Hoboken, NJ: John Wiley & Sons.

Green, S.P. (2007) *Lying, Cheating, and Stealing: A Moral Theory of White-Collar Crime*. New York, NY: Oxford University Press.

Halan, M., Sane, R. and Thomas, S. (2014) The case of the missing billions: estimating losses to customers due to mis-sold life insurance policies. *Journal of Economic Policy Reform* 17(4): 285–302.

Harrison, K. and Ryder, N. (2013) *The Law Relating to Financial Crime in the United Kingdom*. Farnham, UK: Ashgate.

Hill, R.P. and Kozup, J.C. (2007) Consumer experiences with predatory lending practices. *The Journal of Consumer Affairs* 41(1): 29–46.

Hudson, A. (1998) *The uses and abuses of derivatives*. The Paper originally written for Cambridge Symposium on Economic Crime. Available at: http://www.alastairhudson.com/financelaw/useabusederivatives.pdf (Accessed on January 18, 2016).

Huisman, W. (2011) Corporate crime and crisis: causation scenarios. In M. Deflem (ed), *Economic Crisis and Crime* (Vol. 16, pp. 107–125). Bingley, UK: Emeral Group Publishing.

Hyde, D. and Morley, K. (2014) Pension mis-selling: scandal hits 100,000 retired savers a year. *The Telegraph*, November 21, 2014. Available at: https://www.telegraph.co.uk/finance/personalfinance/pensions/11246773/Pension-mis-selling-scandal-hits-100000-retired-savers-a-year.html (Accessed on January 15, 2016).

Ianelli, N. and Hackworth, A. (2007) Botnets as a vehicle for online crime. *The International Journal of Forensic Computer Science* 1: 19–39.

Instefjord, N., Jackson, P. and Perraudin, W. (1998) Securities fraud: it is a matter of incentives from bottom to top. *Economic Policy* 13(27): 585–623.

Jagatic, T.N., Johnson, N.A., Jakobsson, M. and Menczer, F. (2007) Social phishing. *Communications of the ACM* 50(10): 94–100.

Johansson, T. (2010) Regulating credit rating agencies: the issue of conflicts of interest in the rating of structured finance products. *Journal of Banking Regulation* 12(1): 1–23.

Jones, M.J. (2011) *Creative Accounting, Fraud and International Accounting Scandals*. Chichester, UK: John Wiley & Sons.

Kane, E.J. and DeTrask, K. (1999) Breakdown of accounting controls at Barings and Daiwa: benefits of using opportunity-cost measures for trading activity. *Pacific-Basin Finance Journal* 7(3): 203–228.

Khalique, F. (2015) Mis-selling: fix hedges in the spotlight. *Euromoney*, April 30, 2015. Available at: https://www.euromoney.com/article/b12kmzmxk5tzrv/mis-selling-fx-hedges-in-the-spotlight (Accessed on January 17, 2016).

Körnert, J. (2003) The barings crises of 1890 and 1995: causes, courses, consequences and the danger of domino effects. *Journal of International Financial Markets, Institutions & Money* 13(3): 187–209.

Krawiec, K.D. (2000) Accounting for greed: unraveling the rogue trader mystery. *Oregon Law Review* 79: 301–338.

Krawiec, K.D. (2009) The return of the rogue. *Arizona Law Review* 51: 127–174.

La Porta, R., Lopez-de-Silanes, F., Shleifer, A. and Vishny, R.W. (1998) Law and finance. *Journal of Political Economy* 106(6): 1113–1155.

Laffort, E. and Cargnello-Charles, E. (2014) Reducing the risk of fraud in financial market: psychosocial drivers and enactment-based perspective. *World Journal of Social Sciences* 4(2): 1–13.

Leeson, N. (1996) *Rogue Trader: How I Brought Down Barings Bank and Shook the Financial World*. Boston, MA: Little, Brown & Company.

Lehmann, M. (2014) *Civil liability of rating agencies: an insipid sprout from Brussels*. Working Paper 15/2014, LSE Law, Society and Economy.

Levi, M. (2009) Financial crime. In M. Tonry (ed), *Oxford Handbook of Crime and Public Policy* (pp. 223–246). New York, NY: Oxford University Press.

Lewis, M.K. (2012) New dogs, old tricks. why do ponzi schemes succeed? *Accounting Forum* 36(4): 294–309.

Lokanan, M.E. (2014) The demographic profile of victims of investment fraud: a canadian perspective. *Journal of Financial Crime* 21(2): 226–242.

Lomnicka, E. (2008) Investors protection in securities markets. In P. Cane and J. Conaghan (eds), *The New Oxford Companion on Law*: Oxford University Press.

Lovet, G. (2006) *Dirty money on the wires: the business models of cyber criminals*. Paper presented at the Proceedings of the 16th Virus Bulletin International Conference.

Lowenfels, L.D. and Bromberg, A.R. (1999) Suitability in securities transactions. *The Business Lawyer* 45(4): 1557–1597.

Lynch, J. (2005) Identity theft in cyberspace: crime control methods and their effectiveness in combating phishing attacks. *Berkeley Technology Law Journal* 20(1): 259–300.

Maas, D.A. (2011) Policing the ratings agencies: the case for stronger criminal disincentives in the credit rating market. *The Journal of Criminal Law and Criminology* 101(3): 1005–1038.

MacLean, T.L. (2008) Framing and organizational misconduct: a symbolic interactionist study. *Journal of Business Ethics* 78(1–2): 3–16.

Mahoney, P.G. (1995) Mandatory disclosure as a solution to agency problems. *The University of Chicago Law Review* 62(3): 1047–1112.

Markham, J.W. (1995) Protecting the institutional investor: jungle predator or shorn lamb? *The Yale Journal on Regulation* 12(2): 345–386.

Markopolos, H. (2010) *No One Would Listen: A True Financial Thriller*. Hoboken, NJ: John Wiley & Sons.

Marshall, P. (2014) Interest rate swaps and the sale of the unknown: blind alleys, an enfeebled equity and the triumph of certainty over fairness. *Butterworths Journal of International Banking and Financial Law* 29(1): 9–15.

McCoy, P.A. (2005) A behavioral analysis of predatory lending. *Akron Law Review* 38(4): 725–739.

Mitchell, O.S. and Smetters, K. (2013) The market for retirement financial advice: an introduction. In *The Market for Retirement Financial Advice* (pp. 1–10). New York: Oxford University Press.

Moore, T., Clayton, R. and Anderson, R. (2009) The economics of online crime. *The Journal of Economic Perspectives* 23(3): 3–20.

Morley, K. (2015) Is this the worst pension mis-selling ever? Ariva knew this customer was Ill. *The Telegraph*, March 28, 2015. Available at: https://www.telegraph.co.uk/finance/personal finance/pensions/11499715/Is-this-the-worst-pension-mis-selling-case-ever-Aviva-knew-this-cust omer-was-ill.html (Accessed on January 24, 2016).

Mulford, C.M. and Comiskey, E.E. (2002) *The Financial Numbers Game: Detecting Creative Accounting Practices*. New York, NY: John Wiley & Sons.

Mundheim, R.H. (1965) Professional responsiblities of broker-dealers: the suitability doctrine. *Duke Law Journal* 3: 445–480.

Nash, R., Bouchard, M. and Malm, A. (2013) Investing in people: the role of social networks in the diffusion of a large-scale fraud. *Social Networks* 35(4): 686–698.

Naylor, R.T. (2007) The alchemy of fraud: investment scams in the precious-metals mining business. *Crime, Law and Social Change* 47(2): 89–120.

Needleman, M.L. and Needleman, C. (1979) Organizational crime: two models of criminogenesis. *The Sociological Quarterly* 20(4): 517–528.

Nesvetailova, A. and Palan, R. (2013) Minsky in the shadows: securitization, Ponzi finance, and the crisis of northern rock. *Review of Radical Political Economics* 45(3): 349–368.

Nesvetailova, A. and Sandu, A. (2015) The good, the bad and the fraud. In N. Ryder, U. Turksen and S. Hassler (eds), *Fighting Financial Crime in the Global Economic Crisis*. New York, NY: Routledge.

Nguyen, T.H. and Pontell, H.N. (2010) Mortgage origination fraud and the global economic crisis. *Criminology & Public Policy* 9(3): 591–612.

Nguyen, T.H. and Pontell, H.N. (2011) Fraud and inequality in the subprime mortgage crisis. In M. Deflem (ed), *Economic Crisis and Crime* (Vol. 16, pp. 3–24). Bingley, UK: Emeral Group Publishing.

Nolasco, C.A.R.I., Vaughn, M.S. and Del Carmen, R.V. (2013) Revisiting the choice model of Ponzi and pyramid schemes: analysis of case law. *Crime, Law and Social Change* 60(4): 375–400.

Overdahl, J. and Schachter, B. (1995) Derivatives regulation and financial management: lessons from Gibson greetings. *Financial Management* 24(1): 68–78.

Ozaki, K. (2008) *Keynote address*. Paper presented at the The Evolving Challenge of Identity-Related Crime: Addressing Fraud and the Criminal Misuse and Falsification of Identity, Courmayeur Mont Blanc, Italy.

Pardieck, A.M. (2006) Kegs, crude, and commodities law: on why it is time to reexamine the suitability doctrine. *Nevada Law Journal* 7: 301–347.

Partnoy, F. (2002) *Infectious Greed: How Deceit and Risk Corrupted the Financial Markets*. New York, NY: Times Books.

Perri, F.S. and Brody, R.G. (2012) The optics of fraud: affiliations that enhance offender credibility. *Journal of Financial Crime* 19(3): 305–320.

Piskorski, T., Seru, A. and Witkin, J. (2013) *Asset quality misrepresentation by financial intermediaries: evidence from the RMBS market*. NBER Working Paper Series (Working Paper 18843).

Platt, S. (2015) *Criminal Capital: How the Finance Industry Facilitates Crime*. Basingstoke: Palgrace Macmillan.

Podgor, E.S. (1999) Criminal fraud. *American University Law Review* 48(4): 729–768.

Policastro, C. and Payne, B.K. (2014) Can you hear me now? telemarketing fraud victimization and lifestyles. *American Journal of Criminal Justice* 40(3): 620–638.

Pontell, H.N. and Geis, G. (2007) New times, new crimes: "blocking" financial identity fraud. In F. Bovenkerk and M. Levi (eds), *The Organized Crime Community* (Vol. 6, pp. 45–58). New York, NY: Springer.

Pressman, S. (1998) On financial frauds and their causes. *American Journal of Economics and Sociology* 57(4): 405–421.

Ram, C.D. (2008) *Identity related crime as a global issue: the nature, concept and types of identity related crime*. Paper presented at the The Evolving Challenge of Identity-Related Crime: Addressing Fraud and the Criminal Misuse and Falsification of Identity, Courmayeur Mont Blanc, Italy.

Ramamoorti, S. and Olsen, W. (2007) Fraud: the human factor. *Financial Executive* 23(6): 53–55.

Renuart, E. (2004) An overview of the predatory mortgage lending process. *Housing Policy Debate* 15(3): 467–502.

Reurink, A. (2016) *Financial fraud: a literature review*. MPIfG Discussion Paper 16/5. Cologne: Max Planck Institute for the Study of Societies.

Roberts, L. (1996) Suitability claims under rule 10b-5: are public entities sophisticated enough to use derivatives? *The University of Chicago Law Review* 63(2): 801–835.

Rosoff, S., Pontell, H. and Tillman, R. (2014) *Profit without Honor: White-Collar Crime and the Looting of America*. Upper Saddle River, NJ: Pearson Education.

Ryder, N. (2011) *Financial Crime in the 21st Century: Law and Policy*. Cheltenham, UK: Edward Elgar Publishing.

Ryder, N. (2014) *The Financial Crisis and White Collar Crime: The Perfect Storm?* Cheltenham, UK: Edward Elgar Publishing.

Ryley, P. and Virgo, J. (1999) Mis-selling of personal pension plans: a legal perspective. *Journal of Pension Management* 5(1): 18–36.

Schmedlen Jr, D.G. (1995) Broker-dealer sales practice in derivatives transactions: a survey and evaluation of suitability requirements. *Washington & Lee Law Review* 52(4): 1441–1474.

Schulz, J. (2000) The risks of pension privatization in Britain. *Challenge* 43(1): 93–104.

Scopino, G. (2014) Regulating fairness: the Dodd-Frank act's fair dealing requirement for swap dealers and major swap participants. *Nebraska Law Review* 93(1): 31–88.

Selden, S.R. (2006) (Self-)policing the market: congress's flawed approach to securities law reform. *Journal of Legislation* 33(1): 57–98.

Seligman, J. (1983) The historical need for a mandatory corporate disclosure system. *Journal of Corporate Law* 9: 1–61.

Sen, S. (2009) Speculation, scams, frauds and crises: theory and facts. *Economic and Political Weekly* 44(12): 15–19.

Shapiro, D. (2013) Generating alpha return: how Ponzi schemes lure the unwary in an unregulated market. In S. Will, S. Handelman and D.C. Brotherton (eds), *How They Got Away with It: White Collar Criminals and the Financial Meltdown* (pp. 130–147). New York, NY: Columbia University Press.

Shover, N., Coffey, G.S. and Hobbs, D. (2003) Crime on the line. Telemarketing and the changing nature of professional crime. *British Journal of Criminology* 43(3): 489–505.

Shover, N., Coffey, G.S. and Sanders, C.R. (2004) Dialing for dollars: opportunities, justifications, and telemarketing fraud. *Qualitative Sociology* 27(1): 59–75.

Smith, J.C. (2010) The structural causes of mortgage fraud. *Syracuse Law Review* 60: 473–501.

Stein, E. (2001) *Quantifying the Economic Cost of Predatory Lending*. Available at: http://www.selegal. org/Cost%20of%20Predatory%20Lending.pdf (Accessed on January 4, 2016).

Stein, M. (2000) The risk taker as shadow: a psychoanlytic view of the collapse of barings bank. *Journal of Management Studies* 37(8): 1215–1230.

Stolowy, H., Messner, M., Jeanjean, T. and Baker, C.R. (2014) The construction of a trustworthy investment opportunity: insights from the madoff fraud. *Contemporary Accounting Research* 31(2): 354–397.

Summers, L.H. (2014) US economic prospects: secular stagnation, hysteresis, and the zero lower bound. *Business Economics* 49(2): 65–73.

Taibbi, M. (2009) The great American bubble machine. *Rolling Stone*, April 5, 2010. Available at: https://www.rollingstone.com/politics/politics-news/the-great-american-bubble-machine-195229/ (Accessed on November 14, 2015).

Tillman, R. (2002) *Global Pirates: Fraud in the Offshore Insurance Industry*. Boston, MA: Northeastern University Press.

Tombs, S. (2013) Corporate theft and fraud: business as usual. *Criminal Justice Matters* 94(1): 14–15.

Trahan, A., Marquart, J.W. and Mullings, J. (2005) Fraud and the American dream: toward an understanding of fraud victimization. *Deviant Behavior* 26(6): 601–620.

Turner, J.A. and Klein, B.W. (2014) Retirement savings flows and financial advice: should you roll over your 401 (k) plan? *Benefits Quarterly* 30(4): 42–54.

Van Gestel, B. (2010) Mortgage fraud and facilitating circumstances. In K. Bullock, R.V. Clarke and N. Tilley (eds), *Situational Prevention of Organised Crimes* (pp. 111–129). New York, NY: Routledge.

Vishwanath, A., Herath, T., Chen, R., Wang, J. and Rao, H.R. (2011) Why do people get phished? testing individual differences in phishing vulnerability within an integrated, information processing model. *Decision Support Systems* 51(3): 576–586.

Vittal, J.A. (2005) Phishing, pharming, and other scams. *GPSolo* 22(8): 26–32.

Ward, S. (2000) Personal pensions in the UK, the mis-selling scandal and the lessons to be learnt. In G. Hughes and J. Stewart (eds), *Pensions in the European Union: Adapting to Economic and Social Change* (pp. 139–146). New York, NY: Springer Science + Business Media.

Weber, B. (2011) High frequency trading: the growing threat of rogue trading. *Business Strategy Review* 20(2): 50–53.

Wexler, M. N. (2010) Financial edgework and the persistence of rogue traders. *Business and Society Review* 115(1): 1–25.

Will, S. (2013) America's Ponzi culture. In S. Will, S. Handelman and D.C. Brotherton (eds), *How They Got Away with It: White Collar Criminals and the Financial Metldown* (pp. 45–67). New York, NY: Columbia University Press.

Willis, L.E. (2006) Decisionmaking and the limits of disclosure: the problem of predatory lending: price. *Maryland Law Review* 65(3): 707–840.

Young, J. (2013) Bernie madoff, finance capital, and the anomic society. In S. Will, S. Handelman and D.C. Brotherton (eds), *How They Got Away with It: White Collar Criminals and the Financial Meltdown* (pp. 68–81). New York, NY: Columbia University Press.

Zack, G.M. (2013) *Financial Statement Fraud: Strategies for Detection and Investigation*. Hoboken, NJ: John Wiley & Sons.

Zepeda, R. (2013) Derivatives mis-selling by British banks and the failed legacy of the FSA. *Journal of International Banking Law and Regulation* 28(6): 209–220.

5

ESTIMATING INFLATION RISK PREMIA USING INFLATION-LINKED BONDS: A REVIEW

Alexander Kupfer

Department of Banking and Finance University of Innsbruck Austria

1. Introduction

With nominal bonds, investors have transparency on yields in nominal terms. Since inflation would diminish their returns, investors look for compensation on expected inflation in nominal bond yields. Loosely speaking, as expected inflation is uncertain, investors demand an additional premium for this uncertainty (i.e. the inflation risk premium). Obtaining precise information on the inflation risk premium is crucial for several reasons: First, it is possible to extract inflation expectations from nominal bonds and inflation-linked bonds (ILBs). This measure, however, is biased by several factors, including the inflation risk premium. Knowledge of the inflation risk premium's magnitude thus enables more accurate information on inflation expectations derived from market-based measures. Second, sovereign debt management is also interested in the size of the inflation risk premium as they pay this premium when issuing nominal bonds. A positive inflation risk premium and simultaneous absence of any other premium leads to lower costs for the Treasury when issuing ILB (relative to their nominal counterparts). Finally and more generally, the sign of the inflation risk premium offers some intuition about the state of the economy (i.e. supply-side shocks vs. demand-side shocks). While a strictly positive inflation risk premium is commonly assumed,[1] recent research incorporates the possibility of the measure taking on negative values. These emerging discrepancies and current developments in literature evoke the need for a precise measure of the inflation risk premium.

   The current study will demonstrate that the estimation of the inflation risk premium is not as easy a task as it may seem on first glance. First, different sources of data can be used to estimate the inflation risk premium. A considerable body of research literature uses survey inflation forecasts and nominal bond yields to estimate the inflation risk premium (see the beginning of Section 3 for a short discussion). The availability of ILB offered new possibilities to evaluate the premium. With now about 20 years of experience with and a vast amount of

Contemporary Topics in Finance: A Collection of Literature Surveys, First Edition. Edited by Iris Claus and Leo Krippner.

research on ILB (mainly in the USA), a comprehensive overview of the different approaches applied, data used and assumptions made is required. This article provides the aforementioned review, focusing on differences in research designs and approaches as well as highlighting limitations of existing studies, thus striving to answer the following research questions:[2]

- What are advantages and limitations of using ILB data to estimate the inflation risk premium?
- How does existing research cope with these obstacles?
- What are the estimates for the inflation risk premium and how do they differ depending on whether studies do or do not use ILB data?

Several limitations are relevant when the inflation risk premium is estimated using ILB: illiquidity, an indexation lag and an embedded deflation option. These are considered and taken into account to various degrees in different studies, as will be shown in this paper. Thus, this review focuses on how studies have evolved to control and adjust for these limitations and how they have added additional data such as survey inflation forecasts or macro-economic variables to improve their estimation. However, in-depth technical issues, such as parameter restriction or estimation issues, are beyond the scope of this paper.

In this survey, I present and compare existing studies' research designs and data used and finally show their estimates for the inflation risk premium, thus building on the work of Bekaert and Wang (2010) and D'Amico *et al.* (2018), who already compare (their own estimates with) different estimates for the inflation risk premium. A discussion of ILB liquidity and current issues like the zero lower bound complete the summary of existing research designs, liquidity proxies and state of the literature, thus ensuring that the current paper can be used as a convenient starting point for interested reader and future research. This survey is related to an excellent article by Bekaert and Wang (2010) that reviews inflation risk worldwide. While the authors focus on the concept of inflation hedging, they also survey studies that estimate the inflation risk premium by using ILB. In the present review, I (i) update and extend Bekaert and Wang's (2010) review with respect to research design, (ii) provide a detailed overview on the obstacles to using ILB (Bekaert and Wang, 2010, already discussed the problem of ILB illiquidity) and (iii) continue the comparison of different estimates for the inflation risk premium in a comprehensive table.

The remainder of this paper is structured as follows: Section 2 provides an overview of the most relevant concepts discussed: the inflation risk premium (Section 2.1) and the link between ILB and nominal bonds (Section 2.2). Section 3 reviews studies that estimate the inflation risk premium without a term structure model (Section 3.1) and with a term structure model (Section 3.2). Section 3.3 includes an evaluation and comparison of the various estimates for the inflation risk premium. In Section 4, I discuss the impact of liquidity and present a list of liquidity proxies used in previous research. Sections 5 and 6 examine issues in current literature and conclude the paper, respectively.

2. Overview of Relevant Concepts

2.1 *Inflation Risk Premium*

To illustrate the origin of the inflation risk premium more formally, one can start by defining a nominal stochastic discount factor M_t^N and a real stochastic discount factor M_t^R.[3] In an arbitrage-free setting (ensuring consistent pricing), bond prices are defined as follows: The price of a nominal bond that pays one dollar at time τ is given by

$$P_t^N(\tau) = \mathbb{E}_t \left[\frac{M_{t+\tau}^N}{M_t^N} \right] \tag{1}$$

similarly, the price of a real (ILB) bond that pays one unit of the consumption basket (i.e. in real terms) at time τ is

$$P_t^R(\tau) = \mathbb{E}_t \left[\frac{M_{t+\tau}^R}{M_t^R} \right] \tag{2}$$

Given both bond prices, they must be consistent to each other implying the following price level:

$$Q_t = \frac{M_t^R}{M_t^N} \tag{3}$$

Further, decomposition of the nominal bond's price delivers

$$P_t^N(\tau) = \mathbb{E}_t \left[\frac{M_{t+\tau}^N}{M_t^N} \right] = \mathbb{E}_t \left[\frac{\frac{M_{t+\tau}^R}{Q_{t+\tau}}}{\frac{M_t^R}{Q_t}} \right] = \mathbb{E}_t \left[\frac{M_{t+\tau}^R}{M_t^R} \cdot \frac{Q_t}{Q_{t+\tau}} \right]$$

$$= \mathbb{E}_t \left[\frac{M_{t+\tau}^R}{M_t^R} \right] \cdot \mathbb{E}_t \left[\frac{Q_t}{Q_{t+\tau}} \right] + \mathrm{Cov}_t \left[\frac{M_{t+\tau}^R}{M_t^R}, \frac{Q_t}{Q_{t+\tau}} \right] \tag{4}$$

This and all other expressions can be easily converted to yield-to-maturity expressions (see, e.g. Christensen *et al.*, 2010). More importantly, the decomposition of nominal bond prices shows that they basically consist of three terms: The real stochastic discount factor $\mathbb{E}_t[\frac{M_{t+\tau}^R}{M_t^R}]$, expected inflation $\mathbb{E}_t[\frac{Q_t}{Q_{t+\tau}}]$ and the covariance between both terms $\mathrm{Cov}_t[\frac{M_{t+\tau}^R}{M_t^R}, \frac{Q_t}{Q_{t+\tau}}]$. As usual, the sign of the covariance between an asset's return and investors' wealth or consumption defines the sign and the magnitude of the risk premium. In this particular case, the covariance term which defines the riskiness of a nominal bond is known as the inflation risk premium. A negative covariance between the real stochastic discount factor and expected inflation implies a positive inflation risk premium. This happens in times when the real stochastic discount factor is high and purchasing power is low (i.e. high inflation). From a consumption-based view, marginal utility (with low expected consumption growth) occurs at times of high inflation. Since nominal bonds are a poor investment in that case, investors will demand a higher (inflation) risk premium for these assets. On the other hand, if there is a positive correlation between output growth and inflation, nominal bonds are a good hedge implying a negative (or at least lower) inflation risk premium. In a simple sketch, Chen *et al.* (2016) recently estimated the correlation between forward consumption growth and long-run inflation. Similar to the above, a negative correlation indicates a positive inflation risk premium, as could be observed between 1975 and 2009. Nowadays, however, correlation is positive, implying a potentially negative inflation risk premium. The authors trace the change of inflation risk premium's sign back to various types of shocks. More specifically, while formerly shocks have been used to be restricted to the supply side (moving inflation and real growth in opposite directions), they are now increasingly emerging from the demand side (moving inflation and real growth equally). While this exercise by Chen *et al.* (2016) solely serves as an indicator about the sign of the inflation risk premium, a large body of research concentrates on estimating the inflation risk premium. As the focus of this review is on studies using and adding ILB data to achieve this objective, the next section outlines basic knowledge on ILB itself and on the relation between ILB and nominal bonds.

2.2 *Inflation-Linked Bonds and the Break-Even Inflation Rate*

ILBs are considered a popular alternative to nominal sovereign debt and are characterized as debt securities where the bond's principal is adjusted to the changes of a pre-specified (consumer) price index. By linking the principal value to realized inflation, coupon payments as a percentage component of the principal are similarly adjusted. Standard wise, a specific country's consumer price index (CPI), is used as the ILB's underlying. The following features are important to note: First, the indexation exhibits a lag of three months (or even eight months, as used to be the case in the United Kingdom). Hence, inflation protection (in terms of CPI inflation) is not perfect, and a small part of inflation uncertainty remains in ILB. Studies by Evans (1998) and Grishchenko and Huang (2013) explicitly account for the indexation lag and report that the 'indexation premium' is rather small. Second, if CPI growth is negative during the maturity of an ILB (i.e. deflation), the principal is commonly not adjusted. Thus, ILBs contain a deflation option. Christensen *et al.* (2016) and Grishchenko *et al.* (2016) analyse the value of the deflation option in ILB and find that it exhibits considerable time variation with peaks during the financial crisis.

Countries that have issued ILB include the USA, the United Kingdom, Canada, Germany and France. While the USA, the United Kingdom and Canada link their ILB to their respective CPI (or the retail price index in the case of the United Kingdom), German ILBs are linked to the harmonized price index for the euro area. France, on the other hand, offers both: ILB linked to the French CPI and ILB linked to the harmonized price index for the euro area. Regarding the size of the different sovereign ILB markets, of course, the US market naturally represents the largest one in absolute terms ($550 billion of ILB outstanding in the USA in 2017). In relation to total government debt outstanding, on the other hand, the share of ILB is about 25% in the United Kingdom, 12% in France, 8% in the US and 6% in Germany.[4] Comprehensive overviews of the development in the US ILB market and in ILB markets worldwide can be found in Fleming and Krishnan (2012) or Campbell *et al.* (2009) and Deacon *et al.* (2004), respectively.[5]

It is important to discuss the link between nominal bonds and ILB in more detail. Converting the bond prices from Section 2.1 to yield-to-maturity expressions, writing expected inflation as $\mathbb{E}_t[\pi]$ and taking bonds with the same maturity (for readability, I suppress τ), one can show their relation to each other.[6]

This link between nominal bond yields y_t^N and (real) ILB yields y_t^R is called Fisher equation and reads

$$y_t^N = y_t^R + \mathbb{E}_t[\pi] \tag{5}$$

where y_t^N and y_t^R are the yield-to-maturity expression of a nominal and ILB, respectively.[7] To extract a market-implied measure of inflation expectations (of maturity τ), one simply solves Equation (5) for $\mathbb{E}_t[\pi]$ and obtains

$$\mathbb{E}_t[\pi] = y_t^N - y_t^R \tag{6}$$

In fact, subtracting ILB yields from nominal bond yields is often referred to as the break-even inflation rate. However, because expected inflation might deviate from realized inflation, investors could also request compensation for this uncertainty (see Section 2.1). The extended Fisher equation accounts for this compensation and adds an inflation risk premium. For simplicity, I write the inflation risk premia as ϕ^{IRP}. Equation (5) is extended to

$$y_t^N = y_t^R + \mathbb{E}_t[\pi] + \phi^{IRP} \tag{7}$$

If one now calculates the break-even inflation rate by subtracting (real) ILB yields from nominal yields, we have

$$y_t^N - y_t^R = y_t^R + \mathbb{E}_t[\pi] + \phi^{IRP} - y_t^R = \mathbb{E}_t[\pi] + \phi^{IRP} \tag{8}$$

which means that the break-even inflation rate includes not only expected inflation but also the inflation risk premium. Finally, if nominal bonds and ILB differ in liquidity, investors might request a liquidity premium for the illiquid asset. Since (at least US) nominal bonds are known to be highly liquid, a liquidity premium in less liquid ILB might be possible. Given that investors request a liquidity premium for ILB, observed ILB yields y_t^{ILB} are given by

$$y_t^{ILB} = y_t^R + \phi^{LIQ} \tag{9}$$

where ϕ^{LIQ} is the liquidity premium. This add-on again implies that the break-even inflation rate is 'biased' by not only a potential inflation risk premium but also a potential liquidity premium:

$$y_t^N - y_t^{ILB} = y_t^R + \mathbb{E}_t[\pi] + \phi^{IRP} - y_t^R - \phi^{LIQ} = \mathbb{E}_t[\pi] + \phi^{IRP} - \phi^{LIQ} \tag{10}$$

Since only nominal bond yields and ILB yields are directly observable, existing research faces a challenge in decomposing these yields in their respective components. For the break-even inflation rate, in particular, it implies potential biases by both, the inflation risk premium and the liquidly premium. Only in the case of no risk premia (i.e. $\phi^{IRP} = \phi^{LIQ} = 0$) or if both risk premia would cancel each other out (i.e. $\phi^{IRP} = \phi^{LIQ}$), break-even inflation rate would properly represent inflation expectations. On the other hand, positive and differing risk premia bias the break-even inflation rate. To sum up, drawing implications from solely observing the break-even inflation rate (and neglecting the indexation lag and the value of the deflation option) leads to:

- an underestimation of expected inflation if $\phi^{IRP} < \phi^{LIQ}$,
- a correct estimation of expected inflation if $\phi^{IRP} = \phi^{LIQ}$ or
- an overestimation of expected inflation if $\phi^{IRP} > \phi^{LIQ}$.

Two important implications follow: First, the presence of a potential liquidity premium in ILB yields complicates exact estimation of the inflation risk premium via nominal and real (ILB) bond data. Second, obtaining information on both the liquidity premium and the inflation premium is essential before using the break-even inflation rate as a market-implied measure for inflation expectations. The next section surveys articles that focus on the determination of the inflation risk premium with the use of ILB yields. Studies differ in various aspects, such as the way in which ILB liquidity or additional inflation data are accounted for.[8]

3. Estimating the Inflation Risk Premium with ILB Yields

This section surveys articles that include ILB yields in their analysis to estimate the inflation risk premium in US nominal bond yields.[9] A considerable body of the literature has studied the inflation risk premium without using ILB. Because of the plentiful availability of nominal bond data, these studies typically draw on much longer time periods than the studies presented in this section. Among others, Buraschi and Jiltsov (2005) derive a structural model for a (nominal) bond pricing solution that is based on the monetary supply and inflation and that allow the inflation risk premium to be extracted. Ang *et al.* (2008) develop a regime-switching arbitrage-free term structure model for nominal bond yields and inflation and thereby account for the regime-switching properties of inflation and interest rates. Their model also allows the inflation risk premium to be estimated. A detailed discussion of these models, however, is beyond the scope of this survey, but I include their estimates for the inflation risk premium in my evaluation below.

Recently, information from survey inflation forecasts is incorporated in term structure models (see, e.g. Chernov and Mueller, 2012). It has been shown that surveys in general are a useful source of information: For survey inflation forecasts, for instance, Ang *et al.* (2007) show that they outperform a variety of other measures for inflation expectations when predicting inflation. For interest rate surveys, on the other hand, Kim and Orphanides (2012) illustrate that they help to overcome small-sample problems due to persistency of interest rates. Some of studies discussed below that use ILB yields to estimate the inflation risk premium incorporate survey inflation forecasts as well. I firstly consider studies that estimate the inflation risk premium without a complete term structure model (Section 3.1). Section 3.2 then outlines term structure models that estimate the inflation risk premium; in Section 3.3, I provide an aggregate evaluation of studies from both sub-sections.

3.1 *Regression-Based Approaches*

The first study that uses observed ILB yields in the USA to analyse the inflation risk premium is by Roll (2004). However, he addresses the inflation risk premium only indirectly by evaluating yield curves' steepness of nominal bonds and ILB. The fact that yield curves for nominal bonds are steeper than those for ILB might indicate a positive inflation risk premium. The main focus of Roll's (2004) paper is more on diversification effects with ILB than on the inflation risk premium.

Shen (2006) subtracts the (10-year) survey inflation forecast from the observed (10-year) break-even inflation rate. The resulting series can potentially be biased by liquidity and is therefore regressed on two liquidity proxies.[10] Since the regression is estimated in changes rather than in levels, the author calculates cumulative changes in the estimated liquidity risk premium (based on the model's fitted values), which are declining between 1999 and 2006 for 5- and 10-year maturities. While the approach does not allow decomposition of inflation compensation into expected inflation and inflation risk premium, a negative value of survey inflation minus break-even inflation indicates that the liquidity premium is larger than the inflation risk premium (see also Figure 1 above for the relation between liquidity premium, inflation risk premium and break-even inflation rate).

Similarly, Söderlind (2011) calculates so-called break-even deviations for which survey inflation expectations are subtracted from break-even inflation rates for 3- and 10-year maturities. Deviations might mainly be driven by the inflation risk premium and/or by a liquidity premium. To further investigate the origin of these deviation, the author regresses break-even deviations

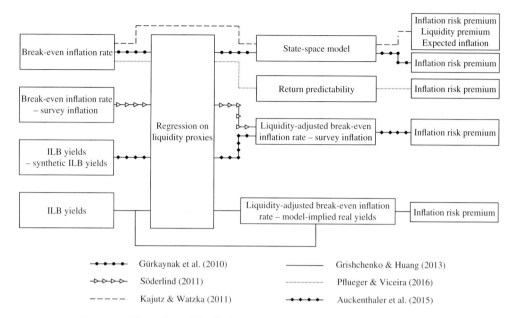

Figure 1. Illustration of Studies' Research Designs Discussed in Section 3.1.
Notes: The figure summarizes the studies' research designs of this subsection. Note that Roll (2004) and Shen (2006) are not included as they do not explicitly estimate the inflation risk premium. Studies can be identified by their unique symbols and shadings. Note that Söderlind (2011) stops at calculating the liquidity-adjusted break-even inflation rate and does not derive the inflation risk premium.

on a set of liquidity proxies as well as measures for inflation uncertainty (i.e. cross-sectional forecast dispersion for the Survey of Professional Forecasters (SPF) and disagreement of inflation forecasts from Michigan survey). For both maturities, liquidity proxies and one measure for inflation uncertainty (SPF forecaster dispersion) have significant coefficients, with signs consistent with intuition. The author presents a premium-adjusted break-even inflation rate but does not decompose the proportion of the inflation risk premium and liquidity premium.

The paper by Auckenthaler *et al.* (2015) does not use the break-even inflation rate but rather builds on the work of Campbell and Shiller (1996) by calculating hypothetical ILB yields. These synthetic ILB yields are compared with their observed counterpart, and in the case of no premia at all, the difference between hypothetical and observed yields should be zero. Since this is not the case for 10-year ILB yields, the authors regress this series (i.e. hypothetical minus observed ILB yields) on a set of liquidity proxies and show that some of the series' variation is due to ILB illiquidity. Applying Gürkaynak *et al.*'s (2010) approach (see below) to extract the liquidity premium (i.e. normalizing the liquidity premium to zero during a period of high ILB liquidity), the authors derive the liquidity premium over time, which is on average 56 basis points from 2001 to 2011. The authors further calculate the liquidity-adjusted break-even inflation rate and subtract SPF survey inflation expectations from it. The resulting series is fully assigned to the inflation risk premium, which amounts to 22 basis points on average during their same sample period. Before the financial crisis and after 2009 again, the inflation risk premium ranges between 0 and 100 basis points, but during the financial crisis, it drops to −200 basis points.

The paper by Pflueger and Viceira (2016) focuses on return predictability. The presence of time-varying premia should make bond returns predictable (see Campbell *et al.*, 2013, for the predictability of nominal bonds). The authors test for return predictability of ILB and the break-even inflation rate. While predictability in ILB returns is attributed to a time-varying liquidity premium, predictability in the break-even inflation rate is assigned to a time-varying inflation risk premium. Pflueger and Viceira (2016) estimate the liquidity premium in the break-even inflation rate by regressing the series on three liquidity proxies. The authors derive a liquidity-adjusted break-even inflation rate and find that it is likewise predictable. This result indicates the presence of an inflation risk premium. The authors assume that the expected liquidity excess return and expected liquidity-adjusted break-even return are fully assigned to the liquidity and inflation risk premium, respectively. Decomposing bond risk premia leads to an average liquidity premium of 92 basis points and to an average inflation risk premium of 163 basis points for the period from 1999 to 2014.

The next three studies apply some structural form (in an arbitrage-free setting) but do not establish a complete term structure model. First, Gürkaynak *et al.* (2010) regress the 5- and 10-year break-even inflation rate on a collection of liquidity proxies to extract the liquidity premium. As already outlined above, the regression's fitted values (i.e. the estimated liquidity premium) are normalized to zero during a period where the liquidity premium is expected to be very low or absent. Using a state space model that includes the liquidity-adjusted break-even inflation rate as well as survey inflation data, inflation expectations are estimated with the use of the Kalman filter. The authors do not derive an inflation risk premium but mention that it could be extracted in the same vein. However, this approach is limited to some extent because of the normalization of the liquidity premium. The paper by Gürkaynak *et al.* (2010) is furthermore important from another perspective since the authors calculate the ILB yield curve for the USA and provide it in a periodically updated fashion on the Federal Reserve's website (in an earlier paper, Gürkaynak *et al.*, 2007, also provide the US yield curve for nominal bonds).

Second, Kajuth and Watzka (2011) use a state space model to estimate the liquidity premium and the inflation risk premium. More specifically, they base their state space model on the (extended) Fisher equation and include proxies for inflation risk and ILB illiquidity. As measures of inflation risk, the authors use (i) the estimated conditional standard deviation of inflation from a GARCH model, (ii) the SPF forecaster dispersion and (iii) the moving standard deviation of inflation. As proxies for liquidity risk, the usual set of measures is used (see Section 4). The model is estimated without information on expected inflation from survey forecasts. Expected inflation is estimated with the Kalman filter and is corrected for the liquidity premium and inflation risk premium. The model-implied estimates for the inflation risk premium are below 60 basis points up to 2006 and increase up to 200 basis points during the crisis. The liquidity premium, on the other hand, is low between 2000 and 2007 (below 50 basis points) and high during the financial crisis (above 100 basis points).

Finally, Grishchenko and Huang (2013) present a 'model-free' approach that does not impose any term structure model (see Evans, 1998, for an antecedent). They take yields as given and estimate (under consideration of the three-month indexation lag and within an arbitrage-free setting) real yields. These estimated real yields are used to calculate break-even inflation rates that are subsequently used to derive the inflation risk premium by subtracting expected inflation. To do so, the authors use three different proxies for expected inflation (i.e. historical inflation average, VAR(1) estimates and survey inflation forecasts). Finally, a liquidity adjustment (13 basis points on average) is added to the inflation risk premium to control for ILB illiquidity. The liquidity adjustment is obtained by the fitted values of regressing difference between break-even and survey inflation rate on a set of liquidity proxies. For the 2000–2008 sample period, the liquidity-adjusted inflation risk premium ranges from −9 to 4 basis points.

While the basic idea of how to extract the inflation risk premium is rather similar among the studies, their 'starting points' differ. Figure 1 provides an overview of how they vary in using different input data. Furthermore, Table 1 in Section 3.3 gives a complete summary of estimated inflation risk premia among the studies discussed in this and the next section. With additional information on expected inflation, one can estimate the inflation risk premium. However, as discussed in Section 1, the inflation risk premium emerges from the covariance between the real stochastic discount factor and inflation. Consequently, for a model-consistent decomposition of the break-even inflation rate in expected inflation, inflation risk premium and a potential liquidity premium, a term structure model is required. The use of a pricing model further allows us to include information from the cross section of both nominal bond yields and ILB yields. Finally, these models also contain a no-arbitrage condition, meaning that there are no opportunities for arbitrage over time and across maturities (i.e. arbitrage-free term structure models).

3.2 Term Structure Models

The arbitrage-free term structure literature started with the founding models of Vasicek (1977) and Cox et al. (1985). All models building on these initial models specify (risk-neutral) dynamics of underlying yield curve factors and risk premia under no-arbitrage conditions over time and across bond maturities. While the original models consist of only one factor (i.e. the short rate), more recent models have at least three factors. With Duffie and Kan (1996), affine arbitrage-free models have become popular, since yields are linear (i.e. affine) functions of the underlying factors. While the risk-neutral Q-world is sufficient for pricing issues, forecasting and decomposing the term structure requires real P-world dynamics. To link both worlds, a functional form for market prices of risk is required. Completely affine risk premia (Dai and Singleton, 2000), essentially affine risk premia (Duffee, 2002) or extended affine risk premia (Cheridito et al., 2007) are most extensively used in the literature. Dai and Singleton (2000) also introduce the notation of $A_m(n)$-models to classify affine term structure models, where m is the number of square-root processes and n is the number of factors in the model.[11] Excellent textbook information on term structure models in general can be found in Singleton (2006) and Piazzesi (2010). Grishchenko and Huang (2012) provide a compact survey on term structure models that focuses on expected inflation, and Rebonato (2016) present a thought-provoking review of current term structure models.

3.2.1 Term Structure Models without Inflation Data

Chen et al. (2010) are among the first to develop a term structure model for the USA that includes both nominal and ILB yields. They develop a two-factor correlated Cox et al. (1985) model in which the first factor represents the real rate and the second factor represents the inflation rate. Hence, the combination of both factors should map the nominal rate. The authors provide a closed-form solution to the nominal and real term structure, which enables a (two step) estimation of the parameters in a state space form. Because of the non-linear measurement equation, the unscented Kalman filter is applied (see the paper for a discussion regarding why the unscented Kalman filter instead of the extended Kalman filter is applied). Market prices of inflation risk for each maturity are estimated within the model's setting. As the difference between nominal and real yields is assumed to be captured by only one factor

Table 1. Overview of Studies' Estimates For the Inflation Risk Premium and the Liquidity Premium.

Paper	Period covered	Model	Min IRP	Max IRP	Min LIQ	Max LIQ	Corrected for Liqu.	Defl.	Lag
ILB-based estimates									
Auckenthaler et al. (2015)	2001–2011	Regression-based approach	−210 (2008)	100 (2004)	0 (2008)	100 (2002)	x		
Kajuth and Watzka (2011)	1997–2009	State space model	10 (1999)	220 (2009)	20 (2006)	130 (2009)	x		
Grishchenko and Huang (2013)	2000–2008	'Model-free' approach	−13 (00–04)	8 (00–04)	−7 (04–08)	33 (00–04)	x		x
Chen et al. (2010)	1998–2007	Two-factor TS model	45 (2000)	70 (2006)					
Adrian and Wu (2009)	2003–2009	Five-factor TS model	10 (2006)	170 (2008)					(x)
Christensen et al. (2010)	2003–2008	Four-factor TS model	−60 (2003)	60 (2004)					
Christensen and Gillan (2012)	2005–2011	Four-factor TS model	−150 (2009)	100 (2008)	0 (2008)	120 (2009)	x		
Andreasen et al. (2017)	1997–2013	Five-factor TS model	−90 (1998)	100 (2004)	−20 (2000)	300 (2009)	x	(x)	
Abrahams et al. (2016)	1999–2014	Six-factor TS model	−40 (2001)	100 (2008)	0 (2005)	210 (2008)	x	(x)	
D'Amico et al. (2018)	1999–2013	Four-factor TS model	0 (2008)	50 (2002)	0 (2005)	220 (2008)	x	x	
Hördahl and Tristani (2014)	1999–2013	Macro-finance TS model	−80 (2008)	100 (2012)	0 (2007)	140 (2009)	x	x	x
Chernov and Mueller (2012, w ILB)	1971–2008	Macro-finance TS model	−30 (2008)	250 (1983)					

Inflation swap-based estimates

Haubrich et al. (2012)	1982–2010	Seven-factor TS model	25 (2009)	59 (1984)
Roussellet (2016)	1990–2010	Four-factor TS model	80 (2012)	−100 (2008)

Other estimates (without ILB and inflation swaps)

Buraschi and Jiltsov (2005)	1960–2000	Macro-finance TS model	25 (1960)	140 (1972)
Ang et al. (2008, 5-year maturity)	1952–2005	Macro-finance TS model	10 (2003)	200 (1982)
Chernov and Mueller (2012, w/o ILB)	1971–2008	Macro-finance TS model	−50 (2008)	600 (1984)

Notes: All estimates are given in basis points and refer to a maturity of (unless noted otherwise) 10 years. Estimates are extracted from respective papers' figures and preferred specification. IRP and LIQ refer to inflation risk premium and liquidity premium, respectively. Minimum and maximum values for both premia are given with the year of realization in brackets. The last three columns indicate whether there is an adjustment for ILB illiquidity (Liqu.), the embedded deflation option (Defl.) and the indexation lag (Lag). A checked option in brackets (i.e. (x)) indicates that a correction is not included in the final specification but part of robustness checks or alternative specifications. Studies are listed as they appear in the main text above. Shen (2006), Gürkaynak et al. (2010) and Söderlind (2011) do not estimate the inflation risk premium. Pflueger and Viceira (2016) derive annualized excess returns rather than yield premia; to avoid confusion, I do not report their (excess return) estimates. Auckenthaler et al.'s (2015) minimum liquidity premium refers to 2008Q1 before the bankruptcy of Lehman Brothers. Kajuth and Watzka's (2011) estimates refer to their model 1. Grishchenko and Huang (2013) only provide summary statistics for their estimates; therefore, minimum and maximum values for both premia can only be listed within a range of four years. For Christensen and Gillan (2012), maximum liquidity premia and minimum inflation risk premium are listed. D'Amico et al.'s (2018) estimates only refer to the period in which ILB yields are included. The estimates from Chernov and Mueller (2012) are based on their model AOT5 (with ILB) and AO5 (without ILB) over their entire sample period. Haubrich et al.'s (2012) and Roussellet's (2016) estimates for the inflation risk premium are over the study's entire sample period. Further, Haubrich et al. (2012) do not explicitly derive a liquidity premium but rather compare swap-based real yields with ILB yields and attributing the difference to a potential liquidity premium.

(i.e. inflation), no further decomposition is possible. Thus, the inflation risk premium is estimated by subtracting the market price of a bond with real (observed) risk parameters from a bond with risk-neutral (model) risk parameters. Chen *et al.* (2010) show that the inflation risk premium's term structure is positive and averages 0.24 basis points for a maturity of three months and 77.24 basis points for a maturity of 20 years during their sample period 1998–2007. However, the authors do not account for ILB illiquidity, which might distort their estimates for the inflation risk premium at least during the first years of the sample period.

In contrast to the two-factor model above, Adrian and Wu (2009) apply a five-factor affine term structure model: two factors explain the real pricing kernel (level and slope) and two factors model inflation expectations. The fifth factor is a variance factor that governs the state variables' variances and covariances dynamics. While the second moments are estimated within a GARCH model, the term structure model is estimated as usual with maximum likelihood, and state variables are obtained with a Kalman filter. The inflation risk premium is then derived by the difference between the (observed) break-even inflation rate and the model-implied estimates for the expected inflation. The inflation risk premium for bonds with a maturity of 10 years varies between 0 and 100 basis points during 2003–2008 and rises sharply during the financial crisis, up to 170 basis points (Adrian and Wu, 2009, figure 5). As in Chen *et al.* (2010) above, there is no explicit consideration of liquidity, but the authors detect a structural break between 2002 and 2003. As the authors' approach does not allow distinguishing between low liquidity or changing economic conditions, their preferred sample period excludes the 'early years' of ILB and starts in 2003. In addition, off-the-run yield curves rather than on-the-run yield curves are used for nominal bond data. Such an indirect consideration of ILB illiquidity might maintain the authors' estimates for the inflation risk premium in a meaningful range. Nonetheless, during the financial crisis, a potential liquidity premium in ILB yields is relevant for their estimates. The inclusion of second moment dynamics increases identification in general and results in an inflation risk premium that is very close to other approaches—at least during financially calm times (see below).

The next three studies are all based on the workhorse model by Christensen *et al.* (2011) (CDR hereafter), which is an arbitrage-free version of the classical model by Nelson and Siegel (1987). CDR show that their model fits in-sample and out-of-sample forecasts quite well. Since the model has affine state and measurement equations and Gaussian errors, maximum likelihood estimation with a Kalman filter can be applied. The feature of their workhorse model is that it includes the benefits of arbitrage-free models and the Nelson-Siegel world in terms of its dynamic extension by Diebold and Li (2006). In essentially affine models, it is common to restrict parameters with low *t*-statistics in pre-estimations to zero in order to overcome problematic model over-parameterization. Such restrictions, however, often lack of theoretical interpretation. The CDR model exhibits (due to the Nelson-Siegel base) a more parsimonious structure and is therefore less problematic to estimate, facilitates model's tractability and allows for factor interpretation (see the textbook by Diebold and Rudebusch, 2013, for a further excellent reference on the CDR model).

To start with, the paper by Christensen *et al.* (2010) extends the CDR model for joint pricing nominal bond yields and ILB yields. According to the authors, the following four factors are adequate to map the joint term structure: two-level factors (one nominal and one ILB), a common slope and curvature factor. To extract the inflation risk premium, model-implied break-even inflation rate is compared with the observed break-even inflation rate. The difference between both series is fully assigned to the inflation risk premium, which can thus have both positive and negative values. The estimates for the premium (for 5- and 10-years' maturity) range between −50 and 50 basis points. Since the sample period starst only four years after the first ILB issuance (in 2003), liquidity concerns are less relevant during this period than during the first years of ILB history. However, as the sample ends in 2008 at the beginning of the financial crisis, ILB illiquidity will play an important role at this time and potentially affects the estimates for the inflation risk premium.

In a follow-up paper, Christensen and Gillan (2012) extend the joint model to allow stochastic volatility and correct ILB yields for the liquidity premium. Since the liquidity premium is not directly observable, the authors use a 'model-independent range' for the ILB liquidity premium: the difference between the break-even inflation rate and the inflation swap rate is calculated. In a frictionless world, both rates should be equal. If these rates are unequal, risk premia are present. By assuming that the spread between both rates is fully attributed to either swap illiquidity or bond illiquidity, the authors derive a range for the potential ILB liquidity premium. Minimum and maximum liquidity-adjusted ILB yields are then used as the input variable for the term structure model. Given that the liquidity premium is assumed to be the maximum, the resulting (minimum) inflation risk premium amounts to 5 and 10 basis points on average between 2005 and 2011 for 5 and 10 years maturity, respectively.

A recent working paper by Andreasen et al. (2017) further extends the CDR model by including ILB (as Christensen et al., 2010), by accounting for the value of deflation protection (as Christensen et al., 2016) and by explicitly including a latent liquidity factor. By comparing the primary dealer transaction volume for nominal bonds and ILB and by observing that the level is quite different but that the pattern of the time series' is rather similar, the authors conclude that one factor that accounts for relative ILB illiquidity is adequate. Their model further allows security-specific liquidity factor sensitives by including raw prices of ILB (with time since issuance and time to maturity). Andreasen et al.'s (2017) model is the only one that accounts for security-specific liquidity risk. They estimate an average liquidity premium of 38 basis points (from 1997 to 2013) with peaks in 2002 (100 basis points) and in 2009 (300 basis points) that includes all issued ILB (Andreasen et al., 2017, figure 5). Alternatively, the liquidity premium for on-the-run ILB is extracted as well: for a 10-year maturity, the average liquidity premium is 30 basis points, with a maximum value of 100 basis points. The authors attribute this dramatic difference in liquidity premia for on-the-run and off-the-run ILB to buy-and-hold investors who 'lock up' the outstanding amount of ILB and limit the amount of ILB available for trading. Thus, security-specific liquidity factor sensitives are vital to account for this characteristic. Finally, break-even inflation rates are decomposed into expected inflation, inflation risk premium and liquidity premium (note that the preferred model by the Bayesian information criterion lacks deflation option adjustment). The inflation risk premium (for a 10-year maturity) is positive on average and varies between −100 and 100 basis points. However, it is only negative during 1998 and 2002, as well as for a short period during the financial crisis (Andreasen et al., 2017, figure 13). While the negative inflation risk premium during the financial crisis is in line with the existing literature, the negative premium in 1998 is typically found only by papers that do not account for ILB illiquidity.

3.2.2 Term Structure Models Including Inflation Data

In a similar vein as above, Abrahams et al. (2016) develop a joint term structure model for nominal and ILB yield curves. Their model is based not on CDR but rather on the more general class of essentially affine term structure models introduced by Duffee (2002). Thus, market prices of risk are less restricted (i.e. they do not have to be consistent with the Nelson-Siegel yield curve). However, for parsimony, their model consists of three nominal pricing factors, two ILB pricing factors and one ILB liquidity factor. While the three nominal pricing factors originate from a principal component analysis, the two ILB pricing factors are derived as follows: First, ILB yields are regressed on the principal components for the nominal yields curve. Second, two principal components are derived from the residuals of the step 1 regression exercise. While this procedure reduces collinearity among the factors, an economic interpretation is impossible. The sixth (liquidity) factor comprises the equally weighted average of two liquidity proxies. The estimation is done with maximum likelihood but uses excess returns rather than zero coupon yields (see Adrian *et al.*, 2013, for a discussion of why returns are favourable against yields). Note that the calculation of nominal bond and ILB excess returns requires both the risk-free short rate and realized inflation. The model allows the break-even inflation rate to be decomposed into expected inflation, the liquidity premium and the inflation risk premium. The authors report the decomposition for the 10-year and 5–10-year forward break-even inflation rate. While the inflation risk premium for the 10-year break-even inflation rate varies between 0 and 50 basis points (with a short peak during the financial crisis), the inflation risk premium for the forward break-even rate is more volatile: It ranges from about 0–100 basis points, again with a peak during the financial crisis (Abrahams *et al.*, 2016, figure 1).

Similarly, the essentially affine term structure model by D'Amico *et al.* (2018) is a joint model of nominal yields, ILB yields and inflation and consists of four factors. As the standard three-factor models exhibit a poor fit of ILB yields (ILB yields are treated as model-implied real yields corrected for the indexation lag), the authors add a fourth factor to their model, which they model as an ILB-specific factor. To test whether this latent factor can be related to ILB illiquidity issues, the authors regress it on a variety of liquidity measures. They also check whether the series is related to certain technical factors, such as the embedded deflation option, seasonality, flight-to-safety effects or Federal Reserve Purchases. When all these controls are included, the effect of ILB illiquidity remains observable implying that the ILB-specific factor actually captures an ILB liquidity premium. Their four-factor model allows the observed break-even inflation rate to be decomposed into its different components. The estimated inflation risk premium is positive and rather stable (even during the financial crisis) at about 30 basis points. Most of the variation during the crisis is covered in the liquidity risk premium, which increases to 200 basis points in 2008 and 2009. Note also that inflation data and survey inflation forecasts are included in their state-space model, which covers the sample period from 1990 to 2013 (prior to the availability of ILB, where ILB yield data are treated as missing data).

3.2.3 *Macro-Finance Term Structure Models*

Hördahl and Tristani (2014) develop a joint model of term structure and macro-economic dynamics in the vein of Ang and Piazzesi (2003). The advantage of jointly modelling inflation, monetary policy, output and term structure movements is given by the fact that the impact of macro-economic variables on the inflation risk premium can easily be analysed. Their model is rather based on the framework developed by Hördahl *et al.* (2006), which allows an additional feedback effect from short-term rates to macro-economic variables. As usual in essentially affine models, risk premia can be linked to the model's state variables. In this case, since the model's state variables are macro-economic variables, the estimated inflation risk premium can be linked to movements in these variables. The authors estimate their model from 1990 to 2013, and ILB yields are included in the estimation as soon as they become available. Hördahl and

Tristani (2014) explicitly correct for illiquidity by regressing ILB yields on a set of liquidity proxies before they are included in the estimation. The model-implied inflation risk premium is obtained by subtracting estimated expected inflation and (liquidity-adjusted) real yields from nominal yields. During 1999 and 2007, the 10-year inflation risk premium ranges between −40 and 50 basis points. After 2007, the inflation risk premium is more volatile for maturities with values between −80 and 100 basis points for 10-year maturity (Hördahl and Tristani, 2014, figures 5 and 6).

Finally, one specification of Chernov and Mueller's (2012) macro-finance term structure model additionally includes ILB yield data. Their (preferred) five-factor term structure model uses data from nominal bond yields, ILB yields, output, inflation and survey inflation forecasts. The authors compare different model specifications and observe that the inclusion of ILB yields increases (decreases) the average model-implied real yields (inflation risk premium). Similarly, volatility of model-implied real yields (inflation risk premium) increases (decreases) as well but model's inflation expectations remain rather stable. Their sample period ranges from 1971 to 2008 but ILB yields are only included from 2003 onwards and are not adjusted for a potential liquidity premium. The estimated inflation risk premium averages 67 basis points without ILB yields and 157 basis points with ILB yields.

3.2.4 *The Use of Inflation Swap Rates Instead of ILB*

As shown above, the paper by Christensen and Gillan (2012) uses inflation swap rates to derive a range for the ILB liquidity premium. Inflation swap rates can also be used to substitute ILB yields, as done in the studies by Haubrich *et al.* (2012) or Roussellet (2016). Haubrich *et al.* (2012) develop a completely affine term structure model with seven factors and four stochastic drivers. Three of the factors are the real interest rate, expected inflation and 'central tendency' of inflation. While these factors determine the cross section of bond yields, they have no direct impact on risk premia. Rather, risk premia depend on the other four factors (i.e. volatility state variables). Such a separation of factors (i.e. one part determines the cross section, the other part determines the risk premia) enables a highly flexible model. The model's input variables are nominal bond yields, survey inflation forecasts and inflation swap rates as soon as they become available in 2004. Thus, it is possible to 'create' inflation-indexed yields without using ILB yields by subtracting inflation swap rates from nominal bond yields with the same maturity.[12] While the model allows nominal bond yields to be decomposed (during their full sample from 1982 to 2009, the 10-year inflation risk premium amounts to 45 basis points on average), the authors also compare their synthetic real yields with ILB yields and confirm the studies discussed above that ILBs were highly mispriced (potentially because of a liquidity premium) in the first years of issuance and during the financial crisis. In line with Haubrich *et al.* (2012), Fleckenstein *et al.* (2014) similarly use inflation swap rates but focus on the mispricing of ILB and the resulting costs rather than on the inflation risk premium (see Appendix B for a discussion). More recently, Roussellet (2016) proposes an affine (four-factor) term structure model that includes macro-economic variables, uses real interest rates from inflation swaps and is consistent with the zero lower bound (see Section 5 for a discussion). The latter is achieved by modelling a Gamma-distributed short rate that accounts for non-negativity but allows the possibility to stay at the zero lower bound. In an empirical implementation, Roussellet (2016) extracts the inflation risk premium by decomposing nominal bond yields and ILB yields. The inflation risk premium in nominal bond yields with a maturity of one year is very volatile and negative over long periods. For a 10-year maturity, however, the premium is considerably less

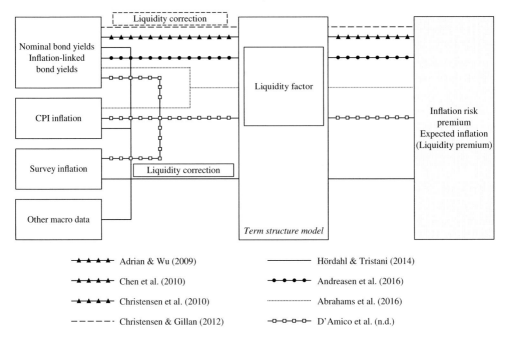

Figure 2. Illustration of Studies' Research Designs Discussed in Section 3.2.
Notes: The figure summarizes the studies' research designs of this subsection. Studies can be identified by their unique symbols and shadings.

volatile and only negative during the financial crisis and in the 1990s. However, it is important to note that both studies by Haubrich *et al.* (2012) and Roussellet (2016) do not use ILB data.

Turning back to ILB, it is obvious that accounting for their illiquidity is essential to obtain unbiased measures for the inflation risk premium and break-even inflation rate. The models discussed in this section apply various strategies in considering liquidity effects. They also differ with respect to the use of additional data such as inflation, survey inflation forecasts or other macro-economic data. Similar to Figure 1 in the section before, Figure 2 now provides an overview of the studies discussed in this section.

3.3 *Evaluating the Use of ILB to Estimate the Inflation Risk Premium*

Both the subsections and figures above show that strategies to estimate the inflation risk premium vary considerable throughout the literature. Not only the approaches differ (i.e. regression-based vs. term-structure model) but also the ways to consider ILB illiquidity, the embedded deflation option or the indexation lag. It is interesting to consider the research's development over time: Studies started with 'simple' term structure models that jointly price the nominal and ILB yield curve. As one observed that ILB yields were too low compared to nominal bond yields, there was the need to consider ILB illiquidity: Studies by Christensen and Gillan (2012) or Hördahl and Tristani (2014) adjusted ILB yields for the liquidity premium and include these liquidity-adjusted yields in their models. Recent papers now include directly a liquidity factor in the term structure model to obtain model-implied estimates for the liquidity premium (see also Figure 2). Among these studies, latent liquidity factors (Andreasen *et al.*, 2017; D'Amico *et al.*, 2018) or liquidity-proxy factors (Abrahams *et al.*, 2016) are used to account for ILB illiquidity.

The indexation lag, another 'feature' of ILB, has shown to be less relevant: Grishchenko and Huang (2013) take explicitly the three-month indexation lag into account and derive an indexation lag premium which ranges between 0.03 basis points (one-year maturity) and 4.2 basis points (10-year maturity). Adrian and Wu (2009) also control for the indexation lag and find no considerable differences. Thus, carry adjustment of yields due to the indexation lag is not very relevant. Moreover, mainly short maturities are affected by the carry effect and the frequently used Gürkaynak *et al.*'s (2010) ILB yield curve data are not available for maturities below two years. The third 'feature' of ILB, which potentially complicates estimations, is the embedded deflation option. Recently, Christensen *et al.* (2016) and Grishchenko *et al.* (2016) analyse the value of this option in ILB yields and find the value to be rather low except during the financial crisis. The increased option value during the financial crisis is rational, given the 'deflation fears' at this time. However, apart from such times of financial turmoil, the embedded deflation option seems to be negligible and studies, like Andreasen *et al.* (2017) for example, show that model fit is better without an option adjustment.

Not only research designs differ, but studies' estimates for the inflation risk premium vary as well. Table 1 gives an overview of the studies discussed and presents their minimum and maximum values for the inflation risk premium. Unless noted otherwise, the values refer to a maturity of 10 years. Moreover, information on the size of the potential liquidity premium and an indication whether the studies control for the above-mentioned features is given. For comparison, I add three major studies (Buraschi and Jiltsov, 2005, for an equilibrium macro-finance term structure model; Ang *et al.*, 2008, for a reduced-form spanned macro-finance term structure model and Chernov and Mueller, 2012, for a reduced-form unspanned macro-finance term structure model) that estimate the inflation risk premium in the USA without using ILB yields.[13] At first glance, minimum and maximum values for the (10-year) inflation risk premium vary considerably throughout the studies. By having a closer look at term structure models, differences across these studies are less massive: Studies that adjust (at least) for ILB illiquidity exhibit similar maximum values for the inflation risk premium (around 100 basis points), but which occur, however, at different points in time. Most of these term structure models also report a negative inflation risk premium, at least once during their sample period. It is noteworthy that term structure models which differ quite considerably in their research design still end up with similar estimates for the inflation risk premium. For instance, as mentioned above, Andreasen *et al.* (2017) do not include any information on inflation or survey inflation forecasts. Abrahams *et al.* (2016) include additionally inflation data and D'Amico *et al.* (2018) use both inflation as well as survey inflation forecast data.

The inflation risk premium's development over time, however, varies considerably across the studies: Some studies' estimates exhibit a peak during the financial crisis (Adrian and Wu, 2009; Kajuth and Watzka, 2011; Abrahams *et al.*, 2016; Pflueger and Viceira, 2016), whereas other studies report a drop of the inflation risk premium during this time (Hördahl and Tristani, 2014; Auckenthaler *et al.*, 2015; Andreasen *et al.*, 2017). And yet others find the premium to be permanently rather stable (D'Amico *et al.*, 2018). Consequently, also the premium's second moment varies considerable throughout these studies. Interestingly, Abrahams *et al.*'s (2016) and Andreasen *et al.*'s (2017) estimates appear to include a similar slight seasonal pattern but a different shape during the financial crisis. Some of the authors kindly provided their estimates for the inflation risk premia. The corresponding figure and a short discussion is included in Appendix C.

The estimated liquidity premium, on the other hand, ranges unanimously between 0 and 300 basis points. More remarkable, minima and maxima liquidity premia occur at similar points in time (see Section 4 for a full discussion). Note, however, that minima and maxima values for the inflation risk premium are rather similar for studies that consider ILB illiquidity and for studies that do not account for it. This would indicate that considering the liquidity premium is more relevant for the extraction of an unbiased break-even inflation rate than for the estimation of the inflation risk premium.

A clear-cut comparison with studies not using ILB yields is difficult due to different sample periods. The studies by Buraschi and Jiltsov (2005), Ang *et al.* (2008) or Chernov and Mueller (2012) have already started in 1960, 1952 and 1971, including periods of high inflation in the 1970s and 1980s. However, estimates at the end of their sample periods are in a similar range as studies using ILB yields. The basic idea of adding ILB yields is to improve the estimation of the inflation risk premium. An improvement can emerge due to more available data (cross sectional in terms of different maturities and time series in terms of frequency) as well as due to a very close proxy for real rates. An explicit study which applies different model specifications including and excluding information from ILB, inflation swap rates and survey inflation forecasts to compare differences between the estimates would be the next step for future research. Furthermore, a recent paper by García and Werner (2010) which analyses euro area term structure with ILB yields (see endnote 6 for an outline) establishes the link between the inflation risk premium and the uncertainty in survey inflation forecasts. Whether there is a link between the survey inflation forecast uncertainty and the inflation risk premium (estimated without the use of survey information at best) for the USA might be subject for future research.

One crucial obstacle concerning the use of ILB yields to estimate the inflation risk premium is liquidity. Since the liquidity premium plays such an important role for an unbiased estimation, the next section is dedicated to discuss this issue.

4. Impact of Liquidity

Although the impact of liquidity is less relevant for nominal bonds, which include this survey's object of interest (i.e. the inflation risk premium), it is important to know the impact of liquidity on ILB yields when these yields are included in the estimation process. From the section above, it is obvious that a potential ILB liquidity premium has to be considered. It is also evident that especially two 'events' have a strong impact on the ILB liquidity premium: the first years of ILB issuance and the financial crisis.

First, ILB illiquidity during the first years of issuance often refers to the fact that ILBs have been a rather new financial instrument. Market participants were unfamiliar with ILB since they have not traded (USA) ILB before (see, e.g. Roll, 2004). As data on ILB yields increase, it might be worthwhile to exclude these years in an analysis, as 'unfamiliarness' is rather difficult to measure with an appropriate proxy and might not be perfectly captured with traditional liquidity proxies. Second, periods of financial crises are crucial because during such a time, it is challenging to the disentangle effects on nominal bond yields or break-even inflation rates. Suppose, for instance, that a drop in break-even inflation rate could be either due to an increased liquidity premium or due to a change in inflation expectations. On the other hand, an increasing break-even inflation rate could be the consequence either of rising inflation expectations or of an increase in the inflation risk premium. Thus, controlling for a potential ILB liquidity premium is vital to estimate at least the liquidity-adjusted break-even inflation rate.

Figures 1 and 2 from the sections above show that studies account quite differently for ILB illiquidity in their research designs. In addition, a variety of proxies for liquidity have been used. Some proxies have been used frequently, whereas other others have been used only once. Proxies can broadly be categorized into (i) ILB-specific liquidity proxies, (ii) relative ILB liquidity proxies, (iii) Treasury liquidity proxies and (iv) proxies for uncertainty. Table 2 below provides an overview of used liquidity proxies, including the articles in which they are applied.

The application of these proxies depends on the research approach. For regression-based approaches or term structure models that use liquidity-adjusted ILB yields as input data, these proxies are used in a regression to estimate the liquidity premium (see, e.g. Hördahl and Tristani, 2014, or Auckenthaler *et al.*, 2015). Term structure models that explicitly incorporate liquidity uses these proxies in a principal component analysis to extract one (or more) liquidity factors (see Abrahams *et al.*, 2016). And still others model a latent factor that is assigned to a liquidity premium. To test this attribution, the latent factor is regressed on a set of liquidity proxies (see D'Amico *et al.*, 2018).

More recent research has started focusing on the ILB liquidity premium itself and how it is affected by Federal Reserves's activities. Both Coroneo (2016) and Christensen and Gillan (2017) analyse how large-scale asset purchases by the central bank—known as quantitative easing—have an effect on the US ILB market. Christensen and Gillan (2017) combine, analogous to Christensen and Gillan (2012), inflation swaps with ILB yields to construct their measure of liquidity premium and apply an event study methodology to analyse the effect of the quantitative easing programme. Without going into detail, the authors find that asset purchases have temporarily lowered the liquidity premium in ILB yields and inflation swaps. Coroneo (2016), on the other hand, identifies an ILB liquidity premium within a state-space model for nominal bond yields and ILB yields. Coroneo's (2016) approach is different to existing studies because the ILB liquidity premium (as a component of ILB yields) is unspanned by nominal bond yields. Thus, it does neither require any liquidity proxy nor the specification of a full-term structure model. While the author does not focus on the inflation risk premium, the extracted liquidity premium still resembles other studies' liquidity premia. Based on a counterfactual analysis (i.e. constructing ILB yields without the asset purchase programme), Coroneo (2016) shows that the quantitative easing programme has only slightly impacted the ILB liquidity premium. Given the size of the ILB liquidity premium and the consequential costs for the Treasury, further in-depth analyses on how the ILB liquidity premium can be lowered represent a promising avenue for future research.

5. Current Developments

5.1 *Inflation Risk Premium and Monetary Policy*

Analysing the impact of 'surprising' monetary policy events is possible without the use of ILB by looking at nominal bond yields or survey inflation forecasts. With a term structure model that is able to decompose yield curves into its single components, however, more detailed interferences can be drawn: By using solely nominal bond yields, for instance, one cannot differentiate between effects on inflation expectations and effects on the inflation risk premium. With survey inflation forecasts, on the other hand, their low frequency does not allow analysing immediate effects. By decomposing the yield curve, both monetary policy effects as well as macro-economic effects, in general, can be analysed very effectively and implications about the origin of the inflation risk premium can be drawn more precisely.

Table 2. Overview of Applied Liquidity Proxies.

Proxy	Frequency	Source	Modifications (studies used in)
ILB-specific liquidity proxies			
ILB fitting errors	Daily	CRSP US Treasury Database	calculation as outlined in Hu et al. (2013) (used by Abrahams et al., 2016; D'Amico et al., 2018; Grishchenko and Huang, 2013)
ILB bid-ask spread	Daily	TradeWeb (ThomsonReuters)	no modification (used by D'Amico et al., 2018)
Relative ILB liquidity proxies			
Outstanding ILB	Monthly	TreasuryDirect	★ relative to all nominal debt outstanding with comparable maturity (used by Kajuth and Watzka, 2011; Shen, 2006) ★ relative to all nominal debt outstanding (used by Auckenthaler et al., 2015)
ILB Primary Dealer Transactions	Weekly	Federal Reserve Bank of New York	★ logarithm of ILB transaction volume (used by Shen, 2006) ★ relative to volume of ILB outstanding (used by Grishchenko and Huang, 2013; Söderlind, 2011) ★ relative to all nominal transactions (used by Auckenthaler et al., 2015; Gürkaynak et al., 2010; Hördahl and Tristani, 2014) ★ relative to all nominal transactions with comparable maturity (used by Kajuth and Watzka, 2011) ★ relative to all transactions and 13-week moving average (used by Abrahams et al., 2016; D'Amico et al., 2018) ★ relative (log) to all long-term nominal transactions and 3-month moving average (used by Pflueger and Viceira, 2016)

ILB asset swap spread—nominal off-the-run asset swap spread	Daily	Barclays	no modification (used by D'Amico et al., 2018)
Inflation swap rate—break-even inflation rate	Daily	Bloomberg	no modification (used by Christensen and Gillan, 2012; D'Amico et al., 2018; Pflueger and Viceira, 2016)
Treasury liquidity proxies			
On-the-run/off-the-run spread	Daily	Bloomberg or CRSP	no modification (used by Grishchenko and Huang, 2013; Kajuth and Watzka, 2011; Pflueger and Viceira, 2016; Shen, 2006; Söderlind, 2011)
Spread between Refcorp strips and nominal Treasury strips	Daily	Bloomberg	no modification (used by Gürkaynak et al., 2010 and Hördahl and Tristani, 2014)
Proxies for uncertainty			
Implied volatility of S&P500 (VIX)	Daily	Chicago Board Options Exchange	no modification (used by Auckenthaler et al., 2015; Söderlind, 2011)
Implied volatility of 10-year future notes	Daily	Bloomberg	no modification (used by Auckenthaler et al., 2015)
Spread between interbank rate and federal funds rate	Daily	Bloomberg	no modification (used by Auckenthaler et al., 2015)

Notes: This table summarizes all ILB liquidity proxies that are used in the studies above. The last column informs about potential modifications and lists studies that use this proxy. Stated frequency refers to the data frequency in general and not to the one used in the respective studies.

Hördahl and Tristani (2014) and Abrahams *et al.* (2016) are among the studies that link the components of the term structure with monetary policy. In a basic analysis, Abrahams *et al.* (2016) show the relation between the inflation risk premium and, among others, the survey inflation forecast disagreement (positive correlation) or the consumer confidence (negative correlation). Similarly, also, Hördahl and Tristani (2014) find a countercyclical inflation risk premium until the financial crisis in 2008. During the financial crisis, the premium has a rather pro-cyclical development which is, however, in accordance with the discussion by Chen *et al.* (2016) about the inflation risk premium's sign (see Section 2.1).

Regarding the effects of monetary policy, Abrahams *et al.* (2016) analyse both the impact of conventional as well as unconventional monetary policy on the yield curve components. Concerning conventional monetary policy, the authors analyse the response of yield curve components during Federal Open Market Committee (FOMC) announcements between 1999 and 2008. While the effect on inflation expectations is negligible, the response of the inflation risk premium is negative and statistically significant. The response is negative over all maturities (from 2 to 10 years) but shows a U-shaped pattern, implying that inflation risk is less relevant in the medium term. This is again in line with the discussion in Section 2.1: Monetary shocks, in this case emerged by FOMC announcements, increase the covariance between inflation and consumption growth leading to a reduction of the inflation risk premium or even to a change in the premium's sign. On the contrary, note that existing studies, such as Hanson and Stein (2015), are unable to explicitly decompose the yield curve and to provide implications for the single curve's components.

5.2 *Estimation Issues*

It is obvious that fully fledged term structure models should be favoured to more simple approaches because of their model-implied (and therefore consistent) estimates for expected inflation and risk premia. However, the more complex (and thus also more flexible) models become, the more relevant estimation issues are. While all studies in Section 3.2 use a maximum likelihood estimation with the Kalman filter (or a modification of it), there might arise estimation problems with canonical term structure models. Loosely speaking, the latent factor specification could lead to multiple maxima during the estimation (because factors can rotate). While the CDR model builds on a theory (i.e. dynamic Nelson-Siegel model), this might be a weak spot of latent-factor models (see, e.g. Kim and Orphanides, 2012, for a discussion). New developments in estimation techniques have emerged and comprise, for instance, a three-step linear regression approach proposed by Adrian *et al.* (2013). In an earlier version of the Abrahams *et al.* (2016) paper, this approach is applied to estimate the model (see Abrahams *et al.*, 2015). Joslin *et al.* (2011) or Hamilton and Wu (2012) are among the studies that present alternative estimation methods. However, as the focus of this survey is more on studies' conceptual structure than on technical or estimation issues, the interested reader should refer to the original studies. Thus, one can say at the bottom line that (i) parsimonious models are needed to make over-parameterization less relevant and (ii) the more flexible in terms of factors and correlation structures term structure models become, the more caution is need during the estimation.

5.3 *Zero Lower Bound*

Recent times with (very) low interest rates cause existing term structure models for nominal interest rates to be revised. The point is that nominal bond yields are expected to approach a lower bound which is zero or slightly negative.[14] The majority of term structure models, however, allow interest rates to be negative which can lead to implausible estimation results. In other words, during times of very low interest rates, standard term structure models face difficulties to account for the non-linearity at the zero lower bound (see, e.g. Kim and Singleton, 2012 for a discussion).[15] Research started to consider this problem by introducing a so-called shadow rate proposed by Black (1995). Including such a shadow rate in a term structure model causes severe estimation issues due to its non-linear structure. Initial studies that include the shadow rate in their term structure models are limited to a maximum of two factors because of estimation complexity. More precisely, if no closed-form solutions are available, one would have to draw on computation-intensive numerical evaluations (see, e.g. Gorovoi and Linetsky, 2004 or Kim and Singleton, 2012 for a discussion). New simulation or approximation techniques to estimate these models are proposed by Ichiue and Ueno (2013), Kim and Priebsch (2013) and Wu and Xia (2016). Recently, however, Monfort *et al.* (2017) propose an affine term structure model which accommodates current challenges and provides closed-form pricing formulas. More specifically, their model includes autoregressive gamma-zero processes which are consistent with non-negative yields and compatible with a short-term rate that stays at the zero lower bound. Monfort *et al.* (2017) demonstrate the model's features for Japanese government bonds.

An alternative way to overcome these computational burdens is proposed by Krippner (2013) with an option-based approach for estimating a shadow rate term structure model. This general procedure allows to estimation of higher dimensional term structure models and mainly serves as a workhorse model for succeeding studies that account for the zero lower bound. The basic idea of this option-based approach is that an observed bond, with a yield constrained by the zero lower bound, may be considered as a combination of a shadow bond that can take on negative yields and a call option that represents the value of the option to hold physical currency rather than being obliged to receive negative shadow rates if they occurred. Christensen and Rudebusch (2015) incorporate this approach into the CDR model and apply it to the Japanese yield curve. Similarly, Christensen *et al.* (2016) apply the shadow rate CDR model to the USA and document a better model fit compared to standard model during times of low interest rates.

To account for the zero lower bond is also important with regard to the estimation of the inflation risk premium since the nominal yield curve is used as input data. Note that the zero lower bond is, however, less relevant for ILB yields since investors accept negative real yields due to the additional inflation compensation. Thus, jointly pricing nominal bond and ILB yields curves in a low interest rate situation requires to account for the zero lower bound as well because break-even inflation rate will be (even further) distorted. More specifically, distortion arises from the option effect in nominal bond yields described above (representing the value to hold physical currency rather than having to invest at negative shadow rates). To the best of the author's knowledge, Carriero *et al.* (2016) is the only study that jointly prices the nominal and ILB yield curve and accounts for the zero lower bound.[16] The authors develop their joint shadow rate model by merging Christensen *et al.*'s (2010) model with the shadow rate model by Christensen and Rudebusch (2015). Carriero *et al.* (2016) apply their model to the UK yield curve and show that the consideration of the zero lower bond is essential in the current low-interest situation. Given the relevance of this topic and the scarcity of existing studies, this is an important issue for future research.

6. Conclusion

Information about the inflation risk premium is crucial for policy makers, investors and sovereign debt management alike. While various possibilities exist to estimate the inflation risk premium in nominal bond yields, this survey focused on studies that additionally use ILB yields. The benefit of using ILB yields are, among others, a high frequency of data and the availability of different maturities. These features are not given for survey inflation forecasts. While this on first glance implies the possibility of improved estimates for the inflation risk premium when ILB yields are taken into account, current research shows an added complexity to this apparently obvious result.

I show that existing studies considerably differ in both their models and their input data. While the categorization of approaches in regression-based and term-structure models can be easily achieved, further classification of the input data proves to be more complex. In addition, a liquidity premium in ILB yields further complicates estimations. This review outlines how existing studies differ in the degree to which they account for the liquidity premium, and presents a list of existing ILB liquidity proxies. Both research designs and studies' estimates for the inflation risk premium are compared. The estimates differ as well considerably among the studies of which some explicitly consider a liquidity premium and others do not. As one main result of the review, the possibility of finding and applying one single and universal approach of IRP estimation can be neglected: factors like estimation and specification uncertainty or how one accounts for the ILB liquidity premium drive the discrepancies between published estimates. Nonetheless, one observers a tendency towards term structure models that account for the liquidity premium in ILB yields. In fact, most recent papers include the liquidity correction within their term structure models.

Current developments in the research area have been outlined in this paper, like the connection of term structure models with monetary policy, developments in term structure estimation strategies and the consideration of the zero lower bound, to give an overview of the state of the art. The survey also presents potential directions for future research like, for instance, term structure models that account for the zero lower bound in nominal yields but allow for negative ILB yields. Similarly, in-depth analyses of the ILB liquidity premium (like Coroneo, 2016 or Christensen and Gillan, 2017, for instance) and its determinations are still necessary because the premium's elimination would allow Treasuries to save an enormous amount of money by issuing ILB. Finally, topics like recent finance-based approaches (rather than macro-economic models) to measure the equilibrium real rate (see, e.g. Christensen and Rudebusch, 2017) or two-(or multi-)country term structure models that additionally include ILB yields represent further important directions for future research.

Acknowledgements

I am grateful to Iris Claus (Editor), the Managing Editor, and three anonymous referees for their constructive comments and helpful suggestions. All comments improved the paper substantially. I thank Tobias Adrian, Jens H. E. Christensen, Olesya Grishchenko, Peter Höhrdahl, Florian Kajuth and George G. Pennacchi for providing me their data. Any remaining errors are the sole responsibility of the author.

Notes

1. Differences in the steepness of the nominal and real term structure, in fact, suggest (in the absence of any other risk premia) a positive inflation risk premium. See also Bekaert and Wang (2010) for a discussion.
2. Since most of the studies use US data, I focus on the USA in the main text. However, Endnote 9 gives an overview of studies using data from the United Kingdom (UK) and the euro area.

3. This derivation is closely related to Christensen *et al.* (2010). Alternatively, one arrives at the same conclusion when using only a real stochastic discount factor with a price deflator (see, e.g. Geiger, 2011).

4. Data are derived from the website of the respective debt management office.

5. Note that in the USA, these securities are called Treasury inflation-protected securities (TIPS). Before and after the first years of issuance, these bonds were typically known as Treasury inflation-indexed Securities (TIIS). For the remainder of the paper, I simply refer to ILB.

6. In fact and more precisely, there is also the real risk premium because, put simply, expected real returns might deviate from realized real returns. The real risk premium is relevant for both, nominal bond yields and ILB yields and cancels out when the break-even inflation rate is calculated. For the sake of readability, I suppress the real risk premium in Equations (5)– (10). If I explicitly introduce a real risk premium ϕ^{RRP}, Equations (7) and (9) would then read as $y_t^N = \mathbb{E}_t[r] + \phi^{RRP} + \mathbb{E}_t[\pi] + \phi^{IRP}$ and $y_t^{ILB} = \mathbb{E}_t[r] + \phi^{RRP} + \phi^{LIQ}$, respectively, where $\mathbb{E}_t[r]$ is the expected real return and ϕ^{RRP} is the real risk premium. Calculating $y_t^N - y_t^{ILB}$ results in $\mathbb{E}_t[\pi] + \phi^{IRP} - \phi^{LIQ}$ which is the same as in Equation (10).

7. More precisely, the Fisher equation is given by $(1 + y_t^N) = (1 + y_t^R) \cdot (1 + \mathbb{E}_t[\pi])$. Multiplying out leads to $(1 + y_t^N) = 1 + y_t^R + \mathbb{E}_t[\pi] + \mathbb{E}_t[\pi] \cdot y_t^R$. Since both $\mathbb{E}_t[\pi]$ and y_t^R are typically rather small values, the cross product gets even smaller and is neglected in the approximation. The approximation is frequently written as equality: $y_t^N = y_t^R + \mathbb{E}_t[\pi]$.

8. Note that for the case that ILB would be as liquid as their nominal counterpart and that there exists a positive inflation risk premium in nominal bond yields, borrowing money would be cheaper with ILB than with nominal bonds for a sovereign. This is one advantage of issuing ILB among others. An overview of ILB benefits is given in Appendix A, and Appendix B discusses whether the US Treasury actually has saved money by issuing ILB.

9. Note that the United Kingdom started to issue ILB already in 1981. As a consequence, studies using ILB yields evolve earlier than in the USA. However, studies by Arak and Kreicher (1985), Wilcox (1985) or Woodward (1990) assume the inflation risk premium to be zero or to be constant. Chu *et al.* (1995) apply a different approach by analysing the correlation between inflation forecast errors and nominal returns. Similarly, Shen (1998) extracts the inflation risk premium for the United Kingdom by subtracting the average expected inflation (based on survey data) from the break-even inflation rate. This computation results in an inflation risk premium sized between 130 (for a maturity of 10 years) to 160 (for a maturity of 25 years) basis points over a two year period (i.e. 1996–1997). Söderlind (2011), Auckenthaler *et al.* (2015) and Pflueger and Viceira (2016) apply regression-based approaches for the USA (see main text) as well as for the United Kingdom and/or the euro area. Kanas (2014) presents a slightly different approach by additionally using bond futures. The author estimates the covariance between both nominal bond yields and bond futures as well as the covariance between ILB yields and bond futures. The difference in covariances is fully attributed to inflation risk and averages 87 basis points between 1985 and 2012. Term structure models have been developed by Risa (2001), Evans (2003), Joyce *et al.* (2010) and most recently, by Carriero *et al.* (2016). Both Risa (2001) and Joyce *et al.* (2010) present essentially affine term structure model that jointly price the nominal and ILB term structure for the United Kingdom. Evans (2003) develops a term structure model that includes a regime-switching property. This feature

allows for a higher flexibility but estimation difficulties at the same time if too many states are included. Carriero *et al.* (2016) extend the term structure model developed by Christensen and Rudebusch (2015) which accounts for the zero lower bound by joint pricing nominal bonds and ILB. For a closer discussion of the zero lower bond issue, see Section 5 in the main text. A rather small research body focuses on the euro area which is mainly due to the limited availability of ILB (France, Germany and Sweden have issued ILB in a considerable amount; Italy and Spain (re)started recently issuing ILB). The paper by Hördahl and Tristani (2014) (outlined in Section 3.2 of the main text) also analyses euro area data. García and Werner (2010) solely focus on euro area and develop a three-factor term structure model for the nominal and real yield curve which includes (among nominal bond yields and ILB yields) inflation and survey inflation forecast data. Most notably, the authors derive proxies for inflation risk (i.e. inflation uncertainty and asymmetry in inflation risks) from survey inflation forecasts and relate these proxies to their estimate of the inflation risk premium. None of these studies has focused on ILB mispricing due to illiquidity indicating that a potential liquidity premium seems to be less relevant in the United Kingdom and the euro area. This could, however, also be driven by a lower availability of liquidity proxies implying that a potential liquidity premium is more difficult to 'detect'. The development of reasonable instrument-specific liquidity proxies (especially for the euro area) describes an avenue for future research.

10. For simplicity and readability, I do not state the specific liquidity proxies throughout this section but list them altogether in Table 2 (see Section 4).

11. See Bekaert and Wang (2010, p. 780) for a typical technique to develop a term structure model.

12. So-called hypothetical ILB yields are also estimated by Campbell and Shiller (1996). However, they estimate ex ante real yields with a VAR system that includes three-month nominal T-bill rates and inflation rates. By forecasting ex ante real yields to the respective maturity, the authors derive hypothetical ILB yields. This procedure, however, requires that the expectations hypothesis holds and that the real term premium is zero (see Auckenthaler *et al.*, 2015, for a discussion).

13. See Bauer and Rudebusch (2017) for an excellent review of macro-finance term structure models.

14. The rationale for the zero lower bound is, loosely speaking, because investors can hold cash. However, investors will, in principle, accept mildly negative yields for the convenience and safety value of electronic balances relative to physical currency. In fact, we observe that several central banks have set slightly negative policy interest rates.

15. Note that practically, also CIR models have to feature of non-zero interest rates due to the square-root process. In these models, however, the zero interest rate rather acts as a reflecting barrier which conflicts with empirical evidence.

16. Note that the paper by Roussellet (2016) discussed in Section 3.2 is similar but uses inflation swap rates rather than ILB data.

References

Abrahams, M., Adrian, T., Crump, R.K. and Moench, E. (2015) Decomposing real and nominal yield curves. FRB of New York Staff Report 570.

Abrahams, M., Adrian, T., Crump, R.K., Moench, E. and Yu, R. (2016) Decomposing real and nominal yield curves. *Journal of Monetary Economics* 84: 182–200.

Adrian, T., Crump, R.K. and Moench, E. (2013) Pricing the term structure with linear regressions. *Journal of Financial Economics* 110(1): 110–138.

Adrian, T. and Wu, H.Z. (2009) The term structure of inflation expectations. FRB of New York Staff Report 362.

Andreasen, M.M., Christensen, J.H.E. and Riddell, S. (2017) The TIPS liquidity premium. Working Paper, Federal Reserve Bank of San Francisco 2017-11.

Ang, A., Bekaert, G. and Wei, M. (2007) Do macro variables, asset markets, or surveys forecast inflation better? *Journal of Monetary Economics* 54(4): 1163–1212.

Ang, A., Bekaert, G. and Wei, M. (2008) The term structure of real rates and expected inflation. *Journal of Finance* 63(2): 797–849.

Ang, A. and Piazzesi, M. (2003) A no-arbitrage vector autoregression of term structure dynamics with macroeconomic and latent variables. *Journal of Monetary Economics* 50(4): 745–787.

Arak, M. and Kreicher, L. (1985) The real rate of interest: inferences from the New U.K. indexed gilts. *International Economic Review* 26(2): 399–408.

Auckenthaler, J., Kupfer, A. and Sendlhofer, R. (2015) The impact of liquidity on inflation-linked bonds: a hypothetical indexed bonds approach. *North American Journal of Economics and Finance* 32: 139–154.

Bauer, M.D. and Rudebusch, G.D. (2017) Resolving the spanning puzzle in macro-finance term structure models. *Review of Finance* 21(2): 511–553.

Bekaert, G. and Wang, X. (2010) Inflation risk and the inflation risk premium. *Economic Policy* 25(64): 755–806.

Black, F. (1995) Interest rates as options. *Journal of Finance* 50(5): 1371–1376.

Bodie, Z. (1990) Inflation, index-linked bonds, and asset allocation. *Journal of Portfolio Management* 16(2): 48–53.

Buraschi, A. and Jiltsov, A. (2005) Inflation risk premia and the expectations hypothesis. *Journal of Financial Economics* 75(2): 429–490.

Campbell, J.Y. and Shiller, R.J. (1996) A scorecard for indexed government debt. *NBER Macroeconomics Annual* 11: 155–197.

Campbell, J.Y., Shiller, R.J. and Viceira, L.M. (2009) Understanding inflation-indexed bond markets. *Brookings Papers on Economic Activity* 40: 79–138.

Carriero, A., Mouabbi, S. and Vangelista, E. (2016) UK term structure decompositions at the zero lower bound. Working Paper 589, Bank of France.

Chen, A., Engstrom, E. and Grishchenko, O. (2016) Has the inflation risk premium fallen? Is it now negative? FEDS Notes.

Chen, P. and Terrien, M. (2001) TIPS as an asset class. *Journal of Investing* 10(2): 73–81.

Chen, R.-R., Liu, B. and Cheng, X. (2010) Pricing the term structure of inflation risk premia: theory and evidence from TIPS. *Journal of Empirical Finance* 17(4): 702–721.

Cheridito, P., Filipović, D. and Kimmel, R.L. (2007) Market price of risk specifications for affine models: theory and evidence. *Journal of Financial Economics* 83(1): 123–170.

Chernov, M. and Mueller, P. (2012) The term structure of inflation expectations. *Journal of Financial Economics* 106(2): 367–394.

Christensen, J.H.E., Diebold, F.X. and Rudebusch, G.D. (2011) The affine arbitrage-free class of Nelson-Siegel term structure models. *Journal of Econometrics* 164(1): 4–20.

Christensen, J.H.E. and Gillan, J.M. (2012) Could the U.S. Treasury benefit from issuing more TIPS? FRB of San Francisco Working Paper Series 2011-16.

Christensen, J.H.E. and Gillan, J.M. (2017) Does quantitative easing affect market liquidity? Working Paper, Federal Reserve Bank of San Francisco (2013-26).

Christensen, J.H.E., Lopez, J.A. and Rudebusch, G.D. (2010) Inflation expectations and risk premiums in an arbitrage-free model of nominal and real bond yields. *Journal of Money, Credit and Banking* 42: 143–178.

Christensen, J.H.E., Lopez, J.A. and Rudebusch, G.D. (2016) Pricing deflation risk with US Treasury yields. *Review of Finance* 20(3): 1107–1152.

Christensen, J.H.E. and Rudebusch, G.D. (2015) Estimating shadow-rate term structure models with near-zero yields. *Journal of Financial Econometrics* 13(2): 226–259.

Christensen, J.H.E. and Rudebusch, G.D. (2017) A new normal for interest rates? Evidence from inflation-indexed debt. FRB San Francisco Working Paper 2017-07.

Chu, Q.C., Lee, C.F. and Pittman, D.N. (1995) On the inflation risk premium. *Journal of Business Finance & Accounting* 22(6): 881–892.

Coeuré, B. and Sagnes, N. (2005) Un bilan de l'émission des obligations françaises indexées sur l'inflation. Diagnostics Prévisions et Analyses Économiques No. 89.

Coroneo, L. (2016) TIPS liquidity premium and quantitative easing. Unpublished Working Paper.

Cox, J.C., Ingersoll, J.E. and Ross, S.A. (1985) A theory of the term structure of interest rates. *Econometrica* 53(2): 385–407.

Dai, Q. and Singleton, K.J. (2000) Specification analysis of affine term structure models. *Journal of Finance* 55(5): 1943–1978.

D'Amico, S., Kim, D.H. and Wei, M. (2018) Tips from TIPS: the informational content of Treasury inflation-protected security prices. *Journal of Financial and Quantitative Analysis* 53, 395–436.

Deacon, M., Derry, A. and Mirfendereski, D. (2004) *Inflation-Indexed Securities*. New York/Chichester, UK: John Wiley & Sons.

Diebold, F.X. and Li, C. (2006) Forecasting the term structure of government bond yields. *Journal of Econometrics* 130(2): 337–364.

Diebold, F.X. and Rudebusch, G.D. (2013) *Yield Curve Modeling and Forecasting: The Dynamic Nelson-Siegel Approach*. Princeton, NJ: Princeton University Press.

Dudley, W.C., Roush, J. and Ezer, M.S. (2009) The case for TIPS: an examination of the costs and benefits. *Economic Policy Review* 15(1): 1–17.

Duffee, G.R. (2002) Term premia and interest rate forecasts in affine models. *Journal of Finance* 57(1): 405–443.

Duffie, D. and Kan, R. (1996) A yield-factor model of interest rates. *Mathematical Finance* 6(4): 379–406.

Evans, M.D.D. (1998) Real rates, expected inflation, and inflation risk premia. *Journal of Finance* 53(1): 187–218.

Evans, M.D.D. (2003) Real risk, inflation risk, and the term structure. *Economic Journal* 113(487): 345–389.

Ewald, C.-O. and Geissler, J. (2015) Markets for inflation-indexed bonds as mechanisms for efficient monetary policy. *Mathematical Finance* 25(4): 869–889.

Fleckenstein, M. (2013) The inflation-indexed bond puzzle. Unpublished Working Paper.

Fleckenstein, M., Longstaff, F.A. and Lustig, H. (2014) The TIPS-treasury bond puzzle. *Journal of Finance* 69(5): 2151–2197.

Fleming, M.J. (2003) Measuring treasury market liquidity. *Economic Policy Review* 9(3): 83–108.

Fleming, M.J. and Krishnan, N. (2012) The microstructure of the TIPS market. *Economic Policy Review* 18(1): 27–45.

García, J.A. and van Rixtel, A. (2007) Inflation-linked bonds from a central bank perspective. ECB Occasional Paper Series 62.

García, J.A. and Werner, T. (2010) Inflation risks and inflation risk premia. ECB Working Paper Series 1162.

Geiger, F. (2011) *The Yield Curve and Financial Risk Premia*. Berlin/New York: Springer.

Gorovoi, V. and Linetsky, V. (2004) Black's model of interest rates as options, eigenfunction expansions and Japanese interest rates. *Mathematical Finance* 14(1): 49–78.

Grishchenko, O.V. and Huang, J.-Z. (2012) Term structure of interest rates and expected inflation. In S. Perrucci and B. Bénaben (eds.), *Inflation-Sensitive Assets: Instruments and Strategies* (pp. 209–253). London: Risk Books.

Grishchenko, O.V. and Huang, J.-Z. (2013) The inflation risk premium: evidence from the TIPS market. *Journal of Fixed Income* 22(4): 5–30.

Grishchenko, O.V., Vanden, J.M. and Zhang, J. (2016) The informational content of the embedded deflation option in TIPS. *Journal of Banking & Finance* 65: 1–26.

Gürkaynak, R.S., Sack, B. and Wright, J.H. (2007) The U.S. Treasury yield curve: 1961 to the present. *Journal of Monetary Economics* 54(8): 2291–2304.

Gürkaynak, R.S., Sack, B. and Wright, J.H. (2010) The TIPS yield curve and inflation compensation. *American Economic Journal: Macroeconomics* 2(1): 70–92.

Hamilton, J.D. and Wu, J.C. (2012) Identification and estimation of Gaussian affine term structure models. *Journal of Econometrics* 168(2): 315–331.

Hanson, S.G. and Stein, J.C. (2015) Monetary policy and long-term real rates. *Journal of Financial Economics* 115(3): 429–448.

Haubrich, J., Pennacchi, G. and Ritchken, P. (2012) Inflation expectations, real rates, and risk premia: evidence from inflation swaps. *Review of Financial Studies* 25(5): 1588–1629.

Hördahl, P. and Tristani, O. (2014) Inflation risk premia in the euro area and the United States. *International Journal of Central Banking* 10(3): 1–47.

Hördahl, P., Tristani, O. and Vestin, D. (2006) A joint econometric model of macroeconomic and term-structure dynamics. *Journal of Econometrics* 131(1–2): 405–444.

Hu, G.X., Pan, J. and Wang, J. (2013) Noise as information for illiquidity. *Journal of Finance* 68(6): 2341–2382.

Ichiue, H. and Ueno, Y. (2013) Estimating term premia at the zero bound: an analysis of Japanese, US, and UK yields. Bank of Japan Working Paper Series 13-E-8.

Joslin, S., Singleton, K.J. and Zhu, H. (2011) A new perspective on Gaussian dynamic term structure models. *Review of Financial Studies* 24(3): 926–970.

Joyce, M.A., Lildholdt, P. and Sorensen, S. (2010) Extracting inflation expectations and inflation risk premia from the term structure: a joint model of the UK nominal and real yield curves. *Journal of Banking & Finance* 34(2): 281–294.

Kajuth, F. and Watzka, S. (2011) Inflation expectations from index-linked bonds: correcting for liquidity and inflation risk premia. *Quarterly Review of Economics and Finance* 51(3): 225–235.

Kanas, A. (2014) Bond futures, inflation-indexed bonds, and inflation risk premium. *Journal of International Financial Markets, Institutions and Money* 28: 82–99.

Kim, D.H. and Orphanides, A. (2012) Term structure estimation with survey data on interest rate forecasts. *Journal of Financial and Quantitative Analysis* 47(1): 241–272.

Kim, D.H. and Priebsch, M. (2013) Estimation of multi-factor shadow-rate term structure models. Unpublished Working Paper.

Kim, D.H. and Singleton, K.J. (2012) Term structure models and the zero bound: an empirical investigation of Japanese yields. *Journal of Econometrics* 170(1): 32–49.

Kothari, S. and Shanken, J. (2004) Asset allocation with inflation-protected bonds. *Financial Analysts Journal* 60(1): 54–70.

Krippner, L. (2013) A tractable framework for zero lower bound Gaussian term structure models. Reserve Bank of New Zealand Discussion Paper Series DP2013/02.

Monfort, A., Pegoraro, F., Renne, J.-P. and Roussellet, G. (2017) Staying at zero with affine processes: an application to term structure modelling. *Journal of Econometrics* 201(2): 348–366.

Nelson, C.R. and Siegel, A.F. (1987) Parsimonious modeling of yield curves. *Journal of Business* 60(4): 473–489.

Pflueger, C.E. and Viceira, L.M. (2016) Return predictability in the Treasury market: real rates, inflation, and liquidity. In P. Veronesi (ed.), *Handbook of Fixed-Income Securities* (pp. 191–209). New York/Chichester, UK: John Wiley & Sons.

Piazzesi, M. (2010) Affine term structure models. In Y. Ait-Sahalia and L.P. Hansen (eds.), *Handbook of Financial Econometrics: Tools and Techniques* (pp. 691–766). Amsterdam/New York: Elsevier.

Rebonato, R. (2016) Structural affine models for yield curve modeling. In P. Veronesi (ed.), *Handbook of Fixed-Income Securities* (pp. 239–264). New York/Chichester, UK: John Wiley & Sons.

Reschreiter, A. (2004) Conditional funding costs of inflation-indexed and conventional government bonds. *Journal of Banking & Finance* 28(6): 1299–1318.

Reschreiter, A. (2010a) Indexed bonds and revisions of inflation expectations. *Annals of Finance* 6(4): 537–554.

Reschreiter, A. (2010b) The inflation protection from indexed bonds. *Applied Economics Letters* 17(16): 1581–1585.

Risa, S. (2001) Nominal and inflation indexed yields: separating expected inflation and inflation risk premia. Unpublished working paper.

Roll, R. (2004) Empirical TIPS. *Financial Analysts Journal* 60(1): 31–53.

Roush, J. (2008) The 'growing pains' of TIPS issuance. FEDS Working Paper 2008-08.

Roussellet, G. (2016) Affine term structure modeling and macroeconomic risks at the zero lower bound. Unpublished Working Paper.

Sack, B.P. and Elsasser, R. (2004) Treasury inflation-indexed debt: a review of the U.S. experience. *Economic Policy Review* 10(1): 47–63.

Shen, P. (1998) How important is the inflation risk premium? *Economic Review* 83(4): 35–47.

Shen, P. (2006) Liquidity risk premia and breakeven inflation rates. *Economic Review* 91(2): 29–54.

Shen, P. (2009) Developing a liquid market for inflation-indexed government securities: lessons from earlier experiences. *Economic Review* 94(1): 89–113.

Singleton, K.J. (2006) *Empirical Dynamic Asset Pricing: Model Specification and Econometric Assessment*. Princeton, NJ: Princeton University Press.

Söderlind, P. (2011) Inflation risk premia and survey evidence on macroeconomic uncertainty. *International Journal of Central Banking* 7(2): 113–133.

UK Debt Management Office (2001) Twenty years of the index-linked gilts market. DMO Annual Review 2001-01.

Vasicek, O. (1977) An equilibrium characterization of the term structure. *Journal of Financial Economics* 5(2): 177–188.

Wilcox, J. (1985) Short-term movements of long-term real interest rates: evidence from the U.K. indexed bond market. NBER Working Paper 1543.

Woodward, G.T. (1990) The real thing: a dynamic profile of the term structure of real interest rates and inflation expectations in the United Kingdom, 1982-89. *Journal of Business* 63(3): 373–398.

Wu, J.C. and Xia, F.D. (2016) Measuring the macroeconomic impact of monetary policy at the zero lower bound. *Journal of Money, Credit and Banking* 48(2–3): 253–291.

Appendix A: Overview of the Advantages of ILB

The reasons for a sovereign state to issue ILB are twofold: First, it can be related to credibly signalling that moderates inflation rates that are put into consideration. This rationale was used, for instance, by Israel in 1955 or the United Kingdom in 1981, while they suffered from high inflation rates in the past and tried to lower these rates in the future. The issuance of ILB reduces the incentive of governments to ease the real value of sovereign debt via higher inflation rates and therefore serves as a credible signalling device. In this context, Margaret Thatcher called these securities a 'sleeping policeman' that helps monitor inflation, and more recently, Ewald and Geissler (2015) present a monetary policy framework that reduces the central banks inflationary bias owing to the availability of inflation-linked debt (see also García and van Rixtel, 2007, who generally analyse ILB from a central banks point of view).

The second argument for issuing ILB is more recent and refers to a cost-saving strategy of sovereigns debt management. As discussed in this survey, nominal bond yields include, besides the real interest rate and expected inflation, an inflation risk premium. If this premium is positive and if ILBs do not include any premium, issuing ILB instead of nominal bonds would lower sovereigns financing costs. These potential savings for the Treasury have been used as an argument for the ILB issuance in, among other countries, the USA or Canada. However, the magnitude of the potential savings is unknown ex ante for two reasons: First, the inflation risk premium cannot directly be observed; second, ILB should be free of any premia. As shown in this paper, both a (most of the time positive) inflation risk premium and a liquidity premium in ILB yields exist. A clear-cut evaluation of whether the Treasury has saved money by issuing ILB is not possible. Appendix B discusses this issue.

While these features are beneficial only for sovereigns, there also exist advantages for policy makers and investors. The most obvious benefit for investors is inflation protection, which is, for instance, not fully given in nominal bonds (in the case of considerable differences between the expected and realized inflation rate). Furthermore, the presence of inflation-linked securities allows a shift in asset allocation and could lead to better diversification of investors portfolios (see, for instance, Bodie, 1990; Chen and Terrien, 2001; or Kothari and Shanken, 2004). Finally, as discussed extensively in the paper, ILBs are useful for policymakers since their yields can be used to extract market-implied inflation expectations. However, as shown, break-even inflation rates are biased by inflation risk premium and liquidity premium, and adjusting for these premia is essential before the break-even inflation rate can be interpreted.

Appendix B: Have ILB Issuances Led to Costs or Savings for the Treasury?

The presence of an inflation risk premium in nominal bond yields and a liquidity premium in ILB yields—as outlined in this paper—raises the question of whether the Treasury has actually saved money by issuing ILB, as was the main argument for the ILB issuance at least in the USA. This appendix focuses on studies that analyse the costs and savings of ILB issuances. Basically, every paper that estimates the (liquidity-adjusted) inflation risk premium can be used to proxy the potential savings for the Treasury.

Based on the calculations of the inflation-risk premium, only Christensen and Gillan (2012) further compute the potential savings for the Treasury owing to the saving of the inflation-risk premium. The authors' so-called 'minimum ly liquidity-adjusted inflation risk premium' is positive on average and therefore implies savings for the Treasury. Christensen and Gillan (2012) furthermore argue that an expansion of the ILB programme in the USA would save the Treasury about $25 billion over a period of 10 years for a constant debt level and an increase of outstanding ILB to 25% of all US government debt outstanding. On the other hand, if the US debt level is increasing constantly (as in the last 10 years) and if the ratio of outstanding ILB would be again 25%, potential savings would amount to about $51 billion. These figures, however, are rather conservative since the calculations are based on the authors' maximum liquidity premium (see also Section 3.2). Given an expansion of the ILB programme, the liquidity premium in ILB yields will likely disappear or at least decrease, implying that the liquidity-adjusted inflation risk premium will increase in the same way.

The paper by Fleckenstein et al. (2014) also investigates the ILB market in the USA by using inflation swap rates. More specifically, the authors rebuild the identical cash flows of a nominal bond by combining the cash flows of an ILB with an inflation swap. Each ILB outstanding is matched with a nominal bond of the same maturity and a similar issue date, and then, by combining ILB with inflation swaps, the mispricing for each bond pair is calculated. Fleckenstein et al. (2014) calculate the average ILB mispricing from 2004 to 2010, which exhibits about 40 basis points until 2008. Doing the time around the Lehman Brothers bankruptcy, however, mispricing increased to about 170 basis points (see Fleckenstein et al., 2014, figure 2). Regarding the costs that emerge from this mispricing, the authors discuss the following option: The Treasury could buy back all outstanding ILB, issue new nominal debt with the same maturity and hedge the inflation risk with inflation swaps. This buy back could save the Treasury about $11 billion at the end of the authors' sample period. At the peak of the mispricing in end-2008, the savings with this procedure would have amounted to about $56 billion. An alternative approach would be to calculate the total costs of the Treasury for issuing ILB instead of nominal bonds, which would amount to about $10 billion during the authors' sample period. Based on these ex post calculations, Fleckenstein et al. (2014) conclude that the issuance of ILB was rather expensive for the Treasury.

Similar to Sack and Elsasser (2004), Fleckenstein et al. (2014) also calculate the ex post costs of the ILB issuance for the Treasury. Sack and Elsasser's (2004) sample period lasts from 1997 to 2003 and therefore mainly covers the early years of ILB issuance, which were characterized by a high liquidity premium. The approach to calculate the costs is different from that of Fleckenstein et al. (2014) and basically compares observed, unadjusted break-even inflation rates with either realized inflation or survey inflation forecasts. The idea is to use realized and survey inflation as a reliable measure for inflation, and the difference between break-even inflation rate and their inflation proxy determines the costs or savings of issuing ILB. Thus, Sack and Elsasser's (2004) approach yields current costs (in 2004) in the amount of about $3 billion (by using realized inflation) and total (expected) costs of about $12 billion (by using survey inflation forecasts). Nonetheless, the authors argue that these costs can be the consequence of different, ILB-specific characteristics such as the fact that ILBs constitute a novel asset class in the USA, ILBs are very attractive for buy and hold investors and ILB might be rather illiquid owing to the low amount issued thus far. In this context, Fleming (2003) documents a smaller trading volume, a longer turnaround time and a wider bid-ask spread for US ILB in comparison with their nominal counterparts.

In a similar vein, the paper by Roush (2008) calculates the savings/costs of the US ILB programme until 2007 and derives a range for the current costs (in 2007) of $5 to $8 billion. Roush (2008) also derives hypothetical savings/costs assuming that ILB would be as liquid as in 2007 over the entire sample period (i.e. 1997–2007). In this case, ILB issuances would have led to savings (in 2007) that amount to about $14 to $17 billion. Therefore, as the author concludes, proving a liquid market is of key importance for the Treasury in order to shift costs of ILB issuances into savings (see also, for instance, Shen, 2009). Similarly, Dudley et al. (2009) investigate the costs and savings of ILB issuance in the USA and apply the same method as Roush (2008) by comparing the auction break-even inflation rate with survey inflation forecasts. Dudley et al. (2009) confirm the findings of the previous study and show for the most recent ILB issuances (in the beginning of 2008, before the Lehman Brothers bankruptcy) that the costs for issuing a nominal bond are ex ante virtually equal to the costs of issuing an ILB. However, as shown in, for instance, Fleckenstein et al. (2014), the costs of ILB considerably increased again during the financial crisis. This period of financial turmoil, however, is not included in the authors' analysis owing to the paper's publication date (i.e. 2009).

Only a few studies provide international evidence on the costs and savings of ILB issuances. Most importantly, in this context, the follow-up paper by Fleckenstein (2013) calculates the ILB mispricing in the vein of Fleckenstein et al. (2014) for the USA and six other countries (i.e. Canada, France, Germany, Italy, Japan and United Kingdom). Mispricing is shown to be rather low on average before the financial crisis but increasing during the crisis for all countries. Interestingly, the mispricing peak around the Lehman Brothers bankruptcy is highest for the USA, followed by the United Kingdom. For the United Kingdom, a publication by the Debt Management Office reveals that ILBs 'have led to a significant reduction in the cost of funding' (UK Debt Management Office, 2001, p. 39) and similarly for France where a publication by the

Minister of the Economy, Finances and Industry summarizes savings owing to ILB issuances up to €120 million for the period 1998–2004 (see Coeuré and Sagnes, 2005). In addition, Reschreiter (2004) studies different risk compensations of nominal bonds and ILB for the United Kingdom and finds that they are different from each other. While the author concludes that ILB could significantly reduce funding costs for the Treasury, there is no analysis of the real (ex post) savings or costs of ILB issuance in the United Kingdom (see also Reschreiter, 2010a and Reschreiter, 2010b).

Appendix C: Comparison of Estimates for the Inflation Risk Premium

The following figure shows estimated inflation risk premia of the following studies: Christensen *et al.* (2010), Kajuth and Watzka (2011), Haubrich *et al.* (2012), Hördahl and Tristani (2014), Auckenthaler *et al.* (2015), Abrahams *et al.* (2016), and Andreasen *et al.* (2017). Time periods (and thus minimum/maximum values as well) may vary to the values in Table 1 since some authors provided updated time series. It is quite impressive that even during the period 2003–2007, the inflation risk premium varies between −50 basis points and +100 basis points. During the financial turmoil in 2008 and 2009, on the other hand, the estimates fluctuate between −200 basis points and +200 basis points. Recalling the interaction between inflation risk premium in nominal bond yields and liquidity premium in ILB yields, Christensen *et al.*'s (2010) low values for the inflation risk premium in 2008 can be attributed to the fact that the paper does not account for ILB illiquidity. Comparing the most recent studies that provided the data for this survey, namely Abrahams *et al.* (2016) and Andreasen *et al.* (2017), one can observe a parallel movements with, however, a level difference of about 100 basis points.

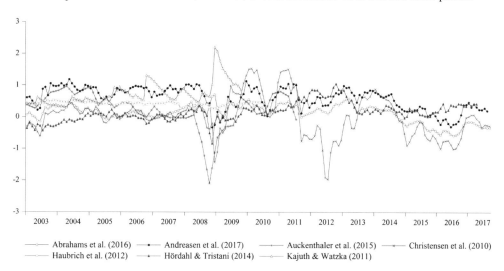

Figure C1. Estimated Inflation Risk Premia of Selected Studies Discussed in the Survey.
Notes: The figure presents estimated inflation risk premia of the following studies: Christensen *et al.* (2010), Kajuth and Watzka (2011), Haubrich *et al.* (2012), Hördahl and Tristani (2014), Auckenthaler *et al.* (2015), Abrahams *et al.* (2016) and Andreasen *et al.* (2017). For inflation risk premia with a daily frequency, monthly averages are calculated (i.e. Christensen *et al.*, 2010 and Abrahams *et al.*, 2016). For inflation risk premia with a quarterly frequency, linear interpolation is applied (i.e. Auckenthaler *et al.*, 2015). Time periods may vary to the time periods described in Table 1 since some authors provided updated series.

6

FINANCE AND PRODUCTIVITY: A LITERATURE REVIEW

Mark Heil

U.S. Department of the Treasury

1. Introduction

Productivity growth is the main contributor to rising prosperity. When productivity rises, economies produce more output for a given level of input, generating gains that increase incomes and improve living standards. However, productivity growth has slowed considerably. Figure 1 shows the evolution of labour productivity growth. In the 1990s, hourly labour productivity growth per year averaged more than 2.0% across Organisation for Economic Co-operation and Development (OECD) countries, and the rate diminished slightly to 1.9% in the 2000–2007 period. Yet, these aggregate figures conceal the changes across regions. In 2000–2007, the euro area and Japan saw substantial drops in their labour productivity growth, which were offset to some degree by increased productivity growth in the United States. However, in the 2007–2014 period, sharp declines in all three regions prompted a more than halving from the previous period in the OECD-wide productivity growth rate to less than 0.9% per year.

In general, the declining productivity growth pattern in developed countries has persisted since the 1970s (OECD, 2017). However, the sharp decline in the latest period raises the stakes for policy makers seeking to support the growth needed for long-run improvements in their residents' quality of life. While the 2007–2014 period coincides with the global financial crisis and sovereign debt crisis in Europe, research suggests that the slowdown in productivity growth reflects both cyclical and long-term structural components (OECD, 2016b).

The author is with the US Department of the Treasury and drafted this paper while he was seconded to the OECD Economics Department. The views expressed in this paper are his own and do not necessarily reflect the perspective of the Treasury Department or the US Government. Acknowledgments: The author is grateful for helpful review comments from Boris Cournéde, Oliver Denk, Priscilla Fialho, Yvan Guillemette, Peter Hoeller, Catherine Mann, Valentine Millot, Paul O'Brien, Sebastian Schich and two anonymous referees. Viktoriya Kuz provided excellent research support.

Contemporary Topics in Finance: A Collection of Literature Surveys, First Edition. Edited by Iris Claus and Leo Krippner.
Chapters © 2019 The Authors. Book compilation © 2019 John Wiley & Sons Ltd. Published 2019 by John Wiley & Sons Ltd.

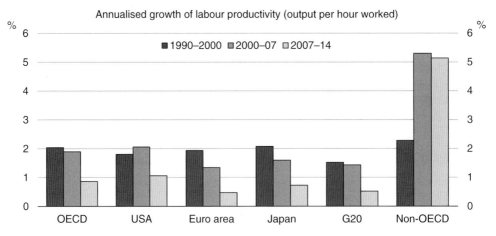

Figure 1. Productivity Growth Has Declined Since the 1990s: Annualised Growth of Labour Productivity (Output Per Hour Worked).
Note: OECD, Euro area, G20 and non-OECD are aggregated using GDP-PPP weights. OECD includes all OECD countries except Estonia. Euro area includes all euro area countries except Estonia. G20 includes all G20 countries except South Africa. Non-OECD is Argentina, Brazil, China, Colombia, India, Indonesia, Latvia, Lithuania, Russia and Saudi Arabia. Data for several countries begin between 1991 and 1995, not in 1990. Labour productivity for non-OECD countries is measured per worker, not per hour worked.
Source: OECD (2016b). [Color figure can be viewed at wileyonlinelibrary.com]

Financial activity has climbed substantially in developed economies over the long term. Figure 2 shows that credit from financial institutions grew over three times as fast as real output in the more than four decades preceding the global financial crisis. Stock market capitalisation expanded nearly six times as fast as real output over the three decades before the crisis.[1] The upward trend of private credit was steady until the financial crisis. Stock market capitalisation's growth path, on the other hand, has been more volatile, as expected, but continues to be well above the levels experienced prior to the internet bubble of the 1990s. Overall, these types of financing have shown remarkable historic growth, and demonstrate that finance has played an ever increasing role in the economy.

Taken together, declining productivity growth and the rising role of finance represent two separate, long-standing forces that shape economic life in OECD countries. However, these diverging trends should not be taken to imply inverse causality. In fact, most studies find that well-functioning systems of finance are highly supportive of productivity growth. Investigating the nexus between productivity and finance, and the policies that influence them, will improve the understanding of researchers and policy makers interested in harnessing appropriate mechanisms to stimulate productivity growth.

This survey of the literature assesses several facets of this nexus, and intends to help inform practitioners so that they may target their future research efforts to extend the current body of work in fruitful directions. It summarises the current state of understanding addressed by empirical studies about how financial factors influence the productivity of non-financial firms and the aggregate economy. It provides a framework for the analysis in the following section. Then, in Section 3, it touches upon the literature on finance and growth, which represents an overarching precursor to studies that specifically focus on productivity. The survey proceeds to

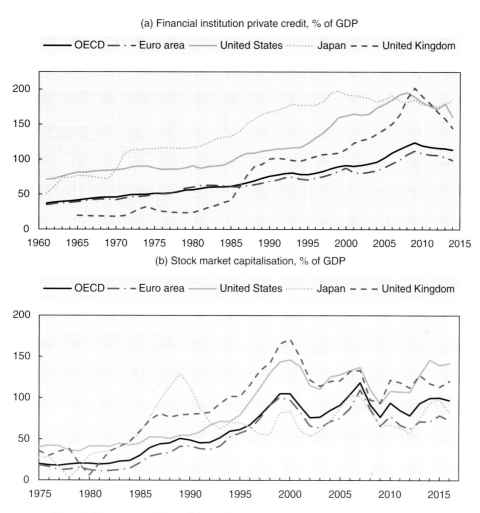

(a) Financial institution private credit, % of GDP

OECD — · — Euro area ——— United States ········ Japan — — — United Kingdom

(b) Stock market capitalisation, % of GDP

OECD — · — Euro area ——— United States ········ Japan — — — United Kingdom

Figure 2. Historic Expansion of Financial Activity: (a) Financial Institution Private Credit, % of GDP; (b) Stock Market Capitalisation, % of GDP.

Note: Financial institution credit refers to credit by depository money banks and other financial institutions to the non-financial private sector. Stock market capitalisation is the value of all listed shares through 28 September 2016. OECD is the simple average of OECD countries for which data are available. Euro area is the simple average of OECD countries that belong to the euro area.
Source: Cournède *et al.* (2015, updated 2016). [Color figure can be viewed at wileyonlinelibrary.com]

review core studies on finance and productivity in Section 4, distinguishing between indirect and direct evidence and discussing interactions with business cycle conditions.

2. A Framework for the Analysis

This section helps frame the literature on productivity and finance by linking financial flows to production inputs and their interactions with policies.

Figure 3 offers a stylised view of key policy mechanisms that affect financial institutions and the financing structure of non-financial firms, which together influence productivity.[2] The solid

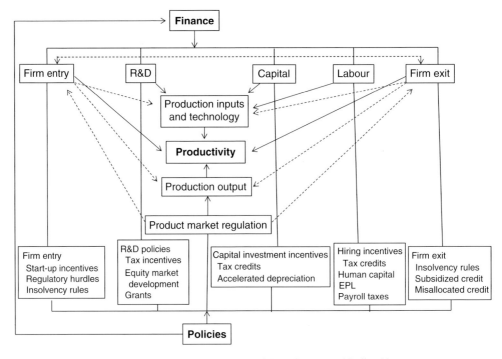

Figure 3. A Synopsis of the Productivity, Finance and Policy Nexus.

lines represent direct paths from one element to another and the dashed lines reflect indirect influences between elements. Starting at the centre, by definition, the combination of production inputs, production technology and outputs co-determine productivity. Production inputs consist of capital and labour, and research and development (R&D) is an input that shapes production technology. All three may be supported by finance of any appropriate type. Finance also supports new firm entry and incumbent firm exit, as both activities incur expenses and influence aggregate productivity. The productivity effect of firm entry may work both through the direct presence of new firms and through their effects on other firms via competitive pressure and potential innovation diffusion, if the entry introduces an innovative production technology or new product. Entering firms may also influence factor and output markets. Likewise, firm exit decisions directly affect productivity and may indirectly influence other firms' productivity through spillover effects on factor and output prices or crowding out (if stagnant incumbent firms remain in the market). Financial market policies will be discussed below.

Public policies influence each of the potentially credit-financed elements of production, sometimes with unintended consequences for productivity. Firm entry policies may encourage (start-up incentives) or discourage (regulatory hurdles) entry, and entry rates may be affected by policies aimed at other objectives (e.g. insolvency rules and product market regulations). R&D policies such as tax incentives aim to encourage the activity, but may favour some types of firms over others in ways that affect productivity gains. Capital investment incentives can encourage investment, but they may also distort incentives and cause overallocation in some areas at the expense of others, if not carefully designed. A range of labour market incentives intended to encourage new hires or worker mobility can influence labour input and productivity, but such marginal incentives can be counteracted by other policies such as permanent payroll taxes. Employment protection legislation (EPL) and employer labour use flexibility may bear substantially on the effect of labour on productivity. Similarly, product market regulations can influence production directly, and indirectly through discouraging new firm entry and reducing competition. Finally, insolvency rules influence firm exit by shaping the costs to be incurred by insolvent firms.[3] When insolvency costs are high, low productivity firms may choose to remain in the market instead of shutting down, impeding reallocation of resources to more productive firms and creating a barrier to entry. At the same time, insolvency regimes that place high burdens on businesses may discourage innovation or new entries, thereby reducing dynamism.

3. Financial Development and Economic Growth

A large number of economic studies have probed the effects of finance and growth, rather than productivity directly, but they provide a useful context as long-term economic growth is largely a reflection of rising productivity. This literature helped to spawn the finance and productivity studies that followed, and one would expect to see effects of finance that are consistent across both bodies of work.

3.1 Conceptual Priors About Finance and Growth

Economic theory suggests that financial development from low levels provides structure and institutions that help to mitigate financial information costs and transactions costs between agents, and facilitates savings, investment and intermediation. This fosters capital accumulation that allows for the development of improved production technologies and feeds economic growth. At higher levels of financial development, capital is more readily available, but its provision may become inefficiently high. Positive and negative channels include the following (Cournède *et al.*, 2015):

- More financial development can support higher economic growth through many channels including:
  - reducing the need for financing projects from own funds;
  - allocating capital to more productive uses;
  - monitoring investments more professionally;
  - providing more insurance, boosting innovation;
  - facilitating the transmission of monetary policy and
  - generating productivity gains within the financial sector.
- On the negative side, too much finance can slow economic growth, particularly by:
  - misallocating capital by funding projects with too low profitability, for instance, when distortions exist in the tax system or in the form of effective public support for too-big-to-fail banks;
  - magnifying the distortionary costs of inefficiencies in financial intermediation such as financial sector wage premia (Denk, 2015a) and
  - heightening the risks of regulatory capture.

The direction of the net effect is therefore an empirical question. To briefly summarise the empirical work, studies from the 1990s and early 2000s found monotonic positive linkages between financial development and economic growth.[4] However, subsequent research suggested that some of them used misspecified models, which generated biased outcomes. More recent empirical research using developed and developing country data find a threshold in the positive economic growth effects of credit finance beyond which additional credit finance can *reduce* economic growth. This threshold effect may be associated with a range of potential channels, including declining efficiency of capital allocation. The limited research on equity finance suggests the relationship is more stable and positive, so that a shift away from credit towards equity appears associated with increased growth rates in more financially developed countries.

4. Finance and Productivity

The research reviewed here suggests that inefficiencies in finance (present in countries with low financial development or through financial frictions) are key factors in explaining the large differences in productivity across countries. The estimated magnitude of the effect of financial frictions on allocative efficiency and productivity growth varies widely in the literature, which is unsurprising given the differences in methods, indicators, sample countries and time periods covered by the studies. This section reviews indirect and direct analyses of the relationship between finance and productivity.

4.1 Indirect Analyses of the Effect of Finance on Productivity

Several country-level studies assessing the relationship between finance and economic growth also provide indirect evidence on resource allocation and productivity. This survey briefly summarises a set of them, touches upon R&D, discusses innovation and firm ownership structures and includes an analysis of potential influences of corporate finance on productivity. Table A1 in the supplementary material summarises the studies in this section.

4.1.1 Studies Providing Indirect Evidence on Finance and Productivity

Rajan and Zingales (1998) note that a mechanism for the higher growth rates of financially dependent industries in more financially developed countries may be the lower cost of finance to firms in these industries. Lower financing costs facilitate more investment. In addition to the direct productivity gain from reducing the cost of a key production factor (capital), the associated potential incremental investment may also improve returns and boost productivity indirectly in the medium or long run.

Early work suggests that finance can boost productivity by promoting the efficient allocation of capital. Wurgler (2000) shows that investment growth is more responsive to value-added growth in more financially developed countries, in a study covering 65 developed and developing market economies over the period 1963–1995. The results offer evidence that financially well-developed countries tend to allocate capital more efficiently than do less developed nations. Financial development is linked to both reducing investment in declining sectors and raising investment in growing ones. The author cites three potential mechanisms for this dynamic: effective management incentives to pursue productive investment strategies (which can be muted in state-owned enterprises), clear signalling of investment opportunities through informative stock prices and strong shareholder rights (which tend to limit investment in declining sectors).

The literature has also pinpointed effects on total factor productivity (TFP). A study using country-level panel data from 1965 to 1985 attempts to assess the economic growth effects of financial development and identifies the main channels through which growth is influenced. Benhabib and Spiegel (2000) offer suggestive evidence that two financial variables in their growth model are positively related to economic growth, after accounting for disparities in factor accumulation rates. These financial variables, a metric of the overall size of the banking sector and a proxy for the share of credit flowing to the private sector, imply that these aspects of financial development fuel economic growth through improvements in TFP. A one standard deviation increase in these metrics increases annual growth by 0.5 and 0.7 percentage points, respectively, in the median sample country.

The allocation of capital shocks may also influence productivity outcomes. Gopinath *et al.* (2017) study the ORBIS-AMADEUS dataset[5] of manufacturing firms of all sizes in Spain from 1999 to 2012 and observe that declining real interest rates appeared to augment capital flows to larger firms (including lower productivity firms), rather than to the most productive firms regardless of size. This reduced sector TFP, as less financially constrained large firms took on more debt and accumulated capital while more constrained smaller firms had limited access to financing. This induced a substantial rise in the dispersion of returns to capital across firms and declining correlations between firm productivity and capital, signalling capital misallocation. Further analysis shows the misallocation occurred in southern European nations but not in northern Europe, suggesting that financial institutions in the southern countries may be less well developed.

4.1.2 *Effect of Finance on Productivity Through R&D*[6]

One channel through which finance can influence productivity is through the funding of R&D. R&D consists of long-run investments with expected positive future returns, features which call for external financing to play a role in their funding. Brown *et al.* (2012) provides empirical support for this hypothesis, based on panel data of 16 European countries from 1995 to 2007. They find that access to equity finance is closely linked to R&D, in a model that includes stock issues and changes in cash holdings to control for endogenous R&D smoothing. This result overturns previous work on the topic that omitted stock issues and cash holdings from the models.

Ilyina and Samaniego (2011) analyse the degree to which different production inputs such as fixed capital or R&D require external finance and how readily different types of firms are able to raise it. They propose that financial development mainly benefits industries with both high need for external finance and a low ability to raise it. Using a sample of 41 countries with data covering the 1970s through the 1990s, the authors first establish that R&D is strongly positively correlated with external financial dependence. Next, they run separate difference-in-differences regressions for each decade to assess how a range of production inputs interact with financial development to determine value added growth. They find that only the R&D input is positive and significant for all three decades for both sets of financial development metrics, implying that it is a persistent and robust contributor to growth.[7] The analysis concludes that industries with high R&D intensity tend to grow faster in more financially developed countries.

Alternative policies that consider the positive spillover effects of private research to warrant public grants to firms for R&D may generate additional favourable impacts to grant recipients. Demeulemeester and Hottenrott (2015) show that public R&D grants to firms tend to lower the cost of private finance for recipients. The study examines nearly 1700 Belgian firms covering 2000–2012 using the average cost of debt as the variable of interest. It finds that firms receiving R&D grants subsequently have lower cost of debt by about 5% on average in the following year. The authors identify three potential channels through which this effect operates. They rule out the 'resource effect' (improved liquidity of firms receiving grants) as a major factor, but find the 'certification effect' (a firm receiving a grant sends favourable signals to credit markets) and the 'preparation premium' for young firms (that the act of applying for grants improves credit outcomes by helping them become more prepared for the loan acquisition process). The study suggests the results offer support for R&D subsidy programmes targeting financially constrained firms.

While R&D may be viewed as a key input to generating productivity gains, some evidence suggests that firm innovation performance may be closely tied to resource allocation and manager incentives. Brav *et al.* (2018) assess the effect of hedge fund activism on corporate innovation using difference-in-differences models that compare treatment firms (those targeted by hedge fund activism) and matched control firms (not targeted), with data from 1991 to 2010. They find that R&D spending fell among target firms by about 20% on average, compared to control firms during the five-year post-intervention period. However, target firms filed 15% more patent applications and each patent received 15% more citations than those filed by control firms, suggesting that innovation activity and quality increased despite lower R&D expenditures. The paper attributes this innovation boost to reallocation through selective patent sales that allow target firms to focus on core expertise areas, performance-enhancing redeployment of staff inventors and stronger incentives for top managers.

4.1.3 *Innovation and Firm Ownership*

There is evidence that institutional ownership of firm equity shares may help to fuel innovation, but the mechanisms underlying the effect remain under some debate. Aghion *et al.* (2013) analyse U.S. firm-level data from 1991 through 1999 to examine whether institutional equity ownership of firms influences innovation activity, with emphasis on firm manager incentives. They find a positive relationship between innovation (proxied by cite-weighted patents) and institutional ownership of equity shares that is enhanced when product market competition intensifies. The authors interpret the results as supportive of a 'career concern' model, in which institutional investment promotes firm innovation by helping to protect managers against reputational damage when revenues are low. Without institutional investment, the market's perception of a manager's skill derives from observing firms' short-run revenues, which can reduce the manager's incentive to innovate. Institutional investors have incentives to monitor manager skill levels independent of revenue outcomes.

Schain and Stiebale (2016) build upon the methods of Aghion *et al.* (2013) by adding 'dependence on external finance' to the models, and challenge their results. They find that the positive association between institutional investment and innovation is substantially greater among firms that are highly financially dependent. A high-dependence subsample of industries shows that the effect of institutional investment on innovation is more than double that of the low-dependence subsample. The paper also notes the effect of competition is not significant after controlling for financial dependence. The authors conclude that financial constraints are a key driver of the effect of institutional investment on firm innovation, and that institutional investment helps to loosen these constraints.

Acharya and Xu (2017) compare publicly traded external finance-dependent and internal finance-dependent firms against privately held firms to assess effects on innovation. Using financial data on U.S. firms for 1994 to 2004, the authors employ regression models and matched firm samples to gain insights. The results show that public firms in external finance-dependent industries invest more in R&D and are more innovative than private firms, but this distinction between public and private firms does not apply to industries dependent on internal finance. The authors believe the positive effect of equity capital on firms in finance-dependent industries is due to the relaxation of financial constraints, but the effect of publicly traded finance on firms in internal finance-dependent industries generates less innovation due to the effect of short termism.

4.2 Direct Analyses of Finance and Productivity

A large set of theoretical and empirical research examines the relationship between finance and productivity in a more direct fashion than those reviewed above. The selected studies reviewed here reflect seminal work and trace the evolution of the field's knowledge. Table A2 in the supplementary material provides a brief summary of the studies discussed in this section.

4.2.1 Productivity Effects of Financial Development

Studies concentrating on periods when the financial sector was less developed tend to uncover stronger productivity benefits of more finance than studies using more recent data or countries where finance is more developed. An early study of the ties between financial development and economic growth also includes analysis of productivity growth: Levine and Zervos (1998) use banking and stock market data as measures of financial development for 47 countries from 1976 to 1993. Running separate models with the dependent variables of output growth and productivity growth, the authors test the influence of financial development by including banking and stock market variables in each model, along with control variables. The results show that both banking and stock market characteristics are positively linked to output and productivity growth, suggesting a complementarity between these forms of financing. The magnitudes of the effects appear substantial. For example, a one standard deviation increase in initial stock market liquidity and initial banking development would accumulate over the period of analysis to yield 24% higher productivity. The authors acknowledge the direction of causality is not established, which is not unusual for studies from this period.

Studies that directly link financial development and productivity generally find that it works through firm dynamism rather than allocation across existing firms. Andrews and Cingano (2014) find that more financial development and lower bank regulation stringency are linked with higher average productivity. The authors interpret this result as working through the mechanism of net firm entry (also known in reallocation studies as the extensive margin), meaning finance helps to improve productivity by reducing the share of lower productivity firms in the economy, consistent with the findings of Midrigan and Xu (2014). Indeed, Andrews and Cingano (2014) detect no clear evidence of a relationship between allocative efficiency and either financial development (using a credit metric) or bank regulation. They consider the potential effects of misallocation of resources linked to a range of policy frictions in 21 OECD nations in 2005 using a difference-in-differences model. They find that some policies, especially employment protection laws, reduce the efficiency of allocation of resources between existing firms.[8]

There is additional indirect evidence of firm dynamics–related productivity benefits of greater financial development. Bravo-Biosca et al. (2013) find such effects in firm-level data covering 10 OECD countries from 2002 to 2005.[9] In industries dependent on external finance, more developed financial institutions are associated with a more dynamic growth distribution of firms (fewer stable firms and more shrinking and growing firms), facilitating the reallocation of capital through the firm churning process. However, they fail to find a significant effect of financial development on multifactor productivity (MFP) in sectors highly dependent on external finance.

4.2.2 Productivity Implications of Financial Frictions

A strand of research investigates the impact of financial frictions on productivity or related outcomes using firm-level data. These studies explore the importance of external financing by testing the effects of borrowing constraints like borrowing ceilings, imperfect contract enforcement and collateral constraints. This literature suggests that financial frictions can slow economic growth and reduce productivity growth, and may be a key determining factor in cross-country productivity differences. They can take different forms:

- limits to contract monitoring and enforcement;
- collateral constraints;
- incentives created by insolvency regimes and
- adverse effects of bank regulatory or supervisory practices.

The rest of the section reviews the literature relating to these sources of financial frictions, before turning to the assessment of their effects that are measured indirectly through:

- differences in borrowing rates and
- accounting ratios.

Obstacles to contract monitoring and enforcement: Difficulties in monitoring or enforcing contracts are a potentially powerful source of financial frictions. A theoretical model put forth by Erosa and Hidalgo Cabrillana (2008) outlines how poor contract enforcement in developing countries may create a pernicious dynamic that results in persistently low aggregate TFP and wide-spread misallocation of resources, marked by the use of low productivity technologies and an unequal distribution of labour productivity across industries. The stylised model suggests that entrepreneurs borrowing from financial intermediaries have little incentive to provide accurate information about the value of their investment projects (due to limited enforcement), and general equilibrium price impacts (inflated output prices and low wages) make it profitable to operate low productivity businesses. Limited contract enforcement impedes factor mobility so that it fails to flow to higher productivity sectors, causing overallocation to less productive industries. Therefore, the financial friction described in the paper has far-reaching effects that distort incentives and results in slow growth and low productivity, which is consistent with the empirical data in some emerging economies.

On the empirical side, a recent study by Cole *et al.* (2016) models firm technology adoption decisions in India, Mexico and the United States with external financing as a critical determinant. They show that a financial system with long-term contracts and efficient performance monitoring promotes the adoption of advanced technologies that fuel higher productivity. Advanced production technologies entail high up-front investment costs (calling for external finance) and generate earnings late in the firm development cycle (requiring careful monitoring by financiers). Thus, only countries with efficient financing institutions and mechanisms can fund advanced technologies. India and Mexico's systems allow adoption of entry-level and intermediate-level technologies, which have lower financing needs and shorter pay-off horizons than does advanced technology. These technology choices help to explain the differences in TFP between these countries. The authors estimate that if India and Mexico had a financial system as well-developed as that of the USA, their TFP would jump by 46% and 43%, respectively, a result of adopting more advanced technologies.

A widely cited study by Buera *et al.* (2011) reveals that financial frictions can account for a large part of the cross-country variation in economic development by increasing gaps in labour productivity, aggregate TFP and capital to output ratios.[10] These frictions create distortions that misallocate capital and skew firm entry and exit decisions, which contribute to low TFP. The authors develop a stylised two-sector model of the effect of poor contract enforcement (financial friction) in developed and developing countries. The quantitative results show that frictions can have substantial effects, potentially reducing labour productivity by half and cutting TFP by one-third on average, relative to a perfect credit benchmark. Consistent with previous studies (e.g. Rajan and Zingales, 1998), it finds that sectors with better developed financing needs are more vulnerable to financial frictions. For example, manufacturing's high fixed costs and large efficient operating scales mean new entries require a large amount of external finance. When availability of finance is distorted through frictions, firm entry and exit diverge from the efficient path, in the more financially dependent manufacturing sector, but less so in the service sector, which has low fixed costs. By acting as a barrier to entry into manufacturing, financial frictions can raise prices of manufactured goods and lower productivity, a symptom of too few firms (therefore, less competition and less production) and too little exit (low productivity firms remain in the market) and entry. This extensive margin dynamic illustrates why the resource misallocation problem in the more financially dependent sectors is greater than in the less financially dependent ones. Misallocation of capital occurs mainly at the intensive margin (between firms) in the service sector, but almost entirely at the extensive margin in manufacturing. Therefore, the frictions are more likely to prevent new enterprises from entering the market when fixed costs are high, and tend to impede between-firm reallocation when fixed costs are lower.

Collateral constraints: Some studies model financial frictions in the form of collateral constraints and distortions.

Midrigan and Xu (2014) examine the productivity effects of misallocation at the intensive and extensive margins associated with financial frictions in the emerging country context, and find minor effects in the modern sector but major losses in the traditional sector. The authors develop a two-sector model calibrated to China, Colombia and South Korea to examine the effects of financial frictions in the form of collateral constraints on TFP. The model includes a traditional sector marked by low barriers to entry and low productivity, and a modern sector with high fixed costs and high productivity. In their model, businesses can self-finance investment from their earnings. However, traditional sector producers are unable to self-finance entry into the modern sector because their low margins preclude saving sufficient funds to meet the high start-up costs of the modern sector. Thus, financial frictions constrain entry into the more profitable modern sector. At the same time, earnings among enterprises in the modern sector are sufficient to self-fund some productive investment when financial frictions impede the acquisition of debt or equity funding. The analysis finds that financial frictions cause relatively modest 5% to 10% TFP losses in the modern sector through capital misallocation (intensive margin). In contrast, the frictions bite much harder in the traditional sector mainly by impeding entry into the more productive modern sector (extensive margin), with productivity losses of up to 40%.

Another form of financial friction related to collateral is discussed by Martin and Ventura (2015), who develop a stylised model of the dynamics of credit bubbles. The authors distinguish between 'fundamental' collateral based on a borrower's expected future production and income, and 'bubbly' collateral based on future borrowing. According to the model, when fundamental collateral is scarce, the conditions for the emergence of bubbly collateral improve. Bubbly collateral allows entrepreneurs to obtain more credit than would be merited by their expected earnings alone. If the bubbly credit is invested productively, it may enhance output and consumption (crowding-in effect), however, large bubbles can raise interest rates and reduce investment (crowding-out). Future productivity levels influence the scale of the crowding-out effects of bubbles. When future productivity is high (low), crowding-out effects will tend to be small (large).

Insolvency regimes, credit supply and productivity: The insolvency regime can generate financial frictions and affect productivity by imposing high costs on shutting down a business. Insolvency costs may take several forms and may have the ex ante effect of complicating the funding of fast-growing-but-risky firms and ex post effects of slowing the exit of low productivity firms and tying capital in low-productivity firms. This mechanism may be particularly important in the post-financial crisis environment due to the large volume of non-performing business debt held by financial institutions and the slow pace of resolution in many countries. At the same time, insolvency regimes with strong creditor protections can increase the supply of credit which may augment productivity enhancing investment, so the net effect on firm productivity remains an empirical question.

Bravo-Biosca *et al.* (2013) use firm-level data on 10 OECD countries from 2002 to 2005 to assess the effects of bankruptcy laws on productivity and find suggestive evidence of a negative relationship. They measure the stringency of bankruptcy laws with an index of creditor rights that incorporates four dimensions of creditors' rights in the event of a debtor's insolvency. Their direct analysis of the effects on productivity by firm characteristics finds that more stringent bankruptcy frameworks are associated with a decline in MFP growth in capital-intensive industries and MFP reduction in sectors with smaller minimum efficient production scales. Additional analysis offers indirect evidence on productivity effects based on firm growth distributions by firm characteristics. Firm growth distributions with relatively large shares of stable firms and small shares of shrinking and growing firms (e.g. Austria) are associated with low dynamism and limited reallocation of resources, whereas distributions with relatively modest shares of stable firms and substantial shares of shrinking and growing firms (e.g. USA) tend to reallocate resources more readily. This reallocation supports productivity growth if, on net, it shifts resources from less efficient firms to more efficient ones.[11] Generally, European countries have larger shares of stable firms than does the United States, but smaller shares of shrinking and growing firms. The study reports differences-in-differences between the 90th percentile (water transport) and 10th percentile (textiles) capital-intensive industries in the countries with the most protective (UK) and the least protective (USA) creditor rights regimes. It shows the difference in the share of high growth firms in the UK between these two sectors is roughly a third smaller than in the USA, and the difference in the share of stable firms is about 20% higher than in the USA, suggesting a less dynamic growth distribution of capital-intensive firms in countries with stronger creditor protections (more costly resolution processes for insolvent firms) in their bankruptcy regulations.

Andrews *et al.* (2014) provide evidence that bankruptcy law can materially affect capital flows to firms holding patents, a proxy for innovative firms. Using firm-level data for 23 OECD countries from 2002 to 2010, their simulation results show a decrease in the cost of the bankruptcy process from the high point (Italy) to the sample mean (France) would yield a 30% greater capital allocation to firms with patents. The results support the view that expectations of costly bankruptcies can discourage entrepreneurs' experimentation with higher risk, higher potential-return investments, and can sequester resources in older, low-productivity firms. These effects help slow growth and dampen firm turnover rates that contribute to productive reallocation in dynamic economies. At the same time, the authors caution that stronger protections for creditors reduces their risk exposure and may increase credit supply, so the net impact of stringent bankruptcy laws is uncertain.

Adalet McGowan *et al.* (2017) show that exit barriers contribute to higher industry shares of lagging firms. Using data on 17 European and Asian OECD countries from 2000–2002 to 2012–2014 they find that countries with high firm exit costs tend to have larger shares of financially unhealthy firms. Likewise, countries with slow-moving commercial courts tend to have more weak firms than do countries with efficient judicial systems. These results suggest that policies and practices that impede firm exit may trap resources in existing low productivity firms and hinder the entry of more productive firms.

While stronger creditor protections may raise insolvency costs for firms, they may also stimulate credit supply by lowering creditor risk, making the net effect on aggregate productivity an empirical question. In contrast to the preceding studies, Arnold and Flach's (2017) analysis focuses on the credit supply response of stronger creditor protections. It examines the 2005 policy reform in Brazil that strengthened creditor protections to test the impacts on allocation of resources across firms. Their model of the determinants of TFP growth includes log employment, initial productivity interacted with the reform, and controls. The study covers 1700 firms from 2000 to 2010. First, the policy reform increased the supply of credit, as predicted by Andrews *et al.* (2014). Second, the results show that firms that were initially more productive have larger post-reform productivity gains than do less initially productive firms, suggesting that the improved access to finance flows towards more productive firms. Third, decomposition of industry-level productivity shows that industries with high dependence on finance saw larger improvements in allocative efficiency (compared to those less dependent on finance) after the reform. The latter two results suggest that the growth in credit supply has productivity enhancing effects. However, the authors do not analyse the potential impacts of the policy reform on bankruptcy costs, which might be less favourable for firm productivity, as outlined by the preceding studies in this section.

Imperfect bank regulatory or supervisory practices: Financial frictions can also arise from imperfect bank regulation or supervision and result in lending practices that reduce productivity. Peek and Rosengren (2005) analyse the misallocation effects of poor regulatory practices and perverse incentives among Japanese banks in the 1990s that caused misallocation through an oversupply of credit to financially troubled firms. Using bank-level and firm-level data from 1993 to 1999, they build a probit model to predict the likelihood of bank lending to firms, while controlling for an array of bank and firm characteristics such as loan demand and firm capital structure. During this period, many Japanese banks faced internal and external incentives to continue lending to financially troubled firms with elevated default risk and low productivity. The internal incentive was to provide more credit to these firms so they could service their existing loans and avoid non-performing loan (NPL) status, which strengthened as a bank's risk-based capital ratio approached its required ratio. External incentives included government encouragement to lend to troubled firms to avoid potential firm bankruptcies (or bailouts) and the associated unemployment, and expectations that banks would continue to lend to firms within their 'keiretsu' corporate groups even when uncreditworthy. Results show robust evidence that supports the influence of each incentive. First, banks were more likely to provide additional funds to financially weaker firms than to financially healthier ones, and this effect was more pronounced among lenders with capital ratios within 2% of their capital requirement thresholds, and among banks with higher credit exposure to the firm. Second, firms that were keiretsu members were more likely to receive additional loans generally, and were likelier still to receive more credit from banks in the same keiretsu group. Third, government-controlled banks were also more likely to increase lending the more financially troubled the borrower firm was, which is suggestive of government complicity in this practice.

Interestingly, unaffiliated non-bank financial institutions behaved differently from banks, as they were less likely to lend more to the financially stressed firms. Overall, the analysis demonstrates the systematic misallocation of credit to the firms that were the least likely to put the funds to productive use, and likely fuelled the stagnation of productivity growth in Japan.

Studies have documented the negative productivity effects that arise when financial systems allow unprofitable firms to absorb excessive capital and labour:

- Caballero *et al.* (2008) find that the substantial market shares of persistently unprofitable Japanese firms ('zombie' firms) that were kept afloat by bank loans in the 1990s dampened productivity growth through two channels.[12] First, these low productivity firms' continued presence in the marketplace directly curtailed aggregate productivity. Second, they reduced the entry of more productive firms. Regressions show that higher industry shares of unprofitable firms are associated with lower investment and employment growth rates among healthy firms in the sector. The difference in productivity between zombie and healthy firms increases substantially as the share of former rises. For industries with high shares of zombie firms, the authors estimate the cumulative losses of investment attributable to their presence. For a typical healthy firm in the wholesale industry over 1993–2002, the cumulative forgone investment compared to the 1981–1992 average ranged between 17% and 43% of capital. Therefore, the evidence suggests that unprofitable firms that remained in business with support from banks crowded out the normal dynamic process of job and firm turnover that promotes productive reallocation. The distortions caused by these firms functioned in part through depressed prices for their products and increased wages, which together reduced incentives for new firm entry.
- Adalet McGowan *et al.* (2017) obtain similar findings when analysing firm-level data for nine European nations from 2003 to 2013.[13] They confirm the existence of spillover effects from zombie firms to healthy ones and find evidence that higher industry shares of zombie firms are linked to greater divergence in MFP between these firms and stronger firms (especially young ones). In a separate cross-sectional analysis of 13 European countries in 2013, the response of firm capital growth to lagged MFP shows more capital investment flows to higher productivity firms, but the flow is abated when industry shares of zombie firms are high, suggesting that resource reallocation may become less efficient.

Financial frictions measured indirectly through borrowing rates: Borrowing rate differentials, especially when they cannot be accounted for by observable risk factors, can serve to measure financial frictions and assess their impact on productivity. Gilchrist *et al.* (2013) develop an accounting framework calibrated to US manufacturing firms to assess empirically how financial frictions affect their factor input decisions and drive resource misallocation. The sample covers 496 firms with access to the corporate bond market from 1985 to 2010, which comprised half of domestic manufacturing sales over the period. Using dispersion in interest rate spreads of publicly traded firm debt to proxy financial frictions, the results suggest that US manufacturing TFP losses due to financial market distortions lie in a relatively modest range between 1.7% and 3.5%, assuming the distortions apply to both capital and labour markets. When the effect of the financial frictions are restricted to distort only capital input decisions, the TFP loss estimates decline by roughly 0.35 percentage points. A simulation wherein the authors increase by 10-fold the dispersion in firm-level borrowing costs yields a nearly 20% loss of TFP due to the associated financial distortion, a level that may be observed in only the least developed countries. The authors also analyse alternative firm structures, factor substitutability scenarios and how widely applicable the distortions are. They find that TFP losses due to financial market distortions are greater when the capital share in the production function is high, when substitutability between capital and other inputs is low and when the financial frictions apply to all production inputs.

Financial frictions measured indirectly through accounting ratios: Accounting ratios, such as book leverage, can provide indications about the cost of external financing and be related to productivity performance. In this vein, a recent study on financial frictions and productivity growth using firm-level data of four European countries from 2000 to 2010 yields a more nuanced finding. Levine and Warusawitharana (2016) estimate the effects of financing frictions on TFP growth due to investments in innovation using a generalised method of moments approach. First, they show that firm-level debt growth (their financing metric) has a positive link with future TFP growth, consistent with previous findings. Next, using the deviation of book leverage from the industry median as a proxy of the cost of debt and lagged deviation of a firm's cash holdings from the industry medians[14] interacted with debt growth to assess the effects of frictions, they find economically meaningful differences. For example, the difference in future productivity growth for a firm at the 25th percentile of financial frictions versus one at the 75th percentile varies from 0.1 to 1.6 percentage points, depending on the exogenous friction metric used. An alternative model using debt growth plus equity growth to proxy financing yields similar results, suggesting that the differences between debt and equity may not be readily discernible in this configuration (the share of capital funded by debt growth far exceeds equity growth in this sample and period).

Summary of the literature on financial frictions and productivity: To summarise this subsection, the evidence is consistent with the view that financial frictions applied to different samples of countries and periods of analysis consistently tend to reduce productivity. The evidence is particularly well developed for the manufacturing sector but it appears to hold for the service sector as well. In broad terms, productivity losses due to financial frictions in a country with a relatively efficient financial system like the USA appear modest (less than 5% of TFP). However, when policies and practices create inefficient incentives in finance, like in Japan in the 1990s, the associated misallocation can exert sharper downward pressure on productivity. In developing countries, financial frictions appear to explain a considerable portion of the productivity gap with developed nations, implying large and persistent productivity losses.

4.3 Studies Investigating Channels Other Than Firm-Level Frictions Through Which Financial Development Influences Productivity

A few studies explicitly examine the underlying channels, beyond firm-level frictions, through which financial development influences the productivity level or growth. Growth theory holds that in steady state, diminishing returns to the capital stock preclude this factor from functioning as the main channel of financial development's influence on long-run rising productivity. Possibly, the innovation channel has constant returns, making it a candidate for the channel that drives the persistent positive effect of financial development on growth and productivity (Madsen and Ang, 2016). Table A3 in the supplementary material summarises the studies in this section.

4.3.1 Direct Analyses of Potential Channels

Some studies have investigated the effect of financial development on TFP versus the accumulation of physical or human capital, with contrasting results:

- Levine and Zervos (1998) find positive effects of bank credit and stock market finance on capital accumulation and productivity growth.

- Beck *et al.* (2000) find that the main channel through which financial development influences economic growth is by fuelling higher TFP.[15] The authors arrive at this conclusion because they find a positive link from finance to growth but not to capital accumulation. Benhabib and Spiegel (2000) report evidence that financial development works through physical capital accumulation but not TFP growth.

One recent paper examines four potential transmission channels using long-run country-level data: knowledge production, savings, investment and education. Madsen and Ang (2016) use data of 21 OECD countries (over 1870–2009) to estimate four sets of models, each using a potential channel as the dependent variable to test the effect of financial development. They find that financial development is strongly positively related to each of the four channels. The central finding suggests that knowledge production is the main driver of financial development's positive effect on growth, contributing 0.43% to the annual average productivity growth rate for sample countries over the full period, compared to 0.18% for savings and 0.02% for tertiary education. The outcomes are robust to alternative metrics of financial development, alternative estimators, a longer time interval period to consider the possible effect of business cycles and allowing for disequilibrium in the housing market. The paper maintains the result is consistent with endogenous growth theory, which holds that long-run productivity growth depends on technology improvement. The authors suggest the policy should place emphasis on knowledge development, given its substantial role on transmitting the effect of financial development to productivity growth.

In summary, there are only few studies that directly examine the potential channels through which financial development influences economic or productivity growth. Broadly, the papers reviewed suggest that financial development boosts economic growth by facilitating productivity improvements. In turn, knowledge production and capital accumulation help fuel productivity. This survey places greater weight on the study by Madsen and Ang (2016) because of its OECD country sample, long time horizon and recent publication.

4.3.2 *Further Evidence on the Human Capital Channel*

Another mechanism through which finance might influence productivity is by facilitating access to higher education. While studies on the effect of education financing on firm or aggregate productivity are scarce, the empirical research shows positive linkages between education and productivity, but evidence of the relationship between finance and education appears mixed.

Both the theoretical and empirical literature suggests that formal education increases the earnings of individual workers. Even when controlling for the potential selection of individuals with higher ability and earnings capacity into higher education, the so-called 'ability bias', empirical studies still find a positive return to education. Harmon *et al.* (2000) review studies estimating the return to education on earnings, using different methodologies and datasets. The literature that studies the causal impact of training on earnings is scarcer and may also be affected by selection bias. Nonetheless, some empirical studies have found a positive impact of lifelong learning on labour income. For example, Vignoles *et al.* (2004) found a positive link between work-related training and earnings in the United Kingdom, using an instrumental variable approach with a model in first-differences to cancel out potential individual fixed-effects. Previously, Lynch (1992) estimated positive returns on earnings from formal employer provided training, previous off-the-job training and apprenticeships in the United States, controlling for the non-random assignment of individuals. To the extent that wages reflect the marginal productivity of workers, a differential in earnings between high-skill and low-skill individuals would indicate a gap in individual productivities.

Among the studies that directly investigate the relationship of education and training with measures of productivity, Black and Lynch (1996) present evidence using establishment-level survey data for the USA. They find that, depending on the econometric specification, a 10% increase in average education of the workforce in the establishment, may lead to an increase in productivity between 4.9% and 8.5% in the manufacturing sector, and between 5.9% and 12.7% in the non-manufacturing sector. They also find evidence on the positive impact of formal off-the-job training on productivity, measured as the dollar value of sales while controlling for the total number of labour hours. Blundell *et al.* (1999) provide a non-technical summary of the evidence on the returns to education for the individual, the firm and the economy at large, mainly for the UK. Among the returns for the firm, they consider the impact on firm productivity. Finally, for the overall economy, they summarise the macroeconomic evidence on the positive impact of education on aggregate productivity growth.

Another strand of the literature, starting with Becker (1967), argues that financial constraints hinder investment in human capital accumulation. This idea relies on the observation that, conditional on ability, college attendance is strongly correlated with family income and wealth, as documented in Lochner and Monge-Naranjo (2011). Lochner and Monge-Naranjo (2012) review studies of the impact of credit constraints on the education decision. They show that incorporating credit constraints in a simple two-period model of human capital investment helps explain observed borrowing, schooling and default patterns in the United States. Nevertheless, there is some ambiguity in the literature on the impact of borrowing constraints on formal education investment. Keane and Wolpin (2001) find that, while youth seem to be severely financially constrained in their consumption decisions, the relaxation of borrowing constraints would barely affect college attendance decisions. The same conclusion emerges in Cameron and Taber (2004) who find no evidence that borrowing constraints generate inefficiencies in the market for schooling. More recently, using a macroeconomic dataset for 21 OECD countries over the period 1870 to 2009 and a reduced form approach, Madsen and Ang (2016) find that financial development, measured by the ratios of credit to GDP, bank assets to GDP and monetary stock to GDP, has a positive impact on gross enrolment rates in secondary and tertiary education. Although financial development may be correlated with lower financial constraints, it should be noted that these are different concepts. As previously mentioned, frictions in a highly developed financial system may still result in significant credit constraints.

Formal education is not the only component of human capital accumulation. However, absent from the literature is research on the potential impact that financial constraints and financial development may have on post-education or lifelong training investment, which has also been shown to positively affect productivity.

Another related issue concerns the impact of student debt on occupational choices and whether this could have an indirect effect on productivity. For instance, Rothstein and Rouse (2011), using a natural experiment in the USA, find that high levels of student debt causes graduates to choose higher salary jobs as opposed to low-paid public sector jobs. Assuming that wages partly reflect the productivity of different occupations, higher levels of student debt could work as an incentive to look for highly productive jobs.

4.3.3 *Potential Influences of Corporate Finance on Productivity*

The literature reported above strongly suggests that the structure of corporate finance has a systematic bearing on firm productivity outcomes. A recent analysis of 11,000 multinational firms covering the period 2002 to 2015 by the OECD (2016a) uses descriptive assessments (not regression based) of firms ordered by deciles of labour productivity growth to consider their relationship with key corporate finance characteristics in order to illustrate some mechanisms through which finance may link to productivity. It finds suggestive evidence that the following practices are associated with firms that have higher productivity growth in advanced economies.

- *Sustained R&D investments.* Firms with higher productivity growth have more sustained growth in their R&D investments than do lower productivity growth firms. The authors regard R&D as an important engine of technological progress and product innovation.
- *Stable equity financing.* Maintaining stable equity financing ratios in the face of external shifts like the financial crisis is a sign that firms concentrate on long-run investment and returns. In advanced economies, the lower productivity growth decile firms substantially increased their debt-to-capital ratios in the post-crisis period, while higher productivity growth firms kept their debt and equity ratios steady across the two periods.
- *Stable free cash flow.* Higher productivity growth firms tend to have greater and more stable free cash flow ratios, than do lower productivity growth firms. Free cash flow can serve as a buffer for firms when short-run fluctuations occur, and allow them to concentrate on their long-run objectives.
- *Merger and acquisition (M&A) activity.* M&A activity was elevated among the lowest productivity growth firms and the highest productivity growth firms. While specific M&A deals may be either productivity-enhancing or productivity-inhibiting depending on the market structure and intentions of the acquiring firm, on the whole, this activity is associated with higher productivity growth. M&A activity frequently requires external financing to execute, so the availability of finance may be a critical factor in realising these potential productivity gains.

The literature provides evidence supporting the favourable productivity effects of M&A activity found by OECD (2016a). There is a vast literature suggesting that M&As create value for the acquirer and target stockholders. These positive returns reflect the market's expectations that mergers will generate efficiency gains, market power gains, or both. Surprisingly, however, there is little evidence on whether such expectations materialise (Kaplan, 2000). A recent study by Li (2013) shows that acquiring firms increase the productivity of targets through more efficient use of investments and labour, as well as through the closure of inefficient plants. The author finds that the target firm's TFP increases relative to comparable firms following the takeover. A similar conclusion is reached by Siegel and Simons (2010), who find that M&As improve the sorting and matching of plants and workers to more efficient uses, using a linked employer–employee dataset that covers all Swedish manufacturing firms and employees.

Since the financial structure of businesses seems to influence the probability that a takeover succeeds, it may indirectly affect productivity gains at the plant level through its impact on M&As. There is evidence that highly leveraged firms are less successful at acquiring targets, starting with Bruner (1988), Clayton and Ravid (2002) and later Uysal (2011). A potential mechanism through which financial structure influences the likelihood of a successful acquisition is the degree to which a potential acquirer firm is leveraged. Less leveraged firms may be able to pay higher premiums than other bidders.

4.3.4 *Studies of Contributions from Efficiency Gains Within Finance to Aggregate Productivity*

Financial development can also contribute to aggregate productivity through the efficiency gains it may generate within the financial sector itself. Some studies have considered that, in the late 1990s, the financial sector improved its own efficiency so much that it contributed substantially to economy-wide productivity growth. Van Ark *et al.* (2003) reckon that the securities-trading industry contributed 0.37 percentage points (and the rest of the financial sector 0.07 percentage points) to the 2.5% per annum increase in labour productivity that the US economy experienced between 1995 and 2000. Van Ark *et al.* (2003, 2008) attribute this strong contribution, which was not observed in the EU economy during the same period, to the deployment of efficiency-enhancing information and communication technologies (ICT) by US brokers and securities dealers. This more efficient use of ICT in securities trading as well as in retail trade was an important driver of the productivity gap between Europe and the United States (Gordon, 2004; van Ark *et al.*, 2008).

However, the huge estimated labour productivity growth within the US brokerage industry in 1995–2001 (9.1% per annum according to Triplett and Bosworth, 2004) seems to owe much to the dotcom bubble and measurement issues (Hartwig, 2008). In particular, the key role played by the number of trades when measuring the US securities industry's output volume strongly boosted volume growth in a period characterised by a rapid rise in trading activity.

4.3.5 *Studies About Productivity Within the Financial Sector*

The rise of very large banks and resulting high concentration in banking has raised questions about whether the cost of weaker competition might be offset by scale economies. Studies on bank economies of scale offer some insight on the productivity implications of bank size.[16] This issue has high salience in the post-recession era as regulatory reform processes may consider placing requirements on large banks that directly or indirectly limit their operating scale. If policy measures lead to the break-up of large banks or effectively limit their size, costs could arise through the loss of economies of scale in the banking sector, but much of the empirical literature finds that financial activities involve no significant economies of scope or scale beyond a relatively small size (see Amel *et al.* 2004, for a survey). Recent research casts doubt on the apparent economies of scale at very large banks and finds they disappear when adjusting for too-big-to-fail subsidies (Davies and Tracey, 2014), although the evidence is not unanimous.[17] This result suggests that systemic risk associated with the failure of large banks may be reduced without efficiency effects from the loss of scale economies of large banks.

Another channel through which too-big-to-fail subsidies arguably have found their way into the real economy, with potential consequences for productivity, is overly high pay in finance. In Europe, the financial sector wage premium (or how much financial employees receive in excess of what similar workers are paid in other industries) is 25% of average earnings (Denk, 2015a). It rises across the earnings distribution, reaching nearly 40% for top-paid workers. High wage premiums are one reason why finance is the industry most disproportionately represented among the top 1% earners (Denk, 2015b). Such financial rents are a symptom of excessive returns to the conduct of banking activities and are likely to reduce productivity, not least considering the importance of banking services as inputs for other industries.

4.4 *Financial Liberalisation and Productivity*

Empirical analyses suggest that financial liberalisation is closely associated with gains in productivity. This evidence comes from cross-country studies using macro data and is corroborated by single-country studies based on micro data. Most of the cross-country papers identify increased investment as a key mechanism through which financial openness fuels productivity growth but they offer limited descriptive detail, given their macro view. Varela (2017) helps to fill this gap by using firm-level data to assess how businesses responded to the lifting of controls on international capital flows in Hungary. Table A4 in the supplementary material summarises the studies in this section.

Bonfiglioli (2008) assesses the relationship between international financial openness and two major GDP growth determinants (TFP and capital investment) based on sample of 70 countries observed from 1975 to 1999. Using instrumented GMM models with panel data that control for a range of factors, she finds a direct positive effect of financial liberalisation[18] on TFP, especially for developed countries. On average, the scale of the effect on productivity is meaningful, with TFP growth of liberalised countries outperforming closed ones by an estimated 11% to 15% over a five-year period. However, the models fail to find direct associations between liberalisation and capital accumulation. Thus, improved access to capital provided through liberalisation does not immediately appear to unleash additional investment, which runs counter to other studies' findings. One potential explanation for these results suggested by the author is that liberalisation may trigger greater specialisation and competition that lead to more efficient allocation of resources which boosts productivity and growth without necessarily increasing capital accumulation. Declining markups and increased firm entry/exit rates observed in liberalised countries are consistent with intensified competition.

Bekaert *et al.* (2011) use country-level data for up to 96 nations from 1980 to 2006 in their regression models examining how liberalisation influences productivity and growth. They find that financial openness[19] is positively associated with both capital stock growth and TFP growth, and the latter accounts for nearly two-thirds of the overall real GDP growth effects. The results support the view that the presence of foreign investors helps to allocate investment capital more efficiently. A test of the persistence of the growth effects of financial liberalisation shows that it imparts both temporary and long-run positive effects on GDP growth rates, suggesting the impacts are not merely transitory. The paper attributes the favourable growth effects of liberalisation to its effects on financial development (stock market and banking development) which increase liquidity, market capitalisation and credit flows.

A study of 25 developing countries by Chari *et al.* (2012) provides further evidence that opening stock markets to foreign capital inflows boosts productivity growth rates. The analysis uses difference-in-differences regression models split into countries experiencing a stock market liberalisation event between 1986 and 1996 (treatment group) and similar nations without market liberalisation (control group). The authors find economically meaningful short-term increases in productivity growth and wage growth associated with liberalisation. The productivity model estimates an average difference in the growth of annual real value-added per worker of 9.7 percentage points in the treatment countries over the control group during a three-year liberalisation impact period.[20] The paper notes that a key mechanism through which open stock markets can boost productivity growth in developing countries is by accelerating physical capital imports that embody efficient production technologies.

Varela (2017) analyses the effects of a relaxation of capital controls on productivity, using firm-level data in Hungary. Prior to liberalisation, capital controls constrained access to international capital markets for domestic firms, while international firms could readily access these markets. Reforms eliminating the capital controls in 2001 substantially improved terms of credit and increased leverage for domestic firms, but not for foreign firms (who were not capital constrained). This reallocation of capital towards domestic firms helped to spur faster growth relative to international firms in capital intensity (by 0.252 log points), labour productivity (by 0.053 log points) and revenue TFP (by 0.032 log points). The paper identifies two likely channels through which increased access to finance improved productivity growth. One, after capital controls reform, domestic firms financed increased investments in technology, as their probabilities of conducting R&D and innovation activities grew by 9% and 12%, respectively. Two, international firms increased their own technology investments in response to the heightened competitiveness of domestic firms, shown by the reduction of the former's price markups. Consistent with this interpretation, the author demonstrates that the impressive post-reform acceleration in Hungary's aggregate productivity growth was driven by within-firm technical efficiency improvements with a minor contribution from reallocation effects.

4.5 Non-Debt Finance and Productivity[21]

As identified in previous empirical work, a substantial presence of younger firms in a market tends to contribute to dynamism both through their high turnover rates and the relatively rapid growth of the survivors among them. Young firms tend to be more dependent on external financing than are older firms as they establish their place in the market and attempt to grow. However, accessing debt financing can be challenging for younger firms for several reasons. For example, they often lack a sufficient capital stock to serve as loan collateral, they typically have volatile revenue histories, and the probability of adverse selection problems may be elevated. These conditions raise the level of uncertainty and risk to potential lenders and may be a barrier to credit provision. In principle, young firms may be better suited to access equity and other forms of non-debt capital. Equity does not add to the firm's leverage (and insolvency risk), it avoids the adverse selection issue, does not require collateral and may allow closer investor monitoring of firm actions and performance (Brown et al., 2009). Table A5 in the supplementary material provides a summary of the studies covered in this section.

4.5.1 Studies of an Indirect Link Between Equity Finance and Productivity

There are few empirical studies looking directly at equity finance and productivity. In order to increase the volume of available studies, this survey widens its scope to include those that may offer indirect insights.

An indirect perspective examines the potential role of equity finance on R&D investment and finds a positive role:

- Brown et al. (2009) develop a model consistent with the endogenous growth literature for US technology firms from 1990 to 2004, a period that witnessed dramatic growth, then downturns, in both equity market capitalisation and R&D investment. In this sector, equity finance dominates debt finance by a large margin. Among young (up to 15 year old) firms, internal and external equity finance are significant drivers of R&D, but no such link exists for older firms. The authors suggest this contrast may be due to the facts that younger firms largely drove the expansion and subsequent contraction in R&D, and that the younger firms may be substantially more financially constrained than older firms, which rely more on internal funding. They note that the observed increase in non-farm labour productivity growth beginning two to three years after the R&D run-up started suggests these equity-aided investments provided a boost to productivity.

- Brown *et al.* (2012) find that stock issuances are consistently positively related to R&D in 16 European countries. The relationship is particularly strong among young firms and small enterprises, which may be more innovative than other firms and in greater need of financing.

A study of 32 developed and developing countries suggests that innovation activity is positively linked to well-developed equity markets but not to credit markets. Hsu *et al.* (2014) use fixed effects panel models with data from 1976 through 2006 to explain five proxies for innovation. Results consistently show that among sectors that are dependent on external finance, more developed equity markets promote increased innovation, but more developed credit markets are associated with *reduced* innovation in these sectors. For example, the number of patents in an industry with average dependence on external finance increase by an estimated 4.2% (fall by 9.9%) in a country with equity market (credit market) development at the 75th percentile relative to a country at the 25th percentile. Likewise, the authors find that equity market development encourages innovation in high-tech industries but credit market development is associated with lower innovation rates in these industries.

Thus, it appears that equity finance plays a prominent role in facilitating activities that support productivity growth, however, the evidence is not unanimous. One study tends to find no specific role of equity finance, though it is not fully developed in this regard. Levine and Warusawitharana (2016) show that financial frictions increase the sensitivity of future productivity growth to debt growth in individual sample countries and in the aggregate. An alternative model using debt plus equity growth to proxy financing yields similar results, suggesting that the differences between debt and equity may not be readily discernible in this configuration (the share of capital represented by debt growth far exceeds equity growth in this sample and period). The authors do not report running the model using equity growth alone to proxy finance.

4.5.2 *Studies of a Direct Link Between Non-Debt Finance and Productivity*

One study uses both equity and debt indicators of financial development in models that assess potential influences on economic and productivity growth. Levine and Zervos (1998) use stock market capitalisation and liquidity indicators in their models. Including both banking and stock market indicators in their models, the results show that bank credit and stock market liquidity and value traded are positively related to GDP and productivity growth (stock market liquidity is the most robust of the equity metrics). A characteristic of stocks is that they allow investors to easily buy or sell shares, and the paper notes that this liquidity may improve efficient allocation of resources, capital formation and growth. The significance of both banking and stock market variables in the regressions signals that both types of financial development may facilitate productivity.

Venture capital (VC) appears to have positive effects on firm productivity, especially for young firms. Chemmanur *et al.* (2011) research the effects of VC on productivity among more than 187,000 US private manufacturing firms from 1972 to 2000. Their analysis offers insights on the effects of VC and the channels through which they operate. The study provides strong evidence that firms receiving VC have better productivity performance both before and after the capital infusions than do firms not receiving it, suggesting that VC firms impart both a 'screening' effect (investing in more efficient firms) and a 'monitoring' effect (assisting and monitoring post-investment performance). On average, over the five years prior to the start of the VC finance, firms receiving VC had 7% higher TFP than non-VC recipient firms (screening effect). In each of the five years after receiving initial VC financing, these firms' TFP growth rates exceeded those of non-VC firms by between 5.5 and 14 percentage points (monitoring effect). Both the estimated screening effect and the monitoring results are economically meaningful and may roughly translate into 24% and 42% higher profits, respectively, according to the study. When dividing the sample into firms receiving initial VC finance at an early start-up stage and those receiving it at a later stage, the evidence shows that while both groups had screening effects of similar magnitudes, the former group shows a substantially greater monitoring effect. This suggests that VC engagement of firms early in their development cycles may yield greater productivity gains later.

Research suggests a positive link between innovation and productivity growth. For example, a simulation analysis using a 2009–2003 long difference model by Andrews *et al.* (2014) shows a 10% rise in the patent stock is associated with a roughly 2% increase in TFP.[22] More resources flow to firms holding patents in countries with better developed financial markets than to firms without patents in those countries. This is consistent with the previous research (which does not distinguish between firms with and without patents) showing that financing plays an important facilitating role in helping capital constrained firms establish themselves in the marketplace. Andrews *et al.* (2014) find that access to VC may be particularly valuable for young firms with patents, wherein patents serve as proxies for firm innovation. Their simulation analysis shows that capital flows to firms with patents would increase by one-third if the country with the lowest VC supply in the sample of 23 OECD countries were lifted to the sample average level.

While equity financing in the form of stock market issuances and VC are well known, private equity financing may also influence firm productivity growth. Private equity entities often aim to acquire control of target firms, implement restructuring plans and then sell or take them public, in an effort to raise the value of the target firm and earn returns for investors. A study by Davis *et al.* (2014) constructs a large dataset of 3200 US firms (target firms) acquired through buyouts between 1980 and 2005 consisting of 150,000 domestic plants and compares them with similar non-acquired firms (control firms) across a wide range of characteristics to assess the potential effects of private equity on productivity. In the two years after a buyout, the study finds that private equity buyouts increase TFP by 2.1 log points among target firms, while baseline TFP growth among control firms is slightly negative. Compared with control firms, target firms are roughly twice as likely to shut down low productivity plants and twice as likely to open new highly productive plants, and this accounts for three-quarters of these TFP gains among target firms.

4.6 *Business Cycles, Finance and Productivity*

The early empirical research on business cycles and productivity, which to a large extent left financial market imperfections aside, concluded that recessions had favourable net effects on resource allocation, supporting Schumpeter's notion of 'creative destruction'. These periods of economic stress were seen as facilitating the process of productivity-enhancing reallocation, in part by sweeping away the least efficient producers, allowing resources to be shifted to more productive uses (e.g. see Davis and Haltiwanger, 1990; Caballero and Hammour, 1994). Table A6 in the supplementary material summarises the studies discussed in this section.

Subsequent analyses reveal a more complex view of business cycle and productivity dynamics by incorporating financial-market imperfections into models. These studies find that under the conditions prevalent during recessions, distortions in credit market incentives can have counterintuitive effects and hamper rather than boost reallocation:

- Barlevy (2003) uses a general equilibrium model to show that well-functioning credit markets during recessions can foster productivity-enhancing *reallocation*. However, in the presence of market frictions, recessions can result in increased *misallocation*. This result emerges from a stylised condition marked by severe liquidity constraints such that creditors have incentives to lend to businesses that require smaller loans, even if they are less productive than businesses seeking larger loans, because lenders perceive their losses in the event of default would be smaller.
- When external funders are imperfectly informed, recessions can have negative effects on reallocation by depriving promising firms of sufficient time to develop and signal their potential. A simulation model by Ouyang (2009) calibrated to the US manufacturing sector uses data on firm entry, exit and productivity to estimate the recessions' potential opposing effects of 'cleansing' and 'scarring'. The cleansing effect of recessions is the notion that recessions improve resource allocation by accelerating the exit of low productivity firms and redirecting their resources to more productive uses. The scarring effect is the idea that recessions induce responses by firms that reduce average productivity. Recessions may force young firms to exit before the firms have sufficient time to learn by doing and reveal themselves to external funders as being potentially efficient. This implies that some share of exiting young firms during a recession would have become high productivity firms had they remained in the market, but the opportunity for them to become productive vanishes when they exit.[23] The model proxies recessions as negative demand shocks causing a drop in prices that shifts firm exit margins leftward. Simulation outcomes show that the long-run scarring effects dominate the cleansing effects, signalling that recessions contribute to net *reductions* in productivity.

The debate is not settled, as other analysis suggests that the positive effects may dominate the negative ones, even in the presence of financial frictions. Osoteimehin and Pappada (2015) develop a model calibrated to the United States from 1994 to 2012 to illustrate firm dynamics with credit frictions and endogenous firm entry and exit to test the cleansing hypothesis of recessions. The model simulates a productivity shock and a financial crisis shock, both with and without financial frictions. The simulations show that in the absence of financial frictions, both types of shocks lead to increased exit rates of lower productivity firms, resulting in higher average productivity among surviving firms and confirming a cleansing effect. The presence of financial frictions modifies the exit and entry decisions of firms by including their net worth (which is not always well aligned with their productive efficiency) in the equation, but both types of shocks still impart a cleansing effect, although a diminished one. One influential factor in the simulations is that more productive firms tend to be larger and therefore need more financing, which makes them more sensitive to the effects of financial frictions than less productive firms. However, this sensitivity is insufficiently strong to overturn the general prevalence for less productive firms to exit before more productive firms.

In contrast to the effect of liquidity *constraints*, finance might also influence productivity growth through rapid *expansion* of credit provision. Borio *et al.* (2015) use one digit sector-level data on 21 developed economies from 1969 to 2009 to shed light on the relationship between credit booms, aggregate productivity and financial crises. The results show that on average, credit booms[24] tend to reduce contemporaneous aggregate labour productivity growth by roughly one-quarter percentage point annually, an economically meaningful decrease. This decline in productivity growth is driven mainly by reallocation of labour to lower productivity sectors during the credit boom period.[25] In combination, employment expansion in the relatively low productivity construction sector and employment shrinkage or slower job growth in the relatively high productivity manufacturing sector account for most of this productivity loss from reallocation. The study also assesses the effect of financial crises after credit booms on labour productivity, and shows that the misallocation effects of boom periods intensify and become considerably more persistent when the credit boom is followed by a financial crisis.

Analysis contends that both cyclical and long-term structural factors have contributed to the slowdown in productivity growth, with each type of factor accounting for half of the decline since the global financial crisis (OECD, 2016b; Denk and Kastrop, 2016). An important cyclical driver for the slowdown in productivity has been very weak investment. Investment rates have yet to recover and remain a drag on productivity growth, especially in Europe. Besides poor demand and world economic growth prospects and a slowing of pro-competitive policy reforms, high financing costs in some markets are a reason why investment remains low.

To sum up this subsection, the literature on business cycles and productivity appears inconclusive, with both evidence to support a cleansing effect of recessions and contrary evidence suggesting that frictions during recessions counteract the cleansing effect. The extent to which these frictions impede improvements in overall productivity depend in part on idiosyncratic characteristics of the models used to identify them. Some of these models use calibrated simulations based on limited empirical data. Fuller empirical cross-country analysis would be helpful in determining how much financial frictions affect the potential productivity improvements generated during periods of recession.

5. Summary

Research on productivity and finance has been evolving rapidly in the current decade, due in part to the heightened priority ascribed to productivity analysis on the policy research agenda and the greater availability of firm-level and plant-level data that are harmonised across countries. This evolution has allowed researchers to analyse interfirm dynamics and the channels that drive them. In turn, the recent empirical literature provides fresh insights that may inform policy development to help enact finance related measures that more effectively promote productivity growth.

5.1 *Finance and Productivity*

Mounting empirical evidence demonstrates that finance is an important contributor to productivity growth, but there are also productivity losses due to financial frictions (eight direct analyses reviewed). Both single-country and cross-country studies agree that a range of different financial frictions can hinder productivity growth by impeding optimal resource allocation. The channels through which this result occurs vary depending on the country and type of financial friction considered. These frictions can reduce competition, impair capital investment, diminish advanced technology adoption and distort incentives to efficient capital allocation. There is some evidence that suggests that financial frictions can explain a sizeable share of the differences in productivity between developed and developing countries (two studies reviewed).

5.2 *Insolvency Regimes and Productivity*

When firm insolvency policies result in high costs for exiting firms, low productivity firms may be less likely to leave the market, thereby tying up resources that could be reallocated to more productive uses. Recent firm-level analyses of firm exit policies show the direct productivity effects of firm exit may be exceeded by the indirect impact of spillovers to factor and product prices. These spillovers can stifle new firm entry, and impede shifts in market shares to more efficient competitors, resulting in missed opportunities for productivity growth. These findings lend further support for reforms of firm exit policies (four quantitative insolvency studies reviewed).

5.3 *Transmission Channels*

The limited direct research on channels suggests that a primary driver of productivity growth is knowledge production, which can have sustained effects on productivity through positive scale effects (four studies on transmission reviewed). Increased human capital through education and training is closely linked to higher labour productivity, yet evidence that the availability of financing facilitates higher educational attainment is tenuous (eight quantitative human capital studies reviewed).

5.4 *M&A and Productivity*

On the whole, M&A activity is associated with gains in productivity. This result comes mainly from higher investment, matching of labour to productive uses and closures of less productive plants after completion of the merger or acquisition (six studies reviewed).

5.5 *Direct Contributions of the Financial Sector to Productivity Improvement*

Efficiency improvements in the US financial sector during the late 1990s were substantial enough to contribute measurably to economy-wide productivity growth. However, these outsized improvements have not persisted and appear tied to the internet stock market bubble (four studies reviewed). More broadly, recent research on bank economies of scale is mixed and does not necessarily support the view that the largest banks realise efficiency gains after controlling for implicit subsidies (two studies on scale economies reviewed).

5.6 *Financial Liberalisation and Productivity*

Cross-country and single-country studies agree that financial liberalisation such as stock market opening and lifting of foreign capital controls is associated with economically meaningful aggregate productivity gains. Most of the recent research finds that improved access to capital via liberalisation boosts investment and improves resource allocation (four studies on financial liberalisation reviewed).

5.7 *Equity Finance and Productivity*

The research suggests that availability of equity financing is particularly valuable for the growth of young and small enterprises and it remains the primary external source for funding R&D. More broadly, equity finance is associated with economic growth while debt financing beyond a certain threshold is linked to declining growth, and equity can improve firm and systemic stability by reducing leverage rates. These characteristics strengthen the case for enacting measures that would help to develop equity markets and removing policies such as debt bias in taxation that favour debt financing (four analyses reviewed).

5.8 *Alternative Finance and Productivity*

A central purpose of risk finance is to provide financial and mentoring support to the type of young, developing enterprises that can yield sizeable productivity gains through new products or production approaches considered too risky by many creditors. Recent evidence shows that the presence of VC investors improves opportunities for young firms to access capital in a marketplace that otherwise may deny them financing, likely due to limited risk appetite among intermediaries and lack of access to capital markets. Firms receiving VC finance have substantially higher post-VC finance productivity growth than similar firms not receiving VC, and this effect is amplified when initial VC flows occur at an early stage of firm development (three studies reviewed).

5.9 *Business Cycles and Productivity*

Recent studies of both periods of economic decline and booms suggest that business cycle influences on productivity are inconclusive. There is evidence of both pro-cyclical and counter-cyclical influences on productivity, with the effects of economic cycles flowing through different mechanisms. One common factor among the studies shows that the presence of financial frictions during cycles can alter the direction and strength of a cycle's productivity impacts. The recent Great Recession saw less productivity-enhancing reallocation than did earlier recessions (five studies reviewed).

The preceding summary highlights some recent areas where the productivity and finance literature has sharpened its focus and improved the understanding of the current conditions and their policy linkages. These studies offer stronger guidance for policy development than did previous generations of research. Nonetheless, this work has not answered all the questions, and ample opportunities for deeper analysis remain, in particular to document how, across countries, financial policies and structures shape the capacity of firms to enhance productivity. Much of the existing research focuses on one or a few countries. For policy advice, it will hence be important to identify empirical regularities, as well as differences across countries.

Notes

1. The private credit growth trend refers to the period 1961 to 2007, and the stock market capitalisation trend covers 1975–2007. Both are based on OECD averages across member countries.
2. This snapshot diagram is in no way an exhaustive explanation of productivity and finance dynamics. To maintain simplicity, it omits several potential influences and linkages between the existing elements. Its intent is to highlight some key interactions between productivity, finance and policy.
3. Related factors such as the efficiency of the judicial system may amplify or counteract the effect of insolvency rules depending on their directions of influence, but this illustrative discussion focuses on the latter for simplicity.
4. See Heil (2017) for a more detailed discussion of the finance and growth literature.
5. This is the Europe component of a large database of finance, corporate structure and other detailed firm-level information on public and private firms, provided by Bureau Van Dijk.
6. This review does not cover studies on intangible capital, but its role should be acknowledged. The growing literature on the productivity impacts of intangible capital (including

R&D) suggests that this investment robustly improves labour productivity growth, and the magnitude of the contribution may vary by sector, period and country. See Corrado *et al.* (2009), Roth and Thum (2013) and Niebel *et al.* (2017) for analyses.

7. The financial development indicators are the domestic private credit to GDP ratio and the domestic stock market capitalisation to GDP ratio.

8. Allocative efficiency is the within-sector covariance between a firm's size and its productivity level.

9. Here, financial development is measured by an index consisting of the sum of stock and bond market capitalisation plus private bank credit all divided by GDP. The metric captures both debt and equity.

10. The paper models financial frictions as endogenous collateral constraints based on imperfect enforceability of contracts.

11. This is the case in the absence of offsetting firm-internal MFP growth.

12. Caballero *et al.* (2008) define zombie firms as those that receive subsidised credit.

13. Adalet McGowan *et al.* (2017) define zombie firms as those more than 10 years old with an interest coverage ratio under one for three consecutive years. Their robustness analysis experiments with alternative time periods and age thresholds.

14. As these firm-level financial friction indicators are endogenous to firms' choices, the authors also use the sovereign debt spread between a country's 10-year sovereign bond and the 10-year German bond as a metric that is exogenous to individual firms.

15. Their main financial development measure is 'private credit' which is the aggregate value of financial intermediary credit to the private sector as a share of GDP. Additional metrics used include 'liquid liabilities' (liquid liabilities of the financial system) and 'commercial-central bank' which measures the scope of commercial banks in the economy. The study does not use an indicator of equity finance.

16. This discussion draws on Cournède *et al.* (2015).

17. Hughes and Mester (2013) also adjust for too-big-to-fail subsidies, and continue to find economies of scale. The contrasting results may be due to distinct methods and substantial differences in the composition of sample banks (banks with assets over $100 billion make up over half of the sample observations of Davies and Tracey (2014), but just 2% of Hughes and Mester (2013)).

18. The paper uses three distinct measures of liberalisation: the IMF indicator of capital account liberalisation from its Annual Report on Exchange Arrangements and Exchange Arrears; the Quinn index of capital account liberalisation and (total foreign assets + foreign total liabilities) / GDP.

19. The paper uses three financial openness metrics: the Quinn capital account liberalisation indicator; a measure of whether foreign investors officially are allowed to invest in domestic equity securities and an intensity equity market liberalisation indicator that gauges the degree to which domestic stocks are open to foreign investors.

20. Based on additional statistical tests, authors believe this effect is unlikely to be caused by domestic economic reforms or by external shocks.

21. Alternative finance here refers mainly to non-debt finance, and includes equity and risk finance.

22. Similarly, Égert (2016) finds higher innovation intensity is positively associated with increased MFP.

23. The model provides no clear mechanism for a firm or its constituent resources to return to the market after exit.

24. The study proxies credit boom periods by the growth rate of private credit to GDP ratio.
25. The analysis does not account for within-sector or within-firm reallocation.

References

Acharya, V. and Xu, Z. (2017) Financial dependence and innovation: the case of public versus private firms. *Journal of Financial Economics* 124: 223–243.

Adalet McGowan, M., Andrews, D. and Millot, V. (2017) The walking dead? Zombie firms and productivity performance in OECD countries. OECD Economics Department Working Papers, No. 1372. OECD Publishing, Paris.

Aghion, P., Van Reenen, J. and Zingales, L. (2013) Innovation and institutional ownership. *American Economic Review* 103: 277–304.

Amel, D., Barnes, C., Panetta, F. and Saleo, C. (2004) Consolidation and efficiency in the financial sector: a review of the international evidence. *Journal of Banking and Finance* 28: 2493–2519.

Andrews, D. and Cingano, F. (2014) Public policy and resource allocation: evidence from firms in OECD countries. OECD Economics Department Working Papers. OECD Publishing, Paris.

Andrews, D., Criscuolo, C. and Menon, C. (2014) Do resources flow to patenting firms? Cross-country evidence from firm level data. OECD Economics Department Working Papers, No. 1127. OECD Publishing, Paris.

Arnold, J.M. and Flach, L. (2017) Who gains from better access to credit? Heterogeneous firm responses and the reallocation of resources. OECD Economics Department Working Papers, forthcoming.

Barleavy, G. (2003) Credit market frictions and the allocation of resources over the business cycle. *Journal of Monetary Economics* 50: 1795–1818.

Beck, T., Levine, R. and Loayza, N. (2000) Finance and the sources of growth. *Journal of Financial Economics* 58: 261–300.

Becker, G. (1967) Human capital and the personal distribution of income: an analytical approach. Woytinsky Lecture No. 1, Institute of Public Administration and Department of Economics, University of Michigan.

Bekaert, G., Harvey, C. and Lundblad, C. (2011) Financial openness and productivity. *World Development* 39: 1–19.

Benhabib, J. and Spiegel, M. (2000) The role of financial development in growth and investment. *Journal of Economic Growth* 5: 341–360.

Black, S. and Lynch, L. (1996) Human-capital investments and productivity. *American Economic Review* (Papers and Proceedings) 86: 263–267.

Blundell, R., Dearden, L., Meghir, C. and Sianesi, B. (1999) Human capital investment: the returns from education and training to the individual, the firm and the economy. *Fiscal Studies* 20: 1–23.

Bonfiglioli, A. (2008) Financial integration, productivity and capital accumulation. *Journal of International Economics* 76: 337–355.

Borio, C., Kharroubi, E., Upper, C. and Zampolli, F. (2015) Labour reallocation and productivity dynamics: financial causes, real consequences. BIS Working Papers, No. 534. Monetary and Economic Department.

Brav, A., Jiang, W., Ma, S. and Tian, X. (2018) How does hedge fund activism reshape corporate innovation? *Journal of Financial Economics* (forthcoming). https://doi.org/10.1016/j.jfineco.2018.06.012

Bravo-Biosca, A., Criscuolo, C. and Menon, C. (2013) What drives the dynamics of business growth? OECD Science, Technology, and Industry Policy Papers, No. 1. OECD Publishing, Paris.

Brown, J., Fazzari, S. and Petersen, B. (2009) Financing innovation and growth: cash flow, external equity, and the 1990s R&D boom. *Journal of Finance* 64: 151–185.

Brown, J., Martinsson, G. and Petersen, B. (2012) Do financing constraints matter for R&D? *European Economic Review* 56: 1512–1529.

Bruner, R. (1988) The use of excess cash and debt capacity as a motive for merger. *Journal of Financial and Quantitative Analysis* 23: 199–217.

Buera, F., Kaboski, J. and Shin, Y. (2011) Finance and development: a tale of two sectors. *American Economic Review* 101: 1964–2002.

Caballero, R. and Hammour, M. (1994) The cleansing effect of recessions. *American Economic Review* 84: 1350–1368.

Caballero, R., Hoshi, T. and Kashyap, A. (2008) Zombie lending and depressed restructuring in Japan. *American Economic Review* 98: 1943–1977.

Cameron, S. and Taber, C. (2004) Estimation of educational borrowing constraints using returns to schooling. *Journal of Political Economy* 112: 132–182.

Chari, A., Henry, P.B., and Sasson, D. (2012) Capital market integration and wages. Working paper.

Chemmanur, T., Krishnan, K. and Nandy, D. (2011) How does venture capital financing improve efficiency in private firms? A look beneath the surface. *Review of Financial Studies* 24: 4037–4090.

Clayton, M. and Ravid, S. (2002) The effect of leverage on bidding behaviour: theory and evidence from the FCC auctions. *The Review of Financial Studies* 15: 723–750.

Cole, H., Greenwood, J. and Sanchez, J. (2016) Why doesn't technology flow from rich to poor countries? *Econometrica* 84: 1477–1521.

Corrado, C., Hulten, C. and Sichel, D. (2009) Intangible capital and US economic growth. *Review of Income and Wealth* 55: 661–685.

Cournède, B., Denk, O. and Hoeller, P. (2015) Finance and inclusive growth. OECD Economic Policy Papers, No. 15. OECD Publishing, Paris.

Davies, R. and Tracey, B. (2014) Too big to be efficient? The impact of implicit subsidies on estimates of scale economies for banks. *Journal of Money, Credit and Banking* 46 (supplement): 1–35.

Davis, S. and Haltiwanger, J. (1990) Gross job creation and destruction: microeconomic evidence and macroeconomic implications. In O.J. Blanchard and S. Fischer (eds.), *NBER Macroeconomics Annual 1990*, Vol. 5 (pp. 123–186). Cambridge, MA: MIT Press.

Davis, S., Haltiwanger, J., Handley, K., Jarmin, R., Lerner, J. and Miranda, J. (2014) Private equity, jobs, and productivity. *American Economic Review* 104: 3956–3990.

Demeulemeester and Hottenrott (2015) R&D subsidies and firms' cost of debt. Dusseldorf Institute for Competition Economics Discussion Paper No. 201. Dusseldorf University Press, Germany.

Denk, O. (2015a) Financial sector pay and labour income inequality: evidence from Europe. OECD Economics Department Working Papers, No. 1225. OECD Publishing, Paris.

Denk, O. (2015b) Who are the top 1% earners in Europe? OECD Economics Department Working Papers, No. 1274. OECD Publishing, Paris.

Denk, O. and Kastrop, C. (2016) Productivity and prosperity: an international perspective. *Wirtschaftspolitische Blätter* 709–719.

Égert, B. (2016) Regulations, institutions, and productivity: new macroeconomic evidence from OECD countries. *American Economic Review* (Papers and Proceedings) 106: 109–113.

Erosa, A. and Hidalgo Cabrillana, A. (2008) On finance as a theory of TFP, cross-industry productivity differences, and economic rents. *International Economic Review* 49: 437–473.

Gilchrist, S., Sim, J. and Zakrajsek, E. (2013) Misallocation and financial market frictions: some direct evidence from the dispersion in borrowing costs. *Review of Economic Dynamics* 16: 159–176.

Gopinath, G., Karabarbounic, L., Kalemi-Ozcan, S. and Villegas-Sanchez, C. (2017) Capital allocation and productivity in South Europe. Working Paper.

Gordon, R. (2004) Why was Europe left at the station when America's productivity locomotive departed? NBER Working Paper, No. 10661.

Harmon, C., Oosterbeek, H. and Walker, I. (2000) The returns to education: a review of evidence, issues and deficiencies in the literature. CEE Discussion Papers, *Centre for the Economics of Education*, 2000–12.

Hartwig, J. (2008) Productivity growth in service industries: are the transatlantic differences measurement-driven? *Review of Income and Wealth* 54: 494–505.

Heil, M. (2017) Finance and productivity: a literature review. OECD Economics Department Working Papers, No. 1374. OECD Publishing, Paris.

Hsu, P.-H., Tian, X. and Xu, Y. (2014) Financial development and innovation: cross-country evidence. *Journal of Financial Economics* 112: 116–135.

Hughes, J. and Mester, L. (2013) Who said large banks don't experience scale economies? Evidence from a risk-return-driven cost function. *Journal of Financial Intermediation* 22: 559–585.

Ilyina, A. and Samaniego, R. (2011) Technology and financial development. *Journal of Money, Credit and Banking* 43: 899–921.

Kaplan, S., ed. (2000) Mergers and productivity. National Bureau of Economic Research Conference Report, University of Chicago Press.

Keane, M. and Wolpin, K. (2001) The effect of parental transfers and borrowing constraints on educational attainment. *International Economic Review* 42: 1051–1103.

Levine, O. and Warusawitharana, M. (2016) Finance and productivity growth: firm-level evidence. Unpublished Working Paper.

Levine, R. and Zervos, S. (1998) Stock markets, banks, and economic growth. *American Economic Review* 88: 537–558.

Li, X. (2013) Productivity, restructuring and the gains from takeovers. *Journal of Financial Economics* 109: 250–271.

Lochner, L. and Monge-Naranjo, A. (2011) The nature of credit constraints and human capital. *American Economic Review* 101: 2487–2529.

Lochner, L. and Monge-Naranjo, A. (2012) Credit constraints in education. *Annual Review of Economics* 4: 225–256.

Lynch, L. (1992) Private-sector training and the earnings of young workers. *American Economic Review* 82: 299–312.

Madsen, J. and Ang, J. (2016) Finance-led growth in the OECD since the nineteenth century: how does financial development translate? *Review of Economics and Statistics* 98: 552–572.

Martin, A. and Ventura, J. (2015) Managing credit bubbles. Working Paper.

Midrigan, V. and Xu, D.Y. (2014) Finance and misallocation: evidence from plant-level data. *American Economic Review* 104: 422–458.

Niebel, T., O'Mahony, M. and Saam, M. (2017) The contribution of intangible assets to sectoral productivity growth in the EU. *Review of Income and Wealth* 63: S49–S67.

OECD. (2016a) Corporate finance and productivity. In *OECD Business and Finance Outlook 2016*, pp. 67–102. Paris: OECD Publishing.

OECD. (2016b) Promoting productivity and equality: a twin challenge. In *OECD Economic Outlook*, Vol. 2016/1. Paris: OECD Publishing.

OECD. (2017) *OECD Compendium of Productivity Indicators 2017*. Paris: OECD Publishing.

Osoteimehin, S. and Pappada, F. (2015) Credit frictions and the cleansing effect of recessions. *Economic Journal* (online posting before print edition). https://doi.org/10.1111/ecoj.12319

Ouyang, M. (2009) The scarring effect of recessions. *Journal of Monetary Economics* 56: 184–199.

Peek, J. and Rosengren, E. (2005) Unnatural selection: perverse incentives and the misallocation of credit in Japan. *American Economic Review* 95: 1144–1166.

Rajan, R. and Zingales, L. (1998) Financial dependence and growth. *American Economic Review* 88: 559–586.

Roth, F. and Thum, A.-E. (2013) Intangible capital and labour productivity growth: panel evidence for the EU from 1998–2005. *Review of Income and Wealth* 59: 486–508.

Rothstein, J. and Rouse, C. (2011) Constrained after college: student loans and early-career occupational choices. *Journal of Public Economics* 95: 149–163.

Schain, J.P. and Stiebale, J. (2016) Innovation, institutional ownership, and financial constraints. Dusseldorf Institute for Competition Economics Discussion Paper No. 219.

Siegel, D. and Simons, K. (2010) Assessing the effects of mergers and acquisitions on firm performance, plant productivity, and workers: new evidence from matched employer-employee data. *Strategic Management Journal* 31: 903–916.

Triplett, J. and Bosworth, B. (2004) *Productivity in the U.S. Services Sector – New Sources of Economic Growth*. Washington, DC: Brookings Institution Press.

Uysal, V. (2011) Deviation from the target capital structure and acquisition choices. *Journal of Financial Economics* 102: 602–620.

Van Ark, B., Inklaar, R. and McGuckin, R. (2003) ICT and productivity in Europe and the United States: where do the differences come from? Economics Program Working Paper Series, No. 03-05, Conference Board, New York.

Van Ark, B., O'Mahony, M. and Timmer, M. (2008) The productivity gap between Europe and the United States: trends and causes. *Journal of Economic Perspectives* 22: 25–44.

Varela, L. (2017) Reallocation, competition and productivity: evidence from a financial liberalisation episode. Working Paper.

Vignoles, A., Galindo-Rueda, F. and Feinstein, L. (2004) The labour market impact of adult education and training: a cohort analysis. *Scottish Journal of Political Economy* 51: 266–280.

Wurgler, J. (2000) Financial markets and the allocation of capital. *Journal of Financial Economics* 58: 187–214.

Supporting Information

Additional Supporting information may be found in the online version of this article at the publisher's website: https://doi.org/10.1111/joes.12297

Table A1. Summary of indirect evidence on finance and productivity

Table A2. Summary of direct analyses of finance and productivity

Table A3. Summary of studies of other channels through which finance influences productivity

Table A4. Summary of studies of financial liberalisation and productivity

Table A5. Summary of studies of non-debt finance and productivity

Table A6. Summary of studies on business cycles, finance and productivity

7

BUSINESS ANGELS RESEARCH IN ENTREPRENEURIAL FINANCE: A LITERATURE REVIEW AND A RESEARCH AGENDA

Francesca Tenca and Annalisa Croce

Politecnico di Milano Dipartimento di Ingegneria Gestionale

Elisa Ughetto

*Politecnico di Torino and BRICK
Collegio Carlo Alberto*

1. Introduction

Since the seminal works of Wetzel (1981a,b, 1983), research on business angels (henceforth, BAs) has emerged as a new and promising research field. BAs are high wealthy individuals, usually former entrepreneurs or professionals, who invest their own money in promising start-ups in which they have no direct connection, in exchange for ownership equity, acting alone or through semiformal networks. They provide seed or growth capital, as well as advice and hands-on assistance (Wetzel, 1983; Mason and Harrison, 2000; Lindsay, 2004).

BAs' research lies at the intersection of economics, finance and business management. The interest in BAs has grown rapidly in consideration of the important role they play in facilitating the growth of new ventures. First, BAs are a crucial component of the entrepreneurial ecosystem: they contribute to bring innovation to the economy, investing at the earliest stages of ventures' lifecycle, long before a typical institutional investor would take interest. Moreover, BAs usually add substantial value beyond cash, becoming active members in the management of the company and providing significant advice. Indeed, BAs' capital is also called 'smart money' because of the value they add through their experience, counselling, and networking, and because they facilitate the raise of additional funding at a later stage (Aernoudt, 2005).

While it is not easy to quantify the size of the angel market accurately, available figures report that the USA (European) BA market is approximately the same size of the USA (European) venture capital (VC) market, totalling $17.7 billion ($5.6 billion) and $18.3 billion

Contemporary Topics in Finance: A Collection of Literature Surveys, First Edition. Edited by Iris Claus and Leo Krippner.

($5.3 billion), respectively (Organisation for Economic Co-operation and Development, OECD, 2011).

Although scholarly interest in BAs has grown in the last decade and some literature reviews exist, they are limited both in their scope (i.e. focusing on specific aspects of BA financing) and adopted methodology.[1] Hence, the cumulative knowledge on BAs lacks a more integrated view on the results achieved so far.

The objective of this review paper is twofold. First, we provide an extensive review of the literature, mapping prior research in the area by including all the main streams of research and a large spectrum of journals. In doing so, we assess the success and future viability of the research field and identify avenues for future research. To date, current research has used a limited number of theoretical perspectives, adopted few rigorous methodologies and has insufficiently accounted for the heterogeneity of BAs within groups/networks, in different national, cultural and institutional contexts, in their relationship with other investors (i.e. VC) and in their approaches to the investment process. In general, this review aims to structure the current knowledge on BAs and to bring some systematization to an area that is poorly organized, in order to identify the main contents and outcomes. Second, we provide a bibliometric analysis to illustrate the evolution of the research field in the last decades, the level of dispersion of the scientific community, the main outlets for publication, the methodological approaches and challenges in doing BAs' research. In particular, through the analysis of backward and forward citations, we depict the current state of knowledge on which BAs' research is grounded and we examine whether it has any impact on other research fields.

We use the Scopus database to run our searches of the reviewed articles. The use of Scopus database allows to follow a bibliometric perspective that adds an important original contribution with respect to other different narratives and to other literature reviews on the topic. In fact, the bibliometric analysis highlights the increasing importance and legitimacy of BAs' research in a formal and objective way, directing scholars, who intend to perform impact research in the field, towards the hottest topics. However, it is important to clarify that the use of Scopus to compute the bibliometric metrics inevitably leads to overlook a number of papers (see next section) that are not included in the database.[2]

Using Scopus, we identify 148 articles published in entrepreneurship, finance, and economics journals and we categorize the prevailing themes addressed by the community of scholars studying BAs into three thematic areas (BA characteristics, BA market and BA investment process) and eleven research lines. We discuss prior works in these three research areas, highlighting the research gaps, as well as the key challenges, and drawing insights that can help to advance BAs' research.

The paper is organized as follows. First we describe the methodology used to select and classify the articles reviewed. Then, we summarize the findings of the prior literature, along the different thematic areas and research lines identified. This is followed by the results of the bibliometric analysis. Finally, we conclude providing some directions for future research.

2. Methodology

This section describes the steps we followed to select and analyse the articles included in our literature review on BA research.

The first stage of the process was setting the inclusion criteria and the strategy for the search and selection of the reviewed studies. We selected articles written in English and published in peer reviewed journals between 1981 (when the first known article on BAs was published) and 2015. Books, book chapters, conference proceedings and unpublished works were excluded.[3]

The primary source for selecting the articles was the online database Scopus, which was used in other literature reviews in entrepreneurship (Ghio *et al.*, 2015). We searched within the title, the abstract, and the keywords the following search strings: 'business angel(s)', 'angel investing', 'angel financing', 'informal risk capital' and 'informal investor(s)', in addition to restricting the search to the Economy and Business research areas of the database. The structured searching process retrieved over 350 papers.[4] We manually checked all the abstracts to exclude those papers that did not clearly refer to BAs, leading to a reduced sample of 148 papers.[5]

We initially recorded for each article the following information: (1) name(s) of the author(s), (2) year of publication, (3) journal, (4) unit of analysis (i.e. individual BA, angel group, angel network, BA market), (5) country, (7) research question(s), (9) data, (10) methodology and (11) key findings. Once the content of the articles was systematically organized, we conducted a first level thematic analysis by coding the abstracts through an inductive approach, that is deriving a set of thematic areas from the data itself (Pittaway *et al.*, 2004; Thorpe *et al.*, 2005). The thematic areas represent the fundamental concepts on which an article's research questions, theoretical basis, models and/or hypotheses are based (Thorpe *et al.*, 2005). The thematic areas were, then, refined and more detailed research lines were identified.

We identified three main thematic areas: BA characteristics, BA market and BA investment process. The research stream on BA characteristics is the first to emerge in the BA literature. It includes the majority of the seminal and early papers that are mainly descriptive in nature. These studies focus on the definition of angel investors and categorize BAs into typologies, based upon their personal characteristics and investing preferences. They also compare individual BAs' profiles across countries, address gender issues and describe the roles played by angel networks and angel groups. We found 37 publications in this area (25%), that we further categorized into four research lines: (1) profiles and types, (2) international differences in profiles, (3) gender and (4) networks and groups.

The second thematic area is BA market, comprising 34 articles (23%). These articles provide estimates of the size of the BA market, examine the dynamics of demand and supply in the informal risk capital market, analyse the role played by BAs in filling regional equity gaps and in stimulating regional economic development and examine the governmental policies implemented or needed to stimulate BA investing activity at both regional and country levels. This thematic area includes three research lines: (1) demand and supply of angel capital, (2) effectiveness of angel financing on regional growth and (3) policies to foster the informal risk capital market.

The last thematic area, which we labelled BA investment process, is the most extensive one, including 77 papers (52%). These studies aim to understand the underlying dynamics of the BAs' investment process. We distinguished four research lines: (1) selection, evaluation and funding, (2) post-investment, (3) impact on investees' performances and (4) overview of the entire investment process. Table 1 illustrates the distribution of the reviewed articles by thematic area and research line.

Figure 1 shows the 148 reviewed articles spanning the period 1981–2015, by thematic area. After the two seminal articles published by Wetzel in 1981 and 1983, the overall distribution of publications shows that BA research has attracted a certain scholarly interest since 2003 and then more consistently beginning from 2007 (with the exception of 2009). We can see that recently, especially beginning from 2011, the growth in the number of publications is

Table 1. Distribution of the Reviewed Articles by Thematic Area and Research Line.

Thematic area	Research line	Description	Year of first publication
BA characteristics (37 articles, 25%)	Profiles and types (22 articles)	Studies that examine BAs' typical profile and categorize BAs into different typologies	1981
	International differences in profiles (8 articles)	Studies that compare BAs' profiles across different countries	1992
	Gender (5 articles)	Studies focusing on gender issues	2006
	Networks and groups (2 articles)	Studies describing the roles played by BA networks and groups	2010
BA market (34 articles, 23%)	Demand and supply of angel capital (15 articles)	Studies that provide estimates of the size of the BA market and that examine the dynamics of demand and supply in the market	1987
	Effectiveness of angel financing on regional growth (6 articles)	Studies that examine the role played by BAs in filling regional equity gaps and in stimulating regional economic development	1991
	Policies to foster the informal risk capital market (13 articles)	Studies that examine the governmental policies implemented or needed to stimulate BAs' investing activity at both regional and country levels	1992
BA investment process (77 articles, 52%)	Selection, evaluation and funding (36 articles)	Studies that examine BAs' decision-making criteria in the screening, evaluation and funding decision of investment proposals	1988
	Post-investment (10 articles)	Studies that examine BAs' post-investment involvement in the invested firms	1996
	Impact on investees' performances (20 articles)	Studies that evaluate the impact of BA financing on invested firms' performances	2002
	Overview of the entire investment process (11 articles)	Studies that examine the different phases of the entire BA investment process	2003

mainly due to a shift in the papers' thematic area, from an early emphasis on BA characteristics towards the understanding of the mechanisms underlying the BA investment process.

3. Main Contributions of BA Research

In this section, we present the main contributions of BA research. We organize the discussion of the literature results along the thematic areas and research lines identified in the methodology section.

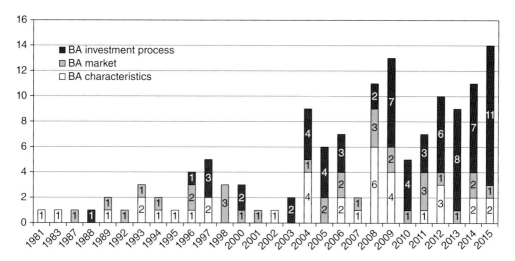

Figure 1. Number of Articles Published per Year, by Thematic Area.

3.1 BA Characteristics

The first thematic area that emerged in BA research is concerned with individual BAs' characteristics. This thematic area accounts for 37 papers describing the profile of BAs in terms of their business background, experience and education, motivations to invest and investing criteria, behaviour and investment activity.

Within this thematic area, we identified four research lines. *Profiles and types* is the most extensive research line, accounting for 22 papers. A first set of papers provides a description of BAs' profiles in terms of portfolio size, investment motivations and preferences, syndication strategies (Wetzel, 1983; Aram, 1989; Moen *et al.*, 2008; Lahti, 2011a), psychological traits (Duxbury *et al.*, 1996), business background and experience, investing criteria and outcomes (Landström, 1992; Paul *et al.*, 2003), factors differentiating professional BAs from non-investors or family and friends capital providers (Maula *et al.*, 2005; Wong and Ho, 2007; Li *et al.*, 2014a,b). Typical BAs are portrayed as male, high net worth, middle-age individuals, with considerable entrepreneurial experience and networks, who prefer early stage investments, in high-tech companies, located in their proximity (Wetzel, 1983; Aram, 1989; Maula *et al.* 2005; Wong and Ho, 2007; Riding, 2008). They are usually patient investors, also driven by non-financial motivations, and willing to be involved in the post-investment management of their companies (Wetzel, 1983; Duxbury *et al.*, 1996). However, these studies have also recognised that BAs can be heterogeneous in their characteristics and investment behaviours. Differences among BAs relate to their demographical characteristics, income and education (Szerb *et al.*, 2007a,b), their motivations and willingness to invest (Freear *et al.*, 1994; Sullivan and Miller, 1996; Robinson and Cottrell, 2007; Szerb *et al.*, 2007a,b), their investing experience and competences (Sørheim and Landström, 2001; Avdeitchikova, 2008) and their investment practices and post-investment involvement (Lathi, 2011b; Landström, 1992). Some recent papers also address the possibility that BAs have dynamic investment patterns, over time or in different contexts (Robinson and Cottrell, 2007; Avdeitchikova, 2008; Avdeitchikova *et al.*, 2008; Lathi, 2011b). A few additional studies focus on particular typologies of BAs, defined as 'technology angels' (Erikson and Sørheim, 2005) or 'founding angels'[6] (Festel and De Cleyn, 2013a).

The second research line *International differences in profiles* counts eight papers, in which BA characteristics and behaviours are compared among different countries and institutional settings. The comparison is often made between the more developed USA financial market and the European one (Harrison and Mason, 1992; Landström, 1993; Wilson, 1995; Brettel, 2003), among different European countries (Bygrave *et al.*, 2003; Stedler and Peters, 2003; Ding *et al.*, 2015) and more recently, between emerging economies and established ones (Li *et al.*, 2014a,b; Scheela *et al.*, 2015).[7] Evidence shows that in comparison to the United States, European BAs invest lower amounts, they are less patient and less risk-adverse investors, while they usually experience higher investment returns (Wilson, 1995; Brettel, 2003). Instead, concerning the differences between emerging economies and developed ones, it has been found that BAs in China, for example, tend to make larger localized investments (by syndication) than BAs in the United States and Europe. They are, also, less patient and less involved in their invested companies in the post-investment phase (Li *et al.*, 2014a,b).

More in general, a significant gap between BAs' research in developed versus emerging economies has emerged. Most of the current knowledge is summarized in a recent review by Scheela *et al.* (2015),[8] focusing on VCs' and BAs' practices in emerging economies of Southeast Asia. The main characteristics of these markets (i.e. high political uncertainty and corruption, lack of supporting institutions for early-stage investment and legal protection for minority shareholders such as BAs) affect BAs' profiles and investment practices in comparison to developed economies. More specifically, the authors identify seven articles exploring the BAs' investment process in Vietnam (Scheela and Nguyen, 2001, 2004), Philippines (Scheela, 2006; Scheela and Isidro, 2008, 2009) and Thailand (Scheela and Jittrapanun, 2008, 2012), concluding that BAs (and VCs) in these countries, in spite of the numerous 'institutional voids', actively support the funding and development of early-stage and high-growth entrepreneurial ventures. They overcome such difficulties by adopting different investment strategies based, primarily, upon significant informal networking and co-investment activities. While BAs in developed countries typically co-invest to reduce financial risk, in emerging countries co-investing is relevant to manage high levels of financial, legal, currency, political, economic and market risks. Informal networking is extremely important because formal institutions, such as clubs and syndicates, are mostly lacking (Scheela *et al.*, 2015).

A third research line, which we labelled *gender*, focuses on the access to angel capital by women (O'Gorman and Terjesen, 2006; Becker-Blease and Sohl, 2007), on the characteristics and investment preferences of women BAs (Harrison and Mason, 2007; Sohl and Hill, 2007) and on the effects of gender diversity on angel group investment behaviour (Becker-Blease and Sohl, 2011). It is found that women BAs are slightly more likely to invest in women-owned businesses, thus exhibiting a certain level of homophile, while gender does not seem to be a major issue in determining the supply of angel financing. However, women seek angel financing at lower rates than men (Becker-Blease and Sohl, 2007) and tend to invest less when they are in small minority as in angel groups (Becker-Blease and Sohl, 2011). Although this research line accounts for only five papers, it seems to have quite a high research impact in terms of citations, as it will be shown in the bibliometric analysis. Indeed, two articles (Becker-Blease and Sohl, 2007; Harrison and Mason, 2007) are included in the top 20 most cited publications in terms of citations per year (CPY).

The last research line *Networks and groups* is limited to two papers, which focus on the new roles played by BAs, emerging from the development of BA networks and groups. These works, which are grounded on social capital and social network theories, describe the function of 'gatekeepers'[9] (Paul and Whittam, 2010) in investment syndicates and of 'nexus angels' (Porter and Spriggs, 2013).

3.2 BA Market

The second thematic area is BA market, which was one of the first topics addressed in BA research, first emerging in 1987 (Wetzel, 1987). This thematic area includes a total of 34 papers, which have been classified into three research lines. The first research line is *Demand and supply of angel capital*, which includes 15 articles. Four papers provide estimates of the total BA market in both the United States (Wetzel, 1987; Gaston, 1989) and the United Kingdom (Mason and Harrison, 2000, 2008), while 10 works specifically concentrate on the understanding of the micro and macro determinants of the demand and supply of angel financing. In general, findings suggest that entrepreneurial activity (i.e. demand for informal investment) generates its own supply of finance, as a result of both micro and macro factors (Burke *et al.*, 2010; De Clercq *et al.*, 2012, 2014). This stream of literature also analyses the impact of economic cycles (Sohl and Rosenbers, 2003; Månsson and Landström, 2006) and of the changes in the national taxation systems and governmental regulations (Månsson and Landström, 2006; Szerb *et al.*, 2007a,b; Tingchi and Chang, 2007) on the evolution of the BA market in several countries (Freear *et al.*, 1995; Manigart and Struyf, 1997; Veselovsky *et al.* 2015). Finally, one last paper (Mason and Harrison, 1997a,b) is the response to the criticisms advanced by Stevenson and Coveney (1996), who attribute inappropriate policies made by the UK government on the informal venture capital market to the influence of Mason and Harrison's misleading research.

The second research line is *Effectiveness of angel financing on regional growth*, which includes six studies that investigate BAs' role in filling regional financial gaps and in stimulating regional economic development. Different studies identify in BAs (Harrison and Mason, 1991) and business angel networks (BANs) (Mason and Harrison, 1995; Aernoudt, 2004) the key to fill the new equity gap left by VCs in seed and early stage investments and stimulate entrepreneurship at the regional level. However, subsequent empirical studies are more sceptical about the role played by BAs and BANs in filling the regional equity market gap. It has been reported that in Sweden BA investments continue to be concentrated in metropolitan and university areas (Avdeitchikova, 2009), while in Scotland a major structural gap for development and expansion capital exists, which is not filled by BANs (Harrison *et al.*, 2010a; Gregson *et al.*, 2013). This is mainly determined by either the withdrawal of VCs from new investments (they tend to concentrate on follow-up rounds), and by BAs that have moved up in deal size, thanks to BA syndicates and co-investments with 'hybrid' financial entities (i.e. public authorities, charitable and academic sectors).

The last research line *Policies to foster the informal risk capital market* evaluates the effectiveness of governmental policies to support BA investing activity (13 papers). This stream of research, despite its relevant implications for entrepreneurs and policy makers, remains far underexplored and quite surprisingly not very successful in terms of citations results (see next section on bibliometric analysis). Papers in this research area are mainly concerned with the evaluation of existing governmental policies (Mason and Harrison, 1997a,b; Lerner, 1998; Mason and Harrison, 2004b; Aernoudt *et al.*, 2007; Knyphausen-Aufse and Westphal, 2008; Collewaert *et al.*, 2010; Christensen, 2011; Romani *et al.*, 2013; Baldock and Mason, 2015). A few suggestions to stimulate the informal risk capital market are proposed in the literature, including policy measures to facilitate the connection between BAs and entrepreneurs, as the introduction of business introduction services and financial match-making services at a regional level (Mason and Harrison, 1992; Mason and Harrison 1993; Mason and Harrison, 1995), to stimulate syndication, promote co-investment schemes and BANs' activities, improve investors' readiness, create BAs' schools or academies (San José *et al.*, 2005), establish corporate partnerships for new ventures and integrate different financing resources (Aernoudt, 2005).

3.3 *BA Investment Process*

The thematic area BA investment process includes a total of 68 articles (54%). It is further divided into four research lines: *selection, evaluation and funding; post-investment; impact on investees' performances and overview of the entire investment process.*

3.3.1 *Selection, Evaluation and Funding*

The first research line *selection, evaluation and funding* is the most explored one within the thematic area BA investment process, totalling 36 papers.

This stream of literature examines the determinants of BAs' decision-making at both individual BAs and BA groups levels (Landström, 1998; Mason and Harrison, 1996b; Saetre, 2003; Sørheim, 2003; Gimmon, 2008; Harrison *et al.*, 2010b; Brush *et al.*, 2012; Mitteness *et al.*, 2012b; Argerich *et al.*, 2013; Ding *et al.*, 2014; Rostamzadeh *et al.*, 2014, 2015), with a specific focus on the criteria employed to reject business proposals (Maxwell *et al.*, 2011; Carpentier and Suret, 2015a), in comparison with the decision-making criteria adopted by other types of investors, such as VCs and bankers (Haar *et al.*, 1988; Fiet, 1995a,b; Guild and Bachher, 1996; Mason and Stark, 2004; Gimmon, 2008; Ibrahim, 2008; Fairchild, 2011; Conti *et al.*, 2013; Hsu *et al.*, 2014, 2015; Hellman and Thiele, 2015).

A more recent stream of literature has also focused on the decomposition of the selection stage in subsequent phases in order to analyse how the criteria applied change. It is generally found that tangible and objective characteristics (i.e. strength of the opportunity and organizational, strategic and technological venture's readiness) are more important during the initial evaluation stage, while intangible and subjective characteristics (i.e. commitment, persuasiveness and passion expressed by the entrepreneur and the top management team) matter most in the subsequent decision stages (Maxwell *et al.*, 2011; Brush *et al.*, 2012; Mitteness *et al.* 2012b).

A significant number of works analyse to what extent the entrepreneur's soft-skill qualities affect BAs' judgements, such as the entrepreneur's personality (Becker-Blease and Sohl, 2015; Murnieks *et al.*, 2015), his/her entrepreneurial passion (Mitteness *et al.*, 2012a; Hsu *et al.*, 2014), his/her presentational skills (Clark, 2008) and the trust established between the entrepreneur and the angel investors (Fairchild, 2011; Nofsinger and Wang, 2011; Wallnöfer and Hacklin, 2013; Douglas *et al.*, 2014; Maxwell and Lévesque, 2014).

A total of three papers develop theoretical models explaining the interaction between entrepreneurs, BAs and VCs in the funding process (Fairchild, 2011; Conti *et al.*, 2013; Hellman and Thiele, 2015). Finally, only a few papers explore the negotiation phase, focusing on how BAs' contracts affect their involvement in invested firms and investments through syndicates (Kelly and Hay, 2003), in comparison with VCs' contractual provisions (Ibrahim, 2008), and

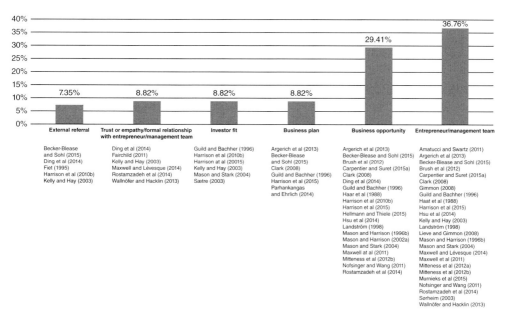

Figure 2. BA's Selection Criteria.

on the challenges faced by entrepreneurs in closing deals with BAs (Amatucci and Swartz, 2011; Douglas *et al.*, 2014).

Figure 2 summarizes the main BAs' selection criteria identified in the literature. The most frequent criteria adopted by BAs in the selection process concern the human capital of the entrepreneur/management team and the business opportunity (i.e. product, market size and potential, strategy, organization) with more than 30% of the papers addressing them. BAs are found to give particular importance to the business plan (i.e. the quality of the business presentation) and to the investor fit (six papers), to the trust and empathy established between a BA and the entrepreneur/management team (five papers) and to external deal referrals, such as other investors or outside advisors (five papers).

3.3.2 *Post-Investment*

We identified 10 articles on the post-investment phase of the BA investment process, plus one study (Amatucci and Sohl, 2004) that we included under the research line *overview of the entire investment process*. Two of these studies are literature reviews (Politis, 2008; Fili and Grünberg, 2014), reporting scholarly works that examine the value-added roles served by BAs and the governance processes of BAs' post-investment involvement.[10]

Research on the post-investment phase is primarily based on case studies (Mason and Harrison, 1996a; Sørheim, 2005; Macht and Robinson, 2009; Macht, 2011; Fili, 2014; Bjørgum and Sørheim, 2015). Only one article by Madill *et al.* (2005) applies a quantitative method, finding that BAs facilitate the investee company to raise additional finance (i.e. VC), along with providing advice and mentoring, networking, assistance in everyday operations, credibility and legitimacy.

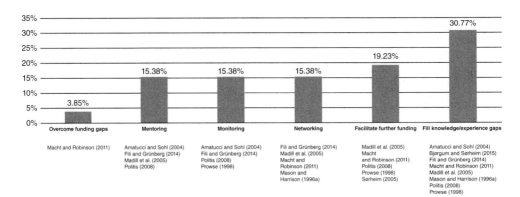

Figure 3. BA's Value-Added Activities.

Figure 3 reports the main value-added activities performed by BAs and the papers in which they are analysed.

3.3.3 *Impact on Investees' Performances*

The research line *impact on investees' performances* includes 20 papers. While extant literature has extensively analysed the impact of individual BAs on both their investment returns and portfolio ventures' performances, the evidence is somehow inconclusive. Results point in the direction of BA funding being associated with enhanced venture performance, but some contrasting evidence exists. Moreover, the effects on the performance of angel groups' returns and their investee companies are still poorly examined.

At the investment level, it emerges that BAs' investment returns have a large variance and are negatively skewed, with many losses and few extraordinarily high returns (Mason and Harrison, 2002b).[11] BAs typically have a relatively short holding period (four years) and trade sale is the most common exit strategy, which is preferred over IPO exit by angel groups too (Roach, 2010; Capizzi, 2015; Carpentier and Suret, 2015b), although angel-backed companies achieve the best performances through IPOs (Mason and Harrison, 2002b).

A few studies question whether formal VC methodologies can be successfully transferred to BAs (Wiltbank, 2005; Wiltbank *et al.*, 2009). It is shown that investing at earlier stages of venture development and providing more post-investment involvement results in fewer negative exits, while doing more due diligence leads to a higher number of failures, but also to more extraordinarily returns (Wiltbank, 2005). Moreover, BAs, who emphasize the use of non-predictive mechanisms (e.g. more post-investment involvement, pursue of possible courses of action based on prior experience) over predictive control mechanisms (e.g. market research, surveys, detailed financial models) in the selection process, experience fewer negative exits (Wiltbank *et al.*, 2009).

At the venture level, prior research has focused on IPO performance (or underpricing) as the primary measure of venture performance, finding contrasting results. A few studies report that BA financing is associated with better IPO performances or lower IPO underpricing (Chahine *et al.*, 2007; Bruton *et al.*, 2009; Hearn, 2014), especially in civil law countries (Bruton *et al.*, 2010). Other studies have instead found that angel-backed IPOs do not outperform non angel-backed IPOs, and may even perform worse (Johnson and Sohl, 2012a,b). A similar positive

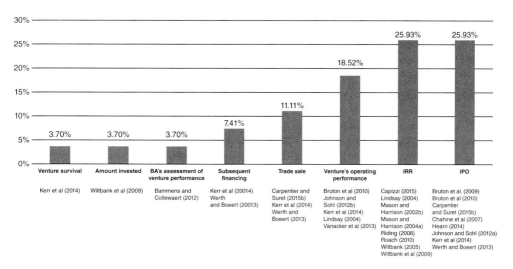

Figure 4. BA's Investment Performance Measures.

effect on ventures' performances is found at the angel group level: companies funded by angel groups experience superior outcomes in terms of higher survival rates, successful exits, employment growth, patenting and web traffic (Kerr *et al.*, 2014). These results demonstrate that there is ample room for researchers to further investigate BAs' exits and clarify apparently contrasting evidence.

Another stream of literature investigates the impact of trust and BA network connections on investees' performance (Bammers and Colleweart, 2012; Werth and Boeert, 2013). It is showed that BAs' trust perceptions lead to higher perceived venture performance up to a certain threshold, beyond which the positive effect is displaced (Bammers and Colleweart, 2012). Moreover, ventures backed by better connected BAs are more likely to receive subsequent funding by VCs and to successfully exit through trade sale or IPO (Werth and Boeert, 2013). Partially connected with this last stream of research, one paper (Colleweart, 2012) examines the angel investor–entrepreneur relationship in their respective exit processes and the impact of different types of conflicts on the intention of the two actors to exit.

Figure 4 shows the main investment performance measures, used in the literature. The most frequent approaches to assess BAs' investment performance are exit through IPO and internal rates of returns (IRRs) with nine papers each, followed by exit through trade sale (four papers). Venture's operating performance is studied only in five papers, while one paper relies on BAs' perceived evaluation of venture performance. Another potential important measure, that is subsequent financing, is almost unexplored, accounting for only two papers.

3.3.4 *Overview of the Entire Investment Process*

The last research line *overview of the entire investment process* includes 11 papers that analyse the entire investment process, 2 of which are literature reviews (Florin *et al.*, 2013; Scheela *et al.*, 2015). Out of 11 articles, 4 papers investigate the role played by different institutional settings on the BA investment process in emerging economies, such as Thailand, China, Philippines (Scheela and Isidro, 2008; 2009; Xiao and Ritchie, 2011; Scheela and Jittrapanun, 2012).

Amatucci and Sohl (2004), Paul *et al.* (2007) and Festel and De Cleyn (2013b) provide a description of the different phases of the BA investment process, focusing, respectively, on the comparison with the VC's process, on the role of gender in the searching, negotiation and post-investment phases, and on founding angels' specific investment practices, while Elitzur and Gavious (2003) develop a theoretical model analysing the interactions between an entrepreneur, a BA and a VC during the investment process, pointing out that, due to a moral hazard problem, the entrepreneur and the VC are incentivized to free ride on the initial investment made by the BAs.

However, it seems that BAs and VCs can also play complementary roles when they co-invest in syndicated deals (Bonnet and Wirtz, 2012). BAs are more involved in the selection phase and first contact with the entrepreneur, while VCs take the lead in the deal-structuring phase. In the post-investment phase, both investors play strong complementary roles, being BAs more engaged in mentoring and VCs in monitoring through contracts and supervisory board involvement (Bonnet and Wirtz, 2012).

4. Bibliometric Analysis

In this section we present the results of the bibliometric analysis, which was performed using the software bibexcel[12] (Persson *et al.*, 2009).[13] The bibliometric analysis includes the analysis of backward and forward citations and the co-authorship analysis.

Table 2 reports the 42 different journals, where the reviewed articles have been published, ordered by number of articles. The Table also includes the total number of forward citations, the incidence of forward citations per article (CPA, representing the average number of citations received by all articles published in the journal and included in the review), and the journal impact factor (last available year, 2015). Following the subject areas classification by Scopus, the publication outlets for the analysed 148 articles refer mostly to Business, Management and Accounting (63.9%), Economics, Econometrics and Finance (23.7%), followed by other minority areas, such as Decision Science (4.1%), Social Sciences (3.1%), Computer Science (2.1%), Engineering (2.1%) and Environmental Science (1.0%). Concerning Business, Management and Accounting the most common journals belong to the following subject areas: Strategy and Management (18.6%), International Management (15.5%) and Management of Technology and Innovation (12.4%). These results seem to suggest that BA research is relevant across different fields of business management.

However, papers are quite concentrated in few journals; the main outlet is Venture Capital with 53 published articles (35.8%), despite its relatively low CPA (2.18%). A total of 17 articles are published in the Journal of Business Venturing (with a CPA of 6.46%), followed by 10 articles published in Small Business Economics and Entrepreneurship and Regional Development. Both journals show a relatively high number of CPA (around 5.40%). Journals with a lower impact factor (below 2.00), such as the Journal of Business Finance and Accounting and the Journal of Banking and Finance are also good outlets for BA research, attaining more than 5% CPA each (corresponding at least to 40 forward citations). Moreover, International Small Business Journal and Entrepreneurship Theory and Practice with just five papers each are, as expected, potentially good outlets, given their discrete CPA above 3%. Thus, we can conclude that the research on BAs potentially offers good publication opportunities if the right journals are targeted.

The papers included in the review have been authored by 187 different scholars. There is evidence of a growing scientific community, because almost half of the scholars (92) joined the

Table 2. Number of Reviewed Articles by Publication Outlet.

Journal	No. articles	No. citations	CPA %	Scopus impact factor (2015)
Venture Capital	53	840	2.18	1.367
Journal of Business Venturing	17	797	6.46	5.657
Entrepreneurship and Regional Development	10	392	5.40	2.109
Small Business Economics	10	391	5.39	2.642
International Small Business Journal	5	164	4.52	3.058
Entrepreneurship: Theory and Practice	5	113	3.11	4.223
Journal of Private Equity	5	18	0.50	0.030
Journal of Banking and Finance	3	132	6.06	1.826
Technovation	3	58	2.66	3.074
Journal of Small Business Management	3	46	2.11	2.495
Asia Pacific Journal of Management	2	9	0.62	2.140
Journal of Developmental Entrepreneurship	2	1	0.07	0.563
MIT Sloan Management Review	1	100	13.78	1.951
Strategic Management Journal	1	94	12.95	4.454
Journal of Business Finance and Accounting	1	41	5.65	1.174
Journal of Small Business and Enterprise Development	1	26	3.58	1.203
Review of Financial Studies	1	25	3.44	3.824
Local Economy	1	25	3.44	0.679
Journal of Business Research	1	23	3.17	2.644
Vanderbilt Law Review	1	19	2.62	0.966
Journal of Economics and Management Strategy	1	15	2.07	0.948
Regional Studies	1	13	1.79	1.939
Journal of Management Studies	1	11	1.52	4.950
International Journal of Entrepreneurial Behaviour and Research	1	9	1.24	1.418
International Business Review	1	7	0.96	0.910
Managerial and Decision Economics	1	7	0.96	0.754
Technological and Economic Development of Economy	1	5	0.69	1.838
International Journal of Technology Management	1	5	0.69	0.221
Industrial Marketing Management	1	3	0.41	2.584
International Journal of Entrepreneurial Venturing	1	3	0.41	0.485
Journal of High Technology Management Research	1	2	0.28	1.109
Journal of Management	1	2	0.28	6.646
Journal of Multinational Financial Management	1	2	0.28	0.687
Team Performance Management	1	2	0.28	1.050
Service Industries Journal	1	1	0.14	0.994
Singapore Management Review	1	1	0.14	0.000
Journal of Management and Governance	1	1	0.14	1.244
International Journal of Economics and Financial Issues	1	0	0.00	0.374
Journal of Entrepreneurship in Emerging Economies	1	0	0.00	0.200
Journal of Financial Economics	1	0	0.00	5.070
Technology Analysis and Strategic Management	1	0	0.00	1.197
International Journal of Entrepreneurship and Innovation	1	0	0.00	0.436
Total	148	3,403	100.00	

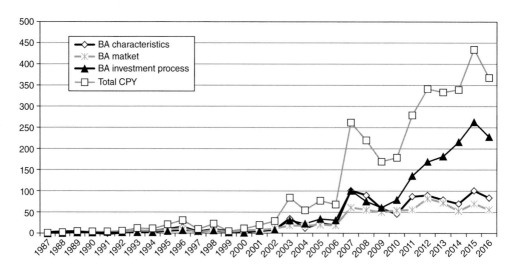

Figure 5. Average Citations per Year, by Thematic Area.

community in the last five years and more than one-third (70) in the last three years. Authors are mainly based in North America (71 authors) and Europe (86 authors, of which around 30% come from the United Kingdom), while a few are from Southeast Asia (19 authors) and other world areas (11 authors).

To analyse the dissemination of BA research, we provide an analysis of forward citations. Figure 5 shows the average number of forward citations per year (CPY) by thematic area, over the time period 1987–2015, considering all the articles included in the current review. CPY are calculated as the total number of forward citations received divided by the number of years of publication. We can see that the thematic area Investment Process has become a hot topic beginning from 2010, when it surpasses the cumulative CPY of the papers on BA character-istics. Papers belonging to the thematic area BA market have always received fewer citations than the other two aforementioned thematic areas (except for 2010), especially from 2011 and besides the potential relevant practical implications for policy makers and entrepreneurs.

Table 3 shows the 20 most cited articles by absolute number of forward citations and by CPY. These papers received a total of 1,492 citations, accounting for the 44% of the total number of forward citations. The bare count of total forward citations provides only partial evidence as a measure of success for scholarly publications, as inevitably favours older studies. Thus, to overcome this bias we also report the top 20 articles by CPY. Articles published after 2010 are now also taken into account.

Looking at the top 20 papers per forward citations some interesting observations can be advanced: first, forward citations are not much concentrated. On average, a paper cites 2.4 of the 20 most cited papers in the field. Second, almost all of the 20 most cited publications consist of empirical studies, rather than theoretical models, methods, or other related phenomena. Third, looking at the topics addressed by the most cited papers we find a confirmation that papers focusing on BA characteristics, in particular belonging to the research lines *profiles and types* and *international differences in profiles*, and BA investment process, in particular belonging to the research lines *selection, evaluation and funding* and *impact on investees' performances*, are well represented, followed by papers on BA market.

Table 3. Top 20 Most Cited Articles by Number of Forward Citations and by CPY.

	Top 20 per forward citations			Top 20 per CPY		
Rank	Authors (year)	Cit.	CPY	Authors (year)	Cit.	CPY
1	Mason and Stark (2004)	112	9.3	Bruton et al. (2010)	94	15.7
2	Aernoudt (2004)	109	9.1	Kerr et al. (2014)	25	12.5
3	Mason and Harrison (2002b)	108	7.7	Wiltbank et al. (2009)	71	10.1
4	Wetzel and William (1983)	100	3.0	Maxwell et al. (2011)	47	9.4
5	Bruton et al. (2010)	94	15.7	Mason and Stark (2004)	112	9.3
6	Mason and Harrison (2002a)	87	6.2	Aernoudt (2004)	109	9.1
7	Freear et al. (1994)	75	3.4	Mason and Harrison (2002b)	108	7.7
8	Mason and Harrison (1996b)	72	3.6	Mitteness et al. (2012a)	29	7.3
9	Wiltbank et al. (2009)	71	10.1	Becker-Blease and Sohl (2007)	60	6.7
10	Fiet (1995a,b)	68	3.2	Mason and Harrison (2002a)	87	6.2
11	Harrison and Mason (1992)	67	2.8	Bruton et al. (2009)	40	5.7
12	Mason and Harrison (1995)	66	3.1	Conti et al. (2013)	15	5.0
13	Landstrom (1993)	64	2.8	Collewaert (2012)	19	4.8
14	Prowse and (1998)	63	3.5	Harrison and Mason (2007)	42	4.7
15	Becker-Blease and Sohl (2007)	60	6.7	Chahine et al. (2007)	41	4.6
16	Haar et al. (1988)	58	2.1	Clark (2008)	35	4.4
17	Sorheim and Landstrom (2001)	57	3.8	Madill et al. (2005)	48	4.4
18	Bygrave et al. (2003)	56	4.3	Bygrave et al. (2003)	56	4.3
19	Lerner (1998)	53	2.9	Politis (2008)	34	4.3
20	Freear et al. (1995)	52	2.5	Fairchild (2011)	21	4.2

If we examine the list of the top 20 papers per CPY, a higher number of articles focusing on the investment process are now clearly accounted for. In particular, one of the most successful research lines for scholars appears to be *impact on investees' performances*, with the article by Kerr et al. (2014) that receives 16 citations in its first year of publication (and a total of 25 cit.). This paper, in fact, is one of the few assessing the impact of BA groups' investments on the performances of invested firms. Of note is the presence of the authors Mason and Harrison, who publish 3 out of the top 20 articles by CPY, accounting for a total of 237 citations. Another interesting new entry is the work by Fairchild (2011), who advances a theoretical model on the entrepreneur's choice between VC and BA financing, based on an original behavioural game theoretical approach. Moreover, two articles that analyse the obstacles faced by women entrepreneurs in accessing informal risk capital (Becker-Blease and Sohl, 2007) and women BA characteristics (Harrison and Mason, 2007) also received a relatively significant number of CPY, along with the literature review on BAs' post-investment value-added activities by Politis (2008).

With regard to the analysis of backward citations (references), the 148 articles count around 4,120 non-duplicated backward citations, of which 62 consist of articles included in the current review. We distinguish between internal and external backward citations. A backward citation is internal (external) if a paper cites another paper included (excluded) in this literature review. Table 4 reports the top 20 most cited articles by both internal and external references.[14]

Among the 20 most cited articles 12 are internal references with the top 4 ones also consisting of internal backward citations (apart from Gaston, 1989). This shows how BA literature

Table 4. Top 20 Most Cited Publications by Number of Backward Citations.

Authors (year)	Backward Cit.	Backward Cit. type
Wetzel (1983)[a]	45	Internal
Freear et al. (1994)[a]	35	Internal
Harrison and Mason (1992)[a]	33	Internal
Landström (1993)[a]	32	Internal
Gaston (1989)	32	External (book)
Mason and Harrison (2002a)[a]	31	Internal
Haar et al. (1988)[a]	29	Internal
Van Osnabrugge (2000)	29	External (article)[b]
Van Osnabrugge and Robinson (2000)	28	External (book)
Wetzel (1981a)	28	External (book)
Mason and Harrison (1994)	26	External (book)
Mason and Harrison (2002b)[a]	26	Internal
Feeney et al. (1999)	25	External (article)[b]
Freear and Wetzel (1990)	24	External (article)[b]
Fiet (1995a,b)	23	External (article)[b]
Mason and Harrison (1996a)[a]	21	Internal
Landström (1998)[a]	21	Internal
Mason and Harrison (1996b)[a]	21	Internal
Sohl and Rosenberg (2003)[a]	20	Internal
Wiltbank (2005)[a]	20	Internal
Lumme et al. (1998)	20	External (book)

[a] Articles included in the present literature review (i.e. internal backward citations).
[b] External articles that are not included in the Scopus database.

is quite a self-referential research field. Precisely, this set of contributions is cited in total 145 times, accounting for nearly the 23% of the total internal references. The two most cited works are two seminal papers on typical characteristics and investment preferences of informal investors in the United Kingdom, while the article in third position provides an assessment of the UK informal venture capital market from a supply side perspective, identifying the main constraints on BAs' ability to invest (Harrison and Mason, 1992). The other most important internal references, again, include articles about BA characteristics in Sweden (Landstrom, 1993) and on the comparison between the UK informal venture capital market with the more sophisticated USA one (Mason and Harrison, 2002a).

As regards external references, the most cited publications (receiving at least 20 citations) ground either on the same topics of internal citations, as BA characteristics and motivations to invest (Wetzel, 1981b; Mason and Harrison, 1994; Van Osnabrugge and Robinson, 2000), or on the VC literature, in particular on the comparison between VCs' and BAs' investment processes and risk avoidance strategies (Fiet, 1995a,b), investment evaluation criteria and funding preferences (Freear and Wetzel, 1990; Feeney et al., 1999). Thus, it emerges that BA research shares some foundation with the VC literature, while there are no apparent links with other research fields. Only if we take into consideration the most recent papers, for example the ones published in the last two years, some contaminations from other research fields are starting to emerge, such as from trust, human and social capital theories (Bammens and Collewaert, 2014; Maxwell and Lévesque, 2014; Parhankangas and Ehrlich, 2014; Ding et al., 2015).

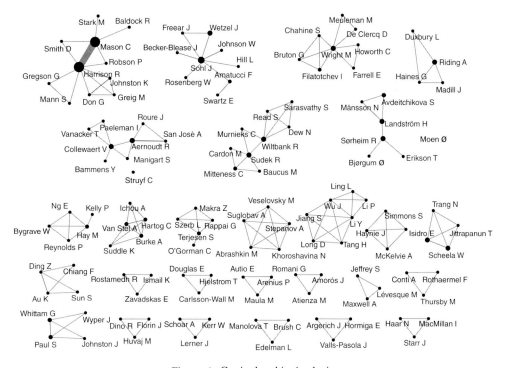

Figure 6. Co-Authorship Analysis.

Finally, once more Mason and Harrison confirm to be the pillars of the scientific community with 6 co-authored articles among the 20 most cited ones.

In Figure 6 we show the co-authorship network, reporting clusters composed by three or more authors for the sake of clarity (15 couples are omitted). First, it is evident that the field is quite fragmented. Five main clusters composed by 8–10 scholars stand out, for the rest collaborations between 3 and 4 authors are the most common ones. Second, the few larger clusters are dominated by founders of BA research, who are still pretty active in the community. In particular, Harrison and Mason are the most prolific researchers with 20 publications each, of which 16 co-authored, followed by Sohl (10 articles), Landström (6 articles), Aernoudt and Wetzel (5 articles), and Wright (4 articles). Third, research collaborations have largely been within the same country or region, and only few cases of collaborations between North American and European researchers exist (Bygrave *et al.*, 2003; Farrell *et al.*, 2008; Brush *et al.*, 2012; Gresgson *et al.*, Harrison *et al.*, 2010a; 2013). Moreover, as one could expect, North America affiliated authors publish more in high-ranking journals, for example 12 articles published in Journal of Business Venturing, 2 articles published in Entrepreneurship Theory and Practice, 1 article published in Review of Financial Studies, with only few exceptions (e.g. Bruton *et al.*, 2010, who published the only article in Strategic Management Journal or Bruton *et al.*, 2009 and Colleweart, 2012, who published in Entrepreneurship Theory and Practice).

Finally, Table 5 illustrates the methodologies used in the reviewed studies, by thematic area. It can be noticed that the quantitative approach is the most frequent methodology used, accounting for 61% of the articles. Among them, surveys represent around 45% of all the methodological approaches, followed by research based on secondary data. Quantitative

Table 5. Methodological Approaches, by Thematic Area.

	BA characteristics	BA market	BA investment process	Total
Quantitative	**30**	**17**	**43**	**90**
survey	29	12	26	67
secondary data	1	5	9	15
observational studies			4	4
content analysis			3	3
experimental studies			1	1
Qualitative (case study)	**3**	**12**	**24**	**39**
ex post interviews	2	4	21	27
observational studies		1	2	3
secondary data	1	7	1	9
Mixed method	**1**	**1**	**1**	**3**
Literature review	**1**		**4**	**5**
Theoretical	**2**	**4**	**5**	**11**

studies also receive a higher number of citations, and 8 quantitative papers rank in the top 10 list of the most-cited publications per citations per year (CPY). Qualitative research represents a modest 26% of the reviewed papers, and it is mostly based on ex post interviews. Only few studies (2.7%) rely on real-time observational techniques (i.e. verbal protocol analysis/policy capturing), although two of them enter the top 10 list of the most-cited papers, demonstrating that these techniques may lead to high-quality and high-impact research. Finally, we identified 5 papers of literature review and 11 theoretical papers, 5 of which develop formal theoretical models on BA market and BA investment process.

In this respect, it is important to highlight the significant methodological obstacles of conducting BAs' research. BAs are very difficult to identify, because of their anonymous and invisible nature, which makes sampling extremely problematic. As a result, the majority of the studies rely on convenience samples (Avdeitchikova et al., 2008). Moreover, BAs are especially invisible in emerging economies compared to developed economies, as they tend to keep a low profile, avoid institutions and rely on personal connections to find investments. Typically, this results in small and non-random samples, especially in emerging countries. Some of these methodological challenges have been addressed in a special issue of Venture Capital (2008, Volume 10, no. 4) in three main papers (Avdeitchikova et al. 2008; Farrel et al., 2008; Mason and Harrison, 2008). We will further discuss these contributions in the next section, when we address the future methodological challenges of BAs' research.

5. Conclusions and Directions for Future Research

This paper provides a literature review of the BAs' literature from the first seminal article published in 1981–2015. As the research field matured, BA research has moved from an early emphasis on the characteristics of BAs and the informal risk capital market, towards an analysis of the BA investment process. The bibliometric analyses show that studies focusing on the analysis of the BA's investment process and, more in general, research using quantitative methods are associated with a consistent number of publications and citations per year. Despite the scientific community is quite fragmented and self-referential, the number of new authors has constantly grown over recent years, indicating that the interest on BA research has expanded and that there are good opportunities to publish high-impact articles.

In this final section, we outline the challenges that remain for future research. From a methodological point of view, the review suggests that BA research is currently using a narrow set of theories and more qualitative than quantitative tools of analysis. There is therefore significant scope to achieve a wider representation in the top journals and this could be done by a cross-fertilization of theories and concepts taken from related disciplines and by the use of new or more sophisticated quantitative methodologies, some of which are widely used in the management and sociology fields. Our review also calls for a need for more longitudinal approaches that could provide valuable insights into the temporal aspects of the BA phenomenon.

A related methodological issue that should be addressed by future research is the construction of high-quality samples of BAs, in order to avoid the exclusive reliance on convenience samples drawn from formalized angel networks or associations that could not be representative of the broad population of BAs. The use of random and multi-sample techniques are, especially, recommended to reduce sample bias, allow for longitudinal analysis (see Avdeitchikova *et al.* 2008; Farrell *et al.*, 2008) and estimation of the overall BAs' market size (Mason and Harrison, 2008). Thus, a combined use of different sources to identify BAs and their investment activity is essential (e.g. BANs, angel syndicates and investment schemes providing tax incentives). Sampling from publicly available business registration data could also improve representative quality, especially in emerging countries, where angel groups and BANs are less developed (Farrel *et al.*, 2008).

Moreover, the review has emphasised that additional research on BAs is needed in emerging economies, especially in some of the fastest-growing markets, such as India, South America or Southeast Asia, which have received very limited attention by prior literature. Indeed, for both developed and emerging economies, we need to implement representative sampling methods that allow to achieve comparable and generalizable results on BAs' characteristics, types of informal investors, BAs' investment preferences and strategies that apply broadly to the institutional context in which they are embedded.

From a content point of view, there are many avenues for future research. We articulate the discussion of the research directions along the thematic areas and research lines previously identified.

5.1 BA Characteristics

5.1.1 Profiles and Types

Although it is the earliest topic addressed by BA research, this research line could be revitalized, especially in connection with other areas of inquiry, such as BA investment process. Researchers have primarily focused on conventional human capital characteristics (i.e. education, experience, geographical location), without in-depth assessments of more intangible aspects (i.e. physical appearance, reputation, commitment, attention to ethical values, cultural norms, passion and network ties). More studies are needed to explore to what extent these intangible human capital aspects impact on the different phases of the investment process and on distinct investment contingencies (e.g. activities performed in the invested firm, holding periods, round of entry and staging strategies). In this regard, it would be interesting to understand whether investors sharing certain soft characteristics would value opportunities differently, add value differently to invested ventures and ultimately influence the overall venture's performances.

Another interesting topic that deserves attention concerns tangible and intangible individual factors (of both investors and entrepreneurs) that shape the matching between entrepreneurs and angel investors. Is there a positive sorting in the BA market, as it happens in the VC market, so that the most reputable investors choose the best entrepreneurs and *vice versa*? Does the heterogeneity (or rather the homogeneity) in entrepreneurs' and investors' individual characteristics allow a better valuation of the deal, allocation of financial sources and access to finance? Which factors moderate the effects on investor–entrepreneur fit (e.g. quality of the venture, investor's resource endowment and conditions of the financial markets)? These are all questions that are likely to be at the leading edge of the academic debate in the next years and that could be addressed with finer grained data and the adoption of a wide range of methods.

5.1.2 *International Differences in Profiles*

Individual BA characteristics, as previously outlined, can impact deal evaluation, funding decisions, value adding activities and exit routes. However, BAs' profiles and types are likely to be influenced by legal, cultural, social norms and habits, which vary across countries and regions. More research is needed to assess both with-in and cross-country differences (similarities) on investors' behaviour in the light of their characteristics. In particular, the differences in BAs' profiles in emerging and developed countries have been marginally addressed so far (Li *et al.*, 2014; Scheela *et al.*, 2015). A further development of this research stream will allow to improve our understanding of BAs' characteristics in emerging economies, where the population of BAs is particularly invisible and where financial markets and BAs' networks are still underdeveloped. In particular, it would be interesting to understand whether BAs' profiles and investment preferences are affected by market inefficiencies and the lack of formal and effective institutions.

Therefore, we call for scholars to address questions like: Do different institutional environments shape BAs differently in their qualifying features? In particular, do BAs have distinct profiles in emerging and advanced economies? Is the matching between entrepreneurs and angel investors easier in certain geographical contexts than in others or does the 'institutional void' in emerging economies make it more difficult? Are BAs' human capital aspects (both tangible and intangible) leading to successful approaches in certain contexts but not in others? Do BAs' types adjust to varied institutional settings? More in general, what type of relationship exists between culture, institutional factors, BAs' investment patterns and outcomes and how does it vary in intensity and directions across countries at different levels of development? Exploring such questions would provide important insights into how the characterization of angel investors diverges within a broad range of institutional contexts.

5.1.3 *Gender*

The theme of gender has been much underexplored, even if it could potentially produce high-impact research, as indicated by two papers (Becker-Blease and Sohl, 2007; Harrison and Mason, 2007) out of the total 5 addressing this theme, which entered the top 20 most-cited list. Future studies could explore a number of interesting issues. Do women BAs have the same human capital characteristics than their men peers? For instance, are women BAs more risk tolerant than men, do they experience higher (lower) failure rates? Are these characteristics affecting their investment behaviour in the same way of men? Do women BAs have different mental constructs to evaluate deals, to take funding decisions and to manage capital and post-investment relationships? Why are women business angels underrepresented in the BA market? Is the rise of women angel groups facilitating the matching between entrepreneurs and women business angels? How is gender shaping the relationship between angels and VCs? How is gender affecting the group thinking behaviour of investors in case of groups of BAs? Each of these questions warrants further exploration.

5.1.4 *Networks and Groups*

As the BA market has matured, BAs have become more professionalized, tend to join together in semiformal or organized networks/groups and their investment process increasingly resembles that of VC funds. However, additional research is needed to improve the overall understanding of the challenges and issues faced by organized angel groups and networks. Future studies can uncover who is attracted by angel networks or groups (e.g. individuals that would have never become solo angels?), how BAs connect to domestic and international networks, how they position into the network and manage their network relationships, how they interact with other members in the investment process and the extent to which investment decisions are influenced by group thinking. Additional questions concern: What role do social capital and the positioning of investors into a network play in driving the selection of which ventures to finance? Does the heterogeneity in terms of competences, experiences, education within the group favour the investment decision? Or rather what drives most the decision making is the homogeneity of BAs? Little is also known about how syndicates operate, if they implement practices and risk reduction strategies similar to VC investors, what are the differences in terms of management and investment practices in different institutional settings. These questions represent a major opportunity for researchers in the entrepreneurial finance field.

5.2 *BA Market*

5.2.1 *Demand and Supply of Angel Capital*

Many of the studies reviewed under this research line have not provided an adequate account of the historical, cultural, economic, social or institutional factors determining the matching between demand and supply of angel capital and little scholarly attention has been devoted to the challenges to overcome to bring the two sides together. The demand and supply of BA financing is influenced by regulatory changes, tax policies, corporate governance regimes, legal environment (e.g. investor protection rights), level of development of financial markets, which greatly vary across nations and between emerging and advanced economies. In particular, the lack of institutions supporting venture financing in emerging economies is expected to hamper the demand and the supply of angel capital, even if recent research seems to suggest that BAs are able, somehow, to overcome these institutional challenges and provide financial resources to new entrepreneurial ventures (Scheela *et al.*, 2015). More extensive research on these issues would further our understanding of which are the consequences for both entrepreneurs and investors of these factors in different institutional settings. Specifically, future studies on emerging markets could support or contradict these preliminary results.

Finally, another theme that has not received much consideration is the impact on the demand side of the changes that have recently taken place in the supply side, namely the organization of angels into angel groups/networks or the adoption by BAs of investment practices similar to the ones adopted by VCs.

5.2.2 *Effectiveness of Angel Financing on Regional Growth*

The geography of BAs' investment activity and the role of BAs in filling the new regional equity market gap, which is deepening at the lower end of the risk capital market, is worth further investigation by future works, for its important policy implications and potential impact on entrepreneurial activity. As prior research suggested, the regional concentration of BAs' investments puts start-ups located in outer regions at disadvantage compared to their equivalents in core economic regions (Avdeitchikova, 2009; Harrison and Mason, 1995). New studies (i.e. outside the United Kingdom) could explore the presence of geographical concentration of BA activity in other settings and to what extent this is determined by institutional, social and economic factors. Further research is needed to assess to what extent the emergence of BA networks and groups can effectively fill the regional equity gap and which legal, institutional, social, regulatory conditions allow BA financing to engage with other sources of financing (i.e. crowdfunding, VC, public sector finance).

5.2.3 *Policies to Foster the Informal Risk Capital Market*

Research on the effectiveness of governmental policies in stimulating BA activities has been limited, despite its important economic implications and benefit for entrepreneurs and BAs alike. Consequently, new studies will have to better clarify in which direction public policy measures should be pointed to stimulate BA risk capital market and to fill the regional equity gap identified in the literature. There is the need to evaluate the efficacy of the introduction of public sector measures to stimulate both the demand and supply side of the BA market, especially in peripheral regions. Are tax reliefs, public guarantees, co-investment schemes and educational initiatives enough to encourage angel investments? Can tax incentives be extended to angels investing in pooled investment vehicles? Is it more effective to sustain the development of BA networks rather than BA groups or *viceversa*? Which measures can be implemented to facilitate the matching between entrepreneurs and BAs, and should these measures be differently shaped for distinct types of investors and entrepreneurs?

5.3 *BA Investment Process*

5.3.1 *Overview of the Entire Investment Process*

Research on BA investment process is still underdeveloped. In general, works establishing patterns of causes and effects in the different sequential stages throughout the entire investment process are very limited. Indeed, only eight empirical papers study the overall investment process, and most of them focus on a particular geographical area or BA's typology. Therefore, we see numerous opportunities to enlarge the overview of the entire investment process, with additional insights into the diverse roles played by individual angels, networks and groups. We detail a number of potential future research lines spanning the overall investment process in the following paragraphs.

5.3.2 *Selection, Evaluation and Funding*

Future research into the selection, valuation and funding stages should examine how investment decisions and patterns change as BAs gain experience and maturity, change their risk-return preferences or syndicate with other investors, controlling for the diversity of the institutional context in which they operate. There is a lack of empirical knowledge on whether evaluation criteria are weighted differently throughout the various stages of the investment process and if this is influenced, to some extent, by BAs' individual characteristics (both tangible and intangible). Little is known about the negotiation phase, and specifically on the determinants of deal terms and deal pricing, which are of crucial importance for both entrepreneurs and BAs, as they determine their relative control over the venture and influence BAs' returns at the exit.

It would be insightful to explore all these issues at the level of both individual angels and BA groups and networks. Indeed, only six papers among those reviewed have examined the investment decision process followed by BA groups. Hence, there is ample room for further research in expanding the number and types of angel groups sampled and in examining how investment groups differing on the size, corporate governance, level of professionalism and maturity differently balance investment criteria in their decision making process and which model likely leads to better decisions.

Finally, the relationship between BAs and VCs represents another promising direction for future research, in particular because empirical research is rather limited. How does the level of engagement of solo angels and BAs networks/groups with VCs influence the selection, evaluation and negotiation of the deals? Who is steering valuations, negotiations and contract terms? Are the inter-relationships between VCs and BAs characterized by complementarity or substitutability and how is this affecting the investment process? Do the characteristics of angels (experience, education, social capital) matter in influencing the decision of VCs to co-invest with BAs or to invest sequentially? Understanding to what extent the interaction with VCs affects the decision making process in all these stages is clearly left for future studies.

5.3.3 *Post-Investment*

The motivations and implications of value-added activities performed by BAs in the post-investment phase are mainly based on limited case studies (a part from Madill *et al.*, 2005). Longitudinal quantitative analyses could expand the current knowledge, in order to understand when and why certain activities performed by angels are perceived as more valuable and how they vary as the post-investment relationship unfolds. More research on the role played by third parties (e.g. other investors, the entrepreneur, board members, management), by certain human capital characteristics, and by the diversity of skills and knowledge within groups on BAs' involvement in invested companies is warranted. In that sense, the use of new methodologies (e.g. dialectical techniques, verbal protocol analysis etc.) could enable a much richer understanding of the post-investment value provided by BAs, compared to self-reported, retrospective questionnaires and interviews.

5.3.4 *Impact on Investees' Performances*

Concerning this research line, there is a need for evidence that could resolve the current contrasting results on the impact of BAs' funding both at the investment and venture level. Also, the distribution of angel groups' financial returns and how syndication affects investment and venture performance are totally underexplored or inconclusive when addressed (Wiltbank, 2005). Thus, future promising research lines could address the following questions: Would ventures that had other sources of financing before the BA investment be better off without them? Would ventures perform better when investments are syndicated or when are invested by individual angels? What does the emergence of angel groups and the function of gatekeepers mean for companies' post-investment performance? Does angel groups provide better invest-ment returns to their members than those obtained by individual angels? What is the impact of co-investment strategies among BAs and VCs on investees' performances? And are there any differential effects when complementary and/or substitute roles between BAs and VCs are envisaged? Moreover, the adoption of more robust methodologies and performance measures would also allow to disentangle the causal effect of BA funding from a priori selection effect of better performing ventures by BAs themselves.

Notes

1. The literature reviews by Politis (2008) and Fili and Grünberg (2014), for example, con-centrate on BAs' value adding activities in the post investment phase on the basis of a limited number of papers (i.e. 14 and 29 papers respectively). Florin *et al*. (2013) analyse BAs' investment process by developing a conceptual framework grounded on prospect theory, without employing a rigorous methodology in the selection of the reviewed pa-pers. Another recent review by Scheela *et al*. (2015) focuses on BA research carried out in Southeast Asia.
2. Given our research objectives, we preferred to perform the bibliometric analysis on a widely recognised formal database like Scopus, which adopts a rigorous and transparent methodology to catalog articles, instead of using a more comprehensive, but less accurate tool (e.g. Google Scholar).
3. We arguably assume that such research products contain less validated knowledge, al-though we are aware that in this way some influential contributions might be overlooked.
4. The query was first run on 02/02/2016 and re-run on 30/08/2016 to check for recent added articles.
5. As said, Scopus excludes a number of articles on the topic. We searched within the main journals included in our sample and we found at least other 35 published articles about BAs that are not reported in Scopus. We decided not to include these papers in the present review to preserve the coherence between the thematic and the bibliometric analysis.
6. Founding angels are BAs who participate in the founding of start-ups, providing pre-seed financing and operational help.
7. One of the main sources of data for these studies is the Global Entrepreneurship Monitor (GEM) survey, a global dataset covering more than 100 countries dedicated to the study of individual-level entrepreneurial behaviours.
8. The paper is formally included under the research topic 'BA investment process' as it analyses BAs' investment process in emerging economies.
9. 'Gatekeepers' manage the outside relationships, especially with entrepreneurs, and pro-vide internal coordination. 'Nexus angels' facilitate entrepreneurs' access to hidden angel groups and support them in the attraction of angel capital.
10. Note that some of the papers analysed by the two aforementioned literature reviews are not included in the post investment category because, either they are published in jour-nals outside the Scopus database, or they have not been attributed to the post-investment phase, as they are descriptive in nature, without having a specific and unique focus on this stage. Therefore, we classified those papers under the thematic area BA characteristics (e.g. Prowse, 1998; Wetzel, 1983; Stendler and Peters, 2003), while we included in the post-investment research line only papers whose research questions are concerned with the identification of BAs' value-added activities.

11. Mason and Harrison (2002b) is the first study that provides an analysis of the distribution of BAs' returns, securing the authors the first place among the most cited papers on BAs (see Table 4). They find that almost half of UK BAs' investments make a loss, around 10% achieve break-even, around 20% report IRRs higher than 50%, while only 10% generate IRRs higher than 100%.
12. http://www8.umu.se/inforsk/Bibexcel/
13. A similar approach is adopted by Ghio *et al.* (2015) and Raasch *et al.* (2013).
14. Note that six of external backward citations refer to books, book chapters or conference proceedings, which are not included in the current review.

References

Aernoudt, R. (2004) Incubators: tool for entrepreneurship? *Small Business Economics* 23(2):127–135.
Aernoudt, R. (2005) Executive forum: seven ways to stimulate business angels' investments. *Venture Capital* 7(4):359–371.
Aernoudt, R., San José, A. and Roure, J. (2007) Executive forum: public support for the business angel market in Europe – a critical review. *Venture Capital* 9(1):71–84.
Amatucci, F.M. and Sohl, J.E. (2004) Women entrepreneurs securing business angel financing: tales from the field. *Venture Capital* 6(2–3):181–196.
Amatucci, F.M. and Swartz, E. (2011) Through a fractured lens: women entrepreneurs and the private equity negotiation process. *Journal of Developmental Entrepreneurship* 16(3):333–350.
Aram, J.D. (1989) Attitudes and behaviors of informal investors toward early-stage investments, technology-based ventures, and coinvestors. *Journal of Business Venturing* 4(5):333–347.
Argerich, J., Hormiga, E. and Valls-Pasola, J. (2013) Financial services support for entrepreneurial projects: key issues in the business angels investment decision process. *Service Industries Journal* 33(9–10):806–819.
Avdeitchikova, S. (2008) On the structure of the informal venture capital market in Sweden: developing investment roles. *Venture Capital* 10(1):55–85.
Avdeitchikova, S. (2009) False expectations: reconsidering the role of informal venture capital in closing the regional equity gap. *Entrepreneurship and Regional Development* 21(2):99–130.
Avdeitchikova, S., Landström, H. and Månsson, N. (2008) What do we mean when we talk about business angels? Some reflections on definitions and sampling. *Venture Capital* 10(4):371–394.
Baldock, R. and Mason, C. (2015) Establishing a new UK finance escalator for innovative SMEs: the roles of the enterprise capital funds and angel co-investment fund. *Venture Capital* 17(1–2):59–86.
Bammens, Y. and Collewaert, V. (2014) Trust between entrepreneurs and angel investors: exploring positive and negative implications for venture performance assessments. *Journal of Management* 40(7):1980–2008.
Becker-Blease, J.R. and Sohl, J.E. (2007) Do women-owned businesses have equal access to angel capital? *Journal of Business Venturing* 22(4):503–521.
Becker-Blease, J.R. and Sohl, J.E. (2015) New venture legitimacy: the conditions for angel investors. *Small Business Economics* 45(4):735–749.
Becker-Blease, J.R. and Sohl, J.E. (2011) The effect of gender diversity on angel group investment. *Entrepreneurship: Theory and Practice* 35(4):709–733
Bjørgum, Ø. and Sørheim, R. (2015) The funding of new technology firms in a pre-commercial industry – the role of smart capital. *Technology Analysis and Strategic Management* 27(3):249–266.
Bonnet, C. and Wirtz, P. (2012) Raising capital for rapid growth in young technology ventures: when business angels and venture capitalists coinvest. *Venture Capital* 14(2–3):91–110.
Brettel, M. (2003) Business angels in Germany: a research note. *Venture Capital* 5(3):251–268.
Brush, C.G., Edelman, L.F. and Manolova, T.S. (2012) Ready for funding? Entrepreneurial ventures and the pursuit of angel financing. *Venture Capital* 14(2–3):111–129.

Bruton, G.D., Filatotchev, I., Chahine, S. and Wright, M. (2010) Governance, ownership structure, and performance of IPO firms: the impact of different types of private equity investors and institutional environments. *Strategic Management Journal* 31(5):491–509.

Bruton, G.D., Chahine, S. and Filatotchev, I. (2009) Founders, private equity investors, and underpricing in entrepreneurial IPOs. *Entrepreneurship: Theory and Practice* 33(4):909–928.

Burke, A., Hartog, C., van Stel, A. and Suddle, K. (2010) How does entrepreneurial activity affect the supply of informal investors? *Venture Capital* 12(1):21–47.

Burke, A., van Stel, A., Hartog, C. and Ichou, A. (2014) What determines the level of informal venture finance investment? Market clearing forces and gender effects. *Small Business Economics* 42(3): 467–484.

Bygrave, W.D., Hay, M., Ng, E. and Reynolds, P. (2003) Executive forum: a study of informal investing in 29 nations composing the global entrepreneurship monitor. *Venture Capital* 5(2):101–116.

Capizzi, V. (2015) The returns of business angel investments and their major determinants. *Venture Capital* 17(4):271–298.

Carpentier, C. and Suret, J. (2015a) Angel group members' decision process and rejection criteria: a longitudinal analysis. *Journal of Business Venturing* 30(6):808–821.

Carpentier, C. and Suret, J. (2015b) Canadian business angel perspectives on exit: a research note. *International Small Business Journal* 33(5):582–593.

Chahine, S., Filatotchev, I. and Wright, M. (2007) Venture capitalists, business angels, and performance of entrepreneurial IPOs in the UK and France. *Journal of Business Finance and Accounting* 34(3–4):505–528.

Christensen, J.L. (2011) Should government support business angel networks? The tale of Danish business angels network. *Venture Capital* 13(4):337–356.

Clark, C. (2008) The impact of entrepreneurs' oral 'pitch' presentation skills on business angels' initial screening investment decisions. *Venture Capital* 10(3):257–279.

Collewaert, V. (2012) Angel investors' and entrepreneurs' intentions to exit their ventures: a conflict perspective. *Entrepreneurship: Theory and Practice* 36(4):753–779.

Collewaert, V., Manigart, S. and Aernoudt, R. (2010) Assessment of government funding of business angel networks in Flanders. *Regional Studies* 44(1):119–130.

Conti, A., Thursby, M. and Rothaermel, F.T. (2013) Show me the right stuff: signals for high-tech startups. *Journal of Economics and Management Strategy* 22(2):341–364.

De Clercq, D., Meuleman, M. and Wright, M. (2012) A cross-country investigation of micro-angel investment activity: the roles of new business opportunities and institutions. *International Business Review* 21(2):117–129.

Douglas, E.J., Carlsson-Wall, M. and Hjelström, T. (2014) Negotiating equity share and management control of the entrepreneurial new venture. *Venture Capital* 16(4):287–307.

Ding, Z., Au, K. and Chiang, F. (2015) Social trust and angel investors' decisions: a multilevel analysis across nations. *Journal of Business Venturing* 30(2):307–321.

Ding, Z., Sun, S.L. and Au, K. (2014) Angel investors' selection criteria: a comparative institutional perspective. *Asia Pacific Journal of Management*, 31(3), 705–731.

Duxbury, L., Haines, G. and Riding, A. (1996) A personality profile of Canadian informal investors. *Journal of Small Business Management* 34(2):44–55.

Elitzur, R. and Gavious, A. (2003) Contracting, signaling, and moral hazard: a model of entrepreneurs, 'angels', and venture capitalists. *Journal of Business Venturing* 18(6):709–725.

Erikson, T. and Sørheim, R. (2005) 'Technology angels' and other informal investors. *Technovation* 25(5):489–496.

Fairchild, R. (2011) An entrepreneur's choice of venture capitalist or angel-financing: a behavioral game-theoretic approach. *Journal of Business Venturing* 26(3):359–374.

Farrell, E., Howorth, C. and Wright, M. (2008) A review of sampling and definitional issues in informal venture capital research. *Venture Capital* 10(4):331–353.

Feeney, L., Haines, G.H. and Riding, A.L. (1999) Private investors' investment criteria: insights from qualitative data, *Venture Capital* 1:121–145.

Festel, G.W. and De Cleyn, S.H. (2013a) Founding angels as an emerging subtype of the angel investment model in high-tech businesses. *Venture Capital* 15(3):261–282.

Festel, G. and De Cleyn, S.H. (2013b) Founding angels as an emerging investment model in high-tech areas. *Journal of Private Equity* 16(4):37–45.

Fiet, J. (1995a) Risk avoidance strategies in venture capital markets, *Journal of Management Studies* 32:551–574.

Fiet, J.O. (1995b) Reliance upon informants in the venture capital industry. *Journal of Business Venturing* 10(3):195–223.

Fili, A. (2014) Business angel–venture negotiation in the post-investment relationship: the use of the good cop, bad cop strategy. *Venture Capital* 16(4):309–325.

Fili, A. and Grünberg, J. (2014) Business angel post-investment activities: a multi-level review. *Journal of Management and Governance* 20(1):89–114.

Florin, J., Dino, R. and Huvaj, M.N. (2013) Research on angel investing: a multilevel framework for an emerging domain of inquiry. *Venture Capital* 15(1):1–27.

Freear, J., Sohl, J.E. and Wetzel Jr., W.E. (1994) Angels and non-angels: are there differences? *Journal of Business Venturing* 9(2):109–123.

Freear, J., Sohlf, J.E. and Wetzel, W.E. (1995) Angels: personal investors in the venture capital market. *Entrepreneurship and Regional Development*, 7(1), 85–94

Freear, J. and Wetzel, W.E. (1990) Who bankrolls high-tech entrepreneurs? *Journal of Business Venturing* 5(2):77–89.

Gaston, R.J. (1989) The scale of informal capital markets. *Small Business Economics* 1(3):223–230.

Gaston, R.J. (1989) *Finding Private Venture Capital for Young Firm: A Complete Guide*. New York: Wiley.

Ghio, N., Guerini, M., Lehmann, E.E. and Rossi-Lamastra, C. (2015) The emergence of the knowledge spillover theory of entrepreneurship. *Small Business Economics* 44 (1):1–18.

Gimmon, E. (2008) Entrepreneurial team-starts and teamwork: taking the investors' perspective. *Team Performance Management* 14(7–8):327–339.

Gregson, G., Mann, S. and Harrison, R. (2013) Business angel syndication and the evolution of risk capital in a small market economy: evidence from Scotland. *Managerial and Decision Economics* 34(2):95–107.

Guild, P.D. and Bachher, J.S. (1996) Equity investment decisions for technology based ventures. *International Journal of Technology Management* 12(7–8):787–795.

Haar, N.E., Starr, J. and MacMillan, I.C. (1988) Informal risk capital investors: investment patterns on the East Coast of the U.S.A. *Journal of Business Venturing*, 3(1), 11–29.

Harrison, R.T. and Mason, C.M. (1992) International perspectives on the supply of informal venture capital. *Journal of Business Venturing* 7(6):459–475.

Harrison, R.T. and Mason, C.M. (1991) Informal investment networks: a case study from the United Kingdom. *Entrepreneurship and Regional Development* 3(3):269–279.

Harrison, R.T. and Mason, C.M. (2007) Does gender matter? Women business angels and the supply of entrepreneurial finance. *Entrepreneurship: Theory and Practice* 31(3):445–472.

Harrison, R.T., Don, G., Johnston, K.G. and Greig, M. (2010a) The early-stage risk capital market in Scotland since 2000: issues of scale, characteristics and market efficiency. *Venture Capital* 12(3):211–239.

Harrison, R.T., Mason, C.M. and Robson, P. (2010b) Determinants of long-distance investing by business angels in the UK. *Entrepreneurship and Regional Development* 22(2):113–137.

Harrison, R.T., Mason, C.M. and Smith, D. (2015) Heuristics, learning and the business angel investment decision-making process. *Entrepreneurship and Regional Development* 27(9–10):527–554.

Hearn, B. (2014) The impact of institutions, ownership structure, business angels, venture capital and lead managers on IPO firm underpricing across North Africa. *Journal of Multinational Financial Management* 24(1):19–42.

Hellmann T. and Thiele, V. (2015) Friends or foes? The interrelationship between angel and venture capital markets. *Journal of Financial Economics* 115(3):639–653.

Hsu, D.K., Haynie, J.M., Simmons, S.A. and McKelvie, A. (2014) What matters, matters differently: a conjoint analysis of the decision policies of angel and venture capital investors. *Venture Capital* 16(1):1–25.

Ibrahim, D.M. (2008) The (not so) puzzling behavior of angel investors. *Vanderbilt Law Review* 61(5):1403–1451.

Johnson, W.C. and Sohl, J. (2012a) Angels and venture capitalists in the initial public offering market. *Venture Capital* 14(1):27–42.

Johnson, W.C. and Sohl, J.E. (2012b) Initial public offerings and pre-IPO shareholders: angels versus venture capitalists. *Journal of Developmental Entrepreneurship* 17(4):1–23.

Kelly, P. and Hay, M. (2003) Business angel contracts: the influence of context. *Venture Capital* 5(4):287–312.

Kerr, W.R., Lerner, J. and Schoar, A. (2014) The consequences of entrepreneurial finance: evidence from angel financings. *Review of Financial Studies* 27(1):20–55.

Knyphausen-Aufse, D.Z. and Westphal, R. (2008) Do business angel networks deliver value to business angels? *Venture Capital* 10(2):149–169.

Lahti, T. (2011a) Categorization of angel investments: an explorative analysis of risk reduction strategies in Finland. *Venture Capital* 13(1):49–74.

Lahti, T. (2011b) Angel investing: an examination of the evolution of the Finnish market. *Venture Capital* 13(2):147–173.

Landström, H. (1992) The relationship between private investors and small firms: an agency theory approach. *Entrepreneurship and Regional Development* 4(3):199–223.

Landström, H. (1993) Informal risk capital in Sweden and some international comparisons. *Journal of Business Venturing* 8(6):525–540.

Landström, H. (1998) Informal investors as entrepreneurs. *Technovation* 18(5):321–333.

Levie, J. and Gimmon, E. (2008) Mixed signals: why investors may misjudge first time high technology venture founders. *Venture Capital* 10(3):233–256.

Lerner, J. (1998) 'Angel' financing and public policy: an overview. *Journal of Banking and Finance* 22(6–8):773–783.

Li, Y., Ling, L., Wu, J. and Li, P. (2014) Who is more likely to become business angels? Evidence of business angels and potential business angels from China. *Journal of Entrepreneurship in Emerging Economies* 6(1):4–20.

Li, Y., Jiang, S., Long, D., Tang, H. and Wu, J. (2014) An exploratory study of business angels in China: a research note. *Venture Capital* 16(1):69–83.

Lindsay, N.J. (2004) Do business angels have an entrepreneurial orientation? *Venture Capital* 6(2–3):197–210.

Lumme, A., Mason, C. and Suomi, M. (1998) *Informal Venture Capital: Investors, Investments and Policy in Finland*. Boston: Kluwer Academic Publishers.

Macht, S.A. (2011) The role of investee company managers in business angels' involvement: empirical insights from dyadic data. *Venture Capital* 13(3):267–293.

Macht, S.A. and Robinson, J. (2009) Do business angels benefit their investee companies? *International Journal of Entrepreneurial Behaviour and Research* 15(2):187–208.

Madill, J.J., Haines Jr., G.H. and Riding, A.L. (2005) The role of angels in technology SMEs: a link to venture capital. *Venture Capital* 7(2):107–129.

Manigart, S. and Struyf, C. (1997) Financing high technology startups in Belgium: an explorative study. *Small Business Economics* 9(2):125–135.

Månsson, N. and Landström, H. (2006) Business angels in a changing economy: the case of Sweden. *Venture Capital* 8(4):281–301.

Mason, C. and Harrison, R. (1992) The supply of equity finance in the UK: a strategy for closing the equity gap. *Entrepreneurship and Regional Development* 4(4):357–380.

Mason, C. and Harrison, R. (1993) Strategies for expanding the informal venture capital market. *International Small Business Journal* 11(4):23–38.

Mason, C.M. and Harrison, R.T. (1994) The informal venture capital market in the UK. In A. Hughes and D.J. Storey (Ed.), *Financing Small Firms* (pp. 64–111). London: Routledge.

Mason, C.M. and Harrison, R.T. (1995) Closing the regional equity capital gap: the role of informal venture capital. *Small Business Economics* 7(2):153–172.

Mason, C.M. and Harrison, R.T. (1996a) Informal venture capital: a study of the investment process, the post-investment experience and investment performance. *Entrepreneurship and Regional Development* 8(2):105–125.

Mason, C.M. and Harrison, R.T. (1996b) Why 'business angels' say no: a case study of opportunities rejected by an informal investor syndicate. *International Small Business Journal* 14(2):35–51.

Mason, C.M. and Harrison, R.T. (1997a) Business angels in the UK: a response to Stevenson and Coveney. *International Small Business Journal* 15(2):83–90.

Mason, C.M. and Harrison, R.T. (1997b) Business angel networks and the development of the informal venture capital market in the U.K.: is there still a role for the public sector? *Small Business Economics* 9(2):111–123.

Mason, C.M. and Harrison, R T. (2000) The size of the informal venture capital market in the United Kingdom. *Small Business Economics* 15(2):137–148.

Mason, C.M. and Harrison, R.T. (2002a) Barriers to investment in the informal venture capital sector. *Entrepreneurship and Regional Development* 14(3):271–287.

Mason, C.M. and Harrison, R.T. (2002b) Is it worth it? the rates of return from informal venture capital investments. *Journal of Business Venturing* 17(3):211–236.

Mason, C.M. and Harrison, R.T. (2004a) Does investing in technology-based firms involve higher risk? An exploratory study of the performance of technology and non-technology investments by business angels. *Venture Capital* 6(4):313–332.

Mason, C.M. and Harrison, R.T. (2004b) Improving access to early stage venture capital in regional economies: a new approach to investment readiness. *Local Economy* 19(2):159–173.

Mason, C.M. and Harrison, R.T. (2008) Measuring business angel investment activity in the United Kingdom: a review of potential data sources. *Venture Capital* 10(4):309–330.

Mason, C.M. and Stark, M. (2004) What do investors look for in a business plan? A comparison of the investment criteria of bankers, venture capitalists and business angels. *International Small Business Journal* 22(3):227–248.

Maula, M., Autio, E. and Arenius, P. (2005) What drives micro-angel investments? *Small Business Economics* 25(5):459–475.

Maxwell, A.L. and Lévesque, M. (2014) Trustworthiness: a critical ingredient for entrepreneurs seeking investors. *Entrepreneurship: Theory and Practice* 38(5):1057–1080.

Maxwell, A.L., Jeffrey, S.A. and Lévesque, M. (2011) Business angel early stage decision making. *Journal of Business Venturing* 26(2):212–225.

Mitteness, C.R., Baucus, M.S. and Sudek, R. (2012a) Horse vs. jockey? How stage of funding process and industry experience affect the evaluations of angel investors. *Venture Capital* 14(4): 241–267.

Mitteness, C., Sudek, R. and Cardon, M.S. (2012b) Angel investor characteristics that determine whether perceived passion leads to higher evaluations of funding potential. *Journal of Business Venturing* 27(5):592–606.

Moen, Ø., Sørheim, R. and Erikson, T. (2008) Born global firms and informal investors: examining investor characteristics. *Journal of Small Business Management* 46(4):536–549.

Murnieks, C.Y., Sudek, R. and Wiltbank, R. (2015) The role of personality in angel investing. *International Journal of Entrepreneurship and Innovation* 16(1):19–31.

Nofsinger, J.R. and Wang, W. (2011) Determinants of start-up firm external financing worldwide. *Journal of Banking and Finance* 35(9):2282–2294.

Organisation for Economic Co-operation and Development (OECD) (2011) Financing high-growth firms: the role of angel investors. OECD Publishing. Available at: http://doi.org/10.1787/9789264118782-en, (accessed on September 30, 2016).

O'Gorman, C. and Terjesen, S. (2006) Financing the Celtic tigress: venture financing and informal investment in Ireland. *Venture Capital* 8(1):69–88.

Parhankangas, A. and Ehrlich, M. (2014) How entrepreneurs seduce business angels: an impression management approach. *Journal of Business Venturing* 29(4):543–564.

Paul, S. and Whittam, G. (2010) Business angel syndicates: an exploratory study of gatekeepers. *Venture Capital* 12(3):241–256.

Paul, S., Whittam, G. and Johnston, J.B. (2003) The operation of the informal venture capital market in Scotland. *Venture Capital* 5(4):313–335.

Paul, S., Whittam, G. and Wyper, J. (2007) Towards a model of the business angel investment process. *Venture Capital* 9(2):107–125.

Persson, O., Danell, R. and Schneider, J.W. (2009) How to use Bibexcel for various types of bibliometric analysis. In: *Celebrating Scholarly Communication Studies: A Festschrift for Olle Persson at his 60th Birthday*, International society for Scientometrics and Informetrics (pp. 9–24). Umeå and Sydney: Aalborg, Copenhagen.

Pittaway, L., Robertson, M., Munir, K., Denyer, D. & Neely, A. (2004) Networking and innovation: a systematic review of the evidence. *International Journal of Management Reviews* 5(6):137–168

Politis, D. (2008) Business angels and value added: what do we know and where do we go? *Venture Capital* 10(2):127–147.

Porter, M. and Spriggs, M. (2013) Informal private equity investment networks: the role of the nexus angel. *Journal of Private Equity* 16(3):48–56.

Prowse, S. (1998) Angel investors and the market for angel investments. *Journal of Banking and Finance* 22(6–8):785–792.

Raasch, C., Lee, V., Spaeth, S. and Herstatt, C. (2013) The rise and fall of interdisciplinary research: the case of open source innovation. *Research Policy* 42(5):1138–1151.

Riding, A.L. (2008) Business angels and love money investors: segments of the informal market for risk capital. *Venture Capital* 10(4):355–369.

Roach, G. (2010) Is angel investing worth the effort? A study of keiretsu forum. *Venture Capital* 12(2):153–166.

Robinson, M.J. and Cottrell, T.J. (2007) Investment patterns of informal investors in the Alberta private equity market. *Journal of Small Business Management* 45(1):47–67.

Romaní, G., Atienza, M. and Amorós, J.E. (2013) The development of business angel networks in Latin American countries: the case of Chile. *Venture Capital* 15(2):95–113.

Rostamzadeh, R., Ismail, K. and Zavadskas, E.K. (2014) Multi criteria decision making for assisting business angels in investments. *Technological and Economic Development of Economy* 20(4):696–720.

Sætre, A.S. (2003) Entrepreneurial perspectives on informal venture capital. *Venture Capital* 5(1):71–94.

San José, A., Roure, J. and Aernoudt, R. (2005) Business angel academies: unleashing the potential for business angel investment. *Venture Capital* 7:149–165.

Scheela, W. (2006) Knowledge transfer: the development of venture capital in South East Asia. In J. Butler, A. Lockett and D. Ucbasaran (Eds.), *Venture Capital and the Changing World of Entrepreneurship* (pp. 75–90). Greenwich: Information Age.

Scheela, W. and Isidro, E.S. (2008) Private equity investing in the Philippines: business angel vs. venture capitalists. *Journal of Private Equity* 11(2):90–99.

Scheela, W. and Isidro, E.S. (2009) Business angel investing in an emerging Asian economy. *Journal of Private Equity* 12(4):44–56.

Scheela, W. and Jittrapanun, T. (2012) Do institutions matter for business angel investing in emerging Asian markets? *Venture Capital* 14(4):289–308.

Scheela, W., Isidro, E., Jittrapanun, T. and Trang, N.T.T. (2015) Formal and informal venture capital investing in emerging economies in Southeast Asia. *Asia Pacific Journal of Management* 32(3):597–617.

Scheela, W. and Nguyen, V.D. (2001) Doing business in Vietnam. *Thunderbird International Business Review* 43:669–687.

Scheela, W. and Nguyen, V.D. (2004) Venture capital in a transition economy: the case of Vietnam. *Venture Capital* 6:333–350.

Sohl, J.E. and Hill, L. (2007) Women business angels: insights from angel groups. *Venture Capital* 9(3):207–222.

Sohl, J.E. and Rosenberg, W. (2003) The private equity market in the USA: lessons from volatility. *Venture Capital* 5(1):29–46.

Sørheim, R. (2003) The pre-investment behaviour of business angels: a social capital approach. *Venture Capital* 5(4):337–364.

Sørheim, R. (2005) Business angels as facilitators for further finance: an exploratory study. *Journal of Small Business and Enterprise Development* 12(2):178–191.

Sørheim, R. and Landström, H. (2001) Informal investors – a categorization, with policy implications. *Entrepreneurship and Regional Development* 13(4):351–370.

Stedler, H.R. and Peters, H.H. (2003) Business angels in Germany: an empirical study. *Venture Capital* 5(3):269–276.

Stevenson, H. and Coveney, P. (1996) A survey of business angels. In R. Blackburn and P. Jennings (eds.), *Small Firms: Contributions to Economic Regeneration* (pp. 37–48). London: Paul Chapman Publishing.

Sullivan, M.K. and Miller, A. (1996) Segmenting the informal venture capital market: economic, hedonistic, and altruistic investors. *Journal of Business Research* 36(1):25–34.

Szerb, L., Terjesen, S. and Rappai, G. (2007a) Seeding new ventures-green thumbs and fertile fields: individual and environmental drivers of informal investment. *Venture Capital* 9(4):257–284.

Szerb, L., Rappai, G., Makra, Z. and Terjesen, S. (2007b) Informal investment in transition economies: individual characteristics and clusters. *Small Business Economics* 28(2–3):257–271.

Thorpe, R., Holt, R., MacPherson, A. and Pittaway, L. (2005) Using knowledge within small and medium-sized firms: a systematic review of the evidence. *International Journal of Management Reviews* 7(4):257–281.

Tingchi, M.L. and Chang, B.C.P. (2007) Business angel investment in the China market. *Singapore Management Review* 29(2):89.

Van Osnabrugge, M. (2000) A comparison of business angel and venture capitalist investment procedures: an agency theory-based analysis. *Venture Capital* 2:91–109.

Van Osnabrugge, M. and Robinson, R.J. (2000) *Angel Investing: Matching Startup Funds with Startup Companies – The Guide for Entrepreneurs and Individual Investors*. San Francisco: John Wiley & Sons.

Vanacker, T., Collewaert, V. and Paeleman, I. (2013) The relationship between slack resources and the performance of entrepreneurial firms: the role of venture capital and angel investors. *Journal of Management Studies* 50(6):1070–1096.

Veselovsky, M.Y., Suglobov, A.E., Khoroshavina, N.S., Abrashkin, M.S. and Stepanov, A.A. (2015) Business angel investment in Russia: problems and prospects. *International Journal of Economics and Financial Issues* 5(3S):231–237.

Wallnöfer, M. and Hacklin, F. (2013) The business model in entrepreneurial marketing: a communication perspective on business angels' opportunity interpretation. *Industrial Marketing Management*, 42(5), 755–764.

Werth, J.C. and Boeert, P. (2013) Co-investment networks of business angels and the performance of their start-up investments. *International Journal of Entrepreneurial Venturing* 5(3):240–256.

Wetzel Jr., W.E. (1981a) Informal risk capital in New England. In K.H. Vesper (Ed.), *Frontiers of Entrepreneurship Research* (pp. 217–245). Wellesley, MA: Babson College.

Wetzel Jr., W.E. (1981b) Technovation and the informal investor. *Technovation* 1(1):15–30.

Wetzel Jr., W.E. (1983) Angels and informal risk capital. *Sloan Management Review* 24(4):23–34.

Wetzel Jr., W.E. (1987) The informal venture capital market: aspects of scale and market efficiency. *Journal of Business Venturing* 2(4):299–313.

Wilson, H.I.M. (1995) Are the business angels of today the venture capitalists of yesterday? *Journal of High Technology Management Research* 6(1):145–156.

Wiltbank, R. (2005) Investment practices and outcomes of informal venture investors. *Venture Capital* 7(4):343–357.

Wiltbank, R., Read, S., Dew, N. and Sarasvathy, S.D. (2009) Prediction and control under uncertainty: outcomes in angel investing. *Journal of Business Venturing* 24(2):116–133.

Wong, P.K. and Ho, Y.P. (2007) Characteristics and determinants of informal investment in Singapore. *Venture Capital* 9(1):43–70.

Xiao, L. and Ritchie, B. (2011) Informal investor investing and networks in China: an exploratory study. *Journal of Private Equity* 14(3):72–85.

Supporting Information

Additional Supporting information may be found in the online version of this article at the publisher's website: https://doi.org/10.1111/joes.12224

Table A1. Summary of the Articles Included in the Review.

8

VENTURE CAPITAL INTERNATIONALIZATION: SYNTHESIS AND FUTURE RESEARCH DIRECTIONS

David Devigne

PMV
Vlerick Business School and Ghent University

Sophie Manigart

Vlerick Business School

Tom Vanacker and Klaas Mulier

Ghent University

1. Introduction

Venture capital is a subset of private equity and refers to investments made for the launch, early growth or expansion of companies.[1] Many high profile companies including Apple, Facebook, Spotify, Google, Gilead Sciences, Starbucks, Airbnb, and Uber raised VC funds in their early years to boost their growth. VC firms are financial market intermediaries, specializing in the management of information asymmetries and high levels of uncertainty (Amit *et al.*, 1998; Gompers and Lerner, 2001). They provide capital to companies that otherwise face severe difficulties to attract financing (Wright and Robbie, 1998; Gompers and Lerner, 2001). The companies that VC firms target are typically small and young, often have negative cash flows, operate in new or volatile markets and possess low levels of collateral (Stuart *et al.*, 1999; Ueda, 2004; Vanacker and Manigart, 2010). VC firms generally invest in these high-risk companies by purchasing equity or equity-linked minority stakes, often take an active monitoring and value adding role, and aim for significant capital gains at exit some 5 to 7 years after an initial investment (Gompers and Lerner, 2001).

Due to the need to reduce information asymmetries and related adverse selection and moral hazard problems, VC investing has long been a local industry (Wright and Robbie, 1998; Cumming and Dai, 2010). The geographical proximity to investment targets was

---

Contemporary Topics in Finance: A Collection of Literature Surveys, First Edition. Edited by Iris Claus and Leo Krippner.
Chapters © 2019 The Authors. Book compilation © 2019 John Wiley & Sons Ltd. Published 2019 by John Wiley & Sons Ltd.

deemed necessary to locate and evaluate target companies (Sorenson and Stuart, 2001) and to efficiently provide postinvestment monitoring and value adding services (Mäkelä and Maula, 2006). As a consequence, investing in nondomestic companies brings liabilities of foreignness for VC investors (Wright *et al.*, 2005), which are "all additional costs a firm operating in a market overseas incurs that a local firm would not incur" (Zaheer, 1995: 343). Compared to domestic VC investments, international VC investments present additional risks and challenges because the geographical, cultural, and institutional distance between portfolio companies and VC investors increases (Devigne *et al.*, 2016).

Given the benefits of local presence, cross-border VC investments were a negligible fraction of the total VC investment activity prior to the early 1990s (Manigart *et al.*, 2010). The enhanced domestic competition in maturing VC industries has, among other factors, increasingly driven VC firms to search for investment opportunities abroad (e.g., Alhorr *et al.*, 2008; Meuleman and Wright, 2011; Tykvová and Schertler, 2011; Aizenman and Kendall, 2012; Vedula and Matusik, 2017). Chemmanur *et al.* (2016) report that cross-border VC investments increased from 10% of all VC investments in 1991 to 22% in 2008 (based on the number of VC investments). Schertler and Tykvová (2011) report that over the period 2000–2008 cross-border VC deals (i.e., deals with at least one foreign VC) accounted for almost one-third of total VC deals worldwide. It is clear that the number of international VC transactions has become non-negligible.

Early research on VC in an international context has focused on comparing domestic VC behavior between different countries (Sapienza *et al.*, 1996; Manigart *et al.*, 2000, 2002; Bruton *et al.*, 2005). This research stream enables to comprehend the differences between VC markets in different countries but it does not provide insights into the challenges faced by VC firms when entering and managing investments in international markets, which is the focus of this paper. While we do not minimize the importance of the numerous papers that have studied various aspects of VC in general and VC internationalization in specific, this paper reviews three major research streams that we identified in the international VC investment literature. A first research stream assesses the country-level and firm-level determinants of international VC investments and the characteristics of favored target countries. A second stream of research focuses on the strategies international VC investors adopt to mitigate liabilities of foreignness. A third research stream examines the outcomes of international VC investments. We then discuss the role of public policy and government VC for VC internationalization. Finally, we discuss several general areas for future research on VC internationalization and specific areas for future research in the three major streams of research that we reviewed within this literature.

2. Determinants of International VC Investment Flows

Given the advantages of proximity between VC investors and portfolio companies (Sorenson and Stuart, 2001; Mäkelä and Maula, 2006), a first important question is why VC firms invest across borders. Below, we discuss both country-level and VC firm-level determinants of international VC flows that have been advanced in the literature.

2.1 *Country-Level Determinants*

Extant research highlights several country-level determinants that impact international flows of VC (e.g., Balcarcel *et al.*, 2010; Guler and Guillén, 2010a; Schertler and Tykvová, 2011,

2012; Aizenman and Kendall, 2012). Selected studies in this domain—that have asked the research question why some countries *import* or *export* more VC than others—are summarized in Table 1.

An important determinant driving the import of international VC is the institutional development of the target country. International VC investors preferably target institutionally developed countries as this creates a more investor-friendly climate with more transparency and fewer information asymmetries between VC owners and their portfolio companies (Balcarcel *et al.*, 2010; Groh *et al.*, 2010; Guler and Guillén, 2010a; Aizenman and Kendall, 2012). VC firms hence invest in target countries characterized by technological, legal, financial, and political institutions that create innovative opportunities, protect investors' rights, facilitate exit, and guarantee regulatory stability. Further, the local presence of qualified human capital is an important factor to attract international VC flows in countries (Aizenman and Kendall, 2012).

Some country characteristics impact both the import and the export of VC (Groh *et al.*, 2010). Specifically, expected economic growth in the home and target country are important factors. Expected GDP growth in the target country is positively associated with the number of deals financed by both domestic and international investors, while expected GDP growth in the country of origin of the VC investor discourages VC exports (Schertler and Tykvová, 2011; Aizenman and Kendall, 2012). These findings suggest that VC firms with more promising investment opportunities in their home country prefer to invest more intensively at home and less intensively abroad. Furthermore, the size of the stock market is a strong determinant of VC import and export. Active stock markets of the target countries provide exit mechanisms for successful portfolio companies (Groh *et al.*, 2010). A country with an active stock market will not only lead to more domestic deals, it will also attract more foreign investors. Interestingly, VC firms operating in a country with an active stock market will also invest more internationally (Schertler and Tykvová, 2011; Aizenman and Kendall, 2012). One potential explanation for this finding is that VC firms located in countries with an active stock market may push their foreign portfolio companies to relocate to the VC firms' country of origin to facilitate IPO exits (Cumming *et al.*, 2009a).

Several studies have also investigated the impact of *differences* between target and investor country characteristics to explain VC flows between these countries. Expected economic growth differences between countries are positively related to a net flow of VC from the low growth to the high growth country (Schertler and Tykvová, 2011). Smaller geographical distance (Colombo *et al.*, 2017), common language, colonial ties (Aizenman and Kendall, 2012) and between-country trust (Bottazzi *et al.*, 2016) increase the flows of VC between countries. When countries' economies become more integrated, as in the European Union, an increase in the amount of international VC investment is likely to follow (Alhorr *et al.*, 2008). Institutional environments hence play an important role in international VC flows.

The presence of strong industry networks between the VC firm's home country and its target country also enhances international VC flows (Madhavan and Iriyama, 2009). Further, "transnational technical communities," which are groups of immigrants active in both home- and host-country technical networks, positively affect international VC flows: higher professional and technical immigration levels from a target nation to the United States predicts higher VC outflows from the United States to the target nation (Madhavan and Iriyama, 2009). Hochberg *et al.* (2010) also show that there is less entry by outside VCs in more densely networked local VC markets within the United States, i.e., markets where network ties among incumbents are strong (Hochberg *et al.*, 2010). Outside VC firms with established ties with local VC firms are able to overcome this barrier to entry, but other local VC firms may react

Table 1. Selected Studies on the Country-Level Determinants of International VC Investments.

Year–Authors	Data sources	Sample	Literature/theory base	Key findings
2008–Alhorr *et al.*	Securities Data Corporation (SDC) Platinum (Thomson Financial Corporation)	24 EU countries for the period between 1985 and 2002	Institutional theory	When countries' economies become more integrated (i.e., adoption of a common market and a common currency), an increase in the amount of international VC investment made into other member countries follows.
2009–Madhavan and Iriyama	Thomson VentureXpert, IMF, Statistical Yearbook of the Immigration and Naturalization Service USA Department of Justice	VC flows from 1982 to 2002 for all nations that have hosted VC flow from the USA as of 2002	Network theory, Social embeddedness perspective	Groups of immigrants active in both the home- and host-country technical networks significantly affect international VC flows. Professional and technical cumulative immigration levels from a given nation to the United States predict VC outflows from the United States to that nation.
2010a– Guler and Guillén	Thomson VentureXpert	216 USA VC firms potentially investing in 95 countries during the 1990–2002 period	Institutional theory	(1) VC firms invest in host countries characterized by technological, legal, financial, and political institutions that create innovative opportunities, protect investors' rights, facilitate exit, and guarantee regulatory stability, respectively. (2) As VC firms gain more international experience, they are more likely to overcome constraints related to these institutions.
2011–Schertler and Tykvová	Zephyr	Worldwide sample of 58,377 VC-portfolio company (PC) links	Institutional theory, Info asymmetry, Macro economics	(1) Expected growth differences between the PC's and VC firm's country are strongly positively related to the number of international deals between the two countries. (2) Expected growth in the VC firm's home country strongly increases the number of domestic deals, while it slightly discourages the number of international deals. (3) A higher market capitalization in the VC firm's home countries leads to more domestic as well as foreign deals. (4) The number of deals financed by foreign investors increases when the expected growth and the market capitalization of the PCs' countries increase.

Author/Year	Data source	Framework/Theory	Findings
2012– Aizenman and Kendall	Thomson VentureXpert	Data on VC investments in over 100 countries covering three decades	Distance, common language, and colonial ties are significant determinants in directing the international VC and VC flows. Moreover, local high end human capital, better business environments, higher levels of military expenditure, and larger financial markets are important factors that attract international VC.
2011–Schertler and Tykvová	Zephyr	Domestic and international VC investments in 15 European countries, the United States, and Canada from 2000 to 2008	Two country demand–supply framework. Most economic factors shape gross and net inflows in a similar way. Two target country economic factors drive gross and net international VC inflow differently. Higher expected economic growth leads to higher gross as well as net international VC inflows, while more developed capital markets and more favorable VC environment results in higher gross inflows, but lower net inflows.
2009– Bottazzi et al.	A survey of 685 VC firms in 15 European countries. Eurostat (trust from the citizens of one country toward the citizens of another country)	107 useable responses on survey	Social capital theory, discrete choice framework. (1) Trust has a significant effect on the investment decisions of VC firms and on how they structure contracts. (2) Trust among nations significantly affects VC firms' investment decisions. Earlier stage investments require higher trust and syndication is more valuable in low-trust situations. (3) Higher trust investors use more contingent contracts.

strategically to increased threats of entry and heightened competition by freezing out local firms that facilitate entry (Hochberg *et al.*, 2010). It would be interesting to examine such potential relationships using a cross-country dataset.

2.2 *VC Firm-Level Determinants*

Besides country-level determinants, several VC firm-level determinants impact individual VC firm's probability to invest in foreign countries. Selected studies in this domain are summarized in Table 2.

Structural and strategic features of VC firms—such as their investment focus, type, and reputation—impact their probability to invest across borders (Gupta and Sapienza, 1992; Fritsch and Schilder, 2008; Cumming and Dai, 2010). VC investment strategies that require higher resource consumption in the form of stronger monitoring are associated with a narrower geographic scope. This includes acting as lead investor or targeting entrepreneurial ventures with very high information asymmetries such as early stage or technology ventures. Corporate VC firms and more reputable VC firms—i.e., older, larger, more experienced, and with a stronger IPO track record—exhibit a broader geographic scope (Gupta and Sapienza, 1992; Cumming and Dai, 2010). These VC investors seem better able to reduce information asymmetries associated with distance. In contrast, government-related VC firms have a narrow geographic scope (Bertoni *et al.*, 2015). Finally, VC firms in which investment managers can devote more time to their portfolio companies (i.e., VC firms with more investment executives per portfolio company) also have a broader geographic scope (Fritsch and Schilder, 2008), consistent with larger distance requiring higher time commitments of the VC investors.

A VC firm's human capital (the nature of the experience of its managers) and social capital (its network of syndication partners) strongly determine its internationalization strategy. First, with respect to a VC firms' human capital, the international investment experience of a VC firm's investment managers impacts its geographic scope (Patzelt *et al.*, 2009; Schertler and Tykvová, 2011, 2012; De Prijcker *et al.*, 2012). VC firms with more managers with foreign experience invest more intensively abroad (Schertler and Tykvová, 2011, 2012) because they are more familiar with the institutional and legal environment in foreign countries and have a better access to international networks. Higher proportions of investment managers with international or entrepreneurial experience also lead to a broader geographic investment scope (Patzelt *et al.*, 2009; De Prijcker *et al.*, 2012). Inherited knowledge through prior foreign work experience of VC firm's management outside the focal VC firm also has a positive effect on internationalization (De Prijcker *et al.*, 2012).

Second, a VC firm's social capital also has a major impact on its geographic scope (Sorenson and Stuart, 2001; Cumming and Dai, 2010; Iriyama *et al.*, 2010; Vedula and Matusik, 2017). Social networks in the VC industry—developed through syndication—diffuse information about potential investment opportunities across boundaries, thereby expanding the spatial investment radius of VC investors (Sorenson and Stuart, 2001). Better networked VC firms hence exhibit less local bias (Sorenson and Stuart, 2001; Cumming and Dai, 2010). These results show that despite communication technology advances, inherent boundaries around the flow of timely, reliable, fine grained and high-quality information still produce localized patterns of exchange. Better networked VC firms are able to reduce information asymmetries associated with distance through interpersonal social relations with local investors. Interestingly, Vedula and Matusik (2017) show that while syndication partners

Table 2. Selected Studies on the VC Firm-Level Determinants of International VC Investments.

Year–Authors	Data sources	Sample	Literature/theory base	Key findings
2009–Patzelt *et al.*	EVCA yearbook of year 2005	TMTs and portfolio strategies of 136 European VC firms	Upper echelon theory	VC firms with higher proportions of TMT members with international or entrepreneurial experience have a broader geographic investment scope.
2010–Iriyama *et al.*	Thomson VentureXpert	50,490 region-nation-year pairs (i.e., 51 USA states, 90 foreign nations and 11 years from 1995 to 2006)	Network theory	The spread of USA international VC investments has a spiky geographical pattern as–driven by the spiky international pattern of human networks–the linkages between certain regions in the United States and some foreign countries is exceptionally intense.
2010–Cumming and Dai	Thomson VentureXpert	Sample of USA VC investments: 122,248 VC company round observations, representing 20,875 companies invested by 1,908 VC firms from 1980 to 2009	Info asymmetry	(1) More reputable VC firms (older, larger, more experienced, and with stronger IPO track record) and VC firms with broader networks prefer a broader geographic scope. (2) VC firm specializing in technology industries and using more staging prefer a narrower geographic scope. (3) VC firms prefer a narrower geographic scope when they are the lead VC and when investing alone.
2011– Schertler and Tykvová	Zephyr	Worldwide sample of 58,377 VC-PC links	Institutional theory, Info asymmetry, Macro economics	(1) VC firms with more foreign and domestic experience invest more intensely abroad since they are more familiar with the institutional and legal environment in foreign countries and have a better access to international networks. (2) VC firms with extensive domestic experience invest internationally more often since they more easily implement a geographical diversification of their portfolios.

(Continued)

Table 2. *Continued*

Year–Authors	Data sources	Sample	Literature/theory base	Key findings
2012–De Prijcker *et al.*	Hand-collected data, questionnaires, archival data, national and European VC associations, Zephyr	110 VC firms from five European countries	Info asymmetry, Agency risk, Network theory	(1) International human capital of VC firms increases the likelihood to operate internationally. (2) VC manager's experience and inherited knowledge have a positive effect on internationalization, but external knowledge has limited impact. (3) Intense international contacts even decrease international activities. (4) Together, these results highlight the importance of VC manager's experience and inherited knowledge to overcome information asymmetries inherent in the internationalization of professional service firms, and of VC firms in particular.
2017–Vedula and Matusik	Thomson VentureXpert	517 first internationalization decisions from 2,160 USA VC firms, representing a sample of 12,654 VC firm-year observations between 1990 and 2012.	Institutional isomorphism	Social cues drive VC firms' first internationalization decisions. A focal VC firm is more likely to internationalize when the number of geographically proximal firms with foreign activities increases. A higher level of foreign investment activity by syndicate partners also positively affects a focal VC firm's first internationalization decision. The economic significance of cues from geographically proximal peers is much larger than cues from syndicate partners.

with foreign experience positively impact USA VC firms' first internationalization decision, social cues from geographically proximal peers have an even stronger impact.

3. Strategies to Compensate for Liabilities of Foreignness

Multiple studies show that portfolio companies differ in the way they are sourced, funded, syndicated and monitored by domestic versus international VC firms (Mäkelä and Maula, 2006).[2] The increased geographical, cultural, and institutional distance that foreign VC firms face, severely limits domestically used strategies to mitigate information asymmetries. In a local context, VC firms manage uncertainty by sourcing favorable investment targets through their entrusted local networks and intensive screening involving face to face meetings (Sorenson and Stuart, 2001). Moreover, VC firms provide their portfolio companies with more than financial resources: after the investment, they provide value adding services and access to other resources (Sapienza et al., 1996; Hsu, 2004). Value adding activities are hindered when investing across borders, because these activities often require proximity and a fine-grained understanding of the local environment, especially for early stage portfolio companies (Devigne et al., 2013). As a result, VC firms investing internationally will have to adapt their investment process rather than merely implementing the "recipes" from their domestic markets. For instance, foreign VC firms in India place greater emphasis on product market factors and accountants' reports than domestic VC firms when selecting investment targets in India (Wright et al., 2002) and they prefer strategic monitoring and advice rather than monitoring of the operational activities because the former is easier to provide across distance (Pruthi et al., 2003).

Table 3 summarizes selected studies that examine how VC investors minimize liabilities of foreignness when investing across borders.

The first step in the VC cycle is to generate deal flow from which to select promising investment targets. A VC firm can either proactively search for deals (solicited deals) or passively wait for deals approaching (unsolicited deals) through the entrepreneur, the VC firm's network or an intermediary (Lu and Hwang, 2010). Generating sufficient deal flow is more challenging for VCs operating across borders, as foreign VC firms originate fewer unsolicited deals from their networks compared to domestic VC firms (Lu and Hwang, 2010). In response, international VC firms mainly draw upon their home country advantages by originating more solicited deals from networks (Lu and Hwang, 2010). Moreover, some VC firms' domestic network advantages, such as their social status advantages, are transferable from the VC firms' home country to the target company's country (Guler and Guillén, 2010b), leading to higher deal flow generation for higher status international VC firms.

Selecting the right investment targets among the deals presented is one of the most important drivers of VC success (Sorensen, 2007). When targeting portfolio companies in a foreign country, a higher geographical and cultural distance and a lower embeddedness in the portfolio companies' environment hampers the transfer of soft information (Devigne et al., 2016). A strategy used by cross-border VC firms to overcome information problems is therefore to select portfolio companies with lower ex ante information asymmetries. Foreign VC firms are more likely to invest in more information-transparent portfolio companies, i.e., in a later stage, in a later round or in larger deals (Schertler and Tykvová, 2011; Dai et al., 2012).

When structuring the cross-border investment, deal features and legal contracts may also be used as a tool to mitigate information problems (Bengtsson and Ravid, 2009; Bottazzi et al., 2009; Balcarel et al., 2010). Cross-border VC investors invest larger amounts in portfolio companies in countries with worse legal protection (Balcarel et al., 2010). This finding

Table 3. Selected Studies on the Strategies Used to Mitigate Liabilities of Foreignness.

Year–Authors	Data sources	Sample	Literature/theory base	Key findings
2002–Wright *et al.*	Interviews with VC executives	31 VC firms investing in India	Institutional theory, Info asymmetry	(1) Foreign (mainly United States) VC firms in India place significantly greater emphasis on product market factors and accountants' reports than domestic firms in India. (2) They place significantly less emphasis on financial contributions of the PC's management in assessing risk and own due diligence and information from entrepreneurs than do USA firms in their domestic market. (3) High levels of employment of Indian nationals afford access to local information networks but foreign firms were also more likely to seek other independent info.
2003–Pruthi *et al.*	Asia Pacific Private Equity Bulletin (VC directory), questionnaire, face-to-face interviews	31 interviews (84% of active VC firms in India in year 2000)	Info asymmetry, Agency theory	(1) Cross-border VC firms are more involved on the strategic level and domestic ones on the operational level of steering PCs. (2) Cross-border VC firms prefer strategic monitoring and advice which is easier to guarantee across distance than monitoring of the operational activities.
2008–Mäkelä and Maula	58 semistructured interviews, observations and several secondary sources (Thomson VentureXpert, company websites, press releases, newspapers,…)	9 PCs from Finland that have their primary market in foreign nations and were invested by at least one cross-border VC	Grounded theory approach, and case study, Institutional theory	Cross-border VC investors preferably invest in companies to which local VC firms have provided operational management advice, introduced local contacts and local market knowledge. The importance of this preparation by local VC firms is mitigated when the entrepreneurs are highly experienced or when the home market is not important for the PC. The domestic VC firms hence have an important signaling value which facilitates cross-border investment and syndication.

2009–Bottazzi et al.	Survey mailed to 750 VC firms, Amadeus, Worldscope, and Thomson VentureXpert	1,431 investments from 124 VC firms in 17 European countries for the period 1998–2001	Double moral hazard, Institutional theory	The VC firm's home country legal system plays a critical role in their behavior when investing abroad. Better legal systems are associated with more VC involvement and the VC investor's legal system is more important than the PC's in determining investor behavior even when investing abroad.
2009–Pruthi et al.	Questionnaire survey with qualitative interviews	37 International VC firms; 31 noninternational VC firms all investing in the United Kingdom	Knowledge-based view (exploratory approach)	(1) When foreign VC firms establish a local branch, the recruitment of local executives is more important than the deployment of expatriates. (2) From all suggested motives in literature, the most important reason for expatriation is to transfer knowledge. (3) Investment committees play a key role in the international decision-making process, they allow international VC firms to manage challenges faced by local branches that otherwise would require the deployment of expatriates.
2010–Lu and Hwang	EDB (Economic Development Board), AVCJ (Asia Venture Capital Journal), Survey in 1999	34 VC firms investing in Singapore responded to survey of which 17 are international VC firms	Liabilities of foreignness, Info asymmetry	Due to liabilities of foreignness, foreign VC firms investing in Singapore originate fewer unsolicited deals from their networks compared to domestic VC firms. In response to this drawback, international VC firms mainly draw upon their home country advantages by attempting to originate more solicited deals from networks.

(Continued)

Table 3. *Continued*

Year–Authors	Data sources	Sample	Literature/theory base	Key findings
2010b–Guler and Guillén	Thomson VentureXpert database, World Bank, Henisz's (2000) Index of Political Constraints, CEPII geographic distance database	All actual and potential investments of 1,010 USA-based VC firms active between 1990 and 2002 in 95 countries	Social network theory, Foreign expansion theory	Home-country network advantages of USA VC firms such as social status advantages are transferable from the home country to the target country.
2012–Dai et al.	Thomson VentureXpert database, SDC Platinum M&As, Global New Issues Database	2,860 PCs receiving 4,254 rounds of VC financing by 468 VC firms in Asia from 1996 to 2006	Info asymmetry	In the Asian VC markets, when investing alone, foreign VC firms are more likely to invest in more information-transparent (later stage, later round) PCs. Partnerships with domestic VC firms help alleviate information asymmetry and monitoring problem and have positive implications for the exit performance of local entrepreneurial firms.
2015–Huang et al.	Thomson VentureXpert	1,095 Chinese PCs, which received 3,365 foreign investments and 696 Chinese investments between 1992 and 2012	Learning perspective	Surprisingly, foreign VC firms are more likely to choose Chinese investors in later rounds and in more mature portfolio companies. Having a Chinese office made foreign VCs less likely to coinvest.

suggests that cross-border VC firms mitigate contracting problems in countries with weak legal environments by taking larger equity stakes (conditional on deciding to invest in a given firm), as this enables them to enforce control rights which courts may not be able to adequately enforce with smaller stakes. Further, when the geographical distance between a VC firm and its portfolio companies increases, investors negotiate contracts which give more high powered incentives to entrepreneurs, such as cash flow contingencies (Bengtsson and Ravid, 2009), thereby more strongly aligning the interests of investors and entrepreneurs. These findings support the view that distance makes monitoring more difficult and that VC investors try to mitigate this issue through contracting.

Furthermore, VC firms' domestic legal system impacts their behavior abroad. For example, VC firms from common law countries are more prone to use downside protection clauses, not only in their domestic investments but also when investing across borders (Balcarel *et al.*, 2010). Bottazzi *et al.* (2009) further show that more developed legal systems in a VC firm's home country are associated with more VC involvement and the VC investor's legal system is more important than the portfolio company's legal system in determining investor behavior even when investing abroad.

Another way to address problems of information asymmetries, monitoring, and resource transfer is to syndicate with local VC firms because this strategy allows to outsource the monitoring and value adding functions to local coinvestors who are not hindered by geographical, cultural or institutional distance (Mäkelä and Maula, 2008; Devigne *et al.*, 2013; Nahata *et al.*, 2014; Huang *et al.*, 2015; Chemmanur *et al.*, 2016). Additionally, a syndicate comprising both local and international VC investors provides a broader skill set, experience, and networks that may generate additional value to companies (Schertler and Tykvová, 2012; Devigne *et al.*, 2013). Coinvesting with domestic VC investors is especially used when entering less institutionally developed countries (Sorenson and Stuart, 2001; Guler and Guillén, 2010b; Meuleman and Wright, 2011; Dai *et al.*, 2012; Chemmanur *et al.*, 2016), although country-level uncertainty decreases the likelihood of coinvestments with local investors (Liu and Maula, 2016).

Yet, not all cross-border VC firms need local firms to mitigate information and resource transfer problems. Organizational learning, including a VC firm's focal country-level experience and its overall multinational experience, reduce its need to rely on local partners over time (Meuleman and Wright, 2011; Liu and Maula, 2016). Further, VC firms with more investment executives per portfolio company learn faster and hence have a lower probability to engage in cross-border syndication (Meuleman and Wright, 2011).

With which domestic VCs do cross-border VCs prefer to syndicate? Cross-border VCs typically prefer domestic VCs with whom they have pre-existing ties. However, high-quality legal frameworks and industry associations facilitate syndication between cross-border and local VCs and diminish the need for cross-border VCs to rely on pre-existing ties (Meuleman *et al.*, 2017).

Finally, the internationalization literature suggests yet another strategy to compensate for liabilities of foreignness, which is to set up a local branch office. This strategy ensures proximity to entrepreneurs, thereby reducing asymmetric information problems (Pruthi *et al.*, 2009). The foreign head office will typically be represented in the branches' investment committee that decides on investments and exits. This strategy allows the foreign head office to manage challenges that otherwise would require the deployment of expatriates (Pruthi *et al.*, 2009). When employing local investment professionals in the branches, cultural and institutional differences are reduced, thereby further facilitating the transfer of knowledge and advice to companies (Pruthi *et al.*, 2009; De Prijcker *et al.*, 2012; Devigne *et al.*, 2016). In the Chinese context,

Huang *et al.* (2015) find that having a Chinese office made foreign VCs less likely to syndicate with local VC firms, thereby suggesting that VC firms with a local branch feel they can address liabilities of foreignness by themselves (through the local office). VC firms' decision to open a branch in a foreign region is strongly driven by the success rate of VC investments in that region (Chen *et al.*, 2010). Research on the use of branch offices in the VC industry remains very limited, however.

4. Outcomes of International VC Investments

What matters for both entrepreneurs and VC investors is the development of the portfolio company, which is ultimately associated with the exit of investors. The exit from portfolio companies is the last and perhaps most important step in the VC cycle (Wright and Robbie, 1998; Gompers and Lerner, 2001). First, the exit route determines the VC firms' returns (Ruhnka and Young, 1987). Second, entrepreneurs are highly involved because the exit route not only impacts their financial return but also their future role within the company. Importantly, a successful outcome for the VC investor is not by definition a successful outcome for the entrepreneur. We will hence discuss the outcomes of international VC investments from the perspective of both the portfolio company and the VC investor.

4.1 *Outcomes from the Perspective of the Portfolio Company*

International VC investors impact their portfolio companies' development differently compared to domestic VC investors. Research has documented that companies backed by cross-border VC investors only grow more strongly in the long term (but not in the short term), while companies backed by a syndicate comprising both domestic and cross-border VC investors outperform all other combinations (e.g., domestic VC or cross border VC investors only) in terms of growth in sales, total assets and employment (Devigne *et al.*, 2013). This finding suggests that domestic and cross-border VC investors can play synergistic roles as their portfolio companies grow and thereby require different resources or capabilities over time.

More specifically, foreign VC investors may help their portfolio companies in their internationalization (e.g., Cumming *et al.*, 2009b; Chahine *et al.*, 2018). Foreign VC firms located in a portfolio company's export market can be especially valuable by legitimizing the unknown new company in that market (Mäkelä and Maula, 2005; Mäkelä and Maula, 2006), by playing a greater advisory and monitoring role (Chahine *et al.*, 2018) or by relocating the company into that market (Cumming *et al.*, 2009a). Local VC firms may actively help their portfolio companies in attracting cross-border VC investors, especially if portfolio companies seek to internationalize (Mäkelä and Maula, 2008) or require large amounts of specialized VC funds that are not always available in the home country (Vanacker *et al.*, 2014a). However, as cross-border investors tend to drive their portfolio companies towards their home markets, the above benefits may turn into disadvantages if portfolio companies' export markets differ from the home markets of the cross-border VC investors (Mäkelä and Maula, 2005).

Moreover, not all portfolio companies develop positively. Mäkelä and Maula (2006) develop a theoretical model which proposes that if a portfolio company's prospects decrease, a cross-border VC firm's commitment will drop more strongly compared to that of a domestic VC investor. Due to their lower embeddedness in the portfolio company's local environment and lower attachment to the entrepreneur, cross-border VC investors have lower attachments to their portfolio companies, thereby easing the abandonment decision (Devigne *et al.*, 2016).

This relationship is magnified with greater geographical distance but mitigated by the relative investment size and the investor's embeddedness in local syndication networks (Mäkelä and Maula, 2006).

In Table 4, we summarize selected studies that have primarily focused on the consequences of international VC investments from the portfolio company's perspective.

4.2 *Outcomes from the Perspective of the VC Firm*

Studies on the investment success of cross-border investors present mixed evidence. On the one hand, controlling for portfolio company quality and VC firm reputation, some studies have shown that cross-border VC firms are less likely than domestic VC firms to have successful exits (Humphery-Jenner and Suchard, 2013; Li *et al.*, 2014). Both institutional and cultural distances decrease the likelihood of a successful exit, although a VC investor's international experience may attenuate the negative effect of institutional distance (Li *et al.*, 2014). This evidence is consistent with liabilities of foreignness inhibiting a successful investment process, hampered by increased information asymmetries and more limited resource transfers (Devigne *et al.*, 2016).

On the other hand, other studies have suggested and shown that cross-border VC investors might bring additional exit opportunities (Bertoni and Groh, 2014). Specifically, controlling for firm performance, investor characteristics and local exit conditions, these studies show that cross-border VC firms have a higher probability of M&A and IPO exit (Cumming *et al.*, 2016), have faster M&A and IPO exits (Espenlaub *et al.*, 2015), and have higher IPO valuations (Cumming *et al.*, 2016; Chahine *et al.*, 2018). Cumming *et al.* (2016) do not find a difference between domestic and international VC M&A exit probability, however. The probability of a successful exit is especially higher for an international VC investor when investing in later stage companies (Humphery-Jenner and Suchard, 2013). Moreover, Knill (2009) shows that international geographical diversification is—on a VC firm portfolio level—the only diversification strategy which has no negative effect on the portfolio company exit performance, in contrast with industry or stage diversification. Nahata *et al.* (2014) show that the cultural distance between countries of the portfolio company and its lead VC investor positively affects exit success.

The above contradicting findings show that more research is needed to fully understand the relationship between international VC investing and exit outcomes. This relationship might, for example, be affected by macro forces such as the (difference in) institutional contexts of both investor and portfolio company, or micro forces such as VC firm and portfolio company characteristics.

Recent studies stress the benefits of local syndication for exit success of cross-border VC investments (thus, combining local and foreign VCs; Cumming and Dai, 2010; Dai *et al.*, 2012; Wang and Wang, 2012; Nahata *et al.*, 2014; Chemmanur *et al.*, 2016). Specifically, portfolio companies with both cross-border and local VC investors are about 5% more likely to exit successfully compared with portfolio companies backed by foreign VC firms only (Dai *et al.*, 2012). Interestingly, while Chemmanur *et al.* (2016) stress that this positive relationship is only present when investing in emerging countries, Nahata *et al.* (2014) find this relationship only in developed economies. Chemmanur *et al.* (2016) show that—in emerging nations and controlling for endogenous participation and syndication by cross-border VC firms—syndicates composed of domestic and cross-border VC firms have more successful exits and higher post-IPO operating performance relative to syndicates of purely domestic VC firms or purely

Table 4. Selected Studies on Outcomes from the Perspective of the Portfolio Company (PC).

Year–Authors	Data sources	Sample	Literature/theory base	Key findings
2005–Mäkelä and Maula	58 semistructured interviews, observations and several secondary sources (Thomson VentureXpert, company websites, press releases, newspapers....)	Nine PCs from Finland that have their primary market in foreign nations and were invested by at least one cross-border VC firm	Grounded theory approach, Case studies, Institutional theory	Foreign VC firms located in a PC's target market of internationalization can be valuable for the venture by legitimizing the unknown new PC in that market. However, foreign investors tend to drive PC toward their home markets, and the benefits may turn into disadvantages if the target market differs from the home markets of the foreign investors.
2006–Mäkelä and Maula	58 semistructured interviews, observations and several secondary sources (Thomson VentureXpert, company websites, press releases, newspapers....)	8 PCs from Finland that were invested by at least one domestic and one cross-border VC firm	Grounded theory approach, Case studies, Commitment theory	Changes in a PC's prospects influence the VC firm's commitment. This relationship magnified by the VC firm's geographical distance and mitigated by the relative investment size and the investor's embeddedness in local syndication networks.
2009a–Cumming *et al.*	Hand collected dataset from VC firms operating in the Asia-Pacific region using Asian Venture Capital Journal's Annual Guides; Asian Venture Capital Journal, Australian Venture Capital Journal, and Thomson VentureXpert	53 VC funds involving 468 PCs and 12 countries in Asia-Pacific region from 1989 to 2001	Institutional theory	(1) Relocations to the United States are motivated by economic conditions as well as an improvement in the laws of the country in which the entrepreneurial company is based. (2) Relocations to the United States yield much greater returns to Asia-Pacific VC firms than investing in companies already based in the United States at the time of VC investment. (3) More experienced Asia-Pacific VC firms have greater success with their PC relocations to the United States, and these relocations yield higher returns relative to staying in their country of origin.

2013–Devigne et al.	VICO dataset, including Thomson ONE, Zephyr, PATSTAT, country specific databases, press releases, press clippings, and websites.	761 European VC backed companies	Resource-based view	Companies initially backed by domestic VC investors exhibit higher growth in the short term compared to companies backed by cross-border investors. In contrast, companies initially backed by cross-border VC investors exhibit higher growth in the medium term. Finally, companies that are initially funded by a syndicate comprising both domestic and cross-border VC investors exhibit the highest growth. Overall, this study provides a more fine-grained understanding of the role that domestic and cross-border VC investors can play as their PCs grow and thereby require different resources or capabilities over time
2016–Devigne et al.	VICO dataset, including Thomson ONE, Zephyr, PATSTAT, country specific databases, press releases, press clippings, and websites.	Longitudinal data on 1,618 unique VC investment rounds in European firms by 1,060 different VC firms. The unit of analysis is the investment decision of each single VC firm in a portfolio company. The data set includes 3,445 investment decisions: 2,399 by domestic VC investors, 568 by cross-border VC investors, and 255 by branch VC investors.	Escalation of commitment	Domestic VC firms have a high tendency to escalate their commitment to a failing course of action. Cross-border VC investors, however, terminate their investments efficiently, even when investing through a local branch.

cross-border VC firms. These findings are again consistent with local VC syndication as a powerful tool to overcome liabilities of foreignness. Still, there is also evidence from USA VC investors, suggesting that the addition of a domestic partner in their cross-border deals is not associated with the probability of an IPO exit and is even negatively associated with an M&A exit (Wuebker *et al.*, 2015). Again, more research is needed to clarify these contradictory findings.

The effect of foreign VC firms' human capital on the exit success of their portfolio companies is not well understood yet. While Hursti and Maula (2007) find that the international experience of the VC management team is positively related to exit performance (more foreign IPOs) in developed markets, Wang and Wang (2011) show that there is little correlation between a foreign VC firms' human capital, such as its experience, networks and reputation, and portfolio companies' exit performance in emerging markets. Instead, the domestic entrepreneurs' experience is crucial for exit performance in emerging markets (Wang and Wang, 2011).

Target country characteristics also impact an international VC firm's exit performance. Superior legal rights and law enforcement as well as better-developed stock markets significantly enhance VC long term exit performance (Nahata *et al.*, 2014). More specifically, foreign VC-backed portfolio companies are more likely to successfully exit through an IPO or an M&A and investment durations are shorter in economically free countries (Wang and Wang, 2012). The legal protection rights of VC firms' country of origin within the VC syndicate of an IPO firm negatively impacts the underpricing of IPOs, which is a sign of higher IPO quality; this negative association is stronger for IPOs involving foreign VC firms (Chahine and Saade, 2011). This finding expands prior research on VC syndication by showing that the shareholders' protection rights of the country of origin of foreign VC syndicate members signal the quality of portfolio companies at IPO.

Surprisingly, cultural distance between the portfolio company's and the lead investor's country positively affects VC success especially in emerging economies: it creates incentives for rigorous ex ante screening, improving VC performance (Nahata *et al.*, 2014). Additionally, Bottazzi *et al.* (2016) find a negative relationship between trust in a country and exit performance, especially for IPOs. However, more sophisticated investors are more likely to make low trust investments, and doing so they achieve superior performance (Bottazzi *et al.*, 2016). Lack of trust in a country is hence a hurdle to making VC investments, but cross-border investors who overcome this hurdle tend to do well.

In Table 5, we provide an overview of selected studies from an increasingly rich literature that has primarily examined the consequences of international VC investors from the VC firm's perspective.

In summary, the increasing occurrence of cross-border investments despite liabilities of foreignness has raised the interesting questions among scholars of *what* drives these investments, *how* they are managed and *what* their outcomes are. So far, we have reviewed and synthesized the extant literature on these three major research streams of VC internationalization. We next discuss the role of public policy as an important and specific type of VC firm, before providing a more in-depth discussion of future research opportunities.

5. Public Policy and VC Internationalization

Governments, both at the national and local level, often try to play an active role in stimulating the development of larger and broader domestic VC markets. They can do so in several

Table 5. Selected Studies on Outcomes from the Perspective of the VC Firm.

Year–Authors	Data sources	Sample	Literature/theory base	Key findings
2007–Hursti and Maula	SDC Platinum New Issues Database, IPO prospectuses (from Pioneer database of perfect information Ltd.), Datastream	2,862 IPOs made by EU VC firms between 1991 and 2001 (of which 163 are foreign IPOs)	Institutional theory	Pre-IPO ownership by cross-border VC investors is positively related to foreign IPOs.
2009–Knill	Galante's Venture Capital and Private Equity Directory and Thomson Financial's SDC Platinum	Investment preferences of the 500 largest USA VC and PE firms + information on PC from Thomson Financial's SDC Platinum	Portfolio theory	Compared to industry, stage and domestic geographical diversification, international geographical diversification is the only diversification strategy which has no negative impact on the PC's exit performance. As such, it is possible that VC firms can use this form of diversification to reduce risk and potentially grow their VC firm without impacting the PC exit performance.
2011–Chahine and Saade	Securities Data Company (SDC) database	410 randomly selected USA VC backed IPOs from 1997 to 2007 (represents 30.5% of all VC backed IPOs)	Institutional theory, Agency theory	(1) USA IPOs' underpricing is negatively related to the weighted average legal protection rights' index of VC firms' country of origin within the VC syndicate of an IPO firm. This negative association is stronger for IPOs involving foreign VC firms. (2) Legal protection rights of foreign VC firms and board independence of IPO firms play a complementary role in reducing underpricing. This suggests that foreign VC firms from countries with a higher legal protection rights are likely to invest in PCs with better governance, and this reduces underpricing. (3) Results are robust when controlling for selection bias of IPO firms by foreign VC firms. (4) Evidence of a positive effect of the legal protection rights of VC firms on the long-term performance of their PCs.

(Continued)

Table 5. *Continued*

Year–Authors	Data sources	Sample	Literature/theory base	Key findings
2011–Wang and Wang	Zero2IPO, Thomson VentureXpert	495 VC investments between 1999 and 2006 by 84 foreign VC firms in 243 Chinese domestic companies	Institutional theory	(1) Foreign VC firms' human capital (experience, networks and reputation) is not correlated with VC performance. (2) Domestic entrepreneurs' experience is crucial to VC performance.
2012–Wang and Wang	Thomson VentureXpert	10,205 cross-border VC investments by 1,906 foreign VC firms in 6,535 PCs from 35 countries between 1995 and 2005	Economic theory, Institutional theory	(1) PC country's economic freedom plays a crucial role in determining cross-border VC performance. In more economically free countries, foreign VC-backed PCs are more likely to be successfully exited (IPO or an M&A), and investment durations are shorter. (2) Cross-border VC performance is also strongly associated with other PC country characteristics. The GDP per capita is negatively correlated to the probability and hazard of a successful exit, legality is positively related to cross-border VC performance and the PC country's entrepreneurial activity is positively related to the probability of a successful exit. (3) PC quality and local VC firms' participation have a positive impact, while early stage investments and VC firms' portfolio size have a negative impact, on the likelihood of a successful exit.
2012–Dai *et al.*	Thomson VentureXpert database, SDC Platinum M&As, Global New Issues Database	2,860 PCs receiving 4,254 rounds of VC financing by 468 VC firms in Asia from 1996 to 2006	Info asymmetry	Partnership with domestic VC firms has positive implication for the exit performance of local PCs. Specifically, PCs with both foreign and local VC partnership are about 5% more likely to successfully exit.

2013–Humphery-Jenner and Suchard	ChinaVenture	4,753 Chinese/Hong Kong portfolio companies that received capital between 1988 and 2011	Networking theory, Info asymmetry, Portfolio theory	(1) The presence of a foreign VC firm by itself does not per se increase the probability of a successful exit. (2) Syndication with local VC firms increases the probability of a successful exit for foreign VC firms. (3) If a foreign VC successfully exits an investment, then, compared with a domestic VC, it prefers to exit via an M&A or a secondary-buyout as opposed to through an IPO. This reflects the significant lock-up periods associated with VC-backed IPOs in China and the difficulty of achieving a foreign listing on Chinese stock markets. (4) The impact of foreign VC firms on performance depends both on the characteristics of the investment as of the VC firm, it is higher when investing in later stage PCs and when the VC is diversified across industries.
2014–Nahata et al.	Thomson VentureXpert, SDC Platinum M&As, Global New Issues Database	9,153 PCs from 32 countries (North America is excluded) invested between 1996 and 2002	Info asymmetry	(1) Superior legal rights (and enforcement) and better-developed stock markets enhance VC performance. (2) Cultural distance between countries of the PC and its lead investor positively affects VC success. (3) Cultural differences create incentives for rigorous ex ante screening, improving VC performance, particularly in emerging economies.
2014–Bertoni and Groh	VICO dataset, including Thomson ONE, Zephyr, PATSTAT, country specific databases, press releases, press clippings, and websites.	422 firms from seven European countries and 1,062 VC investments, including 190 cross-border investments	Socioeconomic and institutional perspectives	Trade sale exits are facilitated by the additional size of the M&A market in the international VC firm's home market. The effect for IPOs is weaker; the IPO volume of the international VC firm's home market is only significant in some specifications. Finally, syndicates with cross-border investors exit underperforming PCs earlier.

(Continued)

Table 5. *Continued*

Year–Authors	Data sources	Sample	Literature/theory base	Key findings
2016–Chemmanur *et al.*	Thomson VentureXpert	30,071 VC backed companies from 41 countries between 1989 and 2008	Institutional theory, Syndication	Controlling for potential endogeneity concerns, PCs (particularly in emerging countries) backed by syndicates composed of international and domestic VC firms have more successful exits and higher post-IPO operating performance than those backed by syndicates of purely international or purely local VC firms.
2016–Cumming *et al.*	SDC Platinum's VentureXpert, M&A and Global New Issues database	67,635 PC/VC investment observations for 31,942 unique PCs, which represents 81 PC domicile nations and 36 VC domicile nations.	Liabilities of foreignness, resources, networks	Syndicates with a cross-border investor base have a higher probability of exiting via an initial public offering (IPO) and higher IPO proceeds. The benefits of cross-border investors in M&A exits are less pronounced.
2018–Chahine *et al.*	Thomson Financial Securities Data Company (SDC), VentureXpert, Datastream, company websites, IPO prospectus, and LinkedIn.	1,086 VC-backed USA IPOs from 1995 to 2011.	Liabilities of foreignness	Mixed syndicates including domestic and foreign VC firms certify the quality of PCs at the time of the IPO, thereby increasing their IPO premium. Foreign VC firms also play an advisory role (thereby increasing foreign business activities of their USA investees) and a monitoring role when the investee's foreign activities originate from the foreign VC's market.

ways, for example, through direct government investment programs or through government programs that foster the formation of partnerships with private VC firms. Several studies provide excellent overviews of the debate if governments have been able to fulfill this role (e.g., Cumming, 2011; Colombo *et al.*, 2016). A key concern, however, is the possibility that private VC may get crowded out by public VC in domestic markets. Government interventions may further reduce cross-border investments by local private VC firms (Cumming, 2011). In this section, we more specifically focus on the potential role of governments in stimulating international VC inflow.

Should governments stimulate investments by cross-border VC firms into their country or region? Our review shows that the empirical evidence on the outcomes of international VC investments is not uniformly positive. Still, recent evidence, taking endogeneity issues into account, suggests that international VC firms, particularly in combination with domestic VC firms, foster firm development, create additional exit opportunities, and create more value at exit (e.g., Devigne *et al.*, 2013; Bertoni and Groh, 2014; Chahine *et al.*, 2018). While these effects are at times more or less statistically and economically significant, even noneffects can be "good news" because governments can pursue to create more active domestic VC markets through fostering international VC flows that do not have detrimental effects for domestic portfolio companies and exit opportunities by domestic VC investors.

Moreover, for companies in particular industries that require considerable amounts of money such as biotech—and that operate in countries with developing VC markets—international VC investments might be crucial to grow into international players. For instance, in the Flemish region in Belgium, investments by international (including UK, United States, French, and Dutch) VC firms have played a critical role in the development of high growth biotech companies (Vanacker *et al.*, 2014a). It is also generally ignored that cross-border VC firms may not only influence the prospects of local companies and exit opportunities in a direct way; they can also stimulate the professionalization of local VC firms. Such prospects may be particularly important in countries with developing VC markets.

Our review has provided a framework of the mechanisms through which governments can facilitate inflows of international VC (from particular countries). In particular, governments can shape the formal institutional (i.e., regulatory, political, and economic) context (Holmes *et al.*, 2016) to foster the inflow of international VC. By stimulating international networks, and international human capital formation, governments may also be influential in shaping the inflow of international VC thereby targeting specific countries that represent, for example, important export markets. Such effects can be realized through their own government-related VC investors or indirectly by providing support (e.g., through a fund of fund investment strategy) to local or foreign independent and other VC investors.

A particular point of concern for policy makers, related to international VC investments in domestic companies, might be that international investors often play an active role in venture relocation (Cumming *et al.*, 2009a) and provide international exit opportunities (Bertoni and Groh, 2014). Policy makers might thereby fear that the best companies (partially) leave their home country. This should not necessarily be problematic, however, as long as a domestic presence is ensured or if the outflow of companies is balanced with a comparable inflow of companies. Moreover, limiting cross-border VC flows to minimize the risk that local firms would relocate may turn out to be ineffective. Recent evidence from USA data suggests that high-tech entrepreneurs in states with limited VC availability are more likely to relocate their activities to states where VC is particularly abundant (De Prijcker *et al.*, 2018). While this evidence represents within country evidence, there is also anecdotal evidence that entrepreneurs move across borders to increase their odds of raising initial international VC.

6. Avenues for Future Research

We structure our discussion of the current state of the international VC literature as follows: we first provide a theoretical integration and an overview of key methodological gaps, we then check for general gaps, and we end with remaining gaps that are specific to each of the three research streams within this literature.

6.1 *Theoretical Integration and Methodological Gaps*

In this section, we provide an integration of the diverse theoretical perspectives that have been employed to understand the VC internationalization phenomenon. We further provide a discussion of important methodological challenges that have characterized the broader VC internationalization literature and beyond.

6.1.1 *Theoretical Integration*

As can be seen in Tables 1–5, different theoretical lenses have been used to examine VC internationalization and the three major research streams of VC internationalization that we have reviewed.

Economic theories and institutional theory have been used to explain the international VC phenomenon both at the micro level (e.g., contract design and investment outcome) and at the macro level (e.g., in explaining international flows of VC). Compared to domestic VC investors, international VC investors are prone to liabilities of foreignness, induced by increased geographic, legal and cultural distance between international investors and portfolio companies. Liabilities of foreignness increase information asymmetries and make monitoring more costly, thereby increasing agency risks. Unsurprisingly, multiple studies have used agency theory and information asymmetry perspectives to increase our theoretical understanding of how international VC investors can minimize these risks.

VC investors are also confronted with heightened difficulties to provide resources to their portfolio companies, although they may provide more diverse and complementary resources. Consequently, the resource-based view of the firm (and related perspectives including social capital theory and the knowledge-based view) has been proposed as an alternative lens to understand the international VC process. Network theory has also received a lot of attention, with (local) syndicate partners being identified as important resource providers enabling to alleviate problems related to access to deal flow, agency risk, information asymmetries and resource access. A VC firm's network of syndicate partners is hence an essential resource, fitting in the resource-based view of the firm as well. It enables access to investment targets, broadens the resource base available for a portfolio company and helps the transfer of resources to the portfolio company.

Taken together, scholars have employed diverse theoretical frameworks to gain better insights into the challenges, drivers, strategies, and outcomes of international VC investments. However, as we detail below, many challenging questions remain underexplored.

6.1.2 *Methodological Issues*

A first important methodological concern that casts a long shadow over the many reviewed studies is that the receipt of international VC is endogenous (for a similar problem in the broader strategy and entrepreneurial finance literature, see Shaver, 1998 and Eckhardt *et al.*, 2006). Companies do not attract financing from international VC firms at random; rather, they may choose specific investors that are optimal given their characteristics and those of their industries. Moreover, international VC firms themselves do not invest at random; rather, they may choose specific portfolio companies, including those that are of higher quality and thus more likely to succeed. When empirical models do not account for such multistage selection on hard-to-measure or unobservable characteristics, this may potentially lead to misspecified models and incorrect conclusions.

Unfortunately, few of the reviewed papers have employed natural experiments or more advanced econometric techniques that are able to disentangle "selection" effects from "treatment" effects. Hence, only few studies truly allow for a causal interpretation to the actual influence of international VC. Notable exceptions are found particularly in the more recent literature. For example, Chemmanur et al. (2016) use an Instrumental Variable (IV) approach to account for endogeneity of international VC participation and endogeneity in the syndication choice of international VCs. They also use natural experiments using bilateral air service agreements and terror activities in India. As another example, Cumming et al. (2016) also use an IV approach. Specifically, they first estimate the level of internationalization in syndication and, then, use this predicted value as the new variable of interest in the analysis of the portfolio company's exit.

A second important concern relates to the secondary data sources that are generally used in the international VC literature and beyond (e.g., Cumming et al., 2009b; Cumming and Johan, 2017). Tables 1–5 show a clear dominance of studies that use commercial databases such as Thomson's VentureXpert and Bureau van Dijk's Zephyr. Despite the strengths of these databases, they also have specific issues. For example, there are often a significant number of "undisclosed" investors (Huang et al., 2015). Moreover, investments attributed to the local subsidiary of a foreign VC firm are often considered domestic (Huang et al., 2015). In addition, these databases also give rise to several biases, including a statistical bias due to differences in variable definitions (e.g., the definition of VC is not always consistent across countries) and collection methods (Cumming et al., 2009b) thereby sometimes under-representing specific types of investments such as early-stage and small VC investments, or specific countries. These databases also lack control groups of companies that either did not search for (international) VC but have similar characteristics as firms that did, or tried to obtain such financing but were unsuccessful (Cumming and Johan, 2017). Previous work has shown that the use of different international datasets can provide different answers to research questions (Cumming et al., 2014), which might explain some of the contradictory findings.

Scholars have addressed these challenges by combining multiple data sources and including research teams from multiple countries. A good example is the VICO database capturing detailed data on companies from seven European countries that raised VC and matched firms that did not raise VC (Bertoni and Martí, 2011). To construct the database multiple data sources have been used, including Thomson ONE (VentureXpert), Zephyr but also national databases. The data was consolidated by a central authority that relied on the data collection efforts and experience from teams in each country. Other scholars have relied on alternative data sources, such as surveys or proprietary data from specific VC firms. But these data sources, obviously, have their own specific shortcomings, including relatively limited response rates or additional selection issues.

6.2 General Gaps

We have summarized an increasingly rich literature on VC firm internationalization, with a focus on international flows of VC, the international VC investment process and the outcome of international VC investments. Yet, many studies have treated VC firm internationalization as a dummy variable: VC firms have either conducted cross-border investments or not (Cumming *et al.*, 2009b). While this represents an important dimension of VC firm internationalization, several other dimensions have been relatively ignored, such as the internationalization intensity and diversity, the entry mode or the impact of the institutional context.

Studies in international business have also explored other aspects of internationalization, such as its intensity (defined as foreign sales to total sales, which in our context could represent the size of foreign investments relative to total investments) and diversity (defined as the number of countries, sometimes weighted by their geographical and cultural difference from the home country, in which a firm generates sales, which in our context could represent the number of foreign countries in which a VC firm has invested) (Fernhaber *et al.*, 2008; Paeleman *et al.*, 2017).

Relatedly, an important area in international business relates to the entry strategy of firms (Zhao *et al.*, 2004). How do they enter foreign markets: through greenfield investments, acquisitions, joint ventures, or other entry modes? VC firms seeking international expansion face a comparable choice. They may either directly invest from their home country or they may set up a local subsidiary. Many VC firms develop a "hub" strategy, whereby they set up a foreign subsidiary which serves a whole region spanning several countries. For example, many foreign VC firms set up a subsidiary in London with the aim to invest across Continental Europe, or invest in East Asia through a subsidiary in Hong Kong or Singapore. Surprisingly, VC firms' entry modes of internationalization have been largely neglected in the VC literature. Both the drivers and impact of the internationalization mode should be further examined (Wright *et al.*, 2002; Pruthi *et al.*, 2003; Guler and Guillén, 2010a). A related interesting question is whether there is a life cycle to these entry modes (Wright *et al.*, 2002). Do VC firms first invest across borders from their headquarters, which is a flexible entry mode that can easily be reversed, and only invest in a local subsidiary at a later stage, for which the investments are larger and more irreversible? Does entry mode depend on the target country?

In addition, while research on VC internationalization is growing rapidly, research on its flip side, namely deinternationalization, is scant. Internationalization moves may fail, leading firms to abandon their international activities and thus de-internationalize. Research focusing on this withdrawing process from international markets is critical as factors that influence the decision to pursue a particular strategic course of action, such as internationalization, and factors that influence the decommitment from that course of action, such as de-internationalization, are expected to be fundamentally different. Moreover, recent events including Brexit (e.g., Cumming and Zahra, 2016) and the election of USA President Trump with his "deglobalization" rhetoric might be additional forces that impact VC deinternationalization. Unfortunately, research on the firm-level (e.g., performance of prior international investments) and macro-level (e.g., Brexit) mechanisms that may drive VC investors to abandon their prior internationalization strategies is completely lacking.

Further, the role of the institutional context, both in the home and the recipient country, warrants further scrutiny. For example, the decision of a French VC firm to invest in a Belgian company (with both countries sharing a border and having a rather comparable institutional context) is expected to be fundamentally different from the decision to invest in a USA or Chinese company. Some studies have indeed reported important differences between international VC behavior in developed and emerging markets (e.g., Dai *et al.*, 2012). A further analysis of the differences in VC firm internationalization between developing and developed markets—and different institutional contexts more broadly (Cumming *et al.*, 2017)—provides an interesting area of future research. This is especially interesting, as there is currently an increased tendency of VC investors from developing markets (e.g., China, Russia) to invest in more developed countries. For example, an important question is whether there are differences between emerging VC markets compared to developed markets in structuring and monitoring investments (Wright *et al.*, 2002).

Many studies on VC internationalization decisions have focused on samples of independent VC firms. Still, in many countries, other types of VC investors are active including government VC, corporate VC, and bank-affiliated VC. Bertoni *et al.* (2015) illustrate that corporate VC investors are 77.4% more inclined to invest across borders. Governments VC investors, however, are especially specialized in domestic companies. They are 73% more oriented to invest domestically than the full sample. Nevertheless, research on how internationalization of corporate or bank-related VC investors might be different, for example, due to the international scope of their parent company, is lacking. Some studies on the outcomes of international VC investments have controlled for VC investor type. However, these studies do not examine how different types of international investors uniquely behave or influence investments outcomes. This raises important questions for future research. For example, how do syndicates comprising local investors and different types of international VC investors influence outcomes?

We further lack insight into micro-level processes in international VC firms. For example, the role of the investment committee in international investment decision-making or the implications of the investment committee's structure and composition for international staffing are still not fully understood (Pruthi *et al.*, 2009). It would also be relevant to investigate in more detail the process of international staffing, especially from the perspective of local offices (Pruthi *et al.*, 2009). Detailed longitudinal case studies might be very instrumental here, to obtain a detailed insight into these processes.

Finally, another general gap in our understanding of VC firm internationalization is how other sources of entrepreneurial finance might work with VC to enable internationalization. The international VC literature, just like the VC literature in general, is largely segmented by the source of financing (Cumming and Johan, 2017). In other words, VC studies generally exclusively focus on VC but ignore the other sources of financing that companies attract. With the growing importance of "new" sources of financing such as crowdfunding (Cumming and Johan, 2016), business angel groups (Shane, 2008) and Initial Coin Offerings, it would be interesting to gain a better understanding of how these other sources of entrepreneurial finance influence the behavior of VC investors and their cross-border activities more specifically. In the case of crowdfunding, for example: Do larger local crowdfunding markets compete with local VC firms for deals, and if so does it push local VC firms to invest across borders? Does the visibility provided by crowdfunding campaigns remove some of the barriers encountered by foreign VC firms? Do international investors syndicate with angel investors, who mainly operate locally, but who may be strongly embedded in their region? While the interaction with other sources of entrepreneurial finance is quite straightforward, it seems not farfetched to assume that also other, more general sources of finance could play a role. However, we know very little so far about the potential that the banking sector might play for VC internationalization. Does an active and well developed bank sector enhance or discourage international VC investment? And what about interfirm credit; do local traditions with respect to trade credit use matter for international VC decisions?

6.3 *Current Gaps in the Determinants of International VC Investments*

Research provides several areas of future research on country-level determinants of international VC flows. Some of the unresolved questions are: Are there temporal variations in the internationalization of the VC industry? For example, the VC industry is cyclical and prone to periodic booms and busts. Could there be differences in global inflow and outflow patterns depending on these cyclical stages (Madhavan and Iriyama, 2009)? What drives the number of countries in which the VC firm has international investments (De Prijcker *et al.*, 2012)? Do international VC firms find foreign countries more attractive based on the characteristics of the available co-investors to syndicate or on the presence of other home-country VC firms (Guler and Guillén, 2010a)? What is the impact of technical immigration as opposed to overall professional immigration on international VC flows? Such refinements would allow scholars to get closer to the drivers of international entrepreneurship in high-technology domains (Iriyama *et al.*, 2010).

Next to country-level determinants, the literature also provides areas of future research on VC firm determinants. Do different VC investors demonstrate different levels of tolerance for risk taking related to a global investment strategy? What are the determinants of such differences, as well as their consequences (Madhavan and Iriyama, 2009)? Finally, country-level and firm-level determinants will not necessarily operate independently (e.g., Vanacker *et al.*, 2014b), which begs the question how country-level factors (including formal and informal country-level institutions) interact with firm-level factors?

6.4 *Current Gaps in the Strategies to Compensate for Liabilities of Foreignness*

Although several studies have started to investigate how international VC investors cope with liabilities of foreignness, there remain unanswered research questions. First, analyzing companies that have tried but failed to raise foreign VC would help to understand more accurately the role of local investors in raising foreign VC (Mäkelä and Maula, 2008). Next, are there differences between domestic and international VC firms in screening and valuing potential portfolio companies? More specifically, to what extent do foreign VC firms adapt their approaches to local market conditions? If so, how do they adapt their approaches to deal with different asymmetric information problems (Pruthi *et al.*, 2003)? Do VC firms, for instance, replicate the network connections present in their home countries in the new markets they enter (Guler and Guillén, 2010b)? Foreign VC firms may also gain external knowledge through domestic syndication partners that have relevant international investment experience or through other network partners, for example, international shareholders or service providers such as lawyers or consultants. To what extent are these other partners substitutes for foreign syndication partners, or do they complement them in different ways (De Prijcker *et al.*, 2012)? Do the technology level of potential investments, the background and experience levels of the VC firm's general partners, and the market for IPOs or other forms of exit available to VC firms impact the investment preferences of VC firms (Gupta and Sapienza, 1992)?

How can mechanisms, such as expatriating staff and hiring local talents effectively overcome hurdles related to information frictions and cultural differences in international VC investments (Dai *et al.*, 2012)? In which environments do local executives effectively substitute for local coinvestors for internationalizing firms seeking to invest in foreign markets (Pruthi *et al.*, 2009)? Is it possible to make the expertise of key people in the home country available through investment committees (Pruthi *et al.*, 2009)? How can VC firms use a mix of strategies—attracting local partners, working with local VC firms or setting up local branches—in order to deal with the peculiarities of the local environment (Meuleman and Wright, 2011)?

6.5 *Current Gaps Related to the Outcomes of International Investments*

Given the mixed evidence presented before, several important questions on the outcomes of international VC investments require further research attention. What is the relation between distance and the probability of nonrational continuation of commitment to a portfolio company that does not meet the initial prospects (i.e., escalation of commitment; Mäkelä and Maula, 2006; Devigne *et al.*, 2016)? Is international VC firm's commitment influenced by country-specific factors other than distance (Mäkelä and Maula, 2006) or by entry mode (Devigne *et al.*, 2016)? Foreign VC firms may help professionalize local entrepreneurial firms given their experience of advising and nurturing portfolio companies in their home countries. Do these local entrepreneurial companies have spillover effects on their peers which are currently not financed by foreign VC firms (Dai *et al.*, 2012)? In the same vein, how does the presence of foreign VC firms, either directly or through a local subsidiary, and their partnership with local VC firms help professionalize local VC firms (Dai *et al.*, 2012)?

Further, can foreign VC firms provide other value-added benefits, such as increased internationalization, even if they are not per se associated with portfolio company success (Humphery-Jenner and Suchard, 2013)? What is the role played by foreign VC firms in portfolio companies after the IPO? Foreign VC firms might provide a better contact with international investors; facilitate the presence of portfolio companies in foreign markets; and they might also provide valuable help in portfolio companies' internationalization process (Chahine and Saade, 2011). Finally, there may be unobserved determinants associated with the relocation of portfolio companies such as tax strategies, the size of VC markets, branch offices in different countries (e.g., Cumming *et al.*, 2009a).

7. Overall Conclusion

Although there has been a recent wave of research on international VC, spurred by the internationalization of the VC industry, many important questions remain unaddressed and warrant further scrutiny. With this paper, we have provided a timely overview of the international VC literature and identified important future research directions. We hope that with this paper we will foster further research on international VC in multiple disciplines (and hopefully also across disciplines) including economics, entrepreneurship, finance, and management.

Acknowledgements

We are grateful to three anonymous reviewers, Mirjam Knockaert, Miguel Meuleman, Tereza Tykvová, and Bruno van Pottelsberghe for their helpful feedback. Financial support of the Belgian Science Policy (BELSPO, SMEPEFI project), the Gimv Private Equity Chair and the Vlerick Academic Research Fund is also gratefully acknowledged.

Notes
1. See Drover et al. (2017), Manigart and Wright (2013), and Vanacker and Manigart (2013) for some recent overviews of the general venture capital literature.

2. In this review, we focus on VC firm internationalization and how VC firms manage the liabilities related to their own internationalization. It is important to acknowledge that other studies have also focused on the internationalization of VC-backed companies and how VC firms manage the liabilities of internationalization of their portfolio companies (e.g., LiPuma and Park, 2014).

References

Aizenman, J. and Kendall, J. (2012) The internationalization of venture capital. *Journal of Economic Studies* 39(5): 488–511.

Alhorr, H.S., Moore, C.B. and Payne, G.T. (2008) The impact of economic integration on cross-border venture capital investments: evidence from the European Union. *Entrepreneurship Theory and Practice* 32(5): 897–917.

Amit, R., Brander, J. and Zott, C. (1998) Why do venture capital firms exist? Theory and Canadian evidence. *Journal of Business Venturing* 13(6): 441–466.

Balcarcel, A.L., Hertzel, M.G. and Lindsey, L.A. (2010) Contracting frictions and cross-border capital flows: evidence from venture capital. Available at SSRN: https://ssrn.com/abstract=1571928 (accessed on June 16, 2018).

Bengtsson, O. and Ravid, S.A. (2009) The geography of venture capital contracts. Available at SSRN: https://ssrn.com/abstract=1361827 (accessed on June 16, 2018).

Bertoni, F. and Martí, J. (2011) Financing entrepreneurial ventures in Europe: The VICO dataset. Available at SSRN: https://ssrn.com/abstract=1904297 (accessed on June 16, 2018).

Bertoni, F. and Groh, A.P. (2014) Cross-border investments and venture capital exits in Europe. *Corporate Governance: An International Review* 22(2): 84–99.

Bertoni, F., Colombo, M.G. and Quas, A. (2015) The patterns of venture capital investment in Europe. *Small Business Economics* 45(3): 543–560.

Bottazzi, L., Da Rin, M. and Hellmann, T. (2009) What is the role of legal systems in financial intermediation? Theory and evidence. *Journal of Financial Intermediation* 18(4): 559–598.

Bottazzi, L., Da Rin, M. and Hellmann, T. (2016) The importance of trust for investment: Evidence from venture capital. *Review of Financial Studies* 29(9): 2283–2318.

Bruton, G.D., Fried, V.H. and Manigart, S. (2005) Institutional influences on the worldwide expansion of venture capital. *Entrepreneurship Theory and Practice* 29(6): 737–760.

Chahine, S. and Saade, S. (2011) Shareholders' rights and the effect of the origin of venture capital firms on the underpricing of US IPOs. *Corporate Governance: An International Review* 19(6): 601–621.

Chahine, S., Saade, S. and Goergen, M. (2018) Foreign business activities, foreignness of the VC syndicate, and IPO value. *Entrepreneurship Theory and Practice*, Forthcoming, https://doi.org/10.1177/1042258718757503.

Chemmanur, T.J., Hull, T.J. and Krishnan, K. (2016) Do local and international venture capitalists play well together? The complementarity of local and international venture capitalists. *Journal of Business Venturing* 31(5): 573–594.

Chen, H., Gompers, P., Kovner, A. and Lerner, J. (2010) Buy local? The geography of venture capital. *Journal of Urban Economics* 67(1): 90–102.

Colombo, M.G., Cumming, D.J. and Vismara, S. (2016) Governmental venture capital for innovative young firms. *The Journal of Technology Transfer* 41(1): 10–24.

Colombo, M., D'Adda, D., Malighetti, P., Quas, A. and Vismara, S. (2017) The impact of venture capital monitoring in Europe. Available at SSRN: https://ssrn.com/abstract=2906236 (accessed on June 16, 2018).

Cumming, D. (2011) Public policy and the creation of active venture capital markets. *Venture Capital*, 13(1), 75–94.

Cumming, D. and Dai, N. (2010) Local bias in venture capital investments. *Journal of Empirical Finance* 17(3): 362–380.

Cumming, D., Filatotchev, I., Knill, A., Reeb, D.M. and Senbet, L. (2017) Law, finance, and the international mobility of corporate governance. *Journal of International Business Studies* 48(2): 123–147.

Cumming, D., Fleming, G. and Schwienbacher, A. (2009a) Corporate relocation in venture capital finance. *Entrepreneurship Theory and Practice* 33(5): 1121–1155.

Cumming, D. and Johan, S. (2016) Crowdfunding and entrepreneurial internationalization. In N. Dai and D. Siegel (eds.), *Entrepreneurial Finance: Managerial and Policy Implications*. Singapore: The World Scientific Publishers. Available at https://ssrn.com/abstract=2711894 (accessed on June 16, 2018).

Cumming, D. and Johan, S. (2017) The problems with and promise of entrepreneurial finance. *Strategic Entrepreneurship Journal* 11(3): 357–370.

Cumming, D., Johan, S., and Zhang, M. (2014) The economic impact of entrepreneurship: Comparing international datasets. *Corporate Governance: An International Review* 22(2): 162–178.

Cumming, D., Knill, A. and Syvrud, K. (2016) Do international investors enhance private firm value? Evidence from venture capital. *Journal of International Business Studies* 47(3): 347–373.

Cumming, D., Sapienza, H.J., Siegel, D.S. and Wright, M. (2009b) International entrepreneurship: Managerial and policy implications. *Strategic Entrepreneurship Journal* 3(4): 283–296.

Cumming, D. and Zahra, S.A. (2016) International business and entrepreneurship Implications of Brexit. *British Journal of Management* 27(4): 687–692.

Dai, N., Jo, H. and Kassicieh, S. (2012) Cross-border venture capital investments in Asia: selection and exit performance. *Journal of Business Venturing* 27(6): 666–684.

De Prijcker, S., Manigart, S., Wright, M. and De Maeseneire, W. (2012) The influence of experiential, inherited and external knowledge on the internationalization of venture capital firms. *International Business Review* 21(5): 929–940.

De Prijcker, S., Manigart, S., Collewaert, C. and Vanacker, T. (2018) Relocation to get venture capital: a resource dependence perspective. *Entrepreneurship Theory and Practice*, Forthcoming, https://doi.org/10.1177/1042258717739003.

Devigne, D., Vanacker, T., Manigart, S. and Paeleman, I. (2013) The role of domestic and cross-border venture capital investors in the growth of portfolio companies. *Small Business Economics* 40(3): 553–573.

Devigne, D., Manigart, S. and Wright, M. (2016) Escalation of commitment in venture capital decision making: differentiating between domestic and international investors. *Journal of Business Venturing* 31(3): 253–271.

Drover, W., Busenitz, L., Matusik, S., Townsend, D., Anglin, A. and Dushnitsky, G. (2017) A review and road map of entrepreneurial equity financing research: venture capital, corporate venture capital, angel investment, crowdfunding, and accelerators. *Journal of Management* 43(6): 1820–1853.

Eckhardt, J.T., Shane, S. and Delmar, F. (2006) Multistage selection and the financing of new ventures. *Management Science* 52(2): 220–232.

Espenlaub, S., Khurshed, A. and Mohamed, A. (2015) Venture capital exits in domestic and cross-border investments. *Journal of Banking & Finance* 53: 215–232.

Fernhaber, S.A., Gilbert, B.A. and McDougall, P.P. (2008) International entrepreneurship and geographic location: an empirical examination of new venture internationalization. *Journal of International Business Studies* 39(2): 267–290.

Fritsch, M. and Schilder, D. (2008) Does venture capital investment really require spatial proximity? An empirical investigation. *Environment and Planning A* 40(9): 2114–2131.

Gompers, P. and Lerner, J. (2001) The venture capital revolution. *Journal of Economic Perspectives* 15(2): 145–168.

Groh, A.P., von Liechtenstein, H. and Lieser, K. (2010) The European venture capital and private equity country attractiveness indices. *Journal of Corporate Finance* 16(2), 205–224.

Guler, I. and Guillen, M.F. (2010a) Institutions and the internationalization of US venture capital firms. *Journal of International Business Studies* 41(2): 185–205.

Guler, I. and Guillen, M.F. (2010b) Home country networks and foreign expansion: evidence from the venture capital industry. *Academy of Management Journal* 53(2): 390–410.

Gupta, A.K. and Sapienza, H.J. (1992) Determinants of venture capital firms preferences regarding the industry diversity and geographic scope of their investments. *Journal of Business Venturing* 7(5): 347–362.

Hochberg, Y.V., Ljungqvist, A. and Lu, Y. (2010) Networking as a barrier to entry and the competitive supply of venture capital. *Journal of Finance* 65(3): 829–859.

Holmes, R.M., Zahra, S.A., Hoskisson, R.E., DeGhetto, K. and Sutton, T. (2016) Two-way streets: The role of institutions and technology policy in firms' corporate entrepreneurship and political strategies. *Academy of Management Perspectives* 30(3): 247–272.

Hsu, D.H. (2004) What do entrepreneurs pay for venture capital affiliation? *Journal of Finance* 59(4): 1805–1844.

Huang, X., Kenney, M. and Patton, D. (2015) Responding to uncertainty: syndication partner choice by foreign venture capital firms in China. *Venture Capital* 17(3): 215–235.

Humphery-Jenner, M. and Suchard, J.-A. (2013) Foreign VCs and venture success: evidence from China. *Journal of Corporate Finance* 21: 16–35.

Hursti, J. and Maula, M.W. (2007) Acquiring financial resources from foreign equity capital markets: an examination of factors influencing foreign initial public offerings. *Journal of Business Venturing* 22(6): 833–851.

Iriyama, A., Li, Y. and Madhavan, R. (2010) Spiky globalization of venture capital investments: the influence of prior human networks. *Strategic Entrepreneurship Journal* 4(2): 128–145.

Knill, A. (2009) Should venture capitalists put all their eggs in one basket? Diversification versus pure-play strategies in venture capital. *Financial Management* 38(3): 441–486.

Li, Y., Vertinsky, I. and Li, J. (2014) National distances, international experience, and venture capital investment performance. *Journal of Business Venturing* 29(4): 471–489.

LiPuma, J.A. and Park, S. (2014) Venture capitalists' risk mitigation of portfolio company internationalization. *Entrepreneurship Theory and Practice* 38(5): 1183–1205.

Liu, Y. and Maula, M. (2016) Local partnering in foreign ventures: uncertainty, experiential learning, and syndication in cross-border venture capital investments. *Academy of Management Journal* 59(4): 1407–1429.

Lu, Q. and Hwang, P. (2010) The impact of liability of foreignness on international venture capital firms in Singapore. *Asia Pacific Journal of Management* 27(1): 81–97.

Madhavan, R. and Iriyama, A. (2009) Understanding global flows of venture capital: human networks as the "carrier wave" of globalization. *Journal of International Business Studies* 40(8): 1241–1259.

Mäkelä, M.M. and Maula, M.V. (2005) Cross-border venture capital and new venture internationalization: an isomorphism perspective. *Venture Capital* 7(3): 227–257.

Mäkelä, M.M. and Maula, M.V.J. (2006) Interorganizational commitment in syndicated cross-border venture capital investments. *Entrepreneurship Theory and Practice* 30(2): 273–298.

Mäkelä, M.M. and Maula, M.V.J. (2008) Attracting cross-border venture capital: the role of a local investor. *Entrepreneurship and Regional Development* 20(3): 237–257.

Manigart, S., Waele, D., Wright, M., Robbie, K., Desbrières, P., Sapienza, H. and Beekman, A. (2000) Venture capitalists, investment appraisal and accounting information: a comparative study of the U.S.A., U.K., France, Belgium and Holland. *European Financial Management* 6(3): 389–403.

Manigart, S., De Waele, K., Wright, M., Robbie, K., Desbrières, P., Sapienza, H. J. and Beekman, A. (2002) Determinants of required return in venture capital investments: a five-country study. *Journal of Business Venturing* 17(4): 291–312.

Manigart, S., De Prijcker, S. and Bose, B. (2010). International private equity flows. In D. Cumming (ed.), *Private Equity: Fund types, Risk and Returns, and Regulation*. New York: Wiley.

Manigart, S. and Wright, M. (2013) Venture capital investors and portfolio firms. *Foundations and Trends*® *in Entrepreneurship* 9(4–5): 365–570.

Meuleman, M. and Wright, M. (2011) Cross-border private equity syndication: institutional context and learning. *Journal of Business Venturing* 26(1): 35–48.

Meuleman, M., Jääskeläinen, M., Maula, M.V. and Wright, M. (2017) Venturing into the unknown with strangers: substitutes of relational embeddedness in cross-border partner selection in venture capital syndicates. *Journal of Business Venturing* 32(2): 131–144.

Nahata, R., Hazarika, S. and Tandon, K. (2014) Success in global venture capital investing: do institutional and cultural differences matter? *Journal of Financial and Quantitative Analysis* 49(4): 1039–1070.

Paeleman, I., Fuss, C. and Vanacker, T. (2017) Untangling the multiple effects of slack resources on firms' exporting behavior. *Journal of World Business* 52(6): 769–781.

Patzelt, H., zu Knyphausen-Aufseß, D. and Fischer, H.T. (2009) Upper echelons and portfolio strategies of venture capital firms. *Journal of Business Venturing* 24(6): 558–572.

Pruthi, S., Wright, M. and Lockett, A. (2003) Do foreign and domestic venture capital firms differ in their monitoring of investees? *Asia Pacific Journal of Management* 20(2): 175–204.

Pruthi, S., Wright, M. and Meyer, K. (2009) Staffing venture capital firms' international operations. *International Journal of Human Resource Management* 20(1): 186–205.

Ruhnka, J.C. and Young, J.E. (1987) A venture capital model of the development process for new ventures. *Journal of Business Venturing* 2(2): 167–184.

Sapienza, H., Manigart, S. and Vermeir, W. (1996) Venture capitalist governance and value-added in four countries. *Journal of Business Venturing* 11(6): 439–470.

Schertler, A. and Tykvová, T. (2011) Venture capital and internationalization. *International Business Review* 20(4): 423–439.

Schertler, A. and Tykvová, T. (2012) What lures cross-border venture capital inflows? *Journal of International Money and Finance* 31(6): 1777–1799.

Shane, S. (2008) Angel groups: an examination of the Angel Capital Association survey. Available at SSRN: https://ssrn.com/abstract=1142645

Shaver, J.M. (1998) Accounting for endogeneity when assessing strategy performance: does entry mode choice affect FDI survival? *Management Science* 44(4): 571–585.

Sorensen, M. (2007) How smart is smart money? A two-sided matching model of venture capital. *Journal of Finance* 62(6): 2725–2762.

Sorenson, O. and Stuart, T.E. (2001) Syndication networks and the spatial distribution of venture capital investments. *American Journal of Sociology* 106(6): 1546–1588.

Stuart, T.E., Hoang, H. and Hybels, R.C. (1999) Interorganizational endorsements and the performance of entrepreneurial ventures. *Administrative Science Quarterly* 44(2): 315–349.

Tykvová, T. and Schertler, A. (2011) Geographical and institutional distances in venture capital deals: how syndication and experience drive internationalization patterns. Available at SSRN: https://ssrn.com/abstract=1810826 (accessed on June 16, 2018).

Ueda, M. (2004) Banks versus venture capital: project evaluation, screening, and expropriation. *Journal of Finance* 59(2): 601–621.

Vanacker, T. and Manigart, S. (2010) Pecking order and debt capacity considerations for high-growth companies seeking financing. *Small Business Economics* 35(1): 53–69.

Vanacker, T. and Manigart, S. (2013) Venture capital. In K.H. Baker and G. Filbeck (eds.), *Alternative Investments: Instruments, Performance, Benchmarks, and Strategies*. Hoboken, NJ: John Wiley & Sons, Inc.

Vanacker, T., Manigart, S. and Meuleman, M. (2014a) Path-dependent evolution versus intentional management of investment ties in science-based entrepreneurial firms. *Entrepreneurship Theory and Practice* 38(3): 671–690.

Vanacker, T., Heughebaert, A. and Manigart, S. (2014b) Institutional frameworks, venture capital and the financing of European new technology-based firms. *Corporate Governance: An International Review* 22(3): 199–215.

Vedula, S. and Matusik, S.F. (2017) Geographic, network, and competitor social cues: evidence from US venture capitalists internationalization decisions. *Strategic Entrepreneurship Journal* 11(4): 393–421.

Wang, L. and Wang, S. (2011) Cross-border venture capital performance: evidence from China. *Pacific-Basin Finance Journal* 19(1): 71–97.

Wang, L.F. and Wang, S.S. (2012) Economic freedom and cross-border venture capital performance. *Journal of Empirical Finance* 19(1): 26–50.

Wright, M. and Robbie, K. (1998) Venture capital and private equity: a Review and synthesis. *Journal of Business Finance & Accounting* 25(5-6): 521–570.

Wright, M., Lockett, A. and Pruthi, S. (2002) Internationalization of western venture capitalists into emerging markets: risk assessment and information in India. *Small Business Economics* 19(1): 13–29.

Wright, M., Pruthi, S. and Lockett, A. (2005) International venture capital research: from cross-country comparisons to crossing borders. *International Journal of Management Reviews* 7(3): 135–165.

Wuebker, R., Kräussl, R. and Schulze, W. (2015) Is venture capital really a local business? Evidence from US cross-border investment. Available at SSRN: https://ssrn.com/abstract=2639282 (accessed on June 16, 2018).

Zaheer, S. (1995) Overcoming the liability of foreignness. *Academy of Management Journal* 38(2): 341–363.

Zhao, H.X., Luo, Y.D. and Suh, T. (2004) Transaction cost determinants and ownership-based entry mode choice: a meta-analytical review. *Journal of International Business Studies* 35(6): 524–544.

9

IS RELATIONSHIP LENDING STILL A MIXED BLESSING? A REVIEW OF ADVANTAGES AND DISADVANTAGES FOR LENDERS AND BORROWERS

Andi Duqi

University of Sharjah

Angelo Tomaselli

*University of Bologna
and University of Amsterdam Business School*

Giuseppe Torluccio

University of Bologna

1. Introduction

Relationship lending is one of the most important lending technologies[1] adopted by banks and their borrowers (Berger and Udell, 2006; Kysucky and Norden, 2016). Although there is still no clear and universally valid definition among scholars of what is considered as relationship lending, the predominant view suggests that under this lending technology banks acquire proprietary information over time through contact with the firm, its owner and its local community on a variety of dimensions and use this information in their decisions about the availability and terms of credit to the firm (Boot, 2000; Berger and Udell, 2002). The alternative lending techniques are commonly grouped under the definition of transaction-based lending (or arm's length lending). Under this approach, banks make mostly use of verifiable and hard information, which is derived from financial statements, credit scoring or guarantees[2] (Berger and Udell, 2006).

The adoption of relationship lending is mainly related to small business lending (Berger and Udell, 2006; Berger, 2015). Granting credit to small firms is different from lending to large corporations because the former are generally informationally opaque, do not present

Contemporary Topics in Finance: A Collection of Literature Surveys, First Edition. Edited by Iris Claus and Leo Krippner.

audited financial statements and do not have traded debt or equity. Relationship lending can be adopted to overcome these difficulties, because bank officers can collect proprietary information through contact over time with firm owners. The bank can use this so-called soft information to provide credit to the firm, which could not access it from other institutions due to the information asymmetries.

The use of relationship lending seems beneficial for banks and firms, but it can also entail some costs for both (Diamond, 1984; Sharpe, 1990). Regarding the borrower, the benefits generally comprise improved availability of credit, less necessity of collateral and better loan terms (Petersen and Rajan, 2002; Berger and Udell, 2006; Bharath *et al.*, 2011). However, the greater is the possibility to not have alternative banking relationships, the greater is the risk that the borrower will be blocked in a relation where the lender exploits all the borrower's information in order to extract rents from her or him. Regarding the lenders, they must be aware that a borrower can have an incentive to hide private information about its real risk of default, to obtain better conditions than the ones deserved. Alternatively, the borrower could practise moral hazard if he anticipates that for some reasons the lender will not interrupt credit or will not increase the borrowing costs (Degryse and Ongena, 2005; Kysucky and Norden, 2016).

The scope of this review is to critically assess how the main determinants of relationship lending impact on benefits and costs for lenders and borrowers. Our novel approach is to employ a two-level framework of determinants, differentiating them in relationship and industry-specific. The first type comprises the bank and firm size, the lender–borrower geographical and functional distance, the duration and the exclusivity of the lending relationship, the presence of a main bank in cases of multiple lending, the importance of lender–borrower trustworthiness and qualitative information. The industry-specific determinants comprise the level of market competition, the regulatory framework and the bank ownership structure. In addition, we try to understand whether the evidence from the recent Global Financial Crisis (2007–2009), has offered novel insights to researchers and policy makers about this lending technology. Last, we attempt to highlight how different financial systems – bank-based compared to market-based – could influence the opportunities for firms to receive a particular type of financing, modulating the financial intermediaries' choice to employ relationship lending.

All the determinants are found to be important factors affecting benefits and costs of relationship lending. In particular, for the relationship-specific ones, we attempt to discern the effect of these variables on three essential elements of the loan contract: the credit provision, the interest rate and the related collateral. We underline possible negative consequences of relationship lending represented by soft-budget constraint, for lenders, and hold-up, for borrowers.

The use of relationship lending has attracted major attention by researchers in the last 30 years. This is the reason why there have been two previous reviews on the topic (Boot, 2000; Elyasiani and Goldberg, 2004) and one meta-analysis study (Kysucky and Norden, 2016). We believe that our review is still necessary for the following reasons. First, Boot (2000) performs a theoretical survey of the literature, whereas our review is mainly based on empirical studies. Second, since the last review of Elyasiani and Goldberg (2004) the literature has grown enormously and has attempted to scrutinize the phenomenon in many more countries, not only developed ones. Last, Kysucky and Norden (2016) in their meta-analysis do not deeply investigate the factors and the theoretical foundations of different studies but rather aim at summarizing in a descriptive way the econometrical impact of different variables that proxy for relationship lending on credit terms.

Other reviews on the literature have investigated related topics but they do not focus exclusively on relationship lending. Beck (2016) surveys the recent literature on the relationship between small-medium enterprises (SMEs), financial deepening and economic development. Steijvers and Voordeckers (2009) review the link between provision of collateral and credit rationing. Moreover, we do not limit our review to the empirical findings evidenced for the USA market (such as Petersen and Rajan, 1994 and Berger and Udell, 1995), but we extend our findings to other papers concerning countries where the prevalent economy is founded on SMEs.

The remainder of the paper is organized as follows. In the next section, we look at the theoretical foundations of relationship lending, its main benefits and principal drawbacks. The third section illustrates our research framework and the analysis of the main determinants of relationship lending, presenting the benefits and costs of relationship lending for borrowers and lenders. In the fourth section, we concentrate on relationship-specific determinants, whereas in the fifth section we focus on industry determinants affecting the adoption and outcomes of relationship lending. In the sixth section, we provide some novel evidence drawn from the Global Financial Crisis (2007–2009). In the seventh section, we highlight differences between bank-based and market-based countries. Finally, in Section 8 we present our final remarks together with suggestions for fruitful research avenues that would enrich the empirical knowledge in this research domain.

2. Theoretical Foundations

Following Boot (2000), before starting our review, we highlight the main benefits and costs of relationship lending based on the theory of financial intermediation. We aim to emphasize that there is clear evidence that banks, by relying on relationship lending can reduce information asymmetry issues in the financial markets and thus screen out bad from good borrowers. The benefits for borrowers appear to depend more on their ability to signal their reputation in the market.

2.1 Positive Side of Relationship Lending

From the lenders' perspective, when banks are not entirely confident about the quality of the borrower they should raise interest rates. The borrowers adjust to this strategy by practicing moral hazard, such as choosing to undertake riskier entrepreneurial projects. Consequently, the bank may not be incentivized to grant loans at a higher interest rate than a certain threshold value, since the higher risk associated with the implementation of the projects undertaken by firms implies lower expected profits (Leland and Pyle, 1977; Keeton, 1979; Stiglitz and Weiss, 1981; Diamond, 1984; Fama, 1985; Besanko and Thakor, 1987).

Within this situation, banks could mitigate information asymmetries in the credit market through monitoring activities, but the incentive to acquire and assess the creditworthiness of the borrower is low in the case of multiple lending, as the cost would be borne by only one lender, whereas the benefits would be spread among all of them. Banks can resolve this information asymmetry by implementing closer relationships with firms, especially smaller ones (Ramakrishnan and Thakor, 1984; Fama, 1985; Rajan, 1992; Fiordelisi et al., 2013).

The problem of information asymmetry tends to be more acute in small firms, since these are more opaque on an information level (Petersen, 2004). External funders cannot readily determine whether the firm will invest in good quality projects (adverse selection problem), or if the funds will be used for purposes other than those financed (moral hazard problem). In this case, long-term banking relationships, such as those typical of relationship lending, could help to mitigate these information problems (Berlin and Mester, 1999; Berger and Udell, 2002; Gambacorta, 2016).

Relationship lending is substantially different from transaction-based forms of financing insofar the latter are associated with the collection of 'tangible' information based on objective criteria such as financial ratios for financial statement lending, or credit scores in the case of credit scoring (Berger and Udell, 2002, 2006). Financial institutions that adopt relationship lending relay extensively on proprietary information which goes beyond the firms' financial statements permitting the bank to overcome problems of information opacity better than transaction based lenders (Cole, 1998; Degryse and van Cayseele, 2000; Berger and Udell, 2002).

When we analyse the borrowers' perspective, the benefits that firms receive in terms of credit allocation appear to depend on their signalling ability. Boot and Thakor (1994) theoretically demonstrate that the cost of debt in relationship lending should decrease over time as a result of signalling and firm reputation. The authors show that following the first success achieved by the firm in terms of an investment project, the bank will grant credit without requiring collateral and at a lower rate of interest than the average market rate in the following periods. Those firms that survive in the market and accumulate a series of payments met on a regular basis significantly reduce liquidity constraints arising from information asymmetries (Holmstrom and Tirole, 1997; Sakai *et al.*, 2010; Kano *et al.*, 2011).

2.2 *Negative Side of Relationship Lending*

The negative effects of a close bank–firm relationship are mainly two, the so-called soft budget constraint, 'creditor capturing', and the hold-up problem, 'debtor capturing'.

The soft budget constraint occurs when the financed firm is in a state of financial distress or the project undertaken becomes more risky and the bank prefers to grant the firm further loans in the hope of avoiding the firm's bankruptcy. Given that the threat to terminate lending is often not credible in a long-term relationship, the entrepreneur may behave opportunistically *ex ante* by, for example, exceeding the risks assumed (Dewatripont and Maskin, 1995; Boot, 2000; Detragiache *et al.*, 2000; Lehmann and Neuberger, 2001). The risk of being captured is higher, the larger the customer requiring a loan is, and the more the bank employs specific resources in a long-term relationship (Gambini and Zazzaro, 2013).

The hold-up problem between the bank and the firm arises when relationship lending gives the bank a monopoly on information, which translates into higher bank rates or conservation strategies (Sharpe, 1990; Rajan, 1992; Von Thadden, 1992; Ioannidou and Ongena, 2010). Banks can learn from their customers in the process of lending. This advantage allows them to capture some of the rents generated by their older borrowers. However, competition forces banks to lend to new firms at interest rates, which initially generate expected losses (Sharpe, 1990). At the same time, borrowers have the possibility to reduce the risk of hold-up by diversifying away from their main bank (Ongena and Smith, 2000). In this way, they tend to forsake a more efficient source of credit in order to optimally circumscribe the power of banks (Rajan, 1992; Von Thadden, 2004). Multiple lending can reduce the risk of a profitable project being prematurely terminated, which is one of the main causes of the credit rationing (Detragiache *et al.*, 2000).

3. Research Framework and Analysis of the Main Determinants of Relationship Lending

In this literature review, we consider studies that cover the period 1990–2016. We adopt a multidimensional framework, which is distinguished within two main levels: relationship-specific and industry-specific (Figure 1).

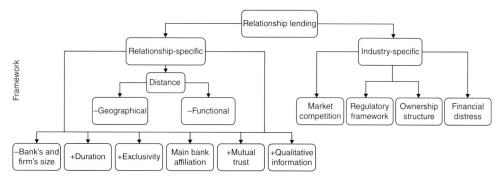

Figure 1. The Multidimensional Framework of Relationship Lending.

At the relationship level, we present how particular features could influence the conditions of relationship lending for lenders and borrowers: namely, the bank and firm size; the lender–borrower distance, which can be geographical or functional; the duration of a relationship; the exclusivity of relationships; the possibility of having a main bank in cases of multiple lending (such as a bank conceding the highest credit share to a firm), the lender–borrower mutual trustworthiness; and the role of qualitative information.

At the industry level, we present how the degree of competition, the regulatory framework, the bank ownership structure and an event of financial distress affect benefits and costs both for lenders and borrowers. In particular, we display some novel results from the literature on relationship lending during the recent Global Financial Crisis.

4. Relationship-Specific Determinants

4.1 *Bank and Firm Size*

As previously mentioned, relationship lending is based on the availability of private or soft information, which allows the bank to identify the most appropriate contractual structure to be proposed to the firm in order to extend credit. This kind of knowledge is generated by a privileged, collaborative and repeated lending relationship with the firm (Cotugno *et al.*, 2013b; Fiordelisi *et al.*, 2013). However, soft information cannot be measured directly, therefore, in the literature it was initially related to the size of the firm and/or the bank. That is, small firms possibly with previous loan delinquencies could be most probably classified as opaque and thus would be the ideal candidate for the adoption of relationship lending by the bank. Moreover, arguments in this strand of literature suggest that small banks are better able to form strong relationships with informationally opaque small businesses, while large banks tend to serve more transparent firms because dealing with opaque firms requires the use of soft information and such information is difficult to quantify and transmit through the communication channels and layers of management of large organizations (e.g., Berger *et al.*, 2001, 2005; Cole *et al.*, 2004; Scott, 2004; Craig and Hardee, 2007). These studies generally use survey data on loan applications from small versus large firms and investigate the link between the amounts of credit granted to the former group by financial institutions of different size.

Even borrowers choose a lending technology based on the quality of information available to them: high quality information will lead to transaction lending, whereas the choice will be relationship lending in case of confidential and private information (Agarwald and Hauswald, 2008). Firms which are more informationally transparent, for example, by maintaining formalized records, find they have a higher probability of their loans being approved (Petersen, 2004).

Although the aforementioned studies empirically support the view that small banks can employ soft information to better evaluate loan requests of informationally opaque borrowers, recent evidence has tried to challenge their results given that those articles did not investigate the lending technology, but inferred it from loan contract terms or the characteristics of the small borrower (Berger and Udell, 2006).

Berger *et al.* (2005) estimate the probability that a small firm gets a credit line from a large versus a small bank given a set of bank and firm characteristics for a sample of USA SMEs. The results show that there are no significant differences among large and small banks in serving opaque firms. Both types of banks provide loans to similar small businesses. The results can be justified by the use of large banks of transaction-based lending technologies such as small business credit scoring, asset-based lending which seem to be suitable for small and opaque firms.

De la Torre *et al.* (2010) provide similar results by analysing data gathered through surveys and interviews with bank officials and SMEs in different emerging countries in the period 2000–2009. The authors provide evidence that any disadvantage in lending to small opaque businesses using relationship lending is offset by the advantages that the large banks have in using certain transaction lending technologies to provide credit. The SME sector is of strategic importance for large banks, therefore these institutions do not only provide different transaction lending technologies to SMEs, but they benefit from economies of scale and scope due to much more advanced and sophisticated risk management systems. Similar results are found by Berger *et al.* (2014) for the USA market.

Berger *et al.* (2011) by using data from a survey on a sample of USA banks of different size point out that small banks do not necessarily rely only on relationship lending. They are using other forms of transaction-based lending such as credit scoring to a much greater degree than expected. Moreover, small banks tend to use credit scoring even for small loans (less than 50,000 USD). Finally, even community banks continue to use relationship lending and employ credit scoring to supplement the use of that technology.

In general (see Table 1), it seems that small banks can employ soft information in order to establish relationship lending and to reduce information asymmetries, but it is also true that in particular cases banks can use soft information to create credit scoring indexes, turning soft information available from local businesses into hard information in a form that is accessible and useful for evaluating SMEs. Moreover, other studies assert that large banks can employ hard information for lending to SMEs.

4.2 *Geographical Distance*

An additional factor that can affect the choice of the borrower and/or the lender to engage in relationship lending and its consequences in terms of pricing, and credit availability is the firm–bank distance. This concept can be defined according to two main dimensions: geographical and functional distance.

The geographical distance is the physical distance between the bank and borrowing firm. Recent advances in communications and information technologies have increased the availability and timeliness of hard information, allowing more impersonal loans by more geographically distant banks. However, there is still debate about the optimal lending choice

Table 1. List of Articles that Discuss How Bank and Firm Size Affect the Use of Relationship Lending versus Transaction-Based Lending and Its Consequences.

Author(s)	Sample	Methodology	Research focus	Results	
				Dependent variable	Main findings
Cole *et al.* 2004 (LP)	USA, 1992; 4637 SMEs	Probit regression	Sharp contrast between RL and TL	Bank's decision to extend or deny credit.	Small banks rely more heavily upon preexisting relationships that provide insights into the "character" of a borrower. Small banks also are less likely to extend credit to firms asking for larger loan amounts, and to firm with past delinquencies of the firm or its primary owner.
Scott, 2004 (BP) (LP)	USA; 2001; 12,500 SMEs	OLS and IV regression	Sharp contrast between RL and TL	Performance (constructed as a factor score depending on the acquisition of soft information).	Community financial institutions (small banks) can rate their bank's performance significantly higher, an outcome consistent with better soft information production. Moreover, CFIs have a niche for small firms in producing soft information; therefore, they give small firms access to capital markets that may not otherwise exist.
Petersen 2004 (LP)	USA: Review; SMEs and large enterprises.	Literature review	RL and TL together in lending technologies	Review-based model discussing feature of hard and soft information in financial decisions.	Credit scoring turns available soft information into hard information, which is quantitative, easy to store and transmit in impersonal ways.

(Continued)

Table 1. *Continued*

Author(s)	Sample	Methodology	Research focus	Results	
				Dependent variable	Main findings
Berger *et al.*, 2005 (BP)	USA; 1993; 131 SMEs	Tobit regression	Sharp contrast between RL and TL	The dependent variable is the fraction of trade credit the firm paid late.	Small banks lend to riskier firms, while large banks lend at a greater distance, interact more impersonally with their borrowers, have shorter and less exclusive relationships and are not as effective as small banks at alleviating credit constraints.
Berger and Udell 2002; 2006 (LP)	USA; Review on SMEs	Literature review	Sharp contrast between RL and TL	Review-based theoretical model identifying key characteristics of relationship lending, as its dependence on soft information about the firm.	Use of hard information. Financial statement lending, asset-based lending, credit scoring.
Craig and Hardee, 2007 (BP)	USA, SMEs; 1998–99	Tobit regression	Sharp contrast between RL and TL	Credit limits as a share of assets banks compared to nonbank financial institutions.	Credit access for small businesses is mainly conceded by small banks and by small financial institutions (capital leasing firms, mortgage companies and financial brokers, etc.) because of frequent interactions with customers.
Berger, Rosen and Udell 2007 (LP)	USA; 1993; 648 SMEs	OLS regression	No contrast between RL and TL	The spread over the prime rate of the bank loan.	Big banks have some advantages from some transaction technologies for serving small, opaque businesses.

Study	Sample	Method	Contrast RL/TL	Dependent variable	Main findings
Agarwald and Hauswald 2008 (LP)	USA; 2002–2003; SMEs and large enterprises; 420 transactional and 915 relationship borrowers.	Logistic regression	Sharp contrast between RL and TL	Decision to offer or deny a loan	Banks disregard publicly available information when they have access to better soft private information through inside lending that becomes the foundation of their relationship-credit decision and pricing.
De La Torre et al. 2010 (LP)	12 countries (USA, South America, EU and Asia); 2006–2009; SMEs	Survey, interviews	No contrast between RL and TL	Banks' attitude towards SMEs	Small businesses strategic sector for big banks. Competitive advantage of big banks in serving small businesses and to overcome the asymmetries inherent in such enterprises.
Berger et al. 2011 (LP)	USA; 2005; Survey on 330 banks; SMEs and large enterprises.	OLS regression	RL and TL together in lending technologies	- Ratio of small Loans to gross total assets. - Return on assets (net income/gross total assets)	Small banks use different lending technologies to reduce the information opacity of firms. This use appears to be associated with higher lending.
Berger et al. 2014 (BP)	USA 2583 firms with less than 500 employees	OLS regression	No contrast between RL and TL	Relationship strength (measured by the length of the relationship).	Big banks do not necessarily serve only transparent firms but also opaque ones. Strength of relationship does not depend on type of bank and firm.

Notes: RL = Relationship Lending; TL = Transaction Lending; RB = Relationship Banking; LP = Lender's Perspective; BP = Borrower's Perspective; SMEs = small–medium enterprises.

for opaque SMEs. A number of studies find that these borrowers tend to have closer credit providers, and most transactions are conducted in person. Therefore, relationship lending is the main credit technology since close-by banks have a competitive advantage by being able to obtain a greater amount of soft information from the borrower at a lower cost (Bonaccorsi di Patti and Gobbi, 2001; Petersen and Rajan, 2002). Other studies highlight that distance is associated with higher probability of credit rationing (Brevoort and Hannan, 2006; Alessandrini *et al.*, 2009; Raterkus and Munchus, 2014). The physical distance from urban areas has an adverse impact on firms' cost of debt because of information disadvantages. Urban banks are unable to carefully monitor firms that are distant from urban areas, and consequently charge higher rates of interest to them (Arena and Dewally, 2012).

Conversely, a second group of contributions argue that physical proximity is important because it allows banks to integrate hard information on borrowers with soft information gathered locally. At the same time, bank–firm proximity may reinforce the market power of the lending bank. The relationship lender may take advantage of the absence of other close-by financial institutions and charge higher interest rates, extracting rents from the borrower (Degryse and Ongena, 2005; Agarwald and Hauswald, 2010). A summary of these studies is presented in Table 2.

4.3 *Functional Distance*

The functional distance is defined as the proximity between the local bank branch, where information is collected and lending relationships are established, and the operational headquarters of the bank, where lending policies are established and decisions whether to allocate credit or not are typically made (Alessandrini *et al.*, 2009). The functional distance is influenced by the asymmetric distribution of information and communication costs within a banking organization, in addition to the economic, social and cultural differences between different communities and places. The increasing distance between decisional and operating centres tends to dissipate soft information gathered by the local offices, increases the monitoring cost of the activities of the local managers, and prevents an effective transfer of best practices from the operating offices to the decisional offices, focusing only on transferring efficiency from the latter to the former (Stein, 2002; Liberti and Mian, 2009; Cotugno *et al.*, 2013a). The information (mainly soft) about local borrowers is in the hands of the local branch manager, and it is not easily transferable to the bank's higher hierarchical levels. In addition, the officers in charge of loans in local banks may seek to influence the final headquarters' loan decisions by distorting the soft information communicated to the central headquarters or by other means (Alessandrini *et al.*, 2009).

Nowadays, the banking centres which make decisions and implement strategic functions are located in a few places in each country due to the intense consolidation in the last 20 years. The spatial concentration of banking power has significantly increased the functional distance of the lending decision control centre from local branches and borrowers, supporting the hypothesis that lengthening functional distance inversely affects the availability of credit to local businesses (Alessandrini *et al.*, 2009). This effect is particularly significant for SMEs in less developed regions. The final outcome of the consolidation trend seems to be a more cost-efficient banking sector. However, this process has also increased the probability of credit rationing for financially opaque firms.

The existing empirical literature on this topic generally finds that banks where managers that are located near their borrowers take the credit decision have some advantages over other

Table 2. List of Articles that Discuss How Geographical Distance Can Affect the Outcome of Relationship Lending.

Author(s)	Sample	Methodology	Results			
			Research focus	Dependent variable	Main findings	
Bonaccorsi di Patti and Gobbi 2001 (BP)	ITA 1990–1998; SMEs and large enterprises.	Weighted least squares	- Geographical distance => + RL's Advantages (BP)	Credit availability	Physical proximity translates into a larger amount of credit for SMEs.	
Petersen and Rajan 2002 (LP)	USA; 1973–1993; 5981 relationships of SMEs and large enterprises.	Weighted least squares	- Geographical distance => + RL's Advantages (LP)	Lender–borrower distance	Banks in the vicinity of firms have an advantage in obtaining soft information at a lower cost. Lender–borrower distance increases with availability of hard information	
Degryse and Ongena 2005 (BP)	BEL; 1995–1997; 13,104 SMEs	Ordinary least squares Panel random effects	- Geographical distance => + RL's Disadvantages (BP) + RL's Advantages (BP)	Loan interest rate	The interest rate required by a bank decreases with increasing distance from a firm but increases with increasing distance of the firm with another bank. Loan rates decrease more for transactional borrowers indicating that the lender may extract rents from close-by firms that engage in RL.	

(Continued)

Table 2. *Continued*

Author(s)	Sample	Methodology	Research focus	Results	
				Dependent variable	Main findings
Brevoort and Hannan 2006 (BP)(LP)	USA: 1997–2001; Small, medium and large banks.	Probit regression	- Geographical distance => + RL's Advantages (LP)	Number of loans to firms in a metropolitan area	The distance between a bank, especially if small, and a firm is negatively associated with the probability of granting a loan.
Alessandrini *et al.* 2009 (BP)	ITA 1995–2003; 526 SMEs.	IV-Probit regression	- Geographical distance => RL's Advantages (BP)	Probability of a firm being credit rationed	Firms face more credit rationing in provinces with lower bank branch density.
Agarwald and Hauswald 2010 (BP)(LP)	USA: 2002–2003; 28,761 loans of SMEs and large enterprises.	Logistic regression	- Geographical distance => Both Beneficial (LP) and Dis-advantageous (BP)	Binary variable for the decision to offer or deny a loan	Distance leads to a trade-off between credit availability and price: physical proximity leads to an increase in credit granted but at a higher price. The use of soft information is determinant for close-by borrowers. The lender can extract rents from them in terms of higher pricing

Study	Data	Method	Finding	Variables	Conclusion
Arena and Dewally 2012 (BP)	USA; 1996–2005: 9134 SMEs and large enterprises.	Panel fixed effects Poisson regression Probit regression	- Geographical distance => + RL's Advantages (BP)	Debt yield spread compared to the USA bonds with similar maturity Number of loans from the main bank Rural bank binary variable	The information disadvantages of firms that are distant from the bank significantly increase their cost of debt. Rural bank rely extensively on RL to overcome their informational disadvantages. Rural firms tend to engage in RL with rural banks closer to them.
Raterkus and Munchus, 2014 (BP)	USA 4240 SMEs with less than 500 employees	Ordinary least squares Probit regression	- Geographical distance => + RL's Advantages (BP)	Lender–borrower distance; Probability of loan denial	Informationally opaque businesses seek out nearby lenders to maximize the value of soft information. Probability of loan denial is not affected by distance. Far away lenders rely on hard information. Firms located in rural areas have higher possibility of loan rejection by banks.

Notes: RL = Relationship Lending; LP = Lender's Perspective; BP = Borrower's Perspective; SMEs = small–medium enterprises.

competitors. They suffer less from agency problems[3] and can make better use of soft information (Berger and Udell, 2002). Large banks are therefore obliged to adopt standard credit policies based on easily observable, verifiable and communicable data. In addition, large banks may choose to avoid relationship lending due to considerable branch–headquarters distance and will probably decide to grant loans to larger firms, located in urban centres. They will be reluctant to extend credit to SMEs located outside urban centres since either the bank branches are much further from the central operational headquarters, or because such firms are characterized by greater information opacity (Arena and Dewally, 2012).

Moreover, Presbitero and Zazzaro (2011) argue that large hierarchical banks have a competitive advantage in using loan technologies based on hard information given the economies of scale in collecting, processing and evaluating it, but are at a disadvantage in using relationship lending because in this case they must handle soft information. Conversely, small institutions with few managerial layers have an advantage in using subjective and uncodified information, and tend to establish exclusive lending relationships with opaque borrowers from an information perspective.

However, De La Torre *et al.* (2010) empirically support an alternative view. That is, large banks use both branches and headquarters to interact with SMEs and the benefits for the latter are not necessarily fewer compared to having close-by lenders. The headquarters typically designate the strategy, both in terms of what types of SMEs will be targeted by the bank and which products they will offer. Branches do not operate as separate or local banks but interact with the central office. Moreover, in the case of international banks, the local branches and subsidiaries can benefit from the information and guidelines of the parent company, which has acquired great experience in dealing with SMEs around the world and can offer personalized services to them at a lower cost compared to relationship lending.

Other recent papers suggest that even adequately decentralized large banks could be able to generate soft information and include it in the credit evaluation process (Canales and Nanda, 2012; Uchida *et al.*, 2012; Bartoli *et al.*, 2013). These articles evidence that it is possible for large banks to engage in relationship lending if they permit their local branch managers to interact frequently with customers, delegate decision making at a lower level and grant branches more autonomy. Therefore, this recent stream of research indicates that relationship lending is not necessarily a monopoly of small financial institutions since even large ones can adopt it in complementarity with transaction-based lending.

In conclusion (see Table 3), the studies under review demonstrate that the reduction of functional distance has positive advantages for borrowers in terms of higher credit availability and lower interest rates and also for lenders in terms of fewer nonperforming loans.

4.4 *The Firm–Bank Relationship Duration*

A further determinant of benefits and costs of relationship lending is the duration of the bank–firm relationship, which has been discussed in the literature both from a lender's and a borrower's perspective. We first evidence the benefits of continued relationships for banks, then the hold-up issues for borrowers and the problem of soft-budget constraints for lenders are discussed.

The impact of a closed and lasting interaction between lender and borrower does not have a univocal effect on the loan conditions. A number of studies find that it impacts negatively on the cost of credit, positively on the amount of credit granted and negatively in the amount of firm guarantees or collateral, since the bank benefits from more and better information

Table 3. List of Articles that Discuss How Functional Distance Can Affect the Outcome of Relationship Lending.

Author(s)	Sample	Methodology	Research focus	Results	
				Dependent variable	Main findings
Alessandrini et al. 2009 (LP) (BP)	ITA: 1995–2003; 526 SMEs.	IV-Probit regression	- Functional distance => RL's Disadvantages (BP)	Probability of a firm being credit rationed. Share of credit line being drawn down per year	Functional distance has hardened firms' credit constraints. It positively affects the probability of credit rationing, and the share of credit lines being drawn down. The adverse effects are particularly higher for small firms.
Liberti and Mian 2009 (LP) (BP)	ARG 1998; 424 medium and large companies	GMM regression	- Functional distance => + RL's Advantages (LP) (BP)	Log of amount of credit approved	The higher the functional distance, the lower the reliance on soft information to make loan decisions. When bank managers are located in the same branch with the loan officer, their use of soft information in loan approval process increases the amount of credit granted to the firm.
De La Torre et al. 2010 (LP) (BP)	12 countries (USA, South America, EU and Asia); 2006–2009; SMEs and large enterprises.	Survey, interviews	-/+ Functional distance => + RL's Advantages (LP) (BP)	Banks' attitude towards SMEs	Large banks that use both branches and headquarters to serve small businesses have competitive advantages over small banks. Due to a large network of branches large universal banks can better capture economies of scale and scope and give SMEs a better personalized service at a lower cost than RL banks.

(*Continued*)

Table 3. *Continued*

Author(s)	Sample	Methodology	Research focus	Results	
				Dependent variable	Main findings
Presbitero and Zazzaro 2011 (LP) (BP)	ITA: 1998–2003; 4121 SMEs	Probit regression	- Functional distance => + RL's Advantages (LP) (BP)	Share of banking credit supplied to the firm by its main bank Binary variable taking value of one if the firm receives at least one-third of bank credit from its main bank	Large and complex banks in which the decision centre is located far away from the borrower tend to rely more on their comparative advantage in transactional lending.
Arena and Dewally 2012 (LP) (BP)	USA: 1996–2005; 9134 SMEs and large enterprises.	Panel fixed effects Poisson regression Probit regression	- Functional distance => + RL's Advantages (BP) (LP)	Debt yield spread compared to the USA bonds with similar maturity Number of loans from the main banks Rural bank binary variable	The information disadvantages of firms that are distant from the bank significantly increase their cost of debt. Rural banks rely extensively on RL to overcome their informational disadvantages. Rural firms tend to engage in RL with rural banks closer to them.
Uchida *et al.* 2012 (BP)	JPN 2005; 2041 SMEs	Logistic regression	Functional distance => + RL's Advantages (BP)	Amount of information collected by the lender and borrower perception of credit rationing	Low turnover of loan officers and high interaction with SMEs increase the quality of the information collected by the bank. Even large banks are able to produce soft information if adequately organized

Study	Sample	Method	Relation	Dependent variable	Findings
Canales and Nanda 2012 (LP)	MEX 2002–2006; 83,930 SME loan applications	Panel fixed effects regression	Functional distance => + RL's Advantages (LP)	Log of loan amount	Decentralized banks can alleviate credit to local SMEs in competitive credit markets
Cotugno et al. 2013a (LP)	ITA; 2007–2009; 4038 bank-year observations	Panel fixed effects regression	- Functional distance => + RL's Advantages (LP)	Ratio of nonperforming loans to gross loan portfolio	Positive relationship between functional distance and loan delinquency. Larger banks, which are geographically and functionally located far away from their borrowers, suffer from a higher proportion of nonperforming loans compared to smaller ones.
Bartoli et al. 2013 (BP)	ITA 2004–2006; 5137 firms	Logistic regression	Functional distance => + RL's Advantages (LP)	Dummy variables for use of different lending technologies. Dummy for credit rationing and dummy for the production of soft information	Even large and foreign banks are able to produce soft information by adopting different lending technologies, by modifying their organizational structure aimed at increasing the degree of delegation and lowering the turnover of the branch managers.

Notes: RL = Relationship Lending; LP = Lender's Perspective; BP = Borrower's Perspective; SMEs = small–medium enterprises.

about the opaque firm and is able to better screen higher from low-risk borrowers. This is demonstrated for the USA (Petersen and Rajan, 1994; Berger and Udell, 1995; Cole 1998; Brick and Palia, 2007), Finland (Peltoniemi, 2007; Peltoniemi and Vieru, 2013), Germany (Harhoff and Körting, 1998)[4] and Italy (Bartoli *et al.*, 2013). Moreover, firms engaging in a long relationship with the same bank experience lower probability of default on previous loans (Fiordelisi *et al.*, 2013).

However, the effects of a long-term relationship between banks and firms may not always be positive. Firms could be exposed to the risk of revenue expropriation through the imposition of high interest rates as a result of a monopoly position on information held by the bank: the so-called 'hold-up' problem. It can be manifested in terms of higher interest rates on loans (Angelini *et al.*, 1998; Stein, 2015), and higher personal or firm guarantees (Lehmann and Neuberger, 2001). These contradictory results could be due to a number of reasons. First, in the case of Angelini *et al.* (1998) the study concentrates on the lending behaviour of cooperative banks. In Italy, these institutions are generally small, they have a different governance model compared to noncooperative banks and operate in a single region. Moreover, the results indicate that the price discrimination occurs only when the bank is lending to nonmembers.[5] In the article of Stein (2015), the discriminatory pricing is observed mainly for bank-dependent SMEs, which rely almost exclusively on banks and therefore have a lower bargaining power. This problem might push the firms to try to switch banks in search for better pricing. Ioannidou and Ongena (2010) provide evidence that the firm's choice to change its relationship bank may initially result in benefits in terms of lower interest rates required by the new bank compared to the old bank. However, after a few years the new bank also raises interest rates even if the firm's credit worthiness has not deteriorated.

Last, the higher value of collateral required by the main bank in Lehmann and Neuberger (2001) is affected by the priority that a lender has over the others. When a bank is the first lender of a firm, it is more likely to get the best collateral. At the same time, it possesses a comparative advantage in evaluating assets for collateralization. Thus, if the firm subsequently applies for a credit at another lender, it may not be able to provide collateral of the same quality or the same extent.

Recently, Gambini and Zazzaro (2013) have shown that a long-term bank–SME relationship does not impact only on loan terms, but might have a significant and adverse effect on firms' growth rate, which is significantly lower than bank-independent small firms.

Reassuming, firms can benefit from better credit availability in a long-term relationship (Petersen and Rajan, 1994; Berger and Udell, 1995; Cole, 1998; Harhoff and Körting, 1998; Brick and Palia, 2007; Peltoniemi, 2007; Bartoli *et al.*, 2013; Fiordelisi *et al.*, 2013), but at the same time they can suffer from the hold-up phenomenon (Angelini *et al.*, 1998; Lehmann and Neuberger, 2001; Ioannidou and Ongena, 2010; Gambini and Zazzaro, 2013; Stein, 2015; see Table 4).

Apart from the hold-up risk in long-term and exclusive relationships between banks and firms, the possibility of a different phenomenon exists: the soft-budget constraint. This situation is verified when the bank continues to grant credit to firms at favourable costs even if the latter are in persistent financial distress (Dewatripont and Maskin, 1995). The lender's decision to prolong financial support to these firms depends on several variables. For instance, Peek and Rosengren (2005), analyse the relationship between main banks and firms in Japan in the period 1993–1999. They find that the amount of credit granted increased with the duration of relationship. This behaviour was due to two factors: the unwillingness of banks to evidence losses in their balance sheets, the pressure from the government and firms' large owners on the

Table 4. List of Articles that Discuss How the Duration Can Affect the Outcome of Relationship Lending and the Hold-Up Problem.

Author(s)	Sample	Methodology	Research focus	Results	
				Dependent variable	Main findings
Petersen and Rajan 1994 (BP)	USA; 1987–1989; 3404 SMEs	OLS regression	+ Duration => + RL's Advantages (BP)	Interest rate Credit availability (total debt/total assets) Amount of trade credit paid late	There is a small decrease in interest rates when the length of relationship increases. The availability of credit increases with length of relationship
Berger and Udell 1995 (BP)(LP)	USA; 1987–1989; 3404 SMEs	OLS regression Logit regression	+ Duration => + RL's Advantages (BP)	Loan interest rate Probability that collateral will be pledged	Small and opaque firms benefit from a longer relationship with the bank in terms of lower spreads on loan interest rates and fewer collateral requests
Harhoff and Körting 1998 (BP)(LP)	GER; 1996–1997; 1127 SMEs and large enterprises.	Probit regression OLS regression	+ Duration => + RL's Advantages (BP)(LP)	Binary variable for firm or personal collateral Interest rates on credit lines Trade credit availability	The duration increases the amount of credit granted and decreases the bank's need for guarantees, while the effect of the relationship duration on the cost of credit, the interest rate, is neither clear nor significant.

(Continued)

Table 4. *Continued*

Author(s)	Sample	Methodology	Results		Main findings
			Research focus	Dependent variable	
Cole 1998 (BP)	USA; 1991– 1994; 5356 SMEs	Logistic regression	+ Duration +RL Advantages (BP)	Decision to extend or deny credit	Preexisting firm–bank relationship positively influence the bank's decision to extend credit
Angelini *et al.* 1998 (BP)	ITA; 1995; 1858 SMEs	OLS regression Probit regression	+ Duration => Hold-up	Loan interest rates Binary variable for decision to extend or deny credit	With the increasing duration of the relationship, the interest rate on loans increases indicating firm capture. However, credit rationing diminishes with increased relationship duration
Lehmann and Neuberger 2001 (BP)	GER; 1997; 1200 banks	OLS regression Tobit regression Probit regression	+ Duration => Hold-up	Loan interest rate Amount of collateral required Credit availability	The main bank receives higher amount of collateral but practices lower interest rates. Credit availability is higher for firms engaged in relationship lending
Farinha and Santos 2002 (BP)	POR; 1980–1996; 1577 FIRMS	Hazard function Panel fixed effects regression Probit regressions	+ Duration => + RL's Advantages/ Hold-up (BP)	Firm investment, profitability, indebtedness	Good quality firms tend to have a long duration with a single bank. Firms decide to initiate a new bank relationship when they are credit rationed from the first one

Peltoniemi 2007 (BP)	FIN; 1995–2001; 768 SMEs	Pooled OLS regression	+ Duration => + RL's Advantages (BP)	Loan interest rate	Loan interest rates decreases with relationship duration. Longer relationships are especially beneficial for high-risk firms in terms of cost of credit.
Brick and Palia 2007 (BP)(LP)	USA; 1990–1994; 766 SMEs	Simultaneous equations – 3SLS	+ Duration => + RL's Advantages (BP)(LP)	Loan rate premium Binary variable for firm collateral Binary variable for personal collateral	The duration of the relationship affects negatively the cost of credit and the probability that firm or personal collateral will be required.
Ioannidou and Ongena 2010 (BP)	BOL; 1999–2003; 2805 enterprises (59% large)	OLS regression	+ Duration => Hold-up (BP)	Spread between new loan interest rate and old loan one	When firms switch banks interest rate initially drops. However, the new bank increases interest rates afterwards.
Peltoniemi and Vieru 2013 (BP)	FIN; 1995–2001; 768 SMEs	Pooled OLS regression	+ Duration => + RL's Advantages (BP)	Effective interest rate including fees and provisions Binary variable if personal guarantee has been used	Transaction-based loans require higher personal guarantees than relationship-based loans. Transaction-based borrowers pay higher loan premiums compared to relationship-based ones.

(Continued)

Table 4. *Continued*

Author(s)	Sample	Methodology	Research focus	Results	
				Dependent variable	Main findings
Bartoli *et al.* 2013 (BP)	ITA; 2004–2007; 5137 firms	OLS regression Probit regression	+ Duration + RL advantages (BP)	Binary variables for the adoption of transaction vs. relationship lending technologies Binary variables for decision to extend or deny credit	Firms may receive credit through different lending technologies. RL lowers the probability of credit rationing
Fiordelisi *et al.* (2013) (BP)	ITA; 2008–2010; 43,338 firms	IV-Probit regression	+ Duration + RL advantages (BP) (LP)	Probability that the firm will default on the loan granted	Longer bank–firm relationship decreases the probability of firm default, even in times of financial crisis.
Gambini and Zazzaro 2013 (BP)	ITA; 1998–2003; About 6000 firms	Quantile regression Logistic regression Heckman sample selection procedure	+ Duration => Hold-up	Firm growth rate	Smaller firms are likely to be captured by the bank in a lasting relationship. They grow less in terms of assets and number of employees compared to bank-independent firms.
Stein 2015 (BP)	GER; 1993–2004; 3741 firms	Pooled OLS regressions	+ Duration => Hold-up	Loan interest rate	Bank-dependent borrowers face a substantial premium after several relationship years.

Notes: RL = Relationship Lending; SMEs = small–medium enterprises; LP = Lender's Perspective; BP = Borrower's Perspective.

bank management in order to help affiliated companies. Similarly, Kawai *et al.* (1996) found for Japan that relationship banks seemed to assist troubled borrowers by applying favourable interest rates during periods of distress. As Dewatripont and Maskin (1995) have theoretically argued, the soft-budget constraint or the capture of the lender should be more observed in bank-based countries like Japan where banks are related with close ties to firms and are reluctant to cut their financing when the firm is experiencing a downturn.

Gambini and Zazzaro (2013) find supporting evidence for a sample of Italian firms indicating that the larger the customer requiring a loan, and the more the bank employs specific resources in a long-term relationship, the greater the possibility of the bank being captured. The captured bank will intervene to curb the decline of a large firm, if the latter is facing temporary difficulties.

Kang *et al.* (2011) offer an alternative explanation of this phenomenon by concentrating on a sample of small banks operating in areas with low population density in the USA. The hypothesis they test is that bank managers in this environment will tend to refinance bad loans to past borrowers because of the fear of losing the customer, but also because of the social pressure from the community, which might blame the bank for the failure of the firm and the loss of jobs. They observe that both the duration and exclusivity of the bank–firm relationship are greater if both the bank and the firm are located in districts with a low population density. In this situation, the risk of banks being captured by firms through the soft-budget constraint is more concrete, given their strong attachment to the community.

In general (see Table 5), the authors reported above, affirm that the relationship duration can increase the possibility of soft-budget constraints for banks when they continue to provide credit to distressed firms (Kawai *et al.*, 1996; Peek and Rosengren, 2005; Gambini and Zazzaro, 2013), but seldom even when the bank is operating in areas with close economic and social ties and low population density (Kang *et al.*, 2011).

4.5 *The Exclusivity and the Main–Bank Affiliation*

The theoretical framework discussed in Section 2 illustrates the benefits and costs that an exclusive bank–firm relationship entails for borrowers and lenders. Alternatively, firms could choose to switch the relationship (main) bank after a number of years or engage in multiple lending with different banks contemporaneously. It is very common for firms to have more than one lender, but at the same time to privilege a long-lasting relationship with one main bank (Hausbank). The main research questions arising from this literature strand are substantially two. First, which firms tend to more frequently adopt switching or multiple lending? Second, does this choice bring any benefits for them in terms of more access to credit, lower probability of distress or lower borrowing costs?

Regarding the first question, Ongena and Smith (2001) find these firms are generally small, young, have high growth opportunities and high leverage. Degryse and Ongena (2001) demonstrate that small and young companies in the early stages of their lives usually have a single banking relationship, typical of relationship lending. When they grow and continue implementing high-quality projects, these firms are more likely to continue the relationship with the same bank. If the future projects of these companies are mediocre, they are likely to change or add banks to try to meet their financial needs, and in doing so send a "low-quality" signal to the credit market. Therefore, companies that maintain a single banking relationship seem to enjoy a better financial profile than companies that rely on multiple lending. Similarly, Farinha and Santos (2002) suggest that firms switch to multiple banking because the incumbent bank

Table 5. List of Articles that Discuss How Duration of Relationship Lending Can Produce the Soft-Budget Constraint Problem.

Author(s)	Sample	Methodology	Research focus	Results	
				Dependent variable	Main findings
Kawai et al. 1996	JPN; 1964–1993; 1412 firms	OLS regression	+ Duration => Soft budget constraint	Interest rate premia paid by firms in financial distress	Firms with stable and long-term relationships with the relationship bank receive favourable financial treatment in periods of financial distress. The main bank appears to extend financial assistance to troubled firms by sacrificing risk premia.
Peek and Rosengren 2005 (LP)	JPN; 1993–1999; 1200 firms	Probit regression	+ Duration => Soft budget constraint	Probability that bank will increase credit to an affiliated troubled firm	Banks extended credit to troubled firms because they were part of the same conglomerate, received pressure from the Government and reduced credit to firms with best prospects
Kang et al. 2011 (LP)	USA; 1994–2002; 640 banks;	Panel random effects regression	+ Duration => Soft budget constraint	(1-Gross charge-offs / Bad loans) Indicator of bad loans that are refinanced	Small banks operating in rural and small communities tend to refinance bad loans, which is an indicator of bank capture by the borrower.
Gambini and Zazzaro 2013 (LP)	ITA; 1998–2003; About 6000 firms	Quantile regression Logistic regression Heckman sample selection procedure	+ Duration => Soft budget constraint	Firm growth rate	Large firms are able to receive adequate financing from the main bank to spur their growth because they can credibly threat the lender of switching to another bank.

Notes: RL = Relationship Lending; SMEs = small–medium enterprises; LP = Lender's Perspective; BP = Borrower's Perspective.

is reluctant to extend more credit to them due to firm's past poor performance and past due loans.

Petersen and Rajan (1994) claim that low-quality firms experience increasing difficulties in getting funded from the existing bank, therefore they adopt multiple banking. Other firms choose this strategy to reap better benefits by putting different banks in competition against each other. Howorth *et al.* (2003) find that one of the most important factors associated with the firm's decision to adopt multiple lending is the fear of being credit rationed. However, some of them cannot switch easily because they are 'informationally captured', due to the difficulty of conveying accurate information about their activities to other lenders. Elsas (2005) provide evidence that banks are more likely to be chosen as relationship lenders by firms when they provide most of the debt financing for the latter. Gopalan *et al.* (2011) find that firms that have existing relationships with small banks are more prone to form new banking relationships to finance their growth.

Regarding the second question, the results from the literature are not conclusive. On the one side, it seems that the lower the number of lenders a firm has relationships with, the lower the cost of credit and/or the lower the probability of credit rationing. The benefits as expected are greater for small and opaque firms which find it difficult to signal their quality to external lenders given lack of audited financial statements (Petersen and Rajan, 1994, 1995; D'Auria *et al.*, 1999; Elsas and Krahnen, 1998; Bharath *et al.*, 2011; Cenni *et al.*, 2015). Multiple lending could also be related to future firm performance. Castelli *et al.* (2012) examine the link between the number of banking relationships and firm profitability. They show that the number of banking relationships affects negatively the performance of a firm. The abovementioned inverse relationship is stronger with regard to small firms. Moreover, the results show that the financing costs increase with the number of relationships.

Nevertheless, contrary to the previous findings, other authors maintain that exclusive lending can also be particularly disadvantageous for borrowers. Generally, these studies show that an exclusive relationship is not necessarily accompanied by higher profits, higher growth rates or lower cost of credit. Apparently, the borrower could suffer an 'informational capture', given that other banks do not know its real value. Therefore, the relationship lender can exercise a monopolistic relationship by extracting rents from him (Weinstein and Yafeh, 1998; Howorth *et al.*, 2003; Cardone *et al.*, 2005; Hernandez-Canovas and Martinez-Solano, 2007; Matias Gama and Van Auken, 2015).

Machauer and Weber (2000) show that the interest rates spreads are not influenced by the number of bank relationships, but generally borrowers with few relationships and a main bank need to provide more collateral. Carmignani and Omiccioli (2007) focus on the benefits and costs of multiple lending on a sample of Italian SMEs. They argue that, on the one hand, exclusive relationship lending reduces the likelihood of a firm running into financial crisis and its subsequent liquidation. They add that these benefits are surpassed by the increasing risk of hold-up for the firm. This effect would explain the widespread adoption of multiple banking relationships by Italian firms.

These contradictory results could depend on the complexity of the phenomenon and on the diversity of datasets under investigation. The relationship between number of banks and credit terms can be affected by a multitude of variables such as bank competition (discussed in Section 5), development of capital markets and several bank and firm characteristics. De Bodt *et al.* (2005) assert that some important variables to be taken into account are the amount of collateral required, the type of financing needed, the type of main bank and bank reputation among others. Gopalan *et al.* (2011) suggest that the firm credit rationing should be studied under a firm life cycle framework. Overall, there seems to be no unique strategy for SMEs in their choice of optimal number of banks or the consequences of this decision for them (see Table 6).

4.6 *The Importance of Lender–Borrow Mutual Trustworthiness and the Role of Qualitative Information*

Most of the abovementioned literature on relationship lending acknowledges the fact that banks using this lending technology benefit from the availability of soft information gathered locally by branch managers. However, since it is not possible to measure the presence and use of this variable, the problem is circumvented by proxying it with relationship duration, lending exclusivity or geographic vicinity. Unfortunately, these criteria could be a necessary but not sufficient condition to generate soft information. Therefore, a number of articles that have tried to integrate this approach with the concept of trust and social capital borrowed from economic sociology (Granovetter, 1973, 1991) on the one side, and the importance of information quality on the other. Regarding the former research body, its main finding is that social networks could remarkably reduce information asymmetries between members. Each member of the network holds social capital deriving from his long-lasting relationships with the other members. Therefore, there will be mutual trust between them, which reduces moral hazard and allows to anticipate the behaviour of the other contractors (Williamson, 1993).

In the banking context, several articles confirm the usefulness of including a measure of trust among explanatory variables. The assessment of trustworthiness of the firm's management is usually captured by specific survey questions or interviews with bank rather than firm directors. The questions aim at assessing the level of mutual trust between relationship bankers and firm owners, or other social aspects such as positive perception of the past interactions, obligation to the counterparty, willingness of the borrower to inform the bank about potential problems, etc. The results indicate that trust and other interactional variables impact negatively on credit costs and collateral requirements (Harhoff and Körting, 1998; Lehmann and Neuberger 2001; Ferrary, 2003; Howorth and Moro, 2012; Moro and Fink, 2013).

The role of qualitative information is emphasized in Uchida *et al.* (2012), Bartoli *et al.* (2013), and Moro *et al.* (2015). In a nutshell, the methodological approach in these papers is based on questionnaires that bank or firm managers are asked to fill. Specific questions aim at measuring the importance of receiving timely, qualitative, quantitative and complete information from the borrowers. The frequency of borrower–lender interaction is another relevant dimension. The results indicate that as information available is considered reliable and complete, and there is a high frequency of loan officer–firm manager contacts, the better are the loan terms that the firm is able to achieve. These papers are summarized in Table 7.

5. Industry-Specific Variables[6]

5.1 *Level of Market Competition*

The level of capital market competition can remarkably affect borrowers and lenders' decisions to employ relationship lending. Closed and continued lender–borrower interactions lead to more credit availability, while lower interest rates depend on banking market competition. If the credit market is competitive and the creditors cannot make a claim on the firm's profits, they cannot afford to demand higher interests rates than the market average in the future,

Table 6. List of Articles that Discuss How Exclusivity and the Main-Bank Affiliation Can Affect the Outcome of Relationship Lending.

Author	Sample	Methodology	Research focus	Results	
				Dependent variable	Main findings
Petersen and Rajan 1994, 1995 (BP)	USA; 1987–1989; 3404 medium and large enterprises	Tobit regression	+ Exclusivity => + RL's Advantages (BP)	Interest rate quoted on recent loan; Total debts dived by the book value of assets.	A long-term relationship with a main bank significantly decreases the probability of rationing and the cost of credit
Elsas and Krahnen 1998 (BP)	GER; 1992–1996; 200 SMEs	OLS regression	Main bank => + RL's Advantages (BP)	Spread: interest rate charged by the bank minus the short-term interest rate	In cases of multiple lending, a main bank can renew a credit offer more easily than other banks.
Weinstein and Yafeh 1998 (BP)	JPN; 1977–1986; 700 SMEs	Pooled OLS	+ Exclusivity => + RL's Disadvantages (BP)	Interest rate of bank loans	SMEs grow more slowly and pay higher interest rates when they have a main bank
D'Auria Foglia and Reedtz 1999 (BP)	ITA; 1987–1994; 2331 firms	Panel fixed effects	+ Exclusivity => + RL's Advantages (BP)	Spread between interest rate charged to the single bank and 3/6/12 month Treasury bill	Having a close relationship with a main bank lowers to cost of credit to the firm. However, firms use multiple banking to avoid risk of hold-up
Machauer and Weber 2000 (BP)	GER; 1992–1996; 190 SMEs	Poisson regression model with random effects; Tobit panel regression	+ Exclusivity => + RL's Advantages (BP)	Loan rate spread Percentage of the credit line that is collateralized	A relationship with a single bank requires more guarantees.

(Continued)

Table 6. *Continued*

Author	Sample	Methodology	Research focus	Results	
				Dependent variable	Main findings
Ongena and Smith 2001	NOR: 1979–1995; 419 SMEs	Hazard functions	+ Exclusivity => + RL's Advantages (BP)	The probability that a firm will switch main bank	The probability of switching a main bank is higher for small, highly leveraged, profitable firms and firms that have multiple lending relationships.
Degryse and Ongena 2001 (BP)	NOR: 1979–1995; 419 SMEs	Cross-sectional regression models.	+ Exclusivity => + RL's Advantages (BP)	Return on assets (ROA)	The profitability of firms that maintain a single relationship is greater compared to those who engage in multiple lending.
Howorth et al. 2003 (BP)	UK; 1996; 2370 SMEs	Multivariate logistic regression	+ Exclusivity => + RL's Disadvantages (BP)	Binary variable for firms that had switched main bank relative to those that were considering switching	Firms decide to switch when they fear credit rationing, are of good quality. Firms that do not switch may be "informationally" captured by the lender
Cardone et al. 2005 (BP)	ESP; 1999; 386 SMEs	OLS regression	+ Exclusivity => + RL's Disadvantages (BP)	Different types of credit rationing, ex: Percentage of financing that the company maintains with credit institutions with respect to total liabilities.	Small businesses that engage in multiple lending have better access to credit.

Study	Sample	Methodology	Hypotheses	Variables	Conclusion
Elsas 2005 (BP)	GER: 1992–1996; 200 medium enterprises	Probit regression	Main bank => + RL's Advantages (BP)	Banks self-assessment of their Hausbank status.	The probability that banks are chosen as Hausbank by SMEs is higher when banks provide a large portion of their debt.
Hernandez-Canovas and Martinez-Solano 2007 (BP)	ESP: 1999–2001; 530 SMEs	GMM regression	+ Exclusivity => + RL's Disadvantages (BP)	Bank Credit: ratio of bank debt to total assets.	Small businesses with an exclusive relationship have a higher probability of rationing and a greater capture risk.
Carmignani and Omiccioli 2007 (BP)(LP)	ITA; 1997–2003; 3597 SMEs	Probit regression	+ Exclusivity => + RL's advantages (BP) vs. + RL's Disadvantages (LP)	Liquidation/Distress: binary variable equal to 1 if the firm runs into liquidation/distress at time $(t+1)$ or $(t+2)$, equal to 0 otherwise.	The cost of single lending, in particular, the hold-up risk, outweighs the benefits.
Gopalan et al. 2011 (BP)	USA; 1990–2005; 12,806 loans of medium–large enterprises.	OLS regression	+ Exclusivity => + RL's Disadvantages (BP)	Yield; Firm investment; Sales growth rate; Leverage, and Analyst coverage.	Firms that have existing relationships with small banks are more prone to form new banking relationships to finance their growth.

(Continued)

Table 6. *Continued*

Author	Sample	Methodology	Research focus	Results	
				Dependent variable	Main findings
Bharath *et al.* 2011 (LP)	USA; 1986–2003; 21,632 loan agreements	Panel fixed effects	+ Exclusivity => + RL's Advantages (BP)	Coupon spread over the LIBOR plus annual fee	Having a relationship lender decreases the cost of borrowing for the firm
Cotugno *et al.* 2013b (BP)	ITA; 2007–2009; 5331 banks; SMEs	OLS regression	+ Exclusivity => + RL's Advantages (BP)	Credit growth rate	During a crisis, firms with exclusive bank relationships are less exposed to credit rationing.
Cenni *et al.* 2015 (BP)	ITA; 2004–2006; 4289 firms of which 2217 are SMEs	Probit regression	+ Exclusivity => + RL's Advantages (BP)	Binary variable if the firm declares it needed more credit; Another binary variable if firm applied for more credit and the credit was denied.	A longer banking relationship decreases the probability of credit rationing
Matias Gama and Van Auken 2015 (BP)	POR; 1998–2006; 468 SMEs	GMM regression	Main bank => + RL's Disadvantages (BP)	The ratio of trade credit to total assets.	A single bank relationship creates a hold up problem and leads to high interest rates

Notes: RL = Relationship Lending; BP = Borrower Perspective; LP = Lender Perspective; SMEs = small–medium enterprises.

Table 7. List of Articles that Discuss the Importance of Lender/Borrower Mutual Trustworthiness and the Role of Qualitative Information.

Author	Sample	Methodology	Research focus	Results	
				Dependent variable	Main findings
Harhoff and Körting 1998 (BP)	GER; 1997; 1399 SMEs	Logistic and OLS regression	Mutual trust =⟩ + RL's Advantages (BP)	Binary variables indicating request of collateral, or interest rate on credit lines	Mutual trust has a significant negative impact on interest rates and collateral requirements.
Lehmann and Neuberger 2001 (LP)	GER; 1997; 1200 banks	Pooled OLS regression	Mutual trust =⟩ + RL's Advantages (LP)	Loan credit terms	Variables measuring trust and social interaction reduce loan interest rates, increase credit availability.
Ferrary 2003 (LP)	FRA	Case study	Mutual trust =⟩ + RL's Advantages (LP)	Credit availability	Banks that engage in social interactions with borrowers, gain their trust, reduce asymmetric information, moral hazard and can establish successful long-term relationships.
Howorth and Moro 2012 (BP)	ITA; 2004–2005; 6 banks and 365 client borrowers	OLS regression	Mutual trust =⟩ + RL's Advantages (BP)	Cost of credit	The cost of credit decreases with trustworthiness.
Moro and Fink 2013 (BP)	ITA; 2005–2007; 9 banks and 449 firms	OLS regression	Mutual trust =⟩ + RL's Advantages (BP)	Log of short-term credit granted by the bank Average credit used by the firm compared to credit line provided by the bank	Credit access improves with the trust the bank manager places on firm owners.

(Continued)

Table 7. *Continued*

Author	Sample	Methodology	Research focus	Dependent variable	Main findings
				Results	
Uchida *et al.* 2012 (LP)	JPN; 2005; 2041 SMEs	Logistic regression	Information quality => + RL's Advantages (LP)	Amount of information collected by the lender and borrower perception of credit rationing	Low turnover of loan officers and high interaction with SMEs increase the quality of the information collected by the bank. Even large banks are able to produce soft information if adequately organized.
Bartoli *et al.* 2013 (LP)	ITA; 2004–2006; 5137 firms	Logistic regression	Information quality => + RL's Advantages (LP)	Dummy variables for use of different lending technologies. Dummy for credit rationing and dummy for the production of soft information	Even large and foreign banks are able to produce soft information by adopting different lending technologies, by modifying their organizational structure aimed at increasing the degree of delegation and lowering the turnover of the branch managers.
Moro *et al.* 2015 (BP)	ITA; 2005–2012; 16 banks	OLS regression	Information quality => + RL's Advantages (BP)	Amount of short-term credit obtained by the firm	More and better information about the borrower will induce the bank to increase credit availability

Notes: RL = Relationship Lending; BP = Borrower Perspective; LP = Lender Perspective; SMEs = small–medium enterprises.

otherwise the firm would abandon the relationship in favour of another bank (Petersen and Rajan, 1994, 1995; D'Auria *et al.*, 1999; Hauswald and Marquez, 2006; Canales and Nanda, 2012). Additionally, the existence of alternative sources of bank credit reduces the bank's ability to threaten a hold-up situation. Firm that rely on multiple banks terminate relationships earlier than single-bank firms. But the multiple-bank firms tend to turn over newer relationships and keep one long-term relationship. Therefore, long-term relationships appear valuable to firms that are unlikely to face credible hold-up threats from one monopolistic bank (Ongena and Smith, 2001).

Nonetheless, Boot and Thakor (2000) emphasize that it is important to consider two types of competition: interbank competition and capital market competition. An increase in interbank competition raises the number of relationship loans, lowering the added value for borrowers. On the other hand, increasing capital market competition reduces the numbers of relationship loans, but each relationship loan has greater added value for borrowers.

Recent empirical evidence shows that the probability of credit rationing for informationally opaque SMEs increases with reduced competition in the banking market (Canales and Nanda, 2012). In a highly competitive environment, small firms tend to have more banking relationships and experience fewer credit constraints (Tirri, 2007; Neuberger *et al.*, 2008). However, this relationship may not be linear. For instance, Vesala (2005) investigates the cost of switching banks as a proxy for competition in the credit market. The author finds that an increase in these costs initially reduces the insider bank's profits, but after a certain threshold the insider bank's mark-up begins to increase again. Therefore, relationship profits resemble a nonmonotonous 'V-shaped' function of the switching costs and, consequently, an 'inverted V-shaped' function of competition.

Bonini *et al.* (2016) point out that the intensity of relationship lending and market competition could jointly influence the cost of borrowing for firms. According to the authors, this outcome could explain the controversial results of previous literature on the impact of relationship lending on the cost of credit. Indeed, if relationship lending measured as duration of relationship with the main bank is interacted with the level of competition in the credit market, the results suggest that duration can affect negatively the cost of credit only when the market is competitive.

Other studies have concentrated on the association between bank competition and firm performance. On the one side, borrowers that receive funding in less competitive markets have lower profitability than those that are financed in a more competitive environment (Agostino and Trivieri, 2010). Conversely, Rogers (2011) argues that in countries with a higher level of banking competition, there is a lower growth rate of SMEs and a lower firm performance. The reason is the difficulty for the bank to establish stable and long-term credit relationships with firms, and the net effect may be that the latter receive lower amounts of funding, preventing the implementation of their projects and their growth.

5.2 *Regulatory Framework – Adoption of Basel II and III*

An overall evaluation of the costs or benefits of relationship lending would not be complete without accounting for differences in bank regulation or legal frameworks across countries. Regarding the latter, a number of articles reach to interesting results. Ongena and Smith (2000) show that in countries that enjoy a high level of creditor protection, firms tend to practice single rather than multiple banking. Similarly, Neuberger *et al.* (2008) show that SMEs tend to adopt single or few banking relationships in countries with high scores of judicial efficiency and law enforcement.

Regarding bank regulation, under Basel II and III banks may have started to adopt new screening technologies based on standardized models that use hard information. These methods could progressively substitute relationship lending or integrate it (Cosci *et al.*, 2009). Adasme *et al.* (2006) show that SME lending might require more provisions for loan losses but less capital given that the distribution of losses in small firms is less skewed than in large ones. Moreover, the creditworthiness of SMEs varies more than that of large enterprises making lending to this segment more problematic especially during economic downturns (Beck, 2016). Other authors are sceptical about the benefits of the Basel approach, which relies heavily on quantitative risk models (Masera, 2011; Haldane, 2012; Admati and Hellwig, 2013). The reliance on risk weights will most probably penalize SMEs as they are perceived as riskier than other counterparties. As an example, an AAA rated firm is assigned a 20% risk weight, whereas an unrated SME is assigned a 75% or 100% risk weight (Beck, 2016).

Another risk related to the Basel approach is that by increasing bank opacity, it will incentivize them to concentrate on assets for which manipulation of risk assessment is relatively easy and will keep them away from small business loans (Bord and Santos, 2012; Ferri and Neuberger, 2014). Moreover, the trend towards loan securitization will reduce the need for banks to engage in relationship lending and invest in the collection of soft information (De Larosière, 2011). The second pillar of Basel II framework requires that the borrower creditworthiness has to be assessed based on scoring system with the use of hard data. This may lead to credit rationing of good borrowers whose quality cannot be observed by the use of hard data alone (Ferri and Neuberger, 2014).

5.3 *Ownership Structure*

As outlined in Section 4.1, there is a preference by small banks towards the use of relationship banking. Additionally, the legal status of banks (commercial/profit oriented vs. cooperative/not-for-profit oriented) might influence their attitude to adopt relationship rather than transaction lending (Delgado *et al.*, 2007). Cooperative banks are deeply embedded in the local communities, where the capital of a small firm is intertwined with the entrepreneur's personal wealth.[7] Therefore, the cooperative bank managers have to encourage discussions of private matters with firm owners, which affect everyday business dealings (Uzzi, 1999). The commercial transaction becomes therefore deeply embedded in social attachments and networks (Neuberger *et al.*, 2008).

There is some evidence that cooperative banks have an advantage over commercial banks in practising relationship lending because of these peculiarities. Angelini *et al.* (1998) find that these banks provide credit at better terms for their members. Ogura (2012) highlights that small cooperative banks provide more credit albeit at a higher cost to their communities in Japan. Ferri *et al.* (2014a,b) find that cooperative banks attempt to smooth financial conditions for their customers by conducting less procyclical loan supply policies than for-profit financial institutions, and by maintaining longer term borrower–lender relationships. Since cooperative banks are major players in the banking landscape of many countries, their role in SME lending and in assisting SMEs' recovery from financial crises should not be understated.[8]

6. Relationship Lending in Times of Financial Distress for Lenders and/or Borrowers

The literature examined so far has mainly dealt with the benefits/costs for lenders and borrowers without considering the impact of financial distress on firms and/or banks. There are some exceptions though. Berger and Udell (2002) and Petersen and Rajan (1995) provide evidence that relationship lenders tend to smooth rates in response to interest rates shocks or changes in the firm's credit risk for distressed borrowers.

The 2007–2009 Global Financial Crisis can be considered as a scenario of distress for both banks and firms (Bongini *et al.*, 2015). It provided a natural experiment to test the use of different lending technologies by financial institutions and the consequences for borrowers and lenders. Most of the related literature is based on European data, probably because of the severity of the crisis in the Eurozone. Predominantly, these studies find that the main benefit of relationship lending under this scenario is a lower level of credit rationing to SMEs compared to arm's length lending (Beck *et al.*, 2014, for Central and Eastern Europe; Malafronte *et al.*, 2014, for Italy; and Dewally and Shao, 2014, for the USA). Relationship banks seem to support their customers even when interbank competition is high (Malafronte *et al.*, 2014). In so doing, they increase their market power, create a competitive advantage and adopt a long-term approach with the borrower which could help banks to potentially extract rents in the future (Santos and Winton, 2008; Mattes *et al.*, 2013).

Hainz and Wiegand (2013) represent a slight exception in literature since their findings evidence some weak sides of relationship lending during the crisis. Analysing SMEs in Germany, they find that firms implementing relationship lending have a lower probability of facing higher information requirements and deteriorating credit terms. However, the banks' decision about credit availability is not affected by relationship lending. This could be a consequence of the fact that banks are starting to make use of hard rather than soft information in their credit risk models when they decide about granting a loan. Moreover, they find that having a second bank (but not more) can be advantageous in terms of lower interest rates for the borrower because it alleviates the hold-up problem with the Hausbank.

Other authors find that relationship lending impacts the borrower probability of default, which influences bank loan losses and its profitability. Fiordelisi *et al.* (2013), focusing on the Italian context, document that small firms experience lower default rates when they can count on a long lending relationship. Cotugno *et al.* (2013b) find that thanks to relationship lending Italian banks were able to maintain a good quality of their loan portfolio in terms of lower borrower default rates. Ono *et al.* (2014) finds that relationship lending reduces default probabilities for Japanese firms. The authors evaluate the *ex post* probability that a borrower might default on a loan granted based on a credit scoring and whether this probability differs when the loan is granted by a relationship lender (the primary bank) or other institutions. Their results demonstrate that relationship lenders are associated with a lower firms' probability of default, which also means that during bad times the provision of small business credit scoring loans by transactional lenders is associated with a deterioration in borrower *ex post* performance. Rosenfeld (2014) finds similar results for the USA, showing that relationship lending can help banks detect which firms are more likely to recover from a temporary shock and eventually support them financially.

Moreover, lender–borrower functional distance and bank organizational structure seem to have played an important role during the last crisis. Banks whose decision centre were far away from local economies in the Italian context experienced larger credit tightening because the distance negatively affected their ability to control credit risk (Cotugno *et al.*, 2013b;

Albertazzi and Bottero, 2014). However, De La Torre *et al.* (2010) reach to opposite results when they study the involvement of international banks in Latin American countries during the crisis. Their results suggest that the banks analysed opted for a continuous financial support to the SME segment because they believed that the shock was transitory or because they were adopting a wide range of lending technologies, risk management and business models, which permitted them to better handle loan credit risk and reduce credit losses.

Another group of papers has taken a slightly different approach. They investigated differences between transaction- and relationship-based forms of lending but put the accent on the *ex ante* situation of the lender (i.e., undercapitalized or adequately capitalized) and the borrower. Bolton *et al.* (2016) theoretically and empirically demonstrate that the positive role that relationship banks can play during a crisis is influenced by the excess equity capital they are able to hold in anticipation of this event. Moreover, relationship banks tend to charge higher interest rates in good times to compensate for better credit terms during a crisis. This behaviour forces safe firms to prefer transaction-based forms of lending and leaves more opaque ones to choose relationship banks.

Sette and Gobbi (2015) provide evidence that relationship lending has a positive effect on the credit conditions applied to small firms. However, this effect vanishes when the financial institution is severely affected by the crisis and when the borrower is financially risky. In this case, the former tends to behave like a transaction-based lender. Their results present similarities with a previous study of Ferri *et al.* (2001) who, focusing on a different time period (the 1997–1998 crisis in Korea), suggest that a more intense pre-crisis relationship between lenders and borrowers reduces the possibility of SMEs' distress during a systemic crisis. However, they also argue that it might be particularly difficult for borrowers to substitute distressed lending banks during a crisis, if they do not have relationship loans with other banks.

Finally, Ferri *et al.* (2014a,b) compare SME credit rationing in the aftermath of the Lehman crisis in several Eurozone countries by transaction- and relationship-based lenders. They show that the use of transaction technology generally reduces credit availability across the sample. In addition, their results suggest that large banks are able to serve opaque SMEs only if they can produce and manage soft information, which is a key element of relationship lending. These results challenge somehow the current Basel regulatory framework. It relies solely on a mechanistic method of risk-weighted approach, and ignores the evaluation of bank business models which could help in properly evaluating banks' level of credit risk (Ayadi *et al.*, 2012).

7. Differences between Financial Systems

Analysing the papers composing our review, we notice that the adoption of relationship lending could be subject to differences in the institutional setting among countries. In countries like Continental Europe, stock markets are underdeveloped compared to Anglo-Saxon economies, firms rely heavily on bank lending and the firm ownership structure is heavily concentrated (La Porta *et al.*, 1998; Ampenberger *et al.*, 2013). Based on this distinction, it seems that relationship lending should be preferred in bank-based economies. However, the empirical evidence in the previous sections acknowledges that even in the USA or UK relationship lending is not uncommon (Berger and Udell, 2002).[9] Relationship lending is usually practised by small banks whose decisional centre is located nearby the borrower (i.e., Petersen and Rajan, 2002; Degryse and Ongena, 2005). Moreover, lenders and borrowers can mutually benefit from closer and long-lasting relationships in bank-based as well as in market-based environments (i.e., Brick and Palia, 2007; Peltoniemi, 2007).

The main differences between financial systems are related to the 'dark' side of relationship lending. From the extant literature, it seems that the risk of hold-up and soft-budget constraint is typical of bank-based economies, where the bond between banks and SMEs is stronger, and firms have fewer financing options than in market-based countries (i.e., Dewatripont and Maskin, 1995; Gambini and Zazzaro, 2013). This could explain why the adoption of multiple banking is widespread in Continental Europe (i.e., Cardone *et al.*, 2005; Carmignani and Omiccioli, 2007). Berger *et al.* (2011) indicate that small banks in USA have started adopting other arm's length lending technologies along with relationship lending. There is still little evidence that this is being replicated in other countries, although as previously mentioned, Basel guidelines encourage a similar approach (Bartoli *et al.*, 2013).

The two types of financial systems differentiate also by their resilience to exogenous shocks. It seems that bank-based systems are more stable where there is no financial crisis, but only recession (Gambacorta, 2016). This is consistent with the idea that when banks are not under distress they can assist their clients to absorb temporary shocks. The opposite is true when there is a financial crisis coincident with a recession (even banks are under distress). In this case, countries that rely mainly on bank financing tend to be more severely hit, whereas more market oriented systems are able to foster a quicker and sustainable recovery (Bech *et al.*, 2012; Gambacorta, 2016).

8. Final Remarks and Suggestions for Future Research

Relationship lending is one of the lending technologies used by banks to cater for SMEs. In deploying this technology, lenders collect soft information about the borrower/entrepreneur over time and use this information in underwriting the loan and monitoring the borrower (Udell, 2015). In this review, we aimed at investigating under which conditions relationship lending is adopted by banks and firms and what are the benefits and costs for both of them. We perform a study on two levels. First, we look at some important determinants at the bank–firm specific level – the bank and firm size, the lender–borrower distance, the duration of a relationship, the exclusivity of relationships, the possibility of having a main bank in cases of multiple lending, the lender–borrower mutual trustworthiness and the role of qualitative information. Then, we include other important variables at the industry level, such as the degree of banks' market competition, their regulatory framework, their ownership structure and the use of relationship lending in times of financial distress such as the recent Global Financial Crisis. We conclude by highlighting possible differences between bank-based and market-based economies. A summary of the articles reviewed for each determinant is presented in Figures 2A(A) and (B).

The literature on relationship lending is vast and it is still growing as the interest on the lending channels of SMEs is of paramount importance for all countries. From the present review we can draw a number of conclusions. Relationship lending is based on the collection of soft proprietary information. This variable cannot be measured directly, and therefore the likelihood that it is included in the loan process of the bank is based on different variables such as firm size, bank size, bank–firm distance, duration of bank–firm relationship, exclusivity of bank–firm relationship, lender–borrower mutual trustworthiness and availability of qualitative information. Each one of these proxies has generated different literature strands.

The early empirical evidence generally acknowledges that relationship lending is practiced by small banks, which are located near their customers and can frequently interact with them. The simple hierarchical structure permits small banks to collect and process proprietary information about the borrowers' creditworthiness, which can be used to offer them better credit

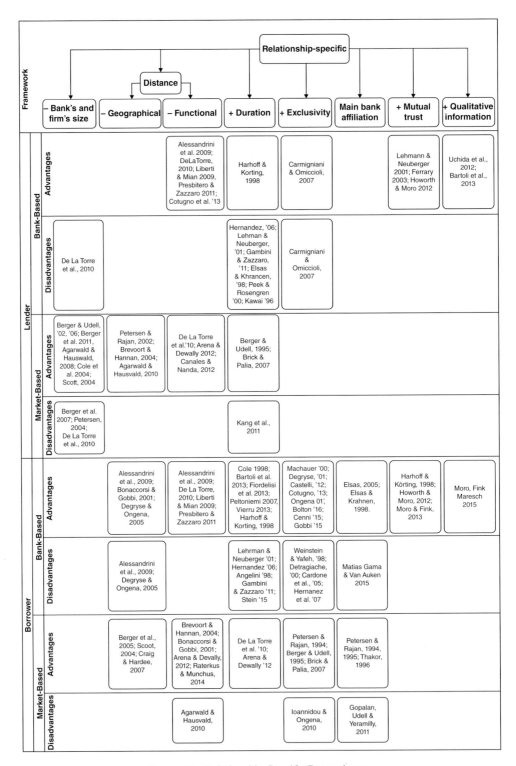

Figure 2A. Relationship-Specific Determinants.

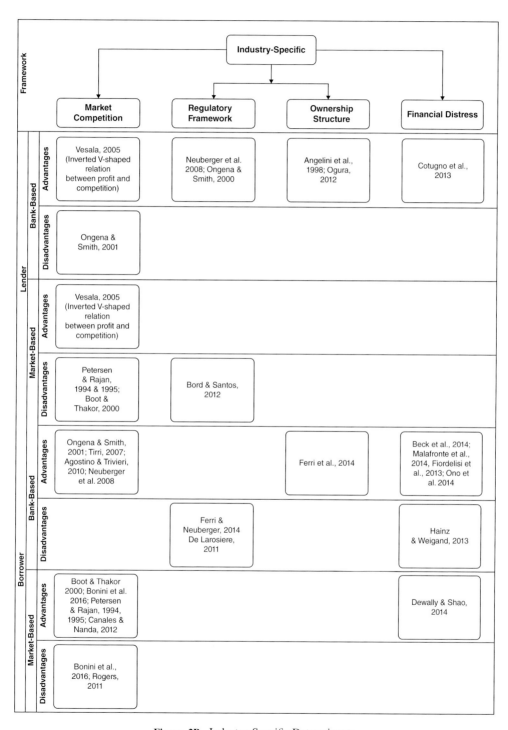

Figure 2B. Industry-Specific Determinants.

terms compared to what other lenders would offer. Therefore, small banks are supposed to serve the SMEs that are unlikely to produce 'hard' information – because of lack of audited financial statements, poor corporate governance and lack of resources – whereas large banks have the chance to deal with more transparent large firms.

The duration of bank–firm relationship is another fundamental element. Here two views co-exist in the literature. On the one side, the longer the relation, the more the bank can overcome information asymmetries about the borrower, and therefore can practise more favourable loan terms. On the other, the bank can extract rents from the SME if it has a monopoly position (hold-up problem). This usually occurs when firms are opaque and they cannot signal their quality to other banks in the market. Even banks can be captured by borrowers if the former cannot avoid granting credit to distressed firms (soft-budget constraint problem).

Regarding the firms' choice to use single or multiple banking, we recognize that it is very rare for firms to rely solely on a single bank relationship, albeit most of the loans are granted by a main lender usually called Hausbank. It seems that firms adopt multiple lending if they have difficulties in getting funded from a single bank or to have better credit terms. The empirical results generally show that it is not optimal for firms to have many banks, as they send a signal of low quality to the market. Moreover, lenders cannot invest in collecting information about the firm if they fear the latter will switch the main bank often. Overall, the funding strategies that SMEs follow depend on many factors and there is no 'one size fits all' option.

The most recent literature has tried to extend the abovementioned views in different directions. A number of papers have suggested that concepts like trust and social capital have to be taken into account, since the mutual trustworthiness between lender and borrower can help them overcome information asymmetries and therefore establish positive long-term relationships for both sides. Then, the use of transaction-based lending technologies seems to not be any more an exclusivity of large banks since small institutions have started to use them along relationship lending. In addition, large banks can adopt relationship lending if they grant their local branches adequate autonomy in the lending decisions. However, it seems that the largest institutions deliberately choose to rely on transaction-based lending, maybe because they possess the necessary tools to get the most benefit from it.

The consequences of the use of relationship lending rather than other technologies cannot be comprehended thoroughly without including in the analysis certain variables that affect the banking industry as a whole. The level of banking competition seems to impact the credit availability and loan terms. A more competitive market leads to lower probability of credit rationing and to lower interest rates, permitting firms to switch lenders more easily and forcing banks to not engage in borrower rent extraction.

The type of financial system where firms and banks operate (bank-based rather than market-based) helps to explain some peculiarities in the use of relationship lending or other technologies. First, in bank-based economies problems such as hold-up or soft-budget constraints are more common as the bond between the main bank and the firm is stronger. Second, in the USA small banks are integrating their credit decisions with transaction-based technologies such as credit scoring, whereas there is still little evidence about this in bank-based economies. In a number of bank-based economies, cooperative banks are important players in the credit market. The empirical evidence shows that they have an advantage over commercial banks in practising relationship lending thanks to their business model.

The empirical evidence from the Global Financial Crisis suggests that relationship lending improved credit availability to the SMEs. Banks whose decision centres were closer to their customers experienced lower credit losses and default rates. However, a number of caveats are worth mentioning here. First, it is important to include in the analysis the *ex ante* situation of the firm and the bank. If the bank is adequately capitalized and is not severely affected by the crisis, it has an advantage over transaction lenders. Otherwise, it will behave similarly to the latter and will not support financially weaker firms. Moreover, relationship banks tend to charge higher loan rates in good times, but can smooth them during recessions to protect their relationship banking investment.

We believe that the relationship lending literature can be further enriched, thus we suggest a number of avenues for future research. The bank ownership type could represent an interesting factor in modulating the firms' choice for long-term relationship with banks. The literature on relationship lending mainly claims that large and foreign banks rely more on hard information and their entry in a market can have negative repercussions for riskier and opaque borrowers if foreign banks crowd out domestic banks. The evidence on this topic is still mixed. It might be true that firms could suffer more financing obstacles in countries with a higher share of foreign banks (Clarke *et al.*, 2006). Nevertheless, the recent evidence indicates that foreign and domestic banks can lend to the same clientele but with different techniques (De la Torre *et al.*, 2010; Claessens and van Horen, 2014). Another related issue is the presence of government banks and their role in lending to opaque SMEs. Although, previous literature finds that government lending is generally inefficient given that government has not only economic but also political goals, we did not find any specific studies linking government ownership of banks with relationship lending.

The adoption of different lending technologies by banks is still a largely unexplored field especially for non-USA firms. Since the paper of Berger and Udell (2006), it is clear that banks rely on different lending technologies for lending to SMEs even to the most opaque ones. There is evidence that small banks in the USA are relying more and more on some of these technologies such as credit scoring, trade credit and asset-based lending. Evidence on other countries is still scant. Bartoli *et al.* (2013), Ferri *et al.* (2014a,b) and Beck (2016) are among the first that investigate the phenomenon and find that all lending technologies are appropriate for SME lending and both small and large banks can cater for SMEs.

The use of different lending technologies and the cost/benefits for lenders or borrowers could be investigated along industry lines. Some sectors could be better served on a relationship basis, whereas for others transaction lending could be more appropriate. In several articles that we reviewed, the industry sector is controlled by including dummy variables, but that is not the focus of those papers, since regression outcomes are not analysed.

The latest evidence on the crisis permits to integrate the relationship lending literature with the regulatory framework in a country and the importance of the financial system. It seems that under Basel II/III, banks are adopting screening technologies that rely on the use of hard information. A great number of eminent scholars are sceptical on the benefits of this mechanistic approach since it does not consider the different business models of financial institutions. Moreover, this will discourage banks from gathering and processing soft information. The recent papers looking at the credit availability for the SME sector during the crisis evidence that relationship banks were able to extend credit at better terms compared to transaction ones. This indicates that when banks are not in distress they are able to handle recessions better when they can use relationship lending. Access to credit for the SME sector especially during bad times is a highly debatable issue in many countries. It is certainly related to the type of business model that financial institutions will adopt in the next future. If banks can know better their customers they can more correctly evaluate their credit risk and decide which firms are meritorious of credit even if the latter are under temporary distress. Therefore, relationship lending via the use of soft information can help attenuate the shocks to the real economy. We believe that future research could further investigate optimal banking practices and their links with regulation, bank stability and the real economy.

Notes

1. In the words of Berger and Udell (2006): 'Lending technologies can be defined as a unique combination of primary information source, screening and underwriting policies / procedures, loan contract structure, and monitoring strategies /mechanisms'.
2. The transaction-based lending technologies comprise: financial statement lending, small business credit scoring, asset-based lending, factoring, fixed-asset lending and leasing (Berger and Udell, 2006).
3. Each hierarchical layer bears a different type of agency problem: borrowers negotiate with the loan officer, who in turn negotiates with the bank director, who in turn negotiates with the bank's shareholders, who in turn negotiate with the bank creditors and government regulators.
4. The authors find that relationship duration has a positive impact on credit availability and negative impact on collateral required, but no effect on interest rates.
5. Cooperative banks have mutualistic governance. Owners (Members) are also customers of the bank. Each member has one vote in the general assembly of the bank regardless of the size of his stake.
6. We decided to not include summary tables in Sections 5 and 6 due to space constraints. However, they are available upon request to the authors.
7. For a review of cooperative bank business model, please refer to endnote 5.
8. The market share of cooperative banks in Western Europe is around 15%. However, in Austria, Finland, France, Germany, Italy and the Netherlands, this number increases to almost 30% (https://economics.rabobank.com/PageFiles/629/cooperatiestudie-200910_tcm64-94102.pdf).
9. Due to space constraints we are not reviewing here all the literature. The reader can refer to previous sections for each firm-specific relationship-lending determinant.

References

Adasme, O., Majnoni, G. and Uribe, M. (2006) Access and risk: friends or foes? Lessons from Chile. Working Paper, World Bank Policy Research.

Admati, A. and Hellwig, M. (2013) *The Bankers' New Clothes: What's Wrong with Banking and What To Do About It*. Princeton: Princeton University Press.

Agostino, M. and Trivieri, F. (2010) Is banking competition beneficial to SMEs? An empirical study based on Italian data. *Small Business Economics* 35(3): 335–355.

Albertazzi, U. and Bottero, M. (2014) Foreign bank lending: evidence from the global financial crisis. *Journal of International Economics* 92(1): 22–35.

Alessandrini, P., Presbitero, A.F. and Zazzaro, A. (2009) Banks, distances and firms' financing constraints. *Review of Finance* 13(2): 261–307.

Ampenberger, M., Schmid, T., Achleitner, A.K. and Kaserer, C. (2013) Capital structure decisions in family firms: empirical evidence from a bank-based economy. *Review of Managerial Science* 7(3): 247–275.

Angelini, P., Di Salvo, R. and Ferri, G. (1998) Availability & cost of credit for small businesses: customer relationships and credit cooperatives. *Journal of Banking & Finance* 22(6-8): 925–954.

Arena, M.P. and Dewally, M. (2012) Firm location and corporate debt. *Journal of Banking and Finance* 36(4): 1079–1092.

Agarwald, S. and Hauswald, R. (2008) The choice between arm's-length and relationship debt: evidence from eLoans. Working Paper, Federal Reserve Bank of Chicago.

Agarwald, S. and Hauswald, R. (2010) Distance and private information in lending. *Review of Financial Studies* 23(7): 2757–2788.

Ayadi, R., Arbak, E. and De Groen, W. P. (2012) *Regulation of European banks and business models: Towards a new paradigm?* Centre for European Policy Studies, unpublished manuscript.

Bartoli, F., Ferri, G., Murro, P. and Rotondi, Z. (2013) SME financing and the choice of lending technology in Italy: complementarity or substitutability? *Journal of Banking and Finance* 37(12): 5476–5485.

Bech, M., Gambacorta, L. and Kharroubi, E. (2012) Monetary policy in a downturn: are financial crisis special? BIS Working Papers 388.

Beck, T. (2016) Bank financing for SMEs – lessons from the literature. *National Institute Economic Review* 225(1): 23–38.

Beck, T., Degryse, H., de Haas, R. and van Horen, N. (2014) When arm's length is too far. Relationship banking over the business cycle. BOFIT Discussion Paper No. 14. http://doi.org/10.2139/ssrn.2489017

Berger, A.N. (2015) Small business lending by banks: lending technologies and the effects of banking industry consolidation & technological change. In A.N. Berger, P. Molyneux and J.O.S. Wilson (eds.), *The Oxford Handbook of Banking, 2nd edn., Oxford Handbooks in Finance* (pp. 292–311). Oxford: Oxford University Press.

Berger, A.N. and Udell, G. F. (1995) Lines of credit and relationship lending in small firm finance. *Journal of Business* 68(3): 351–381.

Berger, A.N. and Udell, G.F. (2002) Small business credit availability and relationship lending: the importance of bank organisational structure. *Economic Journal* 112(477): 32–53.

Berger, A.N. and Udell, G.F. (2006) A more complete conceptual framework for SME finance. *Journal of Banking and Finance* 30(11): 2945–2966.

Berger, A.N., Klapper, L.F. and Udell, G.F. (2001) The ability of banks to lend to informationally opaque small businesses. *Journal of Banking and Finance* 25(12): 2127–2167.

Berger, A.N., Miller, N.H., Petersen, M.A., Rajan, R.G. and Stein, J.C. (2005) Does function follow organizational form? Evidence from the lending practices of large and small banks. *Journal of Financial Economic* 76(2): 237–269.

Berger, A.N., Cowan, A.M. and Frame, W.S. (2011) The surprising use of credit scoring in small business lending by community banks and the attendant effects on credit availability, risk and profitability. *Journal of Financial Services Research* 39(1-2): 1–17.

Berger, A.N., Goulding, W. and Rice, T. (2014) Do small businesses still prefer community banks? *Journal of Banking and Finance* 44(1): 264–278.

Berlin, M. and Mester, L. (1999) Deposits and relationship lending. *Review of Financial Studies* 12(3): 579–607.

Besanko, D. and Thakor, A.V. (1987) Collateral and rationing: sorting equilibria in monopolistic and competitive credit markets. *International Economic Review* 28(3): 671–689.

Bharath, S.T., Dahiya, S., Saunders, A. and Srinivasan, A. (2011) Lending relationships and loan contract terms. *Review of Financial Studies* 24(4): 1141–1103.

Bolton, P., Freixas, X., Gambacorta, L. and Mistrulli, P.E. (2016) Relationship and transaction lending in a crisis. *Review of Financial Studies* 29(10): 2643–2676.

Bonaccorsi di Patti, E. and Gobbi, G. (2001) The changing structure of local credit markets: are small businesses special? *Journal of Banking and Finance* 25(12): 2209–2237.

Bongini, P., Di Battista, M.L. and Nieri, L. (2015) Relationship lending through the cycle: what can we learn from three decades of research? Unpublished Manuscript.

Bonini, S., Dell'Acqua, A., Fungo, M. and Kysucky, V. (2016) Credit market concentration, relationship lending and the cost of debt. *International Review of Financial Analysis* 45: 172–179.

Boot, A.W.A. (2000) Relationship banking: what do we know? *Journal of Financial Intermediation* 9(1): 7–25.

Boot, A.W.A. and Thakor, A.V. (1994) Moral hazard and secured lending in an infinitely repeated credit market game. *International Economic Review* 35(4): 899–920.

Boot, A.W.A. and Thakor, A.V. (2000) Can relationship banking survive competition? *Journal of Finance* 55(2): 679–713.

Bord, V.M. and Santos J.V.C. (2012) The rise of the originate-to-distribute model and the role of banks in financial intermediation. *FRBNY Economic Policy Review*: 21–34.

Brevoort, K.P. and Hannan, T.H. (2006) Commercial lending and distance: evidence from community reinvestment act data. *Journal of Money, Credit and Banking* 38(8): 1991–2012.

Brick, I. and Palia, D. (2007) Evidence of jointness in the terms of relationship lending. *Journal of Financial Intermediation* 16(3): 452–476.

Canales, R. and Nanda, R. (2012) A darker side to decentralized banks: market power and credit rationing in SME lending. *Journal of Financial Economics* 105(2): 353–366.

Cardone, C., Casasola, M.J. and Samartín, M. (2005) Do banking relationships improve credit conditions for Spanish SMEs? Working Paper, Universidad Carlos III de Madrid.

Carmignani, A. and Omiccioli, M. (2007) Costs and benefits of creditor concentration: an empirical approach. Working Paper, Bank of Italy.

Castelli, A., Dwyer, G.P. and Hasan, I. (2012) Bank relationship and firm's financial performance: the Italian experience. *European Financial Management* 18(1): 28–67.

Cenni, S., Monferrà, S., Salotti, V., Sangiorgi, M. and Torluccio, G. (2015) Credit rationing and relationship lending. Does firm size matter? *Journal of Banking and Finance* 53(1): 249–265.

Claessens, S. and van Horen, N. (2014) Foreign banks: trends and impact. *Journal of Money, Credit and Banking* 46(1): 295–326.

Clarke, G., Cull, R. and Martínez Pería, M.S. (2006) Foreign bank participation and access to credit across firms in developing countries. *Journal of Comparative Economics* 34(4): 774–795.

Cole, R., Goldberg, L. and White, L. (2004) Cookie-cutter versus character: the microstructure of small business lending by large and small banks. *Journal of Financial and Quantitative Analysis* 39(2): 227–251.

Cole, R.A. (1998) The importance of relationships to the availability of credit. *Journal of Banking and Finance* 22(6-8): 959–977.

Cosci, S., Meliciani, V. and Sabato, V. (2009) Banks' diversification, cross-selling and the quality of banks' loans. *Manchester School* 77(1): 40–65.

Cotugno, M., Monferrà, S. and Sampagnaro, G. (2013a) Relationship lending, hierarchical distance and credit tightening: evidence from the financial crisis. *Journal of Banking and Finance* 37(5): 1372–1385.

Cotugno, M., Stefanelli, V. and Torluccio, G. (2013b) Relationship lending, default rate and loan portfolio quality. *Applied Financial Economics* 23(7): 573–587.

Craig, S. and Hardee, P. (2007) The impact of bank consolidation on small business credit availability. *Journal of Banking and Finance* 31(4): 1237–1263.

D'Auria, C., Foglia, A. and Reedtz, P.A. (1999) Bank interest rates and credit relationships in Italy. *Journal of Banking and Finance* 23(7): 1067–1093.

De Bodt, E., Lobez, F. and Statnik, J.C. (2005) Credit rationing, costumer relationship and the number of banks: an empirical analysis. *European Financial Management* 11(2): 195–228.

Degryse, H. and Ongena, S. (2001) Bank relationships and firm profitability. *Financial Management* 30(1): 9–34.

Degryse, H. and Ongena, S. (2005) Distance, lending relationships and competition. *Journal of Finance* 60(1): 231–266.

Degryse, H. and Van Cayseele, P. (2000) Relationship lending within a bank-based system: evidence from European small business data. *Journal of Financial Intermediation* 9(1): 90–109.

De La Torre, A., Peria, M.S.M. and Schmukler, S.L. (2010) Bank involvement with SMEs: beyond relationship lending. *Journal of Banking and Finance* 34(9): 2280–2293.

De Larosière, (2011) Risk and balance sheets. Challenges for European Banks, Washington, D.C., G30.

Delgado, J., Salas, V. and Saurina, J. (2007) Joint size and ownership specialization in bank lending. *Journal of Banking and Finance* 31(12): 3563–3583,

Detragiache, E., Garella, P. and Guiso, L. (2000) Multiple versus single banking relationships: theory and evidence. *Journal of Finance* 55(3): 1133–1161.

Dewally, M. and Shao, Y. (2014) Liquidity crisis, relationship lending and corporate finance. *Journal of Banking and Finance* 39: 223–239.

Dewatripont, M. and Maskin, E. (1995) Credit and efficiency in centralized and decentralized economies. *Review of Economic Studies* 62(4): 541–555.

Diamond, D.W. (1984) Financial intermediation and delegated monitoring. *Review of Economic Studies* 51(3): 393–414.

Elsas, R. (2005) Empirical determinants of relationship lending. *Journal of Financial Intermediation* 14(1): 32–57.

Elsas, R. and Krahnen, J.P. (1998) Is relationship lending special? Evidence from credit-file data in Germany. *Journal of Banking and Finance* 22(10-11): 1283–1316.

Elyasiani, E. and Goldberg, L.G. (2004) Relationship lending: a survey of the literature. *Journal of Economics and Business* 56(4): 315–330.

Fama, E.F. (1985) What's different about banks? *Journal of Monetary Economics* 15(1): 5–29.

Farinha, L.A. and Santos, J.A.C. (2002) Switching from single to multiple bank lending relationships: determinants and implications. *Journal of Financial Intermediation* 11(2): 124–151.

Ferrary, M. (2003) Trust and social capital in the regulation of lending activities. *Journal of Socio-Economics* 31(6): 673–699.

Ferri, G. and Neuberger, D. (2014) The banking regulatory bubble and how to get out of it. Center for Relationship Banking and Economics Working Paper Series, No. 01.

Ferri, G., Kang, T.S. and Kim, I.J. (2001) The value of relationship lending during financial crises: evidence from the Republic of Korea. World Bank Policy Research, No. 2553.

Ferri, G., Kalmi, P. and Kerola, E. (2014a) Does bank ownership affect lending behavior? Evidence from the Euro area. *Journal of Banking and Finance* 48: 194–209.

Ferri, G., Murro, P. and Rotondi, Z. (2014b) Bank lending technologies and SME credit rationing in Europe in the 2009 crisis. Centre for Relationship Banking and Business, Working Paper No. 5.

Fiordelisi, F., Monferrà, S. and Sampagnaro, G. (2013) Relationship lending and credit quality. *Journal of Financial Services Research* 46(3): 295–315.

Gambacorta, L. (2016) Relationship and transaction lending: new evidence and perspectives. *Emerging Markets Finance and Trade* 52(1): 70–75.

Gambini, A. and Zazzaro, A. (2013) Long-lasting bank relationships and growth of firms. *Small Business Economics* 40(4): 977–1007.

Gopalan, R., Udell, G. and Yerramilli, V. (2011) Why do firms form new banking relationships? *Journal of Financial and Quantitative Analysis* 46(5): 1335–1365.

Granovetter, M. (1973) The strength of weak ties. *American Journal of Sociology* 78(6): 1360–1380.

Granovetter, M. (1991) *Society and Economy: The Social Construction of Economic Institutions.* Harvard: Harvard University Press, p. 393.

Hainz, C. and Wiegand, M. (2013) How does relationship banking influence credit financing? Evidence from the financial crisis (No. 157). IFO Working Paper.

Haldane, A. (2012) The dog and the frisbee. Proceedings - Economic Policy Symposium - Jackson Hole, pp. 109–159.

Harhoff, D. and Körting, T. (1998) Lending relationships in Germany. Empirical evidence from survey data. *Journal of Banking and Finance* 22(10-11): 1317–1353.

Hauswald, R. and Marquez, R. (2006) Competition and strategic information acquisition in credit markets. *Review of Financial Studies* 19(3): 967–1000.

Hernandez-Canovas, G. and Martinez-Solano, P. (2007) Effect of the number of banking relationship on credit availability: evidence from panel data of Spanish small firms. *Small Business Economics* 28(1): 37–53.

Holmstrom, B. and Tirole, J. (1997) Financial intermediation, loanable funds and the real sector. *Quarterly Journal of Economics* 112(3): 663–91.

Howorth, C. and Moro, A. (2012) Trustworthiness and interest rates: an empirical study of Italian SMEs. *Small Business Economics* 39 (1): 161–177.

Howorth, C., Peel, M.J. and Wilson, N. (2003) An examination of the factors associated with bank switching in the U.K. small firm sector. *Small Business Economics* 20(4): 305–317.

Ioannidou, V. and Ongena, S. (2010) Time for a change: loan conditions and bank behaviour when firms switch banks. *Journal of Finance* 65(5): 1847–1877.

Kang, E., Zardkoohi, A., Paetzold, R.L. and Fraser, D. (2011) Relationship banking and escalating commitments to bad loans. *Small Business Economics* 40(4): 899–910.

Kano, M., Uchida, H., Udell, G.F. and Watanabe, W. (2011) Information verifiability, bank organization, bank competition, and bank–borrower relationships. *Journal of Banking and Finance* 35(4): 935–954.

Kawai, M., Hashimoto, J. and Izumida, S. (1996) Japanese firms in financial distress and main banks: analyses of interest rate premia. *Japan and the World Economy* 8(2): 175–194.

Keeton, W. (1979) *Equilibrium Credit Rationing*. New York: Garland Press.

Kysucky, V. and Norden, L. (2016) The benefits of relationship lending in a cross-country context: a meta-analysis. *Management Science* 62(1): 90–110.

La Porta, R., Lopez-de-Silanes, F., Shleifer, A. and Vishny, R. (1998) Law and finance. *Journal of Political Economy* 106(6): 1113–1155.

Lehmann, E. and Neuberger, D. (2001) Do lending relationships matter? Evidence from bank survey data in Germany. *Journal of Economics Behavior and Organization* 45(4): 339–359.

Leland, H. and Pyle, D. (1977) Information asymmetries, financial structure, and financial intermediaries. *Journal of Finance* 32(2): 371–387.

Liberti, J.M. and Mian, A.R. (2009) Estimating the effect of hierarchies on information use. *Review of Financial Studies* 22(10): 4057–4090.

Machauer, A. and Weber, M. (2000) Number of banking relationship: an indicator of competition, borrower quality or just size? Working Paper, Center for Financial Studies.

Malafronte, I., Monferrà, S., Porzio, C. and Sampagnaro, G. (2014) Competition, specialization and bank–firm interaction: what happens in credit crunch periods? *Applied Financial Economics* 24(8): 557–571.

Masera, R. (2011) Taking the moral hazard out of banking: the next fundamental step in financial reform. *PSL Quarterly Review* 64(257): 105–142.

Matias Gama, A.P. and Van Auken, H. (2015) The interdependence between trade credit and bank lending: commitment in intermediary firm relationships. *Journal of Small Business Management* 53(4): 886–904.

Mattes, J., Steffen, S. and Wahrenburg, M. (2013) Do information rents in loan spreads persist over the business cycle? *Journal of Financial Services Research* 43(2): 175–195.

Moro, A. and Fink, M. (2013) Loan managers' trust and credit access for SMEs. *Journal of Banking and Finance* 37(3): 927–936.

Moro, A., Fink, M. and Maresch, D. (2015) Reduction in information asymmetry and credit access for small and medium sized enterprises. *Journal of Financial Research* 38(1): 121–143.

Neuberger, D., Pedergnana, M. and Räthke-Döppner, S. (2008) Concentration of banking relationships in Switzerland: the result of firm structure or banking market structure? *Journal of Financial Services Research* 33(2): 101–126.

Ogura, Y. (2012) Lending competition and credit availability for new firms: empirical study with the price cost margin in regional loan markets. *Journal of Banking and Finance* 36(6): 1822–1838.

Ongena, S. and Smith, D.C. (2000) What determines the number of bank relationships? Cross-country evidence. *Journal of Financial Intermediation* 9(1): 26–56.

Ongena, S. and Smith, D.C. (2001) The duration of bank relationships. *Journal of Financial Economics* 61(3): 449–475.

Ono, A., Hasumi, R. and Hirata, H. (2014) Differentiated use of small business credit scoring by relationship lenders and transactional lenders: evidence from firm-bank matched data in Japan. *Journal of Banking and Finance* 42(1): 371–380.

Peek, J. and Rosengren, E.S. (2005). Unnatural selection: perverse incentives and the misallocation of credit in Japan. *American Economic Review* 95(4): 1144–1166.

Peltoniemi, J. (2007) The benefits of relationship banking: evidence from small business financing in Finland. *Journal of Financial Services Research* 31(2): 153–171.

Peltoniemi, J. and Vieru, M. (2013) Personal guarantees, loan pricing and lending structure in Finnish small business loans. *Journal of Small Business Management* 51(2): 235–255.

Petersen, M.A. (2004) Information: hard and soft. Working Paper, Kellogg School of Management, Northwestern University.

Petersen, M.A. and Rajan, R.G. (1994) The benefits of lending relationships: evidence from small business data. *Journal of Finance* 49(1): 3–37.

Petersen, M.A. and Rajan, R.G. (1995) The effect of credit market competition on lending relationships. *Quarterly Journal of Economics* 110(2): 407–443.

Petersen, M.A. and Rajan, R.G. (2002) Does distance still matter? The information revolution in small business lending. *Journal of Finance* 57(6): 2533–2570.

Presbitero, A.F. and Zazzaro, A. (2011) Competition and relationship lending: friends or foes? *Journal of Financial Intermediation* 20(3): 387–413.

Rajan, R.G. (1992) Insiders and outsiders: the choice between informed and arm's length debt. *Journal of Finance* 47(4): 1367–1400.

Ramakrishnan, R.T. and Thakor, A.V. (1984) Information reliability and a theory of financial intermediation. *Review of Economic Studies* 51(3): 415–432.

Raterkus, A. and Munchus, G. (2014) Geographical location: does distance matter or what is the value status of soft information? *Journal of Small Business and Enterprise Development* 21(1): 87–99.

Rogers, T.M. (2011) Bank market structure and entrepreneurship. *Small Business Economics* 39(4): 909–920.

Rosenfeld, C.M. (2014) The effect of banking relationships on the future of financially distressed firms. *Journal of Corporate Finance* 25: 403–418.

Sakai, K., Uesugi, I. and Watanabe, T. (2010) Firm age and the evolution of borrowing costs: evidence from Japanese small firms. *Journal of Banking and Finance* 34(8): 1970–1981.

Santos, J.A.C. and Winton, A. (2008) Bank loans, bonds, and information monopolies across the business cycle. *Journal of Finance* 63(3): 1315–1359.

Scott, J.A. (2004) Small business and value of community financial institutions. *Journal of Financial Services Research* 25(2-3): 207–230.

Sharpe, S.A. (1990) Asymmetric information, bank lending, and implicit contracts: a stylized model of customer relationships. *Journal of Finance* 45(4): 1069–1087.

Sette, E. and Gobbi, G. (2015) Relationship lending during a financial crisis. *Journal of the European Economic Association* 13(3): 453–481.

Steijvers, T. and Voordeckers, W. (2009) Collateral and credit rationing: a review of recent empirical studies as a guide for future research. *Journal of Economic Surveys* 23(5): 924–946.

Stein, I. (2015) The price impact of lending relationships. *German Economic Review* 16(3): 367–389.

Stein, J.C. (2002) Information production and capital allocation: decentralized versus hierarchical firms. *Journal of Finance* 57(5): 1891–1921.

Stiglitz, J. and Weiss, A. (1981) Credit rationing in markets with imperfect information. *American Economic Review* 71(3): 393–410.

Tirri, V. (2007) Multiple banking relationship and credit market competition: what benefits the firm? Working Paper, Intesa Sanpaolo Collana Ricerche.

Uchida, H., Udell, G.F. and Yamori, N. (2012) Loan officers and relationship lending to SMEs. *Journal of Financial Intermediation* 21(1): 97–122.

Udell, G.F. (2015) SME access to intermediated credit: what do we know and what don't we know? RBA Annual Conference Volume. In A. Moore and J. Simon (eds.), *Small Business Conditions and Finance* (pp. 61–109). Sidney: Reserve Bank of Australia.

Uzzi, B. (1999) Embeddedness in the making of financial capital: how social relations and networks benefit firms seeking financing. *American Sociological Review* 64(4): 481–505.

Vesala, T. (2005) Relationship lending and competition: higher switching cost does not necessarily imply greater relationship benefits. Research Discussion Paper, Bank of Finland.

Von Thadden, E.L. (1992) The commitment of finance, duplicated monitoring and the investment horizon. Working Paper, CEPR, London.

Von Thadden, E.L. (2004) Asymmetric information, bank lending and implicit contracts: the winner's curse, *Finance Research Letters* 1(1): 11–23.

Weinstein, D.E. and Yafeh, Y. (1998) On the costs of a bank-centered financial system: evidence from the changing main bank relations in Japan. *Journal of Finance* 53(2): 635–672.

Williamson, O.E. (1993) Calculativeness trust and economic organization. *Journal of Law and Economics* 36(1): 453–486.

10

DETERMINANTS OF THE PERFORMANCE OF MICROFINANCE INSTITUTIONS: A SYSTEMATIC REVIEW

Niels Hermes

Groningen Universiteit

Marek Hudon

Universite Libre de Bruxelles

1. Introduction

Research has shown that having access to financial services is crucial for the poor as this helps them to smooth their consumption, generate business opportunities and improve their inclusion in the formal economy in the long run (Collins *et al.*, 2009). Yet, a substantial part of the very poor population (and especially women) in emerging economies is excluded from access to the formal financial system. According to Demirgüç-Kunt *et al.* (2015) in 2014, around 2 billion adults worldwide were still unbanked, that is they did not have an account with or access to credit from a formal financial institution, such as a bank.

Since the late 1970s, the poor in emerging economies have increasingly gained access to financial services offered by so-called microfinance institutions (MFIs). These MFIs have shown significant growth rates in providing financial services to poor households. Whereas in 1997 these MFIs had around 10 million clients, in 2010 this number had grown to over 200 million (Reed, 2015). These MFIs focus on reaching out to the poor, while at the same time being financially sustainable. In the literature, this has been referred to as the microfinance promise (Morduch, 1999).

One important question is whether microfinance really contributes to improving the well-being of the poor. Several studies have looked into this issue by reviewing the results from impact studies. Examples of these review studies are Bauchet and Morduch (2011), Duvendack *et al.* (2011), Van Rooyen *et al.* (2012), Awaworyi (2014), Gopalaswamy *et al.* (2016) and Maitrot and Niño-Zarazúa (2017). These studies refer to the demand side of microfinance. Yet, until now, no study has systematically evaluated the potential of microfinance to reducing

Contemporary Topics in Finance: A Collection of Literature Surveys, First Edition. Edited by Iris Claus and Leo Krippner.
Chapters © 2019 The Authors. Book compilation © 2019 John Wiley & Sons Ltd. Published 2019 by John Wiley & Sons Ltd.

poverty from the supply side. That is, what is the performance of MFIs in reaching out to the poor by providing services poor households need, also referred to as *social* performance, and what determines their success (or failure) in reaching this goal? Moreover, how do MFIs *perform financially*, that is to what extent are they able to reach out to the poor while at the same time being financially sustainable? Only two review papers have dealt with these issues, but they look at specific topics when evaluating the financial and social performance of MFIs (Chakravarty and Pylypiv, 2017; Reichert, 2018).

In this review paper, we focus on the literature that discusses the performance of MFIs. In particular, we provide a systematic overview of research that analyses the determinants of the financial and social performance of MFIs. Research in this field deals with three main topics, that is the determinants of MFI performance related to outreach, financial sustainability and the relationship between the two types of performance.

Reviewing this literature is important. First, in order for MFIs to make a significant and long-term contribution to improving the access of the poor and make them financially inclusive, we need to know more about factors that may help these institutions reaching their financial and social goals. Aiming at maximizing outreach under the condition of being financially sustainable is certainly important, as many MFIs nowadays are still dependent on subsidies from governments, NGOs, etc. In 2010, roughly only 20–25% of MFIs reported not having used subsidies to carry out their activities (D'Espallier *et al.*, 2013a). Having MFIs being dependent on subsidies is not a sustainable long-term business model. The outcomes of a review of the determinants of the performance of MFIs can be an important input for policy advice as to how microfinance can contribute to reducing poverty in a financially sustainable way. Secondly, the research on MFI performance is still in its infancy (Mersland and Strøm, 2014). Although quite a number of papers have been published on this topic since the early 1990s (our systematic review resulted in a list of around 170 papers published in academic journals), there is still controversy about the measurement of MFI performance and the interpretation and importance of outcomes reported in these studies. This is a clear indication of a research gap on this topic.

The remainder of this review is structured as follows. Section 2 briefly summarizes the debate about what MFI performance entails. This section goes into discussing and defining the two main goals of MFIs, that is being financially as well as socially sustainable. Section 3 provides an overview of how performance of MFIs has been measured in the literature. This is followed by a brief discussion in Section 4 of the methodology we followed by systematically reviewing the existing literature. In Section 5, we summarize the main findings with respect to specific categories of determinants of MFI financial and social performance. In particular, we find that the majority of the papers focus on determinants related to MFI characteristics, financing sources for MFIs, organizational governance, the MFIs' external context and the trade-off between financial and social performance. The review ends with discussing a number of research challenges for future research and conclusions.

2. MFI Performance: The Debate

The main business model of MFIs is providing financial services to poor households who are excluded from the formal financial system. This is generally seen as their main (social) mission and is referred to as MFIs' outreach (Morduch, 1999). Reaching out to the poor is usually relatively expensive as compared to the supply of financial services by regular commercial banks, which focus on servicing more wealthy clients. Poor clients may live in rural areas, which makes it usually more costly to supply them with financial services due to higher transaction costs. Moreover, in many cases, they do not have collateral to pledge when obtaining a loan, which may increase the risks, and therefore the costs for the banks. Offering deposit accounts and other savings products is costly, because the amount poor clients can save is very small, while the costs of offering these services for the banks are fixed. Servicing poor clients may also be more costly, because information about their repayment capacity is generally more opaque than for richer clients. This makes the process of screening and monitoring of clients more expensive. Although MFIs have developed methods to reduce these costs (e.g. by offering group loans, making borrowers jointly responsible for the repayment of individual loans)[1], lending to the poor on average is still more expensive and more risky than offering loans to wealthier clients who have a regular income.

The next question is how MFIs finance their activities. As reaching out to the poor is costly, MFIs need a financial strategy enabling them to cover these costs. Given that they have a social mission, donor funding may be one of the sources, next to external commercial funding such as equity and loans, and resources generated through offering savings accounts. The relative importance of these resources may depend on the formal status (or type) of the MFIs. MFIs can be either not-for-profit non-governmental organizations (NGOs), cooperatives, non-banking financial institutions or (for-profit) shareholder-based financial institutions. The amount of financial resources MFIs have access to, in combination with the way these resources are used to offer financial services, ultimately determines the performance of their operations.

Discussing the performance of MFIs is an important issue when evaluating the contribution microfinance can make in reducing poverty and increasing the financial inclusion of the poorest. Financial inclusion refers to individuals, households and firms having access to financial products and services that help them to make transactions, payments, collect savings and pension funds, and obtain credit and insurance (World Bank, 2018). MFIs can make a valuable contribution to increase the financial inclusion of especially the poor by offering products and services that are useful and affordable to them and that are delivered in a responsible and sustainable way.[2] The more efficient MFIs are in turning financial resources they obtain into financial products and services delivered to poor households, the bigger their potential impact can be on increasing financial inclusion of the poor. This may help these poor households to cope with the hardship they experience due to the mismatch between their low, highly fluctuating and uncertain income on the one hand, and their daily basic needs on the other hand (Collins *et al.*, 2009).

What are the choices MFIs make when deciding on how to organize their operations? Should the focus be on outreach to the poor (i.e. *social performance*), given the financial sources available? Or should they focus on generating returns on financial resources (i.e. *financial performance*), given a certain level of outreach? Of course, MFIs can choose various combinations of levels of these two types of performance. Ultimately, answering the above questions is about how to turn (real and financial) resources into the provision of services. In practice, the choice for a particular combination of financial and social performance levels may be linked to the type of MFI. Whereas NGOs may be more inclined to focus on their social mission and prioritize social performance at the cost of reaching financial performance, for-profit microfinance banks on average will most likely attempt to emphasize financial performance, which may result in putting less effort in reaching out to the poor.

The choice MFIs make regarding combinations of financial and social performance and the consequences this has for their operations, has been subject of fierce debate in the microfinance literature and has become known as the *trade-off* discussion. The debate is about whether or not

MFIs can stick to their main social mission of outreach and provide services to poor households (i.e. being socially sustainable), while at the same time being financially sustainable. That is, they should be able to reach out to poor clients without making net losses and/or without being dependent on subsidies over the medium- to long-term. The reason is that, if MFIs provide services to the poor, while making losses at the same time, their business model will not be sustainable in the long-term. The same holds for the dependence on subsidies, because even if subsidies are available, it is recognized that these resources are limited and may decrease in the future. Therefore, in the microfinance literature, people refer to the so-called *double bottom line mission* of improving the lives of the poor while being independent of donor support in the long run (Armendàriz and Labie, 2011).

Until the late 1990s, the role of the microfinance business as being focused on providing financial services to the poor was dominant in the thinking about the main mission of MFIs. Since the early 2000s, however, the debate has moved into the direction of emphasizing the importance of developing financially sustainable MFIs. Nowadays, the importance of striving for financial sustainability has been embraced by most parties in the microfinance debate. Donors, policy makers and other financers of microfinance have recently made a shift from subsidizing MFIs institutions towards an increased focus on financial efficiency of these institutions.

Shifting the focus from social to financial performance coincided with a number of important developments the microfinance business was confronted with, especially since the early 2000s. One important development was the apparent success of the microfinance model. MFIs showed high success rates in reaching the poor, while at the same time reporting low levels of repayment problems. Reported loan recovery rates of 95% or higher were no exception. Microfinance thus appeared to be a thriving, sustainable business model. This triggered the attention of investors, looking for socially responsible investment opportunities. Even commercial banks became interested as they saw providing financial services to the poor as a way to create new markets for their activities. These developments contributed to a fast-growing microfinance sector. During 2000–2005, average annual growth rates in terms of the number of clients served by MFIs amounted to 50%; during 2006–2008 growth rates rose further to 70–100 per year (Sinah, 2010; Assefa *et al.*, 2013). The financial crisis contributed to a substantial reduction in microfinance growth (Wagner and Winkler, 2013). Since 2010, growth has revived albeit not at the pace that was observed before the crisis.

The almost unprecedented growth of the microfinance business also contributed to an increased competition and *commercialization*, revealing itself in private, profit-seeking funding sources entering the business model of MFIs. As the number of MFIs grew fast and they all tried to survive, the pressure to sell financial services led to saturation of markets and over-indebtedness of clients in some countries and regions. Competition and commercialization thus contributed to an increased focus on profit making. In the literature, the recent trend of MFIs shifting their focus from social performance towards a stronger focus on profitability has been referred to as *mission drift* (Copestake, 2007; Mersland and Strøm, 2010; Armendariz and Szafarz, 2011).

At the same time, however, there remains variety in MFIs in terms of their financial sustainability. According to Cull *et al.* (2016), only half of the MFIs listed in the so-called MIX Market data set are financially sustainable.[3] The number of financially sustainable MFI is probably even smaller since the existing data set may be biased towards more profitable and established MFIs. In most cases, these are larger, mature, regulated and relatively well-known MFIs (Deutsche Bank, 2007). The non-profit NGOs are still the main type of MFIs, representing almost half of the total number of MFIs (D'Espallier *et al.*, 2017a). The median level of financial sustainability does not differ much between non-profit and/or NGOs on the one hand and for-profit or microfinance banks on the other hand (Cull *et al.*, 2016). The remaining group of MFIs consists of smaller, start-up organizations, which are still far from being financially sustainable and are therefore (heavily) dependent on subsidies. D'Espallier *et al.* (2013a) show that only 20–25% of MFIs do not receive any donations.

Overall then, during the past three decades, the dominant view regarding the mission of microfinance has shifted from an almost exclusive focus on outreach to the poor, towards an increased focus on profit-making and an emphasis on financial performance. This is at least how thinking among practitioners evolved, making decisions based on their own experience and beliefs, and influenced by the changes that occurred in the microfinance landscape in terms of the financing of MFIs activities and the role played by donors and commercial investors. Yet, what can research tell us about the possible determinants and consequences of both financial and social performance and the potential for a trade-off between these two? Our knowledge on these issues remains scattered, as there is no comprehensive overview of what we know about the performance of MFIs and its determinants. There is thus much room for expanding our knowledge on this topic. The remaining part of this paper is devoted to reviewing the academic literature investigating this question. Before going deeper into this literature, we first discuss how financial and social performance has been measured in microfinance research.

3. Measuring MFI Financial and Social Performance

In the literature, MFI *financial* performance has been measured in various ways. In most cases, researchers use traditional financial ratios such as the return on equity (ROE) or the return on assets (ROAs). These measures are also used in the more general banking literature. ROE is calculated as net operating income divided by the value of outstanding equity; ROA is measured as the ratio of net operating income to the value of total assets of the MFI. In some cases, researchers use other measures of financial performance they borrow from the banking literature, such as loans at risk (a measure of the riskiness of the loan portfolio) or the yield ratio, measured as the total income from interest and fees on the outstanding loan portfolio. However, since detailed, high-quality financial information is usually rather difficult to obtain for MFIs, researchers mostly fall back on using ROA or ROE as a measure of financial performance.

Next to traditional measures, financial performance is also evaluated by using indicators that are more specific to microfinance. These indicators include measures such as the so-called operational self-sufficiency and financial self-sufficiency. Operational self-sufficiency provides information with respect to the ability of MFIs to cover costs with revenues, that is it shows to what extent an MFI is able to break even on its operations. It can be assessed by dividing total operating revenues by the sum of total financial expenses on attracting funding, which includes interest paid to depositors and interest and fees on loans from funds or other financial institutions as well as bondholders, and expenses on loan loss reserves and operations. In some cases, a simpler measure of operational self-sufficiency is used, taking the ratio of operating revenues to operating expenses net of loan loss provision expenses and operating expenses.

Financial self-sufficiency is measured as the adjusted total financial revenue divided by the sum of adjusted financial expenses, loan loss provisions and operating expenses. Adjustments refer to correcting for the country-level inflation rate and the implicit and explicit subsidies. These subsidies include concessionary borrowings, cash donations, and in-kind subsidies. The financial self-sufficiency measure indicates the extent to which MFIs are able to operate without ongoing subsidies, including soft loans and grants (Cull *et al.*, 2007).

In microfinance research, *social* performance is related to the social mission of MFIs, that is reaching out to the poor by lending to individuals, households and small firms having limited or no access to finance. Studies on the social performance of MFIs mostly focus on two dimensions of outreach, that is its breadth and depth (Schreiner, 2003). The breadth of outreach refers to the coverage of MFI and is generally measured by the number of clients served by the MFI. The depth of outreach refers to the type or profile of the clients served by the MFI. The two most widely used measures of the depth of outreach are the ratio of active female borrowers to the total number of active borrowers of an MFI and the average size of the loan divided by the GDP per capita of the country in which the MFI resides. The intuition behind the first measure is that female borrowers are generally considered as being among the poorest of the population and that they are most strongly excluded from taking out loans from formal banks. The second measure is a proxy of the average poverty level of clients taking out a loan from the MFI. The poor are expected to take out smaller loans (relative to their income); MFIs may also not be willing to lend larger sums to poorer clients because of the potential risk of non-repayment. Sometimes, measures related to outstanding (number and size of) deposit accounts are used. However, not all MFIs are offering deposit accounts due to regulatory barriers, meaning that the coverage of studies using these measures is generally lower. A minority of studies also use an indicator of the geographical dimension of outreach by taking the percentage of clients living in rural area. The assumption supporting this measure is that the majority of the poor usually live in rural areas.

A specific and growing branch of literature investigating performance focuses on measuring the efficiency of MFI operations. Studies related to this branch of literature analyse how organizations use resources and turn them into goods and/or services, that is they try to capture the notion of organizational efficiency. This notion of organizational efficiency has been used in the literature discussing non-profit organizations more generally (Callen *et al.*, 2003). The measurement of the efficiency of an organization relates to calculating the maximum level of outputs that can be generated given a certain quantity or costs of inputs. Alternatively, efficiency can be measured by calculating the minimum quantity or costs of inputs to generate a certain output level. The closer the organization is to producing the maximum output level or to minimizing the costs of production, the higher its efficiency.

Most studies use data envelopment analysis (DEA)[4] and/or stochastic frontier analysis (SFA)[5] to measure cost efficiency.[6] DEA and SFA allow for establishing how close the actual costs of the activities of an MFI are to what the costs of a best practice MFI would have been in case it produces identical output under the same conditions. In order to be able to know what the costs of a best practice MFI in producing its services are, a so-called efficient cost function or efficient cost frontier needs to be established. This frontier shows the combinations of output volumes and related minimum levels of input costs. Again, the microfinance literature borrows this approach from studies in banking where this approach has been used extensively.

If an MFI is cost efficient, it is located somewhere on the frontier. In this case, the MFI is said to be both technically efficient (meaning that it maximizes production given available inputs) as well as allocatively efficient (i.e. it uses the optimal mix of inputs given the relative price of each input). If an MFI is located somewhere below the efficient cost frontier, however, it is producing its services (technically and/or allocatively) inefficiently. The distance between the location below the frontier and the frontier is a measure of the extent to which the MFI is considered inefficient.

Both DEA and SFA use data on input prices and output of producing units as their information set. DEA determines the frontier as the curve linking output levels for which costs are minimized. SFA estimates the efficient cost frontier, rather than deterministically establish its position, as is the case for DEA. SFA allows for taking into account several factors that may determine the position of the cost frontier, next to output levels and input prices. It also allows for measurement errors in the underlying information set. DEA does not allow for measurement error and luck factors. These techniques attribute any deviation from the best-practice MFI to technical inefficiency.

Most studies on the measurement of the efficiency of MFIs focus on cost efficiency (Hermes *et al.*, 2011). The main reason is that according to many observers microfinance's mission should be to reduce poverty. Thus, given the available financial resources, MFIs should aim at maximizing their contribution to this goal. Reducing the costs of providing services may maximize their contribution to poverty reduction. Cost efficiency, that is the extent to which MFIs are efficient in using resources and turning them into services, is closely linked to attaining their goal of making a long-term contribution to helping the poor. Studies using DEA and/or SFA to investigate MFI efficiency generally select measures of financial and social performance similar to the ones discussed above.

To conclude this brief overview, we note that there are several ways MFI performance has been measured in the literature. There seems to be no consensus with respect to what is the best way of measuring financial and social performance. Yet, consensus about the correct measurement of these concepts seems to be crucial in order to be able to come to academically founded conclusions about the drivers of MFI performance and to come up with policy relevant recommendations. Developing good and widely accepted measures of financial and social performance is therefore still a challenge.

4. Methodology and Data Description

4.1 *Method of Data Collection*

In this section, we first shortly discuss the method of data collection (i.e. choice of database to search journal papers, key words used, criteria for selecting papers to be included in the data set, etc.). As a first step, we established the topics we want to focus on when discussing the performance of MFIs and its determinants. In order to make this selection, we took the so-called Banana skin reports. These reports are published bi-annually since 2008 and describe the most important challenges MFIs have to deal with based on surveys among representatives of rating agencies, MFI managers and investors asking them what the main challenges are MFIs are confronted with in a given year. A review of these reports shows that some of the most important challenges related to the efficiency of MFIs are the commercialization of and competition within the microfinance business, the governance of MFIs and the type of funding sources MFIs have access to.

Based upon this evaluation of the Banana skin reports, we created a list of key words we used when searching for papers in databases. The list of key words consisted of the following terms:

- Efficiency, performance, productivity, trade-off (all related to the outcome variable in the studies, i.e. measures of efficiency of MFIs);
- Funding, capital, subsidy, financing, grants, aid (all related to the funding sources of MFIs);
- Governance, boards, board characteristics, mission drift, transformation, ownership structure, transparency (all related to the governance of MFIs);
- Market evolution, market structure, commercialization, competition (all related to the market structure and conditions MFIs have to work in).

We used these key words to search in databases of papers. We decided to only select peer-reviewed papers. This ensured that the papers ending up in our database had a minimum level of quality. Moreover, it reduced the scope of the search.[7] We chose using the EBSCO database, which is a widely used search machine for finding peer-reviewed journal papers. We also decided to select papers that were published since 1990. We chose starting the search from this year, because research focusing on the efficiency of MFIs started taking off from the early 1990s. Our paper search stopped in August 2017. Finally, we only selected papers written in the English language.

Using the above described selection criteria, we ended up having 306 papers in our initial sample. We then went through all these papers one-by-one and read the abstracts and introductions to determine what the research was focusing on. We filtered out review papers on microfinance, papers discussing methods of measuring efficiency (instead of reporting efficiency outcomes and their determinants), theoretical and conceptual papers, papers on lending methodologies (such as group lending or individual lending) and individual repayment performance, and papers in which the dependent variable was not MFI efficiency. After carefully evaluating the content of all papers in the database, we ended up having 169 papers. These papers are included in the bibliography and are marked with an asterix (*). This is the set of papers based on which we carry out the systematic review.

We acknowledge that our approach in selecting academic papers only may not provide the full picture of what has been published on MFI performance since the early 1990s. Yet, our survey is not intended to be exhaustive. Instead, it provides a solid sample of published papers, allowing us to describe the most important past developments in the research on MFI efficiency.[8] In this way, our review is also helpful in showing where future research on this subject could, or perhaps even should, focus on, that is it helps identifying research gaps.

4.2 Description of the Data

Table 1 provides an overview of some of the characteristics of the papers in our data set. First, the table presents the number of papers published each year. Although we started searching from 1990, the first paper analysing the performance of MFIs was published only in 2001. While in the first 12 years after the first paper on MFI performance was published, the academic attention for the topic was moderate, from 2013 the research suddenly took off rapidly. Two thirds of the papers were published during 2013–2017. This supports the view that only recently MFI performance and its determinants have gained prominence in academic research. A substantial part of the research focuses on cross-country comparisons of performance and its determinants, as more than half of the papers use data from a worldwide sample of MFIs. At the same time, almost 40% (64 papers) focus on country case studies. The majority of the case studies focus on Asian countries (56%; 36 studies); MFIs in India receive the most attention (21 studies). One third of the country cases (21 studies) deals with MFIs in African countries.

The majority of the papers (51%; 87 studies) in our database analyse both financial and social performance and their determinants. As we will discuss later, in fact several studies discuss the potential trade-off between the two types of performance, as there is a hot debate among academics as well as practitioners about whether or not both these aims of MFIs are substitutes instead of complements. Most studies focus on financial performance when they deal with a single type of performance (33%; 55 studies). Interestingly, attention for social performance of MFIs only really starts from 2010. This may be surprising as the social aims of MFIs were at the forefront of discussions about MFIs, especially during the earlier years of the

Table 1. Characteristics of the Papers in the Database.

Year	Methodology			Geographical			Journal Quality (1 = Scopus)	Type of Performance			Type of Database			Total
	DEA	SFA	Other	Country	Regional	World		Financial	Social	Both	Mix	Rating	Other	
2001			1	1			1	1					1	1
2003			1	1			1			1			1	1
2004			1	1			1			1			1	1
2005			4	2	1	1	4	1	1	2	1		3	4
2006		1		1			1	1					1	1
2007	1		4	1		4	5	2		3	2	1	2	5
2008			4	3		1	4	1		3		1	3	4
2009	1		7	3	2	3	7	3		5	3	1	4	8
2010			12	4		8	12	6	1	5	5	3	4	12
2011		1	7	3		5	8	3	1	4	3	2	3	8
2012	1	1	11	5	1	7	11	4	3	6	11		2	13
2013	2	1	24	6	3	18	24	10	5	12	18	5	4	27
2014	2	1	20	9	2	12	19	7	3	13	13	3	7	23
2015	5	1	24	13	2	15	27	8	6	16	20	2	8	30
2016	7		14	10	4	7	16	6	5	10	16	1	4	21
2017		2	8	1	3	6	8	3	1	6	10			10
Total	19	8	142	64	18	87	149	56	26	87	102	19	48	169

development of the microfinance movement. One reason why attention for social performance increased recently may be the criticism microfinance was confronted with after 2007. MFIs were criticized for their sometimes rather unethical practices, for example in India, and for their increased focus on financial instead of social performance. One example of this was the critique Compartamos was confronted with after their initial public offering in 2007 (Cull et al., 2009).

The vast majority of the studies use quantitative methods to analyse the performance of MFIs (83%; 140 studies). In only 19 studies, qualitative approaches are used to asses MFI performance. With respect to the measurement of performance, most papers use a mix of traditional accounting variables to measure financial and social performance (85%, 142 studies). Popular financial performance variables are, among others, ROA, ROE, operational self-sufficiency, financial self-sufficiency, etc. In more recent studies, researchers started to use more sophisticated measures of performance measurement. Especially since 2012, several studies have used either DEA or SFA in order to measure financial efficiency of MFIs. Still, they account for a minority of all studies investigating the financial performance of MFIs (16%; 27 studies).

Regarding social performance measurement, the average loan size (relative to income of the target population), the number of borrowing clients, the number of loans and saving accounts, the number of branches established and the share of loans to female borrowers are used most often. These measures of social performance have been criticized in the literature (Schreiner, 2003; Manos and Yaron, 2009). They only very roughly and indirectly measure the extent to which MFIs reach their poverty goals. Moreover, they usually measure only one type of outreach, that is the breadth or depth of reaching out to the poor. More sophisticated and complex measures of social performance include the Social Performance Indicators Tool 4 (SPI4) developed by the Social Performance Taskforce (SPTF) and CERISE. This assessment tool provides MFIs the option to perform a detailed self-audit of the extent to which they implement social performance outcomes such as poverty reduction, rural support, reducing gender biases and/or green finance. The tool consists of a large set of standardized questions about the operations of an MFI. These questions are constantly updated, based on the feedback provided by users of the SPI4 tool. The tool was introduced in 2001; by April 2018, some 520 SPI4 audits had been completed covering MFIs in 88 countries (CERISE).[9]

Yet, data allowing for more sophisticated approaches of measuring social performance are often very hard to collect, especially for studies carrying out cross-country comparisons of performance (Hermes et al., 2011), which is why research in many cases relapses into using simpler measures.

Most studies use the MIX market data set as their main source for collecting information with respect to the performance of MFIs (60%; 102 studies). Its extensive nature and easy accessibility makes it a very popular source of data. One potential shortcoming, however, is that it provides data for the larger and more developed MFIs only as it is based on self-reporting, that is the inclusion of an MFI in the data set is voluntary. Several other studies (28%; 48 studies), specifically those focusing on country case studies, use data from national sources. In a number of countries, regulating institutions and/or microfinance associations collect information about the profiles and performance of MFIs. Finally, some studies use data obtained from rating agencies (11%; 19 studies). Specialized agencies such as MicroFinanza, MicroRate, M-CRIL and Planet Rating provide rating services to MFIs, which they need for attracting financial support from donors and investors as well as to regulators, donors and investors, who use the information to monitor their performance. For a substantial number of MFIs, performance data overlap in the MIX Market and the data from rating agencies.

Finally, Table 1 shows information about the outlets in which research on the performance of MFIs has been published. While most papers (53%; 89 studies) are published in journals listed in the Web of Science database (a database that provides information on the impact of a journal using the Social Science Citation Index (SSCI))[10], a substantial part is to be found in journals not covered by this index. A relatively large number of country case studies have been published in outlets outside the list of journals in the Web of Science database (47%; 80 studies). Among the journals listed in the Web of Science database, *World Development* has been used relatively often as an outlet of research on the performance of MFIs (16 studies). Other popular outlets are *Journal of International Development* (8), *Journal of Business Ethics* (5), *Journal of Banking and Finance* (4) and *Applied Economics* (4). In a few cases, microfinance performance research has been published in top finance and economics journals such as *Journal of Finance, Review of Financial Studies, Review of Economics and Statistics, Economic Journal* (2 studies), *Journal of Economic Perspectives* and *Journal of Development Economics* (2).

5. Data Analysis

This section discusses the content of the papers in our database. We discuss papers in various sub-sections based on the topics we have defined as being important in discussion about MFI performance. The discussion of each of these topics starts with an overview of the theory and arguments about how a topic has been related to MFI performance in the literature, that is it shortly describes the underlying reasoning of the hypotheses tested in these papers. The papers are then discussed with respect to what we they do and what they find.

5.1 *MFI Characteristics and Performance*

Several organizational characteristics have been examined in the empirical literature as to how they may impact the performance of MFIs. In our database, 48 papers discuss the impact of MFI-specific characteristics on their performance. We focus on three key characteristics – the size of MFIs, its maturity or age and institutional type – as they are discussed most frequently.

5.1.1 *Organizational Maturity*

The relationship between organizational maturity and performance is not unidirectional. On the one hand, life cycle theory suggests that performance may evolve with the maturity of the organization. More mature MFIs may improve their performance thanks to their accumulated experience (i.e. they profit from a learning curve effect). These MFIs may also benefit from a first-mover advantage, being able to preempt competitors from accessing resources or valuable market niches, but also create long-lasting cost advantages (Suarez and Lanzolla, 2007). On the other hand, however, young organizations may benefit from recent technologies or innovations when they start their operations, that is they have the advantage of backwardness. More mature organizations may be stuck in older and less efficient processes that make them comparatively less efficient. Younger MFIs, for example, may more easily adopt new management information systems and develop mobile banking platforms.

Many papers in our database include the age of the MFI in their empirical analysis. In most cases, however, age is used as a control variable. Most cross-country studies find a positive relationship between the age of the MFI and its financial performance (Cull *et al.*, 2007; Ayayi and

Senne, 2010). One exception is Cull *et al.* (2015) who study Greenfield MFIs and find that they show financial performance comparable to those of the best performing (older) MFIs.

Country studies offer a more mixed picture, however. A few papers study the association between age and the performance of Indian MFIs. Narwal and Yadav (2014) find a negative impact of age on both profitability and outreach. Rai (2015) shows that young Indian MFIs grow faster and hold higher quality assets. Other studies using Indian data find that age positively influences productivity (Rashid and Twaha, 2013) or efficiency (Wu *et al.*, 2016). Wijesri *et al.* (2015) find that age positively influences financial and social efficiency in Sri Lanka, while Wijesri and Meoli (2015) suggest a negative influence on productivity in Kenya. This result may be due to the dynamic and competitive nature of the microfinance sector in this country.

Results are also mixed regarding the influence of age on social performance (D'Espallier *et al.*, 2017a) and more specifically environmental performance (frequently considered as a sub-category of social performance). The evidence on environmental performance depends on the geographical context. Allet and Hudon (2015) show that more mature MFIs perform better environmentally in developing countries. Forcella and Hudon (2016) find no significant impact in a sample of European MFIs.

5.1.2 *Size*

The size of MFIs (measured in terms of their total assets or the value of their loan portfolios) may matter for performance as larger MFIs benefit from economies of scale and scope in providing financial services. Scale and scope economies allow larger organizations to be more efficient, resulting in better financial performance. Larger MFIs may also reach out to the poorer clients, thus increasing the depth of their outreach, once they decide to cross-subsidize such activities by using revenues generated through economies of scale (Armendariz and Szafarz, 2011). At the same time, however, larger MFIs may also generate portfolio growth due to the targeting of less poor clients. This phenomenon is generally referred to as *mission drift* and is associated with lower social performance.

A few papers specifically address the impact of the size of the MFI on their performance. These papers suggest a positive relationship between the size and the efficiency and/or financial performance of the MFI (Cull *et al.*, 2007; Caudill *et al.*, 2009). A few country studies confirm that larger MFIs are more efficient and/or have better financial performance (Gregpore and Tuya, 2006; Rashid and Twaha, 2013; Gohar and Batool, 2015; Bartni and Chitnis, 2016).

Evidence is more mixed with respect to the relationship between size and social performance. While Kar (2013a) finds that larger MFIs have better social performance, Gutierrez-Goira *et al.* (2016) report no significant relationship and both Narwal and Yadav (2014) and Rao and Reda (2015) find that larger MFIs have lower social performance, respectively, in India and Ethiopia. Both surveys on the environmental performance of MFIs suggest that larger MFIs have better environmental performance (Allet and Hudon, 2015; Forcella and Hudon, 2016).

To sum up the above overview, the size or scale of operations has a clear and positive impact on the financial and environmental performance of MFIs but not always on their social performance.

5.1.3 *Institutional Type*

Various institutional types are to be found among MFIs. First of all, MFIs may be classified as not-for profit, NGOs. NGOs do not have a bank license, which means they are not allowed to take voluntary deposits. Owners of these MFIs may consist of a variety of stakeholders such as donors, investors, staff and customers. Second, MFIs also include for-profit shareholder companies such as commercial banks and non-banking financial institutions. Finally, MFIs include credit and savings cooperatives, which are owned by their members. The type of organization may impact MFIs' performance. NGOs are expected to have better social performance than for-profit, commercial organizations since social performance is at the core of their existence and mission (Morduch, 1999). The same holds for cooperatives, which are owned by their members. In contrast, NGOs will have lower financial performance as compared to commercially driven organizations.

Several papers analyse the impact of the type of organization on the performance. Most of them use multi-country data which confirm that NGOs show lower financial performance but perform better when it comes to social performance as compare to their for-profit counterparts (Gutiérrez-Nieto *et al.*, 2007; Cull *et al.*, 2009; Gutiérrez-Nieto *et al.*, 2009; Servin *et al.*, 2012; D'Espallier *et al.*, 2013b; Gutierrez-Goiria *et al.*, 2016). These results are corroborated in a number of country studies showing that for-profit MFIs have lower social performance (Annim, 2012a; Gohar and Batool, 2015). In contrast, however, Mersland and Strøm (2009) and Louis and Baesens (2013) find no significant differences between the two types of MFIs in terms of financial performance. Tchakoute-Tchuigoua (2010) reports that for-profit MFIs have even better social performance than NGOs. Barry and Tacneng (2014), finally, show stronger financial and social performance for NGOs using data from MFIs in a number of Sub-Saharan African countries.

A number of studies focus specifically on the performance of cooperatives. One interesting result is that financial cooperatives are frequently found to be more efficient (Aboagye, 2009; Tchakoute-Tchuigoua, 2010; Abate *et al.*, 2014; Marwa and Aziakpono, 2015). Chidambaranathan and Premchander (2013) show that member-owned MFIs provide better financial and social returns to their members. Kendo (2017) argues that an increase in size can help cooperatives to reduce their costs.

One specific topic discussed in the literature on the type of MFI is the regulation and transformation process from being an unregulated NGO status to a regulated for-profit shareholder organization. Some studies, such as Hartarska and Nadolnyak (2007), Pati (2012) and Pati (2015), compared regulated and non-regulated MFIs and find no significant difference in financial performance and outreach. More recently, instead of comparing different types of MFIs, studies track the evolution of MFIs after transformation. Chahine and Tannir (2010) find that transformation improves financial performance but hinders poverty outreach, which is suggestive evidence for mission drift taking place. D'Espallier *et al.* (2017a) also find that operational efficiency increases after transformation.

Our summary of the above results suggests that the relationship between MFI-specific characteristics and financial and social performance may not be unidirectional, but may actually depend on contextual variables. In particular, the country-level context seems to matter as outcomes from country-specific studies provide contrasting results. Future research may dig deeper in the role of country-level contextual variables, such as macro-economic conditions and formal and informal institutions, to better understand the relationship between MFI-specific characteristics and performance.

5.2 *MFI Performance and Financing Sources*

The financial and social performance of MFIs may be associated with the financing sources to which they have access. In our database, 23 studies address the impact of the type of financing source on the performance of MFIs. MFIs may fund their operations by using debt, deposits, equity and/or various sources of subsidies (Bogan, 2012).

Historically, subsidies were the main sources of financing for microfinance. Many MFIs received large amounts of subsidies to cover their start-up costs. Donors paid for expenses that are particularly difficult to finance for newly created institutions. Several MFIs also received subsidies on a more continuous basis to finance their social mission of poverty reduction (Cull *et al.*, 2009). In particular, it was long assumed that subsidies would always be necessary because of the high transaction costs related to very small loan size and the frequent field visits of loan officers to monitor clients (Armendáriz and Morduch, 2010). Microfinance pioneers mainly relied on these subsidies. Thus, donor funding could be used to finance costs that cannot be priced by the market and/or that are hard for the MFIs to self-finance.

There is, however, a risk of excessive subsidization that may generate inefficiency and thus be detrimental and even counter-productive for the efficient operation of MFIs. Excessive subsidization may be related to the notion of soft budget constraints. With excessively high levels of subsidies, '…the exact relationship between expenditures and earning has been relaxed because excessive expenditure over earnings will be paid by some other institution, typically the State' (Kornai, 1986, p. 4). Access to cheap financing allows inefficient microfinance managers to be bailed out (Morduch, 2000) and decreases the incentive to be efficient.

In trying to reconcile these different views on the role and impact of subsidies, Armendáriz and Morduch (2010) suggest the development of so-called smart subsidies in microfinance. Smart subsidies maximize the social performance of MFIs while at the same time minimizing potential market distortions.

Given the prominence and longstanding focus on subsidies as the main source of finance of MFIs, it may not come as a surprise that most studies on the impact of the sources of financing on MFI performance focus on subsidies. The literature suggests a mixed impact of subsidized funding on financial performance. Several papers support the negative association between subsidies and financial performance. Using the MIX data, Bogan (2012) finds that increased use of grants by large MFIs decreases operational self-sufficiency. Caudill *et al.* (2009) find that MFIs receiving lower subsidies operate more cost effectively over time. Other papers derive opposite conclusions and show that there is a positive relationship between obtaining subsidies and financial performance. Lebovics *et al.* (2016) explain that subsidies help MFIs to achieve high financial efficiency in Vietnam. This result is corroborated in a study by Tahir and Che Tarim (2013) on the efficiency of Vietnamese MFIs. Tchakoute-Tchuigoua *et al.* (2017) also finds that subsidies enhance financial performance. Other authors argue that it is the level of subsidies rather than the simple fact of subsidization that matters. Hudon and Traça (2011) argue that the relationship between productivity and subsidy depends on the level of subsidies: they positively impact productivity until a certain threshold level of subsidies. Mukherjee (2013) reports a similar result. This study shows that excessive subsidies drive out poor borrowers serviced by MFIs in India.

Several papers on subsidized funding address the link with the social performance of MFIs. Most of them find a positive impact. Cull *et al.* (2009) argue that many subsidized MFIs have a strong social mission and serve the poorest customers. In their view, subsidized MFIs may be needed to serve the poorest segment of the market. D'Espallier *et al.* (2013b) find that the lack of subsidies worsens social performance. Lebovics *et al.* (2016) conclude that subsidies allow Vietnamese MFIs increasing their social efficiency. Forcella and Hudon (2016) find that MFIs with better environmental performance also benefit from more donor interest. One exception is Bogan (2012) who finds that there is no relationship between subsidies or any of the other financing variables and the (breath of) outreach of an MFI.

The strong focus on subsidies is accompanied by a lack of studies on the importance of other funding sources, such as deposits, equity and commercial debt for MFI performance. One obvious reason may be that MFIs receiving a large amount of subsidies may not be tempted or pushed to turn to other sources of funding. Subsidies may, for instance, crowd-out savings since MFIs have little incentive to take deposits (Cozarenco *et al.*, 2016). Yet, favoring the use of subsidies instead of deposits as a funding source also has consequences for the social performance of MFIs. Offering savings is a potentially important instrument to help the poor to get out of poverty or deal with uncertainty, perhaps even more than microcredit (Dupas and Robinson, 2013). Offering savings could thus be related to better social performance. Yet, regulatory restrictions limit deposit collection by MFIs, which negatively affects their financial performance (Bayai and Ikhide, 2016). In a similar vein, Caudill *et al.* (2009) find that larger MFIs offering deposits operate more cost effectively over time. Savings mobilization can also help MFIs sustain in times of crisis, such as the Indonesian BRI during the East Asian crisis (Patten *et al.*, 2001).

A few studies focus on the relationship between debt finance and MFI performance. The evidence for this relationship is mixed. Gregoire and Tuya (2006) find that financial leverage is negatively associated with cost efficiency for Peruvian MFIs. Hamada (2010) shows that taking more bank loans is positively related to financial performance among People Credit Banks in Indonesia. Hartarska and Nadolnyak (2007) in a cross-country analysis report that less leveraged MFIs perform better with respect to their financial and social performance. Mersland and Urgeghe (2013) find that commercial lending to MFIs is positively related to financial performance, while subsidized lending is related to better social performance, confirming the general conclusion that subsidies are mainly positive in terms of social performance. Bayai and Ikhide (2016) find that low cost financing sources in terms of equity of Southern African MFIs support their financial sustainability. According to Daher and Le Saout (2015), the most profitable MFIs are also well capitalized and have low costs. Annim (2012b) studies the financing of Ghanaian MFIs and shows that when they use more of their own funding (equity), they also tend to target non-poor clients more, thus reducing their social performance. Finally, some studies look at the determinants of the costs of financing. Garmais and Natividad (2013) find that being rated strongly cuts the cost of financing, particularly for commercial lenders. Rated MFIs also lend more efficiently.

It may seem surprising that, although microfinance has become more commercial over time, the emphasis of the literature on the funding sources of MFIs and the relationship to their performance is still on subsidies. The increased commercialization of the sector also has opened opportunities to diversify their sources of funding. The few papers on savings suggest that the offer of savings seems a promising avenue to improve both financial and social performance of microfinance. Future research therefore could delve deeper into the consequences of a diversification of funding for the financial and social performance of MFIs.

5.3 *MFI Performance and Governance*

One important MFI-specific characteristic that has been discussed quite extensively in the literature dealing with the performance of MFIs is the importance of their governance structure. Governance refers to how the rights/claims and obligations are divided among the stakeholders of the institution. It deals with who owns the institution and who is responsible for the daily management of the institution, and what (internal as well as external) mechanisms are in place to make sure that the interests of the stakeholders are taken care of by the management of the institution. According to the Banana skin reports, published by the Centre of study for

Financial Innovation (CSFI)[11], governance is one of the main concerns MFIs have to deal with when offering financial services to the poor.

Governance has been discussed extensively in the context of publicly listed as well as non-listed private for-profit companies. In this context, researchers refer to corporate governance. The governance of for-profit companies is different from non-profit organizations to which the majority of MFIs belong. Governance of these organizations may be perceived differently as compared to the for-profit corporate sector as non-profit organizations explicitly deal with multiple aims or goals, that is they may have more than one mission. Whereas for-profit corporations usually mainly focus on shareholder interests such as profits and value maximization (e.g. they apply the shareholder model of governance), non-profit organizations have to balance between social and financial performance when taking decisions. This also holds for MFIs. The main challenge for the MFI's management and board is to take into account the interests of different stakeholders when taking decisions. The governance of the organization is an important determinant of how management will be able to deal with this challenge. Consequently, governance may influence MFI performance.

In total, 19 papers in our database discuss aspects of governance and their impact on MFI performance. These papers discuss various aspects such as the role of top management teams and boards in decision-making, the importance of transparency and disclosure in providing information to support screening and monitoring efforts, and the importance of the external regulatory context as a determinant of the performance of MFIs. Most papers discuss the role of boards as determinants of performance. Very few papers concentrate on the importance of transparency and disclosure. A few papers discuss other aspects of governance.

5.3.1 *Boards*

The discussion of boards focuses on the role of board structure and board demographic characteristics, and their impact on MFI performance. One important board characteristic studies focus on is the diversity of board members. In particular, gender and nationality of board members are discussed. According to agency theory, diverse boards are better able to monitor management because a more diverse board is, at least potentially, also more independent from management, allowing for higher quality of monitoring and better organizational performance. According to the resource-based theory, diverse boards may also contribute to better outcomes because they consist of members with different backgrounds and networks, leading to a larger knowledge base and to more ideas to discuss proposals and solve problems.

Several papers in our database exclusively deal with the impact of having female board members. As microfinance is a business model in which the focus is on lending to the poor who in many cases happen to be women, this may be a potentially important topic. Bassem (2009), Mersland and Strøm (2009), Chakrabarty and Bass (2014), Strøm et al. (2014), Augustine et al. (2016) and Vishwakarma (2017) find evidence that having female board members is associated with better financial performance. Gohar and Batool (2015), Hartarska et al. (2014), Mori et al. (2015) and Périlleux and Szafarz (2015) find similar results when focusing on social performance of MFIs. Having women on board thus has positive impact on both financial and social performance! A few studies investigate the importance of independent boards (Kyereboah-Coleman and Osei, 2008; Mori et al., 2015) and find that more independent boards improve both financial and social performance. Similar results are also reported for boards with international board members (Mersland et al., 2011; Mori et al., 2015).

Only a few papers focus on characteristics of the CEO of the institution, for example whether or not he/she is also the chair of the board (i.e. CEO duality) and whether or not he/she is the founder/owner. Moreover, a few studies deal with the remuneration of the management and CEOs in particular. In the literature on corporate governance, CEO duality is generally associated with reduced organizational performance, as it provides CEOs with power to divert resources and use them for their personal benefit. With respect to CEOs being the founder/owner of the organization, evidence from studies on listed companies has shown that the link with performance is non-linear. During the early years, the founder/owner may contribute to improved performance, because as founder/owner the CEO will use his/her expertise and his/her involvement in the success of the organization. Yet, if the founder/owner is CEO for too long, this may be associated with lower performance, since he/she may become too involved and may obstruct necessary changes.

Two studies have looked into the consequences of CEO duality (Kyereboah-Coleman and Osei, 2008; Gohar and Batool, 2015) and find that this negatively affects financial and social performance of MFIs. One study (Mersland et al., 2015) investigates the contribution of the CEO being the founder/owner of the institution, showing that this positively contributes to financial and social performance.

To conclude our discussion on boards, it seems that empirical studies on the role of boards in explaining MFI performance find results similar to studies focusing on the role of boards in listed companies. This suggests that boards of MFIs and the roles they perform within the organization do not differ much from those of corporate organizations.

5.3.2 Disclosure and Transparency

Disclosure and transparency are important topics in governance, also in the context of microfinance. They are particularly relevant when taking an agency perspective regarding governance and its impact on organizational decisions and outcomes. Disclosing information reduces the information asymmetry between management and stakeholders of the organization. This may positively affect organizational performance.

Perhaps surprisingly, only two studies in the microfinance literature have dealt with the importance of disclosure and transparency. Augustine (2012) finds that higher transparency has a positive impact on MFI performance irrespective of the ownership structure or the institutional environment. This result is confirmed in a study by Quayes and Hasan (2014). These studies confirm the general claim in the corporate governance literature about the importance of transparency and disclosure for organizational performance.

Given the potential importance of transparency and disclosure for MFI performance, more research seems desirable. For example, studies may look into the type of information disclosure is particularly relevant for MFI financial versus social performance.

5.3.3 Other Governance Topics

A number of papers take a broader perspective when investigating the relationship between governance and MFI performance, that is they investigate not only ownership, board structure or transparency, but also other governance characteristics. In particular, some studies focus on the remuneration of management, as this is an important topic in the governance literature. In line with agency theory, remuneration can be used to align incentives of management and owners. In particular, performance-based remuneration is used to incentivize management

to focus on maximizing organizational performance. Two studies analyse remuneration policies (among other governance mechanisms) and find no relationship with MFI performance
(Hartarska, 2005; Bassem, 2009). This may suggest that either performance-based pay is not
used extensively in the microfinance business, or that this governance instrument does not
work in the context of microfinance.

Finally, a number of studies address the relationship between what they call external governance and MFI performance. These studies focus on the role of financial market regulations, rating agencies and general institutional quality (such as the rule of law, the quality of
country-level governance, etc.). We discuss these studies when summarizing the literature on
the relationship between external conditions and MFI performance (see Section 5.4).

To conclude, the literature on the relationship between governance and performance is huge
and many governance aspects that may also be relevant for MFIs have until now hardly been
touched upon in research. Examples are CEO remuneration, board dynamics (i.e. the interaction between board members, as well as between boards and management, when taking
decisions), the importance of transparency and disclosure, the role of activism and collective
action among stakeholders in influencing decision making, etc. These and other topics may receive more attention in future research as governance seems an important aspect determining
organizational outcomes, also for MFIs.

5.4 *MFI Performance and the External Context*

In the previous sub-sections we discussed, MFI-specific (or internal) factors that may influence their efficiency. Several studies have investigated whether and to what extent the external
(i.e. country) context has an impact on the performance of MFIs. In our database, 45 studies
discuss the relationship between MFI performance and the country context. This may signal
that the country context is seen as a potentially important factor. Among other things, these
studies focus on macro-economic conditions, the domestic financial system, the institutional
environment and the political context as potential determinants of MFIs performance. Macro-
economic conditions, and especially the country's institutional environment, receive by far the
most attention.

5.4.1 *Macro-Economic Conditions*

The macro-economic context may affect MFI performance in several ways (Ahlin *et al.*, 2011).
A growing economy may increase incentives of small-scale entrepreneurs to invest and/or extend existing projects and business opportunities resulting in higher demand for MFI services
and/or improving repayment performance of MFI borrowers. In both cases, MFI performance
may be positively affected. At the same time, however, a growing economy may also reduce
demand for services from MFIs as households and entrepreneurs are able to finance projects
from profits and/or are able to access finance from formal channels, such as banks. Consequently, MFIs' financial performance may be negatively affected.

In case, the economy is stagnating or experiencing crisis, demand for MFI services may
rise as poor households and micro-entrepreneurs lose their jobs in the formal economy and
have to rely more on their activities in the informal economy. A stagnating or even declining
economy may also lead to deteriorating incomes, however, leading to less demand for savings
accounts and loans, as business opportunities are scarce. Moreover, with deteriorating incomes
accompanying a crisis, borrowers may have more difficulties to repay their loans to the MFI.

Finally, MFI performance may also be unrelated to the macro-economic context. This is the case if most clients of MFIs concentrate their activities in the informal economy and the formal and informal economy are unrelated.

The study by Ahlin *et al.* (2011) is by far the most extensive in terms of analysing the consequences of the macro-economic environment on MFI performance. It shows that the macro-economic context matters for the success of microfinance, but the relationship very much depends on the country-specific macro-economic context. One finding is that MFIs do better in terms of financial performance in times of economic growth, because this reduces defaults. Yet, another finding suggests that MFIs' growth in social performance is slower whenever a country's labor force participation is higher and/or the manufacturing sector is stronger. Under these macro-economic conditions, demand for microfinance is lower. A few other studies also look at the impact of the macro-economic environment, but in most cases this is not their main focus. The results of their findings are mixed. Whereas Ashta and Fall (2012), Sainz-Fernandez *et al.* (2015) and Xu *et al.* (2016) find a positive association between the macro-economic environment and the financial performance of MFIs, Campbell and Rogers (2012) find the opposite.

Several other studies focus on the impact of financial and economic crises on MFI performance. The topics addressed in these studies are quite diverse. Daher and Le Saout (2015) find that financial performance of MFIs declined due to the international financial crisis of 2007–2009. Wagner and Winkler (2013) report similar findings. Monroy and Huerga (2013) add to these findings by showing that listed MFIs seemed to have performed during the financial crisis. Patten *et al.* (2001) find that Indonesian MFIs did financially relatively well during the Asian crisis of the late 1990s thanks to the design of their financial products, which were focused on the ability and willingness to repay of their clients. In addition, as many of these microloan borrowers were active in rural areas, they were also more insulated from the crisis as compared to the corporate loan borrowers in the urban areas. In contrast, Marconi and Mosley (2006), reviewing Bolivian MFIs during the economic crisis of 1998–2004, show that adverse macro-economic conditions adversely affected their financial performance. This was partly due to their focus on lending to the services sector, which was hit hardest by the crisis, as well as due to the fact the government bailed out MFIs that had debt repayment problems, thereby creating moral hazard behaviour.

5.4.2 *The Domestic Financial System*

MFI performance may be positively associated with the level of development of the financial system of a country. First, in a more developed financial system, commercial banks may become engaged in offering financial services for the poor, especially if these activities have been shown to be profitable for MFIs. This leads to increased competitive pressure, forcing MFIs to reduce costs. Second, the presence of commercial banks may lead to positive spillover effects as MFIs may copy modern and more efficient banking techniques. Third, a more developed domestic financial system allows MFIs having better access to financial services themselves.

MFI performance may also be negatively associated with financial system development. First, the presence of commercial banks may lead borrowers substituting their financial services from MFIs for services from commercial banks, because of lower costs, more choice and more flexibility. Second, competition may have an adverse effect on the repayment performance of MFI borrowers, if they take up multiple loans from different financial institutions (McIntosh *et al.*, 2005). This increases costs and thus lowers financial performance of MFIs.

Finally, if formal financial markets are weakly developed, this may increase demand for financial services from MFIs, which help increase the performance of MFIs.

Only a few studies have looked into the relationship between the development of the domestic financial system and MFI performance. The evidence seems mixed. Ahlin *et al.* (2011) argue that MFIs in countries with more developed financial systems show better financial performance. This is corroborated by the findings of Xu *et al.* (2016). These studies suggest that the formal financial and microfinance sector are complements rather substitutes. In contrast, Vanroose and D'Espallier (2013) find that the financial and social performance of MFIs is higher when the country's financial system is weaker, suggesting substitution, rather than a complementarity between the two. Cull *et al.* (2013) draw a similar conclusion. They show that MFIs have stronger social performance when the financial system is more developed.

An issue related to the role of financial system development is the impact of competition in microfinance on their performance. A few studies have investigated this issue. McIntosh *et al.* (2005) show that increased competition reduces financial performance, because clients take out multiple loans. Assefa *et al.* (2013) provide evidence that competition among MFIs is negatively associated with their outreach and repayment performance. This suggests that competition may have a detrimental rather than a positive effect on MFI performance. McIntosh *et al.* (2005) argue this may be due to lacking institutional frameworks, such as credit bureaus that may help MFIs sharing information about delinquent borrowers. In contrast, Halouani and Boujelbène (2015) find that competition boosts financial performance, but has no impact on social performance of MFIs. Their study is based on a one-country case, that is South Africa.

5.4.3 *The Institutional Context*

The country's institutional environment has received a lot of attention as one of the determinants of MFI performance. MFI performance may, at least partly, be driven by formal institutions, such as laws, regulations and market structures, as well as by informal institutions, such as norms, values and cultural beliefs. In particular, the institutional environment may determine the possibilities and/or restraints entrepreneurs are confronted with when operating existing or starting new business activities. This also may have consequences for the performance of MFIs. On the one hand, well-developed institutions such as clear property rights, strong rule of law and an effective government that is able to formulate business-friendly policies and that contributes to reducing corruption may be important prerequisites for successful small-scale businesses. In such an environment, the demand for financial services of MFIs may rise, contributing to their overall performance.

On the other hand, however, well-developed institutions may also make doing business more difficult. In particular, an effective government may also mean a large amount of rules and regulations, leading to higher costs for small-scale entrepreneurs, reducing their demand for financial services. Moreover, effectively reducing corruption means reducing possibilities for small-scale business to avoid all kinds of costly government rules and tax payments and/or may make it more difficult to get access to government services that are difficult to obtain without paying bribes. Once again, this may reduce their demand for financial services of MFIs, thus lowering their performance.

The empirical evidence on the association between the external environment and MFI performance is rather mixed. Several studies focus on the regulatory environment of a country. They refer to the existence and quality of financial regulation for MFIs, as well as to the existence of rating agencies and/or credit bureaus that also target MFIs. Most of these studies find that the regulatory environment has either no or a negative impact, especially on social performance (Hartarska and Nadolnyak, 2007; Mersland and Strøm, 2009; Ahlin *et al.*, 2011; Pati, 2012; Anku-Tsede, 2014; Bakker *et al.*, 2014; Estapé-Dubreuil and Torreguitart-Mirada, 2015; Halouani and Boujelbène, 2015; Pati, 2015). This indicates that regulation of MFI may actually hamper rather than help them in providing their financial services to the poor in a cost-efficient way. A few studies, however, also point at positive associations between financial regulation and MFI performance. Arsyad (2005), Bassem (2009), Boehe and Cruz (2013) and Gohar and Batool (2015) find that financial regulation is associated with better social performance; Bassem (2009) and Emeni (2008) claim this positive association also holds for financial performance. Cull *et al.* (2011) show that the link between regulation and performance may depend on the type of the MFI. They claim that, whereas profit-oriented MFIs respond to supervision by maintaining profit rates and curtailing outreach to women and customers that are costly to reach, NGOs reduce profitability but maintain outreach. With respect to the existence of rating agencies and/or credit bureaus, studies generally find positive effects on both financial (Bassem, 2009; McIntosh *et al.*, 2010; Sainz-Fernandez *et al.*, 2015) and social performance (Annim, 2012b; Bumacov *et al.*, 2014).

A few studies focus on the role of informal institutions as determinants of MFI performance. Some show that MFIs with a religious background have a better social performance (Casselman *et al.*, 2005), but underperform on financial performance, although their funding costs are generally lower than those for profit-oriented MFIs (Mersland *et al.*, 2013). Other studies investigate the role of culture, trust, norms and values, and social capital. Burzynska and Berggren (2015) show that MFIs in countries with higher levels of trust and a more collectivist culture have better financial performance. Arsyad (2005), Churchill (2017) and Postelnicu and Hermes (2016) provide evidence that high social capital is associated with better financial and social performance.

Several studies investigate the importance of the quality of the country's institutional context in a broader context (sometimes referred to as good governance), taking into account the rule of law, the efficiency of governmental institutions and the control of corruption. In particular, they look at the type of law system, the quality (i.e. independence and enforcement) of the law system, the extent to which the government uses financial markets to obtain policy goals, the extent of bureaucratic burden and red tape, etc. Ashta and Fall (2012) find a positive correlation between measures of good governance and the growth of MFIs. Silva and Chávez (2015) make a similar claim by pointing out that MFIs in countries with better governance are affected less by the global financial crisis of 2007–2008. In particular, they point at the importance of a strong rule of law. Quayes and Joseph (2017) corroborate this result. On a closely related issue, Daher and Le Sahout (2015) stress the importance of strong property rights and low levels of government interference in financial markets. Chikalipa (2017) finds a positive relationship between the lack of rules constraining business and MFI performance in sub-Saharan Africa. Finally, Barry and Tacneng (2014) argue that the link between institutional quality and MFI performance depends on the type of MFI. While a weak rule of law results in NGO superiority, stronger institutional quality may encourage banks to cater to more borrowers.

A few studies address a country's political system as part of the institutional context that may influence MFI performance. Two dimensions of a political system are potentially important for the performance of MFIs. First, if politicians can be held accountable, this may lead to policies that are supportive to doing business in general, leading to higher demand for MFI services. In contrast, if the political system is less transparent, economic actors may turn to the informal sector, which increases demand for microfinance. Second, the stability of the system matters for the performance of MFIs. In politically instable environments, doing business becomes more difficult, which may decrease demand for services from MFIs. At the same time, however, political instability may also stimulate economic activity in the informal sector, which increases demand for MFI services.

Only two papers address the importance of the political context for MFI performance. According to Ault and Spicer (2014), NGOs have better social performance than commercial MFIs in weak states. Sainz-Fernandez et al. (2015) show that political stability reduces the likelihood of financial crises for MFIs. They investigate this as part of a broader analysis of the importance of the external environment. Since many MFIs are active in countries with politically weak systems, it seems that more research on the relationship between political factors and MFI performance is definitely needed.

5.5 *Trade-Off between Financial and Social Performance*

Several studies addressing the performance of MFIs focus on the potential trade-off between financial and social performance. Debates on the trade-off between social and financial performance are not recent and became prominent in the 2000s with the commercialization of the microfinance business. There may be several reasons for assuming a trade-off between financial and social performance of MFIs. First, serving very poor people may be costly because of higher operating expenses or more expensive delivery mechanisms to reach them when they live in more remote areas. Second, very poor clients may not be able to cope with expensive financial services or require smaller loans that carry higher unit costs. Therefore, financial sustainability ultimately goes against the goal of serving large groups of poor borrowers. This approach stresses that serving the very poor is not compatible with a focus on financial performance, that is financial and social performance are substitutes. In contrast, however, it has been argued that improved financial performance may go hand in hand with better social performance. The central argument is that reaching a large number of customers allows MFIs to benefit from economies of scale, thus improving their financial performance. Moreover, MFIs showing financial sustainability are better able to attract funding from the private investor, which may be used to improve their outreach.

Results from the literature on the existence of a trade-off between financial and social performance provide a mixed picture. On the one hand, a number of studies suggest a negative relationship between outreach and financial performance (Cull et al., 2007; Hermes et al., 2011; Annim, 2012a; Zerai and Rani, 2012; Abate et al., 2014; Hartarska et al., 2013; Louis and Baesens, 2013; Pedrini and Ferri, 2016; Abdullai and Tewari, 2017). On the other hand, however, several studies find no evidence for a trade-off. In some cases, studies even report a positive relationship between financial and social performance (Gutiérrez-Nieto et al., 2009; Gutiérrez-Nieto et al., 2011; Kar, 2011; Kar, 2013a; Louis et al., 2013; Adhikary and Papachristou, 2014; Gakhar and Meetu, 2013; Kaur, 2016).

Some studies stress that the presence of a trade-off depends on context-specific factors. Hartarska (2005) suggests that the existence of a tradeoff between outreach and financial performance depends whether or not stakeholders are represented on the board of the MFI. Bassem (2009) suggests that the existence of a trade-off depends on the size of the board and on the proportion of unaffiliated directors. Hartarksa et al. (2014) claim that gender diversity in the board is an important contextual variable that may lead to a trade-off. These studies indicate that governance, and especially the board, is an important driving mechanism. Ultimately, the board is responsible for deciding on whether the focus will be on financial or social performance, or a combination of both aims. Other contextual factors are found by Tchakoute-Tchuigoua (2012) who shows it may depend on the loan methodology used. Piot-Lepetit and Nzongang (2014) find evidence for the existence of a trade-off, but only for a minority of MFIs in Cameroon.

Reichert (2018) performs a meta-analysis of the literature on the trade-off between financial and social performance. He synthesizes 623 regression outcomes. His main finding is that the presence of trade-off strongly depends on the measurement of performance used in the empirical analysis. Aggregating all outcomes, he finds that a trade-off is more likely to be reported in studies that use measures of the cost efficiency of MFIs and/or when they focus on the depth and cost of outreach and that there is no evidence for a trade-off when measures of profitability and financial risk are used. This outcome corroborates the observation we made earlier in Section 3, that is that the measurement of financial and social performance is crucial, but also still challenging in the literature on the performance of MFIs.

6. Challenges and Conclusions

The performance of MFIs is a hot topic in the development and finance literature. While most systematic reviews or research reviews tackle microfinance from the demand side and analyse the impact of microfinance on clients, this study offers a review of the literature based on the supply side, focusing on the performance of MFIs.

The empirical literature on the performance of MFIs is rather extensive. Using a systematic review approach, we ended up having a database of close to 170 studies investigating the determinants of MFI performance.

Compared to other types of social enterprises and hybrid organizations, MFI performance has received much more attention. This may be related to the fact that the role microfinance can play in achieving poverty reduction has been at the forefront of discussions in development aid debates at least since the late 1990s. One clear manifestation of this is the fact that in 2006, Grameen Bank and Muhammad Yunus, founder of Grameen Bank, were awarded the Nobel Peace Prize for their efforts to help reducing poverty by developing microfinance solutions. It may also have to with the availability of data available from sources such as the MIX Market platform and rating agencies specializing in analysing MFIs. Thanks to these data sources, performance measurement of MFIs has been carried out using various performance measures and methodologies.

At the same time, however, although many studies have looked into performance measurement and determinants of MFI performance have been published, there is still controversy about how financial and social performance of these institutions can best be measured. As discussed, in many cases, standard measures have been borrowed from the finance and banking literature. Measures of financial performance include simple accounting ratios and measures of cost effectiveness. Some more advanced techniques, such as DEA and SFA, are used more recently, relying on measures of efficiency of operations. These techniques have also been borrowed from the banking literature. Given the heterogeneity of measures used and the lack of consensus about how performance should be measured, there is much room for more research on developing measures that particularly apply to the microfinance business.

There is also a need for improving our measurement of social performance. Most of the measures that are currently used in research are no more than rough proxies (D'Espallier et al., 2017a). Some researchers suggest developing new performance measures that may better capture social performance of MFIs. Yaron (1992), for example, suggests a composite index, 'the outreach index', which takes into account several dimensions of social performance such as the average loan, the number of clients reached, etc., and convert them into one number.

Given the complexity of the concept, we suggest that analyses of social performance should not be restricted to using a single dimension. Instead, social performance should be appraised by using a multidimensional perspective. Analyses of social performance should therefore include a variety of indicators or proxies related to the different groups of clientele of MFIs. Such an approach stresses the need to use various measures of social performance such as measures of outreach, gender and geographical location of poor clients. The recent and holistic methodologies developed by the Social Performance Taskforce (SPTF) in collaboration with CERISE, such as the Social Performance Indicators 4 (SPI4), represents a new opportunity for researchers to improve the analysis of social performance. Yet, we acknowledge it may take time to have comparable data sets that could replace the very extensive databases provided by the MIX Market and rating agencies.

For the future of the research on the financial and social performance of MFIs, it is absolutely crucial that there is consensus about the correct measurement of these concepts. Only then we can to come to conclusions about the drivers of MFI performance that may also help designing policy relevant recommendations. Developing good and widely accepted measures of financial and social performance is one of the major future challenges for researchers in the field of development finance.

Our systematic review summarized the main findings of studies looking into the determinants of financial and social performance of MFIs. One conclusion from this summary is that MFI-specific characteristics such as maturity, size and type of organization, the type funding sources available (and in particular subsidies), governance structures and conditions external to the MFIs are the main drivers of financial as well as social performance. Another conclusion is that the direction of the relationship between these drivers and MFI performance very much depends on the context. In particular, the various outcomes from country-specific and multi-country analyses clearly indicate that country-contextual factors may play a significant role in determining whether the link between the various drivers and MFI performance is positive, negative or non-existent. Future research may dig deeper into developing contextual analyses of MFI performance as most studies until now are one-dimensional, that is they focus on one variable determining MFI performance, without taking into account the possibility of interaction effects with other (contextual) variables and/or carrying out sub-sample analyses.

The review also showed that a substantial number of studies on the performance of MFIs are related to discussing the trade-off between financial and social performance. Results on the presence of such a trade-off are mixed, suggesting that there is no straightforward answer to the question whether or not a trade-off actually exists. One reason explaining the diversity of results may be the multiplicity of measures and techniques used to assess financial and social performance. As discussed, a recent meta-analysis shows that evidence concerning the existence of a trade-off depends on the measures used for financial and social performance. Moreover, the literature suggests that the diversity of results on the presence of a trade-off may depend on context-specific factors, such as the MFIs' governance structure, lending methodology used, etc.

Finally, our research review revealed several areas and issues that have been studied less in the literature. In particular, we highlighted research gaps with respect to the consequences of the diversification of funding available to MFIs for their financial and social performance. Moreover, we pointed at the importance of governance related factors. Examples are the use of incentive-based pay for loan officers, CEO remuneration, board dynamics (i.e. the interaction between board members when taking decisions), the importance of transparency and

disclosure, the role of activism and collective action among stakeholders in influencing decision making, etc. Finally, we suggested more research on the role of the political system and
stability for MFI performance as many MFIs are active in countries with politically weak systems. These topics deserve more attention in future research as they are potentially important
drivers of MFI performance.

As a final remark, one key conclusion of our review is also that MFIs focusing on outreach
and MFIs with a focus on maximizing profits may co-exist in the market, that is there is room
for both types of MFIs in the market. While some MFIs are very profitable and tend to compete
with traditional financial institutions, others still try to maximize outreach and focus on the
very poor clients.

Acknowledgement

We thank Lina Frank for her very helpful research assistance.

Notes

1. See Ghatak and Guinnane (1999) and Armendáriz and Morduch (2010) for overviews of
   the literature on the economics of group lending.
2. Definition of financial inclusion is taken from the World Bank, see: http://www
   .worldbank.org/en/topic/financialinclusion/overview (accessed June 9, 2018).
3. The MIX market is a global web-based microfinance information platform. It provides
   financial data, organizational data and profiles of more than 2000 MFIs located in over
   100 countries around the world. See the following webpage: www.mixmarket.org.
4. See Charnes et al. (1978) and Banker et al. (1984) for a detailed and more technical discussion of this methodology.
5. See Jondrow et al. (1982) for a detailed and more technical discussion of this
   methodology.
6. Next to cost efficiency, DEA and SFA can be used to estimate profit efficiency. While cost
   efficiency is related to the objective of cost minimization, profit efficiency captures profit
   maximization (Maudos et al., 2002).
7. Using the key words and carrying out a search in Pro-Quest, a database that includes
   papers, dissertations and theses, e-books, newspapers, periodicals, historical collections,
   governmental and cultural archives and other aggregated databases, returned almost 2000
   observations.
8. We follow Noussair and Tucker (2013) who took a similar approach in their review paper.
9. Data are taken from the CERISE website; see: http://www.cerise-spi4.org/benchmarking/
   (accessed June 9, 2018).
10. The impact factor of the SSCI is a widely accepted measure of the quality of a journal.
11. The Banana skin reports have been published since 2008 by CSFI. In these reports,
    CSFI ranks the most important challenges MFIs have to deal with, based on surveys
    among various participants in the microfinance business (e.g. practitioners, investors,
    regulators, etc.).

References

*Abate, G., Borzaga, C. and Getnet, K. (2014) Cost-efficiency and outreach of microfinance institutions:
Trade-offs and the role of ownership. *Journal of International Development* 26: 923–932.

*Abdullah, S. and Quayes, S. (2016) Do women borrowers augment financial performance of MFIs? *Applied Economics* 48(57): 5593–5604.

*Abdullai, A. and Tewari, D.D. (2016) Efficiency of MFIs in SSA: An SFA approach. *Ghana Journal of Development Studies* 13(2): 117–139.

*Abdullai, A. and Tewari, D.D. (2017) Determinants of microfinance outreach in SSA: A panel approach. *Acta Commercii* 17(1): a414.

*Aboagye, A. (2009) A baseline study of Ghanian microfinance institutions. *Journal of African Business* 10(2): 163–181.

*Adhikary, S. and Papachristou, G. (2014) Is there a trade-off between financial performance and outreach in South-Asian microfinance institutions?. *Journal of Developing Areas* 48(4): 381–402.

*Aggarwal, R., Goodell, J.W. and Selleck, L.J. (2015) Lending to women in microfinance: Role of social trust. *International Business Review* 24(1): 55–65.

*Ahlin, C., Lin, J. and Maio, M. (2011) Where does microfinance flourish? Microfinance institution performance in macroeconomic context. *Journal of Development Economics* 95: 105–120.

*Alinsunurin, M. (2014) Efficiency of microfinance institutions in the Philippines. *Enterprise Development and Microfinance* 25(4): 1755–1978.

*Allet, M. and Hudon, M. (2015) Green microfinance: Characteristics of microfinance institutions involved in environmental management. *Journal of Business Ethics* 126: 395–414.

*Amersdorffer, F., Buchenrieder, G., Bokusheva, R. and Wolz, A. (2015) Efficiency in microfinance: Financial and social performance of agricultural credit cooperatives in Bulgaria. *Journal of the Operational Research Society* 66: 57–65.

*Anku-Tsede, O. (2014) Microfinance intermediation: Regulation of financial NGOs in Ghana. *International Journal of Law and Management* 56(4): 274–301.

*Annim, S. (2012a) Microfinance efficiency: Trade-offs and complementarities between the objectives of microfinance institutions and their performance perspective. *European Journal of Development Research* 24: 788–880.

*Annim, S. (2012b) Targeting the poor versus financial sustainability and external funding: Evidence of microfinance institutions in Ghana. *Journal of Developmental Entrepreneurship* 17(3): 1–19.

*Arrassen, W. (2017) The determinants of MFIs' social and financial performances in sub-Saharan Africa: Has mission drift occurred? *Annals of Finance* 13(2): 205–235.

Armendáriz, B. and Morduch, J. (2010) *The economics of microfinance*. Boston: MIT Press

Armendáriz, B. and Szafarz, A. (2011) On mission drift in microfinance institutions. In B. Armendáriz and M. Labie (eds.), *The Handbook of Microfinance* (pp. 341–366). London: World Scientific Publishers.

Armendáriz, B. and Labie, M. (2011) *The Handbook of Microfinance*. Singapore: World scientific

*Arsyad, L. (2005) An assessment of microfinance institution performance - the importance of institutional environment. *Gadjah Mada International Journal of Business* 7(3): 391–427.

*Assefa, E., Hermes, N. and Meesters, A. (2013) Competition and the performance of microfinance institutions. *Applied Financial Economics* 23(9-10): 767–782.

*Ashta, A. and Fall, S. (2012) Institutional analysis to understand the growth of microfinance institutions in West African economic and monetary union. *Corporate Governance* 12(4): 441–459.

*Ashta, A. and Hudon, M. (2012) The Compartamos microfinance IPO: Mission conflicts in hybrid institutions with diverse shareholding. *Strategic Change* 21: 331–341.

*Augustine, D. (2012) Good practice in corporate governance: Transparency, trust, and performance in the microfinance industry. *Business & Society* 51(4): 659–676.

*Augustine, D., Wheat, C., Jones, K., Baraldi, M. and Malgwi, C. (2016) Gender diversity within the workforce in the microfinance industry in Africa: Economic performance and sustainability. *Canadian Journal of Administrative Sciences* 33: 227–241.

*Ault, J. and Spicer, A. (2014) The institutional context of poverty: State fragility as a predictor of cross-national variation in commercial microfinance lending. *Strategic Management Journal* 35: 1818–1838.

Awaworyi, S. (2014) Impact of microfinance interventions: a meta-analysis. *Business and Economics* 4(1): 3–14.

*Ayayi, A. and Sene, M. (2010) What drives microfinance institutions' financial sustainability. *Journal of Developing Areas* 44(1): 303–324.

*Ayele, G. (2015) Microfinance institutions in Ethiopia, Kenya and Uganda: Loan outreach to the poor and the quest for financial viability. *African Development Review* 27(2): 117–129.

*Azad, M., Munisamy, S., Masum, A. and Wanke, P. (2016) Do African microfinance institutions need efficiency for financial stability and social outreach? *South African Journal of Science* 112(9-10): 76–83.

*Bakker, A., Schaveling, J. and Nijhof, A. (2014) Governance and microfinance institutions. *Corporate Governance* 14(5): 637–652.

*Balammal, A., Madhumathi, R. and Ganesh, M. (2016) Pentagon performance model of Indian MFIs: A study of institutional enablers. *Paradigm* 20(1): 1–13.

*Banker, R.D., Charnes, A. and Cooper, W.W. (1984) Some models for estimating technical and scale inefficiencies in data envelopment analysis. *Management science* 30(9): 1078–1092.

*Barry, T. and Tacneng, R. (2014) The impact of governance and institutional quality on MFI outreach and financial performance in Sub-Saharan Africa. *World Development* 58: 1–20.

*Bassem, B. (2009) Governance and performance of microfinance institutions in Mediterranean countries. *Journal of Business Economics and Management* 10(1): 31–43.

Bauchet, J., Marshall, C., Starita, L., Thomas, J. and Yalouris, A. (2011) Latest findings from randomized evaluations of microfinance. Access to Finance Forum Reports by CGAP and Its Partners No. 2. Washington, D.C.: Consultative Group to Assist the Poor.

Bauchet, J. and Morduch, J. (2013) Is micro too small? Microcredit vs. SME finance. *World Development* 43: 288–297.

*Baumann, T. (2004) Pro-poor microcredit in South Africa: Cost-efficiency and productivity of South African pro-poor microfinance institutions. *Development Southern Africa* 21(5): 785–796.

*Bayai, I. and Ikhide, S. (2016) Life cycle theory and financial sustainability of selected SADC microfinance institutions. *Journal of Developing Areas* 50(6): 121–132.

*Bhanot, D. and Bapat, V. (2015) Sustainability index of microfinance institutions (MFIs) and contributory factors. *International Journal of Social Economics* 42(4): 387–403.

*Bharti, N. and Chitnis, A. (2016) Size and efficiency of MFIs: A data envelopment analysis of Indian MFIs. *Enterprise Development and Microfinance* 27(4): 255–272.

*Blanco-Oliver, A., Irimia-Dieguez, A. and Reguera-Alvarado, N. (2016) Prediction-oriented PLS path modeling in microfinance research. *Journal of Business Research* 69: 4643–4649.

*Boehe, D. and Cruz, L. (2013) Gender and microfinance performance: Why does the institutional context matter?. *World Development* 47: 121–135.

*Bogan, V. (2012) Capital structure and sustainability: An empirical study of microfinance institutions. *The Review of Economics and Statistics* 94(4): 1045–1058.

*Bolli, T. and Vo Thi, A. (2013) Regional differences in the production processes of financial and social outputs of microfinance institutions. *Economics of Transition* 22(3): 461–495.

*Borden, K. (2009) Microenterprise lending at the Grameen Bank: Effective lending rates on a sample loan portfolio. *B-Quest*: 1–27.

*Bos, J. and Millone, M. (2015) Practice what you preach: Microfinance business models and operational efficiency. *World Development* 70: 28–42.

*Bumacov, V., Ashta, A. and Singh, P. (2014) The use of credit scoring in microfinance institutions and their outreach. *Strategic Change* 23: 401–413.

*Burzynska, K. and Berggren, O. (2015) The impact of social beliefs on microfinance performance. *Journal of International Development* 27: 1074–1097.

*Caballero, K., Melgarejo, M. and Ogliastri, E. (2016) Banco Solidario S.A.: The recovery strategy, 2000–2004. *Journal of Business Research* 69: 4454–4468.

Callen, J. L., Klein, A. and Tinkelman, D. (2003) Board composition, committees, and organizational efficiency: The case of nonprofits. *Nonprofit and voluntary sector quarterly* 32(4): 493–520.

*Campbell, N. and Rogers, N. (2012) Microfinance institutions: A profitable investment alternative? *Journal of Developmental Entrepreneurship*, 17(4), https://www.worldscientific.com/doi/abs/10.1142/S1084946712500240 (accessed on September 15, 2018).

*Casselman, R., Sama, L. and Stefanidis, A. (2005) Differential social performance of religiously-affiliated microfinance institutions (MFIs) in Base of Pyramid (BoP) markets. *Journal of Business Ethics* 132: 539–552.

*Caudill, S., Gropper, D. and Hartarska, V. (2009) Which microfinance institutions are becoming more cost effective with time? Evidence from a mixture model. *Journal of Money, Credit and Banking* 41(4): 651–672.

*Chahine, S. and Tannir, L. (2010) On the social and financial effects of the transformation of microfinance NGOs. *Voluntas* 21: 440–461.

*Chakrabarty, S. and Bass, E. (2014) Corporate governance in microfinance institutions: Board composition and the ability to face institutional voids. *Corporate Governance: An International Review* 22(5): 367–386.

Chakravarty, S. and Pylypiv, M. (2017) Microfinance: What do we know, where do we go? *Annals of Corporate Governance* 2(3): 171–289.

Charnes, A., Cooper, W. W. and Rhodes, E. (1978) Measuring the efficiency of decision making units. *European Journal of Operational Research* 2(6): 429–444.

*Chidambaranathan, M. and Premchander, S. (2013) Community-based microfinance: The potential and challenges of self-reliant, self-help group cooperatives. *Enterprise Development and Microfinance* 24(2): 134.

*Chikalipah, S. (2017) Institutional environment and microfinance performance in Sub-Saharan Africa. *African Development Review* 29(1): 16–27.

*Churchill, S. (2017) Microfinance and ethnic diversity. *Economic Record* 93(300): 112–141.

Collins, D., Morduch, J., Rutherford, S. and Ruthven, O. (2009) *Portfolios of the Poor: How the World's Poor Live on $2 a Day*. Princeton University Press.

*Copestake, J. (2007) Mainstreaming microfinance: Social performance management or mission drift?. *World Development* 35(10): 1721–1738.

*Cornée, S. and Thenet, G. (2016) Efficience des institutions de microfinance en Bolivie et au Pérou: Une approche data envelopment analysis en deux étapes. *Finance Contrôle Stratégie* 19(1): available from https://journals.openedition.org/fcs/1768 (accessed on September 19, 2018).

Cozarenco, A., Hudon, M. and Szafarz, A. (2016) What type of microfinance institutions supply savings products? *Economics Letters* 140: 57–59.

*Cull, R., Demirgüc-Kunt, A. and Morduch, J. (2009) Microfinance meets the market. *Journal of Economic Perspectives* 23(1): 167–192.

*Cull, R., Demirgüc-Kunt, A. and Morduch, J. (2013) Banks and microbanks. *Journal of Financial Services Research* 46: 1–53.

*Cull, R., Demirgüc-Kunt, A. and Morduch, J. (2007) Financial performance and outreach: A global analysis of leading microbanks. *The Economic Journal* 117: 107–133.

*Cull, R., Demirgüc-Kunt, A. and Morduch, J. (2011) Does regulatory supervision curtail microfinance profitability and outreach?. *World Development* 39(6): 949–965.

Cull, R., Demirgüc-Kunt, A. and Morduch, J. (2016) The microfinance business model: Enduring subsidy and modest profit. Policy Research Working Paper 7786. Washington, D.C.: The World Bank.

*Cull, R., Harten, S., Nishida, I., Rusu, A. and Bull, G. (2015) Benchmarking the financial performance, growth, and outreach of greenfield MFIs in Africa. *Emerging Markets Review* 25: 92–124.

*Daher, L. and Le Saout, E. (2013) Microfinance and financial performance. *Strategic Change* 22: 31–45.

*Daher, L. and Le Saout, E. (2015) The determinants of the financial performance of microfinance institutions: Impact of the global financial crisis. *Strategic Change* 24: 131–148.

*de Crombrugghe, A., Tenikue, M. and Sureda, J. (2008) Performance analysis for a sample of microfinance institutions in India. *Annals of Public and Cooperative Economics* 79(2): 269–299.

*de Janvry, A., McIntosh, C. and Sadoulet, E. (2010) The supply- and demand-side impacts of credit market information. *Journal of Development Economics* 93: 173–188.

*Deb, J. and Kar, S. (2016) Financial performance of microfinance institutions in North-East India. *Pranjana: The Journal of Management Awareness* 19(2): 47–57.

*Deb, J. and Purkayastha, M. (2014) Branch-level efficiency and decomposition of Assam Gramin Vikash Bank: An indicative DEA approach. *The IUP Journal of Marketing Management* 15(4): 34–44.

*Delgado, M., Parmeter, C., Hartarska, V. and Mersland, R. (2015) Should all microfinance institutions mobilize microsavings? Evidence from economies of scope. *Empirical Economics* 48: 193–225.

Demirguc-Kunt, A., Klapper, L., Singer, D. and Van Oudheusden, P. (2015) The Global Findex database 2014: Measuring financial inclusion around the world. Policy Research Working Paper No. WPS 7255. Washington, D.C.: World Bank Group. http://documents.worldbank.org/curated/en/187761468179367706/The-Global-Findex-Database-2014-measuring-financial-inclusion-around-the-world (accessed on September 19, 2018).

*D'Espallier, B., Guerin, I. and Mersland, R. (2013a) Focus on women in microfinance institutions. *Journal of Development Studies* 49(5): 589–608.

*D'Espallier, B., Hudon, M. and Szafarz, A. (2013b) Unsubsidized microfinance institutions. *Economic Letters* 120: 174–176.

*D'Espallier, B., Goedecke, J., Hudon, M. and Mersland, R. (2017a) From NGOs to banks: Does institutional transformation alter the business model of microfinance institutions? *World Development* 89: 19–33.

*D'Espallier, B., Hudon, M. and Szafarz, A. (2017b) Aid volatility and social performance in microfinance. *Nonprofit and Voluntary Sector Quarterly* 46(1): 116–140.

Deutsche Bank (2007) Microfinance: An emerging investment opportunity. Deutsche Bank Research. Frankfurt am Main: Deutsche Bank.

*Dutta, P. and Das, D. (2014) Indian MFI at crossroads: Sustainability perspective. *Corporate Governance* 14(5): 728–748.

Dupas, P. and Robinson, J. (2013) Why don't the poor save more? Evidence from health savings experiments. *American Economic Review* 103(4): 1138–1171.

Duvendack, M., Palmer-Jones, R., Copestake, J. G., Hooper, L., Loke, Y. and Rao, N. 2011. *What is the Evidence of the Impact of Microfinance on the Well-being of Poor People?* London: EPPI-Centre, University of London.

*Emeni, F. (2008) Microfinance institutions in Nigeria: Problems and prospects. *Journal of Financial Management and Analysis* 21(1): 69–76.

*Epstein, M. and Yuthas, K. (2013) Rural microfinance and client retention: Evidence from Malawi. *Journal of Developmental Entrepreneurship* 18(1): available from https://www.worldscientific.com/doi/abs/10.1142/S1084946713500064 (accessed on September 15, 2018).

*Estapé-Dubreuil, G. and Torreguitart-Mirada, C. (2015) Governance mechanisms, social performance disclosure and performance in microfinance: Does legal status matter? *Annals of Public and Cooperative Economics* 86(1): 137–155.

*Forcella, D. and Hudon, M. (2016) Green microfinance in Europe. *Journal of Business Ethics* 135: 445–459.

*Gakhar, K. and Meetu (2016) Social and financial performance of microfinance institutions: Is there a trade-off? *Avesha* 9(1): 36–44.

*Gakhar, K. and Meetu (2013) Financial performance and outreach of microfinance institutions: Is there a trade-off? An empirical study of the Indian economy. *Sona Global Management Review* 7(4): 1–7.

*Garmaise, M. and Natividad, G. (2013) Cheap credit, lending operations and international politics: The case of global microfinance. *The Journal of Finance* 68(4): 1551–1576.

*Garmaise, M. and Natividad, G. (2010) Information, the cost of credit and operational efficiency: An empirical study of microfinance. *The Review of Financial Studies* 23(6): 2560–2590.

Ghatak, M. and Guinnane, T. W. (1999) The economics of lending with joint liability: Theory and prac-
tice1. *Journal of Development Economics* 60(1): 195–228.

*Gohar, R. and Batool, A. (2015) Effects of corporate governance on performance of microfinance insti-
tutions: A case from Pakistan. *Emerging Markets Finance & Trade* 51: 94–106.

Gopalaswamy A.K. Babu M.S. and Dash U. (2016) *Systematic Review of Quantitative Evidence on the
Impact of Microfinance on the Poor in South Asia*. London: EPPI-Centre, Social Science Research
Unit, UCL Institute of Education, University College London.

*Gregoire, J. and Tuya, O. (2006) Cost-efficiency of microfinance institutions in Peru: A stochastic fron-
tier approach. *Latin American Business Review* 7(2): 41–70.

*Gutierrez-Goiria, J., San-Jose, L. and Retolaza, J. (2016) Social efficiency in microfinance institutions:
Identifying how to improve it. *Journal of International Development* 29: 259–280.

*Gutiérrez-Nieto, B. and Serrano-Cinca, C. (2010) Factors influencing funder loyalty to microfinance
institutions. *Nonprofit and Voluntary Sector Quarterly* 39(2): 302–320.

*Gutiérrez-Nieto, B., Serrano-Cinca, C. and Molinero, C. (2007) Microfinance institutions and efficiency.
Omega 35: 131–142.

*Gutiérrez-Nieto, B., Serrano-Cinca, C. and Molinero, C. (2009) Social efficiency in microfinance insti-
tutions. *The Journal of the Operational Research Society* 60: 104–119.

*Halouani, N. and Boujelbène, Y. (2015) External governance and dual mission in the African MFIs.
Strategic Change 24: 243–265.

*Hamada, M. (2010) Commercialization of microfinance in Indonesia: The shortage of funds and the
linkage program. *The Developing Economies* 48(1): 156–176.

*Hartarska, V. (2005) Governance and performance of microfinance institutions in Central and Eastern
Europe and the Newly Independent States. *World Development* 33(10): 1627–1643.

*Hartarska, V., Nadolnyak, D. and Mersland, R. (2014) Are women better bankers to the poor?
Evidence from rural microfinance intutions. *American Journal of Agricultural Economy* 96(5):
1291–1306.

*Hartarska, V. and Nadolnyak, D. (2007) Do regulated microfinance institutions achieve better sustain-
ability and outreach? Cross-country evidence. *Applied Economics* 39: 1207–1222.

*Hartarska, V., Shen, X. and Mersland, R. (2013) Scale economies and input price elasticities in micro-
finance institutions. *Journal of Banking & Finance* 37: 118–131.

*Haughton, J., Khandker, S. and Rukumnuaykit, P. (2014) Microcredit on a large scale: Appraising the
Thailand village fund. *Asian Economic Journal* 28–29(4): 363–388.

*Hermes, N., Lensink, R. and Meesters, A. (2011) Outreach and efficiency of microfinance institutions.
World Development 39(6): 938–948.

*Hollis, A. and Sweetman, A. (2007) The role of local depositors in controlling expenses in small-scale
financial intermediation: an empirical analysis. *Economica* 74: 713–735.

*Hudon, M. (2010) Management of microfinance institutions: Do subsidies matter? *Journal of Interna-
tional Development* 22: 890–905.

*Hudon, M. and Traça, D. (2011) On the efficiency effects of subsidies in microfinance: An empirical
inquiry. *World Development* 39(6): 966–973.

*Hup Chan, S. (2010) The influence of leadership expertise and experience on organizational perfor-
mance: A study of Amanah Ikhtiar Malaysia. *Asia Pacific Business Review* 16(1-2): 59–77.

*Janda, K. and Turbat, B. (2013) Determinants of the financial performance of microfinance institutions
in Central Asia. *Post-Communist Economies* 25(4): 558–569.

*Jayashankar, P. and Goedegebuure, R. (2011) Marketing strategies and social performance outcomes:
A field study on MFI clients. *The IUP Journal of Marketing Management* 10(2): 7–32.

*Jia, X., Cull, R., Guo, P. and Ma, T. (2016) Commercialization and mission drift: Evidence from a large
Chinese microfinance institution. *China Economic Review* 40: 17–32.

*Jondrow, J., Lovell, C. K., Materov, I. S. and Schmidt, P. (1982) On the estimation of technical in-
efficiency in the stochastic frontier production function model. *Journal of Econometrics* 19(2-3):
233–238.

*Kar, A. (2011) Microfinance institutions: A cross-country empirical investigation of outreach and sustainability. *Journal of Small Business & Entrepreneurship* 24(3): 427–446.

*Kar, A. (2012) Does capital and financing structure have any relevance to the performance of microfinance institutions? *International Review of Applied Economics* 26(3): 329–348.

*Kar, A. (2013a) Mission drift in microfinance: Are the concerns really worrying? Recent cross-country results. *International Review of Applied Economics* 27(1): 44–60.

*Kar, A. (2013b) Double bottom lines in microfinance: Are they mutually exclusive? *Journal of Small Business & Entrepreneurshi* 26(1): 87–107.

*Kar, A. and Swain, R. (2014) Interest rates and financial performance of microfinance institutions: Recent global evidence. *European Journal of Development Research* 26: 87–106.

*Kaur, P. (2016) Efficiency of microfinance institutions in India: Are they reaching the poorest of the poor? *Vision* 20(1): 54–65.

*Kemonou, R. and Anjugam, M. (2013) Measuring the efficiency of sub-Saharan Africa's microfinance institutions and its drivers. *Annals of Public and Cooperative Economics* 84(4): 399–422.

*Kendo, S. (2017) Do decision variables improve microfinance efficiency? A stochastic frontier analysis for African countries. *Strategic Change* 26: 159–174.

*Khafagi, A. (2013) Towards reasonably priced microcredit: Analyzing Egyptian NGO-MFIs' cost structure and financial performance. *Enterprise Development and Microfinance* 24(4): 1755–1978.

*Kneidig, C. and Tracey, P. (2009) Towards a performance measurement framework for community development finance institutions in the UK. *Journal of Business Ethics* 86: 327–345.

Kornai, J. (1986) The soft budget constraint. *Kyklos* 39(1): 3–30.

*Kusuma, S. and Jaya, W. (2015) The relationship between product diversity and the performance of credit unions and Badan Usaha Kredit Pedesaan in Yogyakarta special province. *Journal of Indonesian Economy and Business* 30(1): 1–16.

*Kyereboah-Coleman, A. and Osei, K. (2008) Outreach and profitability of microfinance institutions: The role of governance. *Journal of Economic Studies* 35(3): 236–248.

*Labie M., Méon, P., Mersland, R. and Szafarz, A. (2015) Discrimination by microcredit officers: Theory and evidence on disability in Uganda. *The Quarterly Review of Economics and Finance* 58: 44–55.

*Lebovics, M., Hermes, N. and Hudon, M. (2016) Are financial and social efficiency mutually exclusive? A case study of Vietnamese microfinance institutions. *Annals of Public and Cooperative Economics* 87(1): 55–77.

*Lønborg, J. and Rasmussen, O. (2014) Can microfinance reach the poorest: Evidence from a community-managed microfinance intervention. *World Development* 64: 460–472.

*Louis, P. and Baesens, B. (2013) Do for-profit microfinance institutions achieve better financial efficiency and social impact? A generalised estimating equations panel data approach. *Journal of Development Effectiveness* 5(3): 359–380.

*Louis, P., Seret, A. and Baesens, B. (2013) Financial efficiency and social impact of microfinance institutions. *World Development* 46: 197–210.

Maîtrot, M. and Niño-Zarazúa, M. (2017) Poverty and wellbeing impacts of microfinance: what do we know? WIDER Working Paper 190/2017. Helsinki: UNU-WIDER.

*Majumder, M., Gopinath, M. and Ramudu, P. (2016) Indian MFIs pattern: Analytical model building. *SCMS Journal of Indian Management* 13(1): 57–66.

*Makarfi, A.M. and Olukosi, J.O. (2011) MFIs as vehicles for sustainable credit access by the poor in Kano State, Nigeria. *European Journal of Finance and Banking Research* 4(4): 34–48.

*Manos, R. and Yaron, J. (2009) Key issues in assessing the performance of microfinance institutions. *Canadian Journal of Development Studies* 29(1-2): 101–122.

Marconi, R. and Mosley, P. (2006) Bolivia during the global crisis 1998–2004: Towards a 'macroeconomics of microfinance'. *Journal of International Development* 18(2): 237–261.

*Marr, A. and Tubaro, P. (2011) Crisis in Indian microfinance and a way forward: Governance reforms and the Tamil Nadu model. *Journal of International Development* 23: 996–1003.

*Marwa, N. and Aziakpono, M. (2015) Financial sustainability of Tanzanian saving and credit coopera-
tives. *International Journal of Social Economics* 42(10): 870–887.

Maudos, J., Pastor, J. M., Pérez, F. and Quesada, J. (2002) Cost and profit efficiency in European banks.
Journal of International Financial Markets, Institutions and Money 12(1): 33–58.

*McIntosh, C., de Janvry, A. and Sadoulet, E. (2005) How rising competition among microfinance insti-
tutions affects incumbent lenders. *The Economic Journal* 115: 987–1004.

*McIntosh, M. (2014) Microfinancing in a commercial bank: impact on firm metrics and mission. *Journal
of Management Policy and Practice* 15(5): 65–81.

*Mersland, R., D'Espallier, B. and Supphellen, M. (2013) The effects of religion on development efforts:
evidence from the microfinance industry and research agenda. *World Development* 41: 145–156.

*Mersland, R., Randøy, T. and Strøm, R. (2015) The impact of entrepreneur-CEOs in microfinance
institutions: A global survey. *Entrepreneurship: Theory & Practice* 39(4): 927–953.

*Mersland, R., Randøy, T. and Strøm, R. (2011) The impact of international influence on microbanks'
performance: A global survey. *International Business Review* 20: 163–176.

*Mersland, R. and Strøm, R. (2008) Performance and trade-offs in microfinance organisations: Does
ownership matter?. *Journal of International Development* 20: 598–612.

*Mersland, R. and Strøm, R. (2009) Performance and governance in microfinance institutions. *Journal
of Banking & Finance* 33: 662–669.

*Mersland, R. and Strøm, R. (2010) Microfinance mission drift? *World Development* 38(1): 28–36.

*Mersland, R. and Strøm, Ø. (2014) Measuring microfinance performance. In R. Mersland and Ø. Strøm
(eds.), *Microfinance Institutions: Financial and Social Performance* (pp. 12–30). London: Palgrave
Macmillan.

*Mersland, R. and Urgeghe, L. (2013) International debt financing and performance of microfinance
institutions. *Strategic Change* 22: 17–29.

*Mia, A. and Chandran, V. (2015) Measuring financial and social outreach productivity of microfinance
institutions in Bangladesh. *Social Indicator Research* 127: 505–527.

*Monroy, C. and Huerga, A. (2013) International for-profit investments in microfinance institutions
equity. *Journal of Industrial Engineering and Management* 6(3): 709–722.

*Morduch, J. (1999) The microfinance promise. *Journal of Economic Literature* 37(4): 1569–1614.

*Morduch, J. (2000) The microfinance schism. *World development* 28(4): 617–629.

*Mori, N., Golesorkhi, S., Randøy, T. and Hermes, N. (2015) Board composition and outreach perfor-
mance of microfinance institutions: Evidence from East Africa. *Strategic Change* 24: 99–113.

*Mori, N. and Mersland, R. (2014) Boards in microfinance institutions: how do stakeholders matter?
Journal of Management Governance 18: 285–313.

*Mukherjee, A. (2013) Microfinance and credit to the ultra-poor. *International Journal of Social
Economics* 41(10): 975–993.

*Musa, A.S.M. and Khan, M.S.R (2010) Benefits and limitations of technology in MFIs. *Journal of
Electronic Commerce Organization* 8(2): 54–65.

*Nanayakkara, G. and Iselin, E. (2012) An explanatory study of the performance of microfinancing insti-
tutions using the Balanced Scorecard Approach. *International Journal of Business and Information*
7(2): 165–204.

*Narwal, K. and Yadav, M. (2014) Impact of characteristics on outreach and profitability of microfinance
institution in India. *International Journal of Financial Management* 4(3): 50–57.

*Nkundabanyanga, S., Opiso, J., Balunywa, W. and Nkote, I. (2015) Financial service outreach correlates.
International Journal of Social Economics 42(4): 404–442.

Noussair, C. N. and Tucker, S. (2013) Experimental research on asset pricing. *Journal of Economic
Surveys* 27(3): 554–569.

*Pati, A. (2012) Regulation versus outreach and sustainability: A study of the performance of microfi-
nance institutions in India. *The IUP Journal of Marketing Management* 11(4): 41–56.

*Pati, A. (2015) Are regulatory microfinance institutions of India better off than non-regulatory ones? A
comparison of performance and sustainability. *Paradigm* 19(1): 21–36.

*Patten, R., Rosengard, J. and Johnston, D. (2001) Microfinance success amidst macroeconomic failure: The experience of Bank Rakyat Indonesia during the East Asian crisis. *World Development* 29(6): 1057–1069.

*Pedrini, M. and Ferri, L. (2016) Doing well by returning to the origin. Mission drift, outreach and financial performance of microfinance institutions. *Voluntas* 27: 2576–2594.

*Périlleux, A. and Szafarz, A. (2015) Women leaders and social performance: Evidence from financial cooperatives in Senegal. *World Development* 74: 437–452.

*Piot-Lepetit, I. and Nzongang, J. (2014) Financial sustainability and poverty outreach within a network of village banks in Cameroon: A multi-DEA approach. *European Journal of Operational Research* 234: 319–330.

*Postelnicu, L. and Hermes, N. (2016) Microfinance Performance and Social Capital: A Cross-Country Analysis. *Journal of Business Ethics*: 1–19.

*Quayes, S. (2015) Outreach and performance of microfinance institutions: A panel analysis. *Applied Economics* 47(18): 1909–1925.

*Quayes, S. and Hasan, T. (2014) Financial disclosure and performance of microfinance institutions. *Journal of Accounting & Organizational Change* 10(3): 314–337.

*Quayes, S. and Joseph, G. (2017) Legal systems and performance of microfinance institutions. *International Review of Applied Economics* 31(3): 304–317.

*Rai, A. (2015) Indian microfinance institutions: Performance of young and old institutions. *Vision* 19(3): 189–199.

*Rao, K. and Reda, T. (2015) The determinants of outreach of microfinance institutions in Ethiopia. *International Journal of Business Insights and Transformation* 8(1): 8–16.

*Rashid, A. and Twaha, K. (2013) Exploring the determinants of the productivity of Indian microfinance institutions. *Theoretical and Applied Economics* 20(12): 83–96.

Reed, L. (2015) *State of the microcredit summit campaign report 2015*. Washington, D.C.: Microcredit Summit.

Reichert, P. (2018) A meta-analysis examining the nature of trade-offs in microfinance. *Oxford Development Studies* 20: 1–23.

*Roberts, P. (2013) The profit orientation of microfinance institutions and effective interest rates. *World Development* 41: 120–131.

*Sainz-Fernandez, I., Torre-Olmo, B., Lopez-Gutierrez, C. and Sanfilippo-Azofra, S. (2015) Crisis in microfinance institutions: Identifying problems. *Journal of International Development* 27: 1058–1073.

*Schreiner, M. (2003) A cost-effectiveness analysis of the Grameen Bank of Bangladesh. *Development Policy Review* 21(3): 357–382.

*Serrano-Cinca, C. and Gutiérrez-Nieto, B. (2014) Microfinance, the long tail and mission drift. *International Business Review* 23: 181–194.

*Servin, R., Lensink, R. and Berg, M. (2012) Ownership and technical efficiency of microfinance institutions: Empirical evidence from Latin America. *Journal of Banking & Finance* 36: 2136–2144.

*Silva, A. and Chávez, G. (2015) Microfinance, country governance and the global financial crisis. *Venture Capital* 17(1-2): 191–213.

Sinah, S. (2010) How to calm the charging bull–an agenda for CGAP in the decade of the 'teenies'. *Microfinance Focus* 15.

*Strøm, R., D'Espallier, B. and Mersland, R. (2014) Female leadership, performance, and governance in microfinance institutions. *Journal of Banking & Finance* 42: 60–75.

*Suarez, F. F. and Lanzolla, G. (2007) The role of environmental dynamics in building a first mover advantage theory. *Academy of Management Review* 32(2): 377–392.

*Tahir, I. and Che Tarim, S. (2013) Efficiency analysis of microfinance institutions in ASEAN: A DEA approach. *Business Management Dynamics* 3(4): 13–23.

*Tchakoute-Tchuigoua, H. (2010) Is there a difference in performance by the legal status of microfinance institutions?. *The Quarterly Review of Economics and Finance* 50: 436–442.

*Tchakoute-Tchuigoua, H. (2012) Active risk management and loan contract terms: Evidence from rated microfinance institutions. *The Quarterly Review of Economics and Finance* 52: 427–437.

*Tchakoute-Tchuigoua, H. (2014) Performance of microfinance institutions: Do board activity and governance ratings matter? *Finance* 35(3): 7–52.

*Tchakoute-Tchuigoua, H., Durrieu, F. and Kouao, G. (2017) Funding strategy and performance of microfinance institutions: An exploratory study. *Strategic Change* 26: 133–143.

*Vanroose, A. and D'Espallier, B. (2013) Do microfinance institutions accomplish their mission? Evidence from the relationship between traditional financial sector development and microfinance institutions' outreach and performance. *Applied Economics* 45: 1965–1982.

Van Rooyen, C., Stewart, R. and De Wet, T. (2012) The impact of microfinance in sub-Saharan Africa: A systematic review of the evidence. *World Development* 40(11): 2249–2262.

*Vishwakarma, R. (2017) Women on board and its impact on microfinance: Evidence from microfinance sector. *Indian Journal of Corporate Governance* 10(1): 58–73.

Wagner, C. and Winkler, A. (2013) The vulnerability of microfinance to financial turmoil–evidence from the global financial crisis. *World Development* 51: 71–90.

*Widiarto, I. and Emrouznejad, A. (2015) Social and financial efficiency of Islamic microfinance institutions: A Data Envelopment Analysis application. *Socio-Economic Planning Sciences* 50: 1–17.

*Wijesri, M. and Meoli, M. (2015) Productivity change of microfinance institutions in Kenya: A bootstrap Malmquist approach. *Journal of Retailing and Consumer Services* 25: 115–121.

*Wijesri, M., Viganò, L. and Meoli, M. (2015) Efficiency of microfinance institutions in Sri Lanka: A two-stage double bootstrap DEA approach. *Economic Modelling* 47: 74–83.

World Bank. (2018) Financial Inclusion, World Bank Website. http://www.worldbank.org/en/topic/financialinclusion/overview (accessed June 9, 2018)

*Wu, Y., Escalante, C. and Xiaofei, L. (2016) Technical efficiency and business maturity: Evidence from Chinese and Indian microfinance institutions. *Enterprise Development and Microfinance* 27(2): 97–114.

*Xu, S., Copestake, J. and Peng, X. (2016) Microfinance institutions' mission drift in a macroeconomic context. *Journal of International Development* 28–29: 1123–1137.

Yaron, J. (1992) Assessing Development Finance Institutions: A Public Interest Analysis (No. 174). World Bank.

*Zerai, B. and Rani, L. (2012) Technical efficiency and its determinants of MFIs in Ethiopia: An SFA approach. *African Journal of Accounting, Economics, Finance and Banking research* 8(8): 1–19.

11

CROWDFUNDING AND INNOVATION

Fabrice Hervé

Université de Bourgogne

Armin Schwienbacher

SKEMA Business School—Université Côte d'Azur

1. Introduction

Finance and financial institutions are important for the economy because they not only play a role in the selection of investment opportunities and the allocation of resources, but also the financing of innovation (Schumpeter, 1912). The function of selecting the best projects is crucial for the economy because innovation is an important source of growth (King and Levine, 1993). Entrepreneurial, high-tech firms (mostly startups), and in particular those financially supported by private sources such as venture capital funds and business angels, contribute significantly to the development of innovation (Kortum and Lerner, 2000; Benson and Ziedonis, 2009; Block *et al.*, 2018a). Therefore, financial institutions participate in the development of innovation not only by providing financial support but also by mitigating the adverse selection of projects. In this paper, we discuss innovation and growth generated in small, entrepreneurial firms by the means of a new form of financing: crowdfunding.

Although it is often claimed that for some forms of innovation, startups are better equipped to innovate, they also face their own difficulties. These difficulties stem from different sources (Lee *et al.*, 2015). First, innovation is strongly related to risk, which in itself makes financing very risky. This can disadvantage small firms, because larger ones can diversify their risk across other activities that either already generate revenues or across other research projects. Second, small innovative firms face more severe information asymmetry problems, which makes financing through traditional sources such as bank finance more difficult than for larger, more established firms (Carpenter and Petersen, 2002). Based on the *pecking order theory* (Myers, 1984), younger and smaller firms therefore need to rely more on equity finance, notably from business angels and venture capital funds, which tend to be more able to evaluate, assist, and monitor these firms. Otherwise, market failures may arise (Akerlof, 1970). Finally, innovation can be very specific and can hardly be transferred nor sold. Often, innovation can only be

Contemporary Topics in Finance: A Collection of Literature Surveys, First Edition. Edited by Iris Claus and Leo Krippner.

implemented inside the firm that developed it in the first place. Thus, innovative startups cannot use their innovation as a form of collateral to secure outside financing in the form of bank finance. Because such startups often do not generate revenues in their first years, they are also not able to service interest payments on a regular basis.

Recently, crowdfunding has developed as a new form of entrepreneurial finance, which aligns with the financing needs of some innovative firms often unable to tap other forms of financing. Its development was accelerated after the financial crisis of 2008, possibly because the supply of traditional financing to small- and medium-sized enterprises (SME) had dried up even more. Crowdfunding has the potential to provide funding to early-stage projects and thereby fill some of the funding gap that plague small, innovative firms (see Cressy, 2002, for a general discussion on funding gaps for SMEs). At first sight, crowdfunding appears as a mixture of other forms of financing (Schwienbacher and Larralde, 2012; Harrison, 2013). Today, we typically distinguish between different types of crowdfunding, ranging from reward-based crowdfunding, donation-based crowdfunding, loan-based crowdfunding, and equity crowdfunding.[1] According to Short *et al.* (2017), the World Bank estimates the volume of crowdfunding to become $300 billion by 2025. Based on a different methodology, Rau (2017) identified over 1,300 platforms worldwide with a total volume of nearly $140 billion in 2015, although the bulk is loan-based crowdfunding. However, all segments exhibit strong growth, including equity crowdfunding. The latter also started a bit later, notably because it is the most regulated type and was therefore forbidden in many countries until recently. An obvious reason why different types of crowdfunding have emerged is because of the broad range of projects seeking money through crowdfunding. In fact, many projects are artistic and social, and thus do not involve an entrepreneurial aspect and are even less likely to include technological innovation. The focus of our paper here is on crowdfunding that involves an entrepreneur with an innovative idea, and not purely, one-shot artistic or social projects. Thus, our discussion will not cover the full range of crowdfunding activities.

Crowdfunding is not a new phenomenon, as illustrated by the financing of the Statue of Liberty in New York. In 1884, due to financing problems in the construction of the Statue of Liberty, the newspaper editor Joseph Pulitzer (publisher of *New York World*) issued an open call to his readers to help finalize the project. This call led 125,000 individuals to donate over $100,000 in total, which was sufficient to cover the remaining costs. As a reward, all the contributors had their names cited in the newspaper. This example shows how the crowd can help in the financing of projects. Another feature of crowdfunding is that the crowd can be solicited to evaluate the project or at least provide feedback on the product to be produced (Mollick, 2014; Vismara, 2016; Strausz, 2017; see also Cumming *et al.*, 2017, for equity crowdfunding). This idea is also not new, because Galton (1907) showed that a crowd may be able to provide an accurate estimation and thus make good decisions when being subject to the right incentives. This phenomenon of *vox populi*, as labeled by Galton (1907; later labeled *wisdom of crowds* by Surowiecki, 2004, although the term was already used by others before him; see Larrick *et al.*, 2011, for a comprehensive discussion), stems from the fact that errors made by individual members of the crowd are cancelled out when the crowd is sufficiently large and diverse, so that on average the crowd may get it right. The big question here though, is whether the crowd is also able to *be sufficiently wise* when it comes to the evaluation of innovation-driven projects, because it requires specific expertise.

For approximately the last 10 years, academic research has been interested in the phenomenon of crowdfunding. Most of the earlier work focused on reward-based crowdfunding and loan-based crowdfunding, mainly because of the quicker availability of data (e.g., on projects funded on the platforms Kickstarter, Indiegogo, Prosper, and Kiva). In addition, the impact of project and entrepreneurial characteristics on campaign success was typically studied. These characteristics include funding goals, project presentation (e.g., the inclusion of a video, the length of the project description, and the complexity of the writing), geography, the size of the entrepreneur's social network and personality traits, and team characteristics (Lin *et al.*, 2013; Leung et Sharkey, 2014; Mollick, 2014; Agrawal *et al.*, 2015; Ahlers *et al.*, 2015; Allison *et al.*, 2015; Colombo *et al.*, 2015; Lin and Viswanathan, 2015; Moss *et al.*, 2015; Bapna, 2017; Bollaert *et al.*, 2017; Buttice *et al.*, 2017; Kuppuswamy and Bayus, 2017). Some of this literature examined whether crowdfunding helps "democratize" access to finance, by investigating whether individuals often discriminated by traditional financial institutions receive more when asking the crowd. This has led some researchers to explore specific individual characteristics of entrepreneurs such as gender and race. Empirical evidence suggests that women benefit proportionately more from crowdfunding, but that discrimination against racial minorities in the United States remains (Pope and Sydnor, 2011; Marom *et al.*, 2016; Greenberg and Mollick, 2017; Younkin and Kuppuswamy, 2017). The crowdfunding's promise of democratization does not alleviate the underrepresentation of minority founders. The dynamics of crowdfunding campaigns have also been studied (Vismara, 2016; Kuppuswamy and Bayus, 2017; Hornuf and Schwienbacher, 2018a), showing that the pattern of contribution over the campaign time period is generally U-shaped for reward-based crowdfunding. For equity crowdfunding, the dynamics are L-shaped for shares allocated on a first-come, first-served basis and U-shaped when allocated by an auction mechanism.

An important economic and public policy question that has been the subject of little research so far is the link between crowdfunding and innovation, with a few exceptions that we discuss later. Our objective is to discuss possible links between crowdfunding and innovation based on the existing literature. More specifically, we raise the questions as to whether and how crowdfunding can spur innovation. We focus on two distinct channels whereby this can occur. The first and more immediate one is that crowdfunding can provide a new source of financing to innovation-driven projects. If crowdfunding provides money to projects that would not be funded otherwise or in a more efficient way than traditional sources of finance, then it may contribute to innovation activities. The second channel is that crowdfunding may enable the participation of the crowd in the innovation process itself. Indeed, crowdfunding is sometimes associated with crowdsourcing (Estellés-Arolas and González-Ladrón-de-Guevara, 2012; Schwienbacher and Larralde, 2012; Harrison, 2013). This aspect makes crowdfunding distinct from traditional sources of finance such as banks and professional equity investors (business angels and venture capital funds). Moreover, as shown by Mollick and Nanda (2015) for artistic projects, the crowd possesses a capacity to evaluate projects that is similar to experts. Whether these findings can be extrapolated to innovation-driven projects remains to be shown, but the fact that the crowd offers funding, ideas, and feedback leaves this question open, especially given that the crowd is often the final consumer of the product that is being put on the market later on. Although professional investors can provide guidance on how to develop the business, the crowd can offer direct feedback on the product. This view is consistent with the theoretical principal-agent model developed by Strausz (2017) that underlines that although crowdfunding is not an effective way to mitigate entrepreneurial moral hazard problems (a task well handled by banks or venture capitalists), the success of reward-based crowdfunding comes from its capacity to reduce the uncertainty about aggregate demand. This argument, however, is specific to reward-based crowdfunding and does not directly extend to other forms.

The remainder of this paper is structured as follows. The next section offers a general discussion on how crowdfunding works, which in recent years has been based on platforms that have emerged on the Internet. Section 3 discusses whether and how crowdfunding can help finance innovative projects and thereby foster innovation. Therein, we also provide a discussion on possible links between crowdfunding and other, more traditional forms of finance. Section 4 presents ways for crowdfunding to foster innovation beyond the pure provision of financial resources. Section 5 concludes with suggestions of avenues for future research.

2. The Functioning of Crowdfunding Platforms

Although the vast majority of crowdfunding campaigns takes place on dedicated platforms, the first campaigns occurred without them. Before the arrival of Kickstarter in 2009 and Indiegogo in 2008, a few entrepreneurs launched a crowdfunding campaign by setting up their own website (Belleflamme et al., 2013). An interesting example is the British software company Trampoline Systems, which aimed at raising £1 million to fund its development without using any platform. Eventually, they only sold securities to accredited investors. The development of platforms has facilitated the launch of campaigns by standardizing the processes and creating greater visibility to projects. This, in turn, has accelerated the development of crowdfunding internationally. Today, there are a large number of platforms operating in various forms. Although some are generalists, others are specialized in specific project categories. Some operate under the all-or-nothing funding model, whereby a funding threshold must first be met, whereas others under the keep-it-all funding model allowing all funding to be kept; others again give entrepreneurs the possibility to choose between the two (Cumming et al., 2016). More recently, some platforms now offer the possibility to choose among different crowdfunding types. For instance, in addition to a reward-based crowdfunding campaign, Indiegogo now offers the possibility to run an equity crowdfunding campaign (https://equity.indiegogo.com/; see also Hornuf and Schwienbacher, 2018a).

The development of social media on the Internet has enabled the emergence of platforms that bring together businesses and potential investors, especially individual investors with little knowledge of finance but each willing to provide a relatively small amount of money (Harrison, 2013). Taken together, these small amounts of money can become large. This development could arise because the Internet has significantly reduced the costs of intermediation so that even small entrepreneurs can rely on the crowd (Belleflamme et al., 2014; Leboeuf and Schwienbacher, 2018; Mollick, 2014).

As mentioned in the Introduction, today the different forms of crowdfunding (donation, reward, loan, equity) coexist in a global ecosystem (Harrison, 2013). At the same time, the fact that crowdfunding takes so many forms makes it appealing to different types of entrepreneurial and innovative projects. When an entrepreneur is not able to obtain the needed funds from traditional sources, he or she can choose the type of crowdfunding that is most suitable to his or her project. Similar to two-sided markets, the platform's role is to match entrepreneurs (or projects) with backers (or contributors) in a way that makes it less costly than without the platform as intermediary (Evans, 2011). These costs may take different forms, such as search costs, costs associated with collecting information on the project and its owner, and costs borne to negotiate a contract between the different parties involved. Although the platform is an intermediary, its role as such is different from traditional intermediaries like banks (Allen and Santomero, 2001; Boot and Thakor, 2000). Although the latter select projects themselves, a crowdfunding platform leaves this decision to the crowd. The platform's intermediation role is restricted to bringing together the two sides of the market. Moreover, in contrast to banks, a platform generally plays no role in the collection of information; it is merely a place where the information provided by the parties is collected so that costs are reduced for everyone (Hornuf and Schwienbacher, 2016).

Given the different forms of crowdfunding available, it is not surprising that they also attract different types of crowdfunders and not just different types of entrepreneurs (Leboeuf and Schwienbacher, 2018; Vismara, 2016). In reward-based crowdfunding, backers generally are compensated by receiving the project's product before everyone else. Thus, backers (at least many of them) make consumption decisions when deciding to contribute. At the other end of the spectrum, equity crowdfunding involves the purchase of financial securities, so that investors become shareholders in the startup. There, backers mainly make investment decisions with the goal of achieving a financial return. Similar objectives are generally targeted for those using loan-based crowdfunding platforms. Backers therefore have different motivations depending on the types of platforms. As we will see later, other motivations may be at play and complement the ones mentioned here.

A characteristic of crowdfunding is that the entrepreneur needs to put a large amount of information in the public domain (the Internet) to convince backers to contribute. Although this can generate problems for the entrepreneur if others aim at replicating the same idea (something we discuss later), the disclosure of relevant information is important to reduce information asymmetry or fraud, and thus risk for the crowd. An accumulation of fraud cases could jeopardize a platform's future or even the entire crowdfunding industry overall. Thus, it is important that platforms are managed to minimize the crowd's risk. Equity crowdfunding has especially attracted much attention by regulators during the last several years, mainly because it involves the public offering of financial securities, which are already heavily regulated. The development of crowdfunding depends on the existence of a supportive legal environment (Dushnitsky *et al.*, 2016). As a way to promote equity crowdfunding while mitigating to some extent the risks for the crowd, different countries have put in place regulations specific to it (Hornuf and Schwienbacher, 2017a). A few countries, such as France and the United Kingdom, have even drafted regulation for loan-based crowdfunding.

The United States was the first country to propose regulations for equity crowdfunding as part of the Jumpstart Our Business Startups (JOBS) Act of 2012, although it was only implemented by the US Securities and Exchange Commission in 2016 (Catalini *et al.*, 2016). Other countries followed their steps, including Italy, France, Germany, Belgium, the United Kingdom, and Austria (Hornuf and Schwienbacher, 2017a). These regulations are often quite different in their approach but also share many similarities. To minimize the crowd's risk in equity crowdfunding (either because of fraud risk or risk specific to this type of investment, especially for innovative startups), regulations generally require a minimum level of information disclosure about the issuer and the company's activities. In addition, there are limits placed both on the amount that each crowd investor can invest, which may depend on the crowd investor's investable wealth, and the maximum amount that any issuer can raise within a period of (typically) 12 months.

3. Crowdfunding and the Financing of Innovation

3.1 *Crowdfunding: A Solution to the Funding Gap?*

Startups often experience difficulties in raising capital, especially if it is meant to finance innovation, a phenomenon generally denoted by "funding gap" (also called equity gap; Cressy, 2002) and which results from important information asymmetry and moral hazard problems investors may face when investing in such firms. But, other sources of difficulty have been identified, such as the lack of sufficient collateral. For instance, firms naturally tend to seek banks to obtain funding, but these require collateral or other guarantees, which innovative startups do not have. Empirical evidence (Cosh *et al.*, 2009) therefore shows that startups do not receive enough external funding and that received funding is often not in the form they would prefer.

Within the financial growth cycle paradigm of Berger and Udell (1998) that considers a linear relationship between investor type and stage of development, crowdfunding would be situated at the beginning of the cycle, coming from friends, family, and professional investors (business angels and venture capital funds). Crowdfunding is generally used by smaller, younger firms with significant problems of information asymmetry. Because this type of firm is often funded by professional investors (Maxwell *et al.*, 2011), crowdfunding can potentially complement or substitute this form of finance.

If one wants to position the different types of crowdfunding within Berger and Udell's (1998) paradigm, one would probably put reward-based crowdfunding first, because it mostly involves small amounts of money (most less than $10,000) for very small firms, and the motivation of backers for pledging is mainly nonfinancial (Cholakova and Clarysse, 2015). The next type would be loan-based crowdfunding, because there too the amounts are often small, whereas the motivation of backers is now financial (Paravisini *et al.*, 2016; Block *et al.*, 2018a). For instance, Prosper.com, a well-known loan-based crowdfunding platform, offers three-year loans for a maximum amount of $25,000 (Leung and Skarkey, 2014). Hildebrand *et al.* (2016) reported that the average amount requested is approximately $8,000. Equity crowdfunding comes last, given that the amount requested is rarely below $50,000.[2] Also, the decision by investors to participate in an equity crowdfunding campaign is mostly driven by financial motivations (Cholakova and Clarysse, 2015; Vismara, 2016). For instance, the average amount raised is £205,000 on the UK platform Crowdcube (Vismara, 2016), €151,000 on the French platform WiSEED (Hervé *et al.*, 2017), and AUD 318,500 on the Australian platform ASSOB (Ahlers *et al.*, 2015). As a result, any type of crowdfunding enables small- and SME to overcome problems of accessing financing, including for innovation projects. This observation is promising because access to external finance is crucial for young firms to survive and develop (Carpenter and Petersen, 2002; Gilbert *et al.*, 2006).

3.2 *Links Between Crowdfunding and Other Forms of Entrepreneurial Finance*

An important question relates to how crowdfunding interacts with other forms of entrepreneurial finance and, in particular, angel finance and venture capital. Although these two other forms appear to be close to crowdfunding in terms of amount provided and stage of development, crowdfunding turns out to be different in many ways. An important difference lies in the contractual arrangements offered by crowdfunding platforms. Professional investors more often make use of contractual covenants that are intended to protect their investment, such as liquidation preferences, preemption rights, veto rights on major corporate decisions, and, in addition to stage financing, milestone financing (Da Rin *et al.*, 2011; Dahiya and Ray, 2012; Hornuf and Schwienbacher, 2016, 2018b; Wong *et al.*, 2009). Because crowdfunding involves many small investments from a large number of individuals, the platforms cannot offer tailored contracts to the same extent as professional investors. Moreover, crowd investors on equity crowdfunding platforms do not purchase equity per se, but often receive other types of securities such as participating notes (Hornuf and Schwienbacher, 2016). In contrast, angel investors and venture capital funds typically purchase common shares and convertible preferred shares. These represent important differences between crowdfunding and professional investors.

Along the same lines, Brown *et al.* (2018) argued that equity crowdfunding will generally be preferred over other forms of equity financing because of weaker control rights required by equity crowdfunders. Thus, equity crowdfunding can be viewed as a diluted form of equity funding due to its weaker capacity to restrain the entrepreneur's autonomy.

Crowdfunding and financing by professional investors generally both occur in the early stage of development, which raises the question whether they are complements or substitutes. Drover *et al.* (2017) showed that startups having completed a successful (reward-based) crowdfunding campaign on a well-established platform were more likely to have venture capitalists perform due diligence on them for follow-up financing. This finding is consistent with the view that a startup that has successfully raised crowdfunding enjoys some form of certification from the crowd, which in turn positively affects the perception of the startup by professional investors.

Colombo and Shafi (2016) examined the links between venture capital financing and crowdfunding in more detail. An interesting point of their focus is the distinction made between firms that have already received venture capital and those which have not. For the latter, they argued that two opposing forces are at play, inducing a tradeoff in the choice of financing. On the one hand, a large amount raised by crowdfunding increases the autonomy of the entrepreneur and gives him/her some indication on the success of the project, even though it is more the venture capitalists who provide indication of success, though in a different way. As a result of the successful crowdfunding campaign, the entrepreneur no longer needs the help of venture capitalists to the same extent as before. This may induce the entrepreneur to rely on other forms of financing in the future, including bootstrap financing. In this case, crowdfunding and venture capital financing are substitutes. On the other hand, a successful crowdfunding campaign reduces the information asymmetry that the firm is generally subject to, because (reward-based) crowdfunding can be viewed as a pretest for commercialization of the ultimate product. This indicates to the venture capital funds that the project may be promising, which in turn induces them to fund the firms themselves. These two opposing forces affect the likelihood of obtaining venture capital financing.

For firms that have already benefited from venture capital, a successful crowdfunding campaign confirms the investment choices made by the venture capital funds and thus further increases the chances of obtaining follow-up venture capital funding. In this case, the outcome is similar to staged financing because the crowdfunding campaign represents a distinct round of financing due to the reduced information asymmetry regarding the quality of the entrepreneurial project. This shows that crowdfunding and venture capital can be complements. Examples of complementarity between the two forms of financing exist. One illustrative example is Oculus Rift, which raised $2.4 million on Kickstarter in 2012, 10 times more than the funding goal. This phenomenal success then attracted the interest of venture capitalists, who provided a further $75 million in 2013, and eventually led to the acquisition of Oculus Rift by Facebook for $2 billion in 2014.

In this vein, Mollick and Kuppuswamy (2016) provided survey evidence indicating that crowdfunding can function as a prelude to traditional funding (venture capital and angel investment). Yu *et al.* (2017) found a correlation between crowdfunded projects and angel funding rounds at the regional level in the United States. Sorenson *et al.* (2016) identified a similar relationship between crowdfunding and venture capital. They suggested that the development of crowdfunding could be at the origin of the development of traditional forms of entrepreneurial finance (venture capital or angel finance) in regions that are traditionally excluded from these forms of financing. These different pieces of evidence are consistent with complementarities between these different sources of financing.

3.3 *Summary: Crowdfunding can Help Finance Innovation*

The relationship between crowdfunding and other sources of finance appears to be complex and needs to be studied in more detail, in particular from an empirical perspective. Research up till now has been theoretical work that has generated different predictions which now need to be tested empirically. What can we conclude so far? On the question as to whether crowdfunding can help alleviate the funding gap of SMEs, the answer is clearly "yes," as evidenced by increased synergies with other sources of entrepreneurial finance. The extent to which this will be the case needs to be seen, because the proportion of crowdfunding going to innovative entrepreneurs (as opposed to artistic and social projects) still remains small. It is however growing fast. Moreover, the way crowdfunding is structured makes it suitable for many startups, also at times as a complement to financing from institutional investors.

As for the question about which type of crowdfunding is most suitable to finance innovation, there is not yet a definitive answer. Reward-based and loan-based crowdfunding for startups mostly involves small amounts, whereas equity crowdfunding is able to attract larger ones. However, the financial motivations present in loan-based and equity crowdfunding limit the possibility to reduce information asymmetry, whereas reward-based crowdfunding can serve as a *proof of concept* or at least as a pretest for assessing market demand. This provides valuable information to the entrepreneur and other investors involved that cannot be obtained from other forms of financing. Although loan-based crowdfunding is by far the most important form of crowdfunding worldwide (Rau, 2017), it seems to offer few opportunities for innovative startups, because the amounts involved are too small and the financial motivations are based on expectations of returns that are too short-term for supporting innovation. In contrast, equity crowdfunding represents more long-term investments and thus is more likely to support innovative projects that require time, while at the same time providing the amounts needed to undertake larger innovation projects.

In this section, we conclude that crowdfunding can constitute a valid form of financing for innovative firms. One related dimension still needs to be explored. Because of its participative nature, crowdfunding involves the participation of a large number of individuals and the disclosure of more information in the public domain than for professional investors. As a result, Harrison (2013) and McKenny *et al.* (2017) highlighted the fact that crowdfunding shares commonalities with crowdsourcing. Therefore, crowdfunding may also help entrepreneurs in carrying out their innovative project by providing other forms of feedback not raised so far. This is what we discuss next.

4. Does Crowdfunding Spur Innovation?

4.1 *Innovation: A Problem of Trust?*

An informational problem may arise when an entrepreneur seeks external finance, a problem called the "Double Trust Dilemma" (Cooter and Edlin, 2013; Hornuf and Schwienbacher, 2016) or the "Paradox of Arrow" (Arrow, 1962). The idea is very simple. When an entrepreneur seeks funding for an idea, he or she needs to engage with an investor. This creates a problem of trust. In order to convince the investor to provide the needed funds, the entrepreneur needs to disclose valuable information about the idea. However, once the idea is revealed, there is a risk that the investor will develop the idea himself/herself causing the idea to be lost for the entrepreneur. In the context of crowdfunding, this problem or paradox is likely to arise because the entrepreneur raises the funds over the Internet where anyone can access the information disclosed. Therefore, there is a risk of the idea being stolen in that someone else replicates it and becomes a direct competitor of the entrepreneur. This, in turn, limits the development of crowdfunding, because entrepreneurs with projects, which are valuable and can be easily replicated, may refrain from using crowdfunding as a source of funding. Projects with innovative ideas are most likely to suffer from this problem because much of their value is based on ideas. Entrepreneurs relying on crowdfunding also generally lack the means to protect their ideas through patents or defend themselves in court in case of patent infringements. Schwienbacher (2017) showed that this affects the types of entrepreneurial projects posted on crowdfunding platforms. Indeed, entrepreneurs may seek to raise more money during the crowdfunding campaign than initially planned as a way to capture part of the aftermarket where the innovative product was intended to be sold (for instance, on Amazon or other online shops, or even in real shops) so as to compete in the aftermarket in the wake of replication. In the extreme case, entrepreneurs may even simply develop a project that is limited to the crowdfunding campaign as opposed to developing a business because of the reduced benefits in the aftermarket. Overall, the Double Trust Dilemma reduces the gains from using crowdfunding so that we expect fewer projects on crowdfunding platforms. However, those using crowdfunding may take whatever they can get during the campaign (even at the cost of not being able to deliver on time) as a way to capture part of the demand that would otherwise have come in the aftermarket. Thus, we would expect fewer but larger projects on these platforms to account for the risk of idea-stealing.

To sum up, the trust problem may limit the types of innovative projects that may use crowdfunding. Projects that are hard to replicate or projects that are only marginally innovative may be more likely to seek crowdfunding. The next subsection will aim at answering two follow-up questions to offer further insights into the type of innovation likely to be fostered by crowdfunding: can crowdfunding contribute to the innovation process? If yes, what type of innovation is likely to benefit most?

4.2 Crowdfunding and Crowdsourcing

Crowdsourcing involves turning to a group (the "crowd"), especially online, to obtain needed ideas, goods, or services. McKenny et al. (2017) pointed out the similarity between the concepts of crowdfunding and crowdsourcing. On a scale of 1 (very similar) to 5 (very different), the participants of their study (the editorial board members of the academic journal Entrepreneurship Theory and Practice) attributed an average value of 2.23, implying they believe both concepts are strongly linked. Harrison (2013) mentioned that crowdfunding can be seen as a mixture of microfinance and crowdsourcing. Schwienbacher and Larralde (2012) even defined crowdfunding as a specific form of crowdsourcing. Estellés-Arolas and González-Ladrón-de-Guevara (2012) undertook a survey of definitions of crowdsourcing provided in academic research. As a conclusion of their work, they provided a definition of crowdsourcing that shares strong similarities with crowdfunding. An important element of their definition is the dimension of partnering with the aim of achieving some mutual benefit. Of course, this may include the provision of financial help, which is close to crowdfunding. However, here we want to go beyond the common financial aspects between the two practices and focus on sharing nonmonetary elements such as ideas and providing advice. This will shed light on other ways in which crowdfunding can contribute to the innovation process. We discuss this in the next subsection.

4.3 The Contribution of Crowdfunding to the Innovation Process

The fact that crowdfunding involves an *open call* affects the relationship between investors and entrepreneurs. First of all, in the case of reward-based crowdfunding, this open call yields an imprecise assessment of the future demand because the interest for the reward (which is generally the final product) during the campaign can provide a hint on the success of the product in the aftermarket. Thus, pledges by the crowd lead to an aggregation of individual preferences. A high demand during the campaign may indicate the entrepreneur's project is promising beyond the crowdfunding campaign. Drover *et al.* (2017) cited a venture capitalist offering a similar view: "If crowdfunding is coming from potential customers it can be a reasonable signal of demand." This is particularly true for reward-based crowdfunding where funding may resemble pre-ordering of the product (Mollick, 2014), but not for loan-based and equity crowdfunding (Schwienbacher, 2017). Indeed, in these latter forms of crowdfunding, backers do not make consumption decisions but rather investment decisions based on their expectations about the startup's profitability, that is, the same criteria as professional investors (Cholakova and Clarysse, 2015; Vismara, 2016; Davis *et al.*, 2017). Thus, the assessment of future demand is likely to be more precise under reward-based crowdfunding. This feedback can be useful to the entrepreneur to decide whether to pursue the project or to adapt his or her strategy, including innovation strategy. The quality of the feedback is even greater if the entrepreneur offers a menu of reward choices in which crowdfunders can choose what they prefer best (this product differentiation can be vertical – in terms of different qualities – or horizontal – in terms of differences in properties such as colors and forms).

Another type of feedback provided by crowdfunders to entrepreneurs takes the form of ideas. Stanko and Henard (2017) and Di Pietro *et al.* (2018) pointed out that the interaction with investors can contribute to the generation and development of new ideas and thus the innovation process. A larger number of backers brings more information, resources, and ideas to mobilize for the development of innovation. Backers can thereby bring *inputs* to entrepreneurs. In this context, Agrawal *et al.* (2014) mentioned the example of the Pebble watch, where crowdfunders have proposed the development of software that can be used with the watch. This software enhances the product and its value to consumers, leading to a true collaboration in the development of the product. This holds for reward-based and equity crowdfunding and perhaps also loan-based crowdfunding because contributors to these crowdfunding forms have an incentive to see the project succeed and are therefore more likely to suggest improvements. Crowdfunders can provide such feedback at any stage of development, although it is perhaps more valuable at a more advanced stage of development when the level of abstraction is reduced (Huizing, 2011). At the time of the campaign, the degree of interaction is however largely determined by the way the crowdfunding platform enables such interactions, irrespective of the type of crowdfunding. Although some platforms restrict the posting of comments at the time a pledge is made, others allow anyone (even those not contributing financially to the project) to post comments. Crowdfunding platforms typically offer ways for entrepreneurs and crowdfunders to interact during the campaign so that this exchange of ideas is possible. However, this may continue beyond the campaign if the entrepreneurs set up own ways to maintain such interactions.

Feedback can also flow the other way from entrepreneurs to investors. Colombo and Shafi (2016) stressed the importance of managerial competencies in innovative firms. These abilities play a major role in the relationship between the startup and investors. As argued by these authors, an open call to the crowd and the dissemination of information on the project can help to better assess the managerial competencies of the entrepreneur, for instance, by observing whether the entrepreneur meets the deadline for delivering the product promised during the reward-based crowdfunding campaign. It also provides information on the capacity of the entrepreneur to convince consumers to purchase the product in the future. Some managerial capacity can also be inferred from equity crowdfunding, because achieving a successful campaign means the entrepreneur has developed a business that is more developed than running a simple project (as is often the case under reward-based crowdfunding). Moreover, many equity crowdfunding platforms offer other expertise, because they carefully select the best projects while at the same time help entrepreneurs structure their firm and prepare it for the campaign. All these managerial competencies are useful and affect how the innovative projects will be managed and developed.

Additional benefits of crowdfunding can come from the ability to develop relationships with other stakeholders. Mollick and Kuppuswamy (2016) reported survey evidence that reward-based crowdfunding helps to find business partners in the industry, recruit talented employees, and enhance the attention of the media/press to the firm. Di Pietro *et al.* (2018) obtained similar survey-based results for equity crowdfunding. They argued that the development of partnerships with industry players, the increased awareness of the venture, and the capacity to attract new employees are all improved thanks to the crowd investors' network. They found that firms exploiting their crowd for such network aspects realized better performance than other firms. This, in turn, suggests that crowdfunding, by way of network development, can play a major role in fostering innovation.

A last characteristic of crowdfunding that can affect the innovation process is based on the way crowdfunders themselves diffuse the information on the project. Crowdfunders may act as ambassadors for promoting the product (Schwienbacher and Larralde, 2012). Such diffusion of information represents a form of "word-of-mouth," which has been shown to be a useful tool in marketing (Kozinets *et al.*, 2010) and in finance (Hong *et al.*, 2005). Several studies have further shown the usefulness of using social networks by entrepreneurs for their crowdfunding campaigns (Ahlers *et al.*, 2015; Buttice *et al.*, 2017). Crowdfunders are then helpful in diffusing the information and letting others know about the product, notably by using their own social networks during and after the campaign. This could facilitate the creation of knowledge and the adoption of new products and services, thereby promoting innovation. Here again, the type of crowdfunding probably does not matter so much because all types induce crowdfunders to use word-of-mouth. The extent to which these arguments are true in practice, however, still needs to be researched.

Despite all these potential benefits, crowdfunding can also hinder the development of innovative projects. One obstacle is that the information and feedback obtained by the entrepreneur from the crowd may become excessive, requiring too much involvement of the entrepreneur into time-consuming activities associated with interacting with the crowd (Agrawal *et al.*, 2014; Brown *et al.*, 2018). This may eventually slow down the entrepreneur. Indeed, the entrepreneur cannot always ignore feedback from the crowd since otherwise, the crowd's view about the project may turn against the entrepreneur and then lead to negative postings on the Internet. Wortham (2012) cited an entrepreneur, who said: "We wanted to make it because it was something we believed in, but we got roped into maintaining a relationship with a lot of people. We weren't prepared to have to deal with that." A second possible obstacle could be the crowd itself, especially if highly diverse (Agrawal *et al.*, 2014; Brown *et al.*, 2018). Entrepreneurs are not always good at coordinating a large number of individuals and thus can end up with contradictory feedback, which can then lead to more uncertainty and again slow down the project's innovation progress.

4.4 *Types of Crowdfunding and Innovation*

We have argued in the previous subsection that crowdfunding has the capacity to help entrepreneurs to innovate by means of both financial and nonfinancial contributions. This however raises the question as to which type of innovation is most likely to benefit from crowdfunding. A commonly used classification of innovation consists in distinguishing between two broad types: incremental and radical innovation (Dewar and Dutton, 1986). Incremental innovation involves improvement or simple adjustment of an existing product or service, whereas radical innovation represents a fundamental transformation of a product or service so that existing products become obsolete.

Two distinct perspectives support the idea that crowdfunding can help these two types of innovation in entrepreneurial firms in distinct ways. First, from the point of view of the consumer, Chan and Parhankangas (2017) considered incremental innovation and presented the following arguments. For the consumer, incremental innovation is more familiar and easier to adopt than radical innovation, which then reduces the consumer's fear for the product's success because less effort to adopt and use it is required. Moreover, a project with incremental innovation may appear easier to implement and thus less risky for the consumer to fund through crowdfunding. Finally, the consumer can more easily provide valuable feedback to the entrepreneur if the innovation is incremental, because assessment requires less knowledge than for radical innovation. All these elements lead to the view that crowdfunders, when being put in the context of consumption, are more likely to fund projects with incremental innovation. Furthermore, an analysis of radical innovation leads to a similar conclusion. Radical innovation is more difficult to understand as it requires specific knowledge, and thus consumers find it more difficult to assess the benefits. Also, given the knowledge needed to appreciate the true value of this type of innovation, it involves more risk and makes interactions with consumers more difficult. This in turn leads to the view that radical innovations are more difficult to crowdfund. Following this consumer perspective (Priem, 2007), it therefore seems that although crowdfunders can provide financial and nonfinancial help, their support is more likely for projects with incremental innovation.

This conclusion may be changed or even reversed if one takes the point of view of the entrepreneur, which represents the second perspective. Davis *et al.* (2017) argued that the level of creativity of the proposed product plays a key role in the competitive advantage of the entrepreneur. These authors developed a measure of creativity which is close to a measure of product innovativeness because it was evaluated with questionnaires asking consumers about the product's degree of originality and "newness." The degree of creativity was seen by consumers as a predictor of the performance of the product on the market. The authors empirically found a positive link between campaign success and product creativity. In this case, crowdfunding favors the highest possible level of innovation, which is the radical one. Stanko and Henard (2017) considered openness in the innovation process and argued that if crowdfunders provided a greater amount of information and ideas and given more sources of external knowledge, then the level of innovation would be increased. This aspect largely compensates for the complexity mentioned above of aggregating the information obtained. Stanko and Henard

(2017) validated the positive effect of the number of external sources on radical innovation through an empirical study on reward-based crowdfunding. The authors did not exclude however that equity crowdfunding may show different effects, because projects funded in this way are quite different.

Finally, the type of innovation featured on the different types of crowdfunding platforms largely results from the fact that equity crowdfunding tends to represent a longer-term investment than reward-based crowdfunding, which assumes that the entrepreneur is able to ship the promised reward within the next few months. Therefore, the entrepreneur needs to be sure to have the product soon ready under reward-based crowdfunding; otherwise, reputational costs may arise for the entrepreneur and hurt him/her in the aftermarket. This may, in turn, reduce the entrepreneur's capacity to pursue radical innovation, because it requires more time. In contrast, investors participating in an equity crowdfunding campaign need to understand that the funds are allocated on a project that will not yield any return in the short run. Thus, an entrepreneur interested in undertaking radical innovation will favor equity crowdfunding.

4.5 *Necessary Conditions for the Development of Innovation*

For crowdfunding to contribute to innovation, it is important to ensure that the campaigns allocate funds in an efficient way and, in particular, to the most promising projects. To ensure this is the case, platforms may need to take an active role by selecting those projects that are most likely to be funded, filtering out the "lemons," and making sure that projects are properly presented. Although reward-based crowdfunding platforms typically filter very little, equity crowdfunding platforms are highly selective. For example, Hornuf and Schwienbacher (2018a) indicated that German equity crowdfunding platforms have an acceptance rate below 5%. Similar rates are reported for France (Hervé *et al.*, 2017). Some equity crowdfunding platforms give the crowd further roles beyond financing projects. These platforms let their registered members vote on projects, and only those with sufficient positive votes and precommitments to invest may launch a campaign (Cumming *et al.*, 2017). One such example is the French equity crowdfunding platform WiSEED. Cumming *et al.* (2017), however, documented that voters are subject to a strong hypothetical bias, because they actually invest only 18% of what they said they would during the voting period.

This further raises questions about the determinants of campaign success. Although we still know very little about the ultimate outcome of crowdfunded projects and the businesses themselves, there exists a significant strand of literature on success drivers of campaigns. Ahlers *et al.* (2015) and Mollick (2014) identified a number of factors that contribute to the success of a campaign, including the entrepreneur's human capital (education level), social capital (size of social network on Facebook and LinkedIn), and intellectual capital (patents). Other relevant factors that are more exogenous to the project itself include the way projects are presented by the entrepreneur and how the platform manages these interactions (Hornuf and Schwienbacher, 2018b). Mollick (2014) showed that including a video that presents the project and the quality of the pitch increase the chances of success. Hornuf and Schwienbacher (2018a) and Block *et al.* (2018b) found that the updates posted by the entrepreneurs and comments posted by the crowd on the platform play a significant role in explaining the success of a campaign. Allison *et al.* (2013) empirically validated these results regarding the rhetoric of the project presentation. Moreover, the platform's marketing effort matters; specific projects highlighted and presented first by the platform on their website ultimately perform better. Although the selection of these projects is not random, it nevertheless gives a role to the platform in promoting individual projects and thereby the innovation outcome of the selected projects.

As mentioned above, a question much less studied deals with the outcome of projects beyond the campaign. One reason is the lack of data, whereas another is the fact that most campaigns are very recent, which makes it often too early to make a judgment about outcomes. This latter reason is particularly true for equity crowdfunding. One of the few exceptions is the study by Signori and Vismara (2016), who examined this question with data from the equity crowdfunding platform Crowdcube. Their results rely however on some strong assumptions. Difficulties in performing such an analysis today include the lack of a secondary market (although a value may be attached to shares of crowdfunded businesses, it remains difficult to sell at any price currently) and the fact that most equity crowdfunded business have not experienced any exit in the form of an initial public offering or being bought by another firm, so that it is still challenging to assess true market values. In any case, studying the question of long-term performance is crucial, not just for the viability of the crowdfunding market itself but also for assessing the impact of crowdfunding on innovation.

5. Conclusions

Crowdfunding appears to offer new financing opportunities to certain types of small, innovative firms. As such, crowdfunding plays a role in filling the funding gap traditionally identified for small businesses. Therefore, it may contribute to the development of innovation in small firms. However, the contribution of crowdfunding to innovation may not be limited to the provision of financial resources. It can also let backers participate in the development of the innovation process by providing feedback and ideas to the entrepreneur. Although research has started to investigate these interactions, whether they ultimately affect the innovation process remains to be studied in more detail.

Agrawal et al. (2014) raised the question as to whether crowdfunding will eventually increase the number and types of innovation. The answer to this important question is complex and is inevitably related to the question if crowdfunding is complementary to other sources of finance and not simply a substitute for them. Research on this question remains inconclusive, but, as discussed in this paper, initial evidence suggests complementarities exist. In terms of types of innovation, the answer is even more difficult, because it is impossible to know the strategies that entrepreneurs would have taken under each of the financing sources. However, because the crowd is likely to make different choices than professional investors, one might expect different types of innovation projects to be funded by the two groups. Also, it remains unclear whether the crowd is better at selecting the most promising projects than professional investors, in particular when it comes to innovation-driven projects. This, in turn, will affect the type of innovation financed by crowdfunding as compared to what professional investors are likely to finance. Further research is needed to offer more reliable answers to these questions. In parallel, crowdfunding will continue to evolve and adapt to improve its operation, including regarding the way projects are selected.

Another open question is which forms of crowdfunding are more likely to spur innovation. Our discussion does not offer a final answer, because it largely depends also on the perspective taken (consumer or entrepreneur). This provides great opportunities for future research in that area. For instance, although the interaction between entrepreneur and crowdfunders has been partially studied (e.g., its impact on campaign outcomes and funding dynamics within campaigns; Block et al., 2018b; Hornuf and Schwienbacher, 2018a), the analysis of the interactions that occur between the two parties during the campaign clearly merits further research, especially concerning the impact on innovation. Content analysis may provide rich insights into how the interactions take place and the value of the discussions, as well as their impact on the innovation process and dynamics.

Finally, an interesting avenue for future research is the role of regulation. As mentioned in this paper, many countries have implemented specific regulations on equity crowdfunding, and we observe a large disparity in approaches to the regulation of equity crowdfunding. Part of this disparity is probably due to different political-economic approaches (some countries consider that the state has an important role to play, whereas others favor some form of laissez-faire). Other reasons for this disparity may be due to different economic structures, which make some countries more prone to promote entrepreneurial activities than others. This may explain why platforms may be more popular in some countries than others. What remains to be seen is which regulatory approaches are more conducive to promote innovation through the different channels studied in this paper.

Notes

1. More recently, real-estate crowdfunding has emerged, offering the possibility to fund large real-estate projects.
2. Hornuf and Schwienbacher (2016) pointed out that some startups have been able to raise several million euros on equity crowdfunding platforms in Germany. The amounts can therefore be at times comparable with those provided by venture capital funds.

References

Agrawal, A., Catalini, C. and Goldfarb, A. (2014) Some simple economics of crowdfunding. *Innovation Policy and the Economy* 14(1): 63–97.

Agrawal, A., Catalini, C. and Goldfarb, A. (2015) Crowdfunding: Geography, social networks, and the timing of investment decisions. *Journal of Economics & Management Strategy* 24(2): 253–274.

Ahlers, G.K., Cumming, D., Günther, C. and Schweizer, D. (2015) Signaling in equity crowdfunding. *Entrepreneurship Theory and Practice* 39(4): 955–980.

Akerlof, G.A. (1970) The market for "lemons": quality uncertainty and the market mechanism. *Quarterly Journal of Economics* 84(3): 488–500.

Allen, F., et Santomero, A.M. (2001) What do financial intermediaries do? *Journal of Banking & Finance* 25(2): 271–294.

Allison, T.H., McKenny, A.F. and Short, J.C. (2013) The effect of entrepreneurial rhetoric on microlending investment: An examination of the warm-glow effect. *Journal of Business Venturing* 28(6): 690–707.

Allison, T.H., Davis, B.C., Short, J.C. and Webb, J.W. (2015) Crowdfunding in a prosocial microlending environment: examining the role of intrinsic versus extrinsic cues. *Entrepreneurship Theory and Practice* 39(1): 53–73.

Arrow, K.J. (1962) Economic welfare and the allocation of resources for invention. In *The Rate and Direction of Inventive Activity: Economic and Social Factors* (pp. 609–626). Princeton, NJ: Princeton University Press.

Bapna, S. (2017) Complementarity of signals in early stage equity investment decisions: evidence from a randomized field experiment. *Management Science*, forthcoming, https://doi.org/10.1287/mnsc.2017.2833.

Belleflamme, P., Lambert, T. and Schwienbacher, A. (2013) Individual crowdfunding practices. *Venture Capital: An International Journal of Entrepreneurial Finance* 15 (4 – Special Issue): 313–333.

Belleflamme, P., Lambert, T. and Schwienbacher, A. (2014) Crowdfunding: Tapping the right crowd. *Journal of Business Venturing* 29(5), 585–609.

Benson, D. and Ziedonis, R.H. (2009) Corporate venture capital as a window on new technologies: implications for the performance of corporate investors when acquiring startups. *Organization Science* 20(2): 329–351.

Berger, A.N. and Udell, G.F. (1998) The economics of small business finance: the roles of private equity and debt markets in the financial growth cycle. *Journal of Banking & Finance* 22(6): 613–673.

Block, J.H., Colombo, M.G., Cumming, D.J. and Vismara, S. (2018a) New players in entrepreneurial finance and why they are there. *Small Business Economics* 50: 239–250.

Block, J., Hornuf, L. and Moritz, A. (2018b) Which updates during an equity crowdfunding campaign increase crowd participation? *Small Business Economics* 50(1): 3–27.

Bollaert, H., Leboeuf, G. and Schwienbacher, A. (2017) The narcissism of crowdfunding entrepreneurs. Working Paper, SKEMA Business School.

Boot, A. and Thakor, A.V. (2000) Can relationship banking survive competition? *Journal of Finance* 55(2): 679–713.

Brown, R., Mawson, S., Rowe, A. and Mason, C. (2018) Working the crowd: improvisational entrepreneurship and equity crowdfunding in nascent entrepreneurial ventures. *International Small Business Journal* 36(2): 169–193.

Butticè, V., Colombo, M.G. and Wright, M. (2017) Serial crowdfunding, social capital, and project success. *Entrepreneurship Theory and Practice* 41(2): 183–207.

Carpenter, R.E. and Petersen, B.C. (2002) Is the growth of small firms constrained by internal finance? *Review of Economics and Statistics* 84(2): 298–309.

Catalini, Ch., Fazio, C. and Murray, F. (2016) Can equity crowdfunding democratize access to capital and investment opportunities? MIT Innovation Initiative, Lab for Innovation Science and Policy Report.

Chan, C.S. and Parhankangas, A. (2017) Crowdfunding innovative ideas: how incremental and radical innovativeness influence funding outcomes. *Entrepreneurship Theory and Practice* 41(2): 237–263.

Cholakova, M. and Clarysse, B. (2015) Does the possibility to make equity investments in crowdfunding projects crowd out reward-based investments? *Entrepreneurship Theory and Practice* 39(1): 145–172.

Colombo, M.G., Franzoni, C. and Rossi-Lamastra, C. (2015) Internal social capital and the attraction of early contributions in crowdfunding. *Entrepreneurship Theory and Practice* 39(1): 75–100.

Colombo, M.G. and Shafi, K. (2016) Does crowdfunding help firms obtain venture capital and angel finance? ENTFIN Conference, Lyon, July 2016, available at www.em-lyon.com/minisiteen/ReCEntFin/ENTFIN-Conference-2016/Papers.

Cooter, R. and Edlin, A. (2013) The double trust dilemma: combining ideas and capital. In R. Cooter (ed.), *The Falcon's Gyre: Legal Foundations of Economic Innovation and Growth* (pp. 3.1–3.18). California: Berkeley Law Books.

Cosh, A., Cumming, D. and Hughes, A. (2009) Outside entrepreneurial capital. *Economic Journal* 119(540): 1494–1533.

Cressy, R. (2002) Introduction: funding gaps: a symposium. *Economic Journal* 112(477): F1–F16.

Cumming, D.J., Hervé, F., Manthé, E., Schwienbacher, A. (2017) The information content of non-binding investment commitments: lessons from equity crowdfunding. Working Paper, https://doi.org/10.2139/ssrn.3114526.

Cumming, D.J., Leboeuf, G. and Schwienbacher, A. (2016) Crowdfunding models: keep-it-all vs. all-or-nothing. https://papers.ssrn.com/abstract=2447567 (accessed on September 30, 2017).

Da Rin, M., Hellmann, T.F. and Puri, M. (2011) A survey of venture capital research. NBER Working Paper No. 17523, National Bureau of Economic Research.

Dahiya, S. and Ray, K. (2012) Staged investments in entrepreneurial financing. *Journal of Corporate Finance* 18(5): 1193–1216.

Davis, B.C., Hmieleski, K.M., Webb, J.W. and Coombs, J.E. (2017) Funders' positive affective reactions to entrepreneurs' crowdfunding pitches: the influence of perceived product creativity and entrepreneurial passion. *Journal of Business Venturing* 32(1): 90–106.

Dewar, R.D. and Dutton, J.E. (1986) The adoption of radical and incremental innovations: an empirical analysis. *Management Science* 32(11): 1422–1433.

Di Pietro, F., Prencipe, A. and Majchrzak, A. (2018) Crowd equity investors: an underutilized asset for open innovation in startups. *California Management Review* 60(2): 43–70.

Drover, W., Wood, M.S. and Zacharakis, A. (2017) Attributes of angel and crowdfunded investments as determinants of VC screening decisions. *Entrepreneurship Theory and Practice* 41(3): 323–347.

Dushnitsky, G., Guerini, M., Piva, E. and Rossi-Lamastra, C. (2016) Crowdfunding in Europe: determinants of platform creation across countries. *California Management Review* 58(2): 44–71.

Estellés-Arolas, E. and González-Ladrón-de-Guevara, F. (2012) Towards an integrated crowdsourcing definition. *Journal of Information Science* 38(2): 189–200.

Evans, D.S. (2011) Platform economics: essays on multi-sided businesses. *Competition Policy International*. http://ssrn.com/abstract=1974020.

Galton, F. (1907) Vox populi (The wisdom of crowds). *Nature* 75(7): 450–451.

Gilbert, B.A., McDougall, P.P. and Audretsch, D.B. (2006) New venture growth: a review and extension. *Journal of Management* 32(6): 926–950.

Greenberg, J. and Mollick, E. (2017) Activist choice homophily and the crowdfunding of female founders. *Administrative Science Quarterly* 62(2): 341–374.

Harrison, R. (2013) Crowdfunding and the revitalisation of the early stage risk capital market: catalyst or chimera? *Venture Capital: An International Journal of Entrepreneurial Finance* 15(4): 283–287.

Hervé, F., Manthé, E., Sannajust, A. and Schwienbacher, A. (2017) Determinants of individual investment decisions in investment-based crowdfunding. https://ssrn.com/abstract=2746398 (accessed on September 27, 2017).

Hildebrand, T., Puri, M. and Rocholl, J. (2016) Adverse incentives in crowdfunding. *Management Science* 63(3): 587–608.

Hong, H., Kubik, J.D. and Stein, J.C. (2005) Thy neighbor's portfolio: word-of-mouth effects in the holdings and trades of money managers. *Journal of Finance* 60(6): 2801–2824.

Hornuf, L. and Schwienbacher, A. (2016) Crowdinvesting – Angel investing for the masses? In C. Mason and H. Landström (eds.), *Handbook of Research on Business Angels*, (pp. 381–397). Edward Elgar Publishing.

Hornuf, L. and Schwienbacher, A. (2017a) Should securities regulation promote equity crowdfunding? *Small Business Economics* 49(3): 579–593.

Hornuf, L. and Schwienbacher, A. (2018a) Market mechanisms and funding dynamics in equity crowdfunding. *Journal of Corporate Finance* 50: 556–574.

Hornuf, L. and Schwienbacher, A. (2018b) *Internet-Based Entrepreneurial Finance: Lessons from Germany*. California: Management Review. https://doi.org/10.1177/0008125617741126 (accessed on September 28, 2017).

Huizingh, E.K. (2011) Open innovation: State of the art and future perspectives. *Technovation* 31(1): 2–9.

King, R.G. and Levine, R. (1993) Finance and growth: Schumpeter might be right. *Quarterly Journal of Economics* 108(3): 717–737.

Kortum, S. & Lerner, J. (2000) Assessing the impact of venture capital on innovation. *Rand Journal of Economics* 31(4): 674–692.

Kozinets, R.V., De Valck, K., Wojnicki, A.C. and Wilner, S.J. (2010) Networked narratives: understanding word-of-mouth marketing in online communities. *Journal of Marketing* 74(2): 71–89.

Kuppuswamy, V. and Bayus, B.L. (2017) Does my contribution to your crowdfunding project matter? *Journal of Business Venturing* 32(1): 72–89.

Larrick, R.P., Mannes, A.E. and Soll, J.B. (2011) The social psychology of the wisdom of crowds. In Joachim I. Krueger (ed.), *Frontiers in Social Psychology: Social Judgment and Decision Making* (pp. 227–242). New York: Psychology Press.

Leboeuf, G. and Schwienbacher, A. (2018) Crowdfunding as a new financing tool. In D. Cumming and L. Hornuf (ed.), *The Economics of Crowdfunding — Startups, Portals and Investor Behavior* (pp. 11–28). Palgrave Macmillan.

Lee, N., Sameen, H. and Cowling, M. (2015) Access to finance for innovative SMEs since the financial crisis. *Research Policy* 44(2): 370–380.

Leung, M.D. and Sharkey, A.J. (2014) Out of sight, out of mind? Evidence of perceptual factors in the multiple-category discount. *Organization Science* 25(1): 171–184.

Lin, M., Prabhala, N.R. and Viswanathan, S. (2013) Judging borrowers by the company they keep: friendship networks and information asymmetry in online peer-to-peer lending. *Management Science* 59(1): 17–35.

Lin, M. and Viswanathan, S. (2015) Home bias in online investments: an empirical study of an online crowdfunding market. *Management Science* 62(5): 1393–1414.

Marom, D., Robb, A. and Sade, O. (2016) Gender dynamics in crowdfunding (Kickstarter): evidence on entrepreneurs, investors, deals and taste-based discrimination. https://ssrn.com/abstract=2442954.

Maxwell, A.L., Jeffrey, S.A. and Lévesque, M. (2011) Business angel early stage decision making. *Journal of Business Venturing* 26(2): 212–225.

McKenny, A.F., Allison, T.H., Ketchen, D.J., Short, J.C. and Ireland, R.D. (2017) How should crowdfunding research evolve? A survey of the *Entrepreneurship Theory and Practice* editorial board. *Entrepreneurship Theory and Practice* 41(2): 291–304.

Mollick, E. (2014) The dynamics of crowdfunding: an exploratory study. *Journal of Business Venturing* 29(1): 1–16.

Mollick, E. and Nanda, R. (2015) Wisdom or madness? Comparing crowds with expert evaluation in funding the arts. *Management Science* 62(6): 1533–1553.

Mollick, E. and Kuppuswamy, V. (2016) Crowdfunding: evidence on the democratization of startup funding. In Dieter Harhoff and Karim Lakhani (eds.), *Revolutionizing Innovation: Users, Communities, and Open Innovation* (pp. 537–559). Cambridge, MA: MIT Press.

Moss, T.W., Neubaum, D.O. and Meyskens, M. (2015) The effect of virtuous and entrepreneurial orientations on microfinance lending and repayment: a signaling theory perspective. *Entrepreneurship Theory and Practice* 39: 27–52.

Myers, S.C. (1984) The capital structure puzzle. *Journal of Finance* 39(3): 574–592.

Paravisini, D., Rappoport, V. and Ravina, E. (2016) Risk aversion and wealth: evidence from person-to-person lending portfolios. *Management Science* 63(2): 279–297.

Pope, D.G. and Sydnor, J.R. (2011) What's in a Picture? Evidence of discrimination from prosper.com. *Journal of Human Resources* 46(1): 53–92.

Priem, R.L. (2007) A consumer perspective on value creation. *Academy of Management Review* 32(1): 219–235.

Rau, P.R. (2017) Law, trust, and the development of crowdfunding. https://ssrn.com/abstract=2989056 (accessed on March 5, 2018).

Schumpeter, J.A. (1912) *Theorie der wirtschaftlichen Entwicklung*. Leipzig: Duncker & Humblot. English translation published in 1934 by Harvard University Press as The theory of economic development.

Schwienbacher, A. (2017) Entrepreneurial risk-taking in crowdfunding campaigns. *Small Business Economics*, forthcoming.

Schwienbacher, A. and Larralde, B. (2012) Crowdfunding of small entrepreneurial ventures. In Douglas Cumming (ed.) *The Oxford Handbook of Entrepreneurial Finance* (pp. 369–391). Oxford University Press.

Short, J.C., Ketchen, D.J., McKenny, A.F., Allison, T.H. and Ireland, R.D. (2017) Research on crowd-funding: reviewing the (very recent) past and celebrating the present. *Entrepreneurship Theory and Practice* 41(2): 149–160.

Signori, A. and Vismara, S. (2016) Returns on investments in equity crowdfunding. https://ssrn.com/abstract=2765488 (accessed on September 25, 2017).

Sorenson, O., Assenova, V., Li, G.C., Boada, J. and Fleming, L. (2016) Expand innovation finance via crowdfunding. *Science* 354(6319): 1526–1528.

Stanko, M.A. and Henard, D.H. (2017) Toward a better understanding of crowdfunding, openness and the consequences for innovation. *Research Policy* 46(4): 784–798.

Strausz, R. (2017) A theory of crowdfunding: a mechanism design approach with demand uncertainty and moral hazard. *American Economic Review* 107(6): 1430–1476.

Surowiecki, J. (2004) The wisdom of crowds: Why the many are smarter than the few and how collective wisdom shapes business. Economies, Societies and Nations 296.

Vismara, S. (2016) Information cascades among investors in equity crowdfunding. *Entrepreneurship Theory and Practice*, forthcoming.

Wong, A., Bhatia, M. and Freeman, Z. (2009) Angel finance: the other venture capital. *Strategic Change* 18(7–8): 221–230.

Wortham, J. (2012) Success of crowdfunding puts pressure on entrepreneurs. *New York Times*, September 17.

Younkin, P. and Kuppuswamy, V. (2017) The colorblind crowd? Founder race and performance in crowd-funding. *Management Science*, forthcoming.

Yu, S., Johnson, S., Lai, C., Cricelli, A. and Fleming, L. (2017) Crowdfunding and regional entrepreneurial investment: an application of the CrowdBerkeley database. *Research Policy* 46(10): 1723–1737.

12

CRYPTO-CURRENCIES – AN INTRODUCTION TO NOT-SO-FUNNY MONEYS

Christie Smith

Reserve Bank of New Zealand

Aaron Kumar

KPMG New Zealand

1. Introduction

This paper provides an introduction to the distributed ledger technology of crypto-currencies. We aim to develop greater public understanding of these technologies, highlight some of the risks involved in using crypto-currencies and discuss some of the potential implications of these technologies for payments systems, financial institutions, markets and regulators.

In Section 2, we provide a brief background discussion of payment mechanisms and describe crypto-currencies in general. We describe the growth of crypto-currencies and the proliferation of new variants. To facilitate understanding of the mechanics of crypto-currencies, we conclude the section by discussing how transactions proceed in Bitcoin, the original and most widely transacted crypto-currency. In Section 3, we examine the 'monetary' properties of crypto-currencies and consider some common uses. We also illustrate some scalability problems that crypto-currencies face by comparing them to the electronic transactions facilitated by traditional financial institutions. We close the section by describing some of the literature on the empirical properties of crypto-currencies (primarily focusing on Bitcoin). In Section 4, we touch on the implications that crypto-currencies have for traditional financial systems, monetary policy and financial regulation. In relation to these issues we draw on work by central banks and international institutions. We then conclude in Section 5.

Contemporary Topics in Finance: A Collection of Literature Surveys, First Edition. Edited by Iris Claus and Leo Krippner.
Chapters © 2019 The Authors. Book compilation © 2019 John Wiley & Sons Ltd. Published 2019 by John Wiley & Sons Ltd.

2. Payment/Exchange Mechanisms

2.1 *Background Context*

The central role of the financial system is to facilitate the exchange of goods and services, through time and space. The financial system contains a diverse range of institutions and mechanisms for enabling such transactions. To provide context for our discussion of crypto-currencies, we briefly discuss three payment mechanisms: (i) legal tender, (ii) e-payments and (iii) e-money.[1]

Legal tender is a payment mechanism recognized by the legal system that can used to extinguish debts in the same units.[2] Typically, the notes and coins issued by a central bank serve as legal tender, which creditors must accept in payment for an outstanding obligation de-nominated in the same currency. For example, a 10 dollar note issued by the Reserve Bank of New Zealand represents 10 New Zealand dollars and can be offered to settle a debt of the same value. Currencies established by government fiat are enduringly useful because they can be used to settle tax obligations – debts to the government.

It should be noted that legal tender does not necessarily need to be used to settle a contract: two parties may stipulate the 'consideration' that will be provided as part of a contractual agreement. For example, it may be agreed that one good or service will be exchanged for another in a barter-type arrangement. Conversely, some firms exclude certain payment mech-anisms. New Zealand corner stores, for example routinely prohibit the use of credit cards, while nevertheless accepting debit cards.

In modern economies, most transactions are conducted via e-payments rather than physical currency. Most e-payments are electronic transfers from deposit and credit accounts facilitated by financial institutions such as commercial banks and credit card companies. These financial institutions use private electronic networks and their own private account ledgers to record account balances that keep track of individuals' purchasing power.

Box 1. Terminology

- Digital currencies represent value electronically. They may or may not be denominated in legal tender.
- Virtual currencies are digital money but are not denominated in units of legal tender.
- Convertible currencies can be converted or exchanged for other currencies if a counter-party can be found.
- Decentralized currencies do not have a central counter-party responsible for the provision of the currency.
- Decentralized ledger technology refers to ledgers that are stored across multiple com-puters, where such computers may be controlled by different people or firms.
- Crypto-currencies are decentralized currencies that use cryptography to secure transac-tions and validate balances.
- Permissioned ledgers restrict the agents able to amend (and possibly view) the ledger of transactions.
- Permissionless ledgers are open-access; all agents can read and, under certain conditions, update such ledgers.

E-money, the third transaction medium mentioned above, is a medium of exchange in which monetary value is stored on hardware or software, enabling people to pay for goods and services bought from third-party merchants (Bank of Canada, 2014b).[3] Contact-less smart cards, such as 'Snapper' cards in Wellington New Zealand and 'Octopus' cards in Hong Kong, are examples of e-money. These cards can be variously used to pay for public transportation, parking metres, taxis, tolls and other retail transactions.[4] E-money does not usually entail a physical exchange of goods. Instead, the e-money device keeps track of a balance of funds that can be used to purchase goods and services.

E-money can be partitioned into two distinct categories: centralized and decentralized. Centralized e-money relies on a central institution – such as Snapper or Octopus – to administer the issuance of the e-money and the facilitation of transactions. Decentralized e-money brings us to the realm of crypto-currencies. (See Box 1 for a brief summary of terminology.)

2.2 What are Crypto-Currencies? How Do They Work?

Crypto-currencies rely on cryptography to facilitate and record transactions on a set of electronic ledgers – databases of financial accounts. Crypto-currencies have no tangible existence, rather they are electronic signals and records that keep track of transactions mediated with the currency. Given their electronic representation, crypto-currencies are also referred to as 'digital' or 'virtual' currencies, though distinctions can be made between all three. See ECB (2012), He *et al.* (2016), and Box 1. The prefix crypto, meaning 'concealed' or 'secret', is derived from the Greek word $\kappa\rho\upsilon\pi\tau\acute{o}\zeta$ meaning hidden. While cryptography is used to secure both individual transactions and the ledger of individual accounts, more properly 'addresses', the ledgers that record all transactions are usually in plain view to everyone who is interested in them. Nevertheless, address owners achieve a degree of anonymity as there is no central authority, such as a bank, tying a particular address to a particular individual.

Like traditional currencies, such as dollar notes or gold coins, crypto-currencies can be used to facilitate 'peer-to-peer' transactions between individuals without the services of a specific financial intermediary. In contrast to commodity currencies such as gold, crypto-currencies, fiat currencies, and bank deposits have no secondary, non-monetary purpose. People transacting using these modern currencies believe that other people will accept them for future transactions and that such currencies will therefore be useful as a temporary store of value. Although crypto-currencies often have no centralized issuer, they are predominantly fiduciary in the sense that they are not backed by precious metal, and require *trust*.[5]

White (2015) refers to crypto-currencies as *competing private irredeemable monies*. Irredeemable crypto-currencies stand in contrast to redeemable private monies, such as bank deposits. With the latter, an issuing bank denominates deposits in fiat currency units and promises to convert or redeem them one-for-one for fiat currency, either on demand or at maturity. Crypto-currencies are not backed by the promises of a similar institution and they are usually denominated in their own units. Bank deposits are liabilities for commercial banks and as such have a well-established place in the accounting and auditing frameworks that banks must legally satisfy as incorporated entities.[6] In contrast, crypto-currencies are not a liability of any given institution, and are not subject to the same accounting scrutiny and assurance.

Decentralized crypto-currencies are designed to facilitate transactions without recourse to a central institution. This decentralization is achieved through the invention of the 'blockchain' – a universal distributed ledger that enables the confirmation of transactions and makes it possible to keep track of individual crypto-currency balances. A distributed ledger is a database of financial records 'distributed' across multiple nodes of a computer network. In the current context a node is a computer attached to the Internet. No single entity, such as a bank, is solely responsible for maintaining the nodes and ledgers.[7]

The ledgers contain a list of *all* transactions previously enabled via the digital currency in the order in which they were undertaken. The ledgers implicitly record the balances of all people using the crypto-currency, ensuring that people cannot spend currency they have not previously earned or obtained. The ledgers accumulate additional 'blocks' of transaction data, which are chained together, hence the name blockchain. Mechanisms are instituted to ensure that the ledgers across different nodes are synchronized, and market participants are incentivized to ensure that the ledgers correctly record transactions.

Cryptographic techniques are used to secure two related elements. First, they are used to secure transactions, to ensure that only an appropriate authority (the 'address holder') can 'spend' the funds attributed to a particular address. Second, cryptography is used to secure the transaction ledgers of the system, ensuring that people cannot fraudulently tamper with their crypto-currency balances. We discuss these cryptographic details in more depth in Section 2.4.

2.3 *Growth in the Supply of Crypto-Currencies*

The idea of transactions by 'blockchain' was first suggested by Satoshi Nakamoto in 2008 on a cryptography mailing list (see Nakamoto, 2008).[8] This suggestion led to the development of Bitcoin in 2009. The number of crypto-currencies is increasing rapidly, in part because the code for Bitcoin is open source. This means that the program code can be copied and altered to create new crypto-currencies relatively easily. In 2014, there were estimated to be 500 crypto-currencies in existence (White, 2015). By 8 November 2016 coinmarketcap.com identified 705 crypto-currencies, which had increased further to 1560 currencies as at 8 April 2018. 'Market capitalizations' in July 2017 ranged from USD 40 billion, for Bitcoin, to essentially nothing. Bitcoin's market capitalization peaked at $326 billion on 17 December, but by 7 April had dropped to USD 112.5 billion. As a point of comparison, the stock of M1 in the United States in the week ending 19, March 2018 was USD 3.6471 trillion, roughly 32 times larger than the USD value of Bitcoin balances. Table 1 reports the top 10 currencies by market valuation as at 8 April, 2018. Only five of these 10 crypto-currencies were among the top 10 by capitalization in June 2017. These new crypto-currency variants are usually substitutes for pre-existing crypto-currencies, posing a competitive threat to pre-existing variants.

A major challenge for currency producers is to ensure that the value of their currencies is not debased by an excessive supply. Limits in the supply of precious metals constrained the supply of currency when coins were made from gold and silver.[9] When metallic coins were used as currency, debasement typically occurred through reductions in the quantity of gold or silver contained in coins. Because fiat money is printed on low-value pieces of paper, it is straightforward to issue more currency, providing central banks or governments with an opportunity to gain control over physical goods and services. When conducted on a large scale, the excessive production of currency can lead to periods of hyper-inflation, in which the value of currency in terms of goods declines rapidly (the price level rises). Inflation targeting frameworks can be thought of as a legislative mechanism to offset this tendency. An independent agent, the central bank, is tasked with ensuring that fiat currency retains a broadly stable value in terms of goods and services, that is inflation is maintained at low levels.

Table 1. Crypto-Currency Capitalizations – Top Ten.

Symbol	Crypto-currency	Mkt cap. (billions)	Price (USD)	Supply (millions)	Volume (24 hours) (USD millions)
	Bitcoin	$118.0	$6,958.19	17.0	$3,767.7
	Ethereum	$38.4	$389.35	98.7	$922.2
	Ripple	$19.1	$0.488821	39,094.5	$159.5
	Bitcoin Cash	$11.1	$647.90	17.1	$210.1
	Litecoin	$6.5	$116.45	56.0	$202.5
	EOS	$4.6	$5.87	778.7	$189.2
	Cardano	$3.9	$0.152333	25,927.1	$45.1
	Stellar	$3.8	$0.202322	18,551.0	$21.7
	NEO	$3.0	$46.91	65.0	$43.6
	IOTA	$2.8	$1.00	2,779.5	$14.4

Notes: Mkt cap. = market capitalization = US dollar (USD) price × supply (millions). Supply is in units of each crypto-currency. Volume = value of transactions in 24 hours, in millions of USD.
Source: coinmarketcap.com. Downloaded 8 April, 2018.

Unlike the fiat monies produced or distributed by central banks, crypto-currencies typically have explicit programmatic rules that prevent an explosion in supply. In the crypto-currency framework exemplified by Bitcoin, 'miners' are rewarded with bitcoins for validating transactions (Peters *et al.*, 2015). With Bitcoin, the validation of transactions is central to growth in the supply of bitcoins. But Bitcoin has a *declining* growth rate in supply – the reward for adding a new block to the blockchain halves with every additional 210,000 blocks (roughly every 4 years, Velde, 2013). Given the programming rules that govern the ledgers, the sum of all bitcoin balances is approaching 21 million bitcoins (Velde, 2013). Each bitcoin is divisible into small units called satoshis: 100 million satoshis equals 1 bitcoin, just as 100 cents equals 1 dollar. Litecoin, another crypto-currency variant, has the same declining reward structure for mining blocks; the supply of Litecoins is approaching 84 million units.

These asymptotic limits ensure that these crypto-currencies will be limited in supply, preventing the infinite debasement of these currencies. In decentralized systems, such as the crypto-currency schemes described here, there is no central authority that could unilaterally alter the protocols that govern crypto-currency supply. Not all crypto-currencies have a fixed level of supply. Crypto-currencies such as Peercoin and Blackcoin have modestly positive growth rates in the supply of 'coins' (Johnson and Pomorski, 2014). Positive growth rates are achieved in the Peercoin and Blackcoin frameworks by minting more coins proportional to all the account balances.

The quantity theory of money suggests that the stock of money (M) multiplied by its 'velocity' (V) equals transactions (T) multiplied by the price level (P): $MV = PT$. As with many other crypto-currencies, Bitcoin and Litecoin have operational constraints that limit the number of transactions that can be processed in a given period of time. The block size for Bitcoin is constrained to be a maximum of 1 million bytes, and blocks usually contain somewhere between a couple of hundred and a couple of thousand transactions.[10] The programming protocols also limit how fast a block can be processed. Bitcoin and Litecoin thus constrain both money supply and velocity.

Superficially, it would seem that crypto-currencies with a fixed M and fixed V should be deflationary, so that changes in price level offset changes in the volume of transactions T; the latter is expected to grow through time in tandem with the economy. In the quantity theory of money, the price level adjusts to equilibrate the supply of money with the demand for money for transactions purposes. This equilibration process presumes that each unit of currency is divisible and each sub-unit of currency (cents when thinking about dollars) has the same velocity as the major units. One cent in a dollar, say, has the same velocity as the dollar itself. If velocity is one transaction per second, then the quantity theory for physical money assumes that 100 cents could be used to implement 100 1-cent transactions per second. However, the transaction velocity constraints for Bitcoin imply that (approximately) 2000 bitcoin transactions could be validated per 10-minute period or 2000 satoshi transactions. Dividing up an electronic currency unit into sub-units does not increase the number of achievable transactions. Consequently, it does not seem that changes in the price level can equilibrate a demand for real transactions with the supply of a given crypto-currency. It seems more likely that equilibration between the demand and supply of electronic transaction media will be achieved by producing additional crypto-currency variants or by crowding out the number of desired transactions.

2.4 *The Mechanics of Bitcoin and the Blockchain*

In the rest of this sub-section we describe the validation process of Bitcoin, the original crypto-currency. While the details for other crypto-currencies may differ, many of the key elements are similar. For a more in-depth treatment of the technical details of Bitcoin transaction, see Narayanan *et al.* (2016, chapters 1–3) and Antonopoulos (2015, chapters 5–7). Vigna and Casey (2015) provide a more informal exposition. Readers less interested in the specific technical details of Bitcoin transactions could skip to Section 3.

In order to transact using Bitcoin, a user usually possesses a 'wallet'. A wallet typically contains:

- 'Addresses'
- Private cryptographic keys
- Public cryptographic keys, and
- A sequence of past transactions.

An address is similar to an identifier for a bank account. It should be noted that there is no physical 'address' within the hardware of some computer that 'stores' crypto-currency coins. Instead, the address is best thought of as specifying an identifier in the duplicate ledgers that record all transactions, similar to an account number in a commercial bank's ledger. In practice, an individual may have multiple addresses, and indeed could use each address for only a single onward transaction. We will return to this issue in a moment. The sequence of past transactions associated with the addresses in a wallet implicitly defines the stock of bitcoins available to the owner of the wallet.

Each address is uniquely associated with a pair of private and public keys. In fact, an address is essentially short-hand for its corresponding public key.[11] These keys are simply strings of letters and numbers used to protect messages cryptographically. The account address is public and the contents of an address can in some sense be viewed by everyone, but only the private key can be used to 'unlock' the address to undertake a transaction. Furthermore, although different address balances are public information, it is not possible, or at least not easy, to connect an address to a specific individual, unless the individual discloses ownership.

A wallet is typically software on an electronic device – such as an app on a smartphone – that helps a person to manage their public and private keys, their addresses, and their balances. Some wallets are 'full nodes' that contain the entire history of all transactions. In principle, these full nodes can use computing power to compete to validate transactions – adding them to the ledgers. Other nodes are 'lightweight' clients that only focus on the addresses and past transactions relevant for a given person or business. In some ways, digital wallets are akin to Electronic Fund Transfers at Point of Sale (EFTPOS)[12] cards that enable one to access a bank account balance, with the EFTPOS card's security pin serving the same role as the private cryptographic key, preventing illegitimate access to an account.

Here, we provide a brief description of a generic transaction using Bitcoin.[13] If person A wants to send crypto-currency to café B, then person A sends a message to the network of 'miners' who undertake the financial book-keeping. This message contains a Bitcoin address for Café B and the amount to be transferred. Person A secures the contents of the message cryptographically by digitally signing it using their private key, so that the miners know that the transaction is correctly authorized. These cryptographic details are discussed in greater depth shortly.

Transactions are characterized as a combination of 'inputs' and 'outputs'. The inputs can be thought of as the 'from' details of the transaction, while the outputs are the balancing details of the 'to' payment. To transact, person A transfers bitcoins from previous transactions on to person B. If the transaction with B is large then A may need to transfer bitcoins from multiple previous inflows (multiple 'inputs' may be required). Conversely, if the transaction is small then a single previous inflow may suffice. Since previous transactions may not be exactly the same size as the current transaction, person A will need to redirect the excess amount, the 'change', back to an address that she or he controls. The output of the transaction 'encumbers' the bitcoins used in the transaction with Café B's public key: B's *private* key needs to be used to 'spend' those coins in their next future transaction. The miners authenticate A's message containing the transaction details – verifying its accuracy – using A's public key, the signature and the message. Person A does not – and should not – reveal the private key that proves he or she is the owner of the address that is being debited.

If Café B is selling a sandwich, they need to provide their address and the amount to A. Café B can convey that information by producing a QR[14] code with the requisite information or by using a phone's NFC[15] capability. A QR code is typically a black-and-white square image, akin to a barcode, that can encapsulate information. See Figure 1 for an example. Buyer A can use a camera on a smart phone to decode the QR code to provide the transaction details directly

Figure 1. Example QR-Code.

1A1zP1eP5QGefi2DMPTfTL5SLmv7DivfNa

Figure 2. Bitcoin Genesis Address.
Source: http://www.theopenledger.com/9-most-famous-bitcoin-addresses/

to the wallet, making it easier to implement the transaction, eliminating the need to write out long addresses and other transaction details by hand. To illustrate why addresses are more convenient than public keys and to show why QR-codes or NFC capabilities are desirable, we replicate the genesis address from the first bitcoin transaction in Figure 2 and report Satoshi Nakamoto's PGP (pretty good privacy) public key in Figure 3. Satoshi used the latter key to digitally sign emails sent to the original Bitcoin developers, making those messages tamper-proof.

Potential transactions are first stored in the Mempool (the Memory-Pool) when they are sent to the peer-to-peer network of nodes. At this point, they have not been verified and incorporated into the blockchain ledger. As illustrated in Figure 4, the network of nodes is connected to each other in a random, non-hierarchical manner, and so transaction messages may take time to disseminate across the entire network. Because of the vagaries of network communication one cannot guarantee that all Nodes (Miners) will have access to the same Mempool of forthcoming, desired transactions. Consequently, the transactions are *not* processed on a first-in-first-out basis. Indeed, different nodes may have received different messages in a different order, given that the nodes are globally dispersed.

Adding blocks to the ledger is performed by the 'miners' associated with the different nodes. The term 'accountant' is a more appropriate label than miner, since the important responsibility of the miners is to *validate* transactions and maintain the integrity of the duplicate ledgers that

```
-----BEGIN PGP PUBLIC KEY BLOCK-----
Version: GnuPG v1.4.7 (MingW32)
```

```
mQGiBEkJ+qcRBADKDTcZlYDRtP1Q7/ShuzBJzUh9hoVVowogf2W07U6G9BqKW24r
piOxYmErjMFfvNtozNk+33cd/sq3gi05O1IMmZzg2rbF4ne5t3iplXnNuzNh+j+6
VxxA16GPhBRprvnng8r9GYALLUpo9Xk17KE429YYKFgVvtTPtEGU1pO1EwCg7FmW
dBbRp4mn5GfxQNT1hzp9WgkD/3pZOcB5m4enzfy1OHXmRfJKBMFO2ZDnsYiGqeHv
/LjkhCusTp2qz4thLycYOFKGmAddpVnMsE/TYZLgpsxjrJsrEPNSdoXk3IgEStow
mXjTfr9xNOrB2OQkOZOO1mipOWMgse4PmIuO2X24OapWtyhdHsX3oBLcwDdke8aE
gAh8A/sHlK7fL1Bi8rFzx6hb+2yI1D/fazMBVZUeOr2uo7ldqEz5+GeEiBFignd5
HHhqjJw8rUJkfeZBoTKY1DKo7XDrTRxfyzNuZZPxBLTj+keY8WgYhQ5MWsSC2MX7
FZHaJddYaOpzUmFZmQhOydulVUQnLKzRSunsjGOnmxiWBZwb6bQjU2FOb3NoaSBO
YWthbW90byA8c2FOb3NoaW5AZ214LmNvbT6IYAQTEQIAIAUCSQn6pwIbAwYLCQgH
AwIEFQIIAwQWAgMBAh4BAheAAAoJEBjAnoZeyUihXGMAnjiWJOfvmSgSM3o6Tu3q
RME9GN7QAKCGrFw9SUDOe9/YDcqhX1aPMrYue7kCDQRJCfqnEAgA9OTCjLa6Sj7t
dZcQxNufsDSCSB+yznIGzFGXXpJk7GgKmX3H9Z14E6zJTQGXL2GAV4klkSfNtvgs
SGJKqCnebuZVwutyq1vXRNVFPQFvLVVo2jJCBHWjbO3fmXmavIUtRCHoc8xgVJMQ
LrwvS943GgsqSbdoKZWdTnfnEq+UaGo+Qfv66NpT3YlOCXUiNBITZOJcJdjHDTBO
XRqomX2WSguv+btYdhQGGQiaEx73XMftXNCxbOpqwsODQns7xTcl2ENru9BNIQME
I7L9FYBQUiKHm1k6RrBy1as8XE1S2jEos7GAmlfF1wShFUX+NF1VOPdbN3ZdFoWq
sUjKk+QbrwADBQgA9DiD4+uuRhwk2B1TmtrXnwwhcdkE7ZbLHjxBfCsLPAZiPh8c
ICfV3S418i4H1YCz2ItcnC8KAPoS6mipyS28AU1B7zJYPODBn8E7aPSPzHJfudMK
MqiCHljVJrE23xsKTCOsIhhSKcr2G+6ARoG5lwuoqJqEyDrblVQQFpVxBNPHSTqu
O5PoLXQc7PKgC5SyQuZbEALEkItl2SL2yBRRGOlVJLnvZ6eaovkAlgsbGdlieOrO
UwWuJCwzZuBDruMYAfyQBvYfXZun3Zm84rW7Jclp18mXITwGCVHg/P5n7QMbBfZQ
A25ymkuj636Nqh+c4zRnSINfyrDcID7AcqEb6IhJBBgRAgAJBQJJCfqnAhsMAAoJ
EBjAnoZeyUihPrcAniVW15M44RuGctJe+IMNX4eVkCO8AJ9v7cXsp5uDdQNo8q3R
8RHwN4Gk8w==
=3FTe
```

```
-----END PGP PUBLIC KEY BLOCK-----
```

Figure 3. Nakamoto's Public PGP Key.
Source: https://bitcointalk.org/Satoshi_Nakamoto.asc

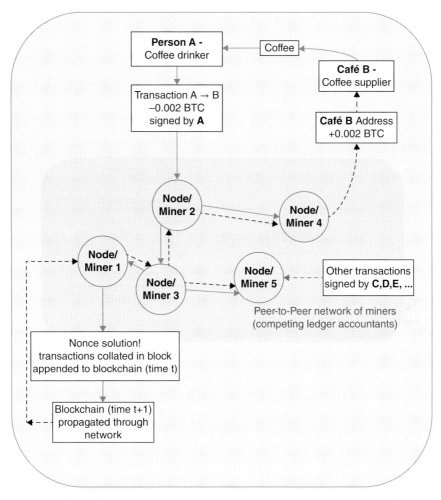

Figure 4. Stylized Bitcoin Transaction. [Color figure can be viewed at wileyonlinelibrary.com]

record transactions. The miners are rewarded with crypto-currency for this validation service as part of the programmed protocols underpinning the currency. Satoshi Nakamoto 'mined' the first block in January 2009 and received 50 bitcoins as a reward. Satoshi later sent coins to Hal Finney, an early developer. Other transactions followed and more users became involved in the mining (validation) process creating the supply of bitcoins. As noted earlier, the reward structure is declining through time. These asymmetric rewards encouraged the early adoption of Bitcoin, as early adopters received larger rewards than later miners. These asymmetric rewards also helped to promote the development of the network of users, ameliorating the 'chicken and egg problem' associated with networks.

The blockchain has the details of all the transactions that a particular account holder has previously undertaken, both additions and subtractions to their implicit account balance (Extance, 2015). By going through the history of transactions, miners verify whether person A and other transactors have enough coins to undertake their transactions. This validation prevents double spending: a transactor cannot use the same inputs in two different transactions. In traditional e-payment systems, financial intermediaries such as banks keep track of ledgers and prevent such double-spending. Although seemingly complicated, validating transactions, ensuring that account balances are non-negative, is relatively simple from a computational perspective.

In Figure 4, the network of miners is an undirected graph, and the blue arrows represent the flow of information about the $A \rightarrow B$ transaction through the network. In this figure, we assume that Node/Miner 1 is the first to solve the computational problem that provides them with the right to augment the blockchain with an additional block. We talk more about this computational problem below. The new extended blockchain propagates back through the network, depicted with the dotted red arrows. We are assuming that Café B learns that the blockchain has been updated from Node/Miner 4 – signalling that payment has been made for the cup of coffee. Each Node has access to a full rendition of the blockchain up to time t, subject to the vagaries of network communication, and has its own version of the Mempool, which we have not depicted in the figure.

A transaction between person A and café B will be visible to the network nearly immediately, but it will only be confirmed once it is collated into a 'block' of transactions that is incorporated into the distributed ledger. The miner who successfully adds the block to the blockchain has their own balance in the ledger increased with an accounting fee – this is the point at which new 'bitcoins' come into existence and the aggregate bitcoin balance is increased. Implicitly, the miner adds the fee transaction to the block. Note that the newly 'minted' bitcoins do not have distinct serial numbers associated with them, as paper notes do. Instead, bitcoins are associated with a given history of transactions over time. In principle, two or more bitcoins could be used for the same transactions, and thus end up with the same transaction history. The minting analogy is a little unfortunate because it is suggestive of a physical existence for bitcoins, which is not the case in practice.

Miners are free to join or leave the network, responding to the relative costs and rewards associated with validating transactions. The exact number of miners competing to validate and authenticate blocks is difficult to ascertain. One estimate from late 2015 suggested that there were around 100,000 miners.[16] Baur et al. (2018, p. 9) identify 135,000 addresses that had received newly minted coins by 2013, which places an upper limit on the number of miners that have been successful in minting coins.

The right to augment the chain proceeds roughly in the following manner. Miners protect the integrity of the ledger(s) by hashing blocks of transaction data. First, to protect the integrity of the message/transaction, miners reduce the message into an encrypted 'hash' – a 64 character representation of the message using hexadecimal numbers, digits 0–9 and letters a–f. As an example, the SHA-256 hash for 'The quick brown fox jumped over the lazy dog'. (with quotes) is:

309eaf49c77e61a70a20b848a494ce13235d13e7297a2033ca18ee3a59b48fd1

while the hash for the same sentence without quotation marks is:[17]

68b1282b91de2c054c36629cb8dd447f12f096d3e3c587978dc2248444633483

Even tiny changes in the underlying message lead to substantial changes in the hash used to represent it. The hash from the first transaction in the block is combined with the next subsequent transaction and the first hash plus the second message are hashed together in turn. This process is conducted a number of times, forming a 'block' of transaction data that is due to be added to the blockchain. Even extremely long 'messages' can be compressed into a hash with a similar number of characters. For example, the hash for an earlier version of this entire paper was:

62acfa1247b7e23d35f6f0a3eb7d683f685b75ac1eea7ae56cd21ec2db128079

Hashing is a one-way function. It is not practically possible to reverse the process, to map from the hash back to the original message. However, if one has a message and its hash (with no counterfeiting concerns for the latter), it is easy to re-compute the hash of the message to ensure that the message replicates the hash, verifying the integrity of the message. Hashes are not necessarily unique. Two different blocks of text could in principle result in the same hash – known as a 'collision' – but such instances are extremely uncommon. Narayanan *et al.* (2016, chapter 1) discusses 'collision resistance', the likelihood of being able to find an alternate message with the same hash. Practical experience with commonly used hash functions suggests that it would take a very long time to identify collisions, though there is no definitive proof of collision resistance. It is even more unlikely that a counterfeit transaction message suitable for Bitcoin, complete with a counterfeit address controlled by a specific individual, would have the same hash as an original, non-counterfeit transaction.

The miners search for a 'block hash' to capture the information in the block that links together with the hash of the previous block in the chain (Extance, 2015). The blockchain hashes are thus recursively connected to each other.[18] If an individual tried to subvert the ledger by revising a transaction message, say to institute a double-spend, it would contaminate that transaction message's hash, the hash of the entire block containing the transaction message, and then the hashes used to link all subsequent blocks together.

The block hash is required by the protocols of the blockchain to have a certain number of zeroes at the beginning of the hash. The only way to generate an acceptable hash is to add a 'nonce' – a made-up segment of text – to the block of messages. The miners search across different nonces to find a hash with the required number of zeroes. A suitable nonce is difficult to find, but once found it is easy to verify that the nonce, in conjunction with the hash of the preceding block and the transaction messages embodied in the block, results in an acceptable hash with the desired number of zeroes. The nonce is referred to as a 'proof of work'.

The time delay introduced by this nonce-search prevents an 'attacker' from falsely amending the history of the ledger and then re-computing all the recursive hashes; to be successful an attacker would need to be able to find hashes faster than all honest nodes combined (Nakamoto, 2008). Importantly, the search for the nonce randomizes the miner who gets to update the chain, which prevents a single miner from monopolizing control over the ledger. Having found the nonce, the miner can augment the blockchain, claiming the reward for updating the ledger. Transactors may also reward miners with additional transaction fees to encourage them to process their transactions. Since the search for the correct solution is something of a lottery, some miners form syndicates to diversify the risk and reward associated with the search for solutions.

With Bitcoin protocols, the difficulty of finding an acceptable nonce is adjusted by changing the number of required zeroes, offsetting changes in the number of miners and changes in computing power. On average, it takes 10 minutes for each new block to be added to the ledger (Narayanan *et al.*, 2016). The delay that results from the proof of work also provides a window of time for an elongated chain to propagate across the network, and reduces the likelihood that different nodes will have different ledgers. Some alternative crypto-currency algorithms generate blocks more quickly. For example, Litecoin, which is based on Bitcoin, adds blocks every two and a half minutes (Adamsson and Tahir, 2015). Miners now use fast, specially-designed computers to evaluate candidate nonces by brute computational force. This computational process literally takes time and energy. Under this scheme, miners incur costs associated with the investment in computing power and electricity to solve the hash problem, to add the new block.

The new block is verified by other miners and the new elongated chain is accepted if the transactions are all valid. Although the longest blockchain becomes the distributed ledger of record, which is then adopted by all computer nodes, distinct blocks will occasionally be added (near) simultaneously creating a 'fork' – two competing chains. One of these chains will ultimately be discarded, for example if another block is successfully added to the second chain it will become clear that the second blockchain is longer. Consequently, the block on the first shorter chain will become 'orphaned'. The transactions in the orphaned block will need to be incorporated into the longer chain that has ultimately become the ledger of record, delaying the validation of these orphaned transactions.

As the reward for finding a suitable nonce and adding the block to the Bitcoin blockchain is automatically decreasing in size through time, the transactions fees that transactors offer for authentication will eventually become important to ensure that miners continue to perform validation services. Even with the current validation rewards, considerable backlogs of transactions requiring validation have occasionally built up – over 180,000 transactions in at least one instance. In such cases, the supply of transactions simply exceeds the validation capacity of the network, and there is little that even the miners can do to rectify this imbalance, as devoting more computational resources leaves the average processing time unchanged.

The proof-of-work reward system keeps multiple parties involved in the validation and ledger process, ensuring that it remains decentralized. While diffusing influence over the ledger, this system also introduces computational costs and expense. In principle, a single, trusted authority maintaining the ledger would reduce the duplication of effort required to update records. However, decentralization reduces the risk that the central ledger fails, either for technical reasons or because of malfeasance. Reliance on the Internet remains a key vulnerability for crypto-currencies.

In this section, we have devoted considerable effort to explain the proof of work schemes used to maintain the integrity of Bitcoin ledgers. Other crypto-currencies, such as Peercoin and Nextcoin, use alternative validation schemes, such as 'proof-of-stake'. In Peercoin's schema, the probability of updating the chain also depends on the 'age' of coins that are staked.[19] The 'stake' is sent to one's self in a transaction, which re-sets the age of the coins to zero. Other variants of proof-of-stake are used by other crypto-currencies. The intention of these alternative schemes is to ensure that no single entity has a monopoly on updating the ledger, protecting the integrity of the ledger at a lower cost than the proof-of-work protocol. For further discussion, see Narayanan et al. (2016, sn. 8.5).

3. What Purpose Do Crypto-Currencies Serve?

3.1 Crypto-Currency and the Basic Functions of Money

In this section, we compare the properties of crypto-currencies to the basic functions of money.[20] Money is traditionally associated with three main purposes: it is a generally accepted form of payment (a medium of exchange); it is a unit of account that can be used to compare prices of different goods; and it acts as a store of value (Lipsey, 1963; Burda and Wyplosz, 1993; Bank of Canada, 2014a).[21] How do crypto-currencies stack up in these terms?

Despite growing popularity, crypto-currencies are far from being a generally accepted form of payment. Once again, we focus on Bitcoin, as the most popular crypto-currency. Weber (2016) reported that 106,000 businesses accepted bitcoins as payment in 2016. While this seems like a non-trivial number of retailers, the scale of Bitcoin is still very small relative to traditional payments systems. In 2010, there were approximately 27.9 million small businesses in the United States alone.[22] Szczepánski (2014) compares the Bitcoin market to Visa and Mastercard in 2014 and notes that Bitcoin undertook less than USD 100 million worth of transactions per day, which is 1% or less of the (daily) USD 16.5 billion and USD 9.8 billion of transactions that were mediated by Visa and Mastercard, respectively.

Next, we compare Bitcoin to transactions mediated by New Zealand's financial system. We first provide a sense of scale and context for the New Zealand economy: New Zealand's population is less than 5 million people, roughly that of Louisiana, and its per capita income in 2016 was roughly USD 39,500, a little less than that of the state of Mississippi or the United Kingdom.[23] New Zealand's financial system is dominated by four large commercial banks. The number of 'un-banked' individuals in New Zealand is comparatively low: 99.4% of adults 15 years old and above have accounts in formal financial institutions.[24] Debit and credit cards are used extensively to conduct transactions in New Zealand, typically at EFTPOS terminals at local retailers.

Between May 2016 and April 2017, approximately NZD 80.6 billion of electronic transactions were processed by New Zealand financial institutions, which corresponds to about NZD 221 million per day in roughly 4.4 million transactions.[25] To process 4.4 million transactions, Bitcoin would need to process $4,400,000 \div (24 \times 6) \approx 30,555$ transactions per 10-minute period, roughly 12 times the number of transactions that Bitcoin can currently handle. Unless the underlying software protocols are amended, Bitcoin could not cope with the volume of transactions undertaken in New Zealand, let alone the world. These scalability issues are particularly acute since part of the appeal of crypto-currencies is that they could facilitate transactions in multiple jurisdictions. The ECB (2015) provides a comparison to a much larger economic region, noting that there were 274 million electronic retail transactions per day in the European Union. In contrast, even with recent data from 1 January to 12 October, 2017, Bitcoin was facilitating around 270,000 transactions per day in the world as a whole.[26] Baur *et al.* (2018) attempt to classify users by the frequency and value of transactions undertaken, identifying also miners that receive newly generated bitcoins. According to their classification, 'currency users', those making just small transactions, were making about 5% of transactions by value, falling to less than half that number in 2014. Based on transaction sizes, they conclude that most Bitcoin transactors have an investment motive.

Scalability issues are already a problem, with an increased number of transactions ending up in the queue awaiting confirmation – the 'Mempool'; see Figure 5. Furthermore, Bitcoin seems to have reached its maximum processing capacity, given the 1 million byte constraint on block size. Gavin Andresen has suggested that the average size of a Bitcoin transaction message is about 250 bytes,[27] implying that roughly 4000 transactions can be squeezed into a block. Given that each block takes 10 minutes to process on average, Bitcoin can process a maximum of $4000 \times 6 \times 24 = 576,000$ transactions per 24-hour period. As of 27 April, 2018, the largest number of Bitcoin transactions processed in a single day, on 4 January, 2018, was 425,000. And 19 December, 2017 had the highest daily average number of Bitcoin transactions/block, 2704, well short of the hypothetical maximum.

Crypto-currencies have been a highly volatile store of value, which is most apparent in the extremely high volatility exhibited by Bitcoin relative to traditional fiat currencies (see

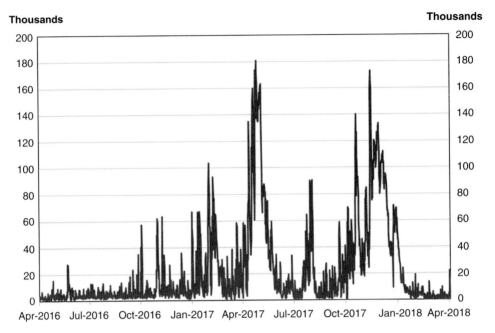

Figure 5. Unconfirmed Transactions in the Mempool. [Color figure can be viewed at wileyonlinelibrary.com]

figure 6). Böhme *et al.* (2015) suggest that the Bitcoin market is relatively shallow and that people attempting to trade large volumes relatively quickly may affect the Bitcoin exchange rate. Yermack (2013) notes that the law of one price does not seem to work very effectively for Bitcoin, with different exchanges transacting at materially different USD/BTC exchange rates; see also Pieters and Vivanco (2017). Böhme *et al.* argue that Bitcoin's exchange rate volatility is of concern to users who are transacting in Bitcoin as well those who are using Bitcoin as a store of value. Using monthly data, we find that the standard deviation of the month-on-month percentage point changes in Bitcoin/USD is 73.1%, while the equivalent for the NZD/USD exchange rate is 3.6%.[28] While there have been a few large (positive) outliers, most percentage point changes have been between −40% and +89% for Bitcoin, cf. −9.7 and +6.6 percentage points for the USD/NZD exchange rate. Yermack (2013) notes that this volatility is large even relative to risky equities.

The volatility of the Bitcoin exchange rate against the USD is particularly problematic if users' assets are denominated in Bitcoin and liabilities are denominated in USD. If, for example Bitcoin users have liabilities such as taxes denominated in USD then volatility in the Bitcoin-USD exchange rate creates volatility in their tax liabilities and hence their net worth. Yermack (2013) discusses Bitcoin as an additional asset class, largely discounting its value as a risk management tool, though see a contrary perspective in Section 3.4.

Volatility in the value of Bitcoin is also a negative feature for real transactions. In principle, any good or service could be used as a unit of account – a common standard for comparing the prices of different goods and services. We could figure out how many hamburgers it takes to obtain a taxi ride home. Or how many kilograms of carrots it would take to purchase an iPhone. In practice, it is helpful to economize on the number of prices one remembers by

USD/Bitcoin

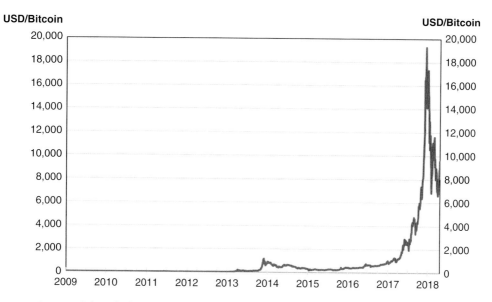

USD/Bitcoin

Figure 6. Price of Bitcoin (USD). [Color figure can be viewed at wileyonlinelibrary.com]

using a single common numeraire to evaluate transactions. A good numeraire will exhibit stable purchasing power with respect to some average of goods and services, though individual prices may fluctuate. Prices in a given numeraire should not fluctuate because of issues specific to the numeraire. For example, carrots would not be a good numeraire if carrot blight suddenly affected the availability of carrots. Suppose we took a Red taxi yesterday and a Blue taxi today, both paid in kilograms of carrots. Ideally, these two prices will be informative when choosing which company to use in future. But if the Blue taxi price in carrots today is high simply because of carrot blight then the allocative signal provided by these two prices is distorted.

In practice, merchants that accept bitcoins usually price their goods in fiat currency units, such as USD, and accept the equivalent number of bitcoins based on the exchange rate at the time of the transaction (Johnson and Pomorski, 2014). Most merchants convert their bitcoin holdings into USD straight away, using a Bitcoin currency exchange such as Coinbase (Davidson, 2015). Bitcoin thus does not really serve as a unit of account. Cheah and Fry (2015, p. 33) argue that Bitcoin's volatility undermines its use as a unit of account.

Rather than focusing on the three traditional monetary attributes described above, the New Monetarist literature described by Williamson and Wright (2010) and Williamson and Wright (2011) emphasizes the simultaneous existence of money and credit markets and the need to be specific about the frictions that motivate these payment mechanisms. One imperfection emphasized by Kocherlakota (1998, 2000, 2002) is the existence of imperfect 'memory' in relation to past transactions. Digital currencies provide memory via the ledger of transactions, providing an alternative to conventional currency balances. But as argued later, they are less adept at replacing the credit services provided by financial intermediaries. Hendrickson *et al.* (2016) make use of the search and matching framework commonly used in the New Monetarist literature, and develop a model that simultaneously contains government legal tender and Bitcoin. They then investigate the conditions under which a government could deter the use of Bitcoin. They find that Bitcoin usage may still occur in equilibrium even if the government refuses to transact in it, provided that some transactors are sufficiently committed to its use.

3.2 *Motivations for Using Crypto-Currencies*

Given that there are alternative methods of payment, why are crypto-currencies being developed and adopted? The original paper that spawned interest in crypto-currencies, Nakamoto (2008), aimed to develop a method of exchange that did not require trust in third party financial intermediaries. The 'genesis block' first verified by Satoshi Nakamoto referenced a 3 January, 2009 *Times* headline 'Chancellor on brink of second bailout for banks'. It is apparent that the crypto-currency movement was in part motivated by the global financial crisis and a lack of trust in traditional financial intermediaries and the regulatory authorities responsible for ensuring financial stability.[29] Nevertheless, as fiduciary currencies, trust is *essential* for the continued acceptability of crypto-currencies. Crypto-currency users must trust the computer programmers who have taken up the design mantle for crypto-currencies; users must trust the miners responsible for validating transactions; and indeed transactors need to trust that others will continue to value and accept crypto-currency units.

Although crypto-currencies arguably fail to satisfy the basic functions of money, their increased popularity is also motivated by genuine economic considerations, including lower transaction costs, 'pseudonymous' payments, transaction irreversibility, and the potential to attract a new customer base. We discuss these reasons further below.

The BIS (2015) identifies transaction costs as an important demand side factor motivating the use of crypto-currencies. Transaction costs are very important to small businesses. For example, high credit card fees (2.5–4.5% of the value of goods and services being exchanged) mean that 55% of American small businesses do not accept credit cards (Kloc, 2014).

Reduced transactions costs may be a particularly important advantage in relation to international transactions. The ubiquitous nature of the internet means that crypto-currencies are relatively unconstrained by geography as physical transportation costs and physical security concerns are negligible for digital currencies. Some early analysis by Goldman Sachs (2014) noted that transaction costs for international remittances were around 1% using Bitcoin, relative to 8–9% for traditional remitters, implying scope for a significant reduction in costs. More recent 2016–2017 data suggest that Bitcoin transactions fees range from 0.35% to 3.1% of the value of transactions, with a median/mean transaction cost around 0.9–1.0%.[30] See Figure 7.

Aside from cost considerations, many users of crypto-currencies are drawn to them because they are thought to be anonymous – or at least more anonymous than electronic transactions facilitated by regulated banks, which are required to adhere to 'know your customer' protocols. Anonymity is of obvious value to individuals undertaking illegal transactions, such as those associated with trade in illegal drugs. Of course, as Szczepánski (2014) and others point out, decentralized ledger systems are not totally anonymous. Although users are not explicitly identified, distributed ledgers typically have a public record of every transaction undertaken (ECB, 2012). If investigators can link a transactor to an address, then they can ascertain all their previous transactions via the public information on the blockchain (Marian, 2015). Such analysis does become more difficult if individuals cycle through multiple addresses, but various techniques can be used to undermine the anonymity of the system, such as tracking the IP (Internet Protocol) addresses of account holders, and data mining the blockchain to try to identify transactors. Narayanan *et al.* (2016, sn. 6.2) discusses mechanisms to deanonymize Bitcoin. Conversely, a number of crypto-currencies, such as Zerocoin and Zerocash for example, have been developed to try to achieve total anonymity. Böhme *et al.* (2015) and Narayanan *et al.* (2016, sn. 6.3) provide details of 'mixing' mechanisms used to achieve anonymity.

Percent

Percent

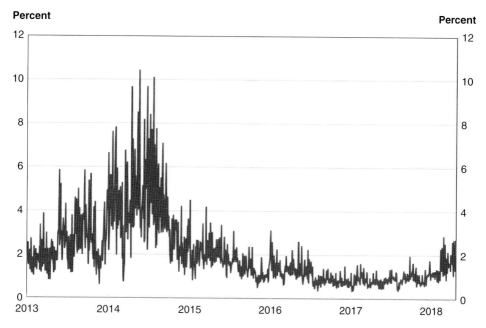

Figure 7. Transactions Costs (Percentage of Transaction Value). [Color figure can be viewed at wileyonlinelibrary.com]

Irreversibility is another motive for using crypto-currencies, one that received considerable emphasis in Nakamoto (2008). There are currently no mechanisms to reverse transactions in the crypto-currency domain. This is an advantage for merchants: in current payment systems involving credit cards, merchants are susceptible to fraud and may have transactions reversed after customers have received goods or services (BIS, 2015). Conversely, irreversibility may deter customers, because they rely on merchants to provide redress if a good or service is faulty. Of course, legal systems and the ongoing value of merchant reputations may help to provide redress, provided transactions are properly documented through conventional means such as receipts.

Merchants may also adopt crypto-currencies to attract new customers. Early adopters of technology may be more inclined to use services of companies that offer crypto-currencies as a payment method simply because they like being involved with new technologies (BIS, 2015). Consistent with this thesis, technology and telecommunication firms have been among the early adopters of crypto-currencies. A number of international companies that accept crypto-currencies for some goods or services are listed below, many of which have strong links with the technology industry.[31]

- Amazon
- WordPress.com
- Bloomberg
- Dell

- Microsoft
- Virgin Galactic
- Expedia.com
- PayPal

3.3 *What are Crypto-Currencies Really Used For?*

Crypto-currencies are regularly associated with four types of transactions or motivations: speculation; illegal transactions; gambling; and cross-border transactions such as remittances. Glaser *et al.* (2014) examine whether users' interest in digital currencies stems from their utility as transaction media or because of their appeal as an asset class and conclude that it is the latter aspect for most holders. Baur *et al.* (2018) reach a similar conclusion based on the frequency and value of transactions being reported in the Blockchain. Fred Ehrsam, a co-founder of Coinbase, one of the leading digital wallet providers, estimated that 80–95% of transactions in 2013 and 2014 using Coinbase were related to speculation (see Goldman Sachs, 2014). In recent months, the value of bitcoins has appreciated rapidly relative to USD. Implicitly, this means that Bitcoin has been deflationary with respect to goods and services – far fewer bitcoins are required to purchase a given consumption bundle of goods and services. If this deflationary impulse is expected to persist, then current holders have an incentive to hold on to their bitcoins, treating the bitcoins as an asset and refraining from using them for transaction purposes.

Regulatory frameworks can be slow to adjust to emerging technologies. As a result, criminals have an incentive to take advantage of new transaction media. Money laundering has been a common financial crime in the crypto-currency domain due to perceptions of anonymity and a lack of regulation (ECB, 2012; EBA, 2013; FBI, 2012). Ponzi schemes are also a threat in the virtual currency domain, prompting attention from the United States Securities and Exchange Commission (SEC, 2013).

Trautman (2014) discusses the regulation of crypto-currencies and provides details on many of the highest profile criminal cases up until 2014. To cite just a few, the Liberty Reserve case involved money laundering; the Western Express International case involved money laundering and servicing criminal transactions in Eastern Europe; and the e-gold case involved money laundering and unlicensed money transfers (Trautman, 2014; Levin *et al.*, 2014). Böhme *et al.* (2015) and Ali *et al.* (2015) discuss the online Silk Road market place, which facilitated transactions in drugs and firearms and other illegal activities until it was shut down by the Federal Bureau of Investigation in 2011. Silk Road used bitcoins to settle transactions and had an estimated revenue of USD 1.2 billion annually (Ali *et al.*, 2015). Crypto-currency transactions, together with the use of the Onion Router, which obscures IP addresses, made it possible for sellers on the Silk Road market place to remain pseudonymous because there was no centralized authority connecting addresses to individuals. However, these safeguards did not prevent Silk Road's founder, Ross Ulbricht, from being caught and sentenced to life in prison.

The pseudo-anonymity of crypto-currency has also increased the rewards associated with Ransomware attacks, by providing a vehicle for ransom payment. In May 2017, a Ransomware attack was implemented by the 'WannaCry worm', which required payments implemented via Bitcoin. Hundreds of thousands of computers were affected. Even law enforcement departments fell victim to the WannaCry worm (Ali *et al.*, 2015, p. 287).

Online gambling has been another prominent source of transactions for crypto-currencies. In a fascinating study using cluster analysis, Meiklejohn *et al.* (2016) undertook transactions with entities known to accept bitcoins and then used the resultant addresses to classify transactions on the Bitcoin blockchain. They found that around 64% of Bitcoin accounts have never been used and 60% of transaction activity occurs through gambling sites. Narayanan *et al.* (2016, chapter 6) discussed this analysis further in the context of anonymity.

Besides Bitcoin, there are other crypto-currencies that have more specialized purposes. Ripple, for example uses a distributed ledger to make cross-border bank-to-bank transactions easier. Ripple is a payment solution that allows users to exchange local currency for a crypto-currency that can be exchanged for a foreign currency. Ripple is thus competing with SWIFT[32] and SEPA,[33] to connect international financial markets. See ECB (2015) for more information.

Other applications have also been proposed for distributed ledgers. Koeppl and Kronick (2017), for example suggest that blockchains could be applied to corporate governance to facilitate shareholder voting or to provide timely updates on firm accounts. Distributed ledgers are being developed to assure the provenance of diamonds, and have also been proposed as mechanisms to reduce the costs of settlement, custody and registration of financial securities (UK Government Office for Science, 2016). Land registries, such as Sweden's Lantmäteriet, are also trialling blockchain ledgers to keep track of land transfers. The Massachusetts Institute of Technology has developed a blockchain to record degrees awarded to students.[34] Tasca (2015) discusses a number of specific projects aimed at asset registry applications. Open access ledgers are a useful mechanism in these applications because they disseminate ownership information to a wide population of potential transactors.

3.4 *Empirical Properties of Crypto-Currencies*

The empirical literature on crypto-currencies, and Bitcoin in particular, is expanding rapidly. Here, we provide a brief introduction to some of this literature, illustrating some of the directions that researchers are exploring in relation to crypto-currencies. One strand of the literature focuses on the time series properties of crypto-currency exchange rates. Given the wild gyrations in crypto-currency/USD exchange rates, it is not surprising that a number of authors examine whether the price (the exchange rate) exhibits characteristics akin to a bubble. A popular approach is to deploy the explosiveness tests of Phillips *et al.* (2014, 2015) or Phillips *et al.* (2011). The explosive component of the series is often interpreted as a bubble. In this vein, Cheah and Fry (2015) find that the Bitcoin exchange rate has a 'substantial speculative bubble component' and suggest that 'the fundamental value of Bitcoin is zero'. Cheung *et al.* (2015) apply this methodology and identify a number of short-lived bubbles during 2010–2014 with three larger and longer-lived bubbles in the latter part of the series, one of which collapsed with the demise of the Mt Gox exchange. Corbet *et al.* (2017) examine Bitcoin and Ethereum pricing and strongly conclude that these crypto-currencies exhibit periods of bubble-like behaviour. They find evidence supporting the view that Bitcoin has been in an explosive phase since the price of Bitcoin increased above USD 1000. Donier and Bouchaud (2015) provide a rationale for price crashes that relates to market liquidity.

The empirical behaviour of Bitcoin and other crypto-currency exchange rates has also come under scrutiny from a finance and time series perspective. Bariviera (2017) and Bariviera *et al.* (2017), for example use various time series statistics, such as the Hurst exponent and detrended fluctuation analysis, to show that the returns of Bitcoin exhibit long memory (a high degree of persistence), implying that Bitcoin prices are not efficient (prices do fully incorporate all information). Urquhart (2016) looks at the efficiency of Bitcoin prices and finds that prices over his full sample are inefficient, though a sub-sample analysis suggests that Bitcoin efficiency may be improving in the latter half of the sample. Nadarajah and Chu (2017) suggest applying a power transform to the return series, and suggest the test results then imply efficiency. Jiang *et al.* (2017) investigate long memory using a rolling window approach to assess whether memory varies over time and conclude that the Bitcoin market is inefficient. Kurihara and Fukushima (2017) find that Bitcoin exhibits trading-day effects, also implying a lack of efficiency, though a sub-sample analysis suggests that the market may be improving in efficiency.

Widening the focus, Phillip *et al.* (2018) examine the returns for 224 crypto-currencies and find that they exhibit long memory and stochastic volatility. Katsiampa (2017) also analyses volatility, using models of generalized autoregressive conditional heteroscedasticity (see also the references therein). Urquhart (2017) looks at the propensity of Bitcoin exchange rates to cluster around round numbers, and shows that price and volume have a significant relationship with price clusters. Brière *et al.* (2015) investigate Bitcoin from a portfolio diversification per-spective. While caveating their results on the basis that past performance may not be indicative of future outcomes, they note that Bitcoin's high volatility is compensated for by high returns, and these returns exhibit low correlation with other asset returns, implying that portfolios may benefit from some exposure to Bitcoin.

Polasik *et al.* (2015) examine the returns to Bitcoin and relate these returns to sentiment in newspaper reports and transaction volumes, and explores the adoption of Bitcoin by mer-chants. Garcia *et al.* (2014) similarly argue for the importance of an interplay between social media communication, Internet search trends and the price of Bitcoin. Urquhart (2018) looks at Google trends data and finds that such data are influenced by realized volatility and the volume of trade, but finds that the Google trends data do not in turn Granger-cause realized volatility or returns.

Adopting a rather different perspective, ElBahrawy *et al.* (2017) employ an ecological model, the 'neutral model of evolution', to describe the crypto-currency market as a whole, and suggest that such a model can reproduce key empirical findings, such as the number of active crypto-currencies, the market share distribution of currencies, the birth and death rate of currencies, and Bitcoin's decreasing market share. Van Vliet (2018) examines the market capitalization of Bitcoin from the perspective of Metcalfe's law, which relates the value of a network to the number of users connected to the system, and additionally accounts for the diffusion of Bitcoin use into the community of possible users.

4. Implications

Since transacting is at the centre of economic activity, crypto-currencies have implications for consumers, producers and financial institutions. Crypto-currencies also raise legislative design issues regarding the treatment of crypto-currency transactions/contracts, law enforcement issues, taxation issues and concerns for monetary authorities and financial regulators. In the re-mainder of this paper, we discuss the implications that crypto-currencies have for consumers, the financial system, and monetary and regulatory authorities, and make a few comments on taxation. Since this domain is very broad, our discussion is necessarily at a very high level.

4.1 *Implications for Consumers*

We noted earlier that there are genuine reasons why consumers may wish to use crypto-currencies to implement transactions. In this section, we highlight some of the risks that consumers face using crypto-currencies.

It is well-understood that the integrity of the blockchain rests heavily on the miners. One concern is that a majority of the miners could collude to control the future evolution of the blockchain, in what is known as a '51% attack'. It is suggested that the miners in control of the blockchain could reverse transactions during the attack (enabling double-spending of balances) and potentially prevent some people from transacting.[35] The sequence of hashes connecting blocks in the blockchain would make it difficult to tamper with the history of transactions embedded in the chain, but the other aforementioned actions might still degrade trust in the currency as a medium of exchange, with the potential to undermine its acceptability.

Böhme *et al.* (2015) observe that Bitcoin miners are incentivized to maintain the integrity of the crypto-currency because they are rewarded in the same currency. However, Eyal and Sirer (2014) argue that colluding miners could attack the currency to obtain a disproportionate revenue share by selectively revealing the blocks that they have discovered, intentionally forking the blockchain. When the colluding group gains a large enough share of computing power, other miners are incentivized to join the colluding group resulting in the collapse of decentralized blockchain validation.

The security of cryptographic systems also relies on algorithms being more complex than current state-of-the-art computers are capable of solving. If quantum computers were developed with much faster speeds and capabilities, then some traditional cryptographic techniques would be susceptible to being cracked, including commonly used public key technologies based on the RSA (Rivest-Shamir-Adleman) algorithm or elliptic curves. Cryptographic techniques are currently being developed to deal with quantum computing challenges and cryptographic standards are being revised to forestall future vulnerabilities (Information Assurance Directorate, 2016). Fortunately, the quantum computers needed to break conventional algorithms are still thought to be a decade (or more) away.[36]

Even if the protocols and cryptography used to implement crypto-currencies are secure, consumers may be vulnerable to errors and exploitation in a number of ways. First, if a transactor unintentionally discloses their private key then the balances associated with their addresses could be depleted of value by unauthorized transactions. Second, if the private key is lost then the balance associated with an address would become permanently inaccessible. Yet another risk is that a transactor could erroneously send crypto-currency balances to an incorrect or non-existent address. As there is no central authority, there is no mechanism to reverse unintended transactions. If there is a non-zero probability of sending transactions to uncontrolled or defunct accounts then the aggregate supply of accessible bitcoins could eventually begin a slow dance towards zero.[37] Third, crypto-currency exchanges and even the providers of digital wallets might be susceptible to fraud. Ali *et al.* (2015) cite research by Dell indicating that 146 strains of malware have been discovered that are designed to steal bitcoins from individuals' computers, by stealing private keys from digital wallets or switching addresses to deliver funds erroneously; half of these malware strands avoided detection from antivirus software.

Yermack (2013) notes that there is no deposit insurance for crypto-currency balances, in contrast to the schemes that exist for bank deposits in most countries (New Zealand being a rather unique exception.) However, the absence of deposit insurance may not be a material issue since crypto-currencies are not a liability of a financial institution, and cannot be extinguished by the failure of a financial intermediary. Of course, mechanical failures or theft as described above could still result in crypto-currency balances disappearing.

A final, deeper concern for consumers is the governance of the currency. Crypto-currency source codes are often contained in Git repositories, which implicitly provides a small number of developers with the ability to amend the source code, subject to an uncertain peer review process. Exactly who has influence over such processes, and the checks and balances on their behaviour, is quite unclear. In contrast, the governance of central banks is typically made explicit in legislation. With respect to Bitcoin, at least one prominent developer, Mike Hearn, has suggested that Bitcoin has failed because of its inability to reach agreement about how to resolve the scalability issues that have contributed to wildly volatile fees and large transaction backlogs, as well as other governance issues.[38] While users of Bitcoin 'vote with their feet' –

by using the currency or not – the role of developers is a source of uncertainty for the durability and longevity of the source code. As Velde (2013) notes: 'the governance of the bitcoin code and network is opaque and vulnerable'. Interestingly, a new variant of Bitcoin was introduced in August 2017 to try to resolve the scalability issues discussed in Section 3.1. This new Bitcoin variant, termed 'Bitcoin cash', changed rules around block size but adopted the Bitcoin ledger at the change-over date, enabling users to spend their traditional Bitcoin balances. This fork in the Bitcoin protocol has not gained universal acceptance and most users continue to use the old protocol, 'Bitcoin'. In April 2018, 'Bitcoin cash' had the fourth highest market capitalization among crypto-currencies, after Bitcoin, Ethereum and Ripple; see Table 1.

4.2 *Implications for Financial Institutions*

Banks and financial institutions provide four main services: (i) they offer access to payment systems; (ii) transform assets (e.g. maturity); (iii) manage risk and (iv) process information and monitor borrowers (Freixas and Rochet, 1997). Crypto-currencies are focused on the payment system function of banks, enabling peer-to-peer exchanges between counter-parties that may not have enduring transactional relationships. The introduction of crypto-currencies clearly increases competitive pressure on financial institutions providing payment services. However, distributed ledgers clearly involve a duplication of effort that is more costly than maintaining a single ledger. Furthermore, maintaining the entire history of transactions instead of simply current balances increases storage requirements of distributed ledger systems based on transactions.[39] It is not clear that crypto-currencies' alleged cost advantage (see the earlier discussion on transactions costs) is in fact large enough to out-compete traditional payments systems providers.

The provision of credit involves ongoing relationships between creditor and borrower. Credit relationships are closely related to banking functions (ii), (iii) and (iv). Credit relationships are largely incompatible with anonymity, since the capacity of Borrower B to repay a loan – and hence Lender W's willingness to lend – depends on expectations of B's future income. As a simple example of functions (iii) and (iv), Lender W might like to diversify exposure across borrowers $B_1, \ldots, B_n$, which increases the analytical burden on W of assessing and monitoring potential counter-parties. Financial institutions can do the same monitoring for many lending individuals, economizing on this analytical cost.

The blockchain's underlying premise of pseudo-anonymity is essentially incompatible with borrowing transactions, as it would invite both adverse selection and moral hazard problems. Adverse selection might arise if good quality borrowers are discouraged from borrowing because high interest rates are required to compensate for risky borrowers, further worsening the average riskiness of borrowers. Moral hazard problems might arise because truly anonymous borrowers would have an incentive to default on their loans; ex ante promises to repay debts would not be credible ex post.

Most crypto-currency frameworks are not currently well-designed to handle credit. Crypto-currencies like Bitcoin are designed so that transactions can only be verified and completed if the sender has enough crypto-currency to make the purchase – account balances must be non-negative. Efforts are being made to amend these characteristics, to make it possible to decentralize credit. Platforms such as Ethereum, and an add-on to Bitcoin called Counterparty, have been developed to implement 'smart contracts'.[40] Smart contracts use computer protocols to ensure that certain features of a contract are executed automatically. For example, Lender W could send 400 coins to Borrower B in exchange for receiving 10 bitcoins from B every month for the next 4 years. However, enforcement of such contracts is still complicated: it is not clear what mechanisms would be put into play if borrower B exhausted their balance of coins before meeting their obligations under the smart contract.[41] Ethereum envisages using arbitrators or courts to resolve such disputes, which again relies on transactors being identifiable.[42] He *et al.* (2016, box 3) raise additional concerns with smart contracts, including concerns about the legal status of such contracts, consumer protection issues, and concerns that smart contracts, like automated high-frequency trading, might adversely affect asset pricing, with possible implications for financial stability. A 'white paper' by the International Swaps and Derivatives Association notes that some contractual obligations can be automated and some parts codified, but others are subjective or require legal interpretation, which creates implementation challenges for smart contracts (ISDA, 2017).

Automated credit evaluation may become possible in future, via 'big-data' techniques, but such evaluations will only be possible if creditor identities can be established with high probability. These issues extend beyond the domain of crypto-currencies and distributed ledgers, but are part of a broader 'fintech' agenda relevant for both market participants and regulators.

The original crypto-currency, Bitcoin, faces competitive pressures on all sides. As discussed in Section 3, the open source nature of Bitcoin has made it comparatively easy to create new variant crypto-currencies. Although Bitcoin has network effects that work in its favour as the first and most famous crypto-currency, emerging crypto-currencies may offer more efficient or cheaper transaction services, potentially eroding the value of bitcoins. Blockchain or distributed ledger technology also has applications in the closed financial networks that are predominantly used to facilitate transactions. Traditional intermediaries such as banks are evolving their business practices to respond to the competitive pressures of crypto-currencies. As an example, the 'R3' consortium of large financial institutions began to develop 'Corda' in September 2015, a platform to facilitate interbank transactions using distributed ledger technology. See http://www.corda.net and Brown *et al.* (2016).[43]

Central banks are also investigating these technologies. In collaboration with private financial institutions, both the Bank of Canada and the Monetary Authority of Singapore are exploring options to use distributed ledger technology to facilitate wholesale transfers.[44] Interestingly, the Bank of Canada has recently concluded that distributed ledger technology is unlikely to yield positive net benefits relative to the centralized system currently employed for wholesale payments, and suggested that the complexity of decentralized systems could increase operational risks (Chapman *et al.*, 2017). Other central banks are investigating digital currencies to replace cash. In 2015, Ecuador introduced a 'Sistema de Dinero Electrónico', a digital currency system implemented via mobile phones, ostensibly in an effort to reduce the costs of using physical USD (the USD has been used as legal tender in Ecuador since 2000).[45] A year later, in November 2016, the People's Bank of China quietly opened a 'Digital Currency Research Institute'.[46] The Swedish Riksbank is also investigating the possibility of issuing a digital 'e-krona', primarily focused on smaller consumer payments, but is not explicitly looking to implement the e-krona as a distributed ledger or crypto-currency.[47] Rather more remarkably, the Republic of the Marshall Islands passed a law in 2018 that authorizes the government to issue a digital decentralized currency as legal tender, with provisions to make an initial currency offering.

4.3 *Implications for Monetary and Regulatory Authorities*

In the near term, the development of crypto-currencies should not materially impact central banks' ability to implement monetary policy in their own fiat currencies. Contracts in most economies are predominantly denominated in fiat currency units and as the residual suppliers of local currency central banks can affect their own local interest rates, influencing private agents' liquidity, short-term debt obligations, and incentives to substitute inter-temporally. However, central banks will not necessarily be able to influence the interest rates charged in 'foreign' crypto-currencies.

If crypto-currencies become more popular as a payment mechanism, central banks' influence on economic activity might be diminished, adversely impacting macro stabilization. The Reserve Bank of Australia (2014) makes essentially the same observation in its submission to an Australian Senate inquiry into digital currencies, noting that wide-scale adoption of digital currencies could hinder the Reserve Bank of Australia's ability to deliver low and stable inflation, because crypto-currency schemes usually have a predetermined supply path that cannot be altered to match the business cycle. These longer run concerns about the growth of crypto-currencies and analytical issues about the relationship between measures of crypto-currency and activity are also discussed by the ECB (2012).

Crypto-currencies pose a challenge for all regulators, because the decentralized ledger system means there is no central authority to regulate. In response to this difficulty, the Financial Action Task Force, initiated by the G-7 countries in 1989 to combat money laundering and the financing of terrorism, has called for the regulation of the exchanges that act as the gatekeepers or interfaces between crypto- and fiat currencies (He et al., 2016). The US Treasury's Financial Crimes Enforcement Network also regulates certain crypto-currency service providers as money transmitters (Marian, 2015). Of course, transactors might still be able to find bilateral counter-parties that enable them to transfer in and out of crypto-currencies, and regulation of the exchanges would not necessarily prevent such transactions. Marian (2015) suggests that the regulatory net could be extended by co-opting legitimate merchants into implementing a sales tax on all crypto-currency transactions, with rebates to be provided to purchasers if they forego anonymity. The aim of this sales tax is to penalize crypto-currency holders that have obtained balances illegally.

One of the largest Bitcoin exchanges, Mt Gox, was hacked in 2014 and had bitcoin balances stolen, reducing trust in the currency and causing the failure of the exchange (Ali et al., 2015). After the Mt Gox debacle, Jiro Aichi, the Japanese minister of finance at the time, made a case for international laws governing crypto-currencies (Knight, 2014). The problem is a familiar one from financial regulation: globally inconsistent laws could result in regulatory arbitrage, favouring some jurisdictions at the expense of others, distorting economic outcomes by prompting exchanges to domicile in low-regulation countries. These low-regulation countries, however, may be at risk of having their access to international financial markets circumscribed by other jurisdictions.[48]

Countries currently take different approaches to taxing and regulating crypto-currencies. The Inland Revenue Service in the United States treats crypto-currencies as property for tax purposes. Wages paid in virtual currency and contracts settled in virtual currencies are both subject to taxation. Gains and losses from the sale of virtual currencies could also be taxed depending on whether it is a capital asset or not (Levin et al., 2014). The Australian Tax Office treats crypto-currencies as an asset for capital gains tax purposes and does not regard crypto-currencies as a currency.[49] Rather, transactions implemented using crypto-currencies are seen as barter arrangements subject to the Australian goods and services tax, and wages paid in bitcoins could be subject to fringe benefit taxes. The European Union Court of Justice has declared that the exchange of fiat currency for 'bitcoin virtual currency' is exempt from value added tax (Court of Justice, 2015), essentially treating Bitcoin as another currency. The Inland Revenue Department in New Zealand regards crypto-currencies as property for tax purposes.[50]

Central banks and other regulatory authorities appear to be relatively sanguine that crypto-currencies do not pose an immediate threat to financial systems, in part because mainstream financial systems continue to predominate. See, for example Reserve Bank of Australia (2014), Ali *et al.* (2014) and Federal Advisory Committee (2014). The European Central Bank's position is similar to that of other central banks (ECB, 2015). The use of virtual currencies remains limited and the European Central Bank sees no immediate threat to the operation of traditional payment systems, monetary policy, price stability and financial stability, though it acknowledges that virtual currencies may have potential advantages over traditional payment systems, especially for cross-border transactions. The European Central Bank's strategy to deal with 'virtual' currencies is to continue to monitor developments and amend the regulatory and supervisory framework in future, as needed. In most jurisdictions, anti-money laundering, taxation, and terrorism issues are of more immediate concern than payment system, monetary policy or financial stability aspects of crypto-currencies (representatively, see Federal Advisory Committee, 2014).

The Reserve Bank of New Zealand's regulatory focus is on systemically important banks, non-bank deposit-takers, insurers and systemically important financial infrastructure.[51] The overall intent of the Reserve Bank's regulatory framework is to promote a sound and efficient financial system for New Zealand. The Reserve Bank does not regulate all non-bank schemes that provide for the storage and transfer of value. For example, the Snapper cards mentioned earlier fall outside the Reserve Bank's regulatory net, since they are small in value and the balances are thought of as a form of pre-payment rather than as deposits per se. Like Snapper, crypto-currency schemes are neither systemically important nor materially important for financial efficiency and have not been brought into the Reserve Bank's regulatory ambit.

5. Conclusion

In this paper, we discussed the growth and usage of crypto-currencies and described a prototypical example of how transactions are facilitated using Bitcoin – the first and most widely traded decentralized crypto-currency. We examined the monetary properties of Bitcoin as a generally accepted means of payment, as a unit of account, and as a store of value. With respect to these monetary properties, we conclude that Bitcoin is not yet generally accepted, it is not typically a unit of account, and its volatility makes it an uncertain store of value. Most crypto-currency addresses lie dormant and many of the active addresses are used only for online gambling or speculative purposes.

Nevertheless, crypto-currencies offer some distinct features, such as quicker cross-border transactions, possibly lower transaction fees, pseudo-anonymity, and transaction irreversibility. These features help to explain the growing demand for crypto-currencies, even though crypto-currencies do not seem to possess the basic attributes of money. Perceptions of anonymity seem to have been particularly important in creating a demand for crypto-currencies to facilitate illegal transactions. However, the anonymity embodied in crypto-currencies has been over-stated. There have been a significant number of crypto-currency prosecutions in relation to money laundering and other crimes, illustrating that there is no guarantee of anonymity.

While crypto-currencies are growing in popularity, they currently facilitate a very small proportion of transactions. Because of their comparatively small role in intermediation, central banks do not presently view crypto-currencies as a material threat to traditional financial systems and intermediaries. Crypto-currencies and decentralized ledger technology could well become an important part of global payment systems, but wide-scale adoption will depend on competition from alternative transaction technologies. And crypto-currencies will also need to address scalability issues if they wish to intermediate the volume of transactions undertaken globally.

Crypto-currencies are primarily focused on providing transaction services, though some efforts have been made to adapt them to the provision of credit. We argue that financial intermediaries will continue to play an important role in facilitating credit, because intermediaries can economize on the analytical burden associated with evaluating and monitoring borrowers.

Proponents foresee an enduring role for crypto-currencies. From our perspective, the future growth of crypto-currencies and their use as transaction media is by no means clear. Even if some of the constructs are enduring, such as distributed ledgers and the use of cryptography, specific crypto-currencies may be supplanted by competing transaction technologies. What does seem clear is that the regulatory and legal status of crypto-currencies must be resolved if crypto-currencies are to play a prominent role in exchange. Regulatory and legal reform will need to account for the decentralized nature of most crypto-currencies, and for their capacity to transcend national borders.

Acknowledgement

We thank Jonathan Chiu and Thorsten Koeppl for sharing their own research on blockchain technology, which helped to improve our understanding of its implementation and the issues that arise. Helpful comments were also received from Angus Barclay, Yuong Ha, Chris Kim, Leo Krippner, Anella Munro, Cavan O'Connor-Close, Roger Perry, Jeremy Richardson, Karam Shaar, Amber Wadsworth and two anonymous referees.

Notes

1. We distinguish e-payments and e-money as per Fung *et al.* (2014).
2. See McBride (2015) for the distinction between 'tender' and payment. To 'tender' is to make a unilateral offer to complete a payment, for example by a consumer, while 'payment' is a bilateral act requiring the consent of both consumer and seller.
3. See also https://www.ecb.europa.eu/stats/money_credit_banking/electronic_money/html/index.en.html, accessed 27 April, 2018.
4. See http://www.snapper.co.nz and http://octopus.com.hk/en, accessed 8 April, 2018.
5. As an exception, e-gold was denominated in physical quantities of gold, and was backed by a corresponding cache of gold bullion. In 2007, e-gold ran afoul of the USA Patriot Act, due to money-laundering concerns, and was eventually closed down.
6. Bank notes in circulation are interpreted as central bank liabilities and are also captured in central bank financial accounts. See, for example the Annual Report of the Reserve Bank of New Zealand, https://www.rbnz.govt.nz/about-us/annual-reports.
7. The idea of a ledger as a substitute for money is a very old one. Lipsey (1963, p. 404) discusses a hypothetical ledger in a government-run store in a communist society.
8. Satoshi Nakamoto is a pseudonym for person or people unknown. In May 2016 an Australian, Craig Steven Wright, claimed to be Nakamoto, but there is public doubt about the truth of his claim. https://www.wired.com/2016/05/craig-wright-privately-proved-hes-bitcoins-creator/, downloaded 8 April, 2018.
9. Sargent and Velde (2001) discuss the 'price revolution' in France – a period of relatively high inflation in the 16th and 17th centuries – which has sometimes been attributed to the expansion of gold and silver supplies in Europe from the New World.

10. See https://blockchain.info/charts, downloaded 8 April, 2018, for the average number of transactions per block.
11. The account address is a transformed, shorter function of the public key. Some of the transformations are to make numbers distinguishable (avoiding lowercase L, uppercase i, capital 'oh' and zero), while others are to provide an internal cross-check on the number (like a 'checksum' for a file), to ensure that the address is valid.
12. EFTPOS cards are debit or credit cards.
13. See Antonopoulos (2015) and Narayanan *et al.* (2016) for more details.
14. Quick response.
15. Nearfield communication.
16. See http://organofcorti.blogspot.co.nz/24May2015, downloaded 27 April 2018.
17. See, for cxample https://quickhash.com/ to generate these hashes.
18. These intertwined sequences of hashes are akin to a 'Merkle tree'. See Narayanan *et al.* (2016) for a more explicit characterization of the differences.
19. 'Age' is the length of time one has owned coins.
20. See also Yermack (2013).
21. Other useful characteristics for money include divisibility, portability, indestructability and 'cognizability', amongst others; see Jevons (1896, chapter 5).
22. https://www.sba.gov/sites/default/files/FAQ_Sept_2012.pdf.
23. https://data.worldbank.org/indicator/NY.GDP.PCAP.CD, accessed 27 April, 2018.
24. See World Bank (2014).
25. Electronic Card Transactions: April 2017. Statistics New Zealand.
26. https://blockchain.info/charts/n-transactions, accessed 27 April, 2018.
27. https://bitcointalk.org/index.php?topic=813324.0, accessed 12 October, 2017.
28. We use data from August 2010 to May 2017 for these calculations. We compute the standard deviation of $100 \times (BTC_t/BTC_t - 1)$, where BTC_t is USD/bitcoin at time t, and compare to the USD/NZD equivalent.
29. Antonopoulos (2016) provides a polemical view of financial and regulatory surveillance. Ali *et al.* (2015) discuss these libertarian motivations further.
30. See https://blockchain.info/charts/cost-per-transaction-percent.
31. See also https://99bitcoins.com/who-accepts-bitcoins-payment-companies-stores-take-bitcoins/, accessed 27 April, 2018.
32. Society for Worldwide Interbank Financial Telecommunication.
33. Single Euro Payment Area.
34. http://news.mit.edu/2017/mit-debuts-secure-digital-diploma-using-bitcoin-blockchain-technology-1017, accessed 26 April, 2018.
35. https://learncryptography.com/cryptocurrency/51-attack, accessed 27 April, 2018.
36. Bill Munro, personal communication.
37. Dowd (2014, p. 42) illustrates the supply of Bitcoin with a hypothetical rate of attrition.
38. See https://blog.plan99.net/the-resolution-of-the-bitcoin-experiment-dabb30201f7, accessed 26 April, 2018.
39. There are, however, mechanisms to try to 'prune' transaction content from ledgers when that content is no longer needed.
40. Ripple introduces the concept of IOUs, whereby a person or company grants credit limits for known counter-parties.
41. The International Chamber of Commerce provides contract terms and conditions to try to facilitate the resolution of contracts agreed electronically, which could perhaps be used

for smart contracts. See http://www.iccwbo.org/products-and-services/trade-facilitation/tools-for-e-business/, accessed 27 April, 2018.
42. http://legal-tech-blog.de/smart-contracts-ethereum-future-of-contracting, accessed 27 April, 2018.
43. In 2016 and 2017, a number of large financial institutions left the R3 consortium to pursue their own distributed ledger initiatives. http://www.reuters.com/article/us-jpmorgan-r3/jpmorgan-chase-co-leaves-blockchain-consortium-r3-idUSKBN17T2T4, accessed 26 April, 2018.
44. For Canada, see http://www.bankofcanada.ca/research/digital-currencies-and-fintech/fintech-experiments-and-projects/ and for Singapore see http://www.mas.gov.sg/Singapore-Financial-Centre/Smart-Financial-Centre/FinTech-Regulatory-Sandbox.aspx; both accessed 27 April, 2018.
45. See Wang (2016) and https://www.cnbc.com/2015/02/06/ecuador-becomes-the-first-country-to-roll-out-its-own-digital-durrency.html, accessed 27 April, 2018. White (2014) suggests that the introduction of the digital currency may be an effort to 'de-dollarize' the Ecuadorean economy.
46. https://www.yicaiglobal.com/news/people%E2%80%99s-bank-china-opens-digital-currency-research-institute, accessed 27 April, 2018.
47. See Riksbank (2017).
48. In 2009, the G20 agreed to develop a blacklist of tax haven countries. The Organization for Economic Cooperation and Development developed criteria and a list of 'uncooperative tax havens'. See http://www.oecd.org/countries/monaco/listofunco-operativetaxhavens.htm, accessed 27 April, 2018.
49. See https://www.ato.gov.au/General/Gen/Tax-treatment-of-crypto-currencies-in-Australia---specifically-bitcoin/, accessed 27 April, 2018.
50. See http://www.ird.govt.nz/income-tax-individual/cryptocurrency-qa.html accessed 26 April, 2018.
51. More details on the Reserve Bank's regulatory responsibilities can be found here: http://www.rbnz.govt.nz/regulation-and-supervision.

References

Adamsson, S. and Tahir, M. (2015) From one to many – The impact of individual's beliefs in the development of cryptocurrency. Master's Programme in Technical Project- and Business Management, Halmstad University.
Ali, R., Barrdear, J., Clews, R. and Southgate, J. (2014) The economics of digital currencies. *Bank of England Quarterly Bulletin* 54(3): 276–286.
Ali, S.T., Clarke, D. and McCorry, P. (2015) Bitcoin: Perils of an unregulated global P2P currency. In Revised Selected Papers of the 23rd International Workshop on Security Protocols XXIII, Vol. 9379 (pp. 283–293). New York: Springer-Verlag.
Antonopoulos, A.M. (2015) *Mastering Bitcoin: Unlocking Digital Cryptocurrency*. Sebastopol, CA: O'Reilly Media.
Antonopoulos, A.M. (2016) *The Internet of Money*. Columbia, MD: Merkle Bloom LLC.
Bank of Canada. (2014a) Decentralized e-money (Bitcoin). *Backgrounders*. Ontario, Canada: Bank of Canada.
Bank of Canada. (2014b) E-money. *Backgrounders*. Ontario, Canada: Bank of Canada.
Bariviera, A.F. (2017) The inefficiency of Bitcoin revisited: a dynamic approach. *Economics Letters* 161: 1–4.

Bariviera, A.F., Basgall, M.J., Hasperué, W. and Naiouf, M. (2017) Some stylized facts of the Bitcoin market. *Physica A: Statistical Mechanics and its Applications* 484: 82–90.

Baur, D.G., Hong, K. and Lee, A.D. (2018) Bitcoin: Medium of exchange or speculative assets? *Journal of International Financial Markets, Institutions and Money* 54: 177–189.

BIS. (2015) Digital currencies. Mimeo, Bank for International Settlements, Committee on Payments and Market Infrastructures.

Böhme, R., Christin, N., Edelman, B. and Moore, T. (2015) Bitcoin: economics, technology, and governance. *Journal of Economic Perspectives* 29(2): 213–238.

Brière, M., Oostelinck, K. and Szafarz, A. (2015) Virtual currency, tangible return: portfolio diversification with Bitcoin. *Journal of Asset Management* 16(6): 365–373.

Brown, R.G., Carlyle, J., Grigg, I. and Hearn, M. (2016) Corda: an introduction. Mimeo.

Burda, M. and Wyplosz, C. (1993) *Macroeconomics: A European Text*. Oxford: Oxford University Press.

Chapman, J., Garratt, R., Hendry, S., McCormack, A. and McMahon, W. (2017) Project Jasper: are distributed wholesale payment systems feasible yet? In *Financial System Review* (pp. 59–69). Ontario, Canada: Bank of Canada.

Cheah, E.T. and Fry, J. (2015) Speculative bubbles in Bitcoin markets? An empirical investigation into the fundamental value of Bitcoin. *Economics Letters* 130: 32–36.

Cheung, A.W.K., Roca, E. and Su, J.J. (2015) Crypto-currency bubbles: an application of the Phillips-Shi-Yu (2013) methodology on Mt. Gox bitcoin prices. *Applied Economics* 47(23): 2348–2358.

Corbet, S., Lucey, B. and Yarovaya, L. (2017) Datestamping the Bitcoin and Ethereum bubbles. *Finance Research Letters*. Forthcoming.

Court of Justice. (2015) The exchange of traditional currencies for units of the 'bitcoin' virtual currency is exempt from VAT. *Press Release 125/15*, Court of Justice of the European Union, judgment in case C-264/14 Skatteverket v David Hedqvist.

Davidson, J. (2015) No, big companies aren't really accepting Bitcoin. *Time Magazine* 10 January, 2015.

Donier, J. and Bouchaud, J.P. (2015) Why do markets crash? Bitcoin data offers unprecedented insights. *PLoS One* 10(10): e0139356.

Dowd, K. (2014) *New Private Monies. A Bit-part Player?* London: The Institute of Economic Affairs.

EBA. (2013) Warning to consumers on virtual currencies. Mimeo EBA/WRG/2013/01, European Banking Authority.

ECB. (2012) Virtual currencies. Mimeo, European Central Bank.

ECB. (2015) Virtual currencies – a further analysis. Mimeo, European Central Bank.

ElBahrawy, A., Alessandretti, L., Kandler, A., Pastor-Satorras, R. and Baronchelli, A. (2017) Evolutionary dynamics of the cryptocurrency market. *Royal Society Open Science* 4(11): 1–9.

Extance, A. (2015) Bitcoin and beyond. *Nature* 526(7571): 21–23.

Eyal, I. and Sirer, E.G. (2014) Majority is not enough: Bitcoin mining is vulnerable. In N. Christin and R. Safavi-Naini (eds.), *Financial Cryptography and Data Security*, Vol. 8437 (436–454). Berlin: Springer.

FBI. (2012) (u) Bitcoin virtual currency: unique features present distinct challenges for deterring illicit activity. *Intelligence Assessment*. Washington, DC: Federal Bureau of Investigation.

Federal Advisory Committee. (2014) *Record of meeting*, Board of Governors, Friday, 9 May, 2014.

Freixas, X. and Rochet, J.C. (1997) *Microeconomics of Banking*. Cambridge, MA: The MIT Press.

Fung, B., Molico, M. and Stuber, G. (2014) Electronic money and payments: Recent developments and issues. *Discussion Paper 2014-2*, Bank of Canada, Ontario, Canada.

Garcia, D., Tessone, C.J., Mavrodiev, P. and Perony, N. (2014) The digital traces of bubbles: feedback cycles between socio-economic signals in the Bitcoin economy. *Journal of the Royal Society Interface* 11: 1–11.

Glaser, F., Zimmermann, K., Haferkorn, M., Weber, M.C. and Siering, M. (2014) Bitcoin – asset or currency? Revealing users' hidden intentions. In *Proceedings of the European Conference on Information Systems (ECIS)*, Tel Aviv Israel: Association for Information Systems.

Goldman Sachs. (2014) All about Bitcoin. *Global Macro Research Top of Mind 21*, Goldman Sachs, 11 March.

He, D., Habermeier, K.F., Leckow, R.B., Haksar, V., Almeida, Y., Kashima, M., Kyriakos-Saad, N., Oura, H., Sedik, T.S., Stetsenko, N. and Yepes, C.V. (2016) Virtual currencies and beyond: initial considerations. *IMF Staff Discussion Notes 16/3*, International Monetary Fund, Washington, DC.

Hendrickson, J.R., Hogan, T.L. and Luther, W.J. (2016) The political economy of Bitcoin. *Economic Inquiry* 54(2): 925–939.

Information Assurance Directorate. (2016) Commercial national security algorithm suite and quantum computing FAQ. *Technical Report, MFQ U/OO/815099-15*, National Security Agency, MD, USA.

ISDA. (2017) Smart contracts and distributed ledger - a legal perspective. *White paper*, International Swap and Derivatives Association and Linklaters, New York, NY.

Jevons, W.S. (1896) *Money and the Mechanism of Exchange*. New York, NY: D. Appleton and Company.

Jiang, Y., Nie, H. and Ruan, W. (2017) Time-varying long-term memory in Bitcoin market. *Finance Research Letters* 25: 280–284.

Johnson, G. and Pomorski, L. (2014) Briefing on digital currencies. *Briefing to the Senate of Canada*, Bank of Canada, Ontario, Canada.

Katsiampa, P. (2017) Volatility estimation for bitcoin: a comparison of GARCH models. *Economics Letters* 158: 3–6.

Kloc, J. (2014) Bitcoin makes the jump to brick-and-mortar in Cleveland. *Newsweek* 162(22), 6 June, 2014.

Knight, S. (2014) Japan says any Bitcoin regulation should be international. *Reuters* 27 February, 2014.

Kocherlakota, N.R. (1998) Money is memory. *Journal of Economic Theory* 81(2): 232–251.

Kocherlakota, N.R. (2000) Creating business cycles through credit constraints. *Federal Reserve Bank of Minneapolis Quarterly Review* 24(3): 2–10.

Kocherlakota, N.R. (2002) Money: What's the question and why should we care about the answer. *American Economic Review: Papers and Proceedings* 92(2): 58–61.

Koeppl, T. and Kronick, J. (2017) Blockchain technology – What's in store for Canada's economy and financial markets. *Commentary 468*, C.D. Howe Institute, Toronto, Canada.

Kurihara, Y. and Fukushima, A. (2017) The market efficiency of Bitcoin: a weekly anomaly perspective. *Journal of Applied Finance and Banking* 7(3): 57–64.

Levin, R.B., O'Brien, A.A. and Osterman, S.A. (2014) Dread pirate Roberts, Byzantine generals, and federal regulation of Bitcoin. *Journal of Taxation & Regulation of Financial Institutions* 27(4): 5–19.

Lipsey, R.G. (1963) *An Introduction to Positive Economics*, fourth impression June 1965. London: Weidenfeld and Nicolson.

Marian, O.Y. (2015) A conceptual framework for the regulation of cryptocurrencies. *The University of Chicago Law Review* 82(1): 53–68.

McBride, N. (2015) Payments and the concept of legal tender. *Reserve Bank of New Zealand Bulletin* 78(6): 3–7.

Meiklejohn, S., Pomarole, M., Jordan, G., Levchenko, K., Mccoy, D., Voelker, G. and Savage, S. (2016) A fistful of bitcoins: characterizing payments among men with no names. *Communications of the ACM* 59(4): 86–93.

Nadarajah, S. and Chu, J. (2017) On the inefficiency of Bitcoin. *Economics Letters* 150: 6–9.

Nakamoto, S. (2008) Bitcoin: a peer-to-peer electronic cash system. Mimeo, Bitcoin.org.

Narayanan, A., Bonneau, J., Felten, E., Miller, A. and Goldfeder, S. (2016) *Bitcoin and Cryptocurrency Technologies: A Comprehensive Introduction*. Princeton, NJ: Princeton University Press.

Peters, G.W., Chapelle, A. and Panayi, E. (2015) Opening discussion on banking sector risk exposures and vulnerabilities from virtual currencies: An operational risk perspective. *Journal of Banking Regulation* 17(4): 239–272.

Phillip, A., Chan, J.S. and Peiris, S. (2018) A new look at cryptocurrencies. *Economics Letters* 163: 6–9.

Phillips, P.C., Wu, Y. and Yu, J. (2011) Explosive behavior in the 1990s NASDAQ: when did exuberance escalate asset values? *International Economic Review* 52(1): 201–226.

Phillips, P.C., Shi, S. and Yu, J. (2014) Specification sensitivity in right-tailed unit root testing for explosive behaviour. *Oxford Bulletin of Economics and Statistics* 76(3): 315–333.

Phillips, P.C., Shi, S. and Yu, J. (2015) Testing for multiple bubbles: historical episodes of exuberance and collapse in the s&p 500. *International Economic Review* 56(4): 1043–1078.

Pieters, G. and Vivanco, S. (2017) Financial regulations and price inconsistencies across Bitcoin markets. *Information Economics and Policy* 39: 1–14.

Polasik, M., Piotrowska, A.I., Wisniewski, T.P., Kotkowski, R. and Lightfoot, G. (2015) Price fluctuations and the use of Bitcoin: an empirical inquiry. *International Journal of Electronic Commerce* 20(1): 9–49.

Reserve Bank of Australia. (2014) Submission to the inquiry into digital currency: Senate Economics References Committee. November 2014.

Riksbank (2017) The Riksbank's e-krona project. Report 1, Sveriges Riksbank, Sweden.

Sargent, T.J. and Velde, F.R. (2001) *The Big Problem of Small Change*. Princeton, NJ: Princeton University Press.

SEC. (2013) Ponzi schemes using virtual currencies. *Investor Alert 153 (7/13)*, United States Securities and Exchange Commission, Washington, DC.

Szczepánski, M. (2014) Bitcoin: market, economics and regulation. Technical Report 11/04/2014, European Parliamentary Research Service, Brussels.

Tasca, P. (2015) Digital currencies: principles, trends, opportunities, and risks. Research Working Paper, Ecurex.

Trautman, L. (2014) Virtual currencies; Bitcoin & what now after Liberty Reserve, Silk Road, and Mt. Gox? *Richmond Journal of Law & Technology* 20(4): 1–109.

UK Government Office for Science. (2016) Distributed ledger technology: Beyond block chain. Mimeo, UK Government Office for Science, London. https://www.gov.uk/government/publications/distributed-ledger-technology-blackett-review

Urquhart, A. (2016) The inefficiency of Bitcoin. *Economics Letters* 148: 80–82.

Urquhart, A. (2017) Price clustering in Bitcoin. *Economics Letters* 159: 145–148.

Urquhart, A. (2018) What causes the attention of Bitcoin? *Economics Letters* 166: 40–44.

Van Vliet, B.E. (2018) An alternative model of metcalfe's law for valuing bitcoin. *Economics Letters* 165: 70–72.

Velde, F.R. (2013) Bitcoin: a primer. *Chicago Fed Letter 317*, Federal Reserve Bank of Chicago.

Vigna, P. and Casey, M.J. (2015) *The Age of Cryptocurrency*. New York, NY: St. Martin's Press.

Wang, S. (2016) Examining the effects of dollarization on ecuador. Mimeo, Council on Hemispheric Affairs.

Weber, W.E. (2016) A Bitcoin standard: lessons from the gold standard. Staff Working Paper 2016-14, Bank of Canada.

White, L. (2014) Defending dollarization in Ecuador. Mimeo, Alt-M.org, 4 December, 2014.

White, L.H. (2015) The market for cryptocurrencies. *Cato Journal* 35(2): 383–402.

Williamson, S. and Wright, R. (2010) New monetarist economics: methods. *Federal Reserve Bank of St. Louis Review* 92(4): 265–302.

Williamson, S. and Wright, R. (2011) New monetarist economics: models. In B.M. Friedman and M. Woodford (eds.), *Handbook of Monetary Economics 3A* (pp. 25–96), San Diego, CA: Elsevier.

World Bank (2014) Financial inclusion. Global Financial Development Report 2014, International Bank for Reconstruction and Development, Washington, DC.

Yermack, D. (2013) Is Bitcoin a real currency? An economic appraisal. Working Paper 19747, National Bureau of Economic Research.

INDEX

ability bias, 166
accounting fraud, 82
accounting ratios, 165
account takeover frauds, 94
advanced economies (AEs), 12, 13. *See also*
 unconventional monetary policy
 (UMP)
 unconventional monetary policies in,
 16–18
AEs. *See* advanced economies (AEs)
affinity fraud, 92
aggressive sales culture, 101
air loans, 86
angel finance, 5. *See also* business angels (BAs),
 research on
arm's length lending, 249
asset-backed securities (ABSs), 88

bad apples theory, 104
balance sheet policies, 15–18
bank
 deposits, 353
 cquity holders, 47
 failure resolution framework, 45, 65
 too-big-to-fail (TBTF), 41, 44, 54–55
bank creditors, benefits from implicit guarantees
 to, 45–47
bank debtors, benefits from implicit guarantees
 to, 47–48
bank owners, benefits from implicit guarantees to,
 47
bank regulation, imperfect, 163
Basel Committee on Banking Supervision
 (BCBS), 65
Basel II and III banks, 282

Bitcoin, 354–355, 363. *See also* crypto-currency
 blockchain, 359–362
 exchange rate volatility, 363–365
 genesis address, 358
 miners, 355, 357–362, 371
 PGP (pretty good privacy) public key, 358
 QR code, 357
 transactions, 357–359
 validation process of, 356–362
 wallet, 356–357
Bitcoin cash, 372
Blackcoin, 355
Black Scholes option pricing approach, 55
blockchain, 353–354, 359–360, 369. *See also*
 crypto-currency
 hashes, 361
bond prices, 118–119
borrowing rate differentials, 164
botnet herders, 95
break-even inflation rate, 121
 liquidity-adjusted, 123
broker-dealers, 89
business angel networks (BANs), 189
business angels (BAs), research on, 183–184
 BA characteristics, 185, 187–189, 201–203
 gender, 188, 202–203
 international differences in profiles, 188,
 202
 networks and groups, 188–189, 203
 profiles and types, 187–188, 201–202
 BA investment process, 185, 190–193,
 204–206
 BAs' selection criteria, 191
 impact on investees' performances,
 192–193, 205–206

Contemporary Topics in Finance: A Collection of Literature Surveys, First Edition. Edited by Iris Claus and Leo Krippner.
Chapters © 2019 The Authors. Book compilation © 2019 John Wiley & Sons Ltd. Published 2019 by John Wiley & Sons Ltd.

business angels (BAs), research on (*Continued*)
  overview of entire investment process,
    193–194, 204
  post-investment, 191–192, 205
  selection, evaluation and funding, 190–191,
    204–205
  value-added activities by BAs, 192
  BA market, 185, 189–190, 203–204
    demand and supply of angel capital, 189,
      203
    effectiveness of angel financing on regional
      growth, 189, 204
    policies to foster informal risk capital
      market, 189–190, 204
  bibliometric analysis, 194–200
  directions for future research, 200–206
  methodology for, 184–186
  overview of entire investment process,
    193–194
  reviewed articles by thematic area and research
    line, 186

capital investment incentives, 154
capital market competition, 281
career concern model, 158
CDSs. *See* credit default swaps (CDSs)
CDS spreads, 55, 64
  fair-value, 55
CE. *See* credit easing (CE)
Centre of study for Financial Innovation (CSFI),
    311–312
certification effect, 157
charter value of bank equity, 50
cleansing effect of recessions, 174
Coinbase, 368
collateral constraints, 161
collateralized debt obligations (CDOs), 88
comprehensive monetary easing (CME), 22
consumer price index (CPI), 120
contact-less smart cards, 353
contingent claims analysis, 59
convertible currencies, 352
cooperative banks, 282
Counterparty, 372
credit bubbles, 161
credit default swaps (CDSs), 55, 89
credit easing (CE), 15
credit losses, 48
creditor capturing, 252
credit rating agencies (CRAs), 90
credit rating agency assessments, 54–55

credit relationships, 372
crowdfunding, 7–8, 331–333
  crowdsourcing and, 339–340
  equity, 336, 343
  and financing of innovation, 335–338
  funding gap and, 335–336
  innovative projects and, 340–342
  loan-based, 336
  necessary conditions for innovation
    development, 343–344
  and other forms of entrepreneurial finance,
    336–338
  platforms, functioning of, 334–335
  and professional investors, differences
    between, 336–337
  reward-based, 336, 340
  trust problem and, 338–339
  types of innovation and, 342–343
  and venture capital, 337
crowdsourcing, 332, 339–340
crypto-currency, 8, 351
  and anonymity, 366
  basic functions of money and, 362–365
  consumers, implications for, 370–372
  decentralized, 353
  description of, 353–354
  empirical properties of, 369–370
  exchange rate, 369
  financial institutions, implications for,
    372–373
  growth in supply of, 354–356
  international companies accepting, 367
  irredeemable, 353
  mechanics of Bitcoin and blockchain, 356–362
  monetary and regulatory authorities,
    implications for, 373–375
  motivations for use of, 366–367
  payment/exchange mechanisms and, 352–353
  pseudo-anonymity of, 366, 368
  top 10 currencies by market valuation, 355
  and transaction costs, 366
  transaction irreversibility in, 367
  use of, 368–369
cryptography, 353, 371
currency crises, 13

data envelopment analysis (DEA), 302
debt of banks, 41
debtor capturing, 252
decentralized currencies, 352. *See also*
    crypto-currency

decentralized ledger technology, 352
deposit funding cost advantages, 53–54
deposit insurance arrangements, 46
    explicit and implicit, 46
detrended fluctuation analysis, 369
digital currencies, 352, 365
disclosure requirements, 80
distributed ledger, 354, 366, 369
    technology, 373
double sales scam, 86
double-spending, 359–360
Double Trust Dilemma, 338–339
dynamic stochastic general equilibrium (DSGE)
    models, 26, 29–30

EBSCO database, 304
ECB. *See* European Central Bank (ECB)
effective lower bound (ELB), 12
efficient cost frontier, 302
Ehrsam, Fred, 368
Electronic Fund Transfers at Point of Sale
    (EFTPOS) cards, 356
emerging market economies (EMEs), 13
e-money, 353
    centralized, 353
    decentralized, 353
e-payments, 352
equity crowdfunding, 332, 335, 336, 343
    platforms, 343
equity finance and productivity, 171–172, 176
equity financing, 5
Ethereum, 372, 373
European Central Bank (ECB), 13, 24–25
European Free Trade Association Court, 46
explicit guarantee, 42–43
    and implicit guarantee, differences between,
        43–44

failure of bank, 44–45
false financial disclosures, 81, 82–90
    in context of loan applications, 84–88
        perpetrators, motivations and opportunities,
            87–88
        prevalence, costs and consequences, 86–87
    in context of structured finance investments,
        88–90
        perpetrators, motivations and opportunities,
            89–90
        prevalence, costs and consequences, 89
    and financial mis-selling practices, 82
    and investment scams, 82

misrepresentations by organizational actors in,
    82
at proprietary trading desks of financial firms,
    82–84
    perpetrators, motivations and opportunities,
        83–84
    prevalence, costs and consequences, 83
Federal Deposit Insurance Corporation (FDIC),
    46
Federal Financial Crimes Enforcement Network
    (FinCEN), 86
feeder funds, 92
fictitious identity frauds, 94
fiduciary duties, 80
finance and productivity, 151–153
    business cycles and, 173–175
    direct analyses of, 159
        financial frictions, productivity implications
            of, 160–165
        financial liberalisation and productivity,
            170–171
        productivity effects of financial
            development, 159
        studies examining other channels, 165–169
    financial development and economic growth,
        155
    framework for analysis, 153–155
    indirect analyses of, 156
        effect of finance on productivity through
            R&D, 157–158
        innovation and firm ownership, 158
        studies on, 156–157
    non-debt finance and productivity, 171–173
    recent empirical literature, and policy
        development
        alternative finance and productivity, 176
        business cycles and productivity, 176
        direct contributions of financial sector,
            176
        equity finance and productivity, 176
        finance and productivity, 175
        financial liberalisation and productivity,
            176
        insolvency regimes and productivity,
            175–176
        M&A and productivity, 176
        transmission channels, 176
    studies on, 155–156
financial activity, expansion of, 152, 153
financial crises, 13
financial deregulation, 104

financial development, 156
    and economic growth, 155–156
    productivity effects of, 159
financial fraud, 3, 79–80, 104–106. *See also*
        specific type
    acts of, 80–81
    definition of, 80
    false financial disclosures, 81, 82–90
    financial scams, 81, 90–96
    fraudulent financial mis-selling, 81, 96–104
    future research perspective, 105
    legal rules and, 80
    in securities markets, 80
    types of, 81
financial frictions, productivity implications of,
        160–165
financial inclusion, 299
financial information, 79
financial liberalisation, 5, 170, 176
financial market policies, 154
financial policy objectives, 42
financial regulatory reform, 61, 62
financial rents, 169
financial scams, 81, 90–96
    financial identity scams, 93–96
        perpetrators, motivations and opportunities,
            95–96
        prevalence, costs and consequences,
            94–95
        proliferation and professionalization of,
            96
        social engineering schemes, 94
        technical subterfuge schemes, 94
    investment scams, 91–92
        perpetrators, motivations and opportunities,
            92–93
        prevalence, costs and consequences, 92
    well-delineated pattern of, 90–91
financial sector wage premium, 48
Financial Stability Board (FSB), 54, 65
financial systemic safety net, 42–43
    traditional definition of, change in, 43, 44
firm entry policies, 154
Fisher equation, 120
five-factor affine term structure model, 128
foreclosure rescue/equity skimming, 86
forward guidance policies (FG), 18
founding angels, 188
fraud, 79. *See also* financial fraud
    financial market activities and, 79
fraud-for-housing schemes, 85

fraud-for-profit schemes, 85, 86
fraud schemes, 81
fraudulent financial mis-selling, 81, 96–104
    financial products in, 97
    of interest rate derivatives, 102–104
    of life insurance and pension schemes,
        99–102
    predatory lending, 97–99
free cash flow, 168
funding gap, 335–336

gatekeepers, 189
general fraud laws, 80
G20 financial regulatory reform agenda, 41–42
global financial crisis, 2, 11, 283. *See also*
        unconventional monetary policy (UMP)
    and financial systemic safety net, 43
    and implicit guarantee, 41
Great Recession, 2
G-SIBs (globally systemically important banks),
        53, 65
    special treatment to, 65–68
guarantees, 42
    effect of, on risky bank debt, 45
    explicit, 42–43
    implicit (*see* implicit guarantee)
guarantor of last resort, 43

hashing, 360–361
Hearn, Mike, 371
helicopter money, 19
hold-up problem, 252
human capital channel, 166–167
Hurst exponent, 369

Icelandic banks case, 45
identity abuses, 94–95
idiosyncratic risk, 52
Iguchi, Toshide, 83, 84
ILBs. *See* inflation-linked bonds (ILBs)
ILB-specific liquidity proxies, 136
impersonal methods, 91–92
implicit guarantee, 3, 41, 69–70
    benefits to
        bank creditors, 45–47
        bank debtors, 47–48
        bank employees, 48
        bank owners, 47
    collective and idiosyncratic risk and, 52
    credit strengths of debtor and guarantor and,
        51–52

economic costs of
  competitive distortions, 50–51
  perceived contingent liabilities for
    sovereign, 51
  risk-taking, increase in, 50
  weakened market discipline, 48–50
ex ante value of, 41
and explicit guarantee, differences between,
  43–44
global financial crisis and, 41
overview of, 41–42
policy makers on, communication by,
  60–63
  financial markets reaction to, 63–65
presence of, cause for, 44–45
special treatment to G-SIBs, 65–68
as subsidy reducing bank funding costs, 46
and TBTF concept, 41
in terms of basis points funding cost
  advantages, 56–57, 60
value of, estimation of, 53–60
indexation lag, 133
indexation premium, 120
inflation crises, 13
inflation-linked bonds (ILBs), 4, 117. *See also*
  inflation risk premium
advantages of, 146–147
issuances as savings for Treasury, 147–149
liquidity premium in, 121
nominal bonds and, link between, 120–121
return predictability, 124
inflation risk premium, 117
estimation issues, 138
estimation of, with ILB yields, 122, 139–140
  comparison of, 149
  evaluation of ILB use for, 132–134
  regression-based approaches, 122–125
  studies on, 126–127
  term structure models, 125–132
impact of liquidity on ILB yields, 134–135
  ILB-specific liquidity proxies, 136
  proxies for uncertainty, 137
  relative ILB liquidity proxies, 136–137
  treasury liquidity proxies, 137
inflation-linked bonds, 120–121
  and break-even inflation rate, 121
magnitude of, knowledge of, 117
and monetary policy, 135, 138
negative, 119
overview of, 118–120
positive, 117, 119

sovereign debt management and, 117
  zero lower bound, 138–139
inflation swap rates, use of, 131–132
inflation targets, 20
information asymmetry, in mis-selling, 96
information specialists, 95
innovation
  financial institutions in, role of, 331
  incremental, 342
  radical, 342
  small firms and, 331–332 (*see also*
    crowdfunding)
insolvency regime, 162
interbank competition, 281
interest-rate hedging product (IRHP), 102
  mis-selling of, 102–104
  over-hedged, 102
  SMEs and, 102–103
interest rate swap, 102
investment opportunity, 92
investment scams, 82, 91–92
  perpetrators, motivations and opportunities,
    92–93
  prevalence, costs and consequences, 92
IRHP. *See* interest-rate hedging product (IRHP)
issuer ratings, 53, 54

joint term structure model, 129–130
Jumpstart Our Business Startups (JOBS) Act of
  2012, 335

Kalman filter, 124, 125
Kerviel, Jerome, 84

labour market incentives, 154
Large-Scale Asset Program (LSAP1), 22–23
lead lists, 90
Leeson, Nick, 83, 84
legal tender, 352
life insurance and pension plans, mis-selling of,
  99–102
liquidity losses, 48–49
liquidity premium, 121
Litecoin, 355, 361
long-term financing operation (LTRO), 24

macro-finance term structure models, 130–131
Madoff, Bernard, 93
malware developers, 95
Maturity Extension Program (MEP), 23
Mempool (Memory-Pool), 358

merger and acquisition (M&A) activity, 168
Merton, Robert K., 93
MFIs. *See* microfinance institutions (MFIs)
microfinance institutions (MFIs), 7, 297
  challenges for future research and conclusions,
    319–321
  characteristics and performance, 307
    institutional type, 308–309
    organizational maturity, 307–308
    size of MFIs, 308
  commercialization of, 311
  double bottom line mission, 300
  external context and, 314
    domestic financial system, 315–316
    institutional environment, 316–318
    macro-economic conditions, 314–315
  financial and social performance, measurement
    of, 301–303
  financial self-sufficiency measure, 301
  financial services to poor, 297, 298
  financing sources, 309–311
  governance, 311–312
    board dynamics, 314
    boards, 312–313
    disclosure and transparency, 313
    external, 314
    remuneration of management, 313–314
  mission drift, 300
  performance of, 298–301
    data analysis, 307–319
    data collection, method of, 303–304
    data description, 304–307
    debt finance and, 311
  social performance of, 298, 302
  subsidies to, 298, 300, 310
  success of microfinance model, 300
  trade-off between financial and social
    performance, 318–319
  trade-off discussion, 299
  types of, 300–301, 308
microfinance promise, 297
Mis-selling agents, 96. *See also* fraudulent
    financial mis-selling
mission drift, 300
MIX Market data set, 300
model-free approach, 124
model-independent range, 129
money laundering, 368
money mule, 95
mooch lists, 90
mortgage fraud, 85

mortgage industry, 84–85
  intermediaries, 87–88
mortgage loans, mis-selling of, 97–99
mortgage origination fraud, 84–88
  consequences of, 87
  definition of, 85
  perpetrators of, 87
mortgage securitization fraud, 88–90

Nakamoto, Satoshi, 354, 366
neutral model of evolution, 370
Nextcoin, 362. *See also* crypto-currency
nexus angels, 189
nominal bonds, 117, 119. *See also* inflation risk
    premium
nonce, 361
non-debt finance and productivity, 171–173

online gambling, 368
open access ledgers, 369
Organisation for Economic Co-operation and
    Development (OECD), 151
originate to distribute (OTD) model, 89–90, 98
Outright Monetary Transactions (OMT) program,
    24

Pebble watch, 340
Peercoin, 355, 362. *See also* crypto-currency
permissioned ledgers, 352
permissionless ledgers, 352
pharming, 94
phishermen, 95
phishing, 94
Ponzi schemes, 91–92, 368. *See also* investment
    scams
predatory lending, 97–99
preparation premium, 157
primary mortgage market, 84
principle of absolute legal liquidation priority, 46
production inputs, 154
production technology, 154
productivity, 154. *See also* finance and
    productivity
productivity growth, 151. *See also* finance and
    productivity
  decline in, 151, 152
  financial system and, 152
  labour, 151
product market regulations, 154
proliferation of mortgage products, 99
proof-of-stake, 362

proof-of-work system, 361, 362
Prosper.com (loan-based crowdfunding platform), 336
proxies for uncertainty, 137

QE. *See* quantitative easing (QE)
qualitative and quantitative easing (QQE), 22
qualitative guidance, 18
quantitative easing (QE), 2, 15, 135
quantity theory of money, 355–356

R&D. *See* research and development (R&D)
real estate title fraud, 86
relationship lending, 6–7, 249–251
   differences between financial systems and, 284–285
   industry-specific variables, 250, 287
      level of market competition, 274, 281
      ownership structure, 282
      regulatory framework, 281–282
   multidimensional framework of, 252–253
   negative side of, 252
   positive side of, 251–252
   relationship-specific determinants, 250, 286
      bank and firm size, 253–254, 255–257
      exclusivity and main–bank affiliation, 271, 273–274, 275–278
      firm–bank relationship duration, 262, 266–271, 272
      functional distance, 258, 262, 263–265
      geographical distance, 254, 258, 259–261
      lender–borrow mutual trust and qualitative information, 274, 279–280
   summary and future research perspective, 285–290
   theoretical foundations of, 251–252
   in times of financial distress for lenders/borrowers, 283–284
relative ILB liquidity proxies, 136–137
research and development (R&D), 154
   finance effect on productivity through, 157–158
   policies, 154
residential mortgage-backed securities (RMBSs), 88
resource effect, 157
return on assets (ROAs), 301
return on equity (ROE), 301
revolving doors policy, 101

reward-based crowdfunding, 332, 335, 336, 340
Ripple, 368–369
rogue traders, 82–84
rolling window approach, 369

scarring effect of recessions, 174
Scopus database, 184
screening effect, 173
secondary mortgage market, 84–85
Securities Markets Program (SMP), 24
security-specific liquidity factor, 129
shadow rate, 139
silent second mortgages, 86
small and medium enterprises (SMEs), 102, 251
smart contracts, 372
smart money, 183
smart subsidies, 310
Snapper cards, 375
social engineering schemes, 94
Social Performance Indicators Tool 4 (SPI4), 306, 320
Social Performance Taskforce (SPTF), 306
Social Science Citation Index (SSCI), 307
Société Général, 84
soft budget constraint, 252
spammers, 95
spoofed e-mails, 94
stand-alone ratings, 53, 54
Stanford, Allen, 93
state space model, 124
stochastic frontier analysis (SFA), 302
stock market capitalisation, 151
stock market wealth, 47
straw borrowers, 87
straw buyer, 86
structured collars, 102
structured investment vehicles, 88
student debt, 167
subprime borrowers, 99
subsidies, 41
   and financial performance, 310
   microfinance institutions and, 298, 300, 310
suitability requirement, 80
superstar environments, 84
survey inflation forecasts, 122
Suspicious Activity Reports (SARs), mortgage-related, 86

TBTF. *See* too-big-to-fail (TBTF)
technical subterfuge schemes, 94

technology angels, 188
term structure models, 125–132
  including inflation data, 129–130
  inflation swap rates, use of, 131–132
  macro-finance, 130–131
  without inflation data, 125, 128–129
too-big-to-fail (TBTF), 3, 41, 44, 54–55, 61–63.
      See also implicit guarantee
  definition of, 62
  ending TBTF, 61, 62
too-big-to-fail subsidies, 169
total factor productivity (TFP), 156
transaction-based lending, 249
transaction costs, 366
transnational technical communities, 217
transparency and disclosure, for MFI
      performance, 313
treasury liquidity proxies, 137

UMP. *See* unconventional monetary policy
      (UMP)
unconventional monetary policy (UMP), 2,
      11–12, 30–31
  in advanced economies, 16–18
  definition of, 15
  impact of, on financial markets
    Europe and, 24–25
    GFC and Aftermath, 22–24
    international spillovers, 25
    Japan's experience, learning from, 20–22
    measurement challenges, 19–20
  macro-economic effects, 26–30
  transition to, 13–19
    2008 GFC, 13–15
  typology of, 15, 18–19
under-priced guarantees, 50
underwriters
  fraudulent misrepresentations by, 89
  job of, 88
unsophisticated investors, 97, 105

vector autoregressive (VAR) mode, 26–29
venture capital (VC) internationalization, 6,
      215–216
  future research avenues, 238–243
    determinants of international VC
      investments, gaps in, 242
    general gaps, 239–241
    methodological concerns, 238–239
    outcomes of international investments, gaps
      related to, 243
    strategies to mitigate liabilities of
      foreignness, gaps in, 242–243
    theoretical integration, 238
  international VC investment flows,
      determinants of, 216
    country-level determinants, 216–220
    firm-level determinants, 220–223
  outcomes of international VC investments, 228
    from perspective of portfolio company,
      228–229, 230–231
    from perspective of VC firms, 229, 232,
      233–236
  public policy and, 232, 237
  strategies to mitigate liabilities of foreignness,
      223–228
virtual currencies, 352, 374–375

'WannaCry worm,' 368
Web of Science database, 307
white collar crime, 85
workhorse model, 128

Zerocash, 366
Zerocoin, 366
zero-interest rate policy (ZIRP), 21, 22
zero lower bound (ZLB), 11–12, 20, 138–139.
      See also unconventional monetary policy
      (UMP)
ZLB. *See* zero lower bound (ZLB)
zombie firms, 164